# ENCYCLOPEDIA OF
# AMERICAN INDIAN CONTRIBUTIONS
# TO THE WORLD

# ENCYCLOPEDIA OF AMERICAN INDIAN CONTRIBUTIONS TO THE WORLD

15,000 YEARS OF INVENTIONS AND INNOVATIONS

EMORY DEAN KEOKE
AND
KAY MARIE PORTERFIELD

Facts On File, Inc.

**Encyclopedia of American Indian Contributions to the World**

Copyright © 2002 by Emory Dean Keoke and Kay Marie Porterfield
Maps pages 316–327 © Carl Waldman and Facts On File, Inc.
Maps pages 328–332 © Facts On File, Inc.

Facts On File, Inc.
132 West 31st Street
New York, NY 10001

**Library of Congress Cataloging-in-Publication Data**

Keoke, Emory Dean.
    Encyclopedia of American Indian contributions to the world : 15,000 years
    of inventions and innovations / Emory Dean Keoke and Kay Marie Porterfield.
        p. cm.
    Includes bibliographical references and index.
    ISBN 0-8160-4052-4 (hardcover)
        1. Indians—Encyclopedias. 2. Inventions—Encyclopedias.
    3. Technological innovations—Encyclopedias. I. Porterfield, Kay Marie.
    II. Title.

    E54.5 .K46 2001
    970'.00497'003—dc21                                              00-049034

Facts On File books are available at special discounts when purchased in bulk quantities for businesses, associations, institutions or sales promotions. Please call our Special Sales Department in New York at (212) 967-8800 or (800) 322-8755.

You can find Facts On File on the World Wide Web at http://www.factsonfile.com

Text design by Joan M. Toro
Cover design by Cathy Rincon
Maps by Dale Williams

Printed in the United States of America

VB FOF 10 9 8 7 6 5 4 3 2

This book is printed on acid-free paper.

For my uncle Francis X. Hairy Chin, for starting me on this project;
for my grandson Jason Keoke, whom I hope will have a better chance
to learn about American Indians than I did; and for Glen Yellow Bird,
a man who always called me brother and whom I respected tremendously.

—EDK

For Hannah Marie White Elk and for Ward E. Porterfield,
who first taught me the difference between corn and beans.

—KMP

# Contents

# PREFACE

What follows is a collection of contributions American Indian peoples have made to the world. The word *contribution* is defined in *The American Heritage College Dictionary, Second Edition* as "to give to the common fund or common purpose." American Indians, from the Arctic Circle to the tip of South America, donated many gifts to the world's common fund of knowledge in the areas of agriculture, science and technology, medicine, transportation, architecture, psychology, military strategy, government, and language. These contributions take the form of inventions, processes, philosophies, and political or social systems. For the most part until the late 19th century, they remained unrecognized outside of the disciplines of anthropology and archaeology. People throughout the world enjoyed the fruits of indigenous American invention—such as rubberized raincoats, POP-CORN, HAMMOCKS, and the drug QUININE—without being aware of their origin. At the same time textbooks, novels, and later movies and television portrayed the first people of the Americas as primitives who were incapable of complex ideas or inventions.

Immediately after initial contact, Europeans from Christopher Columbus on wrote detailed descriptions about the accomplishments of the American Indians they encountered. Often they judged these accomplishments as being superior to anything in the Old World. Nevertheless, as a general rule, within 20 years after contact, conquistadores and colonists alike denied that the American Indians, whom they had begun to call *"savages,"* were responsible for these discoveries. They were so certain that Indian people were incapable of discovering the technology they had encountered that, soon after the voyages of Columbus, they began spreading rumors throughout Europe that the Americas were the site of settlement for a lost colony of Christians or a lost tribe of Israelites. This rumor persisted in popular culture until well into the 20th century.

Later colonists and missionaries in the North American Southeast speculated that the Cherokee, whose way of life they deemed "civilized," spoke a version of Hebrew or Phoenician, "proving" that these people were not Indian. Early European settlers in what would become Virginia theorized that a Welsh prince, Madoc, had wandered to the New World in the 13th century to give the Indian people the technology they possessed. When non-Indians viewed the mounds at Cahokia, an enormous city built by Mississippian people that had flourished in about A.D. 1100 near the site of modern St. Louis, they refused to believe that Indian people had created the city. Anthropologists determined that it had been built by an early vanished race of people that had been vastly superior and completely unrelated to the Indians living at the time of contact.

By the 1800s American history textbooks denied that Indians possessed even a modicum of intelligence or knowledge. This extreme change of attitude about American Indian intellect was not coincidental. Nor was it based on the reality of American Indian intellectual accomplishments, which included an Andean road system more extensive than that of Rome and sophisticated Mesoamerican and North American surgical techniques unheard of in the Old World. Rather, it was grounded in a real and immediate need to justify conquest with a stroke of the pen. "The belief that 'civilization' and 'Indianness' were inherently incompatible, and the failure of Europeans to understand the nature of tribal society, meant that there was little possibility of peaceful coexistence and that the image of the Indian as 'savage,' was used to rationalize conquest and conversion," wrote Colin G. Calloway in *Crown and Calumet: British-Indian Relations, 1783–1815.*

A similar process had taken place in Mesoamerica and in South America in earlier centuries as Spanish conquistadores burned libraries and priests banned even agricultural products such as AVOCADOS and the seed crop AMARANTH because they believed these kept the Indians they sought to convert tied to their "savage ignorance." In order to justify the theft of American Indian ideas, inventions, and land, it was necessary to portray them as less intelligent and less human than Europeans. Use of the terms *savages* and *heathens* were first steps in dehumanizing American Indians; eventually they were equated with animals.

In 1861 American author Mark Twain rode the overland stage across what is now Utah and Nevada. During his journey he encountered what are sometimes referred to as "Digger" Indians—the Shoshone. As a reporter, he recorded his perceptions that the Shoshone were ". . . the wretchedest type of mankind I have ever seen up to this writing." His offhanded condemnation, along with those of countless other authors, led to a stereotype believed by generations of Americans— that the Shoshone and all Indian people had no redeeming social value. This impression is far from the truth. The Shoshone—who invented an effective form of oral CONTRACEPTION years before western medicine came up with one in the mid-20th century—were also masters of ORTHOPEDIC TECHNIQUES. They used ASEPSIS, the practice of creating a sterile field during SURGERY, hundreds of years before this was done in western medicine.

In 1923 *Halleck's History of Our Country,* a popular elementary school text, taught a generation of children, ". . . the Indian was ignorant, and no great teacher had come to him. He had few tools, and most of these were of wood or stone. We could scarcely build a hen coop to-day with such tools."

By the 1980s and 1990s, some school textbooks still showed only a little improvement over Halleck. According to the 1981 edition of *A History of the United States* published by Ginn and Company that was still approved for use in Washington State schools in 1993, "North of Mexico, most of the people lived in wandering tribes and led a simple life. North American Indians were mainly hunters and gatherers of wild food. An exceptional few—in Arizona and New Mexico— settled in one place and became farmers."

In truth, two of the four places where AGRICULTURE independently originated in the world are located in the Americas. After contact the introduction of crops that American Indians had cultivated for hundreds of years provided a nutritional boost that caused a population boom in Europe, which had not fully recovered from the bubonic plague two centuries before. Today POTATOES, CORN, and MANIOC have become a major source of nutrition for people around the globe.

The textbook *World Cultures: A Global Mosaic* published by Prentice Hall in 1993 implies that the WHEEL was invented only one time with the words, "Gradually, the knowledge of the wheel spread around the globe, changing cultures everywhere." No mention is made that the Maya crafted wheeled figurines and that, given the absence of suitable draft animals in the Americas, wheeled vehicles as a mode of transportation would have been inappropriate technology.

Although most textbooks no longer begin their discussion of the history of the Americas in 1492 when Christopher Columbus landed on the island of Hispaniola, some contain only a few pages on precontact American Indian history. The 1991 edition of *A More Perfect Union* published by Houghton Mifflin devotes one page to American history before European exploration. *The United States: Past to Present* published by D.C. Heath and Company in 1989 does not cover precontact history at all.

Authors writing for adults about American Indians before European contact are not immune from perpetuating misconceptions. Erich Van Daniken's popular books, beginning with *Chariots of the Gods* in the 1970s and continuing with *The Arrival of the Gods: Revealing the Alien Landing Sites of Nazca* published in 1998, continue to perpetuate the stereotype that the indigenous people of the Americas were not capable of the engineering feats they accomplished.

Other authors, including Jack Weatherford in *Indian Givers: How the Indians of the Americas Transformed the World,* assert that, along with agricultural, medical, and technological gifts, American Indians presented Europeans with syphilis. He writes: "The accumulation of archaeological and medical evidence has slowly led to the conclusion that in addition to all the medicines that America gave the world, it contributed at least one dreaded disease—syphilis. The Old World had no knowledge of syphilis prior to 1493. . . ."

The facts contradict this conclusion. European accounts from the 1400s document that this sexually transmitted disease was present in Europe at least two decades before Columbus landed in the Americas. (In 1493 Spaniards were already calling it the "French malady.")

Throughout history those who hold power have used it to create definitions that marginalize people who do not hold power. At the same time that they have made use of the technologies and resources of those they dominate, they have minimized them or failed to acknowledge their originators. Sophie Coe, author of *America's First Cuisines,* describes how American Indians failed to receive credit for animal and plant domestication. "The fact that many millennia of patient observations, considered economic decisions, and hard physical work were necessary to assemble the New World crop inventory was brushed aside."

A case can be made that contact with American Indians actually served as one of the catalysts for the Scientific Revolution in Europe. In 1571 King Philip II of Spain commissioned physician Francisco Hernandez to document the medicinal seeds, plants, and herbs that the Aztec used. Spanish physicians exploring indigenous American cures soon published three textbooks based on this information including one on surgery. The study of American Indian medicines and plants that American Indians cultivated for food sparked an unprecedented burst of intellectual curiosity in Europe. The flow of information from Meso- and South America slowed dramatically when a 1577 Spanish decree ordered the destruction of not only American Indian books but also those written by Spaniards about American Indians. However, once the door to intellectual inquiry had been opened, it could not be completely shut.

Although more than 200 of the plants that American Indians used as remedies became part of the *U.S. Pharmacopoeia,* an official listing of all effective medicines, the originators of these remedies often remained unacknowledged. When precontact indigenous origins of medical treatments were mentioned, American Indians were often said to have stumbled on these cures by accident, because they did not use the European scientific method. (Empiricism, sometimes called true science, did not begin in Europe until the time of Francis Bacon in the late 1500s—nearly a century after contact between Americans and Europeans.)

Today more than 120 drugs that are prescribed by physicians were first made from plant extracts, and 75 percent of these were derived from examining plants used in traditional indigenous medicine. Seventy-five percent of the varieties of food grown today are indigenous to North, Meso-, and South America—most of them cultivated by American Indians hundreds of years before European contact.

Most of the entries contained in this encyclopedia of inventions, processes, and ideas came into being in the Americas long before Columbus set foot on Hispaniola in 1492. In instances such as rubber, popcorn, quinine, and hammocks, American Indian contributions became part of everyday life in very tangible ways worldwide. Other contributions were less tangible, but equally important, such as the influence of the Iroquois on the U.S. Constitution and on Frederich Engles's theories of communism.

The transmission of both types of contributions took place in different ways. Some medicines, crops, and techniques, such as the process for making CHOCOLATE, were taken back to Europe by the Spanish conquistadores and explorers. From there, they traveled to European colonies in Africa and Asia. As the conquistadores took over American empires, American Indians lost their land and often their lives, leading some historians to conclude that many of these contributions were stolen goods. Many other contributions were gifts. In the initial stages of contact with European colonists throughout the Americas, Indian peoples often shared their knowledge of AGRICULTURE, home construction, and MEDICINE freely when the newcomers struggled to survive in the unfamiliar environment. This teaching and sharing of information was preserved in diaries and other records of the conquistadores, missionaries, and colonists.

In other instances, the diffusion is undeniable but difficult to clearly trace, since it occurred in subtle ways over time. After 1492 the distinct separation between Europe and the Americas ended forever with the entry of Old World explorers into the New World. Europeans living on the edge of American cultural frontiers took on many of the ways of indigenous people, just as indigenous people living in proximity to Europeans adapted many of their ways. This blending of ideas, technology, dress, food, and language is a primary reason for the unique character of modern nations in the Western Hemisphere today. Certain aspects of indigenous American culture, such as the concepts of democratic freedom contained in the IROQUOIS CONSTITUTION, spread throughout the world.

To be included in the *Encyclopedia of American Indian Contributions to the World,* contributions needed to have (1) originated in North, Meso-, or South America, (2) been used by Indian people, and (3) been in use for some time. A great many were adopted in some way by other cultures. For example corn, which is indigenous to the Western Hemisphere, was cultivated by American Indians, who selectively bred it, developing varieties that have come to be used as a global food source in modern times. Today corn is not only a significant part of world cuisine, but it is used in many products and is a major part of the world economy.

While the great majority of contributions discussed can clearly be shown to be first invented or first used by American Indians, some entries in this book cover things that were invented independently in more than one part of the world, such as the wheel, COTTON cloth, and terraced FARMING. In describing these inventions or processes, the book discusses the unique features of the American Indian version and attempts to compare it to its counterpart. These entries are included for two reasons. First, in the cross-fertilization of ideas that began in 1492, the independent inventions of American Indians became part of the common fund of information humans possessed. This fund was drawn upon by scientists and inventors throughout the world as a source of inspiration and to create new inventions and technologies by synthesizing the ones that have gone before. Vitamin C stands as an example of this process (see SCURVY CURE).

Second, to continue to exclude independent inventions in this encyclopedia would perpetuate the historic unwillingness of non-Indian cultures to share credit for the generation of new ideas and their practical application. The notion that indigenous inventions and technologies must predate the independent creation of similar concepts by other cultures in order to be worthy of notice is flawed. To presume that inventions, technologies, and ways of looking at the world have value only if they have provided significant and obvious benefit to non-Indian cultures is an ethnocentric stance. The idea that something is worth consideration only to the extent that it has been or can be exploited is the very thinking that underlies colonialism. For these reasons this book includes some entries that were unique to American Indians but did not cross cultural boundaries.

The process of cultural and scientific borrowing from American Indian society is not limited to past centuries. During the second half of the 20th century, growing consciousness about nonrenewable natural resources and other environmental concerns spurred a move toward sustainable lifestyles. Western scientists started to reexamine American Indian ideas and inventions that had been ignored in the past. Once termed primitive practices, many of these have been reclassified as "appropriate technology" and are being given serious consideration as solutions to world problems, including hunger, environmental destruction, and the energy crisis.

Ideas such as ECOLOGY, passive solar heating, XERISCAPING, and raised-bed agriculture are "new" only in the sense that they have been borrowed from the vast storehouse of American Indian wisdom only recently. This trend is growing. In the hope of finding cures for cancers and other life-threatening illnesses, medical researchers are currently investigating the botanical remedies that American Indians used for centuries before contact. Agronomists have begun to study previously overlooked crops once grown by indigenous peoples of the Americas in order to solve the problem of world hunger.

Whenever possible, this book provides the time period in which the subject matter of the entry originated. In the last decade of the 20th century, scientific advances in archaeological dating pushed back dates that were accepted for many years. The authors of this book strove in their research to use the most recent dates. Because the vast majority of the contributions included arose in prehistory, these dates can only be approximations. Most come from the work of archaeologists and are, at best, educated guesses that are revised as dating techniques become more sophisticated; for this reason, some of the dates may be obsolete by the time this book is published. In many cases, little is known about the origin of an indigenous technique, idea, or invention, except that it was observed and reported on by the first Europeans in contact with a particular group. Contact occurred starting in 1492. In the case of many groups of Inuit people, first contact occurred as late as the mid-1800s—or even more recently. It is still occurring with tribes in the Amazon Basin of South America today. Thus, although the authors recognize its ambiguity, the only date possible for many entries is "precontact."

Each group of indigenous people in the Americas was highly skilled at adapting to their unique environment in sophisticated ways. Tribes shared not only trade goods but also technologies with each other, so that discovering who came up with the idea first becomes an impossible task. At contact there were an estimated 800 distinct groups of Indians in the Americas. The authors have done their best to credit the tribes or groups of tribes involved in a particular contribution, but undoubtedly many have been missed. Space constraints prevent a comprehensive listing of all tribes connected with each entry. Instead, the authors have tried to be representative, sometimes choosing the short cut of classifying a number of tribes into geographical regions or culture areas. Omissions could not be helped.

At its core, the idea of identifying a single individual or tribe of American Indians with a specific process, technology, or invention is grounded in the Western way of looking at the world. Non-Indians often focus on attributing inventions, intellectual and otherwise, to a particular person. They consider the invention to be the intellectual property of the person who invented it. This property has come to be protected by patent, and the rights to use it are sold. American Indian cultures on the whole were, and continue to be, less concerned with individual accomplishment. Among American Indians, an invention, intellectual or otherwise, was shared by all. Although the invention was valued, the inventor did not seek credit.

At times deciding how to organize the entries was a daunting task, especially for the medical entries. For example, American Indians devised a number of medical treatments that were far more advanced than those of Europeans at the time. Many of these involved botanical remedies. Therefore, entries were labeled by the condition being treated, as in the case of EARACHE TREATMENTS. Every tribe in the Americas had remedies for common medical conditions. To note them all was far beyond the scope of this book. Thus, in each entry only one or two tribes were cited. Readers who desire further information are urged to pursue the ethnobotanical sources listed at the end of these entries.

When treatments were used for more than one condition, the entry was labeled by the action of the medicine; ANTIBIOTIC MEDICATIONS is one such entry. In instances in which the treatment became a significant part of historical or current non-Indian medical practice and gained name recognition, such as JALAP, quinine, and WITCH HAZEL, the medicine is listed by its name.

Whenever possible, technical words have been avoided. Entries on medical and scientific contributions occasionally demanded technical terminology. Whenever these words were used, attempts were made to define them in lay terms within that entry. The glossary also defines terms that appear in several entries.

The authors apologize in advance for anything in this book that might offend any tribe or band of American Indians. Apologies are also offered for any anglicized spellings or misinterpretations of any words or tribes. There has been no intention to speak on behalf of any tribe or to pretend expertise in the ways of all indigenous people. This is a history book—not a cultural or spiritual one—the aim of which is to show the world that prior to contact with Europeans, indigenous people of the Americas were highly civilized and extremely intelligent.

In the course of researching and writing this book, the authors have tried to be as comprehensive as possible. The biggest difficulty in the work has come from the sheer volume of contributions American Indians have made. Although not deeply buried, the information is scattered throughout hundreds of works, many of which mention only one or two contributions in passing. In the course of carrying out the detective work, an overwhelming number of leads to academic sources was encountered. While striving to be as thorough as possible, it was necessary to limit research in order to complete the project in a timely manner.

To compile a definitive catalog of American Indian contributions would take more than one lifetime to accomplish. At best, only broad brush strokes can be used to paint this picture. Each entry stands on its own, while leading to others. The authors hope that taken together the collection as a whole provides a glimpse of the broader panorama of little-known information about the rich inventiveness of the indigenous peoples of the Americas.

# A to Z
# ENTRIES

# A

**abacus** (A.D. 900–1000) *Mesoamerican cultures*

An abacus is a portable calculating device using a frame with rods that are strung with beads. Aztec and Maya who lived in Mesoamerica performed mathematical calculations using an abacus made from maize kernels, instead of beads, threaded on strings. It provided a faster and more accurate way of adding and subtracting than relying on memory alone. This abacus, which was called a *nepohualtzitzin,* had three beads on the top deck and four beads on the bottom. Archaeologists have dated the presence of such counters at about A.D. 900 to 1000. The Aztec abacus, which was devised without any knowledge of the Chinese abacus (invented about 500 B.C.) required the same level of critical thinking and knowledge of mathematics to develop.

The Inca, whose empire was established in what is now Peru in about A.D. 1000, were also known to have a type of abacus. This consisted of a tray with compartments that were arranged in rows in which counters were moved in order to make calculations.

See also BASE 20 SYSTEM; QUIPUS; ZERO.

## Sources/Further Reading

Bankes, George. *Peru before Pizarro.* Oxford, Eng.: Phaidon Press Limited, 1977.

Fernandes, Luis. "The Abacus: the Art of Calculating with Beads." URL: http://www.ee.ryerson.ca:8080/~elf/abacus/intro.html. Updated on March 9, 1999.

Hildago, David Esparza. *Computo Azteca.* Mexico City: Diana, 1976.

Mason, J. Alden. *The Ancient Civilizations of Peru.* New York: Penguin Books, 1988.

Maya Numerals. URL: http://saxakali.com/historymam2.htm. Downloaded on August 28, 1999.

Murguia, Elena Romero. *Nepoualtaitain: Matematica Prehispanica.* Mexico City: UNAM, 1985.

**abstract art, American Indian influence on**
(ca. 1930–present) *North American, Mesoamerican, South American Andean cultures*

Abstract art consists of works that are not subject to the limits imposed by representation. The emphasis in abstract art is on form rather than subject matter. Some abstract designs have no recognizable subject matter. In the late 1930s and early 1940s, pre-Columbian and post-Columbian abstract art that is indigenous to the Americas served as inspiration for the modern American abstract art movement. This reversed the stance of early ethnographers who had termed American Indian art primitive, often because the works were executed on buildings, pottery vessels, clothing, and textiles, rather than on canvas or in marble as was done in the European tradition.

Modern ethnologists and art historians, reflecting on the major artistic contributions of American Indians from the Arctic Circle to South America, now view these indigenous abstractions as both powerful and sophisticated. The split depiction of animals made by artisans of the Tsimshian tribe living on the coast of what is now British Columbia is one example frequently cited. These works were collected and written about by anthropologist Franz Boas. Another example is the progressively abstracted depiction of birds and animals in Mesoamerican glyphic writing (see also WRITING SYSTEMS) and patterned textiles produced by the Aztec, whose civilization arose in Mesoamerica about A.D. 1100. The Maya, who also lived in Mesoamerica starting in about 1500 B.C., produced abstract textile designs, as did the Inca Empire that was established in what is now Peru in about A.D. 1000. (See also WEAVING TECHNIQUES.) The mounds built by the Adena and Hopewell cultures that occupied the Mississippi River Valley of what is now the United States from 1000 B.C. to A.D. 200 and 300 B.C. to A.D. 1250, respectively, are huge abstractions. The Nazca Lines, huge designs made in the earth of the Ingenio Valley in what is now Peru, are also examples of abstraction on an enormous scale. The Nazca culture flourished starting about 600 B.C.

For American Indian artists, as for modern abstract artists, even the simplest designs, such as stripes or a series of triangles, had meaning. Their designs are what modern art critics call "visual syntax"—literally, a language of design. "The fundamental unity of the metaphors that inform the arts of all these non-Western cultures—The 'archaic,' as well as the 'tribal'—essentially manifests itself in the shaping of symbols, monuments, ritual paraphernalia, and semantic signs that were widely absorbed by the societies," writes art theorist Cesar Paternosto in *The Stone and the Thread: Andean Roots of Abstract Art.*

Non-Indian artists first turned their attention to these works by Indians in the early 1930s. Art historian and abstract painter Barnett Newman believed so much in the power of these abstract metaphors that by 1945, in an article he wrote comparing two artists who were painting in Paris, he said, "They have roots deep in the tradition of our American aborigines" and added that "only by this kind of contribution is there any hope for the possible development of a truly American art." Adolph Gottlieb, who painted a series of pictographs based on artistic concepts that he learned from textiles and paintings made by indigenous people living along the Pacific Northwest Coast, cosigned a letter to the *New York Times* in 1943. Along with Newman and fellow artist Mark Rothko, he publicly claimed "spiritual kinship with primitives and archaic art." In 1946 Newman organized an exhibit of paintings by Indians of the Northwest at a prestigious art gallery. Many of these paintings had come from the American Museum of Natural History. Newman said that the move had declassified the pieces as scientific specimens and reclassified them as art.

Sculptor John Storrs, who made towerlike structures of stone and metal, based his designs on some of the patterns of the Navajo (Dineh) rugs that he collected. Sculptors Henry Moore and Josef Albers incorporated indigenous Mesoamerican designs into their works. Painter Richard Pousette-Dart, who lived in New York City in the 1940s, wrote that he had an inner vibration comparable to American Indian art and acknowledged that prehistoric American cave painting and rock art had inspired his own works. Painter Jackson Pollock, who grew up in the West, was knowledgeable about American Indian art and borrowed themes from indigenous artifacts during the early part of his career.

See also ARCHITECTS; BOOKS; EMBROIDERY; POTTERY; STONEMASONRY TECHNIQUES.

### Sources/Further Reading

Boas, Franz. *Primitive Art.* 1927. Reprint. New York: Dover Publications, 1955.

Dockstader, Fredrick J. *Indian Art in South America.* Greenwich, Conn.: New York Graphic Society, 1967.

Goldwater, Robert. *Primitivism in Modern Art.* Cambridge, Mass.: Harvard University Press, 1986.

Kubler, George. *Esthetic Recognition of Ancient Amerindian Art.* New Haven, Conn.: Yale University Press, 1991.

Levinson, Jay A., ed. *Circa 1492: Art in the Age of Exploration.* Washington, D.C.: National Gallery of Art and Yale University Press, 1991.

Newman, Barnett. *Barnett Newman: Selected Writings and Interviews.* New York: Alfred A. Knopf, 1990.

Paternosto, Cesar. *The Stone and the Thread.* Austin: University of Texas Press, 1996.

### achiote  (annatto, bixin, *Bixa orellana*)  (precontact)
*Mesoamerican, South American Tropical Forest cultures*

The achiote *Bixa orellana* is a shrub that is indigenous to the tropics of America. Its seed covering, when ground, was used by the ancient Aztec to flavor CHOCOLATE drinks and to dye clothing. The Aztec civilization arose in Mesoamerica about A.D. 1100. Bixin, the bright red, oily DYE contained in the husks, was used as body paint by Indians in South America's Amazon Basin and served double duty as an INSECT REPELLENT. It was used to color pottery as well. The dye, also known as annatto, is employed today as food coloring, primarily for butter, margarine and cheeses, and as a seasoning.

### Sources/Further Reading

Coe, Sophie. *America's First Cuisines.* Austin: University of Texas Press, 1994.

R.C.I. International. "Productos Organikum S.A." URL: http://www.foodcolors.com/achiote.html. Posted 1998.

### acid etching  See ETCHING, ACID.

### acoustics  (precontact)  *South American Andean cultures*

The science of sound is known as acoustics. Precursors of the Inca were well versed in acoustics, as demonstrated by their production of POTTERY *silvatos* (whistles). (The Inca established an empire in what is now Peru in about A.D. 1000.) These *silvatos* were shaped like small human figurines and were hollow with holes in front and in the back. A hole in the top of the head served as the blowhole for the whistle. These whistles were similar in tone and sound to ocarinas. (See also MUSICAL INSTRUMENTS.)

Unlike an ocarina, each *silvato* produced a distinct harmonic sound that was rich in tone. Upon examining a broken *silvato,* archaeologists found the source of the harmonic tone. Inside were two spherically configured, partially enclosed resonance compartments, each connected to a sound hole. When the whistle was blown, the air exiting the sound holes stimulated vibrations from the resonance compartments. This overall effect produced a fuller tone than that of whistles without this ingenious feature. Pino Turolla, author of *Beyond the Andes: My Search for the Origins of Pre-Inca Civilization,* stated about the *silvatos,* "What incredible technical mastery these people had; their expertise embraced even acoustics."

**Sources/Further Reading**
Benson, Elizabeth P. *The Maya World.* New York: Thomas Y. Crowell Company, 1967.
Turolla, Pino. *Beyond the Andes: My Search for the Origins of Pre-Inca Civilization.* New York: Harper & Row Publishers, 1970.

**adobe** (ca. 3000 B.C.) *South American Andean, Mesoamerican, North American Southwest cultures*

A mixture of clay and water called adobe was one of the primary building materials used by American Indians of pre-Inca Peru (see also PYRAMIDS), Mesoamerica, and the North American Southwest of what is now the United States. Applied wet as plaster or mortar, or mixed with plant fiber and dried into bricks, adobe enabled builders to construct vast APARTMENT COMPLEXES, referred to as *pueblos* by the Spaniards, throughout these regions.

The Moche, who lived on the northwest coast of what is now Peru from about 200 B.C. to A.D. 600, built enormous temples using adobe bricks. One of the most impressive examples of Moche adobe construction is the larger of two pyramids built at Moche near the modern city of Trujillo. The largest of these pyramids, the Huaca del Sol, consists of about 130 million bricks. These bricks are inscribed with what archaeologists believe are the names of individual workers or teams of workers. Archaeologists have found a number of smaller adobe pyramids as well as adobe forts scattered throughout what is now Peru. Often these structures were decorated with clay relief and painted with murals.

The Hohokam, whose culture arose in what is now Arizona in about 300 B.C. and who are the ancestors of the Akimel O'odham (Pima) and Tohono O'odham (Papago), built massive mud-walled structures that Spanish conquistadores compared to castles. One of the foremost examples of Hohokam architecture, Casa Grande, is located outside of what is now Phoenix, Arizona. Thought to have been built about A.D. 1300, Casa Grande is four stories tall, and at least 1,500 cubic yards of soil was used in its construction. It has adobe walls that are more than four feet thick at their base, tapering to about two feet at the top, with no reinforcing beams. Casa Grande's ceilings were framed with more than 600 juniper, pine, and fir beams cut from mountains more than 50 miles away. The Hohokam often used I-beam construction for such framing. Archaeologists do not know the exact purpose of Casa Grande and other huge Hohokam buildings but believe that they were designed to protect against attack. Window openings in upper levels of Casa Grande are aligned to the position of the sun at the time of equinox and at solstices, so they might have served as OBSERVATORIES as well.

Initially archaeologists speculated that Casa Grande's thick walls were built in stages, with mud packed into wattle and daub forms made from woven branches plastered with mud, and then compacted by applying pressure. However, recent study has shown that Hohokam builders mixed mud to the proper consistency in large holes they dug in the ground, then piled it up, or "puddled" it, by hand in 26-inch courses. Each layer was allowed to dry before the next one was laid. The process was repeated layer by layer. After nearly 700 years, the walls of Casa Grande are weathered, but they still stand. Their durability can be credited to the fact that the original ARCHITECTS selected caliche for the adobe. Caliche is a soil layer in which earth particles have been bonded by carbonates of calcium or magnesium, which cause the adobe to harden, almost like cement, as it dries. (See also CONCRETE.)

In addition to the Hohokam, the Anasazi—who lived in the Southwest of what is now the United States from 350 B.C. to about A.D. 1450, and who are the forerunners of modern Pueblo people—relied on adobe for the construction of their homes. In about A.D. 700 they traded the pit houses that they had previously occupied for above-ground cubicle homes, built so that adjoining units shared walls. As their population grew, the Anasazi added stories to their dwellings. Families slept in the upper front units, where they would be warmed at night by a form of passive solar heating provided by the adobe. Heat absorbed from the sun by the adobe walls throughout the day radiated into the rooms at night. Food was stored in the cooler interior rooms.

The most skilled Anasazi adobe builders lived in the pueblos of Chaco Canyon in what is now New Mexico. According to the National Park Service, the agency in charge of the site, buildings in the Chaco community were originally constructed in A.D. 700 from a central design that was added onto later. That, combined with the construction techniques used to build the structures, has led archaeologists to believe that the Anasazi had architects whose job it was to plan the structures before they were built.

In Pueblo Bonito, the main complex in Chaco Canyon, an average room required about 50,000 tons of stone and 16,500 tons of clay for its construction. The adobe walls were built on top of mortar- and rubble-filled trenches in order to keep the walls from settling. The walls themselves, which tapered from three feet at the base to one foot at the top, were made of rough, flat stones mortared with adobe. This core was covered with flat pieces of rock called *ashlar.* A layer of adobe was plastered over this. When the building was expanded, Anasazi builders bonded new walls to old ones by interlocking the new stones with those in the existing walls. Some of the walls in the Chaco complex had a rubble and adobe core and were faced with stone.

The Anasazi builders who lived in areas along the Rio Grande River often could not find enough suitable rock for construction of their homes. There was, however, an abundance of water. Instead of using adobe as plaster over a rock core, they made fat adobe bricks called "turtle backs," slapping and shaping them, then setting them atop each other and smoothing over the surface with a finish coat of adobe.

Often historians mistakenly credit the Spaniards with teaching the Pueblo people how to make uniform adobe bricks that are molded in forms. (The Spanish learned adobe construction from the Moors, who migrated from Africa to Spain in A.D. 711.) Two archaeological sites that have been dated to

Casa Grande, built by the Hohokam in about A.D. 1300, is one of the largest prehistoric structures constructed in North America. Made of adobe formed from caliche (soil that is high in calcium or magnesium), the ruins at Casa Grande National Monument are protected today by a canopy to preserve them. *(Photographer: Grant U.S. Department of the Interior. National Park Service)*

about A.D. 1300 show evidence that precontact American Indians poured wet mud into stone or wooden forms and allowed it to sun-dry. These sites are the pre-Hopi site of Homol'ovi and the Fourmile Ruin near Taylor, Arizona.

The most famous of the adobe pueblos still occupied today is Taos Pueblo in New Mexico, which was started before the 1500s. The walls of the two clusters of units that make up this pueblo are two feet thick at the bottom tapering to about a foot thick at the top. Each spring the pueblo's residents replaster the exterior walls of their homes with a new coat of adobe. Adobe is also used as a roofing material at Taos and in other pueblos. Cedar beams, whose ends protrude through the walls, support the roofs. Branches are placed on these log beams, or *vigas,* and are next covered with grass. A layer of adobe plaster serves as a sealant.

Today adobe architecture has come to be known as one component of the Santa Fe style and is popular throughout the Southwest. However, modern builders, who must meet mandated building codes, find it more expensive to build with adobe than to construct frame houses and plaster the exteriors with adobe to make them look authentic.

See also CARPENTRY TECHNIQUES; INSULATION, HOME.

**Sources/Further Reading**

Folsom, Franklin and Mary Elting Folsom. *America's Ancient Treasures,* 4th ed. Albuquerque: University of New Mexico Press, 1993.

Kidwell, Clara S. and Peter Nabokov. "Directions in Native American Science and Technology." In *Studying Native America: Problems and Prospects.* Edited by Russell Thornton. Madison: The University of Wisconsin Press, 1998.

Mason, J. Alden. *The Ancient Civilizations of Peru.* New York: Penguin Books, 1988.

Nabokov, Peter and Robert Easton. *Native American Architecture*. New York: Oxford University Press, 1989.

Noble, David Grant. *Ancient Ruins of the Southwest: An Archaeological Guide*. Flagstaff, Ariz.: Northland Publishing, 1991.

Preston, Julia. *Re-Engineering Tequila, the Other Cognac*. New York Times News Service. URL: http://www.latinolink. com/biz/teq0103.html. Posted 1995.

Smith, Michael E. *The Peoples of America: The Aztecs*. Cambridge, Mass.: Blackwell, 1996.

## agave  (century plant, *Agave*)  (precontact)

*Mesoamerican, North American Southwest cultures*

Agave (*G. Agave*), a succulent plant that is also known as century plant, is native throughout the arid regions of what is now Mexico and the southwestern United States. The best known species of agave is the American aloe that is also called aloe vera. The agave plant consists of a thick cluster of gray-green leaves that are 10 to 18 inches long and arranged in a rosette shape. The large, thick, fleshy leaves of agaves soak up moisture, storing it for the plant's use during dry periods. A tall stalk grows from the center of the leaves. It is topped with clusters of yellow flowers during the summer months. These flowers distinguish the plant from the YUCCA, which has white flowers.

American Indians from a number of tribes in the region used agave root and leaf pulp for DETERGENT. The Aztec boiled sap from agave to make syrup and sugar. They also fermented the syrup into a drink called *pulque*. In addition, the Aztec used fermentation to make vinegar from agave. In the 1600s the Spaniard Francisco Hernandez listed indigenous uses for agave that included roofing tiles, plates and dishes, and fences for fields when planted around the perimeter. The thorns were used for nails and tacks.

Medicinally, the sap from the aloe heart, an ANTIBIOTIC, served as a laxative and as a treatment for chapped lips, burns, rashes, and sunburns. Mesoamerican cultures used fiber from agave or maguey leaves to make a PAPER that resembled papyrus. Fiber from a species of agave called henequen was also used to make twine, which was sometimes used for sandals and was also woven into coarse cloth. Indigenous people of the desert Southwest used the tops of the stalks of various types of agave to make black body paint.

The two most common uses for agave today are the production of aloe vera, the juice of the American aloe, which is still used as a skin soother; and the manufacture of mescal and tequila. Tequila is made in Mexico from a species of the plant called the blue agave, which grows in the region of Jalisco. The hearts, which take 10 years to mature, are harvested from the plants with machetes. After the spines are cut off, the hearts are steamed and ground. As they ferment, they are distilled twice, which gives tequila its high alcohol content.

See also DISTILLATION; PUBLIC DRUNKENNESS LAWS.

### Sources/Further Reading

*Arizona Cactus and Succulent Research*. URL: http://www. primenet.com/~azcactus/medicine.htm. Downloaded on January 13, 1999.

Coe, Sophie. *America's First Cuisines*. Austin: University of Texas Press, 1994.

## agricultural experiments  See ZONED BIODIVERSITY.

## agriculture  (8000–7000 B.C.)  *Mesoamerican; South American Andean and Tropical Forest; North American Southeast, Northeast, and Southwest cultures*

Agriculture, the science of cultivating the soil to produce crops, arose independently in four areas of the world, two of them in the Western Hemisphere. In Meso- and South America, farming based on CORN, SQUASH, and BEANS began in the flood plain of the Tehuacan Valley of what is now Mexico in about 8000–7000 B.C. At about the same time, MANIOC and SWEET POTATO cultivation arose in the tropical forests of what is now Brazil and Guatemala, and POTATO-based farming developed in mountainous highlands of the Andes in what is now Peru.

Indigenous people living in the Eastern Woodlands of what is now the United States independently began cultivating chenopod (goosefoot), marsh elder (sumpweed), squash, and SUNFLOWERS. Erect knotweed, little barley, and maygrass—all seed-producing grasses—were also domesticated. All of these plants grew along river flood plains. By 2000 B.C. Native Americans in eastern North America were planting and harvesting at least four of these plants and were well on the way to depending on agriculture, rather than gathering, for their livelihood. Corn seeds were brought into the area from what is now Mexico about A.D. 200, but maize (another word for corn) remained a minor crop for eastern farmers until about A.D. 800. Recent discoveries about North American agriculture are exciting to researchers because they provide the clearest record available of agricultural origins anywhere in the world.

The transition from hunting and gathering food to growing crops was a complex one, taking place over thousands of years. It required knowledge of plants, growing cycles, and seed selection as well as understanding how temperature, moisture, and soil composition affect plants. Archaeologists believe that American Indian women, whose responsibility it had been to gather plant foods, brought about this revolutionary transformation. They were the ones who made the first agricultural discoveries and began the centuries-long process of domesticating crops.

Agriculture was an important development, not only because it supplied steady nutrients to keep people alive, but also because it allowed people to invest less time in obtaining food than hunting and gathering required. The new ability to remain in one place enabled settled villages to flourish and indigenous Americans eventually to develop political systems now called chiefdoms. Some chiefdoms evolved into complex political and social structures, as is the case with the Maya and Aztec Empires that arose in about 1500 B.C. and A.D. 1100, respectively, in Mesoamerica. The Inca Empire that arose about A.D. 1000 in what is now Peru is also an example of this. The Iroquois League, which originally consisted of the Mohawk, Oneida, Onondaga, Cayuga, and Seneca tribes (and later the Tuscarora) and was formed sometime between A.D. 1100 and A.D. 1450, could be established because of agriculture.

### MESO- AND SOUTH AMERICAN AGRICULTURE

Meso- and South American indigenous farmers first raised bottle GOURDS and PUMPKINS as early as 8000 B.C. They began selecting seeds, and by 5200 to 3400 B.C. their crops included corn; tepary (similar to lima), black, and common beans; CHILE peppers; AVOCADOS; AMARANTH; bottle gourds; and two kinds of squash. By 3400 to 2300 B.C. their agricultural productivity was high enough to create a surplus, enabling them to live in permanent villages within walking distance of the fields.

Between 2200 and 500 B.C., they began to cultivate sunflowers and manioc, and they began to grow lima beans, squash, TOBACCO, and COTTON between 1500 B.C. and 999 B.C. By about 1000 B.C. Mesoamerican Indians had become full-time farmers. Between 900 B.C. and A.D. 700 they became experts at irrigation and added runner beans, TOMATOES, PEANUTS, and GUAVA to their produce. At that time they also started cotton WEAVING, TURKEY BREEDING, and salt production.

The agricultural way of life spread to the Southwest of what is now the United States. Between 100 B.C. and A.D. 100, the Hohokam, who are believed to have lived on the northern frontier of Mesoamerican culture, began to cultivate the common, or kidney bean. As early as A.D. 630, western farmers may have sown tobacco seeds. Soon they wood be growing corn, which became a staple crop. By A.D. 900 squash cultivation had spread throughout the Southwest.

One of the most impressive aspects of Mesoamerican and South American agriculture is the sheer number of crops American Indian farmers produced—more than 300 of them. Before Columbus returned with New World foods, the European diet had consisted mainly of wheat, rye, oats, barley, cabbage, and dried peas. The Spanish and Portuguese, the first Europeans to view and taste the crops the Mesoamerican farmers grew, were astounded at the bounty and took seeds and plants back not only to Europe but also to their Asian and African colonies. Seventy-five percent of the varieties of food grown around the world today was first discovered by indigenous farmers in the Western Hemisphere thousands of years ago. Most of these discoveries were made by agriculturists in Meso- and South America, whose technology was so advanced that they established the equivalent of agricultural research test stations. (See also ZONED BIODIVERSITY.)

A few of the more familiar varieties of crops cultivated by Mesoamerican farmers were:

### Food

AMARANTH, ARROWROOT, AVOCADOS, BEANS of all varieties (except for the European broad bean, the mung bean and soy bean), BRAZIL NUTS, CACAO, CASHEWS, chayote, CHIA, CHILE peppers, CORN, GUAVA, HICKORY nuts, JERUSALEM ARTICHOKES, JICAMA, MANIOC, PAPAYAS, PEANUTS, PINEAPPLES, POTATOES, PUMPKINS, QUIONA, SAPODILLA, SQUASH, SWEET POTATOES, TOMATOES, VANILLA, YAMS

### Fiber

AGAVE, COTTON

### Flowers and shrubs

cantua, DAHLIAS, MARIGOLDS, MORNING GLORIES, NASTURTIUMS, POINSETTIAS, tiger flowers, tuberoses, YUCCA, ZINNIAS

### Stimulants

COCA, TOBACCO

### Containers and Utensils

bottle GOURDS, CALABASH

### Dyes

ACHIOTE, INDIGO

In addition to the above-listed plants, American-Indian farmers grew hundreds of others that are not well known today. They also cultivated medicinal herbs (see GARDENS, HERB).

### EASTERN WOODLAND AGRICULTURE

Between 3000 and 2000 B.C., American Indians living in the Eastern Woodlands developed different varieties of domesticated squash, including bottle gourds, which were used for utensils. In addition, they cultivated sunflowers, marsh elder, and chenopod. By 2000 B.C. American Indian agriculture was well established in areas known today as Tennessee, Arkansas, Illinois, Kentucky, Ohio, Missouri, and Alabama. In time, more seed-bearing grasses were domesticated, including erect knotweed, little barley, and maygrass, so that between 250 B.C. to A.D. 200 Hopewell villages centered on farming were established in river valleys where the soil was most fertile.

The crops grown—first by the Adena and then by the Hopewell people, who lived on small farmsteads and cultivated small plots—do not have high name recognition. For years archaeologists and ethnobotanists chose not to study them. Even though these crops are relatively unknown to most people today, they once provided a balanced diet for American Indian people. The plants that they chose to domesticate had high yields. Five people could harvest a 200-square-foot field, planted equally with marsh elder, or sumpweed, and chenopod in a little more than a week. A field such as this would have provided half the caloric requirements in the form of oil and starch for 10 people over a period of six months.

By about A.D. 800 North American Indian farmers began cultivating corn, or maize, in large fields, developing varieties that would mature in 90 days to fit the growing season where they lived. They grew corn from what is now northern Florida to Ontario and from the Atlantic coast to the Great Plains. American Indians living in what is now the United States and Canada also cultivated HICKORY nuts and chestnuts as well as several varieties of berries.

Despite the fact that farming was taking place throughout the East, European colonists often described the land as a vast, empty tract, a myth that has persisted in American history books. One reason for this was their claim to ownership of the land through eminent domain. This concept, a part of English common law, operated under the premise that if property or possessions were unoccupied or unused, they belonged to the Crown. In order for the rule of eminent domain to apply, it was necessary for British colonists to portray the New World as an uninhabited area where the soil was untilled. Although the population density in the New World was much lower than that of Europe, the notion that North America was a wild and empty place was far from the truth. By their own accounts, the explorers and colonists—English, French, and Spanish—encountered tilled fields rather than a vast wasteland.

As early as A.D. 1535, French explorer Jacques Cartier reported that Indians living near Montreal cultivated cornfields and that they stored surplus corn from their harvests. Four years later, when the Spaniard Hernando de Soto landed in what is now Florida, he found that the Indians in the Apalachee region (modern-day Tallahassee) were raising large quantities of corn, beans, pumpkins, and other vegetables—literally enough to feed an army. Near present-day Ocala, Florida, de Soto's men took a three-month supply of corn from the Apalachee fields. The Indian farmer's yields were so high because they were planting two crops and rotating their fields, practices respectively called DOUBLE CROPPING and MILPA. During their explorations, de Soto's army passed through fields of corn said to be 12 miles long.

Colonists near Roanoke, Virginia, reported in 1584 that the Indians were growing white corn and a number of varieties of beans. In 1607, when the Jamestown colony was established in Virginia, the Algonquian tribes along the coast and on the Piedmont, Interior Low, and Cumberland Plateaus were expert farmers. They cultivated beans, two types of pumpkins, and sunflowers, as well as two varieties of corn (flint and dent) in fields that varied from 20 acres to 200 acres in size. In 1614 the Chickahominy Indians in Virginia agreed to supply colonists with 1,000 bushels of corn each year as part of a treaty.

French explorer Samuel de Champlain reported in 1610 that Indians near Lakes Erie and Ontario grew corn both for their own consumption and as a trade commodity. The Huron, who depended on agriculture to meet 75 percent of their food needs, tried to grow enough each year to provide a two- to four-year surplus against crop failure. One technique that they developed to increase crop production included soaking corn seeds in water for several days to speed germination. They supplied corn for other tribes in the region. Given population estimates, modern ethnobotanists believe that the tribe had as many as 23,300 acres in cultivation. Reports from the time describe Huron cornfields so large that a member of a French exploration party became lost in them while walking from village to village. Mohawk agriculture was so sophisticated that they treated their seed

Indians throughout the Americas were expert farmers. This engraving of the village of Secotan in what is now Virginia depicts the variety of crops Eastern farmers of North America grew. Europeans such as Theodore De Bry, who made this engraving between 1590 and 1598, were impressed by corn, beans, sunflowers, squash, and other crops that were unknown in Europe.

by coating it with hellebore, a plant containing a substance that poisoned the crows.

Indians in North, Meso-, and South America demonstrated to the colonists which seeds to plant and where to plant them. They shared techniques such as using FERTILIZERS, natural INSECT REPELLENTS to control pests, INTERCROPPING and double cropping. Once the colonists learned to farm, they viewed the Indian fields as prime agricultural property, because this land was already cleared and proven to be fertile. By the early 1600s European colonial governments began writing treaties that took the land from the American Indian farmers and put it beneath the plows of the colonists.

See also AGRICULTURE, RAISED BED; COCHINEAL; CROP STORAGE; DYES; FARMING, TERRACED; FOOT PLOWS; GARDENS, BOTANICAL; IRRIGATION SYSTEMS; ORCHARDS; PASSION FRUIT; PAW PAWS; PECANS; POTTING SOIL; SAFFLOWER; SEED SELECTION; SETTLEMENT PATTERNS.

## Sources/Further Reading

Cowan, C. Wesley and Patty Jo Watson, eds. *Prehistoric Plant Husbandry in Eastern North America in The Origins of Agriculture, An International Perspective.* Washington D.C.: Smithsonian Institution Press, 1992.

Driver, Harold E. *Indians of North America.* Chicago: University of Chicago Press, 1969.

Hurt, R. Douglas. *American Indian Agriculture: Prehistory to Present.* Lawrence: University Press of Kansas, 1987.

Nabhan, Gary. *Enduring Seeds: Native American Agriculture and Wild Plant Conservation.* San Francisco: North Point Press, 1989.

Selig, Ruth and Bruce D. Smith. "Quiet Revolution: Origins of Agriculture in Eastern North America," in *Anthropology Explored: The Best of Smithsonian Anthro Notes* edited by Ruth Selig and Marilyn London. Washington, D.C.: Smithsonian Institution Press, 1998.

Smith, Bruce, D. *The Emergence of Agriculture.* New York: Scientific American Library, 1995.

———. *Rivers of Change, Essays on Early Agriculture in Eastern North America.* Washington, D.C.: Smithsonian Institution Press, 1993.

Trigger, Bruce G. *Case Studies in Anthropology: The Huron Farmers of the North.* New York: Holt Rinehart and Winston, 1969.

Weatherford, Jack. *Indian Givers: How the Indians of the Americas Transformed the World.* New York: Fawcett Columbine, 1988.

## agriculture, raised-bed (*chinampas*) (ca. 1500 B.C.)
*Mesoamerican cultures*

Growing plants in soil that has been enriched and heaped into raised garden plots is called raised bed agriculture. It is an effective way to increase crop yield. American Indians in South and Central America invented one of the most productive methods of farming ever to be devised when they began building artificial islands called *chinampas* in swamplands and lakes as early as 4,000 years ago. These plots were more sophisticated than the raised bed agriculture that became popular in the United States and Europe in the 20th century. First developed by the Maya, who lived in the lowlands of southern Yucatán Peninsula of what is now Mexico and in parts of Belize and Guatemala starting in about 1500 B.C., this system of farming revolutionized agricultural production in South America.

First, American Indian farmers partially drained swamps by digging long, straight canals, or ditches, and used gravity to clear them of as much water as possible. Next they piled soil and vegetation between the canals. When they had finished this, they blocked the outlets of the ditches and allowed them to fill with flood water during the rainy season. The *chinampas* were built four or five feet above the waterline to make sure that the roots of crops did not become waterlogged. Resembling artificial islands, these *chinampas* not only provided fertile and moist ground for crops but also were part of a highly efficient environmental system.

As the soil eroded from the raised beds, it collected in the canals, where it became a source of nutrients for aquatic plant growth. (See AQUACULTURE.) Each season before planting, indigenous farmers would harvest the water plants and add them to the raised beds' soil to enrich it. In addition, they also collected soil that had washed into the canals and replaced it on the beds, so that no potential plant nutrients were lost to erosion. When the soil of their raised fields begin to lose its fertility, they gathered more organic matter from the lake to use as FERTILIZER. In addition to providing an ideal environment for crops, chinampas plots created a haven for birds, while the canals served as an ideal environment for fish—yet another food source.

Perhaps the most impressive use of *chinampas* agriculture was that of the Aztec in the Valley of Mexico, who constructed their raised bed plots by transporting canoe-loads of earth from the mainland and depositing it in Lakes Chalco and Xochimilco, which were shallow. By A.D. 1200, large areas of both lakes were covered by these artificial islands. Trees planted on the *chinampas* sunk roots into the lake bed and stabilized the fields. Increased population in the city of Teotihuacán on the lakeshore spurred further expansion of the plots in the 14th and 15th centuries in order to provide food for the area's residents. These agricultural plots reached their height of sophistication in the 1500s, when they nearly covered the lakes. Farmers, who maintained the chinampas by adding more soil each year, built their homes on raised beds in the middle of the swamps and traveled to their fields in canoes. These farmsteads were grouped in small communities, and the buildings were set on artificial foundations. In addition to providing water for the crops, the wider canals doubled as local "shipping" lanes for rafts bearing trade goods for farmers living on the raised beds.

So sophisticated was Aztec agricultural technology that farmers converted a large bay of the saline Lake Texcoco into a freshwater lake by building a network of sluiced dikes and AQUEDUCTS fed by a freshwater spring. This area was then covered with *chinampas*. By 1519 the combination of *chinampas* agriculture, canals, floodwater *irrigation systems,* and terracing (see also FARMING, TERRACED) supported the densest population in the history of the culture area. Crops that the farmers grew on the *chinampas* met the nutritional needs of the 100,000 to 250,000 people who resided in the vicinity surrounding the lakes. Archaeologists estimate that the gross area of reclaimed swamps, excluding islands, eventually amounted to more than 46 square miles. The islands themselves equaled over 22,230 acres of productive soil.

Early European explorers reported that Aztec farmers set CORN seedbeds on the *chinampas,* later transplanting the seedlings to the fields. (See also TRANSPLANTING, AGRICULTURAL.) They marveled at the idea of transplants, a technique they had not seen before. Farmers often germinated the seeds on floating woven rush-and-cattail frames piled with earth. These nurseries were as long as 20 to 30 feet long and were towed from bed to bed for planting. The first Europeans saw these "floating gardens" and believed that the *chinampas* plots themselves floated on woven mats, a myth that persisted to the 1980s.

Most of the *chinampas* plots in Meso- and South America were abandoned after Spanish conquest. The conquistadores did not realize how productive this farming method was and did not maintain the plots or the canals. Late in the 16th century, after the Spanish Mexico City had replaced the Aztec city of Tenochtitlan, the lakes were drained as a form of flood control. Even so, indigenous farmers still tended their *chinampas* plots on the outskirts of the city. Today, the freshwater springs that fed Lake Xochimilco have been diverted to provide Mexico City's drinking water. The canals are filled with treated sewage and industrial waste. Modern *chinampas* farmers in Mexico City have survived economically by growing flowers to sell to the tourists rather than vegetables. Although today the raised beds have become little more than a tourist attraction, the ideas behind their development live on. Agricultural scientists currently are studying this farming method as a way to increase soil productivity in a more ecologically sound manner.

See also AGRICULTURE; CANALS, SHIPPING.

**Sources/Further Reading**

International Ag-Sieve. "Elevating Agriculture to Old Heights." *Ancient Farming* 5, no. 3. URL: http://www.enviroweb. org/publications/rodale/ag~sieve. Downloaded on January 15, 1999.

McDowell, Bart. "The Aztecs." *National Geographic* (December 1980): 704–752.

Smith, Michael E. *The Peoples of America: The Aztecs.* Cambridge, Mass.: Blackwell, 1996.

von Hagen, Victor Wolfgang. *The Aztec: Man and Tribe.* New York: The New American Library, Inc., 1961.

**allspice** (precontact) *South American Circum-Caribbean and Tropical Forest, Mesoamerican cultures*

Allspice is a seasoning with a flavor that resembles a blend of cinnamon, pepper, juniper, and cloves. It is made from the dried, unripe fruit and seeds of a large evergreen tree indigenous to the Caribbean Islands and the tropics of Mesoamerica and South America. The scientific name for this tree is *Pimenta dioica.* Powdered allspice is an important part of apple pie for modern Americans. It is also one of the ingredients of CURRY powder and is used in many Jamaican dishes such as jerked chicken. Allspice is valued for medicinal purposes as well as for the flavor it imparts to food.

The medicinal uses for allspice go back centuries and have a scientific basis. Both allspice fruit and seeds contain a volatile oil similar to clove oil, which has eugenol, a substance that provides the plant's value as an indigestion remedy and a topical ANESTHETIC. Eugenol helps digestion by enhancing the activity of the digestive enzyme trypsin. Although clove oil contains more eugenol than allspice does, causing dentists to favor it as a pain reliever, allspice also works as a home remedy to soothe aching teeth until the dentist can be seen. (Concentrated allspice oil should not be swallowed because it can cause vomiting and even convulsions.)

The tree from which allspice comes reaches a height of about 30 feet. Its large, leathery leaves resemble those of a laurel tree. The first European to describe allspice, a physician who accompanied Christopher Columbus to Hispaniola, mistook the trees for laurels even though he found them to smell like cloves. On another voyage, men from Columbus's crew found the trees covered with round fruits about a third of an inch in diameter growing in clusters at the ends of their branches. Thinking these were black peppercorns, they named the trees *Pimenta.* Throughout the years allspice has also been called pimento and Jamaica pepper. More than half of the world's supply of the spice today comes from Jamaica, where it grows so abundantly that it does not need to be cultivated except for clearing away brush surrounding the trees.

Although it is primarily used to spice foods, allspice is also used as a home remedy in many areas. Modern Jamaicans drink hot allspice tea for colds, menstrual cramps, and upset stomachs. Costa Ricans also use the spice to treat upset stomachs, flatulence, and diabetes. Guatemalans apply crushed berries to bruises and painful joints and muscles.

**Sources/Further Reading**

*Botanical.com, a Modern Herbal by Mrs. M. Grieve.* URL: http://www.botanical.com/botanical/mgnh/a/allsp025. html. Downloaded on January 24, 1999.

*Center for New Crops and Plants Products/Purdue University.* URL: http://www.hort.purdue.edu/newcrop/Crops/ Allspice. Downloaded on January 24, 1999.

Trager, James. *The Food Chronology: The Food Lover's Compendium of Events and Anecdotes from Prehistory to Present.* New York: Henry Holt, 1995.

**almanacs** (A.D. 600) *Mesoamerican cultures*

Almanacs are BOOKS containing astronomical and meteorological information. Many facets of Mesoamerican life were influenced by almanacs that were based on observations of the planet Venus. These almanacs—invented by the Maya, whose culture arose in Mesoamerica about 3,500 years ago—were invented independently of similar books in other parts of the world. Europeans created written almanacs at a much later date. (Before A.D. 1150, no specific mention of almanacs exists in Europe.)

Mesoamerican almanacs were made up of 260-day cycles called "day counts." Each of the days was assigned a meaning based on a cycle of 20 day names and 13 numbers. When the 260-day-long count ended, the cycle repeated itself. Some ethnoastronomers believe that this numbering system may have been based on the length of human gestation. Because the first day of the almanac is dedicated to Venus, a more plausible explanation for the number 260 is that these almanacs were based on a calculation involving a cycle of Venus, an important planet in Mesoamerican ASTRONOMY.

The sacred almanacs were gathered into books, some of which survived burning by the Spanish conquerors. Anthropologists believe Mesoamerican books were first made in about A.D. 600 and continued after contact. The Codex Borgia is a precontact ritual almanac that survived Spanish book burnings. Special calendar priests who understood which deities governed which days interpreted almanacs like these, which the Aztec called *tonalpohualli*. The almanacs were used to name children based on their birthdates, set the dates of rituals, and determine which days might be lucky or unlucky for certain activities. Like modern horoscopes, sometimes they were used to divine the future. Some Maya people continue to use similar almanacs today.

See also CALENDARS; OBSERVATORIES; WRITING SYSTEMS.

## Sources/Further Reading

Hoskin, Michael, ed. *Cambridge Illustrated History of Astronomy.* New York: Cambridge University Press, 1997.

Krupp, E. C. *Echoes of the Ancient Skies: The Astronomy of Lost Civilizations.* New York: Harper and Row, 1983.

Sharer, Robert. *Daily Life in Maya Civilization.* Westport, Conn.: Greenwood Press, 1996.

Smith, Michael E. *The Peoples of America: The Aztecs.* Cambridge, Mass.: Blackwell, 1996.

**aloe vera**  See AGAVE.

**alpacas (*Lama pacos*)**  (ca. 4000 B.C.) *South American Andean cultures*

Alpacas, like LLAMAS, are mammals that are members of the camel or dromedary family. The animals, whose scientific name is *Lama pacos,* weigh about 150 pounds, half as much as llamas do, and stand about three feet tall. The first known record of alpacas was found drawn on the walls of Andean Mountain caves in South America. The ancestors of the Inca domesticated alpacas more than 6,000 years ago. Over the centuries they selectively bred the alpaca for its silky wool, unlike the llama, which served them primarily as a source of food and as a beast of burden. (See WEAVING TECHNIQUES.)

Alpaca wool was so highly prized that the Inca, who lived in what is now Peru from about A.D. 1000 to A.D. 1519, measured wealth by the number of these animals they owned. Compared to wool from sheep, the fiber from alpacas has five times the insulation properties. This is because alpaca fibers are partially hollow. Fine and lightweight, these filaments are five to six inches long and are exceptionally strong. Because of the length and the structure of alpaca wool, garments made from it are extremely soft and light. Alpaca wool comes in over 20 natural shades, from white to silver, rose-gray, brown burgundy, and black. Shorn every year or two, each animal produces five to nine pounds of wool per shearing.

When Spaniards invaded the region, they moved the alpaca from their traditional area to make room for the sheep

they had brought from Europe. The number of alpaca subsequently declined. The animals that survived were relocated to higher elevations in the mountains. Alpaca fiber was not introduced to the European market until the mid-1800s and quickly commanded high prices because of the small number of animals being raised. Today it is used to make luxury and designer clothing items such as sweaters and coats that sell for high prices.

Introduced to North American livestock growers in the mid-1980s, alpacas are currently being touted as an investment opportunity for ranchers there, in Europe, and in Australia. Alpacas of the Suri breed, which produce the longest fur, sell for the highest prices. In 1997 an Oregon physician spent more than $50,000 on a single alpaca at an Ohio auction. That same year in Sydney, Australia, a stud alpaca was sold for $190,000. In the United States, breeding animals average between $10,000 and $30,000 per animal. Although world interest in alpaca breeding is growing, 98 percent of the world's alpacas are still raised in South America, and most of the wool they produce is shipped to Japan and Europe.

See also ANIMALS, DOMESTICATED; VICUNAS.

## Sources/Further Reading

*Alpaca Breeders Association.* URL: http://alpaca breeders.org. Downloaded on January 24, 1999.

*Alpacanet.* URL: http://www.alpacanet.com. Downloaded on January 24, 1999.

Tannahill, Reay. *Food in History.* New York: Stein and Day, 1973.

Whyte, Murray. "Alpaca ranchers know what many may discover: the woolly beasts are kind, clean and cost a fortune." *Seattle Times,* (July 8, 1997).

**amaranth (*Amaranthus spp.*)**  (ca. 3400 B.C.) *Mesoamerican cultures*

A plant that thrives in heat and low moisture, amaranth (*Amaranthus spp.*) produces seeds that are 13 to 18 percent higher in protein than other cereals. Early Mesoamerican farmers domesticated wild amaranth about 3400 B.C. These seeds served as a dietary staple for indigenous people in the region, including the Aztec, who established an empire in what is now Mexico in about A.D. 1100. Although 10 varieties of wild amaranth are native to Asia and Africa, they were used as potherbs or vegetables and not as a cereal because those varieties contain fewer seeds than do the 45 amaranth varieties native to Mesoamerica.

Amaranth, called *huahtli* by the Aztec, played such an important role in their culture that the Codex Mendoza, an Aztec BOOK of accounts, reported that Montezuma, the emperor of Mexico prior to Spanish conquest, received annual tributes of 20,000 tons of amaranth. (See TAX SYSTEM.) In addition to serving as a foodstuff and a way to pay taxes, amaranth played an important role in religious ceremonies. Ground seeds were mixed with maguey sap (see also AGAVE) or honey (see also BEEKEEPING) and shaped into replicas of Huizilpochtli, the Aztec war god. These were paraded through the streets of Tenochtitlán, the seat of the Aztec Empire. Priests distributed pieces of the statue to the people to eat as representations of the flesh and bones of the god.

The first European to describe amaranth was Pedro de Alvarado, who was sent by Hernán Cortés on a two-year-long campaign to subdue the Aztec living in what is now Guatemala. When he saw them eating amaranth TAMALES as a form of worship, he decided that the practice was a mockery of Catholic communion. Soon afterward, the Spaniards outlawed amaranth cultivation, sale, and consumption under penalty of death in an effort to stop Aztec religious practices. Within years, amaranth decreased in popularity as a foodstuff, but its use did not stop completely. Mexican street vendors made, and still continue to make, candy from amaranth seeds that have been popped then mixed with boiled sugar syrup and finally pressed into molds.

Today the seeds that were once a central part of the Aztec diet are making a comeback. In addition to being high in protein, they contain as much of the amino acide lysine as is found in milk and twice the lysine as contained in wheat, making amaranth's proteins more balanced than those of most other plants. Amaranth also contains high levels of calcium, magnesium, potassium, iron, zinc, vitamin E, and vitamin B complex. New World amaranth varieties have been introduced around the world. Currently the seeds are an important part of the diet for people living in India, China, Pakistan, Tibet, and Nepal. Amaranth is still relegated primarily to the shelves of health food stores in the United States.

See also AGRICULTURE.

## Sources/Further Reading

Coe, Sophie. *America's First Cuisines.* Austin: University of Texas Press, 1994.

Gepts, Paul. *Crop of the Day.* 1996. URL: http://agronomy. ucdavis.edu/gepts/pb143/crop/amaranth. Downloaded on January 26, 1999.

National Research Council. *Lost Crops of the Incas.* Washington, D.C.: National Academy Press, 1989.

Segura-Nieto, M., A.P. Barba de la Rosa, and O. Paredes-Lopez. "Biochemistry of Amaranth." In *Amaranth Biology, Chemistry and Technology.* Edited by Octavio Paredes-Lopez. Boca Raton, Fla.: CRC Press, 1994.

Weatherford, Jack. *Indian Givers: How the Indians of the Americas Transformed the World.* New York: Fawcett Columbine, 1988.

## American hemp   See HEMP, AMERICAN.

## American history, recorded   (ca. 31 B.C.)

*Mesoamerican; South American Andean; North American Paleo-Indian, Great Plains, and Northeast cultures*

History is a written record of the events that have taken place in a culture. Although knowledge of these events was primarily preserved within an oral tradition in the Americas before European conquest, indigenous people in North, Meso-, and South America also recorded them. These historical records ranged from petroglyphs carved onto rocks by Paleo-Indians throughout the Americas to the sophisticated BOOKS created in about A.D. 600 by the Maya culture that began its rise in Mesoamerica starting in about 1500 B.C. and later the Aztec, whose empire was established in about A.D. 1100. The oldest writing (see also WRITING SYSTEMS) that has been found in Mesoamerica is a bar-and-dot date, 31 B.C., that was carved onto a stele, an upright stone slab used as a monument, by the Olmec. The Olmec inhabited Mesoamerica from 1700 B.C. to 400 B.C.

The Moche, who lived on the northern coast of what is now Peru from 200 B.C. to A.D. 600, preserved their historic record in detailed POTTERY that is painted with realistic scenes of everyday life as well as diplomatic gatherings. Later the Inca, whose empire was established in about A.D. 1000 in the same area, used the QUIPU, a knotted-string device that served to record accounts as well as other information.

In North America, Eastern Woodlands cultures used WAMPUM belts, or sashes made from shells, to commemorate important historical events. Indians of the northern plains had a profound sense of history as well, painting records of their past onto buffalo hides. These were called winter counts because they were made in the winter when people had more time to spend on such projects than in summer when hunting, gathering, and food preservation were of primary importance. Each winter marked one year that had passed. These winter counts were meant as mnemonic devices, or memory aids, so the pictures that composed them were not detailed. The events they portrayed included good and poor hunting years, disputes both inside and outside of the tribe, the deaths of leaders, and unusual natural events. Usually the counts were recorded and kept by elders who were entrusted to pass their knowledge of history on to future generations. When the hides wore out, the counts were copied onto new hides.

After the arrival of Europeans, American Indian historians began using paper for winter counts, drawing pictures with pens, pencil, and watercolor. Ledger books used by military storekeepers and traders became highly prized for recording tribal and personal history.

See also ALMANACS; CALENDARS.

## Sources/Further Reading

*American Treasures of the Library of Congress: Memory.* "The Winter Count." URL: http://www.loc.gov/exhibits/treasures/trm054.html. Downloaded on March 29, 1999.

Catherine, Janet. "Plains Indian Drawings 1865–1935." *The Drawing Center.* URL: http://www.artseensoho.com/Art/DRAWINGCENTER/plains96/plain sintro.html. Downloaded on March 29, 1999.

Hassrick, Royal B. *The Sioux: Life and Customs of a Warrior Society.* Norman: University of Oklahoma Press, 1964.

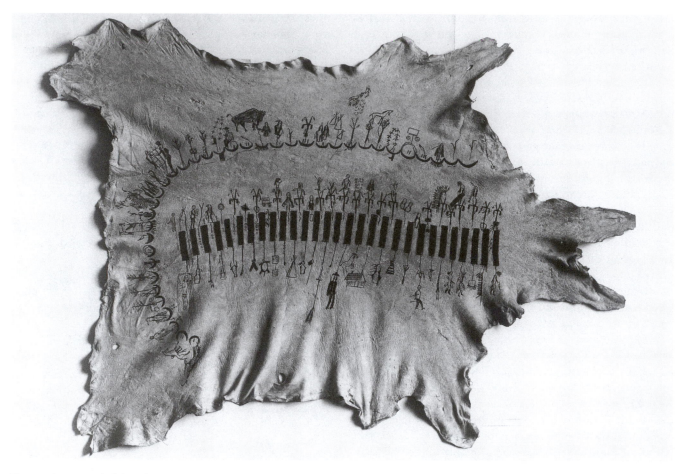

Plains tribes recorded their history in winter counts, such as this Kiowa painting on buckskin that was made between 1871 and 1907. *(Photograph No. NWDNS-106-IN-78/National Archives and Records Administration at College Park)*

**amputation** See SURGERY.

**anatomical knowledge** (ca. A.D. 1100) *Mesoamerican cultures*
Anatomical knowledge, the understanding of the structure and function of the parts of the human body, is the foundation of medical practice. In order to successfully treat illness and injuries, ancient American Indian physicians needed a broad knowledge of human anatomy, including the skeletal system. The Aztec, whose civilization arose about A.D. 1100 in Mesoamerica, were so expert in MEDICINE compared to European physicians that reportedly the Spanish conquistadores preferred to seek help from them instead of barber-surgeons who accompanied the Spaniards to the New World.

Aztec physicians understood the workings of the heart and circulatory system long before Europeans possessed such knowledge. They were familiar with the main details of the internal parts of the heart as well. (Historians generally credit William Harvey, an Englishman who lived between 1578 and 1657, with putting forth the first theory describing the circulatory system.) The Aztec language, Nahuatl, even contained a word to describe the throbbing of the heart: *tetecuicaliztli.*

The Aztec not only developed sophisticated anatomical terminology but also classified the parts of the human body, organizing them into systems. In his book *Indian Givers: How the Indians of the Americas Transformed the World,* anthropologist Jack Weatherford states, "The Nahuatl-speaking doctors developed an extensive vocabulary that identified virtually all of the organs that the science of anatomy recognizes today."

The terms that follow are only a small sample of the terms routinely used by the Aztec physicians.

| English | Nahuatl (Aztec) |
| --- | --- |
| skin | *cuatl* |
| thorax | *elpantli* |
| head | *totzontecan* |
| tongue | *nenepilli* |
| lungs | *tochichi* |
| stomach | *totlatlalizan* |
| spleen | *elcomalli* |
| wrist articulation (joint) | *maquechtli* |
| elbow articulation (joint) | *maliztli* |
| shoulder articulation (joint) | *acolli* |
| knee articulation (joint) | *tlanquaitl* |

In contrast to the Aztec, Europeans had less understanding of the internal organs and their functions. Physicians in the Middle Ages relied on a medical text written by Galen, a Greek who lived from A.D. 130 to A.D. 200. He taught that blood filled the arteries, and he described the chambers of the heart. Considered to be scholars, physicians did not make practical application of this anatomical information, nor did they do anatomical research, since they viewed the body as "worldly" and of little consequence. For the most part they focused on Galen's unfounded theories that taught that illness was caused by an imbalance of four bodily fluids called humours. Surgeons, who were viewed as craftspeople, treated patients mainly by bloodletting. Medieval Europeans, who believed illness was a punishment for sin, treated most sickness with prayer and penance.

See also DENTISTRY; ORTHOPEDIC TECHNIQUES; PHARMACOLOGY; SURGERY.

## Sources/Further Reading

Driver, Harold E. *Indians of North America.* Chicago: University of Chicago Press, 1969.

Ortiz de Montellano, Bernard. *Aztec Medicine, Health, and Nutrition.* New Brunswick, N.J.: Rutgers University Press, 1990.

Peredo, Miguel Guizman. *Medical Practice in Ancient America.* Mexico City: Ediciones Euroamericanas, 1985.

Viola, Herman and Carolyn Margolis. *Seeds of Change: 500 Years Since Columbus.* Washington, D.C.: Smithsonian Institution Press, 1991.

Vogel, Virgil. *American Indian Medicine.* Norman: University of Oklahoma Press, 1977.

Weatherford, Jack. *Indian Givers: How the Indians of the Americas Transformed the World.* New York: Fawcett Columbine, 1988.

## anesthetics (ca. 1000 B.C.) *Mesoamerican, South American Andean, North American Northeast cultures*

Anesthetics are substances that cause partial or total loss of sensation or loss of consciousness. They were used by pre-Columbian physicians in the Americas for a number of medical problems, such as bone fractures, gout, rheumatism, and neuralgia. American Indians also used anesthetics for SURGERY, including brain surgery (see also TREPHINATION) as early as 1000 B.C. COCA, PEYOTE, and datura (see also ARTHRITIS TREATMENTS) are three of the many anesthetics American Indians used to numb feelings of pain.

Coca (*Erythroxylon coca*), or cocaine as it is known today, was used both as an external and an internal anesthetic by Inca physicians who understood the drug's anesthetic property. The Inca culture arose about A.D. 1000 in what is now Peru. When they used coca externally, they prepared it as a poultice and applied it to the painful areas of the patient's body. Inca physicians also had their patients ingest coca before any surgery. Not until Carl Kohller's 1884 experiments in Germany did the non-Indian world discover co-

caine's anesthetic properties. Soon after the modern medical community stumbled upon cocaine's ability to suppress sensation, the plant-derived drug became popular among physicians.

The Aztec, who established an empire in Mesoamerica and what is now Mexico in about A.D. 1100, employed peyote (*Lophophora williamsii*) as an anesthetic for many years before contact with Europeans. Aztec physicians used a lotion made from the root of the plant for health problems such as sore feet and headaches. Taken internally, a decoction of peyote served as a fever reducer. Indians of southern Arizona and northern Mexico used peyote to dull the pain of large open wounds, snakebites, and fractures. They ground the root of the peyote plant, prepared it as a poultice, and applied it to the injured area. Peyote's anesthetic properties were so effective that in the 1800s U.S. Army surgeons used the plant as a painkiller as well.

Indians living in the area of what is now Virginia used "Jamestown weed" (*Datura stramonium L.*), or jimson weed, as it was later called. Like coca and peyote, this plant was used both externally and internally. Indian healers ground the root to form a plaster that was applied to wounds, bruises, and cuts. They had their patients take the plant internally as an anesthetic prior to setting broken bones and fractures as well as for general debility and paralysis. After contact with American Indians, colonial doctors adopted jimsonweed as an anesthetic.

Prior to the mid-1800s, non-Indian doctors who performed surgery did not have effective anesthetics. As a result, surgery was often both a last resort and a barbaric practice. Some physicians resorted to knocking patients out by hitting them in the jaw. Before 1847 and the discovery of ether, alcohol and opium were the most reliable ways non-Indian physicians had to numb their patients' pain. The high dosages of alcohol or opium required to kill pain sometimes killed the patients.

See also MEDICINE; PHARMACOLOGY.

## Sources/Further Reading

Mason, J. Alden. *The Ancient Civilizations of Peru.* Rev. ed. New York: Penguin Books, 1988.

Ortiz de Montellano, Bernard. *Aztec Medicine, Health, and Nutrition.* New Brunswick, N.J.: Rutgers University Press, 1990.

Peredo, Miguel Guizman. *Medical Practice in Ancient America.* Mexico City: Ediciones Euroamericanas, 1985.

Sullivan, John T. "Surgery before Anesthesia." *Neurosurgery Home Page.* URL:http://neurosurgery.mgh.harvard.edu/History/beforeth.htm. Downloaded on July 27, 1999.

Vogel, Virgil. *American Indian Medicine.* Norman: University of Oklahoma Press, 1977.

Weatherford, Jack. *Indian Givers: How the Indians of the Americas Transformed the World.* New York: Fawcett Columbine, 1988.

**animal calls** See CALLS, ANIMAL AND BIRD.

**animals, domesticated** (ca. 13,000 B.C.–10,000 B.C.)
*North American, Mesoamerican, South American Southernmost
Paleo-Indian cultures*
Animals are considered to have been domesticated when they are kept for clear purposes, the traits that they exhibit in the wild have been modified, their breeding is controlled, and their survival depends on the humans who keep them. Animal domestication is more complex than simply taming them; it necessitates selecting types of animals that have the temperament to remain close to humans and those that will provide benefit to humans. Indians began to domesticate animals in the Americas from 15,000 to 12,000 years ago. These animals included DOGS, GUINEA PIGS, TURKEYS, LLAMAS, ALPACAS, and VICUNAS. The Muscovy duck (see also DUCKS, MUSCOVY), PARROTS, and bees (see BEEKEEPING) were also domesticated.

Throughout the Americas, the domestication of animals was far surpassed by agriculture or plant domestication. One reason for this was the lack of native animals suitable for draft purposes such as pulling plows or carts. (Although paleontologists believe a horse evolved in the Americas, it became extinct long before humans began domesticating animals.) The BISON, or buffalo, that ranged throughout North America had an extremely strong herd instinct and were unlikely beasts of burden or draft animals. Llamas, which were domesticated in South America, were more suitable for pack animals than for draft purposes.

**Sources/Further Reading**
Driver, Harold E. *Indians of North America.* Chicago: University of Chicago Press, 1969.
Farb, Peter. *Man's Rise to Civilization as Shown by the Indians of North America from Primeval Times to the Coming of the Industrial State.* New York: E. P. Dutton & Company, 1968.
Weatherford, Jack. *Indian Givers: How the Indians of the Americas Transformed the World.* New York: Fawcett Columbine, 1988.

**annatto** See ACHIOTE.

**annealing** (ca. 5000 B.C.–4000 B.C.) *North American
Paleo-Indian, Mesoamerican, South American Andean cultures*
Annealing is the process of heating metal until it is red-hot and then slowly allowing it to cool in order to make it soft and malleable. About 7,000 years ago, Paleo-Indians of the Great Lakes Region of North America discovered the process that allowed them more versatility than that of previous metallurgical technology, such as cold hammering, bending or rolling, all of which cause metals to lose tensile strength and become more brittle. Although other cultures used annealing, recent evidence points to the fact that these early Americans were the first metalworkers in the world and the first to invent annealing.

James Maxwell wrote in *America's Fascinating Indian Heritage:* "For decades archaeologists had examined the well made Wisconsin artifacts of copper—including chisels, spear points, axes, and knives—and pronounced them extraordinary, since they must have been made in the seventh or sixth century B.C. But in recent years Carbon-14 testing has yielded astonishing results: the Old Copper Culture of the Great Lakes area actually flourished between six and seven *thousand* years ago!"

Pre-Columbian Indians of Central and South America also developed a working knowledge of annealing, including the Chavin, who lived in what is now Peru from 1000 B.C. to 200 B.C., and the Moche, who lived in what is now Peru about 200 B.C. to A.D. 600. Archaeologists consider the Moche to have been the most sophisticated metalworkers in the Americas. Because annealing creates stronger and more flexible metal, the process allowed pre-Columbian American metalworkers to create highly detailed objects from metal, such as JEWELRY, tweezers, and SCALPELS.

See also METALLURGY; SINTERING; TOOLS.

**Sources/Further Reading**
Benson, Elizabeth P. *The Maya World.* New York: Thomas Y. Crowell Company, 1967.
Driver, Harold E. *Indians of North America.* Chicago: University of Chicago Press, 1969.
Mason, J. Alden. *The Ancient Civilizations of Peru.* Rev. ed. New York: Penguin Books, 1988.
Maxwell, James A. *America's Fascinating Indian Heritage.* Pleasantville, N.Y.: Reader's Digest Books, 1978.

**antiasthmatic medication** (precontact) *North
American Southwest and California cultures*
Asthma is a chronic disease of the respiratory tract that is often triggered by allergies. People with asthma frequently experience a feeling of tightness in their chests and have difficulty breathing. American Indians living in what are now California, Arizona, southern Utah, and northern Mexico used a tonic of yerba santa (*Eriodictyon californicum*) to treat this pulmonary problem. The herb, which grows in dry, rocky places, was also chewed and smoked for the same effect. In addition, American Indians used this herb—which is sometimes called mountain balm, tarweed, consumptive's weed, or bearsweed—to treat bronchitis, chronic laryngitis, and colds. The first Spanish priests in California thought so much of its curative powers, that they gave yerba santa its name, which means "holy herb" in English.

See also MEDICINE; PHARMACOLOGY.

**Sources/Further Reading**
Lust, John. *The Herb Book.* New York: Bantam Books, 1974.
Vogel, Virgil. *American Indian Medicine.* Norman: University of Oklahoma Press, 1977.

Weiner, Michael A. *Earth Medicine, Earth Food: Plant Remedies, Drugs, and Natural Foods of the North American Indians.* New York: Fawcett Columbine, 1990.

## antibiotic medications (precontact) *Mesoamerican; North American Southwest, Northwest Coast, and Northeast cultures*

Substances that destroy bacteria—microorganisms, some of which cause disease—are called antibiotics. The Aztec used sap from the maguey varieties of AGAVE, to dress wounds, demonstrating a clear knowledge of its ability to prevent and cure infection. Although penicillin was discovered in 1927, modern medical science did not begin treating or curing infections with this antibiotic until 1941.

Even in very small doses, substances contained in maguey provide an antibiotic environment by increasing cell osmosis, the movement of water through the cell membranes of bacteria. When a semipermeable membrane, such as a cell membrane, separates two solutions that contain different amounts of dissolved particles, water passes from the solution with the fewest particles to that containing the most. The presence of maguey sap literally pulls water from bacterial cells, which are composed of mainly water and proteins, causing them to die from dehydration. Pre-Columbian Aztec physicians also added salt to the maguey sap to enhance its effectiveness against bacteria that were resistant to the maguey alone.

In 1983 Bernard Ortiz de Montellano, author of *Aztec Medicine, Health, and Nutrition,* and a collaborator ran tests on maguey sap and found that it was effective in inhibiting the growth of some gram-negative and gram-positive bacteria, including *Shigella sonnei, Escherichia coli, Pseudomonas aeruginosa, Sarcina luta,* and *Salmonella paratyphi.* These are the most common bacteria known to infect wounds. The researchers found that compounds called polysaccharides and saponins in the plant were the basis for maguey's antibiotic effect. The experiments confirmed that mixing maguey sap with salt made it effective against the bacteria *Staph aureus,* unlike the sap alone.

The Aztec were not the only pre-Columbian Indians to understand and use antibiotic plants to treat bacterial infections. The Makah people who lived on the Olympic Peninsula of what is now Washington State used yarrow (*Achillea millefolium*) as an antibiotic. The Yurok of California used rhizomes, or rootlike underground stems, of a fern plant (*Polypodiaceae*) as an antibiotic, as well. The Zuni of the Southwest used sage (*Asteraceae*) to treat foot infections. American Indians living in the Eastern Woodlands and those living in what is now New England relied on CRANBERRIES and BLUEBERRIES for infection cures. Both berries contain arbutin, a chemical that modern medical researchers have found to be antibiotic as well as diuretic.

See also ANTI-VIRAL MEDICATIONS; MEDICINE; PHARMACOLOGY.

### Sources/Further Reading

Camazine, Scott and Robert A. Bye. "A Study of the Medical Ethnobotany of the Zuni Indians of New Mexico." *Journal of Ethnopharmacology* 2 (1980): 365–388.

Duke, James A. *The Green Pharmacy.* New York: St. Martins Press, 1997.

Moerman, Dan. *Native American Ethnobotany Database: Food, Drugs, Dyes and Fibers of Native North American Peoples.* URL: http://www.umd.umich.edu/cgi-bin/herb. Downloaded on March 31, 1999.

Ortiz de Montellano, Bernard. *Aztec Medicine, Health, and Nutrition.* New Brunswick, N.J.: Rutgers University Press, 1990.

## antihelmintics (intestinal worm medications)

(precontact) *North American Northeast and Southeast cultures*

Antihelmintics are medications used for combating parasitic intestinal worms, especially roundworms, a problem that has plagued human beings since the beginning of time. One of the most effective and widely used antiworm herbs of American Indians was the pinkroot (*Spigela marilandica L.*). Sometimes this plant is called the Indian pink, the Carolina pink, worm grass, or wormroot. A beautiful wildflower, it grows two feet tall and has about 12 flowers. The Cherokee and Creek of the Southeast discovered that the roots, which contain an alkaloid, would kill intestinal parasites. They also knew that ingesting too much pinkroot could be fatal since it becomes toxic in large doses.

Early American colonists learned to use pinkroot to eliminate intestinal worms, mixing it with laxatives. It was either taken powdered or made into a tea and was a standard home remedy for Americans until the early 20th century, when it was replaced with derivatives of the alkaloids found in this American Indian biopharmaceutical discovery.

See also CASCARA SAGRADA; MEDICINE; PHARMACOLOGY.

### Sources/Further Reading

Lust, John. *The Herb Book.* New York: Bantam Books, 1974.

Vogel, Virgil. *American Indian Medicine.* Norman: University of Oklahoma Press, 1977.

Weiner, Michael A. *Earth Medicine, Earth Food: Plant Remedies, Drugs, and Natural Foods of the North American Indians.* New York: Fawcett Columbine, 1990.

## antispasmodic medications (A.D. 1100)

*Mesoamerican; North American Northeast, Southeast, and Southwest cultures*

Drugs that combat seizures or convulsions are called antispasmodics. Epilepsy is the most common seizure disorder. It was referred to more than 4,000 years ago in ancient Greek texts and in the Bible. The Aztec, whose civilization arose in Mesoamerica in about A.D. 1100, developed the oldest known medical treatments and medications for epilepsy. According to Bernard Ortiz de Montellano, author of *Aztec Medicine, Health, and Nutrition,* epilepsy was common enough among the Aztec to be part of their mythology and cosmology. They used the steam bath as part of their therapy, as they did for treating almost all pathologies. (See also STEAM ROOMS.) They also administered wild YAM (*Dioscorea villosa*) to treat epilepsy. Yams, called *Chipahuacxithuitl* in Nahuatl, the Aztec language, contain a chemical sedative called sapongenin. The Aztec steeped wild yam roots in hot water and administered the resulting tea orally.

At the same time the Aztec were using medications for epilepsy, Europeans believed that seizures were caused by demons. They feared those who suffered from the disease so much that epileptics were often subjected to exorcisms. Others were locked away, and some were persecuted and killed. Not until the mid-1800s did non-Indian physicians seriously study the disease. In 1857, hundreds of years after the Aztec, Sir Charles Locock introduced, what medical historians termed the first sedative to help control seizures.

Michael Weiner states in *Earth Medicine, Earth Food;* ". . . epilepsy was not common among the aboriginal Indians. Several 'cures' are reported, but these were usually performed for white patients by an Indian practitioner." Dr. Virgil Vogel cites an example of an American Indian successfully treating a white epileptic patient, as reported by Pierre Charlevoix, an early French writer in the New World: "He spoke of a French soldier cured of epilepsy by an Indian woman who administered a pulverized root."

Even if epilepsy was not prevalent, a number of North American tribes had discovered pharmaceutical treatments for the disease. In the eastern part of the present-day United States, the Iroquois used several different plants for treating epilepsy. These were club moss (*Huperzia lucidula*), crowfoot (*Ranunculus abortivus*), and yellow pond lilly (*Acorus calamus*). The Lenni Lenape (Delaware), who also lived in the Northeast, used lambsquarter, or pigweed (*Chenopodium album*), to treat convulsions. The Hopi, a tribe of the Southwest, used sage (*Asteraceae*) and the Chippewa (Anishinabe), who lived in the upper Midwest, used heart seed (*Polygonum pensylvanicum*). The Cherokee of the Southeast used Indian pipe (*Monotropa uniflora*). The Creek Indians, also from the Southeast used passionflower (*Passiflora incarnata*). The Creek also prepared a hot bath in which the patient was immersed. They steeped boneset (*Eupatorium perfoliatum*) in hot water and added it to the bath water.

See also MEDICINE; PHARMACOLOGY.

### Sources/Further Reading

Hutchens, Alma R. *Indian Herbology of North America.* Boston: Shambhala, 1991.

Lust, John. *The Herb Book.* New York: Bantam Books, 1974.

Ortiz de Montellano, Bernard. *Aztec Medicine, Health, and Nutrition.* New Brunswick, N.J.: Rutgers University Press, 1990.

Vogel, Virgil. *American Indian Medicine.* Norman: University of Oklahoma Press, 1977.

Weiner, Michael A. *Earth Medicine Earth Food: The Classic Guide to the Herbal Remedies and Wild Plants of the North American Indians.* New York: Fawcett Columbine, 1980.

**antiviral medications** (precontact) *North American Great Plains cultures*

Viruses are disease-causing agents that reproduce within human cells. They are so small that an electron microscope is required in order to view them. Only in the last decade of the 20th century has medical research made breakthrough discoveries of a small number of antiviral drugs, including interferon and azido thymidine (AZT) to combat the HIV (the virus that causes AIDS) and acyclovir to counter herpes. Although these tiny pathogens frustrate modern physicians, for centuries the Indians of the northern and southern plains used a plant called echinacea to effectively treat viral infections. Many Great Plains tribes relied on the remedy, more commonly known as purple coneflower, to treat viral illnesses, including systemic infection, or blood poisoning. According to medical historian Virgil Vogel, the Sioux (Dakota, Lakota, Nakota) even used it to treat hydrophobia, more commonly known as rabies, a disease caused by a virus. Today echinacea has become a popular over-the-counter cold and influenza remedy.

Biochemists have found that two compounds in the root of the echinacea plant, echinacin and caffeic acid, fight viruses by boosting the effectiveness of interferon, an antiviral compound that the human body manufactures on its own to combat infections. Chicoric acid, also found in echinacea, inhibits the ability of viruses to reproduce. Additional chemicals strengthen the body's natural immune system by raising the level of properdin in the body. Properdin is a compound that directs white blood cells to the site of the infection to fight viruses.

Based on scientific evidence supporting echinacea's antiviral properties, the official German committee that evaluates herbal remedies for that government has approved the use of purple coneflower extracts to treat flu symptoms. Although the U.S. medical community has not given its assent to the herb's antiviral properties, popular demand for it is rising. Commercial herb growers have begun to plant echinacea, but fear demand will eventually outstrip supply because the plant must mature several years before its roots can be harvested. Interest in the herb is so great that a black market has developed in echinacea roots illegally dug from federal land and sold for $20 to $30 a pound. Federal park rangers are investigating cases such as one in Wyoming's Black Hills that involved the theft of 18,000 plants that had been growing 30 to 40 years. Federal officials fear these entrepreneurs will endanger the survival of the plant in the region.

See also ANTIBIOTICS; MEDICINE; PHARMACOLOGY.

### Sources/Further Reading

Duke, James A. *The Green Pharmacy.* New York: St. Martin's Press, 1997.

Hutchens, Alma R. *Indian Herbology of North America.* Boston: Shambhala, 1991.

Moerman, Dan. *Native American Ethnobotany Database: Food, Drugs, Dyes and Fibers of Native North American Peoples.* URL: http://www.umd.umich.edu/cgi-bin/herb. Downloaded on June 3, 1998.

Sanderson, Jim. "Thieves Uproot Hills Forest Herb." *Rapid City Journal* (July 9, 1998).

Vogel, Virgil. *American Indian Medicine.* Norman: University of Oklahoma Press, 1977.

Weiner, Michael A. *Earth Medicine Earth Food: The Classic Guide to the Herbal Remedies and Wild Plants of the North American Indians.* New York: Fawcett Columbine, 1980.

## apartment complexes (multiple family dwellings) (ca. A.D. 1) *Mesoamerican, North America Southwest and Northeast cultures*

Indigenous people from tribes in both North America and Mesoamerica lived in groupings of multiple family dwellings that contained living quarters for families as well as areas shared in common with other families. Although multiple family dwellings were built by other cultures, American Indians constructed some of the largest and most impressive in the world.

The residents of the first urban center in the New World built the oldest of such major complexes in the Americas—the city of Teotihuacán, which was located in what is now central Mexico on the site of Mexico City. This city flourished in the first thousand years after A.D. 1, and it is the only Mesoamerican city to have multiple family dwellings. Archaeologists—who are unsure of who the people of Teotihuacán were, where they came from, and what happened to them—have found the remains of block after block of one-story stuccoed ADOBE apartment buildings.

The Anasazi, ancestors of modern Pueblo peoples, built apartment complexes further to the north. The Anasazi lived in what are now New Mexico, Arizona, Utah, and Colorado. Anasazi adobe cliff dwellings consisted of hundreds of rooms

Multiple family dwellings, the first American apartment complexes, were common throughout the Southwest. Taos Pueblo, still occupied today, is a prime example of the Pueblo style of architecture invented by the Anasazi, who began building the structures in the Southwest in about A.D. 700. This photograph was taken in 1941. *(Photograph No. NWDNS-79-AA-Q02/National Archives and Records Administration at College Park)*

and several stories. The remains of many of these vast complexes, which were built about A.D. 700, still stand throughout the American Southwest today. The Spaniards called the contiguous masonry rooms covered with adobe *pueblos,* a word that means *towns.*

The two most impressive examples of Anasazi architecture are Mesa Verde in the southwestern part of what is now Colorado and Pueblo Bonito at Chaco Canyon in what is now New Mexico. Mesa Verde's Cliff Palace contains 200 rooms. In the early 10th century, Pueblo Bonito consisted of about 100 rooms. A century later it covered almost two acres and contained 800 rooms. At its highest point, the D-shaped pueblo was four stories high.

In the Northeast of what is now the United States, the Iroquois lived in bark-covered longhouses. Although many families belonging to the same matrilineal clan lived in each dwelling, every family had its own separate sleeping area complete with bunk beds. These 20-foot long apartments were considered private, with two families living across from each other sharing the same cooking fire. When young people married, sometimes an addition was built onto the end of the long house to accommodate their new family unit. Longhouses ranged between 90 and 100 feet in length. Enclosed porches at the ends held firewood and served as storage for possessions. The houses, which would later serve as an inspiration for QUONSET HUTS, were enclosed by a high log STOCKADE, making them the first secured apartment complexes on the continent.

See also CITIES, AMERICA'S FIRST.

## Sources/Further Reading

Nabokov, Peter and Robert Easton. *Native American Architecture.* New York: Oxford University Press, 1989.

Nobel, David Grant. *Ancient Ruins of the Southwest: An Archaeological Guide.* Flagstaff, Ariz.: Northland Publishing, 1991.

———. *New Light on Chaco Canyon.* Santa Fe: School of American Research, 1985.

Stuart, George. "The Timeless Vision of Teotihuacán." *National Geographic* 188, no. 6 (December 1995): 2–35.

Trigger, Bruce G. *Case Studies in Anthropology: The Huron Farmers of the North.* New York: Holt Rinehart and Winston, 1969.

## Appaloosa horse breed  (ca. A.D. 1710)  *North American Plateau culture*

Appaloosa horses are a breed characterized by a light gray coat that is dappled with darker gray spots. The breed shares other characteristics, including mottled skin pigmentation and striped hooves. These horses were portrayed in European cave drawings 20,000 years ago. The Spaniards introduced the horse to the North American continent, but by 1710 the Indians of the Northwest had adopted the animal as their own. The Nez Perce favored spotted horses over the others. They are credited with developing the strong, sure-footed breed recognized today. Although they were not the first people in the world to care

for the spotted horse, they were the first to begin selectively breeding their mounts for speed and intelligence by mating only the best stallions with mares. They traded the horses that they considered inferior to other tribes who prized them for their outstanding qualities compared to other horses.

For years the Nez Perce maintained friendly relationships with early white settlers to the Wallowa Valley of what is now Oregon, where they lived. Those pioneers also recognized the superiority of the Nez Perce's horse herds. They called the animals *Palouse* after the river where the tribe grazed many of their horses. In time *Palouse horse* became shortened to *Appalousey* and then *Appaloosa,* the name that is used for the breed today.

By 1858 the U.S. government had confined the tribe to a 10,000-square-mile reservation. Ten years later a gold rush led the government to shrink the size of the reservation to 1,000 square miles, driving the people from their ancestral homeland. The lower Nez Perce refused to leave. In 1873 President Ulysses S. Grant declared the Wallowa Valley a Nez Perce reservation, but in 1877, under pressure from settlers, the government ordered Nez Perce to move to the Lapwai Reservation in Idaho. Reluctantly, the chiefs agreed, but on their way to the new location, tensions erupted that led to the deaths of four white men. The U.S. Army retaliated with force. Under the leadership of Chief Joseph, the Nez Perce evaded the soldiers for more than 1,000 miles, riding their Appaloosa horses through the Bitterroot Mountains and across Montana. Not far from the Canadian border, the army stopped them. Chief Joseph, knowing that his people were too weak to fight or flee, surrendered.

Most of the tribe's Appaloosa horses were confiscated and sold to local ranchers. The horses that escaped capture were hunted down and shot by soldiers, who were rewarded by the army with one bottle of whiskey for each Indian horse they killed. Over the next 50 years the remaining horses were bred with other types of horses so that the distinct Appaloosa breed nearly became extinct.

In 1938 a group of concerned horsemen formed the Appaloosa Horse Club to preserve the breed and make its history known. Today the club, located in Moscow, Idaho, maintains the official Appaloosa registry. Members of the Nez Perce Tribe, as well, are working to reconnect their people with the breed of horse they created. In 1991 the Chief Joseph Foundation was established on the Nez Perce reservation to promote cultural pride and community healing through activities centering on the horses.

See also ANIMALS, DOMESTICATED; MILITARY TACTICS.

## Sources/Further Reading

Appaloosa. URL: http://ansi.okstate.edu/breeds/horses/app. Updated on May 20, 1996.

Greasley, George. "Appaloosa: an Outstanding Breed." *Horse Previews Magazine.* URL: http//www.horse-previews.com/1295 articles/appyoutstanding.html. (December 1995).

Pavia, Audrey and Bob Langrish. *Appaloosa Spirit (Spirit of the Horse).* Mission Viejo, Calif.: BowTie Press, 1998.

Pony Boy, GaWaNi and Gabrielle Boiselle. *Horse Follow Closely: Native American Horsemanship.* Mission Viejo, Calif.: BowTie Press, 1998.

Waldman, Carl. *Atlas of the American Indian.* Rev. ed. New York: Facts On File, 2000.

**aquaculture** (precontact) *South American, Circum-Caribbean, Mesoamerican cultures*

The practice of raising food crops in water instead of soil is called aquaculture. The Mesoamerican Indians practiced raised bed agriculture (*chinampas*) beginning as early as 1500 B.C. (See also AGRICULTURE, RAISED BED.) In the process of mounding earth on lake beds and swamps, they dug extensive networks of canals. These canals became nutrient-rich havens for fish, mollusks, and other aquatic life. Some archaeologists believe the fish were as well cared for as the crops that grew on the garden plots. The Maya, whose culture arose in about 1500 B.C., and the Aztec, whose empire was established around A.D. 1100, followed the same practice.

One of the amazing feats of the Aztec *chinampas* farmers was to turn saltwater into freshwater by building an enormous dike that separated the salty water of the biggest lakes. Father Francisco de Garay, a contemporary observer, wrote: "As the lakes of fresh water to the south poured their surplus water into the lake of Mexico through the narrows of Culhuacan and Mesicaltzingo, those waters spread through the western lake, the lake of Mexico and completely filled it. . . . In this way the basin of fresh water was converted into a fish pond and a home for all sorts of aquatic fowl."

The Aztec also harvested BLUE-GREEN ALGAE from lakes and shaped it into bricks for drying. Algae, which is high in protein, was a staple in the Aztec diet. After the bricks were dry, they were light in weight and could be stored for about a year. The Aztec also ate dried algae as a part of their daily diet. It was often eaten with TORTILLAS. The Aztec military carried bricks of blue-green algae as rations. The algae also became a valuable TRADE item.

Long before Christopher Columbus arrived on the island of Hispaniola, which is now Haiti and the Dominican Republic, the Arawak who lived there had created large ponds in which they cultivated stocks of fish and turtles. The underwater corrals that they constructed out of reeds held up to 1,000 large sea turtles, or terrapin. This many turtles yielded the same amount of meat as 100 head of cattle, the animals Europeans relied upon as a meat source. Aquaculture was a highly efficient way to provide nutrition, since it required much less time and energy than hunting. Because female sea turtles lay about 500 eggs a season, this food resource was renewable.

The Arawak harvested these turtles in a unique way. They observed that the remora, or suckerfish (*Echeneis maucrates*), attached itself to the body of a shark and other types of large fish by means of a suction disc in its head. They caught and fed remoras, training them to tolerate a light cord fastened to their tails and gills. When a turtle was sighted, the Arawak turtle hunters would release a remora, which swam to the turtle, attaching its suction disc to the under side of the carapace, or shell. Holding the line to the remora, the hunter would follow in a canoe and gaff the turtle or tie it to the canoe.

**Sources/Further Reading**
Olsen, Fred. *On the Trail of the Arawaks.* Norman: University of Oklahoma Press, 1974.

Sauer, Carl Otwin. *Early Spanish Main.* Berkeley: University of California Press, 1966.

Sharer, Robert. *Daily Life in Maya Civilization.* Westport, Conn.: Greenwood Press, 1996.

Stannard, David E. *American Holocaust: Columbus and the Conquest of the New World.* New York: Oxford University Press, 1992.

**aqueducts** (ca. 1700 B.C.) *Mesoamerica, South American Andean cultures*

Aqueducts are pipes or channels designed to carry water from long distances. Most work on the principle of gravity. The Olmec, whose civilization arose in Mesoamerica in about 1700 B.C., were the first people to build aqueducts in Mesoamerica. (In contrast, Roman aqueducts date to about 300 B.C.)

The Olmec constructed their amazing engineering feats, including PYRAMIDS, out of basalt, a volcanic rock that is very dense, hard, and heavy. Olmec engineers used stone tools to build their aqueducts. A portion of the work was done at the basalt quarry, and the rest was done once the stones had been transported to the building site. The stoneworkers carved basalt blocks into U-shaped containers and laid them end-to-end from the water source to the locations where the water was needed. Once the U-shaped blocks were completed, they set them into clay in ditches. They carved capstones to lay on top of the U-shaped blocks that completely enclosed the water running through them. Archaeologists discovered that the capstones also served as altars or monuments, suggesting that the Olmec may have considered the water sacred. Water was piped through aqueducts for agricultural purposes. (See also IRRIGATION SYSTEMS.) Recent research at the San Lorenzo site indicates that the systems were used to pipe drinking water as well. (See also PLUMBING.)

The Moche, whose culture flourished on the northern coast of what is now Peru from about 200 B.C. to A.D. 600, built extensive aqueducts to carry their irrigation canals across ravines. An aqueduct in the Chicama Valley is nearly 50 feet high and a mile long. Nearly every valley contained water-engineering projects. The Inca, whose empire was established in what is now Peru in about A.D. 1000, built stone aqueducts to irrigate terraced fields and to carry water into city centers. When the terrain required it, they built causeways to carry water over low or marshy spots. They also built stone-lined and stone-covered conduits to bring water into buildings in Cuzco, a major population center.

**Sources/Further Reading**
Coe, Michael. *America's First Civilization.* New York: American Heritage Publishing Co., 1968.

Grove, David C. *The Olmec.* URL: http://www.stevensonpress. com/Maya/Olmec.html. Downloaded on August 15, 1999.

Mason, J. Alden. *The Ancient Civilizations of Peru.* Rev. ed. New York: Penguin Books, 1988.

## arches, corbeled (ca. A.D. 300–A.D. 600)

*Mesoamerican, North American Southwest culture*

The corbeled arch is made by setting layers of braces or stones, each row projecting further inward from the vertical line of the wall below until they meet at the center. Unlike a true arch, the corbeled arch cannot carry a significantly heavier load of weight than a horizontal beam. The lowland Maya invented the corbeled arch during the Classic period, between ca. A.D. 300 to A.D. 600. Their invention of corbeling was completely independent of the same discovery by the Hittites in Asia Minor in about 2000 B.C. The Maya used corbeled arches in the construction of stone buildings, often incorporating the technique in doorways. Ancient American Indian ARCHITECTS in Uxmal, a Maya city in the Yucatán built between A.D. 800 and 1400, as well as Navajo (Dineh) architects in the Southwest used corbeled vaults to cover their buildings.

See also STONEMASONRY TECHNIQUES.

### Sources/Further Reading

Benson, Elizabeth P. *The Maya World.* New York: Thomas Y. Crowell Company, 1967.

Mesoamerican architects designed buildings with corbeled arches such as this structure at Uxmal. The Maya built a series of cities on this site in the Yucatán Peninsula during the late Classic period between the seventh and 10th centuries A.D. *(Abbye A. Gorin Collection from the Latin American Library Photographic Archive, Tulane University)*

Nabokov, Peter and Robert Easton. *Native American Architecture.* New York: Oxford University Press, 1989.

## architects (A.D. 600) *North American Northwest Coast and Southwest, Mesoamerican, South American Andean cultures*

Architects are professionals who design and supervise the construction of buildings. Many of the buildings of American Indians show evidence of sophisticated architectural planning. Examples range from the large wooden buildings of the Tlingit, Tsimshian, and Haida on the southern coast of what is now Alaska and the Queen Charlotte Islands of British Columbia (see also CARPENTRY TECHNIQUES) to the pre-Inca and Inca cities built of stone in what is now Peru (see also STONEMASONRY TECHNIQUES) and the Olmec, Maya, Aztec, and pre-Peruvian PYRAMIDS. Massive Hohokam buildings made of ADOBE, such as Casa Grande in what is now Arizona, and Anasazi cliff dwellings of the American Southwest (see also APARTMENT COMPLEXES) also serve as evidence of specialized planning professionals, expert at mathematics and engineering principles.

The earliest clear archaeological evidence for architecture as a specialized profession in the Americas exists in Peru. Before any temple, palace, city, or village was built, the Quecha, predecessors of the Inca, constructed models of buildings called maquettes. (Quecha culture arose in about A.D. 600.) A number of these models, made of stone or pottery, can be found in museums today.

One of the oldest stone buildings in Peru is the *castillo* (castle) at Chauvin in the northern highlands. Built in about A.D. 300 to 800, it is 245' x 235' and contains many rooms. "The plan is complex and it must have been built from the first stone with the finished structure in mind, if not according to a drawn plan or a model," wrote anthropologist J. Alden Mason in his book *The Ancient Civilizations of Peru.* "The building even contains a system of ventilating shafts [see also VENTILATION SYSTEMS], both vertical and horizontal, so efficient that it is said they still provide fresh air for the interior rooms—surely the work of no amateur masons."

In the past, archaeologists often evaluated the buildings of American Indians from an ethnocentric perspective of Euclidean geometry. They ascribed sloppy workmanship and a lack of planning to buildings that were quadrangular rather than square. This was the case with the buildings with walls that do not form right angles at Uxmal, a city built by the Maya in Yucatán between A.D. 800 and 1400. Only in the last decades of the 20th century have researchers discovered that the walls of a building in Uxmal called the Nunnery form sight lines to the rising and setting of celestial bodies including Venus, one of the most important planets in Mesoamerican astronomical observations. That the Maya builders were able to lay out structures along survey lines and accommodate all the necessary astronomical angles to come up with a building with such structural integrity is a feat of drafting.

See also ARCH, CORBELED; ASTRONOMY; OBSERVATORIES; URBAN PLANNING.

## Sources/Further Reading

Josephy, Jr., Alvin M., ed. *America in 1492: The World of the Indian People Before the Arrival of Columbus.* New York: Random House, 1991.

Mason, J. Alden. *The Ancient Civilizations of Peru.* Rev. ed. New York: Penguin Books, 1988.

Nabokov, Peter and Robert Easton. *Native American Architecture.* New York: Oxford University Press, 1989.

## aromatherapy (ca. A.D. 1100–A.D. 1519)
*Mesoamerican, North American cultures*

The idea that scents can affect mood and health is called aromatherapy. This notion is not a new one. Ancient Aztec, whose civilization arose in Mesoamerica about A.D. 1100, believed that pleasant aromas were connected to the gods and that to smell them would increase a person's well-being. Aztec physicians routinely prescribed that patients smell the fragrances of certain flowers to alleviate depression and fatigue. They planted vast public gardens with fragrant flowers valued for their healing effects. The Maya living in Mesoamerica at the time of conquest had similar practices. Landa, the Spaniard who chronicled Maya life shortly after the Spanish invasion, reported that they used perfumes as well as bouquets of flowers and "odoriferous" herbs, "arranged with great care."

Copal incense, made from the gum of the copal tree (*Buresera fugaroides*) was an important part of Aztec life. The Aztec believed it could alleviate the symptoms of epilepsy. (See also ANTISPASMODICS.) Using incense burners that resembled long-handled frying pans, priests burned copal incense to purify both temples and houses of negative spiritual influences. Similar burners found in the remains of private homes indicate that copal burning was a routine part of daily life for Aztec people. Copal was traded to the Maya, who called it *pom,* and who also used it for purification and prayer. North American tribes to the further north burned dried sage, sweetgrass, or cedar for similar purposes. The Choctaw, a Plains tribe, used medicinal herbs in their STEAM ROOMS, sometimes steeping them in water that was used to make the steam.

See also GARDENS, BOTANICAL.

## Sources/Further Reading

Benson, Elizabeth P. *The Maya World.* New York: Thomas Y. Crowell Company, 1967.

Ortiz de Montellano, Bernard. *Aztec Medicine, Health, and Nutrition.* New Brunswick, N.J.: Rutgers University Press, 1990.

Smith, Michael E. *The Peoples of America: the Aztecs.* Cambridge, Mass.: Blackwell, 1996.

## arrowroot (*Maranta arundinacea L.*) (ca. 2000 B.C.)
*South American Andean and Circum-Caribbean, Mesoamerican cultures*

By about 2000 B.C. the indigenous people of what is now Peru had cultivated arrowroot (*Maranta arundinacea L.*). The Inca, whose empire was established in what is now Peru used it as food, as did the Maya, whose culture arose in Mesoamerica in about 1500 B.C. The Arawak and Taino, who lived in the Caribbean, also used arrowroot as a food and made a poultice of arrowroot to draw poison from arrow wounds. Arrowroot is a good source of starch, a form of energy-giving substance found in plants. Non-Indians used arrowroot as a food for children who were convalescing from illness and used it to make teething biscuits.

## Sources/Further Reading

Vogel, Virgil J. *American Indian Medicine.* Norman: University of Oklahoma Press, 1970.

von Hagen, Victor Wolfgang. *Royal Road of the Inca.* London: Gordon Cremonesi, Ltd., 1976.

## arthritis treatments (precontact) *North American Northeast, Southeast, and Southwest; Mesoamerican cultures*

Arthritis is a disease characterized by joint inflammation and pain that can lead to degeneration of the bones and related structures. This condition can be either chronic or acute. Without treatment, the disabling and disfiguring disease can be extremely painful and can impede a person's mobility. Pre-Columbian American Indians experienced arthritis as well as other forms of muscle soreness, inflammation, pain, and joint stiffness. They developed a number of treatments for these conditions. Often these were used in conjunction with steam baths. (See also STEAM ROOMS.)

The Potawatomi, a tribe living in the North American upper Midwest, used the plant spikenard (*Aralia racemosa*) externally as a poultice to reduce inflammation in painful joints. The Cherokee, a southeastern tribe, made a tea of the rootstock of this plant and drank it for the analgesic (pain-killing) effect it produced. This herb was so effective that between 1916 and 1965 spikenard was listed as an analgesic and anti-inflammatory in the *National Formulary,* a standard reference for pharmacists. The Rappahannock, who lived in what is now Virginia, used a tea made from the roots of the bloodroot (*Sanguinaria condenses*) plant to treat arthritis. This herb also acts as a sedative.

The Aztec, whose empire was established in Mesoamerica in about A.D. 1100, used steam baths and bathing as part of their treatment regimen (see HYGIENE, PERSONAL). They also used datura (*Datura stramonium*), a sedative that relieves pain, administering it orally during or after the bath or steam bath. (See also ANESTHETICS.) Aztec physicians applied a poultice of datura to the painful and inflamed joints as well. Atropine, the pain-relieving chemical in datura, was absorbed through the skin, providing relief as a local anesthetic. (Atropine is used in some modern topical drugs for arthritis pain.) Aztec physicians were likewise familiar with the analgesic properties of capsicin, the chemical responsible for the spicy taste of CHILES. Many analgesics used for arthritis treatment today contain capsicin.

Indians from tribes living in the North American Southwest heated PRICKLY PEAR CACTUS pads, applying them to the affected joints, much like the modern electric heating pad. Other North American Indian tribes used hot baths as treatment, steeping boneset (*Eupatorium perfolatium*) in the bath water.

See also ARTHROCENTESIS; MEDICINE; PHARMACOLOGY.

## Sources/Further Reading

Hutchens, Alma R. *Indian Herbology of North America*. Boston: Shambhala, 1991.

Lust, John. *The Herb Book*. New York: Bantam Books, 1974.

Ortiz de Montellano, Bernard. *Aztec Medicine, Health, and Nutrition*. New Brunswick, N.J.: Rutgers University Press, 1990.

Taylor, Norman. *Plant Drugs That Changed the World*. New York: Dodd, Mead, and Company, 1965.

Vogel, Virgil. *American Indian Medicine*. Norman: University of Oklahoma Press, 1977.

Weiner, Michael A. *Earth Medicine Earth Food: The Classic Guide to the Herbal Remedies and Wild Plants of the North American Indians*. New York: Fawcett Columbine, 1980.

## arthrocentesis (precontact) *Mesoamerican culture*

Arthrocentesis is an operation performed to remove fluid from the knee joint. An excessive amount of fluid causes difficulty in mobility, range of motion, and flexion of the joint. This common condition is also very painful. Modern physicians treat it by puncturing the area with a needle to drain the fluid. Most are unaware that the Aztec, whose empire was established in Mesoamerica in about A.D. 1100, invented this treatment in pre-Columbian times. Hundreds of years before Western doctors, ancient Mesoamerican physicians used a thorn to lance or puncture the knee to drain excess fluid accumulated in the joint.

See also ARTHRITIS TREATMENTS; ORTHOPEDIC TECHNIQUES; SURGERY.

## Source/Further Reading

Ortiz de Montellano, Bernard. *Aztec Medicine, Health, and Nutrition*. New Brunswick, N.J.: Rutgers University Press, 1990.

## asepsis (precontact) *North American Great Basin, South American Andean cultures*

Asepsis is the absence of disease-producing microorganisms. Non-Indian historians usually credit Joseph Lister, an Englishman who lived between 1827 and 1912, with inventing the theory that microorganisms cause infections and other illnesses. Lister introduced to the non-Indian world the use of asepsis in SURGERY, thus creating a sterile environment during operations. (Prior to Lister, in the 1300s French surgeon Guy de Chauliac advocated aseptic treatment of wounds, but his advice was ignored for 500 years in Europe.)

Yet asepsis was practiced by American Indians long before Lister discovered it. The Shoshone and Paiute, who lived in

what is now Nevada, used cough root (*Apiaceae*) as the basis for a number of antiseptics, or disinfectants. Balsam fir served as an antiseptic for other North American tribes. One of the important South American antiseptics is the Peruvian balsam (*Mypoxylon pereirae*). "It was capable of destroying the bacteria commonly encountered in wounds and thus protected the body from suppuration [forming or discharging pus], scabies, eczema and inflammatory skin reactions," wrote Dr. Virgil Vogel in his book *American Indian Medicine*. Bernard Cobo, a Spaniard, observed in 1653 that the indigenous people of South America pounded leaves of Peruvian balsam and used them to treat fresh wounds.

Indian healers routinely dressed wounds with boiled water at a time when Western physicians did not see a need to clean wounds or to wash their hands before treating patients or performing operations. Today the practice of asepsis, known by American Indians for centuries, is a basic tenet taught in medical and nursing schools throughout the world. Aseptic technique is responsible for saving many lives by preventing infections and keeping outbreaks of contagious diseases to a minimum, especially those diseases caused by bacterial or viral pathogens.

See also ANTIBIOTIC MEDICATIONS; ANTIVIRAL MEDICATIONS; CHIA; HYGIENE, PERSONAL; MOUTHWASHES; PHARMACOLOGY; SANITATION.

## Sources/Further Reading

Lust, John. *The Herb Book*. New York: Bantam Books, 1974.

Peredo, Miguel Guizman. *Medical Practice in Ancient America*. Mexico City: Ediciones Euroamericanas, 1985.

Train, Percy, James R. Henrichs, and W. Andrew Archer. *Medicinal Uses of Plants by Indian Tribes of Nevada*. Washington, D.C.: U.S. Department of Agriculture, 1941.

Vogel, Virgil. *American Indian Medicine*. Norman: University of Oklahoma Press, 1977.

Weiner, Michael A. *Earth Medicine Earth Food: The Classic Guide to the Herbal Remedies and Wild Plants of the North American Indians*. New York: Fawcett Columbine, 1980.

## asphalt (asphaltum) (8000 B.C.) *North American California and Northeast cultures*

The lowest grade of crude oil is called asphalt. Brownish black in color, it is solid or semi-solid. Evidence exists that cultures east of the Missouri River were using it as a WATERPROOFING agent as early as 8000 B.C. The Chumash of Southern California used and traded asphalt so extensively that some archaeologists have deemed them to have an "asphaltum culture." The tribe obtained the asphalt from the area now known as the La Brea tar pits located in what is now the Los Angeles area. The oil there had been formed by the action of pressure and time on marine plankton deposited millions of years earlier. According to scientists, the petroleum took about 40,000 years to migrate to the surface. Asphalt was formed naturally when the lighter, more volatile substances such as kerosene evaporated.

Caulking for CANOES was one of the most important uses for the substance. The Chumash crumbled dry asphalt and heated it in a stone vessel, mixing it with pitch to make a sealant. This was then thickened with red ochre. The mixture was poured onto the boat's surface from soapstone ladles. The Chumash spread it on the canoes with willow-bark brushes and scraped the excess off with bone scrapers. When boats needed to be recaulked, a hot stone was applied to melt the seam.

The Chumash also used asphalt to seal long-necked baskets (see also BASKET WEAVING TECHNIQUES) that they used as water containers. They coated the insides by filling them with pebbles that they had dipped into hot asphalt and then shaking the basket. They used asphalt to coat the exterior of these baskets as well. The Chumash also used asphalt to plug up the holes in abalone shells so that they could be used as dishes, and as a glue to fasten spear points and arrow points to shafts. Just as the ancient Sumerians of the Middle East had done, the Chumash independently discovered how to use the substance to glue shell inlay as a decoration on stone, bone, and wood. Asphalt was in such high demand among other West Coast tribes that the Chumash traded it for goods such as soapstone, salt, fur, and food. (See also TRADE.)

Most of the asphalt used today is a byproduct of petroleum distillation. It is used to line reservoirs and swimming pools as well as to surface roads. The use of asphalt for road surfaces did not begin in the United States until 1870. In the mid-1960s highway engineers discovered that when asphalt was blended with about 18 percent RUBBER, another American Indian invention, the new substance provided increased resistance to melting in hot weather and cracking in cold weather.

See also PETROLEUM REFINING.

**Sources/Further Reading**
Doyle, Thomas W. *The Saga of An Old Spanish Land Grant—Its Authentic Legends And the Colorful People Who Shaped Its History.* Mailbu, Calif.: The Malibu Lagoon Museum, 1985.
Hazen-Hammond, Susan. *Timelines of Native American History: Through the Centuries with Mother Earth and Father Sky.* New York: Berkeley Publishing Company, 1997.
Natural History Museum of Los Angeles County Foundation. *Answers to Commonly Asked Questions.* URL: http://www.tarpits.org/faq-asphalt.html. Downloaded on March 10, 1999.
Rubberized Asphalt Concrete Technology Center. *The History of Rubberized Asphalt.* URL: http://www.rubberized asphalt.org/history/phoenix.htm. Downloaded on March 10, 1999.
Shupp, Mike. *Gabrielino Material Culture.* URL: http://www.csun.edu/~ms44278/gab.htm. Downloaded on January 6, 1999.

**aspirin** See SALICIN.

**astringents** (precontact) *North American Northeast cultures*
Astringents are substances that draw together or tighten tissue; they also work to stop bleeding or diarrhea by coagulating proteins on the surface of cells. North American Indians compiled an extensive list of plants with astringent properties that were used to treat a number of health problems.

The Menominee, who lived in and around the area known as Wisconsin today, used alum root (*Huechera Americana*) as an astringent. They administered this plant, found in the eastern half of North America, both internally and externally. They prepared it by pounding the moist root into a pulp that was then eaten to treat bloody diarrhea. To treat dysentery, they steeped the rootstock in water and drank the resulting tea. Members of the Menominee also used alum as an astringent for bleeding hemorrhoids by administering "tea" rectally with a bulbed SYRINGE. (See also ENEMAS.) The Mesquaki used alum root to treat obstinate sores and wounds. They pounded the dry root into a powder and applied it directly into the open wounds, which would soon begin to heal.

Cranes bill (*Geranium maculatrum, L.*), which grows throughout North America, except for the coldest areas, was another astringent that American Indians used. The Ottawa and Chippewa (Anishinabe) in the Great Lakes area boiled the whole plant and used it to stop intestinal and external bleeding as well as for a diarrhea and dysentery cure. They also used cranes bill to effectively treat nosebleeds, internal bleeding, sore throats, and bleeding gums. Sometimes it was used to stop excessive menstrual blood flow.

The Oneida, who lived in the Northeast of what is now the United States, used another astringent, the blackberry, for treating dysentery. In his book *Earth Medicine, Earth Food,* author Michael Weiner writes: "Five hundred Oneida Indians cured themselves of dysentery with this plant while the neighboring white settlers succumbed to the disease."

See also BLACKBERRIES; PHARMACOLOGY.

**Sources/Further Reading**
Hutchens, Alma R. *Indian Herbology of North America.* Boston: Shambhala, 1991.
Lust, John. *The Herb Book.* New York: Bantam Books, 1974.
Vogel, Virgil. *American Indian Medicine.* Norman: University of Oklahoma Press, 1977.
Weiner, Michael A. *Earth Medicine, Earth Food: Plant Remedies, Drugs, and Natural Foods of the North American Indians.* New York: Fawcett Columbine, 1990.

**astronomical observatories** See OBSERVATORIES, ASTRONOMICAL.

**astronomy** (ca. 1500 B.C.) *North America Southwest, Northeast, and Great Plains; Mesoamerican; South American Andean cultures*
Astronomy is the study of the position and movement of planets, stars, and constellations. Unlike astronomical observers in

other parts of the world, American Indian astronomers focused on events that happened at the horizon, including the rising and setting of stellar constellations, the sun, the moon, and Venus. They used a sophisticated system of astronomy developed independently from that of other cultures, which could calculate celestial events like solar eclipses. They also created CALENDAR systems, complete with corrections that were based on detailed observations of the cycles of the sun and moon.

Indians built structures throughout North and South America that aligned to the planets and the solstices. For example, Casa Rinaconada, a kiva (chamber) built by the Anasazi in the Chaco Canyon area of what is now New Mexico about A.D. 1100, has irregularly placed windows and niches that, modern astronomers have discovered, align with the light of the summer solstice. Only in the last decades of the 20th century did researchers discover that the angled walls of a building in Uxmal, a city built by the Maya in Yucatán between A.D. 800 and A.D. 1400, form sight lines to the rising and setting of celestial bodies including Venus, one of the most important planets in Mesoamerican astronomical observations. (See also ARCHITECTS.) Modern astronomers believe that structures such as these either served as calendars or OBSERVATORIES. The Bighorn medicine wheel in Montana, whose spokes align to the rising of the stars Aldebaran and Rigel weeks before the summer solstice, also shows that ancient North Americans were well aware of the cyclical nature of planetary and stellar movements.

Both the sun and the constellation Pleiades served to mark the planting season for agricultural people in North America. Seneca communities living in what is now New York State observed that the constellation Pleiades rose by the middle of October, and they timed their midwinter ceremony to occur when the constellation was directly above them. They planted their corn, a variety that requires 120 frost-free days, when the Pleiades disappeared below the horizon in mid-May. The Sac (Sauk), Mesquaki, and the Dakota, Lakota, and Nakota people of the Great Plains all have legends about this constellation. The appearance and disappearance of the Pleiades also held special significance for Mesoamericans. When it appeared at its apex in the night sky on the 52nd year of the Aztec and Maya long count calendar, it marked the time of the New Fires Ceremony, when old fires were extinguished and new ones kindled. The Maya culture arose in what is now Mexico in about 1500 B.C. The Aztec, who conquered the Maya and used many of their discoveries, established their empire in about A.D. 1100.

Both the Maya and the Aztec made observations of Venus. From evidence found in Maya writings, archaeoastronomers know that the Maya, and later the Aztec, followed the movements of Venus through the sky closely and recorded them accurately. These ancient North American astronomers knew that Venus was present as the morning star for 236 days then disappeared for 90 days; that it reappeared as an evening star for 250 days; and that it was then invisible again for eight days. Much of the content of the surviving Maya and Aztec BOOKS consists of astronomical records in the form of ALMANACS.

## Sources/Further Reading

Aveni, A. F., ed. *Archaeoastronomy in the New World: American Primitive Astronomy.* London: Cambridge University Press, 1982.

Folsom, Franklin and Mary Elting Folsom. *America's Ancient Treasures,* 4th ed. Albuquerque: University of New Mexico Press, 1993.

Hoskin, Michael, ed. *Cambridge Illustrated History of Astronomy.* New York: Cambridge University Press, 1997.

Iseminger, William, R. "Mighty Cahokia." *Archaeology* (May/June 1996): (30–37).

Jennings, Francis. *The Founders of America: How Indians Discovered the Land, Pioneered in It, and Created Great Classical Civilizations; How They were Plunged into a Dark Age by Invasion and Conquest; and How They are Now Reviving.* New York: W.W. Norton, 1993.

Krupp, E. C. *Echoes of the Ancient Skies: The Astronomy of Lost Civilizations.* New York: Harper and Row, 1983.

Sharer, Robert. *Daily Life in Maya Civilization.* Westport, Conn.: Greenwood Press, 1996.

Smith, Michael E. *The Peoples of America: The Aztecs.* Cambridge, Mass.: Blackwell, 1996.

**atropine**    See ARTHRITIS TREATMENTS.

**auditory decoys**    See CALLS, BIRD AND ANIMAL.

**avocados (*Persea Americana*)**    (ca. 8000–7000 B.C.)
*Mesoamerican, South American Andean, and Circum-Caribbean cultures*
The avocado is a wild fruit that grows on trees indigenous to the areas now known as the West Indies, Guatemala, and Mexico. Archaeological evidence shows that American Indians gathered and ate wild avocados in the Tehuacán Valley of Mexico as early as 8000–7000 B.C. The cultivation of avocado trees began in the region between 3400 and 2300 B.C. About 900 B.C. farmers began selectively planting and raising avocado trees along streams and then irrigation ditches. Although these trees did not bear fruit for seven years, they needed to be kept well-watered while they matured, so it is clear that the farmers had made detailed observations of the plant's life cycle before attempting to domesticate it. Although avocado seeds have been found on Peruvian seacoast archaeological sites dating to 2400–2000 B.C., ethnobotanists believe the fruits were first cultivated in Huaca Prieta, Peru, in about 750 B.C.

The Aztec, whose empire was established in Mesoamerica in about A.D. 1100, called these leathery-leafed trees *ahuacacuauhitl,* or testicle trees. Little is known about how the Aztec served avocados, except that they made a sauce of mashed avocados called *huaca-mulli,* GUACAMOLE today. The Maya, whose culture arose in Mesoamerica about 1500 B.C., sliced avocados and ate them wrapped in a TORTILLA or chopped them and added them to stews that had already been cooked. Rich in unsaturated fats, avocados contain no cholesterol and are high in fiber as well as vitamins A, B$_6$, and C. Ounce for ounce they contain more potassium than do raisins, bananas, broccoli, carrots, and other more popular sources of this mineral.

Spanish priests—who believed the fruits were aphrodisiacs because of the tree's name and their appearance—frowned on eating them and forbade them from being grown in mission gardens. Because avocados did not remain fresh on long ocean voyages, they remained an oddity to Europeans for many years. The British termed them "alligator pears" because of their green, bumpy skin. Europeans who did taste avocados often were not sure of what to do with them. Some culinary experts advised mixing them with lime juice and sugar, while others said they were best eaten salted. Still others swore they should be eaten plain. Avocados did not become popular in the United States until the 1900s. By 1993 people in the United States were eating an average of two pounds of avocados per person each year. California and Florida are currently the primary avocado-producing states in the United States. According to the U.S. Department of Agriculture the annual value of U.S. avocado production is about $200 million.

See also AGRICULTURE.

## Sources/Further Reading

Coe, Sophie. *America's First Cuisines.* Austin: University of Texas Press, 1994.

Gepts, Paul. *The Crop of the Day.* 1996, URL: http://agronomy. ucdavis.edu/gepts/pb143/crop/avocado. Downloaded on January 16, 1999.

Hurt, R. Douglas. *Indian Agriculture in America: Prehistory to Present.* Lawrence: University of Kansas Press, 1987.

Trager, James. *The Food Chronology: The Food Lover's Compendium of Events and Anecdotes from Prehistory to Present.* New York: Henry Holt, 1995.

U.S. Department of Agriculture. *An Economic Assessment of Avocados: Executive Summary.* URL: http://www.act.fcic. usda.gov. Downloaded on January 16, 1999.

**axes, copper** (ca. 5000 B.C.–4000 B.C.) *North American Copper Culture Paleo-Indians*

Axes are TOOLS with blade-shaped heads mounted on a handle. They are used for chopping and in previous centuries they were sometimes thrown as weapons in battle. Paleo-Indians living in the southern Great Lakes area of what is now the United States made a technological leap when they invented the first metal axe blade made in the Americas, 6,000 to 7,000 years ago. They created these axes from copper found in nuggets around the area. According to archaeologists, before this time Paleo-Indians had chipped axe blades from stone. Metal axes were a valuable technological improvement over stone axes because they could be sharpened. They were also heavier and more effective for cutting wood than stone axes. These Paleo-Indians, whom archaeologists call the Old Copper Culture of the Great Lakes Region, are considered to be the world's first metalworkers.

See also ANNEALING; METALLURGY.

## Sources/Further Reading

Driver, Harold E. *Indians of North America.* Chicago: University of Chicago Press, 1969.

Francis, Lee. *Native Time: A Historical Time Line of Native America.* New York: St. Martin's Press, 1996.

Mason, J. Alden. *The Ancient Civilizations of Peru.* Rev. ed. New York: Penguin Books, 1988.

Maxwell, James A. *America's Fascinating Indian Heritage.* Pleasantville, N.Y.: Reader's Digest Books, 1978.

# B

**baby bottles**  See SYRINGES.

**baby carriers**  See CRADLE BOARDS.

**backstrap looms**  See LOOMS.

**balloons**  See TOYS.

**balls, rubber**  (ca. 1700 B.C.)  *Mesoamerican cultures*
The Olmec were the first people to produce and play with rubber balls, spherical objects that are widely used in many sports and games today. A rubber ball dated to 1000 B.C. has been found in the Olmec site of La Venta. Rubber is made from the sap, or latex, of a tree indigenous to the area. The Olmec, whose culture flourished from 1700 B.C. to 400 B.C., were the first to manufacture objects made of rubber. They, and later the Maya and Aztec, made hollow and solid rubber balls that were used for playing a team sport on huge ball courts. (See also BAS-KETBALL.) The Maya culture arose in about 1500 B.C.; the Aztec Empire was established in about 1100 A.D. Rubber balls were so highly valued that the Codex Mendoza, an Aztec book of accounts, listed 16,000 rubber balls being paid by the coastal provinces to the Aztec emperor.

One version of Mesoamerican basketball was played with a solid rubber ball that varied in size from 2 to 10 inches in diameter. This version could produce bodily damage without the protective gear worn by players. Even with padding, ballplayers were not immune from bruises and other injuries because, in one version of the game, they could use only their shoulders, thighs, knees, head, and hips to hit the ball in order and get it through a high hoop.

This hollow clay whistle in the shape of a Maya ballplayer shows him holding a rubber ball. Rubber balls that American Indians made before contact with Europeans have been found throughout Mesoamerica. The earliest date to 1000 B.C. *(Photograph courtesy of the Milwaukee Museum)*

The hollow rubber ball was lighter and bounced higher. Spaniards, who observed the game and the technology for making the balls, introduced rubber balls to Europe. An Olmec modification of the hollow rubber ball, the rubber-bulbed SYRINGE, was used to administer medication and for ENEMAS.

See also HELMETS, SPORTS.

### Sources/Further Reading

Benson, Elizabeth P. *The Maya World.* New York: Thomas Y. Crowell Company, 1967.

Farb, Peter. *Man's Rise to Civilization as Shown by the Indians of North America from Primeval Times to the Coming of the Industrial State.* New York: E. P. Dutton & Company, 1968.

Scarborough, Vernon L. and David R. Wilcox, eds. *The Mesoamerican Ballgame.* Tucson: University of Arizona Press, 1991.

**balsa rafts**  See RAFTS, BALSA.

**balsa wood**  (precontact) *Mesoamerican; South American Andean and Tropical Forest; Circum-Caribbean cultures*
The wood from the balsa tree (*Ochroma lagopusis*), indigenous to the American tropical forest, is stronger than Mediterranean cork. Because of its buoyancy, it was used by indigenous Americans to construct BRIDGES and RAFTS. Those who worked with balsa included the Mesoamerican Maya, whose civilization began in 1500 B.C., and the Inca, whose empire arose in what is now Peru in about A.D. 1000.

Balsa trees grow wild in lowlands and jungle clearings. Today they are also cultivated on plantations, reaching heights of up to 90 feet. Under ideal conditions they reach maturity in as short a time span as six years. At six to nine pounds per cubic foot, balsa is the lightest weight wood in the world. It is also one of the softest and most porous, making it extremely useful in a number of applications in the modern world.

Although today balsa wood is best known for its use in model airplanes and boats, it is primarily used as a core for lightweight sandwichlike composites in building, boat building, and airplane construction. Taking a hint from Mayan traders, who transported their goods on balsa wood rafts, the modern marine industry uses the wood, laminated with fiberglass or other material, for hulls for speedboats and sailboats. In the 1950s, surfers began constructing boards of this wood, and although most surfboards today have foam cores, the ones made of balsa are still considered the best.

Modern uses for balsa wood are varied. In World War II it was a major component of plywood-skinned British Mosquito attack bomber planes. Today the U.S. Army uses it for combat-ready cargo containers and for chemical containment tanks, because it resists corrosion better than stainless steel. Balsa wood was even used on the National Aeronautics and Space Administration's (NASA) ranger Moon-landing vehicle. The aircraft industry uses the wood in airplanes for flooring, over-head compartments, and cabin partitions, where it reduces vibration and serves as a sound insulator. Those same sound-insulating properties are used in the construction of theaters and recording studios. Industrial uses for balsa include wind turbine blades, stacks, scrubbers, and storage tanks. In building it is used for concrete forms and for the bottoms of shower stalls. Balsa is also used for artificial limbs.

See also TRADE.

### Sources/Further Reading

Baltek Balsa Home Page. URL: www.baltek.com. Downloaded on January 9, 1999.

von Hagen, Victor Wolfgang. *Realm of the Incas.* New York: New American Library, 1957.

**barbecues**  (ca. A.D. 1100) *Mesoamerican, Circum-Caribbean cultures*
The term *barbecue* refers to an outdoor pit or grill for cooking meat over a fire. The word can also mean the method of cooking or a social gathering where food is cooked in this manner. The Maya, whose civilization arose in about 1500 B.C. in Mesoamerica, and the Aztec, whose empire was established in the same area beginning in about A.D. 1100, were known to roast meat over an open fire on a framework of greenwood sticks. The Taino of the Caribbean, whom Columbus and his crew encountered, introduced the barbecue to Europeans. Early engravings by explorers show indigenous people from this area roasting meat on woven frames of greenwood. (Although there is no evidence the indigenous people of the West Indies were cannibals, one of these engravings shows them cooking a human leg, perhaps to make the artist's voyage seem more exciting and to dehumanize the Indian people encountered.) The Spanish called the open-fire cooking method *barbacoa,* from which the English word BARBECUE is derived.

Barbecues began making their way northward during the early 1600s, when runaway bonded servants, shipwrecked sailors, and outcasts from the new colonies began to filter into the sparsely settled areas of Hispaniola, bringing pigs and cattle with them. They had learned from the Taino who had survived the diseases brought by the Europeans not only how to cook but also how to dry meat, making JERKY on green wood frames over a fire constructed of animal bones and hides. The Indians called this food-preservation technique *boucan.* When the new residents of Hispaniola, now Haiti and the Dominican Republic, began drying their surplus livestock in this manner, the French called them *boucanier.* Eventually the word became BUCCANEER, meaning "pirate." Today barbecues are not only an important part of southern cooking but have become a popular summer pastime for people throughout the United States.

### Sources/Further Reading

Coe, Sophie. *America's First Cuisines.* Austin: University of Texas Press, 1994.

Tannahill, Reay. *Food in History.* New York: Stein and Day, 1973.

Weatherford, Jack. *Indian Givers: How the Indians of the Americas Transformed the World.* New York: Fawcett Columbine, 1988.

## barbershops  (ca. A.D. 1100–A.D. 1519) *Mesoamerican cultures*

Long before contact with Europeans, the Aztec patronized barbershops established in large, thriving urban centers. Ancient Aztec barbers differed from the Old World barbers, who were referred to as barber-surgeons and who performed bloodletting and crude surgery. Instead, their work more closely resembled that of present-day hair stylists. Aztec barbershop patrons either had their heads shaved or had their hair trimmed or washed in these establishments.

See also DETERGENT; HAIR CONDITIONERS; HYGIENE, PERSONAL.

### Source/Further Reading

Peredo, Miguel Guizman. *Medical Practices in Ancient America.* Mexico City: Ediciones Euroamericans, 1988.
Soustelle, Jacques. *Daily Life of the Aztecs.* Stanford, Calif.: Stanford University Press, 1985.

## base 20 mathematical system  (31 B.C.)
*Mesoamerican cultures*

In mathematics a base is the number that, when raised to certain powers, makes up the basic units used for counting. For example, the components used as placeholders in the Arabic base 10 system that is common throughout the world today are ones, 10s, 100s, 1000s, and so on. Mesoamericans invented a mathematical system using a base 20 system. Some ethnologists speculate that the 20 was used as the base of the indigenous American system because early Mesoamerican people initially used both fingers and toes for performing calculations.

The Maya, whose culture arose in about 1500 B.C., have often been credited with inventing the base 20 system. Maya mathematicians are considered to have been the most sophisticated in the New World. However, the Olmec may have invented the system much earlier. An Olmec stele, or stone pillar, carved with the equivalent of the date 31 B.C. in bar and dot notations, is the oldest proof for a mathematical system and a CALENDAR in the New World. The Olmec civilization arose in the Yucatán Peninsula of what is now southern Mexico in about 1700 B.C. to 400 B.C.

In the Mesoamerican system of numeric notation, a dot stood for one unit and a bar stood for five. A shell symbolized ZERO, a concept invented by Mesoamerican mathematicians. Like the numbers in the Arabic numeral system, the first nine in the Mesoamerican system were unique. Combining the symbols for one through nine with the symbol for 10 formed the numerals 11 through 19. After that, numbers were organized in multiples of 20. The numbers were written from top to bottom, and the value of these bars and dots were determined by the positions in which they were written.

In addition to being used for calendar calculations, mathematics was used by the Maya and Aztec to figure daily transactions in the marketplace. Maya merchants used CACAO beans or other counters arranged on a flat surface to do the math. Evidence exists that the Maya and Aztec used an ABACUS as well. They performed addition and subtraction by adding or subtracting counters from the proper row. Because the system contained a zero, multiplication and division could also be performed, making it more versatile than the system of Roman numerals used in Europe at the time.

Although the Mesoamerican mathematical system could not handle fractions, it was sophisticated and allowed extremely accurate calculation, so much so that the Maya and Aztec calendar systems that were constructed using it are some of the most precise in the world.

The base 10 system of mathematics is a relatively new numeric system to Europe, having been introduced by the Moors who invaded Spain during the 11th century. Islamic mathematicians had learned the concept of place value and base 10 in about A.D. 850. Olmec mathematicians invented the concepts at least 200 years before. The Chinese also adopted the Arabic system. Before the 11th century Europeans practiced Greek mathematics that used a base 60 system, borrowed from the Hittites, who invented it.

The Zuni, a Pueblo people living in what is now the southwestern United States, independently invented a base 10 system before contact with Europeans. The Pomo living in what is now Southern California also used a base 10 system for counting and record-keeping and were able to express numbers in the thousands.

### Sources/Further Reading

Closs, Michael P., ed. *Native American Mathematics.* Austin: University of Texas Press, 1986.
*Maya Mathematics.* URL: http://www.astro.uva.nl/~micheileib/maya/math.html. February 11, 1999.
Sharer, Robert. *Daily Life in Maya Civilization.* Westport, Conn.: Greenwood Press, 1996.

## basketball  (ca. 1000 B.C.) *Mesoamerican, North American Southwest cultures*

Basketball, a team sport in which points are scored by throwing a rubber ball through a hoop, is an all-American game that most people believe was invented about 100 years ago. In truth, it was played by American Indians about 3,000 years ago. The Olmec, who lived in what is now southern Mexico and Central America from about 1700 B.C. to 400 B.C., originated the game because LATEX-producing trees grew in their area and they had developed the technology to create BALLS made from rubber. Because this game is the first one known to have used a rubber ball, many anthropologists consider it to be the forerunner of all modern games that use bouncing balls, including basketball, soccer, and football.

Both nobles and commoners played the game, and nearly every adolescent male participated. The nobility sponsored professional basketball teams that played on feast days. So important was the ball game to Olmec culture that huge stone ball courts were built in the central, ceremonial areas of Olmec and, later, the Maya and Aztec. Evidence of these impressive courts has been found from Honduras to Arizona; the archaeological remains of 600 ball courts have been found in Mexico alone. They typically contain large circular stones with a hole in the center that were mounted high on the side walls of the playing field. Instead of being horizontal, these pre-Columbian hoops were mounted vertically. Many anthropologists think the game, which involved making goals by getting the ball through a stone or (sometimes) wooden hoop, spread throughout the Americas when the Indians of different areas visited one another. Archaeologists have found about 200 Hohokam ball courts in what is now Arizona. The Hohokam culture arose in about 300 B.C. Both solid and hollow rubber balls have been found near the old courts.

As basketball spread, it eventually became more of a ritual than a recreational pastime. Some anthropologists who have studied hieroglyphs believe that the Maya impersonated the Gods as they played, making the match a form of theater. The precise details of how pre-Columbian basketball was played remain a mystery, but glyphs and small statues offer some clues. For years archaeologists thought that the players were not allowed to touch the ball with their hands or feet, instead moving it from one end of the court to the other with their shoulders, elbows, hips, and knees in play that must have resembled a very intense soccer game. Recently some scholars have begun to disagree, among them archaeologist Nicholas Hellmuth. Based on the evidence of two eighth century Maya sculptures and several Maya vases that show players with their hands on the ball, he believes players could in fact touch the ball and that the Maya played two types of games—a form of handball using a small, solid rubber ball, and what he calls "big ball," a ritualized form of the game using a larger rubber ball.

The notion that two distinct games developed is supported by the fact that pre-Columbian basketball courts were built in two shapes, one like a capital T and the other a capital I. Both courts were large, 20 to 30 feet wide and 40 to 50 feet long. They were surrounded by 8 1/2-foot whitewashed walls on which the hoops were mounted. A line on the ground divided the court in half. Tiered stone seats built into the walls indicate that the games attracted large crowds. The ancient basketball courts also had facilities where the teams prepared and dressed for the game. Locker rooms seem to have been as necessary an adjunct to basketball in ancient times as it is today.

Early Spanish explorers who watched the basketball game that the Aztec called *tlachitli* admired the way the sport was played and commented on how dexterous and skilled the players were. Because the ball was so hard and the play so rough, the team members wore padding much like a goalie on an ice hockey team does today. Hernán Cortés liked the Indian sport so much that he took two teams back to Spain to play exhibition matches before European audiences. However, basketball

Basketball courts similar to this one at XochIcalco in what is now Mexico served as the playing fields for the game invented by the Olmec, whose culture arose in about 1700 B.C. Players earned points by passing a rubber ball through vertical stone rings on the walls at each end of the court. *(Abbye A. Gorin Collection from the Latin American Library Photographic Archive, Tulane University)*

never caught on in Europe. As the conquistadores spread through the Aztec and Maya Empires, under the direction of the Catholic Church, they suppressed all "heathenish practices" of the indigenous people, including the game.

James Naismith, a non-Indian teacher of Bible studies and physical education at the Young Men's Christian Association (YMCA) Training School in Springfield, Massachusetts, reinvented basketball in the United States. Faced with a gym class full of bored and rebellious students, he was desperate to keep them occupied during the winter of 1891. He tried to modify the rules of LACROSSE, another game invented by American Indians, so that it could be played indoors. When that failed, he came up with a game in which points were scored by players getting the ball in peach baskets mounted on the end walls of the gym. His version of the game borrowed some of the offenses, fast breaks, and defenses from the strategies of lacrosse.

See also HELMETS, SPORTS.

## Sources/Further Reading

Blanchard, Kendall and Alyce Cheska. *The Anthropology of Sport, an Introduction.* South Hadley, Mass.: Bergin Garvey Publishers, 1985.

Coe, Michael D. *Mexico from the Olmecs to the Aztecs.* London: Thames and Hudson, 1994.

Gabriel, Kathryn. *Gambler Way: Indian Gaming in Mythology, History and Archaeology in North America.* Boulder, Colo.: Johnson Publishing, 1996.

Houston, Stephen. "Hoop Shots and Hieroglyphs." Presentation at the Fourth Annual Maya Symposium, Brevard Community College, February 8–11, 1996, Cocoa, Fla.

Scarborough, Vernon L. and David R. Wilcox, eds. *The Mesoamerican Ballgame.* Tucson: University of Arizona Press, 1991.

Stern, Theodore. *The Rubber-Ball Games of the Americans. Monographs of the American Ethnological Society,* No. 17. New York: J. J. Austin, 1950.

von Hagen, Victor Wolfgang. *The Aztec Man and Tribe.* New York: The New American Library, Inc., 1961.

**basket-weaving techniques** (ca. 8000 B.C.) *North American California and various, Mesoamerican, South American cultures*

Baskets are containers woven from plant fibers and materials such as twigs and grass. Although basketry is a craft that was and continues to be practiced throughout the world, American Indians, with their fine workmanship and unique designs, raised basket weaving to an art form. As early as 8000 B.C., Shoshone people of the North American Great Basin were making baskets of twine that they were able to cook in. American Indian basket makers used a number of styles as they wove containers. One technique was wickerwork, an over-and-under interweaving of horizontal (weft) fibers on a vertical frame made from sturdier material. This frame was known as the warp. Variations of wickerwork basket making such as plaintwining, three-strand braiding, and lattice-twining produced sturdy and tightly woven baskets that were beautifully designed as well as utilitarian. The second technique, coiling, was accomplished by twining together weft fibers and coiling them several times around a simple foundation. Plaiting, a technique similar to braiding, was also used for baskets. Many American Indian basket makers used a variety of styles, choosing the one based on the individual basket's intended use.

Usually women made baskets, crafting them from the fibers at hand. In the Northwest, basket makers used cedar; in the Northeast they used CATTAILS to weave mats that served as insulation for their homes. In the North American Southwest, fibrous plants such as the AGAVE provided basket material. Basket makers in what is now southern California used grass and rushes to weave their containers. They made patterns by choosing different WEAVING TECHNIQUES or by coloring, or dying, the fiber. (See also BLACK WALNUTS; DYES.) Sometimes basket makers used reeds that were treated with ashes and left to dry in the sun to give them a white color. They also dyed reeds with plant pigments or buried them to absorb mineral pigment from the soil.

The Pomo, a tribe living in what is now southern California, were known for their basket-weaving craftsmanship. They wove feathers, down, and shells into their designs. When English explorer Sir Francis Drake saw the feather baskets, he

American Indians found many uses for the baskets they made. The Pomo, a California tribe considered to be the most highly skilled basket makers in North America, wove these baskets. They were used to prepare mush and bread made from acorns.
*(Photograph No. NRHS-75-SAO-CODED-150FRESNO-16/Survey report of Fresno and Madera counties by L. D. Creel ca. 1920/Department of the Interior/Bureau of Indian Affairs Sacramento Area Office Sacramento/National Archives and Records Administration—Pacific Region)*

noted that they were so well made they held water. To challenge their skills, some Pomo weavers wove baskets the size of the head of a pin. Unlike the practice of other North American tribes, both Pomo women and men made baskets. They were known as the finest basket makers in all of the Americas.

American Indians took care when they made baskets because these items were such a necessity to daily life. Some baskets were made for gathering food. Others were intended for the preparation, serving, and storage of food. Loosely woven baskets were used as sifters or strainers. Southern California tribes, including the Pomo, used coiled baskets that were coated with ASPHALT both on the inside and the outside to carry and store water. These containers typically had long necks and stoppers. Open coiled baskets were often used for cooking. The food to be cooked was placed inside the basket and covered with water that was then heated by dropping hot rocks into it. Larger baskets were used to store food such as acorns. In areas where wood was scarce, CRADLEBOARDS were woven of wickerwork; sometimes even houses were constructed in this manner.

At the beginning of the 1900s, non-Indians in the United States began collecting American Indian baskets as curios to display in their homes. Indian women began making baskets for the tourists as a source of income. Soon non-Indian manufacturers began imitating the traditional Indian designs. Many of the baskets sold in home decorating stores today are based on traditional designs Indian basket makers created hundreds of years ago. Regarded as an art form, today baskets made by enrolled members of Indian tribes skilled in the technique have once again become popular collectors' items.

See also BOXES.

## Sources/Further Reading

Hoxie, Frederick E., ed. *Encyclopedia of North American Indians.* New York: Houghton Mifflin Company, 1996.

Hurst, David, Jay Miller, Richard White, Peter Nabokov, and Philip Deloria. *The Native Americans.* Atlanta: Turner Publishing, Inc., 1993.

Mason, Otis Tufton. *American Indian Basketry.* New York: Dover Publications, 1989.

Maxwell, James A. *America's Fascinating Indian Heritage.* Pleasantville, N.Y.: Reader's Digest Books, 1978.

Peterson, James B. *A Most Indispensable Art: Native Fiber Industries from Eastern North America.* Knoxville: University of Tennessee Press, 1996.

Porter, Frank W. *The Art of Native American Basketry.* Westport, Conn.: Greenwood Press, 1990.

Shupp, Mike. *Gabrielino Material Culture.* URL: http://www.csun.edu/~ms4427/gab.htm. Downloaded on January 6, 1999.

**bathing**   See HYGIENE, PERSONAL.

**beakers**   See KEROS.

**beans**   (ca. 5200 B.C.–3400 B.C.) *Mesoamerican; South American Andean; Circum-Caribbean; North American Southwest, Northeast, Great Plains, and Southeast cultures*
Beans are plants known as legumes that bear pods with edible seeds. Along with CORN and SQUASH, beans were among the earliest plants American Indians domesticated. By 5200–3400 B.C., farmers in the Tehuacán Valley of what is now Mexico were growing tepary beans (*Phaseolus acutofolius*) and a black variety of common beans (*P. vulgaris*). American Indians also domesticated common beans in the highlands of what is now Peru. Between 900 B.C. and A.D. 700, runner beans (*P. coccineus*) were added to the list of crops being grown in Mesoamerica; about 200 B.C. Lima or sieva beans (*P. lunatus*), were domesticated in the Andean Mountains. Although evidence exists that indigenous people gathered scarlet runner beans in the regions of Oaxaca and Tehuacan in Mexico at about 8750 B.C., these beans were not cultivated until 100 B.C.–A.D. 100.

Through indigenous TRADE networks, common beans made their way to the American Southwest, where they were cultivated along with tepary beans and jack beans (*Canavalia ennsiformes*) by about 1500 B.C. Careful SEED SELECTION enabled southwestern farmers to develop bush varieties that, unlike the twining kind, did not compete for water with other plants, such as corn growing in the same plot. Between 100

B.C. and A.D. 100, the Hohokam people, who lived in what is now the Arizona desert from 300 B.C. to A.D. 1100, began growing the variety of common bean known today as a kidney bean as well as jack beans. Sometime later lima beans were introduced to the Southwest. Tepary beans were the favored variety for Hohokam farmers because they had a high yield and were drought-resistant.

American-Indian agriculturists living in what is now called the Ohio Valley began growing common beans around A.D. 800. Northern Plains Indian farmers and those of the Eastern Woodlands began growing beans around A.D. 1000. Farmers on the plains developed the variety known today as great northern beans.

The most common way of cooking beans in both North America and Mesoamerica was to soak and boil or bake them. The Maya, whose culture flourished starting in about 1500 B.C. in what is now Mexico, often ate them cooked with CHILE peppers and accompanied by corn TORTILLAS, standard Mexican fare today. Sometimes beans were cooked with greens, such as chenopod (see also AGRICULTURE) and flavored with ACHIOTE. Beans were also parched and ground into flour, then reconstituted with the addition of water (see INSTANT FOOD). The Algonkin, who lived along the northern east coast of the United States, combined beans and corn for a dish they called SUCCOTASH. The combination of beans and corn as dietary staples, an American Indian tradition, provided a balanced diet. Beans contain lysine and tryptophan, two amino acids that corn lacks. Together, these two foods provide protein of high nutritional value. American colonists adopted the Algonquian dishes succotash and baked beans. Today these foods are considered New England traditions.

String beans, snap beans, pinto beans, common beans, butter beans, lima beans, navy beans, pole beans, French beans, Rangoon beans, Burma beans, and Madagascar beans all originated in the Americas. Although garbanzo beans (chickpeas) were grown in the Middle East, and adzuki and mung beans were cultivated in the Orient, at the time Columbus arrived in the New World, Europeans grew only fava beans. These were not a major part of the European diet. The first American beans to reach Europe were sent by Hernán Cortés to King Charles I of Spain in 1528. According to some reports, the king gave the beans to the pope, who passed them along to yet another benefactor. By 1532 they were being grown in Italy. Although the European colonists began eating beans, this uniquely American food never became tremendously popular in Europe.

## Sources/Further Reading

Coe, Sophie. *America's First Cuisines.* Austin: University of Texas Press, 1994.

Driver, Harold E. *Indians of North America.* Chicago: University of Chicago Press, 1969.

Hurt, R. Douglas. *Indian Agriculture in the Americas: Prehistory to Present.* Lawrence: University Press of Kansas, 1988.

Trager, James. *The Food Chronology: The Food Lover's Compendium of Events and Anecdotes from Prehistory to Present.* New York: Henry Holt, 1995.

Trigger, Bruce G., and Wilcomb E. Washburn, eds. *The Cambridge History of the Native Peoples of the Americas: Vol. I, Part I, North America.* New York: Cambridge University Press, 1996.

Weatherford, Jack. *Indian Givers: How the Indians of the Americas Transformed the World.* New York: Fawcett Columbine, 1988.

## beekeeping (precontact) *Mesoamerican cultures*

People who care for honey-producing insects in human-made hives in order to harvest honey are called beekeepers, or apiarists. Indigenous people throughout North-, Meso- and South America gathered wild honey to use as a sweetener, but the Maya have the distinction of being the first beekeepers in the Americas. (See also ANIMALS, DOMESTICATED.) Maya culture arose in what is now southern Mexico and in parts of Mesoamerica in about 1500 B.C.

Initially the Maya took honey from wild bee colonies, and then cut tree trunks containing wild hives, relocating these under the eaves of their houses, where they cared for them until the honey was harvested. The bees that they raised (*Apis meliponini*) did not have the ability to sting. The Maya called them *Xuna'an-Kab, Kolel'Kab,* or *Po'ol-Kab.* After closely studying the insects, the beekeepers learned what types of plants helped their bees produce the best honey and how to better protect the bee colonies. In time they learned to increase honey production by building special huts to shelter the hives. Each hut, or apiary, contained from 100 to 200 hive-logs. Maya beekeepers then began to breed many varieties of native, honey-producing, stingless bees.

The *Madrid Codex,* one of four surviving Maya BOOKS that were written prior to Spanish conquest, discusses beekeeping and its importance. The Maya used the honey harvested to sweeten CORNMEAL drinks and for a ceremonial fermented drink called *balche* that included honey, herbs, and water. Maya beekeepers were required to pay government tributes in honey. Both honey and beeswax were traded with the Aztec and other culture groups. (See also TRADE.)

The beekeeping technology that the Maya devised was just as sophisticated as that used in Europe until the 1700s. According to Gonzalo Fernandez de Oviedo, who wrote the *General Natural History of the Indies* (published 1535), Maya beekeeping was much more extensive than that taking place in Europe. Early Europeans in the Yucatán described bee yards containing thousands of hives.

Soon after their arrival, the Spaniards tried to stop local honey production in order to ensure that sugar from their newly established sugarcane plantations would be the sweetener of choice. Under these circumstances, production might have ended altogether were it not for the Catholic Church's requiring more beeswax for its candles than Spain could provide. As a result, the colonial government in the Yucatán Peninsula of what is now Mexico began encouraging bee culture and demanded beeswax tributes, as well as honey, from the Maya. In 1549, the first year such a tribute was levied, about 95 percent of the towns in the Yucatán Peninsula paid the Spanish colonial government a total of 7,293 pounds (or more than 26 pounds for every 20 people) of honey and 64,753 pounds of beeswax.

European bees were not introduced to the New World until they were sent to Florida in the late 1600s. These beekeeping experiments were a failure. In 1764 the Spaniards tried beekeeping again, this time in Cuba. Shortly afterward, bees of European origin made their way into Mexico. However, by 1821 they had not yet become established in the Yucatán, where traditional beekeepers, who continued to produce wax, undoubtedly preferred to work with stingless bees. Not until the end of the 1800s was the European bee finally introduced to the area.

### Sources/Further Reading

Coe, Sophie. *America's First Cuisines.* Austin: University of Texas Press, 1994.

History of the Beekeeping in Mexico. URL: www.metcall.com.mix. Downloaded on March 12, 1999.

Weatherford, Jack. *Indian Givers: How the Indians of the Americas Transformed the World.* New York: Fawcett Columbine, 1988.

## bee sting remedies See INSECT BITE AND BEE STING REMEDIES.

## bell peppers See PEPPERS, SWEET OR BELL.

## bells (ca. 1000 B.C.) *South American Andean, Mesoamerican cultures*

Bells are hollow metal instruments that emit a tone when struck. Indians of the New World invented several types of bells independently from cultures in other parts of the world. According to some sources, the Chavin, who lived in the northern part of what is now Peru starting in about 1000 B.C., made the first small bells. The Moche, whose culture arose in the same region in about 200 B.C., also made bells. In appearance these bells resembled the jingle bells used today as Christmas decorations, but the South American bell casings were solid, and the pellet was permanently enclosed inside. These bells were soldered (see also SOLDERING) together and then attached to ear plugs (jewelry that was worn in the ear lobes much like earrings). The bells were also used as ornaments for pendants, necklaces, nosepieces, and other decorative items. The Moche metalworkers (see METALLURGY) made these bells of copper, gold, silver, and from combinations of these metals.

The second group of indigenous people to produce bells were the Toltec, who lived in the Yucatán peninsula of what is now Mexico around A.D. 800. They invented a copper bell that resembled the European sleigh bell. It was larger than the Moche bells and had thin, cold-hammered walls with slits in them. A copper pellet was placed inside of it to make the sound.

Archaeological evidence exists that the Toltec made bells from an alloy of copper using the LOST-WAX CASTING TECHNIQUE. It is believed they traded these bells, which have been found in Aztec archaeological sites on the western coast of what is now Mexico (see TRADE). In turn, the Aztec traded the bells to the Indians of the North American Southwest, such as the Anasazi whose culture flourished from 350 B.C. to A.D. 1450.

See also WELDING, SWEAT.

## Sources/Further Reading

Benson, Elizabeth P. *The Maya World.* New York: Thomas Y. Crowell Company, 1967.

Driver, Harold E. *Indians of North America.* Chicago: University of Chicago Press, 1969.

Mason, J. Alden. *The Ancient Civilizations of Peru.* Rev. ed. New York: Penguin Books, 1988.

**bindweed**   See JALAP.

**bird calls**   See CALLS, ANIMAL AND BIRD.

**birth control**   See CONTRACEPTION, ORAL.

**bison**  (buffalo, *Bison bison*)  (precontact)  *North American Great Plains cultures*

Bison are hoofed mammals that have curved horns and a dark brown, shaggy coat. They are distinguished by a shoulder hump. Larger than cattle, bison have 14 pairs of ribs compared to the 13 that cattle have. Long before the first Europeans arrived in North America, American bison roamed the continent from Great Slave Lake in what is now Canada to what is now Mexico. They were found in the Eastern Woodlands in the areas that are now New York, Pennsylvania, and in Georgia and Florida. They also grazed the river valleys of the Pacific Northwest. An estimated 60 to 70 million bison—or buffalo, as they are commonly called—ranged North America in 1492. The heaviest concentration was in the Great Plains of the United States and Canada, from the Rocky Mountains to the Mississippi River and south to what is now Texas. Although indigenous people from many regions used the American bison for food, leather, and other purposes, the tribal people of the plains developed an entire culture centered on the animals. Plains tribes including the Cheyenne, Arapaho, and Dakota, Lakota, and Nakota, and others used every part of the bison and considered it an integral part of their religious belief system.

A variety of bison, sometimes erroneously termed the *aurochs,* existed in Europe and was the subject of ancient cave paintings on that continent. Small bands of these bison (*Bison bonasus*) survived in the forests of England, continental Europe, and parts of Asia but had long been extinct by the 1400s, when Europeans set sail to the Americas. The word *buffalo* is actually the Italian spelling of the Spanish and Portuguese word *bufalo* and was used for the animals that roamed North America as early as 1544, when the Spanish explorer, Hernando de Soto, described them. Zoologists do not consider the American bison a true buffalo like the beasts of burden found in Asia and Africa. Although bison existed in other parts of the world, no other continent produced a single wild game animal in such large numbers.

The indigenous people of North America used rawhide for shields, containers (see also BOXES), MOCCASIN soles, ropes, boats, SNOWSHOES, drums, and even splints for fixing broken limbs (see ORTHOPEDIC TECHNIQUES). Buckskin, the hide which had been tanned with the animals' brains and sometimes the liver (see TANNING, BRAIN), was made into moccasin tops, bedding, clothing, tipi covers (see also TIPIS), bags, backrests, dolls (see also TOYS) and mittens. American Indians transformed bison horns into cups, fire carriers, spoons, headdresses, medicines (see also MEDICINE; PHARMACOLOGY), and, after the arrival of the Europeans, powder horns. The meat was eaten fresh or dried into JERKY, which decreased its weight by five-sixths of that of fresh meat, making it an ideal traveling food. Jerky, which could be stored for three years, or more, was also pounded to make PEMMICAN, another trail food. Indian people also ate the brain and used bison blood in soups and puddings as well as for paints. The animal's fur was used to line moccasins, as pillow stuffing, and for headdresses. Bison sinew and muscles became glue, thread, arrow ties, and bowstrings. Some tribes used sinew to laminate bows. (See BOWS, LAMINATED.) Fat was rendered to make tallow, hair pomade, cold weather balm, a skin protector, and soap. (See also HYGIENE, PERSONAL.) Bison bones were turned into sled runners, splints, scrapers, dice (see also GAMES, DICE), SHOVELS, arrowheads, awls, and knives. Internal organs, such as the stomach and bladder, were used as containers. The paunch liner was used to wrap meat, for a canteen, and as a collapsible drinking cup. Buffalo skulls were used in religious ceremonies, and the hooves were used for rattles. Even bison chips—dried dung—were useful. They could be burned as fuel or used as an absorbent filler for a DISPOSABLE DIAPER. No part of the animal was wasted. Even the tail was used as a fly swatter and as a hairbrush.

American Indian buffalo-hunting methods, developed over thousands of years, were complex, and required group cooperation. Sometimes these involved surrounding the buffalo herd then driving it into some type of natural or quickly constructed corral. Frequently the bison, which stampede when they sense danger, were driven over a cliff. The Indians often assigned one person to watch from the bottom; once the estimated number needed had been driven over the cliff, he would signal those herding the buffalo to stop. At Head-Smashed-In Buffalo Jump, a United Nations Educational Scientific and Cultural Organization World Heritage Site located in what is now Alberta, Canada, this hunting technology was very sophisticated. The site includes a gathering basin, a natural grazing area with water, where buffaolo were attracted. American Indian hunters built drive lanes made of many piles of stone that led to the edge of the cliff in order to help them direct the stampeding herds. While buffalo grazed in the gathering basin, young men called buffalo runners, who were trained to imitate the sound of a lost calf, lured the herd to the lanes. Hunters shouted and waved from behind to scare the animals into stampeding and falling to their deaths from the buffalo jump. The campsite and meat processing area were located just below the kill site at the bottom of the cliff. Here the women butchered the meat from the carcasses and dried it to make JERKY. From jerky they made PEMMICAN. They also cracked the bones and boiled them by dropping hot stones into hide-lined pits filled with water to render the marrow. In this way hundreds of animals could be killed and processed at one time. Similar jumps and processing sites existed throughout the plains of North America, but without gathering areas and driving lanes. Although Indian hunters killed many animals, the numbers they killed were small in comparison to those killed by non-Indian buffalo hunters in the 1800s.

The reintroduction of the horse to the northern plains by the Spaniards in the 1600s made American Indians more mobile and efficient hunters. By the 1840s, despite 200 years of mounted hunting by Indians and the incursion of European settlers, an estimated 40 to 50 million bison still inhabited North America.

The 1840s marked the beginning of professional buffalo hunting that ended the indigenous plains buffalo economy forever. White adventurers first began killing buffalo to supply the needs of the railroad crews laying track throughout the West. Later they provisioned U.S. Army troops with bison meat. Because buffalo robes (hides with the fur on them) were in high demand, both on the East Coast of the United States and in Europe, hunters often killed thousands of buffalo a day, skinning them and leaving the carcasses to rot. The introduction of the long-range, high-powered Sharps rifle allowed hunters to kill the buffalo from a distance and to kill them in great numbers. A buffalo hunter could slaughter as many as 100 to 300 of the animals in a day.

Soon it became clear to U.S. policymakers that the Plains Indians would not stop fighting the U.S. Army troops trying to force them onto reservations unless the buffalo herds that were the Indians' source of food, clothing, and shelter were destroyed. Columbus Delano, President Ulysses Grant's secretary of the interior said in 1873, "The civilization of the Indian is impossible while the buffalo remains upon the plains." Although it was an unwritten policy, the U.S. Army encouraged the extermination of the buffalo as a military tactic to rid the plains of Indians. During the 1870s, after about 30 years of commercial hunting, and the U.S. Army policy an estimated 20,000 buffalo hunters drove the once vast herds to near-extinction. By 1887 less than a thousand of the animals were left on the Great Plains. Today, through the efforts of ecologists and American Indian tribes, bison are making a comeback. These animals are now raised commercially, and their meat is sold in restaurants and grocery stores. Because bison meat contains less fat than beef, it is marketed to health-conscious consumers.

## Sources/Further Reading

"The Buffalo Culture of the Plains Indians." *The Wind River Rendezvous* 8, no. 2, (Spring, 1983).

Dary, David. *The Buffalo Book: The Full Saga of the American Animal.* Lancaster: Ohio University Press, 1990.

Geist, Valerius. *Buffalo Nation: History and Legend of the North American Bison.* New York: Voyageur Press, 1998.

Haines, Francis. *The Buffalo: The Story of American Bison and Their Hunters from Prehistoric Times to the Present.* Norman: University of Oklahoma Press, 1995.

*Head-Smashed-In Buffalo Jump Archaeological Facts.* URL: http//www.headsmashed-in.com/frmarchaeol2.htm. Downloaded on July 2, 2001.

Schult, Milo J. and Arnold O. Haugen. *Where the Buffalo Roam.* Interior, South Dakota: The Badlands Natural History Association in cooperation with Badlands National Park. (undated)

**bixin**  See ACHIOTE.

**blackberries (*Rubus*)** (precontact)  *North American Northeast and Subarctic cultures*
Blackberries are a type of prickly, fruit-bearing bush that grows throughout the world. Blackberry fruits consist of a number of black or dark red drupelets (tiny seeded fruits). The varieties that grew in what is now Canada and the northern part of the United States were used as food by many tribes such as the Potawatomi, the Mohawk, and the people of the subarctic, who gathered and dried them for winter storage. Some North American tribes understood that blackberries had ASTRINGENT properties and used the berries to treat diarrhea. They also used tea made from the root or leaves to treat excessive menstrual bleeding and fevers. Early European settlers used blackberries that grew in North America for jams, jellies, vinegar, and brandy.

## Sources/Further Reading

Hutchens, Alma R. *Indian Herbology of North America.* Boston: Shambhala, 1991.

Moerman, Dan. *Native American Ethnobotany Database: Food, Drugs, Dyes and Fibers of Native North American Peoples.* 16 March 1999 http://www.umd.umich.edu/cgi-bin/herb.

**black walnuts (*Juglans nigra*, L.)** (precontact)  *North American California, Great Plains, and Southeast cultures*
Black walnuts grow on a tree native to the United States and Canada. The nuts are covered with a green husk about the size of a golf ball. Indians from a number of tribes used the pulp of the husk, which turns black once the nut falls from the tree, for dyeing (see also DYES) and tanning (see also TANNING, BRAIN). The Pomo, who lived in what is now California, used the hulls to dye the rushes that they used for basket

making. (See also BASKET WEAVING TECHNIQUES.) Some California Indians used the shells for gambling games. (See also GAMES, DICE.)

The Comanche used a poultice made from black walnut leaves to treat ringworm. Modern herbal practitioners sometimes use the hulls to treat ringworm today. The hulls are believed to contain a substance that is effective against the fungus that causes the condition. Although American Indians used black walnut to treat a number of illnesses from headaches to toothaches to constipation, parts of the tree are poisonous, so they were very cautious about the dosage.

Indians throughout North America, including the Pomo of California, the Cherokee of the Southeast, and Mesquaki of the Northeast, shelled and ate the nuts that are high in magnesium. The Iroquois and Narragansett, Eastern Woodlands tribes that lived in New England, used crushed nutmeats and black walnut oil in CORNBREAD and pudding. The Plains tribes, including the Dakota, Omaha, Ponca, and Pawnee, ground the nuts and made them into soup or ate them with honey. Today black walnuts are a popular ingredient in candy and ice cream throughout the world. The black walnut tree produces a hardwood that is valued by modern woodworkers for making fine furniture and other projects.

## Sources/Further Reading

Carson, Dale. *New Native American Cooking.* New York: Random House, 1996.

Duke, James A. *The Green Pharmacy.* New York: St. Martins Press, 1997.

Hutchens, Alma R. *Indian Herbology of North America.* Boston: Shambhala, 1991.

Moerman, Dan. *Native American Ethnobotany Database: Food, Drugs, Dyes and Fibers of Native North American Peoples.* URL: http://www.umd.umich.edu/cgi-bin/herb. Downloaded on February 5, 1999.

*Rancho Santa Ana Botanic Garden Web Page.* URL: http://www.cgu.edu/inst/rsa/education/teachers/iu/html. Downloaded on February 5, 1999.

## blowguns (1500 B.C.) *North American Southeast, Mesoamerican, South American Tropical Forest cultures*

Blowguns are long, hollow tubes through which a pointed dart is propelled with a strong puff of breath. The Maya, whose culture arose in what is now Mexico in about 1500 B.C., were the first to invent the blowgun in precontact America. The Aztec, whose civilization arose in what is now Mexico and in parts of Mesoamerica starting in about A.D. 1100, and the Indians of South America used them for hunting and as weapons. The Indians of the Amazon region of South America relied on them extensively and continue to use them today. The blowgun did not find widespread use among North American Indians except for the Choctaw, Cherokee, and Seminole peoples, all of whom lived in the Southeast.

All of the tribes that utilized the blowgun used small darts as ammunition. In the Amazonian region the darts were tipped with the natural poison CURARE. Montezuma, the Aztec emperor at the time of Spanish conquest, referred to the blowgun as a blowpipe. He used it in his personal gardens for sport and fired small pieces of baked clay shaped like marbles as missiles. Some Mesoamerican blowguns or blowpipes were made of copper.

Not all blowguns were constructed in the same way. Although they appear simple, these weapons demonstrate a working understanding of physics. The Indians of the Amazon region, particularly the Shuar, Achuar, and Aguaruna tribes, relied on master technicians to produce their blowguns because the engineering technique used required an experienced specialist. These blowguns were made from two equal lengths of hardwood fitted together to form a longer tube. The seam where the two pieces joined had to be perfectly fitted so that there would not be a ridge on the inside of the bore to skew the trajectory of the missile.

The blowgun used by tribes in the southeastern part of what is now the United States was about five or six feet long. Because of this length, it bowed slightly when a hunter held it in the ready position. To compensate for this bend in the blowgun, it was made with the hole bored so that the ends of the hole bowed slightly upward when it lay on a flat surface. In the ready position, the bore became perfectly straight.

## Sources/Further Reading

Closs, Michael P. *Native American Mathematics.* Austin: University of Texas Press, 1986.

Driver, Harold E. *Indians of North America.* Chicago: University of Chicago Press, 1969.

Mason, J. Alden. *The Ancient Civilizations of Peru.* Rev. ed. New York: Penguin Books, 1988.

Soustelle, Jacques. *Daily Life of the Aztecs.* Stanford, Calif.: Stanford University Press, 1985.

## blueberries (*Vaccinimum*) (precontact) *North American Northeast and Great Plains cultures*

Blueberries are bushes that bear small blue to black globes of very sweet fruit. American Indians gathered wild blueberries indigenous to North America for both food and medicine. They added dried or fresh blueberries to soups and stews. The Indians who lived on the shores of what is now called Lake Huron mixed powdered, dried berries with water, CORNMEAL, and wild honey to make a pudding, reported French explorer Samuel de Champlain in the early 17th century. Following the example set by the American Indians, the Pilgrims, who landed on the coast of what became New England, learned to dry blueberries. Later, explorers Meriwether Lewis and William Clark relied on a mixture of pounded blueberries and meat that had been dried over a fire to provide nourishment on their journey to find a passage to the Northwest. This food was called PEMMICAN.

Utilized as a restorative by Indian people for years, blueberry tea was soon relied upon by Colonial women as a tonic during childbirth (see also OBSTETRICS). Soon settlers were using blueberry juice as a cough medicine. Civil War soldiers kept their strength up by drinking sweetened blueberry juice. Today blueberries have been found to be a healthy food containing high levels of iron; vitamins A, C, and E; bacterial inhibitors; and folic acid. They also contain antioxidants, chemicals that neutralize DNA-damaging free radicals that scientists believe may play a role in cancer and aging.

Anthocyanin, a naturally occurring chemical in blueberry pigment, is currently being researched as a cataract prevention substance. (See also CATARACT REMOVAL.) In addition, researchers believe anthocyanin may be an antibacterial agent. (See also ANTIBIOTICS.) Blueberry juice has been shown to be as effective a treatment for bladder infections as cranberry juice is. (See also CRANBERRIES.) In Sweden dried blueberries are used to treat diarrhea in children. Some researchers believe that anthocyanin works by killing *Escherichia coli,* a bacteria that can cause diarrhea.

Although blueberries also grow in Asia and Europe, it is the wild highbush American variety, a staple of the diet of many American Indians, that was domesticated in the United States at the turn of the century. By 1935, 30 new varieties had been developed, and a major industry had begun. In 1995, 183 million pounds of blueberries were grown in the United States. Today blueberries are grown commercially in 30 states. Michigan, Indiana, New Jersey, North Carolina, Georgia, Oregon, and Washington are the highest producers. British Columbia is the largest blueberry producer in Canada. About 60 to 70 percent of the blueberries sold in North America are cultivated; the rest are wild. Half of the commercial blueberries are turned into jams, pies, and other bakery products and processed food. According to the North American Blueberry Council, more than 10 new food products containing blueberries are introduced to the market every month.

## Sources/Further Reading

Duke, James A. *The Green Pharmacy.* New York: St. Martins Press, 1997.
Kowalchuk, J. "Antiviral Activity of Fruit Extracts." *J Food Science* 41 (1976): 1013–1017.
*North American Blueberry Council Web Page.* URL: http://webcom/bberry/welcome.html. Downloaded on February 6, 1999.
Vander Kloet, S. P. *The Genus Vaccinium in North America.* Publication 1828. Ottawa: Research Branch, Agriculture Canada, 1988.

## blue-green algae (spirulina, *Spirulina geitleri*)

(A.D. 1000–A.D. 1519) *Mesoamerican cultures*
Blue-green algae is a primitive aquatic plant that has no leaves, stems, or roots but contains chlorophyll. A popular item in health food stores today, blue-green algae was a staple in the diet of the Aztec, who skimmed it from lakes in the Valley of Mexico, including Lake Texcoco, with nets or shovels. The Aztec Empire was established in Mesoamerica starting in about A.D. 1100.

Once it was harvested, the Aztec sun-dried the algae and cut it into bricks. When preserved this way, it would remain edible for a year. The Aztec, who called the algae *tecuitlatl,* ate it with TORTILLAS or toasted CORN. Sometimes it was combined with CHILES and TOMATOES to make a sauce. The Inca, who established an empire in what is now Peru in about A.D. 1000, also ate freshwater algae, either fresh or dried.

Some of the Spanish conquistadores referred to blue-green algae as slime; most refused to eat it. After the Spanish conquest of the Aztec Empire, the lakes in the Valley of Mexico were drained. Indigenous people stopped eating the algae that had once been a major part of their diet. Rediscovered in the 1970s, spirulina is sold as a health food today. Blue-green algae has been found to contain 70 percent protein and an essential amino acid, linolenic acid. Combined with corn, another Aztec dietary staple, it makes a complete protein that the body can easily absorb. Blue-green algae is also high in vitamin $B_{12}$ and beta carotine and has a high vitamin content, including phosphorus, thiamin, riboflavin, and niacin. A fast-growing crop, the algae from the surface of Lake Texcoco alone has been estimated to have been enough to meet the protein needs of the 1.5 million people who lived in Tehnochtitlan and the surrounding area before Spanish conquest. (See CITIES, AMERICA'S FIRST.)

Drought-proof and independent of rainfall, spirulina has been investigated as a solution for famine in various parts of the world. The World Health Organization found that eating one gram of blue-green algae a day would decrease the incidence of blindness caused from vitamin A deficiency in malnourished children. As a result, the organization is encouraging its cultivation throughout the world.

See also AQUACULTURE.

## Sources/Further Reading

Coe, Sophie. *America's First Cuisines.* Austin: University of Texas Press, 1994.
Diet and Nutrition Resource Center, Mayo Clinic. URL: http://www.mayohealth.org/mayo/askdiet/htm/new/qd970618.htm. Posted on June 18, 1997.
Ortiz de Monteljano, Bernard. *Aztec Medicine, Health and Nutrition.* New Brunswick, N.J.: Rutgers University Press, 1990.

## board games (1500 B.C.–A.D. 1519) *Mesoamerican, North American Southwest cultures*

Board games are played by moving counters, or "men," over a pattern drawn or painted on a flat surface. A roll of the dice (see also GAMES, DICE) usually determines the number of spaces a player may move. *Patolli* and *bul,* two board games played by ancient Mesoamericans, were engaged in recreationally, as a form of gambling, and for religious purposes. These games, blending strategy and chance, were just as challenging and entertaining as those devised in Europe or Asia. Boards for *patolli* have been found scratched into building floors and on benches at Aztec archaeological sites; the Florentine Codex (see also BOOKS) shows a picture of two people playing *patolli*. (The Aztec Empire was established in what is now Mexico and parts of Mesoamerica in about A.D. 1100.) Although *bul* is certain to have originated with the Maya, who were playing it by the time the Europeans arrive, no game boards have been found. (Maya culture flourished starting in about 1500 B.C.)

*Patolli* is often credited with having Aztec origins; however, some archaeologists believe that both games are Maya in origin. *Patolli* boards have been discovered throughout the Maya world.

Both *patolli* and *bul* could be played on round or square boards, but the rules were different. *Patolli* was similar to modern-day backgammon or Parcheesi. Generally it was played on a marked board or bark PAPER, with BEANS for counters. The first person to travel around the board and return home safely would be the winner. Whether or not the Aztec originated the game, they played it frequently and bet high stakes on who would win.

*Bul,* the Maya word for playing with dice, utilized grains of CORN for markers and involved throwing other grains of corn that had been burned on one side as dice. Players advanced their markers by throwing the dice. If they landed on a space occupied by another player's marker, or "warrior," they could capture it, then change direction to drag it back to the other end of the board. At that point the opponent's warrior would be officially dead. The game ended when all of one of the player's men had been "killed." When more than two people played, the rules were more complex. Some Maya still play a version of the game today.

Board games were popular throughout North America as well. Much like modern board games, they were played with dice and counters, or "men," that were moved around a course marked out on a board. For example the Hopi, a tribe living in what is now Arizona, played a game called *totolospi,* using dice made of two pieces of cane with designs burned into the round side. Players placed stones that they called *animals* on a board marked with a square design, including a number of circles around the perimeter. Usually these boards were inscribed on sandstone slabs. The opponents would take turns dropping the cane pieces and moving their animals around the board. The number of spaces they moved was determined by the number of blank and inscribed canes that were visible after each throw. The object of the game was to be the first to travel around the board and reach "home."

## Sources/Further Reading
Culin, Stewart. *Games of the North American Indians.* Reprint. Lincoln: University of Nebraska Press, 1992.

Gabriel, Kathryn. *Gambler Way: Indian Gaming in Mythology, History and Archaeology in North America.* Boulder, Colo.: Johnson Books, 1996.

*A Mayan Game of Chance.* URL: http://www.halfmoon. org/bul.html. Downloaded on January 10, 1999.

von Hagen, Victor Wolfgang. *The Aztec: Man and Tribe.* New York: The New American Library Inc, 1961.

**bolas** (ca. 13,000 B.C.) *North American Arctic, South American Southern cultures*

Bolas—ancient weapons used for hunting or warfare—are made with weights affixed to cords. The bolas used by Argentine gauchos, or cowboys, on the Pampas today were in use in Peru as early as 15,000 years ago according to some archaeologists. Inuit people of what is now Alaska also used bolas for hunting. Unlike the atlatl or the sling, which are independent inventions, the bola is indigenous to the Americas. Archaeologists believe the earliest targets of bolas were the mastodons at the end of the Paleolithic era.

*Bolas* is Spanish for "balls." The South American version of the bola is made of two or three golf ball-sized, grooved stones tied to leather thongs, or cords. These cords are about two to three feet in length, and their free ends are joined together. The Mapuche people, who continue to live in the southern part of South America today, used bolas to hunt LLAMA, deer, and rhea. When the Spaniards introduced horses to what is now Chile and Argentina, bola hunting was done on horseback, and the era of the gaucho began.

Early explorers to the Arctic regions found Inuit people using what they called the *qilamitautit* to hunt birds. These were believed to have been invented by people of the Thule culture about A.D. 1000. Inuit *qilamitautits* contained four to

Bolas, a weapon unique to the Americas, were used both for hunting and for warfare by American Indians in South America and the North American Arctic. This drawing is based on one made by Indian artist and historian Felipe Guamán Poma de Ayala, prior to A.D. 1615. (Nueva Coronica y Buen Gobierno)

eight carved ivory weights connected to a wooden handle by sinew cords about 30 inches long. These were carried in a leather bag around the hunter's neck. The range of these weapons was reported to be 35 yards.

Throwing a bola so that it would meet its mark took considerable skill. The weapon was used by holding one of the weighted ends and twirling the other two ends overhead. Before releasing the bola, the thrower needed to have a clear line of sight to the target. Once the bola was thrown at the target, the weights would spread out and spin, much like helicopter blades. When the bola hit its target, the loose weights wrapped themselves around the target from two different directions, effectively entrapping the target and rendering it immobile until the hunter or warrior could reach the prey, either man or animal.

## Sources/Further Reading

Josephy, Jr., Alvin M., ed. *America in 1492: The World of the Indian People Before the Arrival of Columbus.* New York: Random House, 1991.

Mathiassen, Therkel. *Archaeological Collection From The Western Eskimos.* Copenhagen: Gyldendalske Boghandel, 1945.

Oswalt, Wendal N. *Eskimo and Explorers.* Novato, Calif.: Chandler & Sharp, 1979.

## books (ca. A.D. 660) *Mesoamerican cultures*

A book is a set of written pages that have been bound together. Many Mesoamerican cultures compiled their writing into books well before the Europeans reached the Americas. They include the Maya, whose culture arose in about 1500 B.C.; the Toltec; the Mixtec, who followed the Toltec; and the Aztec, who established their empire in about A.D. 1100. Because the books that existed at the time of Spanish conquest threatened the Spaniards' rule by keeping indigenous culture alive, they ordered most of them destroyed shortly after seizing power.

The Toltec, the first Mesoamericans known to have created books, are believed to have written a religious encyclopedia as early as A.D. 660. Mixtec language, which was spoken by the precursors of the Aztecs, is preserved in the Codex Nuttall. Anthropologists believe that because Mixtec books were intended to serve only as a memory aid for oral historians, they recorded a narrow range of historical and ritual events. (See also AMERICAN HISTORY, RECORDED.)

Many of the early Maya books contained the histories of cities, lists of rulers, genealogies, notations of deaths, and descriptions of wars. Some books written by the Maya were filled with accounts of ownership for personal objects such as jewelry. Texts from the later period survive in four codices. These concern themselves more with astronomy and religion than matters of state.

Aztec books were produced for a variety of reasons. Some, like the Codex Borgia, consisted of depictions and descriptions of gods and rituals and contained information about the 260-day CALENDAR. The Aztec historical books included a list of years in the year-count calendar, with the key events that happened in those years. Codex Mendoza and the *Tira de la Peregrinacion* are examples of historical books. Administrative books, like section two of the Codex Mendoza, consisted of tribute lists, maps of the territories, and land-holding records. Often these books were collected into libraries. Bernal Díaz del Castillo, who accompanied Hernán Cortés in Mexico, reported that Montezuma, the Aztec emperor at the time of conquest, had a "great house full of books."

The Aztec called the scribes who made the books *tlacuilo.* Of them, Fray Bernardo Sahagun would later write that they not only had to be artists but also had to grind pigment to make the colors. Aztec scribes often specialized in one type of book. The profession was hereditary, passing from parent to child. An honored art among the Aztec, book painting and inscribing was practiced by both men and women. Several codices show scribes of both sexes doing their work.

Mesoamerican books were recorded on long sheets of PAPER made from the soft inner bark of the amate, or tropical fig tree, and were folded like a screen. Both sides of the paper were coated with a sizing made of fine lime plaster. The hieroglyphs were painted in black and red inks with a fine brush, and the texts were lavishly illustrated. As time threatened disintegration, Mesoamerican scribes preserved books by recopying them.

Fray Díaz del Castillo, one of the first Europeans to see the books, was impressed by their quality and quantity, remarking that he had seen great stacks of them near the Aztec city-state of Compala. He wrote: "Then we came on some towns and found idol houses and many paper books doubled together in folds like Spanish cloth, that I do not know how to describe it, seeing things as we did that had never been heard or seen before or even dreamed about." Two of the books were sent back to Spain with the first gold that Hernándo Cortés and his men collected.

For a time early Spanish missionaries encouraged the scribes to create more books to enable the priests to become familiar with the people they hoped to convert. Continuing to use their own languages, the *tlacuilos* continued copying pre-Columbian documents, sometimes changing them to fit the missionaries' demands and even writing tribute registers from what they remembered had been collected during the rule of Montezuma. The work continued until a royal decree from Spain demanded that not only Native books but also works by conquistadores and missionaries about Native peoples, such as Fray Bernardo de Sahagun's *General History of the Things of New Spain,* be destroyed. The 1577 decree ordered delivery to the representatives of the crown of all originals and copies of writings about pre-Columbian society and culture so that they could be burned. It also forbade further writing in any language containing the "superstitions and way of life these Indians had."

The books that the Spaniards destroyed contained records from original books that were hundreds of years old. Diego de Landa, a Franciscan priest who was named bishop of Yucatán, recorded the reaction to the destruction of the Maya books in the Yucatán: "We found a large number of books in these characters and, as they contained nothing in which there were not to be seen superstition and lies of the devil, we burned them all, which they regretted to an amazing degree and which caused them much affliction."

To their credit, some priests attempted to save books from the flames. Fray Juan de Zumarraga collected all the Aztec books he could find, especially in the royal library at Texcoco, east of Mexico City, which was a repository of national archives for the Aztec. Most of the books that escaped burning by the Spaniards were ruined or lost to the ravages of time. Only 12 authenticated pre-Columbian Aztec books, or codices, remain.

Four pre-Columbian Maya books are in existence today: The Dresden, Madrid, Paris, and Grolier Codices. All four focus on religion and deities rather than secular history. The Dresden and Grolier codices served as ALMANACS, which gave information such as tables for Venus rising. Books of Maya literature, such as the Popol Vuh, the sacred book of the highland Quiche Maya, were recorded during colonial times from oral tradition. About 500 Mesoamerican manuscripts prepared by scribes after conquest survived. Most of the surviving Maya and Aztec records exist on stone or POTTERY.

See also WRITING SYSTEMS.

**Sources/Further Reading**
Brotherson, Gordon. *Painted Books from Mexico.* London: British Museum Press, 1995.
Fagan, Brian M. *Kingdoms of Gold, Kingdoms of Jade: The Americas Before Columbus.* New York: Thames and Hudson, Inc., 1991.
Jennings, Francis. *The Founders of America: How Indians Discovered the Land, Pioneered in it, and Created Great Classical Civilizations; How They Were Plunged into a Dark Age by Invasion and Conquest; and How They Are Now Reviving.* New York: W. W. Norton, 1993.
Josephy, Jr., Alvin M. *The Indian Heritage of America,* Rev. ed. Boston: Houghton Mifflin Company, 1991.
Sharer, Robert. *Daily Life in Maya Civilization.* Westport, Conn.: Greenwood Press, 1996.
Smith, Michael E. *The Peoples of America: The Aztecs.* Cambridge, Mass.: Blackwell 1996.
von Hagen, Victor Wolfgang. *The Aztec: Man and Tribe.* New York: The New American Library, Inc., 1961.

**botanical gardens** See GARDENS, BOTANICAL.

**bottles** See ASPHALT; BASKET WEAVING TECHNIQUES; KEROS.

**bow drills** See DRILLS, BOW.

**bows, laminated** (precontact) *North American Great Basin, Arctic, and Subarctic cultures*
Lamination is the process of covering an object with thin sheets of material that are bonded together. Bows are curved weapons that are used to launch arrows. American Indian tribes of the Great Basin region, located in what are now western Oregon,

southern Idaho, Utah, and Wyoming discovered that by laminating their bows with sinew (the tendons of animals) they could dramatically increase the efficiency of their bows. These first compound, laminated bows in precontact America were an important discovery, since the indigenous people of this area hunted on foot for the large game they depended on for food.

To shape the bow, they first heated mountain mahogany (not a true mahogany) or another hard wood over an open fire. Next, they bent the wood into a double curve. Afterward, they polished and smoothed the bow with a piece of obsidian flint. (See also FLINTKNAPPING.) Once the shaping and polishing were completed, the next step was to laminate the bow. The bow maker placed wet strips of deer sinew along the concave and convex sides of the bow's length. One layer was thus positioned and allowed to dry, and then another layer was placed on the opposite side of the bow. When it was dry, the sinew became like plastic or fiberglass. It was also just as pliable. Next, wet sinew strips would be wound around the bow, across the grain of the two layers that had already been fixed to the bow. After this had dried, the bow maker attached bowstrings to the ends of the outward curves of the bow. When the bow had been strung, the archer held it halfway between the ends at the inward central curve in order to use it to propel arrows at game.

The laminating process made the bow incredibly powerful. A laminated bow could send an arrow completely through a deer at close range. In some instances, European observers reported that American Indians shot BISON with such force that their arrows passed through and projected out the other side. The power of this bow was comparable to the English crossbow. Lamination also increased the distance from which the hunter could place a projectile into a target.

Inuit people living in the Arctic and subarctic regions of North America used a similar process to make their bows. In the far North there are few trees, so they used pieces of short wood and mountain sheep and goat horns. They then employed wet rawhide to hold the pieces of the bow together. The horns were heated until they straightened and then were pierced together using a lamination process similar to that used by the indigenous people of the Great Basin.

**Sources/Further Reading**
Folsom, Franklin and Mary Elting Folsom. *America's Ancient Treasures,* 4th ed. Albuquerque: University of New Mexico Press, 1993.
Laubin, Reginald and Gladys Laubin. *American Indian Archery.* Norman: University of Oklahoma Press, 1980.
Marriott, Alice, and Rachlin, Carol K. *American Indian Epic: The Story of the American Indian.* New York: New American Library, 1970.

**boxes** (precontact) *North American Northwest Coast, Northeast, and Great Plains cultures*
In addition to being sophisticated carpenters who constructed impressive cedar buildings (see also CARPENTRY TECHNIQUES), the American Indians of the Northwest Coast excelled at

smaller projects as well. One of their specialties was wooden boxes used for storage. Some of these were made by hollowing out blocks of wood and fitting them with covers, but others were made of bent wood. Box makers carefully grooved a cedar plank then steamed it so that it could be bent into a square or rectangle with three seamless corners. They would often sew the joint and make it watertight with clamshell paste. Other boxes were made by coating one surface of the joint with pigment and then pressing the two pieces together to form a bond. The bottom was grooved around the rim so that the sides would fit tightly into it, and the joints were reinforced with pegs fitted into drilled holes (see also DRILLS, BOW) and sealed with clamshell paste. These wooden boxes were used for storing food preserved in fish oil (see also FOOD PRESERVATION) and as cooking pots. Food was cooked by placing it in the box with water and adding red-hot stones to raise the temperature so that the water would boil.

In the Eastern Woodlands, birch bark was used for food containers as well as for covering CANOES. The containers served both for storage and for food preparation. Readily available, waterproof, and rot resistant, the bark was cut to shape and sewn together with spruce roots. These boxes were so finely constructed that they were watertight. Like the Northwest Coast tribes, Northeast tribes cooked food by dropping hot stones in water-filled containers.

Indigenous people of the Plains sewed together pieces of BUFFALO rawhide to make *parefleche* containers used to store PEMMICAN, buffalo JERKY, and small items.

See also BASKET WEAVING TECHNIQUES.

### Sources/Further Reading

Driver, Harold E. *Indians of North America.* Chicago: University of Chicago Press, 1969.

Maxwell, James A. *America's Fascinating Indian Heritage.* Pleasantville, N.Y.: Reader's Digest Books, 1978.

## Boy Scouts of America, American Indian influence on (20th century) *North American Northeast and Great Plains cultures*

The Boy Scouts of America, founded in 1908 by Lord Robert Stephenson Baden-Powell, is one of the largest organizations for young men in the world. The direction of the organization was profoundly affected both directly and indirectly by American Indian culture in the United States.

Ernest Thompson Seton, an author of nature books, began the Woodcrafter movement in July 1902. It was a major inspiration for modern scouting in the United States. Seton formed boys' clubs based on Indian culture and called them Woodcraft Indian societies. Members worked on projects such as animal tracking and tipi making. When the boys finished a project, they earned a feather and a "WAMPUM badge" that was worn on a sash. Members joined the group as "braves" and worked their way up to "warriors" and then "sagamores." These levels were similar to the ranks in scouting today. Each individual group of Woodcrafter boys was called a tribe. The role

model the young Woodcraft Indians were encouraged to emulate was Tecumseh, an important Shawnee leader. The Shawnee are a tribe of the Great Plains.

Although Seton tried to export the Woodcraft Indian movement, it never caught on in England. In that country Lord Baden-Powell, a veteran of the Boer Wars in Africa, began Boy Scouts, an organization that used many of Seton's ideas, but without the Indian characteristics. The new British organization overtook the Woodcraft movement in popularity in that country. In North America, however, the two groups merged. Boy Scouts in the United States retained many American-Indian themes, while English Boy Scouts remained more closely tied to Powell's military themes.

Charles Eastman, a Dakota physician and advocate of American-Indian rights, became involved with the American scouting movement in 1910, when he began working for the organization, lecturing at scouting camps and leading nature walks. He also wrote a guidebook for the Scouts called *Indian Scout Tales,* published in 1914.

### Sources/Further Reading

Badt, Karin Luisa. *Charles Eastman, Sioux Physician and Author.* New York: Chelsea House Publishers, 1995.

Weatherford, Jack. *Native Roots: How the Indians Enriched America.* New York: Fawcett Columbine, 1991.

## brain surgery See TREPHINATION.

## brain tanning See TANNING, BRAIN.

## Brazil nuts (precontact) *South American Tropical Forest cultures*

Brazil nuts grow on huge rain forest trees indigenous to what is now Brazil, Ecuador, Colombia, and Venezuela. The trees reach heights of up to 160 feet or more. Each year an individual tree produces up to 300 fruit pods that weigh two to five pounds. Twelve to 25 Brazil nuts are arranged inside each of these hard, woody pods like the segments of an orange. From January to June, the ripe pods fall from the branches to the ground, where indigenous people gather them as they have been doing for thousands of years.

Historically, tribes living in the tropics used the nuts for food, eating them raw or grating them and combining them with MANIOC to make a kind of gruel. Because the nuts are 17 percent protein and high in both selenium and amino acids, they were an excellent source of nutrition and considered a valuable TRADE commodity. Indigenous people used the wood as well as the empty seedpods, which were turned into vessels for collecting LATEX from rubber and SAPODILLA trees. They would also light small fires in the pods and carry them to repel black flies.

Brazil nuts are 70 percent oil, so high in it that the nuts themselves will burn when lit. Indigenous people extracted the oil and used it for cooking, lamps, and soap-making (see also DETERGENTS). Today it is also used as an ingredient in shampoo, skin creams, and HAIR CONDITIONERS throughout the world.

As it has been for centuries, most Brazil nut production today comes from wild trees. Dutch traders began exporting the nuts in about 1600 from the Amazon region, and today they are second only to rubber as a Brazilian export. In addition to serving as a source of nutrition for humans, Brazil nuts are used in South America to feed livestock.

## Sources/Further Reading

Heywood, V. H. *Flowering Plants of the World.* New York: Oxford University Press, 1993.

Schultes, R. and R. Raffauf. *The Healing Forest.* Portland, Oreg.: Dioscordes Press, 1990.

Smith, Nigel, J. Williams, Donald Plucknett, Donald and Jennifer Talbot. *Tropical Forests and Their Crops.* New York: Comstock Publishing, 1992.

**bridges** (ca. A.D. 1000) *South American Andean cultures*
Structures built to span gorges or rivers in order to provide passage are called bridges. As part of their extensive ROAD SYSTEM, the Inca constructed a variety of types of bridges, or *chacas*, that were adapted to the characteristics of the land as well as to the building materials that were available near the bridge sites. The Inca Empire existed in what is now Peru starting in the central highlands about A.D. 1000 and spreading throughout the entire area by A.D. 1440.

Bridges were so critical to the Inca system of transportation that laws existed setting the death penalty for anyone who tampered with one. Upkeep of the bridges was one of the labor taxes imposed on villages as part of the *mit'a*, or TAX SYSTEM, by the Inca government.

Some Inca bridges were quite simple, such as a log or stone slabs positioned across a river and set onto piers. Stringing a thick hemp guide rope across a river and affixing either end to sturdy trees or large boulders made a type of bridge called a *huarao, uruya,* or *oroya*. Goods and even people were placed in a large basket with a thick wooden handle placed over the guide rope and were then slid across. Today this concept is called a *breeches bouy*. Other Inca bridges were more highly complex, including cantilevered suspension and pontoon bridges.

Some of the stone bridges were cantilevered, creating corbeled arches (see also ARCHES, CORBELED), such as the 30-foot one built east of Lake Titicaca about 1450. Cantilevered bridges were impractical for spans greater than 40 feet but were permanent structures. Some of these exist even today.

Floating, or pontoon, bridges were sometimes used to cross relatively calm water. Often these were made with braided fibers, including reeds, over a hemp frame that was tied to BALSA WOOD floats. One of the most famous of these was used by Incas to cross the river that drains Lake Titicaca. Built more than 800 years ago, it was used until 1875. Bridges of this type, as recorded by Spanish explorers, were made in

Bridges were an integral part of the Inca road system. The Inca built pontoon bridges and cantilevered bridges as well as suspension bridges. Many were more complex than the one in this drawing by Felipe Guamán Poma de Ayala, an Indian historian and artist who lived in Peru in the early 1600s. (Nueva Coronica y Buen Gobierno)

sections and linked together with a thick rope. Replacing pontoons when they became waterlogged was a project that fulfilled the *mit'a* labor tax requirements Inca emperors levied on citizens.

In the 1300s the Inca built suspension bridges called *simp'achaka*, which means "braided bridges." Many were hung on ropes made of hemp that were as thick as a person's body. Others used cords braided with wild bunch grass or the fibers from AGAVE, or aloe plants. Llama leather provided more reinforcement when it was needed. Workers made the cables at the site where the bridge was to be erected, a technique that would be used centuries later for steel cables when the Brooklyn Bridge was constructed in New York City in 1864.

Inca builders buried rope supports for suspension bridges deeply underground for about 20 feet on each end of the bridge. These were anchored with heavy wooden beams. The ropes were then raised over wooden pillars on either bank of the river. Cables were tied between the pillar bases to form the foundation for the walkway. Wooden supports covered the cables, providing solid footing. The result was a narrow but extremely sturdy bridge. The Inca road system contained more than 40 large bridges of this type and over 100 small ones. Some of the larger ones spanned about 150 feet.

Miguel de Estete, who traveled with Francisco Pizarro, later described a bridge at yurmarca in his memoirs: "Next day [Pizarro] reached a large village in a valley, and a very rapid river intercepted the road. it was spanned by two bridges close together, made of network in the follwing manner. They build a foundation near the water and raise it to great height; and from one side of the river, there are cables as thick as a man's thigh. They are held up by the towers and at the ends buried in the gournd with greate sto0nes. the width is that of a cart's width."

An example of a suspension bridge can be found over the Apurimac River near Cuzco. This bridge became famous as the Bridge of San Luis Rey. It has been called the most spectacular engineering feat in the Western Hemisphere. Workers changed the fiber cables on this bridge every two years, enabling it to last from before A.D. 1400 to 1880.

Tolls were charged to cross some bridges in the Inca Empire. In 1553, when Francisco Pizarro and his men were on the march, they encountered two suspension bridges spanning what they called the Santa River. He reported that guards at the bridge exacted a toll from those who would cross it, and that the toll-taking was customary. Many early explorers, not used to anything resembling the Inca suspension bridges in the Old World, wrote letters home detailing their fear of crossing them because they swayed in the wind. The building of suspension bridges in Europe did not begin until 1810.

## Sources/Further Reading

Bankes, George. *Peru Before Pizarro.* Oxford, Eng.: Phaidon Press Ltd., 1977.
Davis, Nigel. *The Ancient Kingdoms of Peru.* New York: Penguin, 1998.
Morris, Craig and von Hagen, Adriana. *The Inka Empire and Its Andean Origins.* New York: Abbeville Press, 1993.
Moseley, Michael E. *The Incas and Their Ancestors: The Archaeology of Peru.* New York: Thames & Hudson, 1993.
von Hagen, Victor Wolfgang. *Realm of the Incas.* New York: New American Library, 1957.
———. *The Royal Road of the Inca.* London: Gordon Cremonesi, Ltd., 1976.

**briquettes** (600 B.C.–A.D. 200) *North American Southeast cultures*

Briquettes are small bricks. Today they are made from charcoal or coal dust and are used for BARBECUES. American Indians who were part of the Poverty Point Culture in what is now Louisiana between 600 B.C. and A.D. 200 made theirs from clay. They molded clay balls into briquettes of different sizes and shapes with their hands. Once the balls were dried, they were heated in a fire until they became red hot. Then up to two hundred of them were placed in a roasting pit. Archaeologists believe that the different shapes may have been used to control temperature and cooking time. Similar briquettes have been found in what is now Florida. Archaeologists have excavated long trenches that served as cooking pits in which American Indians had used tennis ball-sized clay briquettes.

## Sources/Further Reading

Milanich, Jerald T. *Florida's Indians from Ancient Times to the Present.* Gainsville: University Press of Florida, 1998.
*Louisiana Prehistory Poverty Point.* URL: http://crt.state.la.us/arch/laprehis/ppt.htm. Downloaded on March 21, 1999.

**buffalo** See BISON.

**bunk beds** (precontact) *North American Northeast cultures*

Bunk beds are arranged one on top of the other, usually in order to save space. Tiers of such beds were lashed to the interior walls of Iroquois and Algonkin long houses (see also APARTMENT COMPLEXES). The residents covered these platforms with bark sheeting and then with hides and furs. Arthur C. Parker, an Iroquois writing in the early 20th century, said that the bunks were similar in appearance to upper and lower beds in a train's sleeping car. The lower bunks were used mainly in winter so that sleepers would be nearer to the fire. Often the top bed was used for the storage of personal items. In the summer it would be occasionally used for sleeping.

See also HAMMOCKS.

## Sources/Further Reading

Nabokov, Peter and Robert Easton. *Native American Architecture.* New York: Oxford University Press, 1989.
Trigger, Bruce G. *Case Studies in Anthropology: The Huron Farmers of the North.* New York: Holt Rinehart and Winston, 1969.

# C

**cacao  (*Tobroma cacao*)**  (ca. 200 B.C.)  *Mesoamerican, South American Tropical Forest cultures*

The cacao tree is native to the tropics of Central America as well as parts of Brazil and the Orinoco Valley of what is now Venezuela. It earned its Latin name, which means food of the gods, from the fact that CHOCOLATE, which is made from cacao beans, was used in Maya and Aztec religious ceremonies. The Maya, whose culture arose in Mesoamerica about 1500 B.C., began cultivating the trees about 200 B.C., using the beans for food and medicine.

Cacao cultivation is no easy task because the trees are delicate, requiring shade and protection from winds for the first two to four years of growth in order to flourish. Often they are planted in the shelter of other trees, such as plantain or rubber trees, for shade and shelter from the wind. Needing evenly distributed rainfall and rich, well-drained soil, they require constant care. Properly pruned, they begin bearing fruit in the fifth year after they are planted. At maturity, cultivated trees reach about 15 to 25 feet tall.

Although thousands of small pink and white blossoms cover the branches of the three varieties of cacao grown commercially today, only about 10 percent of them mature into fruit. Cacao pods are maroon or reddish colored, woody-shelled, and shaped somewhat like footballs. Because the bark of the cacao tree is soft and the tree's roots are shallow, harvesting of ripe pods is still done by hand on cacao plantations throughout the world today. Growing and harvesting cacao has changed little from 2,000 years ago.

Once the harvesters remove the pods from the trees, they are split with machetes, and 20 to 50 cream-colored seeds that look similar to almonds are scooped out and dried. Exposed to air, the seeds turn lavender. They do not obtain their dark brown color or chocolate flavor until they are fermented, roasted, and ground. About 400 beans are required to produce a pound of chocolate.

Because cacao is a labor-intensive crop, the Maya used cacao beans as a medium of exchange, trading them for other goods. (See also TRADE.) The Aztec could not grow the trees in what is now central Mexico, which was the seat of their empire. They imported beans from the Maya and also levied tributes of cacao beans from Maya people they had conquered. The annual tribute during the reign of Montezuma, the Aztec emperor at the time of conquest, totaled about 24 tons of beans. (See also TAX SYSTEMS.) Like the Maya, the Aztec used cacao beans as a medium of exchange. Spaniards who were part of the expedition led by Hernán Cortés reported that 100 beans could buy clothing or a canoe of fresh water. Cacao beans were also used to purchase PUMPKINS, slaves, prostitutes, and more. Cacao was such a valuable medium of exchange that it was counterfeited; filling empty shells with dirt was one method used. One of the moneymaking ideas Cortés proposed to the Spanish court was to use cacao beans instead of coins as money in Spain. Although that idea was ignored, the notion of drinking chocolate became accepted.

After conquest, the Spanish began cacao plantations in their colonies, and eventually cultivation expanded throughout the world in a strip 10 degrees north and south of the equator. Today the top cacao-producing countries are Brazil and Ecuador, and in West Africa—Nigeria, Ghana, and Côte d'Ivoire. Although cacao is a fairly recent crop in Malaysia and Indonesia, cultivation there is rapidly increasing. In addition to chocolate, cacao beans are used in medications and soft drinks. (See also SOFT DRINK INGREDIENTS.) Cocoa butter, the stearic acid pressed from beans, is used by the cosmetics industry.

## Sources/Further Reading

*Cadbury's Chocolate History and the Growing of Cocoa.* URL: http://cadbury.co.uk/facts/html/cocoa2.htm. Downloaded on January 11, 1999.

Coe, Sophie and Michael D. Coe. *The True History of Chocolate*. London: Thames & Hudson, 1996.

Feltwell, John. "Cacao Plantations." In *The Book of Chocolate*. Edited by Ghidlaine Bavoillot. Paris: Flammarion, 1995.

**cactus**  See AGAVE; PRICKLY PEAR CACTI; YUCCA.

**calabash** (*Crescentia alata* and *C. cujete*) (ca. 5000 B.C.) *Mesoamerican; South American Tropical Forest and Andean; Circum-Caribbean cultures*

The calabash is a large gourdlike fruit. (See also GOURDS.) Unlike true gourds, the calabash grows on trees belonging to the same family as catalpa and jacaranda trees. Calabash trees grow wild in Mexico, Mesoamerica, and South America, producing as many as 100 fruits up to 10 inches in diameter. For thousands of years, indigenous people of the Americas have cultivated and used calabashes for a number of purposes. The earliest calabash seeds were found in Peru and dated to about 5000 B.C. When dried, the calabash was very practical as a container and had many uses. Indigenous people used it for food and water containers and as bowls and drinking vessels. Often they decorated the large gourds, which were also used for storing non-food items. When bored with small holes, calabashes were used as COLANDERS. Indians also used them as floats for fishing nets.

**Sources/Further Reading**

Armstrong, W. P. "The Wild and Wonderful World of Gourds." *Zoonooz* 69 no. 10 (1996): 24–27.

Benson, Elizabeth P. *The Maya World*. New York: Thomas Y. Crowell Company, 1967.

Mason, J. Alden. *The Ancient Civilizations of Peru*. Rev. ed. New York: Penguin Books, 1988.

**calendars** (600 B.C.) *Mesoamerican; South American Andean; North American Great Plains, Southwest, and Southeast cultures*

American Indians throughout North America, Mesoamerica, and South America used astronomical observations to create calendars, systems of reckoning the passing of time. The oldest of these calendars are the stone "medicine wheels" in what are now Montana and Saskatchewan. The stone "spokes" of these wheels have been shown to align to the rising of stellar constellations at the time of the summer solstice. One of these stone wheels, the Bighorn medicine wheel, in Montana, is estimated to be several hundred years old, based on astronomical calculations. Features of the Bighorn medicine wheel align to the sunrise at the summer solstice. Other features are aligned to the rising of the constellations Aldebaran and Sirius. A wheel at Moose Mountain in Canada with similar alignments has been carbon-dated to be about 2,600 years old. Many such medicine wheels have been found throughout the northern plains of the United States and Canada. Located in relatively remote areas,

they were built on high hills or bluffs that would have offered ancient astronomers unobstructed stargazing.

Mesoamerican calendars were extremely sophisticated and accurate. Archaeologists believe the Maya, whose culture arose about 1500 B.C. in Mesoamerica, calculated these calendars. The Aztec, whose empire was established in the same region about A.D. 1100, adopted them. This Mesoamerican system was composed of several calendars, each of which served a different purpose. The *day count* was a 260-day ritual almanac used primarily to time religious ceremonies, name children, and predict the future. The earliest known stone carving to display elements of the 260-day calendar is Monument 3 from San José Mogote, located in the valley of Oaxaca nine miles north of the ruins of the ancient Zapotec city of Monte Albán. This carved stone is between 2,600 and 2,500 years old.

The Maya and Aztec also kept an annual calendar based on the Sun. Containing 365 days that were arranged into 18 months of 20 days each, this calendar was used to determine the seasons and to schedule events such as market gatherings and crop planting. Without telescopes or the mathematical concept of fractions, early Mesoamerican people by the fifth century B.C. had calculated a year's length so precisely that it was only 19 minutes off. Only the Chinese equaled this amazing feat of observation and calculation. The scientific tools the Mesoamerican astronomers used to construct their calendars were shadow-casting devices, accurate observation, and meticulous record-keeping.

In addition to the solar, or sidereal, calendar, the Maya devised a lunar calendar. This calendar consisted of alternating periods of 29 and 30 days in order to compensate for the actual time it took for one lunar cycle. Like their solar calendar, it was accurate. Modern ethnoastronomers have not yet discovered its purpose.

The 260-day and 365-day calendars were used side by side at least 2,400 years ago. Their interlocking combination produced a cycle of dates that did not repeat for 52 years; this was called the calendar round, beginning with the start of the Maya world. Calendar rounds were used to keep track of historical events and consisted of 52-year-long cycles, which the Maya called *xiuhmolpilli* or "year bundles." The Maya "long count," a unique calendar system that kept track of 5,128 years, had fallen out of use before the Europeans came. The "long count" cycle, according to some archaeoastronomers, is supposed to end on December 21, 2012.

The Inca, who established an empire in the Andes and along the coast of what is now Peru in A.D. 1000, devised a calendar that was more tied to agricultural purposes than other Mesoamerican calendars. They timed the first plowing and planting seasons to the Sun's nadir (lowest point) and the summer solstice. Phases of the Moon determined the dates that were set for Inca religious festivals. Inca calendars integrated both lunar and solar counts. Several Inca roads leading from the Temple of the Sun are arranged astronomically, serving as a sort of calendar. Some archaeologists believe that many of the Nazca lines on the pampas of what is now Peru, which were created between about 400 B.C. and A.D. 600, may have astronomical

Mesoamerican calendars were extremely accurate. By the fifth century B.C., American Indian astronomers had calculated a year's length so precisely that it was off by only 19 minutes. This mosaic is a reproduction of an Aztec calendar. *(Neg. No. 315090. Photo Rice & Bierwert. Courtesy of Library Services American Museum of Natural History)*

meaning and might have served calendar functions. The Anasazi, whose culture arose in the desert Southwest of what is now the United States in about 350 B.C. and lasted until about A.D. 1450, built a calendar at Chaco Canyon in what is now New Mexico. They arranged large rock slabs atop a high butte so that shafts of sunlight fell between them on a carving of a spiral drawn onto a cliff. As the angle of the sunlight changed with the seasons, shafts of light fell on different parts of the carving, enabling those who knew how to read them to tell important dates. Called the Sun Dagger Calendar, it is at least 700 years old and has been termed a work of genius by archaeologists.

In Cahokia, the largest settlement built by the Mississippian Culture in about A.D. 1100 near the site of modern St. Louis, Missouri, archaeologists have found a calendar device they call "Woodhenge." It consists of large, oval-shaped pits that once contained posts arranged in a circle. These were aligned to the position of the sun at equinoxes and solstices.

Ochre (a natural iron oxide pigment) found in the holes indicates that the poles were painted red. Each circle had a center post where, perhaps, an astronomer stood to observe sunrises on the eastern horizon.

The Hopi people of the American Southwest have used horizon calendars for centuries, timing their annual ceremonies to the position of the sun as it rises over the San Francisco Peaks to the southwest of their home. The geographical features of their mountains, such as notches and mesas, serve as the markers on this ingenious landscape calendar. This calendar served a very practical agricultural purpose. By watching the sky and noting the rising and setting positions of the sun and moon, the Hopi could tell when crops were ready to plant. Archaeological experiments have shown that by predicting the spring solstice, Hopi farmers could avoid freezing crops with great accuracy.

In more modern times, a Ho-Chunk (Winnebago) spiritual leader carved a calendar stick in the 1800s that served to mark both lunar and solar calendars based on his observations. The stick has been determined by some astronomers to be the most sophisticated and accurate calendar device made in North America.

See also ALMANACS; ASTRONOMY; OBSERVATORIES, ASTRONOMICAL; ROAD SYSTEMS.

**Sources/Further Reading**

Aveni, A. F., ed. *Archaeoastronomy in the New World: American Primitive Astronomy.* London: Cambridge University Press, 1982.

Folsom, Franklin and Mary Elting Folsom. *America's Ancient Treasures,* 4th Ed. Albuquerque: University of New Mexico Press, 1993.

Hoskin, Michael, ed. *Cambridge Illustrated History of Astronomy.* New York: Cambridge University Press, 1997.

Iseminger, William R. "Mighty Cahokia." *Archaeology* (May/June 1996): (31–37).

Jennings, Francis. *The Founders of America: How Indians Discovered the Land, Pioneered in It, and Created Great Classical Civilizations; How They Were Plunged into a Dark Age by Invasion and Conquest; and How They Are Now Reviving.* New York: W. W. Norton, 1993.

Krupp, E. C. *Echoes of the Ancient Skies: The Astronomy of Lost Civilizations.* New York: Harper and Row, 1983.

Malpass, Michael A. *Daily Life in the Inca Empire.* Westport, Conn.: Greenwood Press, 1996.

Sharer, Robert. *Daily Life in Maya Civilization.* Westport, Conn.: Greenwood Press, 1996.

Smith, Michael E. *The Peoples of America: The Aztecs.* Cambridge, Mass.: Blackwell, 1996.

**calls, bird and animal** (precontact) *North American Northeast cultures*

Calls, or auditory decoys, make sounds that attract wild game or fowl. For the pre-Columbian American Indians, hunting involved more than just stalking prey and attempting to kill it. They studied the lay of the land and the habits of the animals they hunted. They also took into consideration the weather, the time of the year, and the type of weapon they would use. Throughout the Americas, indigenous hunters used animal calls to attract prey to within a range close enough to ensure that the weapon of choice could do its job. Auditory decoys saved hunters time and energy that would have been lost during the pursuit of prey.

The materials used in auditory decoys—sticks, antlers, and blades of grass—were simple, but the technique was a sophisticated one. Attracting wild game by emulating their sounds is not accidentally stumbled upon; the task took a great deal of observation and experimentation. Once the concept was developed, the next step was to find the appropriate material to produce the needed sound. Finally, a test period was required to determine which sounds would attract the target animal. One of the most widespread and simplest calls was the whistle, which was used throughout North America. Other calls were more sophisticated and specialized. Although today's auditory decoys would not be recognizable to American Indians of the past, the technology of animal calls used by modern hunters is essentially the same as that used by American-Indian hunters for thousands of years.

### DEER AND ELK CALLS

American Indians placed a blade of grass between the thumbs and blew over it to imitate the cry a fawn would make when in distress, a sound that would attract a doe. This form of call is one of the first examples of the ribbon-reed concept being used in the Americas. The Menominee sucked on a dogbane stalk to imitate a fawn that wanted its mother. Rubbing deer scapula, or shoulder bones, against a tree to imitate a doe rubbing her horns against a tree when she is in heat was another auditory decoy. Indigenous hunters also attracted deer by banging two sets of antlers together. This duplicated the sound of two stags fighting over territory or a doe.

### MOOSE CALLS

Algonkin hunters made moose calls resembling a megaphone from birch bark. These calls imitated the sound a cow moose would make during the mating season.

### CARIBOU CALLS

Caribou—large, antlered land animals found in the northern part of North America—were a source of food as well as many tools and daily items necessary for the existence of American Indians. The hide, for example, was used for shelter, clothing, and footwear. Indigenous hunters of the Eastern Woodlands observed caribou and determined what notes, tones, and pitches would produce a sound that would be appealing to animals. As a result of these experiments, they rolled a tube of bark so that one end was larger than the other, making it look somewhat like a megaphone, and used it to make sounds to call their prey.

### WILD SHEEP CALLS

The Shoshone residing in the Great Basin region invented a unique form of auditory decoy based on astute observations of the environment and extensive knowledge of animal behavior. They created a decoy that simulated the sound of rams butting heads, a behavior that took place during mating season. Shoshone hunters produced an imitation of the sound of butting heads by banging rocks or sticks together that was very effective in attracting wild sheep.

### SEAL AND WALRUS CALLS

Aware that seals and walruses use their claws to scratch breathing holes in sea ice and revisit those holes often, an Inuit hunter would wait by one of these air holes. When the animal came up to breathe the hunter would harpoon it, let it thrash, and then pull it to the surface and kill it with a blow from his fist. To lure the prey closer, a hunter would sometimes place a pick into the ice and whistle along the shaft to imitate the sounds a seal makes, or he would drag an ice pick or specially designed scratcher along the ice to rouse the seal's curiosity.

See also DECOYS, DUCK.

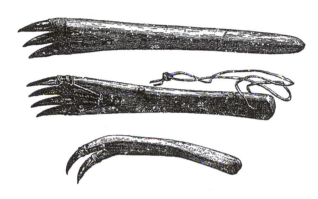

Inuit seal hunters scratched the ice with scrapers like these to lure their curious prey close to holes they had made in the ice. (U.S. Bureau of Ethnography)

### Sources/Further Reading

Driver, Harold E. *Indians of North America.* Chicago: University of Chicago Press, 1969.

Josephy, Jr., Alvin M., ed. *The Indian Heritage of America.* Rev. ed. Boston: Houghton Mifflin Company, 1991.

Murdoch, John. *Ethnological Results of the Point Barrow Expedition Annual Report of the U.S. Bureau of Ethnology 1887–1888.* Washington, D.C.: U.S. Government Printing Office, 1892.

Weatherford, Jack. *Indian Givers: How the Indians of the Americas Transformed the World.* New York: Fawcett Columbine, 1988.

**camouflage** (precontact) *North American, Mesoamerican, Circum-Caribbean, South American cultures*
Camouflage equipment, such as headgear, clothing, and face paint, is designed to make hunters more invisible to the animals by helping them blend into the environment. Pre-Columbian American Indians used camouflage in warfare and hunting for hundreds of years before the arrival of Europeans.

Indian hunters in both North and South America camouflaged themselves with animal hides for clothing and heads as headgear. They also painted their faces. In the Amazon, hunters rubbed the fruit of the picho huayo shrub over their bodies to mask their odor, so that animals would not detect them. The Inuit of the North American Arctic built snow walls when they hunted polar bears. They would position themselves behind these white, portable walls downwind from their prey. Because it was made from hides, the day-to-day clothing of peoples of the Arctic also served to mask the fact that they were human and not deer or elk. (See also PARKAS.) Archaeologists believe that some Shoshone people may have hunted waterfowl by placing DUCK DECOYS (see also DECOYS, DUCK) on their heads in order to get close enough to their prey in the water to capture them. Hunters of the Great Basin and California culture areas used the pigeon blind, a different sort of snare to catch birds. They built these blinds in much the same way that modern hunters' duck blinds are built today, locating them in areas where pigeons were abundant. Sometimes they built them on scaffolds. American Indian hunters waited inside the blind and grabbed pigeons as they came to rest on it.

Many military historians credit the victory of the American colonists over British troops in the American Revolution to the lessons about camouflage and guerrilla fighting they learned from American Indians (see also MILITARY TACTICS). Armies throughout the world today issue clothing in several earth-toned colors and irregular patterns to help break up the visual pattern of the soldier in the enemy's vision. Face paint does the same by breaking up the symmetry of the face.

### Sources/Further Reading

Driver, Harold E. *Indians of North America.* Chicago: University of Chicago Press, 1969.

Duke, James A. *The Green Pharmacy.* New York: St. Martins Press, 1997.

Hurst, David, Jay Miller, Richard White, Peter Nabokov, and Philip Deloria. *The Native Americans.* Atlanta: Turner Publishing, Inc., 1993.

Maxwell, James A. *America's Fascinating Indian Heritage.* Pleasantville, N.Y.: Reader's Digest Books, 1978.

Powell, J. W. *Ninth Annual Report of the Bureau of Ethnology to the Secretary of the Smithsonian Institution 1887–88.* Washington, D.C.: Government Printing Office, 1892.

Weatherford, Jack. *Native Roots: How the Indians Enriched America.* New York: Fawcett Columbine, 1991.

**canals, irrigation** See IRRIGATION SYSTEMS.

**canals, shipping** (ca. A.D. 1100) *Mesoamerican cultures*
The Aztec dredged canals through the *chinampas,* or artificial islands, on which they grew food crops and flowers. This dredging allowed canoes bearing heavy loads to pass through the waters surrounding the raised beds.

See also AGRICULTURE, RAISED BED; TRADE.

**Source/Further Reading**

Josephy, Jr. Alvin M., ed. *America in 1492: The World of the Indian People Before the Arrival of Columbus*. New York: Random House, 1991.

**canoes** (precontact) *North American Northeast and Northwest Coast, Mesoamerican, Circum-Caribbean, South American Tropical Forest cultures*

Slender, long, narrow, keelless boats with pointed ends are called canoes. They are moved through the water with paddles. The word *canoe* came into the English language from *kenu*, a word the Taino people living in the Caribbean taught Columbus, meaning a boat carved out of a tree. Later explorers used *canoe* to describe any America Indian boat.

Northeastern peoples of North America traditionally made dug-out canoes, but by the 1500s they had begun constructing lightweight white cedar frames that were covered with birch and occasionally elm bark. These watercraft could float in as little as four inches of water and were ideal for travel in shallow rivers and streams. Because a dry, 15-foot canoe weighed only about 40 pounds, a traveler could easily carry it over a portage. Despite its weight, a relatively small canoe could hold loads of up to a ton. Canoes were built in all sizes—from small ones for a single person to large ones that could carry up to 50 paddlers.

The Algonkin made their canoes from bark that they stripped from birch trees early in the summer by making a perpendicular slit along the tree trunk. This allowed the bark to be peeled off in a roll large enough to cover a canoe. After soaking the bark to soften it, the Indians sewed it together at the ends. Because the brown-colored inside of the bark was smoother and more waterproof than the outside, they faced it outside on the canoe when they stitched it to the gunwales, the bow, and the stern. Women did the sewing, using tamarack, spruce, ash, or jack pine roots for the lashing. Men made the canoe ribs from white cedar, steaming them to bend them to the proper shape. While the ribs were still pliable, the builders forced them into the hull. As they dried, the ribs pushed outward on the hull, making it rigid. Finally the canoe makers caulked the seams on the covering with hot pine, spruce, or balsam pitch and grease. Larger canoes often had laminated frames. (See also BOWS, LAMINATED.)

Like the Taino canoes and the first ones built by Eastern Woodlands Indians, canoes made by Northwest Coast tribes were mostly dugouts. Carved from one log, they were made in many shapes and sizes depending on whether they were used for the ocean or in the river. The largest of these canoes could hold as many as 50 people and was used to transport war parties. The Haida, who were known for their carpentry skills (see also CARPENTRY TECHNIQUES), excelled in canoe making. In the Arctic, where birch trees were not available, the Inuit peo-

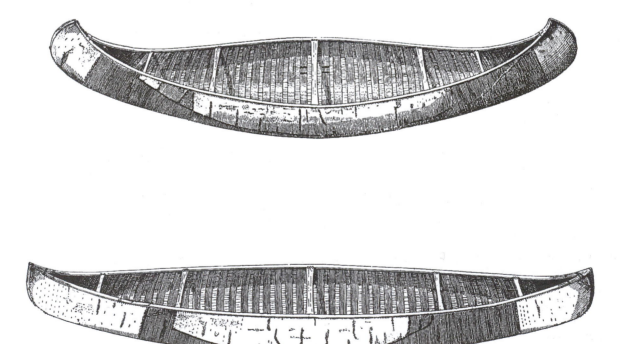

Although Indians throughout the Americas made canoes, the best known today are the birch-bark canoes of Northeast North American culture groups. A canoe that weighed about 40 pounds could easily be carried between rivers or streams. Europeans quickly adapted this mode of travel. *(U.S. Bureau of Ethnography)*

ple covered canoes with hides, developing a unique boat called the KAYAK.

Europeans quickly adopted canoes, which could be constructed from materials at hand and were easily portaged. French fur traders, who immediately saw the benefits of canoe travel, began the first factory at Trois-Rivières, Quebec, in about 1750. American Indians designed canoes so elegantly that the unique style of the boat remains basically unchanged today, except for the materials used to construct it.

See also KAYAKS.

## Sources/Further Reading

Adney, Tappan, and Howard I. Chapelle. *Bark Canoes and Skin Boats of North America.* Washington, D.C.: Smithsonian Institution Press, 1993.

Flexner, Stuart Berg. *I Hear America Talking: An Illustrated History of American Words and Phrases.* New York: Simon and Schuster, 1976.

Forest Preserve District of Cook County. *Nature Bulletin No. 463 A.* Nov. 1970.

Josephy, Jr. Alvin M. *The Indian Heritage of America.* Rev. ed. Boston: Houghton Mifflin, 1991.

Maxwell, James A. *America's Fascinating Indian Heritage.* Pleasantville, N.Y.: Reader's Digest Books, 1978.

Oswalt, Wendell. *Eskimos and Explorers.* Novato, Calif.: Chandler & Sharp Publishers, 1979.

## "caramel" corn (precontact) *North American Northeast cultures*

American Indians living in what is now New England dipped popped POPCORN and PEANUTS into MAPLE SYRUP to make a snack food similar to Cracker Jack. The Chippewa (Anishnabe) and other tribes of the present-day Great Lakes region made a similar product. Anthropologists believe that, like PEMMICAN, some was saved for the winters. In case the weather got too bad or game became scarce Indian people could rely on the "caramel" CORN to sustain them until conditions improved. The corn provided bulk, and the maple syrup provided a source of energy and calories. Corn and maple syrup in this form could be stored all winter without losing any of its nutritional value.

## Sources/Further Reading

Davis, Emily C. *Ancient Americans.* New York: Cooper Square Publishers, 1975.

Porter, C. Fayne. *The Battle of the 1,000 Slain; and Other Stories Selected from Our Indian Heritage.* New York: Scholastic Book Service, 1964.

Weatherford, Jack. *Indian Givers: How the Indians of the Americas Transformed the World.* New York: Fawcett Columbine, 1988.

## cardiac medications See DOGBANE; FOXGLOVE; HEMP, AMERICAN; WAHOO.

## cariole sleds See SLEDS, CARIOLE.

## carpentry techniques (ca. 3000 B.C.) *South American Tropical Forest, North American Northwest Coast, Mesoamerican cultures*

Indians throughout North, Meso-, and South America found many innovative ways to construct homes of wood. For example, indigenous builders in the Amazon jungles of South America used cashew wood for home construction because it repelled termites and other damaging insects (see INSECT REPELLENTS). They joined the wood together with vines that, when dry, created a stronger bond than nails and lasted up to 20 years, withstanding the humidity of the tropics.

Northwest Pacific Coast tribes of North America are noted for their beautiful homes and the craftsmanship that went into the construction of these dwellings. Their building material of choice was red cedar, which modern builders use for siding and shingles. Western red cedar (*Thuja*), with its tiny scale-like evergreen leaves and drooping branches that resemble ferns, are not true cedars. Although European colonists called these trees cedars, true cedars have spiny needles and are native to the Mediterranean and Himalayan regions of the world. Like true cedar wood, that of the western red cedar trees is aromatic. It contains a natural resin called thujic acid that repels termites, moths, insects, and vermin. The thujic acid also makes red cedar relatively water-resistant, a useful characteristic in one of the wettest regions on the earth, with a rainfall of 80 inches a year.

American Indian builders of the Northwest Coast were well aware of the insect- and water-repelling properties of this wood, as well as its superior insulating properties compared to other available wood and its resistance to warping. Cedar was used as the basis of a sophisticated architecture that housed an estimated 75,000 indigenous people living from what is now the Alaskan Panhandle to southern Oregon. All the tribes of the region constructed huge plank-covered post-and-beam houses of varying shapes and designs. They sometimes felled these huge trees by making a large hole in the side of the tree and setting a slow fire in it so that the trunk would eventually burn through and the tree would fall. They split the trunk into planks with wooden wedges. (See also TOOLS.)

The Haida, who lived in the northern Queen Charlotte Islands off the western coast of what is now Canada, perfected the art of plank-home building. They were masters of mortise and tenon joining. A mortise is a hole drilled into wood that is prepared to accept a projection (a tenon) that has been carved into another piece of wood. Haida houses had six roof beams. These were not supported on central posts but rested instead on angled gable plates, with slotted corner posts and three beams that were flattened on the lower side. The result was an interior uncluttered by supports. Vertical wall planks fitted into slots on both of the gable plates that ran above the ground to form the mortise and tenon joint. Sometimes the Haida, whose homes had cellars, shaped the wood by steaming and bending it so that it would overlap and produce weather-tight walls.

Haida builders of the North American Northwest constructed their homes and community buildings from cedar, a material that remains popular with homebuilders today. This Haida house in Skedans Village on one of the Queen Charlotte Islands, B.C., was photographed in 1878. *(National Archives of Canada/PA-038148/Geological Survey of Canada Collection)*

Roofs were gabled and covered with planks that were fastened so that they could be moved to form skylights that would let in fresh air and light or let out smoke. Tlingit and Tsimshian homes were of similar construction.

In 1792 French explorer Etienne Marchand was impressed by the Haida houses he saw on his journeys. He wrote: "Is not our astonishment increased when we consider the progress these people have made in architecture? What instinct, or, rather, what genius, it has required to conceive and execute solidly . . . these edifices, those heavy frames of buildings of fifty feet in extent by eleven in elevation."

In order to construct these buildings, the Haida and other Northwest tribes invented a number of specialized woodworking tools. The carpentry of the indigenous builders of the Northwest is remarkable because, for the most part, they did not make their tools of metal. Some non-Indian anthropologists could not believe that this was possible and claimed that building in the Northwest only flourished after Europeans in-troduced metal tools. An experiment conducted by archaeologists at Canada's Museum of Man in the 1970s, however, suggests that it was possible for the Indians to build their magnificent structures with clamshell-edged adzes and chisels, bone awls and bores, and hardwood or sheephorn wedges.

Hafted beaver-tooth and mussel-shell knives as well as stone drills have been found in Washington State at the Ozette site, which has been dated to A.D. 800. Here some metal tools of later date have been found that were in use in pre-Columbian times. Archaeologists believe they might have been crafted from the iron in meteors. (See IRONWORKING.) When British navy captain James Cook sailed into Nootka Sound on Vancouver Island, he was the first European the Nootka had seen. Yet when his men examined a Nootka carpenter's tool box, they found a maul, metal chisels, wedges, adzes, simple drills, sandstone grindstones for finishing, and sharkskin, which served as fine sand paper. (See also TOOL KITS; TOOLS.)

Because the Northwest's humid climate eventually rots the wood, remains of ancient houses are scarce. Archaeologists in the Skeena River Canyon on what is now British Columbia's mainland have found evidence of villages composed of rectangular wooden houses that are nearly 5,000 years old. Similar finds have been uncovered on Prince Rupert Island in British Columbia.

In addition to homes, carpenters of the Northwest constructed CANOES from red or yellow cedar. Red cedar was used for arrow shafts and bentwood BOXES because of its fine, straight grain. Bowls and dishes were made from red alder, which does not contain thujic acid like cedar; nor does it split as easily. Boxes were made of white cedar. Clubs, bows, harpoon shafts (see also HARPOONS) and canoe paddles were made from Pacific yew, which is extremely strong.

See also ARCHITECTS; AXES, COPPER; INSULATION, HOME; STONEMASONRY TECHNIQUES.

## Sources/Further Reading

Josephy Jr., Alvin M., ed. *America in 1492: The World of the Indian People Before the Arrival of Columbus.* New York: Random House, 1991.

Nabokov, Peter and Robert Easton. *Native American Architecture.* New York: Oxford University Press, 1989.

Oregon State University. "False Cedars." URL: http://www.orst.edu/instruct/for241/con/cedrgen.html. Downloaded on January 12, 1999.

Weatherford, Jack. *Indian Givers: How the Indians of the Americas Transformed the World.* New York: Fawcett Columbine, 1988.

## cascara sagrada (*Rhanimus purshiana*) (precontact)
*North American0 Northwest Coast, Plateau, and California cultures*

Cascara sagrada is one of the most common ingredients in over-the-counter laxatives today. Centuries ago, Pacific Coast Indians discovered the laxative properties of its shrub, which grows from California to British Columbia. Brewed into a tea, cascara sagrada was used by the Kutenai people who lived in the Plateau region, the Karok who lived on the California coast, and other tribes. This herbal laxative works when glycosides contained in the bark of the plant are acted on by bacteria naturally present in the colon. The result is increased peristalsis, or intestinal contractions. Its gentleness made it an effective treatment for both children and the elderly.

The Spaniards called the plant cascara sagrada, or the "sacred bark," perhaps because, despite the existence of some cathartics in the Old World, cascara sagrada was much milder and created almost no discomfort to the user. Although it is very effective, cascara sagrada is also very bitter, so bitter that it is sometimes used today as a deterrent to thumb-sucking in children. In order to tolerate the laxative, Native people mixed it with a sweetener. After contact, Indians added CHOCOLATE to mixtures containing this laxative, predating modern chocolate-flavored laxatives by many years. Since 1878 cascara

sagrada has become one of the most widely used laxatives in the world.

## Sources/Further Reading

Moerman, Dan. *Native American Ethnobotany Database: Food, Drugs, Dyes and Fibers of Native North American Peoples.* URL: http://www.umd.umich.edu/cgi-bin/herb. Downloaded on February 2, 1998.

Weatherford, Jack. *Indian Givers: How the Indians of the Americas Transformed the World.* New York: Fawcett Columbine, 1988.

## cashews (*Anacardium occidentale*) (precontact)
*Mesoamerican, South American Tropical Forest, Circum-Caribbean cultures*

The cashew tree is native to Mexico, Brazil, Peru, and the West Indies. Requiring less water than other nut trees, cashews produce nuts that when shelled, roasted, and salted are popular throughout the world. Indigenous people used them not only as food but also as medicine for hundreds of years. American Indians in the Amazon Basin used cashew wood to construct their homes because it repelled insects. (See also CARPENTRY TECHNIQUES; INSECT REPELLENTS.)

Europeans did not encounter the tall cashew trees, with their thick trunks and twisted branches, until 1558, when the Portuguese saw them in what is now Brazil. There the Cuna Indians used cashew bark to make teas for asthma, colds, and congestion. Cashew bark tea was used for thrush and severe diarrhea. Old cashew leaves were applied to burns and a tea made of leaves was used for sore throats. In fact, the cashew tree was considered a virtual pharmacy; its bark, juice, and nut oil was said to cure warts, corns, and calluses as well.

Shortly after the Portuguese saw cashews, they transported trees to their colonies in East Africa, India, and Indonesia. There, as well, the trees became an important source of medicine. Today India's Ayurvedic medicine practitioners consider cashew fruit an aphrodisiac. They also use it to treat dysentery, fever, piles, tumors, and obstinate ulcers. In Africa cashew bark and leaves are used for gingivitis and toothaches. Cashew bark tea is used in Malaysia to cure diarrhea. In Indonesia cashew leaves provide poultices for burns and skin diseases. Juice from the fruit is a remedy for dysentery in the Philippines. Both the cashew nut and the shell are sold throughout the world for their medicinal uses. Cashawa gum, the clear, sticky liquid that oozes from the stems of the fruit, is used by the pharmaceutical industry today as a substitute for gum arabic that is used to make emulsions and PILLS.

Modern industry has found a number of other uses for cashew tree products. Cashew Nut Shell Liquid (CNSL), a black oil that is a by-product of the cashew nut industry, is an alternative to petrochemically derived phenol, a caustic compound. CNSL serves as a WATERPROOFING agent and preservative. Because of its toughness and high resistance to chemicals, CNSL friction dust is used for brake linings, clutch facings, and also magneto armatures in airplanes. This oil is also used to termite-proof lumber. The tree's bark is used as a tanning agent. Its juice, which turns black in the air, makes indelible ink. Cashew wood is used for constructing buildings and boats and for making furniture.

Today, as in the past, cashew harvesting must be done by hand. After the mature fruit has fallen to the ground and the fleshy parts have dried away, the nuts are gathered and roasted in the shell. They are removed by workers who are skilled in breaking the shells with wooden hammers without damaging the nuts inside.

The primary appeal of cashews today is as food. The nuts are made up of about 45 percent edible oil. Although high in fat, they are also high in protein, providing nearly 17 grams of it per 100 grams of nuts. They are also high in vitamin A, calcium, phosphorous, iron, and fiber. In addition to eating the cashew's nuts people who live in South America eat the applelike fruit that surrounds the nut or make it into jam. Modern Brazilians make a juice from cashew fruit that is sometimes fermented.

## Sources/Further Reading
Duke, James A. *Handbook of Energy Crops.* Unpublished, 1983. URL: http://www.hort.purdue.edu/newcrop/duke_energy. Downloaded on March 3, 1999.
Johnson, D. 1973. "Cashew Cultivation in Brazil." *Agronomy* 7, no. 3: 119–129.

**cassava**  See MANIOC.

**casseroles** (precontact) *Mesoamerican cultures*
Casseroles, dishes consisting of vegetables and meat cooked in a sauce, were popular among the Aztec, according to the Spanish priest Fray Bernardo de Sahagun, who described those that were sold in the Aztec marketplaces. One of these casseroles, called *pipia'n,* was made with red CHILES, TOMATOES, and ground SQUASH seeds. A fish casserole he detailed was made with yellow chiles and tomatoes. Frogs, tadpoles, locusts, and shrimp also found their way into the casserole dishes of Aztec cooks. Another casserole called for small white fish, unripe plums, yellow chiles, and tomatoes. The Aztec Empire flourished in Mexico and parts of Mesoamerica starting about A.D. 1100.

## Sources/Further Reading
Coe, Sophie. *America's First Cuisines.* Austin: University of Texas Press, 1994.
Ortiz de Montellano, Bernard. *Aztec Medicine, Health, and Nutrition.* New Brunswick, N.J.: Rutgers University Press, 1990.

**cataract removal** (ca. A.D. 1100) *Mesoamerican cultures*
Cataracts, which are caused by the aging process, cloud the lens of the eyes. Left untreated, this condition can lead to partial or total blindness. The surgical removal of cataracts from the eyes was one of the more remarkable pre-Columbian medical procedures. Aztec physicians used small, thin pieces of obsidian flint as SCALPELS. These were extremely sharp and were called *iztli* in Nahuatl, the Aztec language. Anthropologist Harold Driver in *Indians of North America* described the ancient practice of cataract surgery as ". . . removing growths and white opacities from the eyes. . . ." The Aztec Empire was established about A.D. 1100 in Mesoamerica.

See also EXCISION; EYES, MEDICAL TREATMENT OF; FLINTKNAPPING; SURGERY.

## Sources/Further Reading
Driver, Harold E. *Indians of North America.* Chicago: University of Chicago Press, 1969.
Ortiz de Montellano, Bernard. *Aztec Medicine, Health, and Nutrition.* New Brunswick, N.J.: Rutgers University Press, 1990.
Vogel, Virgil. *American Indian Medicine.* Norman: University of Oklahoma Press, 1970.

**cat's cradle (string games)** (precontact) *North American Arctic, Subarctic, Northwest Coast, Great Plains, and Southwest cultures*
Cat's cradle, a string game, is the practice of making figures by looping string on the fingers. American Indians invented string games independently from indigenous people in other parts of the world. Inuit people, who lived in the northern part of the North American continent, were so adept at making figures with reindeer sinew that they demonstrated 139 distinct figures, all of which they had named, to an early anthropologist who studied their culture in the late 1800s. Some of the figures were so complex that they included moving parts. One of these was a representation of a reindeer that could be made to move downhill from one hand to the other by the movement of the player's fingers. Other moving figures included fighting reindeer, dancing shamans, and a mink running along the seashore.

Unable to believe that American Indians were capable of making complicated figures with string, at least one anthropologist stated that they must have been taught the art after contact with Vikings. Later anthropologists found that the game of cat's cradle was not isolated to the eastern Inuit. Anthropologist Franz Boas, who wrote the definitive work on string figures, reported that cat's cradle was known from Greenland to the Pacific coast. Each group of Inuit developed their own local string figures, such as whales, walrus, wolves, and ravens, a circumstance that argues in favor of independent Indian invention from Old World games of cat's cradle.

Caroline Furness Jayne, author of *String Figures and How to Make Them,* also dismisses the Viking theory as "untenable," writing: "Though cat's cradle is now known through all Western Europe, I find no record of it at all in the ancient part of our world." Cat's cradle is believed to have been introduced to Europe from eastern Asia.

In addition to the Inuit, the Tlingit, Tsimshian, and Kwakiutl, who lived in the Pacific Northwest, all played string games. Cat's cradle has also been recorded among the Salish of the Northwest as well as the Cherokee of the Southeast, the Omaha and Pawnee of the Great Plains, and the Navajo (Dineh) and Pueblo Indians of the Southwest. The Teton Lakota of the Great Plains played string games, as did the Sac (Sauk) and Mesquaki (Fox) of the Midwest. The Apache of the Southwest and the Hupa of what is now northwest California played them as well. Evidence exists that the Maya of Mesoamerica made figures as well.

In the Southwest, the Zuni called the pastime *pichowainai* or *pishkappoa*, which means "netted shield." According to their legends the game was originally taught to the twin war gods by their mother Spider Woman for their amusement. According to one of the informants that anthropologist Stewart Culin consulted for his 1907 ethnographic report, the Navajo used the games to teach children the position of the stars. Several of the figures they made represented constellations, including Pleiades, a constellation important in indigenous ASTRONOMY of the Southwest.

The Navajo, who also believed that string games came from Spider Woman, called their games *na-ash-klo*, which means "continuous weaving." The manual dexterity required for the games and the string used to play them is similar to the technique and material used for finger weaving, the practice of making cloth without a loom. (See also WEAVING TECHNIQUES.)

**Sources/Further Reading**

Boas, Franz. "The Game of Cat's Cradle." *Internationales Archiv fur Ethnographie*. 1 (1888).

———. "The Central Eskimo." *Sixth Annual Report of the Bureau of Ethnology 1884–85*. Washington, D.C.: U.S. Government Printing Office, 1888.

———. "The Eskimo of Baffin Land and Hudson Bay." *Bulletin of the American Museum of Natural History*. New York 15 (1901).

Culin, Stewart. *Games of the North American Indians*. Reprint. Lincoln: University of Nebraska Press, 1992.

Jayne, Caroline Furness. *String Figures and How to Make Them: A Study of Cat's Cradle in Many Lands*. Reprint. New York: Dover Publications, 1962.

Murdoch, John. "Ethnological Results of the Point Barrow Expedition." *Ninth Annual Report of the Bureau of Ethnology, 1887–1897*. Washington, D.C.: U.S. Government Printing Office, 1892.

cal head densely covered with tiny brown flowers. American Indians who lived in the Northeast and the Great Lakes regions used cattails for food starting in about 2000 B.C. They also used them as medicine and as a source of cordage for making mats and baskets. (See also BASKET WEAVING TECHNIQUES; WEAVING TECHNIQUES.) Cattails were also used to make dolls and small figures used as TOYS. In addition they were used to make duck DECOYS.

Because cattails contain 10 times the amount of starch as that in an equal amount of POTATOES, they provided a good source of food energy. American Indians, including the Paiute of the Great Basin, picked and peeled cattail shoots in the springtime. In the winter, Indian people dried the roots and pounded them into flour. They also used mashed roots for TOOTHPASTES.

Root flour that was made into tea was used to stop diarrhea. Because cattail pollen is hemostatic and an ASTRINGENT, it was placed on cuts to control bleeding. Fresh, pounded root was applied as a poultice for blisters and insect stings. (See also INSECT BITE AND BEE STING REMEDIES.) The Mesquaki, a Northeast tribe, boiled the root and applied it to skin that had been burned. American Indians gathered fuzz from female cattail flower heads and used it to make DISPOSABLE DIAPERS. American Indians also used cattail pollen as a HAIR CONDITIONER.

To make cordage, Indians of many tribes pounded or shredded cattail leaves and then soaked them to further separate the fibers. They twisted two strands together by rubbing them on the top of the thigh with the palm of the hand. Women sewed double-layered cattail mats to cover wigwams. English colonist William Wood was impressed by the effectiveness of this method of construction, writing in 1634 that the wigwams covered with these mats were "very strong and handsome, covered with close-wrought mats of their one weaving, which deny entrance to any drop of raine, though it come both fierce and long, neither can the piercing North winde find a crannie, through which he can conveigh his cooling breath, they be warmer than our English houses."

See also INSULATION, HOME.

**Sources/Further Reading**

Densmore, Frances. *How Indians Use Wild Plants for Food, Medicine and Crafts*. New York: Dover Publications, Inc., 1974.

Prindle, Tara. *NativeTech: Cattails*. 1994–1998. URL: http://www.nativeweb.org/NativeTech/cattail/. Downloaded on April 10, 1999.

Wood, William. *Wood's New England's Prospect*. Boston: Publications of the Prince Society, 1865.

**cattails (*Typha latifolia*)** (2000 B.C.) *North American Northeast cultures*
The cattail (*Typha latifolia*) is a type of marsh plant that grows throughout the temperate zone of North America. Its most distinguishing characteristic is a tall stalk topped by a cylindri-

**caucus** (precontact) *North American Northeast cultures*
*Caucus*, the word for a closed-door political meeting often held to discuss strategy, was first used by English speakers in 1773. It comes from the Algonquian word *caucauasu*, meaning "counselor." The Iroquois and other Algonquian-speaking

tribes, who lived in the Northeast of what is now the United States, were politically sophisticated. Between A.D. 1100 and A.D. 1450, they joined together to form the Iroquois League, a confederation of tribes that originally consisted of the Mohawk, Oneida, Onondaga, Cayuga, and Seneca; the Tuscarora joined later. Many parts of the Iroquois confederacy's constitution served as foundations to the form of democracy practiced in the United States today and greatly influenced the contents of the U.S. Constitution.

See also IROQUOIS CONSTITUTION; UNITED STATES CONSTITUTION, AMERICAN INDIAN INFLUENCE ON.

### Sources/Further Reading

American Heritage Dictionary, Second College Edition. Boston: Houghton Mifflin Company, 1985.

Flexner, Stuart Berg. I Hear America Talking: An Illustrated History of American Words and Phrases. New York: Simon and Schuster, 1976.

### caulking compound  See ASPHALT.

### cayenne  (postcontact) *Mesoamerican cultures*

*Cayenne* is the term for several varieties of red CHILE peppers indigenous to the Americas that have been dried and ground into powder. When cayenne pepper is mixed with other ingredients such as garlic powder, it is called chili powder.

### Source/Further Reading

American Spice Trade Association. *Capsicum Spices and Oleoresins.* URL: http://astaspice.org/sp_cap.htm. Downloaded on February 17, 1999.

### cedar shingles and siding  See CARPENTRY TECHNIQUES.

### census  (ca. A.D. 1000)  *South American Andean cultures*

In order to be able to manage their *mit'a,* or work TAX SYSTEM, the Inca, whose empire was established in what is now Peru, needed to know their exact population. As new territory was brought under their rule, they conducted periodic censuses so that work-tax levies, or *mit'a,* could be modified to meet changing demographics. Each year the Inca gathered vital statistics on their population to determine who was widowed, who was poor, and who could not pay taxes. The annual census was also used to determine manpower available for defense of the villages. Census records were gathered using the *quipu,* a counting and record-keeping device that utilized a system of knots tied on colored strings to store information (see also QUIPUS).

### Sources/Further Reading

Josephy, Jr., Alvin M., ed. *America in 1492: The World of the Indian People Before the Arrival of Columbus.* New York: Random House, 1991.

Moseley, Michael. *The Inca and their Ancestors.* London: Thames and Hudson, 1992.

### century plant  See AGAVE.

### ceramics  See POTTERY.

### cesarean section  See OBSTETRICS.

### chemical fishing  See FISHING, CHEMICAL.

### chewable dentifrices  (precontact)  *Mesoamerican, South American, North American Southeast and Great Plains cultures*

A dentifrice is a substance used to aid in cleaning the teeth in order to maintain healthy teeth and gums. During 1998, chewable dentifrices were marketed in the United States as "new" products and advertised as a breakthrough in dental care. However, chewable dentifrices are prehistoric in origin. The American Indians of South and Mesoamerica relied on chewable dentifrices for routine preventative dental care for hundreds of years before the present-day dental aid made its debut. For example, the Aztec, who established an empire in Mesoamerica in about A.D. 1100, used plain unsweetened CHEWING GUM made from chicle as a preventative measure against tooth decay. This demonstrated a high level of medical knowledge of dental care.

In North America many Indian tribes in the South used Indian cup, or ragged cup (*Silphium perfoliatum*), for the plant's resinous sap. After extracting the sap, the Indians chewed it not only to clean teeth but also to treat other medical conditions. Ragged cup sap has stimulant, tonic, ANTISPASMODIC, and diaphoretic (perspiration-producing) properties. The practice of chewing ragged cup to aid in cleaning the teeth was adopted from the Indians by the early European immigrants to America. The Choctaw of the South also used button brush (*Cephalanthus occidentalis*) as a chewable dentifrice.

In addition, gum served medicinal purposes such as easing headaches, toothaches, and indigestion. In North America, Indians chewed pine needles, for example, to relieve sore throats and coughing. Besides soothing the symptoms, the needles provided vitamin C. The Dakota, Lakota, and Nakota people of the northern plains chewed on pieces of sweet flag to moisten the mouth and ease the pain of toothaches. Some Indian people chewed charcoal as a breath freshener. Charcoal served as an excellent breath freshener because of its ability to absorb odors.

See also DENTISTRY; TOOTHPASTES AND POWDERS.

### Sources/Further Reading
Lust, John. *The Herb Book.* New York: Bantam Books, 1974.

Ortiz de Montellano, Bernard. *Aztec Medicine, Health, and Nutrition.* New Brunswick, N.J.: Rutgers University Press, 1990.

Vogel, Virgil. *American Indian Medicine.* Norman: University of Oklahoma Press, 1977.

**chewing gum** (precontact) *North American California and Northeast, Mesoamerican, South American Tropical Forest cultures*

For thousands of years Indians throughout the Americas chewed the sap or LATEX of plants for the same reasons people chew gum today—to relieve hunger and thirst and to freshen breath. Indian peoples also relied on chewing gum for routine dental hygiene. (See also CHEWABLE DENTIFRICES.)

The Gabrielino people of Southern California boiled milkweed sap and chewed the result for gum. Other American Indians used several substances for chewing gum, such as licorice and marshmallow roots, sweet gum, and hollyhock. Plantain roots were sometimes chewed to relieve thirst. American Indians taught New England colonists to chew spruce sap as a breath sweetener. The practice quickly became a fad. Spruce gum was being sold by the lump in eastern United States by the early 1800s, making it the first commercial chewing gum.

Chicle, the original basis for modern chewing gum, is the milky latex of the tropical SAPODILLA tree (*Manilkara zapota van Royen*) that is native to northern Brazil, Mesoamerica, and parts of Mexico. The Maya, whose culture began in Mesoamerica in about 1500 B.C., discovered how to tap the sapodilla tree. The Aztec, whose empire was established in Mesoamerica in about A.D. 1100, later adopted gum chewing. Although people from cultures throughout the world chewed gum, without the introduction of chicle, the multimillion dollar U.S. chewing gum industry would not exist.

Mexican general Santa Anna introduced chicle to the United States after being exiled from Mexico in 1855 and bringing a block of it among his belongings. When he showed it to Thomas Adams, the inventor thought it would be the perfect substance from which to manufacture rubber as the Olmec had done for centuries. (Olmec culture arose in Mesoamerica in about 1700 B.C.) Adams began importing chicle to the United States from the Yucatán Peninsula. When that experiment failed, he shaped the chicle into small pieces he called "Adams New York Gum" and began marketing them in 1891 at a New Jersey drug store.

Although the gum was unflavored at first, it worked better than chewing paraffin, which had become a popular substitute for the pine sap Indians had taught the early colonists to chew. A few years later another inventor, Henry Fleer, coated chicle squares with white candy, calling them Chiclets. He and inventor William Wrigley Jr. added latex to the gum to make it stretch and added extracts of mint, including WINTERGREEN, another American Indian contribution, to their product. Today the chicle in chewing gum has for the most part been replaced with synthetic polymers made from oil and latex from tropical trees.

**Sources/Further Reading**

Hendrickson, Robert. *The Great American Chewing Gum Book.* Radnor, Penn.: Chilton, 1976.

Sharp, Mike. *Gabrielino Material Culture.* URL: http://www.csun.edu/~ms4427/gab.htm. Downloaded on January 6, 1999.

Weatherford, Jack. *Indian Givers: How the Indians of the Americas Transformed the World.* New York: Fawcett Columbine, 1988.

**chia** (precontact) *Mesoamerican; North American California, Great Basin, and Southwest cultures*

Chia is a generic name for several species of related plants, including *Salvia hispanica, S. Labiatae,* and *S. columbariae,* that are native to the deserts of Mexico and the U.S. Southwest. (Because of its square stems and oblong leaves, chia is sometimes mistaken for sage.) For many people today the word *chia* calls to mind the green "hair" or "fur" that sprouts on clay statues after they are sprinkled with seeds and watered. Yet, far from being novelty items, the seeds from the chia plant were such an important part of the Aztec diet that they were brought as tribute to the capitol city, Tenochtitlán (see also TAX SYSTEMS). The Aztec Empire was established in Mesoamerica about A.D. 1100.

For the Aztec, chia served as a source of nutrition in the form of drinks and gruels that were sweetened or flavored with CHILES. The seeds were also used as medicine, as an oil base for paints and a varnish, and as an ointment that served as a skin protectant on the legs and feet of hunters and fishermen.

American Indian tribes living in what are now Arizona, Utah, and Southern California—including the Akimel O'odham (Pima), Paiute, Kawaiisu, Diegueño, Tataviam, Gabrielino, and Cahuilla—routinely ate chia seed porridges or used the seeds as the basis for drinks. The Pomo, a California tribe, parched seeds to make a flour called *pinole.* Early Spanish settlers in the region also came to depend on chia for their nutrition.

Chia seeds are the most highly concentrated source of linolenic acid known. They are also high in other omega 3 fatty acids and naturally occurring antioxidants as well as calcium. The seeds contain a great deal of fiber, so much so that ingesting too many can have a laxative effect. The small gray seeds are higher in protein than other grains and seeds. Because they contain all of the essential amino acids, the protein they provide is nutritionally complete.

The effects of chia's nutritional potency were legendary. Aztec warriors and hunters lived on chia seeds in the field. The Tahuamara Indians of what is now northern Mexico are said to have credited chia seed for their ability to hunt by outrunning their prey. American Indian runners who carried messages and traded throughout the Southwest also relied on it. (See also RUNNING.) When the Spaniards forced California Indians to march long distances to missions where they were forced to live, the Indians often subsisted on a spoon of chia seeds mixed with water to see them through a 24-hour march.

This mixture was said to quench thirst in addition to providing energy.

Modern researchers believe chia's power to sustain comes from the fact that each seed can absorb more than 12 times its weight in water. When this absorption takes place, the mucilloid gel within the seed mixes with the water and causes it to gel—nature's way of keeping the seeds moist and anchored in desert soil. This property means that drinking chia causes the body to conserve water and retain electrolytes even during exercise. Chia gel may also slow the conversion of carbohydrates into sugar, providing added stamina.

Members of the Cahuilla of what is now California and the Kawaiisu tribes of what is now Utah placed a chia seed in irritated eyes to reduce inflammation and to remove foreign matter. (See also EYES, MEDICAL TREATMENT OF.) The Cahuilla used it to purify alkali drinking water and as a disinfectant for wounds. Spanish missionaries who encountered chia seeds were so impressed by the medicinal uses they observed that they adopted a mixture of the seeds and water as a fever remedy and packed chia poultices into gunshot wounds in order to prevent infection. (See also ASEPSIS.)

Ignored as a food source in modern times, chia began making a comeback in the late 20th century. Today it is grown primarily as a food crop, but its potential for use in the cosmetic and other industries is currently being explored. In Argentina chia has overtaken beans as a profit-making crop, prompting farmers to significantly increase acreage devoted to chia.

See also SALVE, DRAWING; SUN SCREEN, MEDICINAL.

**Sources/Further Reading**

Coe, Sophie. *America's First Cuisines.* Austin: University of Texas Press, 1994.

Moerman, Dan. *Native American Ethnobotany Database: Food, Drugs, Dyes and Fibers of Native North American Peoples.* URL: http://www.umd.umich.edu/cgi-bin/herb. Downloaded on January 6, 1999.

Nabokov, Peter. *Indian Running: Native American History and Tradition.* Santa Fe, N.M.: Ancient City Press, 1981.

Ortiz de Montellano, Bernard. *Aztec Medicine, Health, and Nutrition.* New Brunswick, N.J.: Rutgers University Press, 1990.

Shupp, Mike. *Gabrielino Material Culture.* URL: http://www.csun.edu/~ms4427/gab.htm. Downloaded on January 6, 1999.

**chicle**  See CHEWING GUM.

**chiles**  (7000 B.C.–5500 B.C.) *Mesoamerican, Circum-Caribbean, South American and North American Southwest cultures*

After salt, the chile pepper, which is indigenous to the Americas, has become the most frequently used seasoning worldwide. Chile and sweet, or bell, pepper plants belong to the *Capsicum* genus. (*Capsicum* comes from the Greek word that means "to bite.") They are part of the Solanaceae family and are related to TOBACCO, TOMATOES, and POTATOES that are also indigenous to the Americas. Neither chile nor sweet peppers are related to black peppers (*Piper nigrum*), which are not indigenous to North or South America. Christopher Columbus, the first European to encounter chiles, assumed that because of their pungency they must be a kind of pepper. His mistake stuck and has been a source of confusion ever since.

Indigenous Americans began cultivating chile peppers in northeastern Mesoamerica by between 7000 to 5500 B.C. This makes chiles one of the oldest crops on the continent. By 5200 to 3400 B.C., Indians were cultivating at least three varieties in the Tehuacan valley of what is now Mexico, where the Coxcatlan people, who predated the Aztec, grew them. By the time Columbus landed in Hispaniola, American indigenous farmers had developed dozens of types of chiles and their cultivation had spread to the Caribbean.

*Chile* comes from the Nahuatl, or Aztec, word *chilli.* (The Aztec Empire arose in what is now Mexico and in parts of Mesoamerica in about A.D. 1100.) To say that chiles were an important part of the Aztec diet is an understatement. Friar Bartolomé de Las Casas commented in the 1500s that "without the chile, [the Aztec] don't believe that they are eating." Other early European observers reported that the Aztec people used chiles in much the same way as Europeans used salt. According to some accounts, the Aztec ate them for breakfast, lunch, and dinner and even spiced their CHOCOLATE drinks with them. They made *chillatolli,* a thick cornmeal with yellow chile and honey (see also BEEKEEPING), to cure coughs. They also made a hot drink from salt and chile. They dried peppers and made them into pickles to take on journeys. About 20 types were sold in the marketplace in the capitol city. The Aztec also collected tributes in the form of chiles. The town of Ixtapa in Michoacan paid the emperor eight loads of them every 20 days. (See also TAX SYSTEMS.)

Chile eating was not limited to the Aztec. The Maya, whose culture arose about 1500 B.C., were such chile connoisseurs that they had a word, *hu'uyb,* which meant to draw a breath with puckered mouth after eating them. By the time Columbus landed in the West Indies, the Arawak and Taino people who lived there were growing and eating chiles as well.

During Columbus's first voyage, he observed that the Taino endured the cold weather of the mountains by eating meat with very hot spices. He brought what they called *aji,* but what he believed to be peppers, to Spain on his return in 1493. That year Peter Martyr wrote that Columbus had brought back "pepper more pungent than that from the Caucasus." Portuguese explorers took chiles to their colonies in India and Malaysia. Soon plants were growing there, so that by 1548 cayenne pepper was introduced to Britain from India. By the middle of the 1500s the chile trade was booming and the flavorful spice was becoming an integral part of cuisines in West Africa, Thailand, India, and the Szechwan and Hunan regions of China, in addition to Spain. The first commercial chile cultivation in what would later become the United States began in 1600 when Spanish colonists planted seeds in the Chama river region of northern New Mexico. Flavor was only one reason chile spread so rapidly; compared to other spices it was inexpensive and so could be enjoyed by common people as well as the wealthy.

Botanists believe that more than 100 varieties of wild and cultivated capsicum were native to what is now Mexico. These grew in a variety of colors, including red, green, yellow, and black. They varied in size from tiny chiles that were 1/4-inch long to those that measured a foot. Their shapes were as varied as the degree of heat they produced when eaten. Scientists continue to discover even more native varieties as they explore the tropical regions more thoroughly.

From curry powder and paprika to salsa, capsicums have become an everyday flavoring for many people throughout the world. It is chile that gives ginger ale its bite (see also SOFT DRINK INGREDIENTS) and four-alarm CHILI its punch. Botanists number the total of known chile varieties at over 200 throughout the world today. From the Anaheim and ancho to the chipotle, jalapeño, Jamaican hot, and poblano, chiles derive their spicy flavor from capsaicin, a substance in the seeds and membranes. As a rule, small chiles are hotter than larger ones because they contain more seeds and veins than the larger ones do. A dominant gene, one that sweet peppers lack, controls the amount of capsaicin in a pepper. Through SEED SELECTION, Mesoamerican chile growers were able to regulate the amount of capsaicin in the peppers they raised, a technique that continues today. Stress, in the form of poor soil or hot temperatures, also causes the peppers to develop more of the fiery chemical, a fact that indigenous farmers knew and used to produce the type of pepper they desired.

Chiles are the most concentrated source of vitamin C available, containing twice the amount found in citrus fruits. Cooking destroys only a third of the vitamin C in chiles, but it is lost completely during the drying process. In addition to vitamin C, chiles contain vitamins A, $B_1$, and E.

For thousands of years capiscums have been used as medicine as well as food. The Maya and the Aztec used them for treating coughs and colds. They also used them as a topical pain reliever. On initial contact with the skin or mucous membranes, capsaicin works as a powerful irritant that causes the release of a neurotransmitter called substance P, which tells the brain something painful is occurring. Eventually substance P is depleted and pain from that area of the body is no longer registered by the brain. That is why some people may notice numbness in their lips and mouth after they come in contact with the hotter varieties of chiles. The Aztec, who were familiar with the numbing properties of capsaicin, used chiles to treat toothaches. (See also DENTISTRY.)

In more recent times, chiles have been used in the United States in over-the-counter analgesic balms such as Heat and Sloan's Liniment. The U.S. Food and Drug Administration (FDA) has approved the use of capsaicin in creams used to reduce phantom limb pain experienced by amputees and to control post-operative pain for mastectomy patients. Medical research has shown capsaicin to be effective in reducing pain from cluster headaches, shingles, and arthritis. When used repeatedly, it reduces inflammation. In high concentrations, capsaicin can destroy the nerves. Because of the chemical's potency, the FDA has set the highest concentration allowed for medicinal purposes at 0.075%. Taken orally, chile peppers have also been used as a digestive aid and a laxative because they stimulate the production of gastric juices. Too much chile, however, can cause pain, vomiting, and gastrointestinal distress. In addition to nutritional and medical uses, chile has been painted on children's thumbs for years to discourage thumb-sucking. The same principal is used to produce preparations that discourage squirrels from eating underground cable, flower bulbs, and birdseed.

Today chile is also used commercially as a barnacle repellent on ships and as a rodent and INSECT REPELLENT. Oleoresin capsicum, a compound in chiles, forms the basis for the pepper spray carried by on-duty police patrol officers. This spray temporarily incapacitates a person by causing the eyes to swell shut and breathing to become difficult. Postal workers also use the spray to repel attacking dogs.

An important industrial application of chile is as a DYE. In addition to being used in cosmetics, it is used to color processed lunch meats, sausage, and salad dressings. (See also FOOD COLORING.) Chickens fed red chile produce eggs with a reddish yellow yolk, a color preferred by consumers. Some zoos feed chile peppers to flamingos in order to make their feathers more brilliant.

Today chile peppers are grown primarily in Asia, Africa, and parts of the U.S. South and Southwest. According to the U.S. Department of Agriculture, China is the top chile producer in the world, followed by Turkey, Nigeria, and Mexico. The United States ranks sixth, with New Mexico as its top chile-pepper producing state.

See also CAYENNE; PAPRIKA; PEPPERS, SWEET OR BELL; SALSA.

## Sources/Further Reading

American Spice Trade Association. *Capsicum Spices and Oleoresins.* URL: http://astaspice.org/sp_cap.htm. Downloaded on April 2, 1999.

Andrews, Jean. *Peppers: The Domesticated Capsicums.* Arlington: University of Texas Press, 1995.

Bosland, Paul. "Capsicums: Innovative Uses of an Ancient Crop." In *Progress in New Crops.* J. Janick, ed. Arlington, Virginia: AHHS Press, 1996.

Coe, Sophie. *America's First Cuisines.* Austin: University of Texas Press, 1994.

Database of the known varieties of capsicum: The largest Internet database of all the known varieties of the Capsicum species (with photographs). URL: http://easyweb. easynet.co.uk/~gcaselton/chile/var-l.html. Posted on August 22, 1998.

Hurt, R. Douglas. *Indian Agriculture in the Americas: Prehistory to Present.* Lawrence: University Press of Kansas, 1988.

Hutchens, Alma R. *Indian Herbology of North America.* Boston: Shambhala, 1991.

Sokalow, Raymond. *Why We Eat What We Eat: How the Encounter Between the New World and the Old Changed the Way Everyone on the Planet Eats.* New York: Summit Books, 1991.

Tannahill, Reay. *Food in History.* New York: Stein and Day, 1973.

Trager, James. *The Food Chronology: The Food Lover's Compendium of Events and Anecdotes from Prehistory to Present.* New York: Henry Holt, 1995.

Weatherford, Jack. *Indian Givers: How the Indians of the Americas Transformed the World.* New York: Fawcett Columbine, 1988.

**chili**  (precontact)  *Mesoamerican, North American Southwest cultures*

The word *chili,* like *chile,* comes from the Nahuatl, or Aztec, word *chilli.* It was first used in the English language in the 1600s. Today *chili* has come to mean a spicy dish of beans, chile powder, and meat. (CHILE refers to the hot peppers used in the dish.) Although no one can be certain whether or not chili originated with the Aztec, whose empire was established in about A.D. 1100, they did make sauces of chile powder and shredded meat. Beans were also a part of their diet. It is not improbable that they combined the ingredients and were eating chili long before Hernán Cortés and his men arrived in what would become Mexico. The dish called chili is popular in Mexico and the North American Southwest today.

## Sources/Further Reading
Coe, Sophie. *America's First Cuisines.* Austin: University of Texas Press, 1994.

Flexner, Stuart Berg. *I Hear America Talking: An Illustrated History of American Words and Phrases.* New York: Simon and Schuster, 1976.

**chinampas**  See AGRICULTURE, RAISED BED.

**chips, potato**  See POTATO CHIPS.

**chisels, metal**  (ca. 5000 B.C.–4000 B.C.)  *North American Northeast Paleo-Indian cultures*

A chisel is a tool that has a sharp, beveled edge, which is used to shape wood, metal, or stone. The first metal chisel appeared in North America approximately 6,000 to 7,000 years ago. In the southern Great Lakes area of present-day Wisconsin, the Paleo-Indians produced copper implements and tools, one of which was the chisel. Once the chisel was made, it was placed in a fire and then allowed to cool. (See also ANNEALING.) This caused the copper to harden, and in this state it was capable of chipping harder substances than it could in its natural state.

See also METALLURGY; TOOLS.

## Sources/Further Reading
Driver, Harold E. *Indians of North America.* Chicago: University of Chicago Press, 1969.

Maxwell, James A. *America's Fascinating Indian Heritage.* Pleasantville, N.Y.: Reader's Digest Books, 1978.

**Chisholm Trail**  (A.D. 1832)  *North America*

One of the most popular cattle trails used by cattlemen to drive herds from Texas to the Kansas railheads was originally blazed by Cherokee/Scottish trader and interpreter Jesse Chisholm. Chisholm established the route as a wagon road in 1832 to haul freight from Kansas in order to stock his trading posts. Some western historians credit him with being the father of the first chain of convenience stores, since his posts sold provisions to the cattlemen on their way north.

The trail began in southwestern Texas; crossed the Nueces, Colorado, Brazos, Trinity, Red, Washita, Canadian, North Canadian, Cimarron, and Arkansas rivers into Abilene; and ended at Ellsworth, Kansas. U.S. Highway 81 follows the route today. Sometimes it is confused with the Chisum Trail, a different cattle trail in Texas.

Although some western history experts believe he never actually drove cattle over the route, evidence exists that in 1866 Chisholm traveled from Kansas to his trading post on the North Canadian River with furs, buffalo (see also BISON) robes, and 250 head of cattle. Although cattle were not his favored item of trade, he occasionally accepted them, selling them at Fort Gibson. Jesse Chisholm died on March 4, 1868.

See also PLACE-NAMES; ROAD SITES; SETTLEMENT PATTERNS.

## Sources/Further Reading
Gard, Wayne. *The Chisholm Trail.* Norman: University of Oklahoma Press, 1984.

Waldman, Carl. *Atlas of the North American Indian,* Rev. New York: Facts On File, 2000.

Worcester, Donald Emmet. *The Chisholm Trail: High Road of the Cattle Kingdom.* Lincoln: University of Nebraska Press, 1980.

**chocolate**  (A.D. 1)  *Mesoamerican cultures*

Chocolate is the result of grinding and roasting CACAO beans. When sweetened, this popular substance is used to flavor many foods, including candy and beverages. In 1997, per capita chocolate consumption in the United States was 11 1/2 pounds. The Maya, whose culture arose in Mesoamerica about 1500 B.C., discovered the process to transform the beans of the cacao tree into chocolate in about A.D. 200, although they had cultivated the trees earlier. In 1502, near what is now Nicaragua, Christopher Columbus encountered a Maya trading canoe (see TRADE) and obtained some cacao beans that he took to King Ferdinand and Queen Isabella. The Spanish court, uncertain about how the beans could be used, at first ignored them.

By the time Columbus met the traders, the Maya had been chocolatiers for centuries. They processed cacao beans by first opening the pods and scooping out the seeds that are covered with a white, sweet pulp. Next they fermented the seeds for several days to convert the sugar content to lactic and acetic acid. This removed the bitterness and released compounds that produce chocolate flavor when the beans are roasted. After the Maya roasted the beans, they removed the thin shells. Finally, they ground the beans several times to make a paste. Archaeologists believe the Maya developed this technology about A.D. 1; without it, the beans are bitter and unpalatable. The Maya made chocolate into hot and cold beverages, believing they were medicinal and had spiritual properties. Some Maya were buried with clay chocolate vessels.

The Aztec, whose empire was established in Mesoamerica in about A.D. 1100, consumed chocolate, as did the Toltec and Mixtec. Since cacao trees did not grow in the Valley of Mexico, they imported their beans from the Maya. They also obtained the raw material for chocolate by levying tributes of cacao beans from Maya villages they had conquered. (See also TAX SYSTEMS.) In Aztec society, chocolate beverages were the drinks of the ruling class because the beans were relatively scarce. One of the Aztec drinks was called *xocoatl,* the Nahuatl word from which the term *chocolate* is derived.

Aztec chocolate was sometimes flavored with VANILLA, ALLSPICE, and cinnamon-like barks that were native to South America. The Aztec thickened their chocolate with flour made from CORN or spiced it with CHILE, a taste combination present in mole today. Although Europeans are usually credited with creating sweet chocolate, the Maya and later the Aztec sweetened their chocolate drinks with honey for hundreds of years before Europeans knew that chocolate existed. (See also BEEKEEPING.) Whether served hot or cold, most of the Mesoamerican drinks were beaten until foamy. The Aztec ate the roasted beans and solid chocolate as well, possibly in a form that was the forerunner of today's candy bars. They also made chocolate tablets that were dissolved in water to make "instant" chocolate drinks. (See also INSTANT FOOD.)

The Aztec believed that in addition to its food value, chocolate had medicinal properties. It was used as an aphrodisiac as well as to treat diarrhea and dysentery. Modern research has shown that chocolate contains phenylephylamine, a substance nearly the same as the neurochemical produced by the human brain when a person falls in love. Other scientific research indicates that chocolate contains high levels of antioxidant chemicals called phenolics, which slow the oxidation of LDL, the saturated fat that clogs arteries when it is oxidized.

In 1519 Hernán Cortés observed the Aztec practice of chocolate drinking. The Aztec emperor Montezuma, who was rumored to drink as many as 50 or more of the beverages daily, served chocolate in golden goblets to those who would soon lay waste to his empire. Cortés returned to Spain with cacao beans and processed powder. He wrote to Charles I of Spain that chocolate fought fatigue and built up resistance to disease. Bernardo de Sahagun the Spanish chronicler of Mesoamerican life wrote that in moderation chocolate invigorated, refreshed, and consoled. He cautioned, however, that the drink could be addictive.

Perhaps because of his comments, Europeans at first viewed chocolate as intoxicating. The early reviewers said that it was a drink fit for pigs. In 1569 Pope Pius V described chocolate as being so disgusting that he could not imagine anyone wanting to drink it. By 1580, however, members of the Spanish aristocracy were drinking chocolate and were flavoring it with lemon peel, musk, and ambergris, orange, rose water, or anise seed. Although Spain established cacao plantations in its colonies, they kept the chocolate-making process they had learned from the Maya a secret for almost 100 years. When the Spanish monks, whose job it was to make the chocolate, revealed the secret, chocolate manufacturing swept through Europe. The invention of the steam engine enabled mechanical grinding, dropping the price of chocolate so low that it became available to common people as well as the wealthy. By 1765 the first U.S. chocolate factory had been founded.

By the 20th century, chocolate had become a part of daily life. During World War II, soldiers were issued chocolate bars in their rations. The morale-boosting power of the candy and nutritional value was so recognized by the U.S. government that valuable shipping space was reserved for cacao beans during the war effort. Chocolate is also on the menu for the astronauts in the U.S. space program. According to a recent Gallup poll, people in the United States reported 3 to 1 that their favorite flavor was chocolate; collectively, they eat 2.8 billion pounds of chocolate each year. Every day nine out of ten Americans eat some form of chocolate, according to the Chocolate Manufacturers Association.

## Sources/Further Reading

*Cadbury's Chocolate History and the Growing of Cocoa.* URL: http://cadbury.co.uk/facts/html/cocoa2.htm. Downloaded on January 11, 1999.

Chocolate Manufacturers Association. URL: http://www.candyusa.org. Downloaded on January 11, 1999.

Coe, Sophie. *America's First Cuisines.* Austin: University of Texas Press, 1994.

Coe, Sophie and Michael D. Coe. *The True History of Chocolate.* London: Thames & Hudson, 1996.

Hershey Foods Corporation. URL: http://www.hersheys.com/totally/history/chocolate. Downloaded on January 11, 1999.

Lavanne, Pierre. "The History of Chocolate." In *The Book of Chocolate.* Ghidlaine Bavoillot, ed. Paris: Flammarion, 1995.

Trager, James. *The Food Chronology: The Food Lover's Compendium of Events and Anecdotes from Prehistory to Present.* New York: Henry Holt, 1995.

**cigarettes** (precontact) *Mesoamerican, Circum-Caribbean cultures*

Rolling shredded tobacco in paper or similar material produces cigarettes. When Hernán Cortés invaded Mexico in 1519, he found the Aztec smoking perfumed reed cigarettes. Before banquets, Aztec dinner guests were presented with smoking tubes containing TOBACCO. According to early accounts of such feasts in the time of Montezuma, the Aztec emperor at the time of conquest, cigarette smoking was a ritual event. The tubes were said to represent the warrior's darts. They were offered again the next day when a second banquet would begin.

Europeans did not smoke cigarettes until the early 1600s when, in Seville, beggars rolled them from tobacco, gleaned from used CIGARS, in bits of paper. Not until 1847 did Philip Morris set up a shop to sell hand-rolled cigarettes. Machine-manufactured cigarettes were not introduced until 1860. The invention of the first mechanized cigarette-rolling machine in the late 1880s spurred cigarette smoking's growth. Awareness of the health risks of smoking caused the number of cigarette smokers in the United States to drop from 40% to 25% in the late 20th century. The number of cigarettes smoked has not declined, however. Based on an analysis of tobacco company annual reports, the total 1996 U.S. cigarette sales volume was 24,165 billion packs.

See also PIPES, TOBACCO.

### Sources/Further Reading

Borio, Gene. *The History of Tobacco.* URL: http://www. historian.org/bysubject/tobacco.htm. Posted 1997.
CNN. *A Brief History of Tobacco.* URL: http://www.cnn.com/ US/9705/tobacco/history/index.html. Downloaded on February 7, 1999.
Coe, Sophie. *America's First Cuisines.* Austin: University of Texas Press, 1994.

### cigars (ca. A.D. 1000) *Mesoamerican, Circum-Caribbean cultures*

Cigars are rolls of TOBACCO leaves that are smoked. American Indians smoked cigars at least 1,000 years ago. A picture on a POTTERY vessel found in Guatemala dated from before A.D. 1000 shows a Maya man smoking a roll of tobacco leaves tied with a string. (Maya culture arose in what is now Mexico and in parts of Mesoamerica in about 1500 B.C.) The Maya word for smoking was *sik'ar,* which became the Spanish word *cigarro.* Rather than smoking cigars as part of daily life, as is done today, the Maya used cigars in their religious ceremonies.

Cigar making and smoking was practiced in the Caribbean as well. Members of Christopher Columbus's crew were the first Europeans to see the West Indies version of the cigar. The Spaniards, who introduced tobacco to Europe, soon established plantations in what is now Cuba for the growing tobacco market in Spain. European demand for cigars did not truly boom until the early 1800s. In 1821 King Ferdinand VII of Spain issued a decree urging a state monopoly on cigar production in what had become Cuba.

Settlers in New England learned to cultivate tobacco from the Indians. An early cigar factory in Conestoga, Pennsylvania, gave the name "stogie" to the U.S. version of the rolled tobacco leaves. Cigar use began to boom in the early 1800s and

again after the U.S.-Mexican War (1846–48). Cigar store owners once placed wooden statues of Indians outside of their shop doors to advertise their wares. Today cigar smoking is once again on the rise in the United States. In 1997, 5.1 billion cigars were smoked in the United States, an increase of 68 percent from 1993. Like CIGARETTES, however, cigars pose health hazards.

See also PIPES, TOBACCO.

### Sources/Further Reading

Borio, Gene. *The History of Tobacco.* URL: http://www. historian.org/bysubject/tobacco.htm. Posted 1997.
CNN. *A Brief History of Tobacco.* URL: http://www.cnn.com/ US/9705/tobacco/history/index.html. Downloaded on February 7, 1999.
Josephy, Jr., Alvin M. (ed.) *America in 1492: The World of the Indian People Before the Arrival of Columbus.* New York: Random House, 1991.
U.S. Department of Agriculture. *Tobacco Situation and Outlook Report.* Washington, D.C.: U.S. Department of Agriculture Trade and Economics Division Economic Research Service, April 1998.

### cinchona   See QUININE.

### cinnabar   See MERCURY.

### cities, America's first (1200 B.C.–precontact) *Mesoamerican, South American Andean, North American Southeast and Southwest cultures*

Cities are centers of population. In addition to being places where people live, they tend to be a focal point for commerce and culture. Many of the 75 to 100 million indigenous residents of the Western Hemisphere were urban dwellers before European colonists established their cities in what they would call the New World. The oldest city site that has been found is El Aspero in what is now Peru. It was built in 3000 B.C. and is famous now for its PYRAMIDS. Some indigenous urban centers, or cities, included the culture center Poverty Point in what is now Louisiana; the Hohokam city Snaketown in the Southwest desert; the Inca city of Machu Piccu; the Maya towns of Tikal, Copán, and Chichén Itzá in the Yucatán; large villages along the Northwest Pacific coast of North America; Monte Albán, which was founded by the Olmec and later developed by the Zapotec; and the pueblos of the Southwest. Many more existed.

America's indigenous agricultural revolution enabled permanent settlement and as these settlements grew, towns and then cities were founded throughout North, Meso-, and South America in areas where sophisticated AGRICULTURE had become an established way of life. With increasing agricultural production, not as much labor was required to supply food as hunting and gathering had required. This freed a number of people to focus on other forms of work, such as building, tool-making, and other crafts. (See also TOOLS.) These services and goods could be traded for food. In some towns marketplaces were established where both local and distant TRADE goods were sold—precursors of the modern shopping mall. Leisure time increased as this new way of life became more prevalent, enabling the arts to flourish. Craftspeople began to make decorative luxury items and spent more time and attention than previously possible on the crafting of life's necessities, such as pottery vessels, baskets, and cloth. (See also POTTERY; BASKET WEAVING TECHNIQUES; WEAVING TECHNIQUES.)

One of the oldest urban areas in the Americas are of Olmec origin. The Olmec culture arose in Mesoamerica in about 1700 B.C. The most notable of these urban centers are La Venta, San Lorenzo, and Tres Zapotecs. They are said to have flourished between 1200 B.C. and 700 B.C. The Olmec had already developed a wide trading network by this time. Another of the oldest cities in the Americas was the pre-Inca community of Samapaita in what is Bolivia today. Traces of this settlement are dated at 1500 B.C. This community is surrounded by a very picturesque environment, including sandy beaches around lagoons and waterfalls.

In about A.D. 1, major urban centers began to flourish in the Americas. The Moche, who lived in what is now Peruvian South America from 200 B.C. to A.D. 600, built Huaca del Sol (Pyramid of the Sun) dated to 100 B.C.–A.D. 100. The central pyramid in this worship complex that was surrounded by dense settlement is the largest pre-Columbian edifice in South America.

The city of Teotihuacán, established in what is now central Mexico, is the oldest urban area in Mesoamerica. Founded in the first millennium A.D., it was as large as Rome at the time, covering nearly eight square miles, but fell into decline 500 years later.

Cahokia, a Mississippian culture city constructed eight miles east of the site of modern St. Louis, Missouri, was a center of a trade network that ranged from the Gulf Coast to the Great Lakes and from the Atlantic Coast to Oklahoma. The city, which covered over five square miles and contained over 120 earthen mounds that supported civic buildings and the homes of the city's ruling class, is considered the largest and most influential American Indian settlement north of Mesoamerica. Located on a floodplain at the confluence of the Mississippi and Missouri Rivers known as the American Bottom, the city's site ensured an abundance of wildlife and fertile soil for agriculture. Settlement began with temporary Paleo-Indian camps as early as 950 to 800 B.C. Between 600 B.C. and A.D. 800, the birth of agriculture in the region resulted in the permanent town of Cahokia and settlements in outlying regions. During its peak, from A.D. 1050 to A.D. 1250, the city's population was estimated to be between 10,000 and 20,000 residents.

The residents of Cahokia lived in single-family dwellings made of pole frameworks, covered with thatched roofs and mat walls. They clustered these homes into extended family compounds that were arranged around courtyards. These small

groups were arranged around larger community plazas that could be considered distinct neighborhoods. Ceremonial buildings formed Cahokia's center. Like modern cities, Cahokia had suburbs in addition to its thriving downtown. A number of smaller mound centers were distributed throughout the American Bottom. Many smaller farmsteads were scattered throughout the area as well. For unknown reasons the city began to decline about A.D. 1200 and was virtually empty by A.D. 1400.

The Anasazi, the ancestors of today's Pueblo people, built many settlements throughout the North American Southwest desert. The urban settlement of Chaco Canyon, located in what is now New Mexico, is one of the largest and most-studied Anasazi cities. This population center was home to an estimated 6,000 people and its influence extended for hundreds of miles in every direction. The first permanent residents of Chaco Canyon began living there about 900 B.C. By about A.D. 700, they began building ADOBE pueblos on the site of Pueblo Bonito. (See also APARTMENT COMPLEXES.) By A.D. 1115 the Anasazi had constructed between 125 and 150 outlying pueblos within the 60,000 square miles of the San Juan Basin. Some of these smaller towns, called outliers, were connected to Pueblo Bonito, the capitol, by more than 400 miles of ROAD SYSTEMS. Although the houses were built of adobe, their beams were logs. Between 100,000 and 200,000 huge ponderosa pine logs had to be transported from distant mountains for their construction. Pueblo Bonito alone contains more than 600 rooms. Trade was an important enterprise in Chaco Canyon. Shells, copper bells, and macaw skeletons have been found, indicating that the trade goods came from long distances. Recently archaeologists have hypothesized that large rooms in Pueblo Bonito and in the Anasazi city Mesa Verde, built in what is now southwestern Colorado, were storage facilities for grain. (See also CROP STORAGE.) They speculate that these pueblos served as food distribution centers for large areas of the Southwest.

Teotihuacán, a Mesoamerican city that fell in A.D. 800, had a population as large as 200,000 in the fifth century A.D. Tenochtitlan, the Aztec city that has now become the site of modern Mexico City, was founded in A.D. 1325. (See also SETTLEMENT PATTERNS.) The city, which in the Aztec language Nahuatl means "place of the cactus fruit," became the largest metropolis in the Americas; its population was an estimated quarter of a million. The center of the Aztec Empire, which was established in about A.D. 1100, Tenochtitlan was the capital of an empire that ruled several million people. Surrounded by water, it was the site of artificial islands, or *chinampas,* on which crops were grown to feed the residents. (See also AGRICULTURE, RAISED BED.) Tenochtitlan was filled with temples, palaces, schools (see also COMPULSORY EDUCATION), and a huge marketplace. Tenochtitlán also contained ZOOS and botanical gardens. (See also GARDENS, BOTANICAL.) When conquistador Hernán Cortés and his men first saw the huge city and the roads leading from it, they could not believe their eyes. Bernal Díaz Castillo, who wrote an account of Cortés's travels, noted: "Some of the soldiers among us who had been in many parts of the world, in Constantinople, and all over Italy and Rome, said that so large a marketplace and so full of people, and so well regulated and arranged, they had never seen before."

South American cities continued to be built at the same time. Chan Chan, which would become the largest pre-Columbian city in Peru, is one of the most well known. At its height Chan Chan is believed to have housed about 50,000 people in approximately 10,000 dwellings. It was built by the Chimu culture (A.D. 1000 to A.D. 1475), which was conquered by the Inca, who had established their empire in about A.D. 1000. Cuzco, the seat of the Inca Empire, was also a large urban area. Like most ancient cities, it was laid out on a grid. Cuzco served as the center point of the extensive road network built by the Inca. The Inca not only paid attention to roads but also paved the streets of their cities with basalt cobblestones.

Flourishing urban areas were not limited to Meso- and South America at the time of contact. The Iroquois and other Iroquoian-speaking peoples of what are now the northeastern United States and Canada, had been living in villages for hundreds of years by the time the colonists arrived. Early European visitors were so impressed by these American Indian settlements with their surrounding STOCKADES that they called them castles. Evidence gathered at the Draper site, a Huron village near modern Toronto, indicates that by A.D. 1500 the community had 45 to 50 structures, covered 15 acres and supported at least 2,000 residents inside its palisade. In 1535 French explorer Jacques Cartier reported that 3,600 people lived in 50 bark longhouses in Hochelaga, an Iroquois town near what is now Montreal. During the early phases of European colonization, the villages continued to flourish. By the late 1600s, the Iroquois settlement of Gannagaro in Ontario County, New York, consisted of 150 longhouses with thousands of residents. By this time 25 major Iroquois towns existed. One of the largest was a two-village settlement called Cahiague between Lake Simcoe and the Georgian Bay in Ontario. It was composed of 200 longhouses and about 4,000 residents. As European colonists claimed more land, many towns were either destroyed or abandoned.

See also CIVIC CENTERS; STONEMASONRY TECHNIQUES; URBAN PLANNING.

## Sources/Further Reading

Donnan, Christopher B. "Masterworks of Art Reveal a Remarkable Pre-Inca World." *National Geographic* 177, no. 6 (June 1990): 17–33.

Iseminger, William R. "Mighty Cahokia" *Archaeology* (May/June 1996): 31–37.

Jennings, Francis. The *Founders of America: How Indians Discovered the Land, Pioneered in it, and Created Great Classical Civilizations; How They were Plunged into a Dark Age by Invasion and Conquest; and How They are now Reviving.* New York: W.W. Norton, 1993.

Nabokov, Peter and Robert Easton. *Native American Architecture.* New York: Oxford University Press, 1989.

Nobel, David Grant. *New Light on Chaco Canyon.* Santa Fe: School of American Research, 1985.

Stannard, David E. *American Holocaust: Columbus and the Conquest of the New World.* New York: Oxford University Press, 1992.

Stuart, George E. "The Timeless Vision of Teotihuacán." *National Geographic* 188, no.6 (December 1995): 5–35.

Trigger, Bruce G., and Wilcomb E. Washburn, eds. *The Cambridge History of the Native Peoples of the Americas, Vol. I, Part I, North America.* New York: Cambridge University Press, 1996.

Viola, Herman J. and Carolyn Margolis. *Seeds of Change: 500 Years Since Columbus.* Washington, D.C. Smithsonian Institution Press, 1991.

**civic centers  (plazas)**  (precontact)  *Mesoamerican, South American Andean, North American Southeast and Southwest cultures*

Many population centers throughout the pre-Columbian Americas were arranged around a main plaza or civic center. Often these plazas were laid out based on astronomical observations. (See also ASTRONOMY.) The Olmec, the first great Mesoamerican civilization, which arose in about 1700 B.C., constructed cities with ball courts in the center. (See also BASKETBALL.) Archaeologists believe that the civic centers flanked by PYRAMIDS, such as those located in the Aztec cities of Tenochtitlan and Teotihucan, were used primarily for ceremonial purposes. The Aztec culture arose in Mesoamerica in about A.D. 1100.

Mississippian towns in North America were also arranged around a central plaza. The Grand Plaza at Cahokia, located in what is now southern Illinois, encompassed 40 acres and was surrounded by temples and the homes of leaders. The construction of Cahokia was begun in about A.D. 800. Compounds of dwellings surrounded smaller community plazas scattered throughout the site. The Natchez, another mound-building Mississippian people living in what is now Louisiana, also built plazas. Mississippian culture began about 1500 B.C. and flourished from A.D. 900 to A.D. 1250 in the North American South and lower Midwest.

Plazas were also an integral part of North American southwestern cities. Anasazi builders who constructed Pueblo Bonito and the other multistoried ADOBE buildings in Chaco Canyon, located in what is now New Mexico, arranged them around large courtyards that served as common areas. The Anasazi, the ancestors of today's Pueblo people, lived in the North American Southwest starting in about 350 B.C. They began to build cities filled with adobe apartment complexes in about A.D. 700.

A more modern example of the civic center approach to urban living is that of the Creek, who lived in what are now Georgia, northern Florida, and the Carolinas. They built their wattle and daub dwellings around a civic plaza known as a square ground. It was here that residents held green corn ceremonies and here where the village leaders met in the Great Council to decide community matters. In the summer they would sit in the open, but in winter they gathered in a communal townhouse located near the square ground. They called these townhouses *chakofas*. Round and with high cone-shaped roofs, the *chakofas* ranged from 30 to 60 feet in diameter. As many as 500 people could be seated on rows of raised platforms. These tiers resembled bleachers. In the wintertime, townhouses provided shelter for the elderly or people who found themselves without a place to live.

The building of these community halls was a communal effort. According to a report by artist John Mix Stanley, who traveled among the Creek in 1843, the town spiritual leader made a model of the planned building and distributed the sticks he had used to construct it among residents. They were responsible for cutting the logs the twigs represented. (See also ARCHITECTS.) The Yuchi, Cherokee, and Chickasaw, who lived in North America's Southeast, also constructed townhouses that served as the center of religious and governmental activities for the people in their villages. These, along with the plaza, were the central focus of the villages.

In addition to the square ground, towns built by Southeast tribes typically featured a central field covered with fresh sand, called the swept area. This served as a ball court and was used for games such as chunkee and one that resembled field hockey. Chunkee, which was played throughout the Southeast, involved rolling a stone across a field and trying to hit it with a pole. The games were sometimes played to resolve disputes between towns and to make political alliances.

See also CITIES, AMERICA'S FIRST; HOCKEY, FIELD AND ICE; URBAN PLANNING.

### Sources/Further Reading
Iseminger, William, R. "Mighty Cahokia." *Archaeology* (May/June 1996): 31–37.
Josephy, Jr., Alvin M., ed. *America in 1492: The World of the Indian People before the Arrival of Columbus.* New York: Random House, 1991.
Nabokov, Peter and Robert Easton. *Native American Architecture.* New York: Oxford University Press, 1989.

### clambakes (precontact) *North American Northeast cultures*
Steaming clams in a fire pit dug on the beach is considered a New England tradition. Although the clambake has come to symbolize New England regional cuisine, few people know that it was an American Indian invention. At first European settlers on the East Coast were resistant to the idea of eating clams, believing that the seafood that was a regular part of the American Indians' diet was poisonous. Indians taught colonists to dig a pit, line it with flat stones, and build a fire on it. When the rocks were white-hot, the embers were brushed away and a layer of seaweed was placed on the stones. They placed alternate layers of clams and CORN and more seaweed on top of this. Then they covered it with a wet blanket or hide and allowed it to cook from the heat of the rocks for about an hour. After the clams and corn were finished cooking, the Indians removed the blanket or hide. Once the colonists had tried this traditional In-

dian way of cooking clams, they adopted the clambake as their own.

### Sources/Further Reading
Tannahill, Reay. *Food in History.* New York: Stein and Day, 1973.
Weatherford, Jack. *Indian Givers: How the Indians of the Americas Transformed the World.* New York: Fawcett Columbine, 1988.

### classifications, plant  See PLANT CLASSIFICATIONS.

### cloth  See WEAVING TECHNIQUES.

### clothing, fringed  See FRINGED CLOTHING.

### coca (*Erythroxylon coca*) (precontact) *Mesoamerican, South American Andean, and Circum-Caribbean cultures*
The cultivation and use of the coca bush, which is indigenous to the Americas, extended from Argentina in the south to Nicaragua and the West Indies in the north. The plant grows to a height of eight feet. Coca is best known today as the plant from which cocaine is manufactured. Coca leaves played an integral role in the lives of the Inca. They grew it on the slopes of the Andes and harvested and dried the leaves. The Inca Empire was established in what are now Peru and parts of Bolivia in about A.D. 1000. Archaeologists believe that the ancestors of the Inca used coca for thousands of years prior to that time.

The Inca chewed coca with a pinch of lime, made by burning seashells or limestone, in order to release the chemical methylbenzyl contained in the leaves. This alkaloid, one of 14 present in the leaf, is the one that is processed to make cocaine today. Although cocaine is considered an addictive drug and is included in the U.S. Drug Enforcement Administration's schedule of controlled substances, the Inca did not use coca leaves as a recreational drug. Rather, they regarded them as a gift from the gods, and the Inca government regulated them.

Because the juice from the coca leaves took away feelings of fatigue, cold, and hunger, leaves were rationed to workers, especially miners in the Andean mining camps, so that they would be more productive. (See also LABOR LAWS.) Coca was also used as a medicine and as an ANESTHETIC. In fact, its hunger-suppressing properties are a result of anesthetizing the stomach. Archaeologists believe that, in addition to being used by the miners, coca was used only by Inca nobles and the foot messengers, or *chaski*. (See also RUNNING.)

The first European reference to the cultivation and use of coca leaves came in 1499 when Thomas Ortiz, a Dominican missionary, saw it being grown along the Venezuelan coast. When the Spaniards colonized what is now Peru, they deposed the Inca government and enlarged the existing coca plantations. Once Europeans controlled coca, they began selling the leaves, not only to those who had been nobles but also to everyone who would buy it. By 1550 Spaniards had made fortunes in the coca trade. Seeing the negative impact of coca's wholesale use and fearing that its close association to indigenous religion would slow conversions, the Catholic Church began to lobby for a ban on coca. Priests called chewing the leaves a form of idolatry. At the same time, the church itself profited from coca speculation. At one point most of the cathedral revenues in some provinces came from the tithe of the Spanish coca traders. A number of Spanish administrators argued that the practice of chewing coca leaves should be kept in order to enable Indian miners to work even harder and to prevent them from revolting.

The coca leaves that were taken back to Europe were first used primarily by physicians in Spain. By the late 1800s Europeans had learned to synthesize cocaine, and its use spread throughout the continent. Because the alkaloid methylbenzyl interrupts the transmission of electrochemical signals in the nerves, it became highly effective as the first local anesthetic used in Western medicine. Sigmund Freud, sometimes known as the father of psychiatry, used cocaine frequently for the feelings of euphoria it produced. He believed that it promoted health. In the United States, coca became the basis of a number of patent medicine "nerve tonics," including Coca-Cola, which is named after the plant. Cocaine was removed from the popular soft drink after the FDA banned the drug in 1903. (See also MEDICINES, PATENT; SOFT DRINK INGREDIENTS.)

Today coca leaves remain a part of the indigenous religion of the Andean people and are used as offerings to the gods. Medicinally, they are used for dizziness, headaches, sore throat, indigestion, and as an anesthetic. Peru's legal cocaine cultivation is controlled by the government through the Coca National Enterprise (ENACO). This agency attempts to buy all the coca leaves produced in the country. The leaves are then sold to the people for religious purposes and to the pharmaceutical industry. Illegal growers in Peru, Colombia, and other South American countries sell the drug to processors who furnish cocaine for the illegal drug trade.

See also PEYOTE; SURGERY; TREPHINATION.

**Sources/Further Reading**

Karsh, Steven B., M.D. *A Brief History of Cocaine.* Boca Raton, Fla.: CRC Press, 1997.

Mason, J. Alden. *The Ancient Civilizations of Peru,* Rev. ed. New York: Penguin Books, 1988.

von Hagen, Victor Wolfgang. *Realm of the Incas.* New York: New American Library, 1957.

**cochineal** (precontact) *Mesoamerican, South American, Circum-Caribbean cultures*

Tiny coccid insects (*Dactylopius coccus*) that produce craminic acid are processed to make a brilliant crimson DYE called cochineal. The Maya, whose civilization arose in what is now Mesoamerica in about 1500 B.C., gathered these insects from PRICKLY PEAR cactus plants that grew where they lived. They developed the technology for making this dye hundreds of years before the arrival of the Spanish.

First the Maya dye makers removed the mature insects from the tents they spun on cactus pads where they lived on the juice. Next the dye makers sorted the insects. Only the female bugs, which reach only two to five millimeters in length, were used to produce the dye. These were killed in boiling water and then dried in the sun. The dried insects turned a silver color resembling metal chips. Finally, they were ground into a powder that could be used to produce not only reds but also shades of orange, pink, and purple for textiles. The Maya also used cochineal powder as a flavoring for food.

The Aztec, whose empire arose in what are now Mexico and parts of Mesoamerica about A.D. 1100, learned cochineal dye-making from the Maya they had conquered. When Spanish conquistador Hernán Cortés and his men arrived in the New World, they saw brilliant red COTTON cloth and yarn spun of rabbit fur being sold in the marketplaces of the Aztec cities. They were impressed by the quality of the color. Although Asians and Europeans knew how to make red dyes, the pigments were expensive to obtain. European commoners were limited to reds produced by "madder," a loud rather than rich color that was obtained from the roots of plants similar to the common weed bedstraw. When they encountered cochineal, the Spaniards immediately knew that they had hit upon an economic bonanza. Soon cochineal became the most widely traded and most valuable product of the West Indies after gold and silver. In England the dye was used to produce the red coats that were part of the military uniform. (British soldiers were called "red coats.")

The trade in cochineal dyes began to decline in the 1870s when the textile industry began using synthetic fabric dyes. Today cochineal is a luxury dye for weavers and other textile artisans. Cochineal insects are now raised or harvested in South, Central America, and Mexico, where they serve as a cash crop for indigenous people. The red dye produced from the insects continues to be used in cosmetics and for artist's pigments. One of cochineal's main modern uses is in the food industry, where it is used to color processed meats, jams, gelatin deserts, candy, baked goods, dairy products, and alcoholic beverages such as Campari and red vermouth. Recently physicians have discovered that cochineal extract can cause anaphylactic shock in people who are allergic to bee stings or other insect bites.

See also FOOD COLORING; TRADE.

**Sources/Further Reading**

Forest Preserve District of Cook County Illinois. *Nature Bulletin* No. 203 (1981).

Grae, Ida. *Nature's Colors: Dyes from Plants.* New York: Macmillan Publishing Company, Inc., 1974.

Grupo Inca. URL: http://www.grupoinca.com/colorantes.htm. Downloaded on February 6, 1999.

University of Michigan Health Services. URL: http://www.med.umich.edu/opm/newspage/dye.htm. Downloaded on February 6, 1999.

**cocoa** (precontact) *Mesoamerican cultures*

The invention of the cocoa—the powdered by-product that remains when the fat, or cocoa butter, is removed from chocolate—was a milestone in CHOCOLATE production. This process enabled candy makers to boost the amount of cocoa butter contained in candy, making the taste richer and the texture creamier. The invention of the cocoa press is usually credited to Conrad Van Houten, a chemist from Holland who came up with the idea in 1828. Although he was the first to invent this particular piece of equipment, the Maya had been removing cocoa butter from beans and adding it to chocolate drinks for centuries before this. Their mastery of the process was mentioned by Diego de la Landa, a Franciscan Friar who chronicled Maya life in the 1570s, well over 200 years before the Dutch began to manufacture cocoa. The Maya culture arose in Mesoamerica in about 1500 B.C.

See also CACAO.

**Sources/Further Reading**

Coe, Sophie. *America's First Cuisines*. Austin: University of Texas Press, 1994.

Lavanne, Pierre. "The History of Chocolate." In *The Book of Chocolate*, Ghidlaine Bavoillot, ed. Paris: Flammarion, 1995.

**codes** (A.D. 1917–1945) *North American Southeast, Great Plains, and Southwest cultures*

A code is a system of symbols used to represent letters or numbers. Often codes are used to transmit information secretly. During World War I, Choctaw soldiers in the United States Army's 36th Division, who spoke their own language fluently, were chosen to communicate with each other in it, in order to keep the messages they transmitted secret from the Germans. At least one Choctaw soldier was placed in each field company

The Navajo Code Talkers served with the U.S. Marines on Saipan in World War II. They landed with the first assault waves to hit the beach. Code Talkers could communicate secret information in a code that they had developed based on their own language and translate the code into English in 20 seconds. Other codes took hours to translate. Unlike other codes, the Navajo code was never broken by the enemy. *(Photograph No. NWDNS-127-N-82619/Department of Defense, U.S. Marine Corps June, 1944. National Archives and Records Administration at College Park)*

headquarters, taking messages, translating them into his native tongue, and then writing field orders that were carried by runners to the other companies. Although the German army captured several of these messengers, they were never able to crack the code.

The Choctaw were so successful in World War I that others of their tribe served the same purpose for the army during World War II, when Comanche, Navajo (Dineh), and Sioux (Dakota, Lakota, Nakota) soldiers were also selected for signal corps service. The Comanche used their word *posah-tai-vo,* or "crazy white man," to mean Adolf Hitler. Because they had no word for bomber, they made a phrase that literally translated "pregnant airplane."

In the Pacific theater during World War II, when communication leaks caused military setbacks, 29 Navajo who were fluent in both Navajo and English were recruited to construct a written code from their language, which before that time had been oral. Only an estimated 30 non-Navajo in the world were fluent in the language at the outbreak of the war. They invented an alphabet using words that described nature to talk about military subjects. The Navajo word for potato meant "grenade," and submarines were called "iron fish." Military units were designated by clan names. This code completely baffled the Japanese, who were never able to decipher any of it.

By the end of the war, 420 Navajo had served in the Code Talker program with the U.S. Marines. The Code Talkers participated in combat, taking part in every assault the U.S. Marines conducted in the Pacific theater from 1942 to 1945. They faced a special danger because some others—both Allies and enemies—thought they appeared Japanese. In fact, at some points they were assigned bodyguards to avoid any confusion. They communicated by field telephone and walkie-talkie to call in air strikes, artillery bombardments, direct troop movements, report enemy locations, direct fire from American positions, and transmit sensitive military information. During the first 48 hours at Iwo Jima, they relayed all the orders directing the strike. Six Navajo radio nets operated around the clock, sending and receiving more than 800 messages without making any mistakes. Major Howard Connor, Fifth Marine Division signal officer who served at Iwo Jima and commanded the six Code Talker networks, said afterward, "Were it not for the Navajos, the Marines would never have taken Iwo Jima." Years later, in September 1992, the U.S. Pentagon honored the Navajo Code Talkers.

See also MILITARY TACTICS.

## Sources/Further Reading

Department of the Navy, Naval Historical Center. *Navajo Code Talkers: World War II Fact Sheet.* URL: http://history. navy.mil/faqs/faq61-2.htm. Downloaded on October 30, 1999.

Durrett, Deanne. *Unsung Heroes of World War II.* New York: Facts On File, 1998.

Hirshfelder, Arlene and Martha Kreipe de Montano. *The Native American Almanac: A Portrait of Native America Today.* New York: Prentice Hall, 1993.

Marine Corps History. *Navajo Code Talkers.* URL: http://www. usmc.mil/History.nsf. Downloaded on October 30, 1999.

Nies, Judith. *Native American History: A Chronology of a Culture's Vast Achievements and their Links to World Events.* New York: Ballantine Books, 1996.

**code talkers**  See CODES.

**colanders**  (A.D. 1)  *Mesoamerican cultures*
Many times when people need to rinse pasta, fruit, or vegetables, they reach for a colander. Colanders are containers that are perforated in order to rinse or drain food. This common and highly useful utensil was known and used by indigenous Americans by A.D. 1 or perhaps earlier. The Maya, whose culture arose in Mesoamerica in about 1500 B.C., used the colander in nixtamalization, which is the processing of CORN with lye to produce HOMINY. This technology allowed the niacin and amino acids present in the corn to be more readily absorbed by the body, avoiding the disease pellagra (niacin deficiency). American Indians made their colanders out of CALABASHES, large gourds that they also used for bowls, cups, and food and water containers. Holes were bored in the large calabashes, and the corn was placed inside of it to be rinsed off—a very simple and valuable piece of culinary technology.

## Source/Further Reading

Benson, Elizabeth P. *The Maya World.* New York: Thomas Y. Crowell Company, 1967.

**colonial confederacy**  See UNITED STATES CONSTITUTION, AMERICAN INDIAN INFLUENCE ON.

**community service**  See TAX SYSTEMS.

**companion planting  (intercropping)**  (precontact)
*Mesoamerican; North American Southeast, Northeast, and Southwest cultures*
The Maya, whose culture arose in Mesoamerica in about 1500 B.C., practiced companion planting, the practice of cultivating different crops together in the same plot. In North America, the people in the Southeast, Northeast, and Southwest used this technique as well. Throughout the Americas, Indians frequently planted CORN, SQUASH, and pole BEANS in the same hill or midden, or grouped them together in flat fields. Planting several types of crops together not only maximized yield through more effective land use but also fostered better growth because the plants complimented each other. Companion planting also often served as a natural form of pest control, a concept touted by today's organic gardeners. (See also INSECT REPELLENTS.)

Corn stalks provided a place for the bean runners to climb and partial shade for squash plants that covered the ground.

This ground cover prevented moisture from evaporating as quickly as it would otherwise do. Because squash plants provided competition for weeds, farming became less labor-intensive, since there was less weeding to do. Modern agricultural researchers have discovered why the bean plants helped the other plants: bacterial colonies on the roots of bean plants store nitrogen from the air, releasing some of it to the soil. Corn needs large amounts of nitrogen in order to prosper.

In the southwestern region of North America, American Indian farmers did not rely so extensively on companion planting as did those in other areas. They developed varieties of bush beans that did not need corn stalks to support them. Plants in that semi-arid environment did better when they were spaced far enough apart so that they would not compete for moisture in the soil with other plants. (See also SEED SELECTION.)

The concept of companion planting was so much a part of American Indian culture that people of many tribes called corn, beans, and squash the "three sisters." Not only were these three crops interdependent during their growth, they complimented one another nutritionally as well. Together the amino acids in corn and beans provide a complete protein, something neither food does on its own. The nutrients in squash, such as beta carotene and vitamin C, compliment those provided by the other two vegetables in the trio.

Today Maya farmers continue to practice companion planting as their ancestors did, sometimes cultivating as many as 60 to 80 species of crops in one family plot. Typically, even tiny plots contain a dozen or more types of plants, including coconut and palm trees, citrus and papaya trees, cacao, corn, beans, and squash.

See also AGRICULTURE; MULTIPLE CROPPING.

## Sources/Further Reading

Hurt, R. Douglas. *American Indian Agriculture: Prehistory to Present.* Lawrence: University Press of Kansas, 1987.

Oneida Tribe. *Three Sisters Cookbook.* URL: http://www.one-web.orgt/oneida/food-index.html. Downloaded on January 5, 1998.

**compasses** (pre-1000 B.C.) *Mesoamerican cultures*
A compass is a device that uses a lodestone, or a piece of iron that has been magnetized by contact with a lodestone, to determine magnetic north. The Olmec are believed to have discovered that a lodestone will align itself in a magnetic north-south position, and they are credited with developing a compass before 1000 B.C. Olmec civilization arose in the Yucatán Peninsula of what is now Mexico in about 1700 B.C.

The American Indian discovery of the compass occurred about 1,000 years before the Chinese developed a compass, according to Mesoamerica expert Michael Coe and other archaeologists. The earliest date for a compass in China is A.D. 1100. Western Europeans did not use them until A.D. 1178.

Coe found an oblong, grooved, magnetic base during an archaeological dig at San Lorenzo in the Yucatán Peninsula of what is now Mexico in 1967. Believing that this evidence indicated the Olmec used a magnetic compass, he tested his theory by placing the lodestone on a piece of cork large enough to float. When he placed the cork in water, it consistently pointed a little west of magnetic north. He next turned the lodestone upside-down, and it consistently pointed a little east of magnetic north. Further scientific experiments performed six years later confirmed that a simple compass was probably made and used by the Olmec.

## Sources/Further Reading

Coe, Michael D., and Richard A. Diehl. *In the Land of the Olmecs: The Archaeology of San Lorenzo Tenochtitlan.* Vol. 1. Austin: University of Texas Press, 1980.

Reader's Digest Association. *Mysteries of the Ancient Americas.* Pleasantville, N.Y.: Reader's Digest Books, 1986.

**compulsory education** (precontact) *Mesoamerican, South American, North American Arctic cultures*
Compulsory education is formal schooling that has mandatory attendance. All Aztec young people between the ages of 10 and 20 received compulsory formal schooling. The Aztec Empire was established about A.D. 1100 in Mesoamerica. Male Aztec children who did not come from the ruling classes lived at schools called *telpochalli,* which meant "youth's house" in Nahuatl, the Aztec language. Female children also attended these schools, but historians are not certain whether they boarded there or attended them as day schools. The young men and women were instructed separately; however, both received training in singing, dancing, and playing MUSICAL INSTRUMENTS.

According to Father Diego Duran, who observed the schools in the 1500s, students were taught "to be well-mannered, to respect their elders, to serve, to obey, given papers on how they were to serve their lords, to move among them and be polite to them." Oratory was also taught in these schools.

During their schooling, the boys worked on projects such as carrying firewood for the temples, making roads, and repairing buildings. The main focus of their training was learning military skills. (See also MILITARY TACTICS.) These skills included archery and sword fighting. Children of nobles attended *calmecas,* exclusive schools that were connected to a large temple. Here they received leadership training with an emphasis on self-control, obedience, and discipline. Promising youths from the lower classes were also sometimes selected to attend these special schools. In addition to being groomed for government administrative positions, students were trained for the priesthood and the military. According to Fray Duran, the classes taught at the *calmecas* included instruction in the arts, military skills, religion, technological skills, and astronomy. Etiquette was also a major focus of the curriculum. In addition to hands-on instruction methods, students learned from studying textbooks. (See also BOOKS.) Students who attended the *calmecas* were expected to perform community service. Unlike the manual labor engaged in by boarding school students, the children of the nobility helped the priests during ceremonies and engaged in other tasks that would prepare them for the responsibilities that they were expected to shoulder as adults.

In South America the Inca, whose empire was established in what is now Peru in about A.D. 1000, also had compulsory schooling for the sons of nobility. The Inca did not provide education for children of the lower classes. Teachers—called *amautas* in Quecha, the Inca language—instructed their students in a wide range of subjects, including astronomy, music, philosophy, history, religion, martial arts, poetry, and government. Students learned how to encode and read information from QUIPUS, knotted strings that were used for accounting and to record laws and history. They were also given military training. Boys typically received four years of schooling at a school in Cuzco, the Inca capital. The teachers lived in the schools, which were called *yacha huaci,* or teaching houses.

Girls of conquered people that showed special talents were selected as Chosen Women at the age of 10. They were brought to Cuzco and taught cooking, weaving, spinning, and other domestic arts as well as religion. After this training, the Inca emperor decided whether they would be placed to work in a temple or spend their lives serving him.

Although not compulsory in the sense of Aztec and Inca schooling, other American Indian tribes had formal education systems long before the arrival of Europeans. For example, the Inuit of East Greenland received instruction in specific skills like whale hunting and kayak making from specialized instructors for a fee. Feats of strength and drum singing were also taught.

**Sources/Further Reading**

Malpass, Michael A. *Daily Life in the Inca Empire.* Westport, Conn.: Greenwood Press, 1996.

Oswalt, Wendell. *Eskimos and Explorers.* Novato, Calif.: Chandler & Sharp Publishers, 1979.

Salmoral, Manuel Lucena. *America in 1492: Portrait of a Continent 500 Years Ago.* New York: Facts On File, 1990.

Smith, Michael E. *The Peoples of America: The Aztecs.* Cambridge, Mass.: Blackwell, 1996.

**concrete** (ca. 300 B.C.–A.D. 300) *Mesoamerican cultures*
Concrete, a mixture of sand and/or gravel, lime, and water, is used in construction projects including buildings and roads. Because of the lime, concrete is more durable than ADOBE. The Maya, whose culture arose in Mesoamerica in about 1500 B.C., are the first indigenous Americans to make concrete, inventing it independently of the Egyptians and the Romans. During the late pre-classic period of their cultural development, which lasted from 300 B.C. to A.D. 300, the Maya used concrete as mortar to adhere blocks to each other, and plaster or stucco (a thicker version of plaster) to cover stone or adobe surfaces in their masonry projects and in their art. They called this plaster *sacbe.* The Maya used stucco in their sculpture as well. (See also STONEMASONRY TECHNIQUES.)

One of the main ingredients in these building materials is lime (calcium oxide). Maya builders mixed dry powdered calcium and clay with water, sand, gravel, and/or crushed stone.

They extracted the calcium oxide from limestone by first burning it on special piles of wood that had been stacked in a circle. More wood was placed on top until it resembled a cylindrical building. Constructing the fire in this manner prevented impurities from getting into the resulting calcium oxide. The calcium oxide was used to make mortar and concrete. Plaster and stucco were two uses for mortar and concrete. Maya builders applied the stucco to wooden frames that they placed on temples and buildings in order to give them the appearance of height without the weight of stone. They also used limestone stucco on building facades and in their roads.

In about A.D. 1100 the Aztec used concrete and mortar in the same manner and for the same reasons the Maya did. Aztec builders added wooden frames to the tops of their buildings, temples, and pyramids. These frames were covered with concrete and mortar. Archaeologists believe this was done to make the buildings appear taller.

See also CARPENTRY TECHNIQUES; ROAD SYSTEMS.

**Sources/Further Reading**

Benson, Elizabeth P. *The Maya World.* New York: Thomas Y. Crowell Company, 1967.

Soustelle, Jacques. *Daily Life of the Aztecs on the Eve of the Spanish Conquest.* Stanford, Calif.: Stanford University Press, 1961.

**conditioners, hair** See HAIR CONDITIONERS.

**consensus management** (precontact) *North American cultures*
Management by consensus is the practice of making decisions based on the general agreement of the group. Many business leaders in the late 20th century believe this form of management is an enlightened one because it results in workers having a vested interest in corporate policy. However, Indian tribes throughout North America practiced management by consensus.

Although leaders governed Indian peoples, these leaders did not command people to carry out orders. Instead they generally served by example. Decision making for matters affecting the tribe generally took place in council meetings that often lasted until complete consensus was reached, so that even those who did not totally agree with the choice had a chance to resign themselves to it. The process, although sometimes lengthy, drew on the collective wisdom of tribal members and created a unified sense of community.

See also CAUCUS.

**Source/Further Reading**

Josephy, Jr., Alvin M., ed. *America in 1492: The World of the Indian People Before the Arrival of Columbus.* New York: Random House, 1991.

**conservation, water** See WATER CONSERVATION.

**Constitution, Iroquois** See IROQUOIS CONSTITUTION.

**Constitution, U.S.** See UNITED STATES CONSTITUTION, AMERICAN INDIAN INFLUENCE ON.

**contraception, oral (oral birth control, birth control pill)** (precontact) *North American Great Basin cultures*

Oral contraceptives are substances taken by mouth to prevent pregnancy. They work by suppressing ovulation. North American Indians were using oral birth control in the 1700s, more than 200 years before Western medicine invented the birth control pill. John Lawson, who wrote *A History of North Carolina* in 1714, told his readers that the Indians living there "have an Art to destroy Conception." The indigenous people of North America discovered birth control independently from the Egyptians.

Western physicians, who had dismissed the Egyptian recipes as useless nostrums, or home remedies, ignored anthropological reports of the American Indian oral contraception as well. They continued to instruct patients on barrier contraception, which blocks the sperm from reaching the egg, and on the "rhythm method," timing intercourse so that it does not coincide with ovulation. Many dismissed the idea of oral contraception altogether. As late as 1936, Norman Himes, the American author of *The Medical History of Contraception,* reviewed literature on the American Indian use of oral contraception and wrote, ". . . for no drug has yet been discovered which when taken by mouth will induce temporary sterility."

One of the herbs used as an oral contraceptive by the Shoshone Indians, who lived in the Great Basin of North America, was the stone seed (*Lithospermum suderale*). Medical researchers tested this and other American Indian oral contraceptive plants in the 20th century and found them to be effective oral contraceptives. For example the Potawatomi of the Northeast used the herb DOGBANE.

When scientists invented an oral form of birth control in the 1950s, the high-dose, hormone-based pills that were first prescribed were shown to have many side effects, including the chances of cancer. In the late 20th century, pharmaceutical researchers began to explore the medical uses of plants containing substances that act in ways similar to hormones. One day they may reinvent a plant-based contraceptive similar to those that American Indians used.

See also OBSTETRICS; MEDICINE; PHARMACOLOGY.

**Sources/Further Reading**

Josephy, Jr., Alvin M. *The Indian Heritage of America,* Rev. ed. Boston: Houghton Mifflin Company, 1991.

Ortiz de Montellano, Bernard. *Aztec Medicine, Health, and Nutrition.* New Brunswick, N.J.: Rutgers University Press, 1990.

Vogel, Virgil. *American Indian Medicine.* Norman: University of Oklahoma Press, 1977.

**corbeled arches** See ARCHES, CORBELED.

**corn (Indian corn, maize, *Zea mays*)** (8000– 7000 B.C.) *North American Southwest, Northeast, and Great Plains; Mesoamerican; Circum-Caribbean; South American Andean cultures*

The term *corn* is commonly used to refer to the principal cereal grain of the Americas. Europeans called this crop *maize* or Indian corn. Mesoamerican farmers in the Tehuacán Valley of Mexico first began domesticating corn (*Zea mays*) at about 8000 to 7000 B.C. Although some modern ethnobotanists believe that the ancestor of corn was a type of wild corn that is now extinct, most think that American Indian agriculturists cross-pollinated and saved seeds from a wild grass called teosinite (*Zea mexicana*), which grows in the Sierra Madre of what is now Mexico. Teosinite bears seeds that can be ground into flour or popped like popcorn.

Corn as Americans know it today came about because of the American Indian practice of planned SEED SELECTION, a revolutionary agricultural development that transformed the world. Mexican anthropologist Arturo Warman calls corn a cultural artifact because it is a species that does not grow in the wild and can only survive if planted and tended by human beings. The deliberate creation of corn, which requires extensive weeding and watering to flourish, led to terraced farming (see FARMING, TERRACED) and the building of IRRIGATION canals throughout Mesoamerica and the Southwest of what is now the United States. American Indian domestication of corn helped the Mississippian cultures to flourish along the riverine bottomlands of what is now the United States, in addition to the Iroquois and other farming tribes of the Eastern Woodlands. Although it served primarily as animal feed in some areas of Europe, eventually corn greatly improved nutrition. As caloric intake increased, rapid population growth occurred, according to author Jack Weatherford.

The oldest surviving entire ear of corn, which is dated 5000 B.C., was found by archaeologists in the Tehuacán Valley of Mexico, but the plant was domesticated in several other areas of Mesoamerica as well. The first corn that American Indians grew had small ears that contained only six to nine kernels per cob. By 3000 B.C. more varieties had been developed, and corn had become a dietary staple for the people of Mesoamerica, along with BEANS and SQUASH.

The Maya, who lived in Mesoamerica beginning in about 1500 B.C., learned many ways to use the corn plant. The leaves contain a large amount of sugar and the Maya used them as the first CHEWING GUM. They ate immature corn as a fresh vegetable. The dry, mature kernels of corn were ground into flour, parched, or popped (see also POPCORN). Eventually corn would make up 80 percent of the Maya diet and become so central to the culture that the Maya creation story tells of the first people being made from corn.

At the same time that corn cultivation spread southward into South America, *Zea mays* seeds were brought northward to the American Southwest. By about 1500 B.C. farmers in the

Southwest were cultivating corn. By 300 B.C. southwestern farmers had used seed selection in order to adapt corn to growing and climate conditions throughout the arid region. Corn seeds were brought into the Mississippi and Ohio Valley floodplains about A.D. 200 but remained a minor crop for eastern farmers until about A.D. 800. By the early 1600s Indians near Lake Erie and Lake Ontario grew corn both for their own consumption and as a TRADE commodity. The Huron, who depended on AGRICULTURE to meet 75 percent of their nutritional needs, grew enough in vast fields each year to provide a two- to four-year surplus against potential crop failure. The Mohawk, who stripped cornhusks from the dried cobs with a wooden peg, used every part of the corn plant. Husks were used to make moccasins, mats, and baskets, while medicine was stored in hollowed-out corn stalks.

By the time Columbus landed in the New World, Indians in Meso- and North America, had created more than 700 varieties of corn through crossbreeding and seed selection, and they were growing it from the Andes mountains to as far north as

Corn, first domesticated by Indians in central Mexico, was grown by indigenous farmers throughout the Americas. This drawing, after one by Felipe Guamán Poma de Ayala, depicts Inca corn harvesters in the early 1600s. (Nueva Coronica y Buen Gobierno)

what is now Ontario, Canada. These varieties included the types of corn still grown today:

**popcorn**  the type of corn that was originally domesticated.

**flint corn**  a type similar to popcorn but with a larger grain size and a bigger yield. American Indians adapted it to cold climates.

**flour corn**  a variety with kernels containing soft starch that can be easily ground and made into meal or tortillas.

**dent corn**  a type combining the properties of both flint and flour corn.

**sweet corn**  a variety with kernels that contain more soluble sugar than starch. It is picked when the ears have not yet turned hard and is eaten as a vegetable.

In 1492, two of Columbus's men were the first Europeans to see maize. They returned from the interior of an island in the northern Antilles with a grain that the Taino, who lived in the Caribbean, called *mahis,* which meant "source of life." The sample the sailors brought their captain had been baked, dried, and turned into flour. Columbus noted the find in his journal, remarking that it was "well tasted."

Europeans who referred to many different types of grain as "corn" and who had never seen anything like this new one called it *maiz.* English speakers spelled it *maize* but were soon referring to it as Indian corn rather than by its Taino name. When Carl Linnaeus, the Swedish botanist who developed today's binomial classification system, devised a name for maize, he used a combination of the Taino name and its translation into Greek in order to come up with the genus and species of the plant: *Zea mays.* Tribes throughout North and Central America had different names for corn, many of which can be translated as "our mother" or "our life." In Nahuatl, the Aztec language, corn was called *centli.* The Aztec, whose empire was established in Mesoamerica about A.D. 1100, believed that the god Quetzalcoatl, the feathered serpent, turned himself into an ant to steal maize as a gift for humans.

At first the Europeans considered corn a botanical curiosity to be planted in the gardens of the wealthy, but later they tried eating it. From Europe corn spread to the Philippines, where it was known in the 1500s, and then to Africa and Asia. By 1555 corn was an important crop in China. In Europe corn was grown in the Mediterranean, where wheat and rice are not easily produced. Northern Europeans tended not to like the taste of corn. One commentator wrote in 1597 that although the "barbarous Indians" who did not known any better could consider it good food, "civilized people" looked upon corn as food for swine. For many years, corn remained primarily an animal food in northern Europe, boosting the supply of meat, milk, butter, and cheese and thereby an increase in the population, which had been severely affected by bubonic plague.

People who lived in southern Europe and Africa began depending on corn to meet most of their nutritional requirements, but they soon began to suffer from a deficiency of the essential amino acids lysine and tryptophan. Italians called the condition pellagra. In Africa it was known as the mealies. Because Indians in Mesoamerica and in North America knew how to process corn in order to allow its vitamin content to be more readily absorbed by the human body, they did not suffer from pellagra. In addition to this technology, called *nixtamalization,* they routinely ate corn with squash and beans, which together form a complete protein.

Indigenous people taught the European colonists in North and Mesoamerica, not only how to grow corn, but how to cook it. New England and southern colonists quickly adopted Indian foods in their diets, including CORNBREAD, corn puddings, chowders, SUCCOTASH, corn on the cob, and other dishes that became the basis of regional cuisines. In Mesoamerica the Maya and Aztec made corn TORTILLAS and TAMALES that have been eaten for thousands of years became the basis for Mexican dishes that are popular today.

Today corn is the third most planted crop throughout the world after wheat and rice. Together, China, the United States, and Brazil account for 73 percent of the world's production of this crop, which is used for human consumption, animal feed, and industrial purposes. According to the U.S. Department of Agriculture, corn is planted on 70 to 80 million acres in the United States each year. Annual U.S. production is about 9 billion bushels, which has a value of 30 billion dollars. About three-quarters of the corn grown is of the dent type, which has a hard outer portion about the thickness of a fingernail. The inner portion of the corn kernel is soft and floury. Dent corn is used to make starches and oils as well as CORN SYRUP sweeteners and other ingredients that appear in all kinds of foods from soft drinks to baked goods.

Taking the lead provided by the indigenous people of the Americas, modern scientists have found a way to utilize every part of the corn plant. According to the National Corn Growers Association, more than 3,500 different uses for corn have been found. More environmentally friendly than phosphate, corn-derived citric acid increases the cleaning power and decreases the volume of laundry detergents. It is used for biodegradable "packing peanuts." One hundred percent biodegradable plastics are being made from corn, which may help with the problem of overflowing landfills. Corn-based ink is now replacing the printer's ink formerly made from petroleum products. Hydrosorb, a super absorbent cornstarch that was discovered in one of USDA's regional laboratories, absorbs 300 times its weight and is used in some disposable diapers (see also DIAPERS, DISPOSABLE) and automobile fuel filters. Calcium magnesium acetate, or CMA, is a noncorrosive road deicer made from corn. CMA does not contain sodium or chloride, so it is safe in watersheds and agricultural areas and will not damage roads and bridges. CMA is also used as a runway deicer at airports. Ethanol, an alcohol that can be made from corn, is being blended with gasoline to help reduce air pollution.

See also CORN BREAD; CORNMEAL; CORN, PARCHED; HOMINY.

**Sources/Further Reading**

Coe, Sophie. *America's First Cuisines.* Austin: University of Texas Press, 1994.

Fagan, Brian M. *Kingdoms of Gold, Kingdoms of Jade: The Americas Before Columbus.* New York: Thames and Hudson, Inc., 1991.

Heiser, Charles B. *Seed to Civilization: The Story of Food.* Cambridge: Harvard University Press, 1990.

Hurt, R. Douglas. *American Indian Agriculture: Prehistory to Present.* Lawrence: University Press of Kansas, 1987.

Iowa State University. *The Maize Page.* URL: http://www.ag.iastate.edu/departments/agronomy/cornpage.html. Downloaded on February 16, 1999.

Nabhan, Gary. *Enduring Seeds: Native American Agriculture and Wild Plant Conservation.* San Francisco: North Point Press, 1989.

National Corn Growers Association. *World of Corn On-Line.* URL: http://www.ncga.com. Downloaded on February 16, 1999.

Salvador, Ricardo. "Maize." In *The Encyclopedia of Mexico: History, Culture and Society.* Chicago: Fitzroy Dearborn Publishers, 1997.

Selig, Ruth and Bruce D. Smith. "Quiet Revolution: Origins of Agriculture in Eastern North America." in *Anthropology Explored: The Best of Smithsonian Anthro Notes* edited by Ruth Selig and Marilyn London. Washington, D.C.: Smithsonian Institution Press, 1998.

Tannahill, Reay. *Food in History.* New York: Stein and Day, 1973.

Trager, James. *The Food Chronology: The Food Lover's Compendium of Events and Anecdotes from Prehistory to Present.* New York: Henry Holt, 1995.

Trigger, Bruce G. *Case Studies in Anthropology: The Huron Farmers of the North.* New York: Holt Rinehart and Winston, 1969.

Weatherford, Jack. *Indian Givers: How the Indians of the Americas Transformed the World.* New York: Fawcett Columbine, 1988.

**corn bread** (precontact) *North America Northeast and Southeast cultures*

A thick, unleavened CORN flatbread was a staple of the diet of Eastern Woodland Indians. Frequently this bread was cooked in the embers of a fire. The bread soon became a mainstay in the diet of New England and southern colonists, who called it corn pone.

The Iroquois made corn bread from HOMINY flour (see also CORNMEAL) mixed with boiling water until it formed a stiff paste. The dough was kneaded, shaped into a ball, and then flattened so that it was about an inch and a half thick and about seven inches in diameter. Each piece was put into a pot of boiling water with a special bread paddle. When the cakes were cooked, they were removed from the water. Eaten hot or cold, they were sometimes covered with CORN SYRUP. Because the Indians, and later the colonists, took these loaves with them as they traveled, they were called journey cakes. Eventually the colonists modified them to make what were called johnnycakes as well.

Indians living in the Southeast taught colonists to make fried corn bread by dropping spoonfuls of cornmeal dough into hot bear fat to make what became known as hushpuppies.

## Sources/Further Reading

Tannahill, Reay. *Food in History.* New York: Stein and Day, 1973.

Weatherford, Jack. *Indian Givers: How the Indians of the Americas Transformed the World.* New York: Fawcett Columbine, 1988.

**cornmeal (grits, hominy grits)** (precontact) *North American Northeast and Southeast, Mesoamerican, South American cultures*

Grinding hard kernels of CORN into fine pieces makes cornmeal. Indigenous cooks of Mesoamerica and the Southwest ground corn, or maize, by rubbing a handheld stone that the Spaniards would later call a *manojh* over corn heaped on a flat stone called a *metate*. Unlike modern cornmeal eaten in North America today, this had been soaked in a mixture of water and ashes or ground limestone, so that it was more like grits, or HOMINY grits, than the cornmeal sold in stores today. This process, called *nixtamalization,* prevented pellagra, a niacin deficiency. First the Maya and then the Aztec used a finely ground cornmeal, or corn flour, to make TORTILLAS and TAMALES and also used cornmeal to make atole, a thin gruel; and posole, a soup or stew. The Aztec started their day with a breakfast of maize porridge sweetened with honey (see also BEEKEEPING) or spiced with red peppers (see also CHILES). Maya culture arose in Mesoamerica in about 1500 B.C. The Aztec Empire was established in the same area in about A.D. 1100.

*Grits* is the generic term applied to a gruel made from coarsely ground corn. In the United States the word usually means ground hominy, corn that has been treated by soaking in a solution of lye in order to soften it and make the amino acids more readily absorbed by the body. The Choctaw of Mississippi boiled ground hominy and called the resulting gruel *ta-fula.* It was made by soaking the corn long enough to loosen the hulls and then winnowing the grains in a basket. The winnowing continued until each kernel was broken into three or four pieces, or grits. These were boiled in water in which wood ashes had been soaked, in order to provide the lye to release the amino acids. Porridge made from hominy grits became a staple of the southern colonial diet and remains an important part of the regional cuisine of the American South today. In the American South cooks also make hushpuppies from cornmeal or corn flour.

Indians of the Eastern Woodlands also made meal by pounding corn that had been soaked overnight in wood ashes and water to soften it. The pounding took place in an oversized wooden mortar made from a tree stump. They tied a heavy wooden pestle to a nearby sapling that served as a spring pole, which served to help lift the pestle. The resulting cornmeal was used to make samp, a corn, BEAN, and dried meat porridge that soon became a central part of the colonial diet. The colonists, who substituted salted beef for the dried meat, copied the design of the American Indian samp pounder and often installed a communal samp pounder in the central squares of their villages. Colonists used cornmeal in a number of dishes. These included mush, also known as hasty pudding or Indian pudding, one variation of which is a sweetened cornmeal custard that is baked and eaten with a spoon; corn dodger, a cake that is fried, baked, or boiled as a dumpling; CORN BREAD; and corn muffins.

## Sources/Further Reading

Coe, Sophie. *America's First Cuisines.* Austin: University of Texas Press, 1994.

Domestic West–Food URL: http://xroads.virginia.edu/ ~HYPER/HNS/Domwest/food.html. Downloaded on March 3, 1999.

For centuries Indians of the North American Northeast used log mortars for pounding corn that had been soaked in wood ashes and water into cornmeal as this Iroquois man did in 1912. European colonists adopted cornmeal as part of their diet, borrowing many recipes from the Indians. *(National Archives of Canada/PA181637/R. F. Waugh Collection)*

Ingrassia, Michele. "Dinner, and a Snack, Too." *Long Island Our Story.* URL: http://www.lihistory.com/2/hs204a.htm. Downloaded on March 3, 1999.

Koph, Bobbie. *Preparing Tash-lubona and Ta-fula.* URL: http://www.yvwiiusdinvnohii.net/history/cook.html. Downloaded on January 22, 1999.

Smith, Michael E. *The Peoples of America: The Aztecs.* Cambridge, Mass.: Blackwell, 1996.

Tannahill, Reay. *Food in History.* New York: Stein and Day, 1973.

## corn, parched (precontact) *North American Northeast and Great Plains, Mesoamerican cultures*

North American Indians of many tribes prepared dried CORN, or maize, by using dry heat. This is called parching. They put the kernels into a clay pot that was placed on a fire. The heat made the kernels break open but not actually pop (see also POP-CORN). The result was similar to modern corn nuts and was carried as traveling food. (See also PEMMICAN; SNACK FOODS.) The Iroquois, who lived in what is now called New York State, ground parched corn and mixed it with maple sugar or MAPLE SYRUP for their traveling food. The Hidatsa, who lived along the upper Missouri River, sometimes parched entire ears of corn at a time by holding them over the fire on a stick. Another method they used for parching corn was to heat a clay pot full of sand gathered from the Missouri River, then stir ears of corn together with the sand until the skin broke open. The Hidatsa, who grew many types of corn, ground parched corn, mixed it with animal fat, and shaped it into balls.

The Aztec, whose empire was established in what are now Mexico and parts of Mesoamerica in about A.D. 1100, used parched or toasted corn that had been ground as a basis for drinks. They called this parched corn meal *pinolli*. Sometimes they ate the ground parched corn plain. In the Northeast, the Iroquois mixed parched corn with MAPLE SYRUP to carry as a trail food. New England colonists adopted this sweeter corn and ate it with milk as a breakfast food.

### Sources/Further Reading

Coe, Sophie. *America's First Cuisines.* Austin: University of Texas Press, 1994.

Oneida Tribe. *Three Sisters Cookbook.* URL: http://WWW.one-web.orgt/oneida/food-index.html. Downloaded on January 5, 1998.

Weatherford, Jack. *Indian Givers: How the Indians of the Americas Transformed the World.* New York: Fawcett Columbine, 1988.

Wilson, Gilbert L. *Buffalo Bird Woman's Garden: Agriculture of the Hidatsa Indians.* Reprint. St. Paul: Minnesota Historical Society Press, 1987.

## corn syrup (precontact) *North American Northeast, Mesoamerican cultures*

Corn syrup is a sweetening agent for food that is made from CORN. Indians in both North and Mesoamerica used corn syrup as a sweetener. When Hernán Cortés described the marketplace in the Aztec capital of Tenochtitlán, he mentioned seeing a maize stalk sweetener for sale there. The Aztec Empire was established in what are now Mexico and parts of Mesoamerica in about A.D. 1100. In the 1700s colonists reported that Indians in the eastern part of what is now the United States were using a clear, sweet syrup from corn stalks to sweeten their food. They increased the sugar content of the stalks by removing the newly developed ears from the corn they had planted for that purpose.

Today corn syrup is manufactured from corn kernels. Because it resists crystallization and holds moisture, it has become the most popular sweetener for processed foods, including baked goods, ice cream, catsup, syrups, and candy. Less expensive than cane sugar, corn syrup accounts for half of the nondiet sweeteners used in the United States and is an ingredient in every nondiet soft drink on the market. Crystallized fructose made from corn is also used in powdered drinks, like lemonades and fruit drinks. One of the more unusual uses for corn syrup is as a movie prop. Hollywood producers dye it red and use it for fake blood because of the slowness with which it dries.

See also MAPLE SYRUP.

### Sources/Further Reading

Coe, Sophie. *America's First Cuisines.* Austin: University of Texas Press, 1994.

National Corn Growers Association. *World of Corn On-Line.* URL: http://www.ncga.com. Downloaded on February 16, 1999.

Weatherford, Jack. *Indian Givers: How the Indians of the Americas Transformed the World.* New York: Fawcett Columbine, 1988.

## cotton (6000–5000 B.C.) *Mesoamerican, South American Andean, North American Southwest cultures*

Cotton is a plant that produces a mass of fiber around the seeds; this fiber is used to make textiles. (See also WEAVING TECHNIQUES.) American Indians domesticated a variety of cotton indigenous to the Americas (*Gossypium barbadense*) in the Tehuacán Valley of what is now Mexico and on the eastern slope of the Andes in what is now Peru between 3500 and 2300 B.C. This occurred independently from cotton domestication in the Indus valley of what is now India in about 3000 B.C. Cotton was not cultivated in Egypt until about 700 B.C.

Archaeologists have found 7,000- to 8,000-year-old Peruvian MUMMIES wrapped in cotton textiles. Some believe that wild cotton was used for clothing in Peru as early as 10,000 B.C. These were made by a people known as the Chinchoros. They estimate that as much as 10 percent of the land under cultivation in Peru was devoted to cotton growing. The plant was used primarily for textiles, but it was also a source of oil and food, and in some cases it was considered medicine. Recent research has shown that cottonseeds are high in ANTIBIOTICS.

The Maya, whose culture arose in about 1500 B.C. in what are now Mexico and parts of Mesoamerica, grew cotton in household garden plots as well as village fields. They developed extensive TRADE in woven cotton goods throughout Mesoamerica. The Aztec, whose empire was established in what are Mexico and parts of Mesoamerica in about A.D. 1100, valued cotton so highly that they used it, along with CACAO beans, as a form of money. The Maya also made mattresses from cotton.

The American cotton species *Gossypium barbadense* is characterized by medium fibers and is distinguished from Egyptian cotton, as well as that cultivated in India, by its many shades, including beige, brown, mauve, rust, and chocolate. This fact so amazed the Spaniard Barbabe Cobo that he concluded in his *History of the New World,* written in the 17th century, that the indigenous people of the Americas had devised a way to dye cotton while it remained on the plant. Later European writers copied his error, and in some circles the myth still persists today.

American Indians in the Southwest began growing cotton sometime after 1500 B.C. The earliest woven cotton found in that region comes from New Mexico and has been dated to about A.D. 700. The Hohokam, whose culture flourished in the desert of what is now Arizona starting in about 300 B.C., began growing cotton about A.D. 500. They built extensive IRRIGATION SYSTEMS to boost production so that they could harvest crops two to three times each year. After A.D. 1000, the Anasazi and Mogollon people of the North American Southwest began to cultivate cotton as well, planting it on alluvial fans (silt deposits) and flood plains. Using the process of SEED SELECTION, these southwestern people developed a variety called *Gossypium Hopi* that has the shortest growing season of any variety in the world.

Although Alexander the Great (king of Macedonia from 336 to 323 B.C.) had introduced cotton to Europe, the plants could not be grown there, and therefore items made from cotton cloth were considered luxuries. The Spaniards first encountered cotton in the Americas when Taino Indians of the Caribbean Islands offered it to Columbus as a trade good. The cotton textiles of both the Aztec and the Maya impressed early Spanish explorers. Conquistador Francisco Vásquez de Coronado, who traveled in the North American Southwest, noted that Indians grew cotton from the Rio Grande in the south to Hopi country in the north. The Zuni planted it in irrigated gardens and hand-watered it as well. They were experts at separating the fiber from the bolls by flailing them between blankets.

During colonial times in what would become the United States, planters in the South began growing indigenous cotton in the hope that it would replace the TOBACCO that quickly depleted soil nutrients. Cotton did not become a viable cash crop until seeds from a variety with long, fine fibers from the Bahamas were introduced to Georgia. This variety was called Sea Island cotton because it grew best along the sandy coastline and on Georgia's Sea Islands. These seeds are believed to be of the same type that Columbus brought back to Spain from his first voyage in 1492. Eventually Sea Island cotton was taken to Egypt in the mid-1800s. There plant breeders crossed it with varieties indigenous in the Middle East to produce plants with an extremely long staple, or fiber. With the invention of the cotton gin in 1793, the tedious and time-consuming job of removing cottonseeds from the fiber by hand was mechanized. By 1803 southern planters were growing $10 million worth of cotton annually. This increased each year until the economy in the South became dependent on cotton.

At the start of the 20th century, a cross of Egyptian and American cotton was introduced to the Southwest. Seeds were selected, and eventually a superior long staple variety, which came to be called *Pima cotton,* was developed. Its name came from the Pima (now known as Akimel O'odham) Indians, descendants of the Hohokam, who helped raised the cotton on a U.S. Department of Agriculture farm in Sacaton, Arizona. Ironically, their own traditional cotton fields had become almost completely supplanted by the introduction of sheep to the area by early colonizers.

Today, cotton serves as a fiber, animal feed, and a food crop. More than 75 percent of the people in the world wear cotton clothing. About two thirds of the harvested crop is composed of the seed. Much of this is used for animal feed. Cottonseed oil is a common component of many food items. The United States uses about 3.5 billion pounds of cotton per year, an average of 14 pounds per person. China is the world's leading cotton producer, followed by the United States. American Pima cotton is grown primarily in Arizona, California, New Mexico, and Texas.

See also AGRICULTURE.

### Sources/Further Reading

Adams, Richard E. W. "Rio Azul." *National Geographic* 169, no. 4 (April 1986): 420–451.

———. Fibers, Dyes and Tannins. URL: http://www.isc.tamu.ed/FLORA/328FALL96/fiberdye.html. Downloaded on July 4, 1998.

Hurt, R. Douglas. *American Indian Agriculture: Prehistory to Present.* Lawrence: University Press of Kansas, 1987.

Schuster, Angela M.H. "Colorful Cotton! An Ethnoarchaeologist tries to revive a 5,000-year-old Peruvian Textile Tradition." *Archaeology* (July/August 1995): 40–45.

Sharer, Robert. *Daily Life in Maya Civilization.* Westport, Conn.: Greenwood Press, 1996.

Smith, Michael E. *The Peoples of America: the Aztecs.* Cambridge, Mass.: Blackwell, 1996.

Supima Association of America. URL:sumpimacotton.org/supima/cotton.htm. Downloaded on April 24, 1999.

**countertraction**   See TRACTION AND COUNTERTRACTION.

**cradleboards** (precontact) *North American Great Plains, Northeast, California, Southwest, Arctic, and Subarctic; South American Andean cultures*
A cradleboard consists of a rigid frame with a softer pouch attached in which a baby is placed. The baby carrier that became so popular in the late 1960s and early 1970s because it allowed women to be more active while remaining close to their children

to keep the baby from slipping. Many had a wooden frame that projected enough from where the baby's head would be so that the child would be protected if the board accidentally tipped over while sitting on the ground.

Tribes throughout what are now the United States and Canada made use of this convenient way to care for a child. Indians of the southern plains and the Southwest tribes used wood and leather to construct their carriers. California tribes wove their carriers like baskets. Inuit mothers carried their infants strapped on their backs beneath the PARKAS they wore. Many of the infant carriers were elaborately decorated with quillwork and, after contact, beads as a way of showing how important the child was to the family and the tribe.

By using a cradleboard, a mother could carry her baby on her back as she walked. After the introduction of the horse by the Spaniards, northern plains mothers tied their babies' cradleboards to their saddles or to the travois pulled behind the horses. Often children were propped in cradleboards inside the home or leaned against a tree. From a very young age, North American babies were able to observe the world around them while remaining safe from harm. Being raised this way taught them the value of observation.

Cradleboards served as a comfortable and convenient way to carry babies. Many Plains tribes made cradleboards similar to the Kiowa cradleboard shown here. Although Indian mothers throughout the Americas relied on these first baby carriers, styles varied from region to region. *(Kansas State Historical Society, Topeka, Kansas)*

was not a new invention. Traditional American Indian mothers had devised a way of tending babies while freeing their hands for work long before contact with Europeans. Northern Plains and Eastern Woodland mothers would strap their infants snugly into soft leather pouches, called moss bags, a few weeks after the child was born. Various materials—including moss—were used to keep the baby dry and comfortable. (See also DIAPERS, DISPOSABLE). The moss bags were then attached to wooden frames. Most cradleboards were made with safety features, including support for the baby's head and a hood or shade to shield the child's face from the sun, and some had a narrow shelf on the bottom

The Inca of what is now Peru invented a cradleboard with legs that could also be used as a crib. *(After Felipe Guamán Poma de Ayala. Nueva Coronica y Buen Gobierno.)*

The Inca, who established an empire in what is now Peru in about A.D. 1000, made a unique baby carrier that served as a cradle for newborns and a crib as they became older. It was a unique design because it had six legs—four at the head and two at the foot. The four legs at the head were made of two long branches that were bent so that they formed two large Us. These were crossed with the ends serving as the legs. When a mother placed a blanket over these legs, a small dome was formed, protecting the infant's face and head from insects and the sun. The legs at the foot of this cradle were attached separately. Mothers tied a long strip of cloth or leather around each end of the cradleboard to use as a shoulder strap, or TUMPLINE, in order to carry the child. Because the carrier had six legs, it did not have to be placed on a smooth surface. Similar carriers are still used by the indigenous people of Peru.

## Sources/Further Reading

Bankes, George. *Peru before Pizarro.* Oxford, England: Phaidon Press Ltd., 1977.

Capps, Benjamin. *The Indians.* New York: Time Life Books, 1973.

Dupree Cradle Board Collection, Kirkpatrick Center, University of Oklahoma. *The Culture Areas: A Survey.* Ottawa, Canada: Minister of Indian Affairs and Northern Development, 1996.

## crampons (snow creepers) (ca. 1000 B.C.) *North American Arctic cultures*

Crampons are devices attached to the bottom of the shoe to prevent slipping when walking, especially on snow or ice. The Paleo-Indians of the North American Arctic invented crampons made of bone or ivory and began attaching them to the bottom of their footwear in about 1000 B.C.

In the spring, when melting made the surface of the snow slippery, the Inuit people of Point Barrow in what is now Alaska, sewed double strips of sealskin to the soles of their MUKLUKS over the ball of the foot and the heel area. Bent into a half moon or horseshoe shape, these patches provided the traction necessary for keeping one's balance on the icy crust. Other Inuit people attached carved chips of ivory to the soles of their mukluks with leather straps in order to provide traction when walking.

See also SNOWSHOES.

## Sources/Further Reading

Paterek, Josephine, Ph.D. *Encyclopedia of American Indian Costume.* Denver: Colo.: ABC Clio, Inc., 1994.

Powell, J. W. *Ninth Annual Report of the Bureau of Ethnology to the Secretary of the Smithsonian Institution 1887–88.* Washington, D.C.: Government Printing Office, 1892.

## cranberries (*Vaccinium vitis-idaea*) (precontact) *North American Northeast, Northwest Coast, Subarctic cultures*

Cranberries are the tart fruit of a bushy plant that grows in the acidic soil of bogs in the upper United States and parts of Canada. American Indians gathered them for DYES and MEDICINE as well as for food. The berries were often mashed and mixed with dried deer meat to make PEMMICAN. In what is now British Columbia, the upper north Wakashan and southern Tsimshian Indians mixed high bush cranberries with pacific crab apples to make what would be called a cranberry juice cocktail today. Inupiaq Indians further north mixed low bush cranberries with frozen fish eggs or blubber for a frozen dessert high in Vitamin C.

For American Indians of many tribes, the berries' pigment provided color for blankets, clothing, and rugs. The Lenni Lenape (Delaware) Indians, who lived in the Northeast, regarded the hardy plants so useful that they used the cranberry as a symbol of peace.

American Indians throughout cranberry-growing areas used the berries to make poultices to draw infections from wounds. The medicinal use of cranberries persists today. Physicians often recommend drinking cranberry juice as a way to help prevent and cure bladder infections. In 1998 researchers from Rutgers University studied why this folk remedy worked so well. After a five-year-long study, they isolated substances called condensed tannins, or proanthocyanidins, from cranberries that were found to prevent E. coli bacteria from attaching to the cells of the urinary tract. This property enables the bacteria to be flushed from the body. Rutgers researcher Amy B. Howell, Ph.D., estimated that drinking one 10-ounce glass of cranberry juice a day could ward off both bladder and kidney infections. Published in the *New England Journal of Medicine,* her study confirmed what American Indians knew long ago—that cranberries, and other fruits that contain the same tannins, such as blueberries, are an effective way to prevent bladder and kidney infections. (See also ANTIBIOTICS.)

Although it is not certain, the red berries may have been a part of the THANKSGIVING feast held in Plymouth, Massachusetts, in 1620. Later German and Dutch settlers termed the fruits "crane berries," because their blossoms look like a crane's neck, head, and bill. That word became cranberry. Recipes for the wild berries began being included in colonial cookbooks in the 1700s, but European settlers did not cultivate them until 1816, when they were planted on Cape Cod.

Today cranberries raised for commercial purposes are grown on low-lying bushes with a long life span. It is common to find 75- to 100-year-old bogs still producing berries for the market. Massachusetts is the leading cranberry producer. The berries are also grown in Wisconsin, Washington, Oregon, Rhode Island, New Jersey, Quebec, and British Columbia. In the United States, more than 5 million barrels are produced annually at a value of about $300 million according to the U.S. Department of Agriculture.

## Sources/Further Reading

Canada News Wire. "Rutgers Researchers Find E. Coli Inhibitor in Cranberries." October 7, 1998. URL: http://www.newswire.ca/releases/October1998/07/c1657.html. Posted October 7, 1998.

Compton, Brian Douglas. *Upper North Wakashan and Southern Tsimshian Ethnobotany: The Knowledge and Usage of Plants.* Ph.D. dissertation, University of British Columbia, 1993.

Jones, Anore. *Nauriat Niginaqtuat: Plants That We Eat.* Kotzebue, Alaska: Maniilaq Association Traditional Nutrition Program, 1983.

National Agricultural Statistics Service (NASS), Agricultural Statistics Board, U.S. Department of Agriculture, 1997.

**crochet** See KNITTING.

**crop storage** (precontact) *Mesoamerican; South American Andean; North American Southwest, Northeast, Circum-Caribbean and various cultures*

One of the main goals of crop cultivation for American Indians was to produce a surplus of food that would enable them to eat during the winter and times of crop failure. Tribes in Meso-South, and North America devised ingenious ways to store these harvests. At the outset, they understood the principles of cold storage, keeping grain, especially seeds they had saved for future planting, in caves where they would remain cool. When these natural storage lockers were not readily available, they devised their own systems.

The Maya, whose culture arose in about 1500 B.C. in Mesoamerica, constructed large granaries, as did the Inca, whose culture arose in what are now Peru and part of Bolivia about A.D. 1000. The Aztec, who established their empire about A.D. 1100 in Mesoamerica, built elaborate granaries as well. The Hohokam, who lived in what is now Arizona starting in about 300 B.C., stored shelled corn and dried SQUASH in baskets and POTTERY vessels. The Anasazi, who lived in the Four Corners region of the North American Southwest from about 350 B.C. to A.D. 1300, used storage pits and made storerooms. They built these granaries along overhangs in canyons, lined with flat rocks or clay, even though they initially lived in pit houses that were partially underground. Anthropologists believe that food storage was the primary factor that impelled them to begin building aboveground rooms and the pueblos where they eventually lived. (See also APARTMENT COMPLEXES.) They also think that the Anasazi pueblos, such as Mesa Verde in what is now Colorado and Pueblo Bonito in what is now New Mexico, had the capacity to store thousands of bushels of grain and served as regional food distribution centers.

By A.D. 1200, American Indian farmers in the Ohio Valley were constructing sophisticated underground silos that could hold 30 to 40 bushels of shelled CORN. These cylindrical storage tanks were lined with grass and rawhide and covered with caps made of grass. Eastern Woodlands Indians dug storage pits about two to three feet in diameter and lined them with bark to keep their corn dry and safe from rodents. These caches were not safe from marauding Pilgrims, however. Only a few days after the *Mayflower's* landing, a party of starving immigrants discovered food the Indians had stored. "We marched to the

The Inca stored their crops in large stone granaries. From there they were distributed to soldiers and people in need. *(After Felipe Guamán Poma de Ayala. Nueva Coronica y Buen Gobierno)*

place we called Cornhill, where we had found the corn before," one of them wrote. "At another place we had seen before, we dug and found some more corn, two or three baskets full, and a bag of beans . . . In all we had about ten bushels, which will be enough for seed. It was with God's help that we found this corn, for how else could we have done it, without meeting some Indians who might trouble us." Far from troubling the English, the Indians provided them with food and taught them not only to plant corn but also to fertilize it and to build corn cribs to store it.

See also AGRICULTURE; BEANS; SEED SELECTION.

**Sources/Further Reading**

Hurt, R. Douglas. *American Indian Agriculture: Prehistory to Present.* Lawrence: University Press of Kansas, 1987.

Josephy, Jr., Alvin M., ed. *America in 1492: The World of the Indian People Before the Arrival of Columbus.* New York: Random House, 1991.

Lowen, James W. *Lies My Teacher Told Me: Everything Your American History Textbook Got Wrong.* New York: The New Press, 1995.

Trigger, Bruce, and Wilcomb E. Washburn, eds. *The Cambridge History of the Native Peoples of the Americas, Vol. I, Part One: North America.* Cambridge: Cambridge University Press, 1996.

**curare** (precontact) *South American Tropical Forest, Circum-Caribbean cultures*
Curare is the Portuguese and Spanish version of the Carib word *kurari,* the name for the vines that produce a chemical that American Indians used in warfare and that is used in modern medicine as a muscle relaxant. American Indians extracted curare from *Stryclinos toxifera,* a woody vine of the *chondodendren* genus and similar herbs that grew throughout the Amazon jungles. The Indians cooked the plants that contained poison and used the resulting gum to coat the tips of their weapons. The secret of these plants remained a mystery to non-Indians until 1807, when German baron and naturalist Alexander von Humboldt is credited with discovering the source of curare.

The first European invader to die from curare poisoning was a member of Francisco de Orellana's party while they were seeking El Dorado, a mythical city of gold. What they found was the Amazon River. When the Indians of the area discovered these European intruders in their homelands, they defended themselves. The Spaniards were armed with metal weapons and the Indians with their stone-age implements, including arrows and BLOWGUNS. In his book *Indian Givers,* Jack Weatherford states: "The simple wooden weapons of the Indians seemed to offer little threat against the sophisticated European arsenal of metal." The Indians may have appeared to be a minor inconvenience to the invaders, but they possessed something that would level the playing field—curare. Even though Orellana's man received a minor wound from a small projectile, he died quietly and quickly. The tip of the arrow had been dipped in curare.

Curare is harmless when taken orally. However, it is lethal when it enters the bloodstream through a break in the skin. It works by blocking the electrical impulses traveling along the nerve cells that cause the muscles to flex or extend. Once the muscles that control the lungs stop working, death by suffocation results. Modern medicine uses small dosages of curare for surgical purposes because it provides complete muscular relaxation without the use of excessively deep anesthesia. (See also ANESTHETICS.) The derivative form in which curare is administered medically today is called *tubocurarine chloride.* It is used in abdominal SURGERY, including gall bladder and stomach operations, and for hysterectomies as well as thoracic surgery and tonsillectomies.

Curare is also used to treat tetanus, or lockjaw, a disease that is caused when the exotoxin *Clostridium tetani,* a highly toxic by-product of the tetanus bacteria, causes involuntary, sudden, and severe muscle spasms including contraction or cramping in the jaw and throat muscles, as well as other voluntary muscles. Prior to treatment of tetanus with curare derivatives, most tetanus victims died from the disease. Today the death rate is 30 percent.

### Sources/Further Reading
Josephy, Jr., Alvin M., ed. *America in 1492: The World of the Indian People Before the Arrival of Columbus.* New York: Random House, 1991.
Vogel, Virgil. *American Indian Medicine.* Norman: University of Oklahoma Press, 1977.
Weatherford, Jack. *Indian Givers: How the Indians of the Americas Transformed the World.* New York: Fawcett Columbine, 1988.

### curry, American Indian influence on
(postcontact) *Mesoamerican cultures*
Curry is a fiery mixture of spices including CHILE peppers, which are indigenous to the Americas. The Portuguese colonizers brought the chiles they found at trading posts in Pernambuco, Brazil, to India and China (and eventually to Japan and the Philippines) through their colony at Goa, on India's west coast. Although East Indians were making curried dishes before this time, soon after tasting chiles, they added the ground peppers to their curry powder, which already contained black pepper and ginger. The resulting fiery-tasting curry sauces have become standard in East Indian cooking today. The word *curry* is derived from *kari,* a Tamil word meaning sauce.

### Sources/Further Reading
Naj, Amal. *Peppers: A Story of Hot Pursuits.* New York: Knopf, 1992.
Sokalow, Raymond. *Why We Eat What We Eat: How the Encounter Between the New World and the Old Changed the Way Everyone on the Planet Eats.* New York: Summit Books, 1991.
Trager, James. *The Food Chronology: The Food Lover's Compendium of Events and Anecdotes from Prehistory to Present.* New York: Henry Holt, 1995.
Weatherford, Jack. *Indian Givers: How the Indians of the Americas Transformed the World.* New York: Fawcett Columbine, 1988.

**cuy** See GUINEA PIGS.

# D

**dahlias** (precontact) *Mesoamerican cultures*
Known for their large colorful blooms, dahlias are flowers indigenous to the mountains of Mexico, Colombia, and Guatemala. Pre-Columbian Indians, who used them for ornamental landscaping, were the first to domesticate them. Botanists accompanying the Spanish conquistadores noted that the stems of these flowered plants, known as "tree dahlias" (*D. imperialis*), sometimes grew more than 20 feet tall. The Aztec used the hollow stems for carrying water from place to place, and thirsty travelers would sometimes drink the water sap contained in the stems of growing plants. The Nahuatl, or Aztec, name for the flowers was *acocotli*, or "water cane."

About 200 years after Hernán Cortés marched through Mexico, dahlia seeds and roots were sent to Europe, where they were planted at the Royal Botanical Gardens in Madrid. The first European dahlia breeders experimented with the plants as a food source, but their trials failed. More experiments produced the flowers with double blooms that are popular with gardeners today.

In 1872 a shipment of dahlia roots sent from Mexico to Holland failed to survive the crossing except for one root. When planted, this root produced a bright red blossom with rolled back and pointed petals. Botanists cross-bred this new variety (*D. Dares*) with earlier varieties to form the basis for the hybrids grown in gardens today.

See also GARDENS, BOTANICAL.

## Sources/Further Reading

Killingsworth, Brian. *Dahlia Basics, Chapter 1.* URL: http://dahlia.com/basic.html. Downloaded on April 22, 1999.
Driver, Harold E. *Indians of North America.* Chicago: University of Chicago Press, 1969.
Virginia Co-operative Extension. *Flowers of Pre-Columbian America.* URL: http://www.ext.vt.edu/departments/envirohort/articles/herbaceous _plants/pr ecoll.html. Downloaded on April 22, 1999.

**datura** See ANESTHETICS.

**debridement** (precontact) *Mesoamerican, North American cultures*
Debridement—the removal of dead, damaged, or foreign tissue from wounds—was practiced by pre-Columbian Aztec physicians as well as those in other North American tribes. This technique, which is still used by modern medical practitioners, increased the speed at which wounds heal. Indigenous doctors used several methods to perform debridement. One of these was to apply clean white cotton bandages to the wound and to change them daily. Sometimes they packed the wound with eagle down, the contents of a puffball, or a spider's web. Changing these dressings also removed scabs from the wound and allowed it to heal faster. Irrigating the wound, flushing it with a liquid by using a SYRINGE, was another technique that they frequently used.

The process of debridement allowed ancient American Indian physicians to aid patients by increasing the speed at which they recovered from injuries and is an indication of the advanced medical knowledge and skills they possessed. Colonists to the Americas remarked on the fact that American Indians excelled at wound care and copied the innovations, procedures, and supplies that Indian physicians used.

See also DRAINAGE, SURGICAL AND WOUND.

## Sources/Further Reading

Ortiz de Montellano, Bernard. *Aztec Medicine, Health, and Nutrition.* New Brunswick, N.J.: Rutgers University Press, 1990.

Vogel, Virgil. *American Indian Medicine.* Norman: University of Oklahoma Press, 1977.

## decoys, auditory   See CALLS, ANIMAL AND BIRD.

## decoys, duck   (ca. 1000 B.C.)   *North American Great Basin cultures*

Decoys, figures that resemble ducks, are a standard part of the duck hunter's equipment today. The duck decoy was invented about 3,000 years ago by American Indians living in what is now northwest Utah. Decoys that archaeologists found in the Lovelock caves of Nevada have been dated to about 1000 B.C. "Made by desert foragers some 3000 years ago, the decoys were used to attract migrating ducks to nearby marshes," wrote James A. Maxwell in *America's Fascinating Indian Heritage.* Many anthropologists believe indigenous hunters made similar decoys much earlier. Visual decoy technology attracted the prey, conserving time and energy that would be spent pursuing ducks, which were a food source. The development of decoys required advanced intelligence and knowledge of hunting technology and the behavior of birds.

American Indians made duck decoys from materials such as reeds and CATTAILS. Some of the decoys were painted. Others were made to appear more lifelike by skinning a real duck and placing the feathered skin over a reed or cattail frame. These decoys were almost indistinguishable from the real thing.

Some archaeologists suggest that indigenous hunters wore the decoys on their heads while submerged in water and breathed through a hollow reed. They would grab ducks that were attracted to the decoys and pull them under water. Another possible hunting method was to lure the ducks close enough to be disabled by various projectiles such as rocks or arrows. Yet another method of capturing ducks might have been to throw a net over them. The Indians, who utilized more sophisticated hunting technology than did their European counterparts at the time, also used auditory decoys when hunting waterfowl and animals.

See also CALLS, ANIMAL AND BIRD.

### Sources/Further Reading

Driver, Harold E. *Indians of North America.* Chicago: University of Chicago Press, 1969.

Hurst, David, Jay Miller, Richard White, Peter Nabokov, and Philip J. Deloria. *The Native Americans.* Atlanta: Turner Publishing, Inc., 1993.

Maxwell, James A. *America's Fascinating Indian Heritage.* Pleasantville, N.Y.: Reader's Digest Books, 1978.

Weatherford, Jack. *Indian Givers: How the Indians of the Americas Transformed the World.* New York: Fawcett Columbine, 1988.

## decoys, fish (olfactory)   (precontact)   *North American Northeast cultures*

Olfactory fish decoys rely on scents to lure fish. American Indians living in the upper Midwest of what is now the United States invented this technology. It elevated fishing to a science and was a concept that was many years ahead of its time. From careful observation American Indians knew that smell and sight are often equally significant as cues to fish seeking food. American Indians boiled the rootstock of the herbs sarsaparilla (*Smilax officinalis*) and sweet flag (*Acorus calamus L.*) and applied the resulting broth to fishing decoys. (See also DECOYS, FISH [VISUAL].) They used the herbs individually and in combination.

See also FISHING, CHEMICAL.

### Sources/Further Reading

Josephy, Jr., Alvin M., ed. *America in 1492: The World of the Indian People Before the Arrival of Columbus.* New York: Random House, 1991.

Kimball, Art and Brad Kimball. *Fish Decoys of the Lac Du Flambeau Ojibway.* Boulder Junction, Wisc.: Aardvark Publications, 1988.

Weatherford, Jack. *Native Roots: How the Indians Enriched America.* New York: Fawcett Columbine, 1991.

## decoys, fish (visual)   (ca. A.D. 1000)   *North American Northeast cultures*

Unlike hooked fishing lures of today, fish decoys were designed to resemble the smaller fish that game fish eat or to resemble fish of the same species. American Indians were known to use fish decoys as a way to entice fish within range so that they could spear them. These visual decoys were being used by about 1000 A.D., but many archaeologists believe their invention might have come earlier. The oldest fish decoys that have been found were made of shell. Later fish decoys were made of wood. The decoys were crafted so well that at a distance they were difficult to distinguish from a real fish. The Chippewa (Anishinabe), Menominee, Ottawa, Santee Dakota, and Potawatomi used them primarily in the winter for ice fishing. (See also FISHING, ICE.)

The fisher would lower the decoy through a hole in the ice and then maneuver it to imitate a swimming fish by connecting a line to a hole in the dorsal part of the wooden fish. A weight was tied to a line attached to the ventral part of the fish decoy. This line was long enough to keep the weight out of the fish's line of sight. The fisher moved the decoy through the water with approximately the same pitch and attitude of a real minnow or bait fish. Sometimes the decoys were soaked in a special scent designed to attract fish. (See also DECOYS, FISH [OLFACTORY].) When a game fish came near the decoy, the fisher would spear it. Fish were an excellent source of protein and vitamin A, and the invention of fishing decoys enabled the American Indians to ensure a constant supply of it. This, in turn, ensured the health and well-being of the tribe.

### Sources/Further Reading

Josephy, Jr., Alvin M., ed. *America in 1492: The World of the Indian People Before the Arrival of Columbus.* New York: Random House, 1991.

Kimball, Art and Brad Kimball. *Fish Decoys of the Lac Du Flambeau Ojibway.* Boulder Junction, Wisc.: Aardvark Publications, 1988.

Weatherford, Jack. *Native Roots: How the Indians Enriched America.* New York: Fawcett Columbine, 1991.

**democracy** See UNITED STATES CONSTITUTION, AMERICAN INDIAN INFLUENCE ON.

**dental inlays** (ca. 1000 B.C.) *Mesoamerican cultures*

A dental inlay is a solid filling made to the precise shape of a cavity in a tooth and cemented into place. The Maya, whose culture arose about 1500 B.C. in Mesoamerica, were doing dental inlays before Columbus landed in the New World. They used jade for inlays as well as jet, gold, hematite, and turquoise. Sometimes these inlays were set into incisors and canines, and in some cases they were set into premolars. Lower and upper teeth also had inlays set into them. Archaeological evidence suggests that most inlays were done for aesthetic purposes and that decorative inlays were a practice among the upper class of ancient Maya society.

Mesoamerican dentists drilled teeth with a bow drill (see also DRILL, BOW), another American Indian precontact invention. The DRILL BIT was mounted on a shaft that was rotated by means of a bow. Drill bits were hollow and made of copper. They came in different diameters and were about an inch in length. The diameter of the drill bit that the dentist chose to use varied depending on the size of the tooth and the size of the inlay desired.

Archaeologists are not certain of the type of adhesive used by the Maya dentists to secure the inlays. They do know of two types of adhesive that were used for other purposes, one of which was made from liquid amber and the other from the maguey plant. (See also AGAVE.) Either could have been used to cement the inlays into place.

In order for ancient Maya dentists to do dental inlays, they had to possess a knowledge of dental anatomy. They knew that they should not drill too deeply into the tooth, or they would hit the pulp, something which could also cause an abscess. Although fillings were not as common as decorative inlays, the ancient Maya dentists did make them for teeth that had decayed. They drilled out the tooth, shaped a jade filling, and cemented it into place in the tooth.

The sophisticated practice of ancient American DENTISTRY resembles the work of present-day Western dentistry. It arose at a time when Europeans' only recourse for toothaches was extraction. In Europe, decayed teeth were filled with wax or gum starting in the Middle Ages. Gold was not employed until about A.D. 1450. Yet Maya inlays were so well done that after over 2,000 years, inlays are still securely in place in teeth from Maya human remains.

See also JADE WORK; JEWELRY, TURQUOISE AND SILVER.

**Sources/Further Reading**

Benson, Elizabeth P. *The Maya World.* New York: Thomas Y. Crowell Company, 1967.

Fastlicht, Samuel. "Dental Inlays and Fillings among the Ancient Mayas." *Journal of the History of Medicine* 17, no. 2 (July 1962): 393–340.

———. *Tooth Mutilations and Dentistry in Pre-Columbian Mexico.* Mexico City: Quintessense Books, 1971.

Vogel, Virgil. *American Indian Medicine.* Norman: University of Oklahoma Press, 1977.

**dentifrices, chewable** See CHEWABLE DENTIFRICES.

**dentistry** (ca. 1000 B.C.) *Mesoamerican cultures*

Dentistry is the field of medicine that focuses on the diagnosis and prevention of diseases of the teeth. A sophisticated form of dentistry evolved among several ancient Mesoamerican culture groups. The Maya, whose culture arose about 1500 B.C. in Mesoamerica, practiced an amazing type of dentistry, as did the Aztec, whose empire was established in the same region in about A.D. 1100.

Ancient American Indian dentistry covered many areas. Indigenous dentists had names for various types of teeth; for tooth conditions, such as decay; and for procedures, such as tartar removal. Pre-Columbian dentists removed tartar with metal instruments and knew how to prevent and treat gum and mouth sores and lesions. They also knew how to prevent and treat halitosis, or bad breath, and used alum to whiten teeth. (See also DISTILLATION.)

Mesoamerican dentists performed tooth extractions and filled cavities. They also set decorative DENTAL INLAYS in the anterior portion of the front teeth. After treating a dental condition, the ancient American Indian dentists made a saline, or salt, solution to use as a mouth rinse—something that is done today.

Aztec dentists, who were called *tlantonaniztli* in Nahuatl, the Aztec language, developed standard PRESCRIPTIONS for preventing halitosis and tooth decay as well as gum lesions and inflammations. They were able to identify the fever blister and treated this condition with herbal remedies as well. They were also able to develop CHEWABLE DENTIFRICES and a type of TOOTHBRUSH that contained astringent properties, and they instructed patients on the use of the toothpick, or *netlantataconi*.

The Spanish conquistadores were impressed by the sophistication of Aztec dental practices. In 1571 King Philip II dispatched Francisco Hernandez, a physician, to document the medicinal seeds, plants, and herbs he could find there. In 1790 Casimiro Gomez Ortega reviewed his works and found eight references to treatment for halitosis, 10 references to oral hygiene, and 49 plants used for the prevention of dental caries, or tooth decay. In contrast, Western dentists did not understand preventative dentistry until the mid-18th century and did not stress it until the 20th century.

See also MOUTHWASH; TOOTHPASTES AND POWDERS.

**Sources/Further Reading**

Fastlicht, Samuel. "Dental Inlays and Fillings among the Ancient Mayas." *Journal of the History of Medicine* 17, no. 2 (July 1962): 393–340.

————. *Tooth Mutilations and Dentistry in Pre-Columbian Mexico.* Mexico City: Quintessence Books, 1971.

Ortiz de Montellano, Bernard. *Aztec Medicine, Health and Nutrition.* New Brunswick, N.J.: Rutgers University Press, 1990.

Vogel, Virgil. *American Indian Medicine.* Norman: University of Oklahoma Press, 1977.

Weatherford, Jack. *Indian Givers: How the Indians of the Americas Transformed the World.* New York: Fawcett Columbine, 1988.

## deodorants (precontact) *Mesoamerican, North American Great Plains cultures*

Deodorants are substances applied to the body to neutralize or mask body odor. The Aztec wore or carried fragrant flowers for this purpose. (The Aztec Empire was established about A.D. 1100 in what are now Mexico and Mesoamerica.) Unlike their European contemporaries, the Aztec practiced daily bathing. Their use of deodorants was an adjunct to personal hygiene. (See also HYGIENE, PERSONAL.)

The Aztec used several substances as underarm deodorants, including copal gum, liquid amber oil, and American balsam oil. Liquid amber and American balsam *(Abies balsamea)* were boiled to remove the oil from the plant and then distilled to extract the oil from the water mixture. They applied the result both as an underarm deodorant and as a perfume.

Indians who lived on the Great Plains of North America were concerned about odor as well. Often they stored sweetgrass with their buckskin clothing in order to make it smell fresh. Daily bathing was routinely practiced to prevent body odor.

See also DISTILLATION.

### Sources/Further Reading

Benson, Elizabeth P. *The Maya World.* New York: Thomas Y. Crowell Company, 1967.

Ortiz de Montellano, Bernard. *Aztec Medicine, Health, and Nutrition.* New Brunswick, N.J.: Rutgers University Press, 1990.

Paterek, Josephine, Ph.D. *Encyclopedia of American Indian Costume.* Denver, Colo.: ABC Clio, Inc., 1994.

Vogel, Virgil. *American Indian Medicine.* Norman: University of Oklahoma Press, 1977.

## detergents (shampoo; soap) (precontact)
*Mesoamerican; North American California, Great Basin, Southwest, and Southeast cultures*

Laundry detergent is a modern term that is commonly used for cleansing agents. Unlike Europeans, who tended to eschew personal hygiene (see also HYGIENE, PERSONAL), American Indians washed their clothing as often as practical when it became soiled, including both cloth and hide garments. They also used plant-based detergents as body soap and as shampoo.

The Aztec, who established an empire in what is now Mexico in about A.D. 1100, used several plants as effective detergents. One of these was a tree that they called *copalxocatl.* The Spanish later called this the soap-tree. The *copalxocatl* produced small fruits that contained a chemical capable of producing lather when mixed with water. The Aztec also used the *Saponaria americana* and *Sapindus saponarius.* The roots of these plants contain a substance called saponin, which produces suds that result in a cleansing action. The Aztec crushed these roots before adding them to water.

North American Indians used a number of plants as laundry and personal detergents. These plants contained saponin as well. The Karok, a California tribe, pounded the bulbs of the soap plant (*Chlorogalum pomerindianum*) to clean both clothing and buckskin blankets while the Mahuna used them whole as soap bars. The Karok also rubbed the roots and crushed leaves of saltbrush (*Atriplex lentiformis*) on their garments to clean them. The Diegueno, a California tribe, and the Kawaiisu, a Great Basin tribe, used the mashed or grated root of the soap plant (*Chenopodium californicum*) to both clean and whiten articles of clothing. The above-mentioned plants served as shampoos as well.

Wild gourd, or buffalo gourd (*Curcubita foetidssima*), was used as laundry detergent and bleach for the Cahuilla and Diegueno. (See also INSECTICIDES.) They used both the root and the mashed pulp and seeds. The Tohono O'odham (Papago), who lived in the Arizona desert, washed clothing with wild gourd, as did the Pueblo peoples of the Southwest. Sometimes they cut the gourd in half and rubbed it on garments as a stain remover.

Wherever they lived, American Indians found plants containing saponin. Tribes throughout the Southwest and in the Great Basin used roots from a number of varieties of YUCCA plants for the same purpose as well as a body wash and shampoo. (Several modern shampoos contain yucca.) Often they roasted the roots in order to release the saponin. In the Southeast the Cherokee used bear grass roots (*Yucca filamentosa L.*) as a detergent.

See also HAIR CONDITIONERS.

### Sources/Further Reading

Dunmire, William W. and Gail D. Tierney. *Wild Plants of the Pueblo Province: Exploring Ancient and Enduring Uses.* Santa Fe: Museum of New Mexico Press, 1995.

Lust, John. *The Herb Book.* New York: Bantam Books, 1974.

Moerman, Dan. *Native American Ethnobotany Database: Food, Drugs, Dyes and Fibers of Native North American Peoples.* URL: http://www.umd.umich.edu/cgi-bin/herb. Downloaded on December 26, 1999.

Sahagun, Fray Bernardino de. *General History of the Things of New Spain* (Florentine Codex). Trans. Charles E. Dibble and Arthur J. O. Anderson. Santa Fe: The School of American Research and the University of Utah, 1963.

Soustelle, Jacques. *Daily Life of the Aztecs on the Eve of the Spanish Conquest.* Stanford, Calif.: Stanford University Press, 1955.

Vogel, Virgil. *American Indian Medicine.* Norman: University of Oklahoma Press, 1977.

## diabetes medication (A.D. 1938) *North America Northwest Coast cultures*

Diabetes is an endocrine disease caused by an inability of the pancreas to make sufficient amounts of insulin. Insulin is a hormone that regulates glucose, or sugar, levels in the blood. Medical researchers believe that diabetes was not a problem among American Indians prior to the arrival of Europeans. Today it has become epidemic among the North American Indians, an event blamed on dietary changes and other changes in lifestyle imposed by conquest and caused by assimilation. Before contact, American Indians used several herbs for medical conditions that are used today by modern practitioners of herbal medicine to regulate the level of glucose in the blood. One example of one of these herbs is Devil's Club (*Fatsia horrida*).

Since the 1930s researchers have performed tests on Devil's Club that have demonstrated its ability to regulate blood sugar. When the plant was tested on rabbits, it performed like insulin. In 1938 a Canadian physician learned that the American Indians of British Columbia had been using Devil's Club for the control of diabetes for many years. When a Prince Rupert doctor examined an American Indian male, it was noticed that the man exhibited all the signs of diabetes yet was not experiencing any ill effects of the disease. The patient explained that he had been taking a mixture of Devil's Club and hot water. No one knows how many years prior to 1938 the Canadian Indians were using this herb, but it is reasonable to assume that the time could be considerable. Modern physicians did not find plant-based oral medications for diabetes until the 1940s, and these did not become a standard part of diabetes treatment until the 1960s.

See also MEDICINE; PHARMACOLOGY.

### Sources/Further Reading

Weiner, Michael A. *Earth Medicine Earth Food: The Classic Guide to the Herbal Remedies and Wild Plants of the North American Indians.* New York: Fawcett Columbine, 1980.

Vogel, Virgil. *American Indian Medicine.* Norman: University of Oklahoma Press, 1977.

## diapers, disposable (precontact) *North American Great Plains and Northeast cultures*

North American Indians of many tribes used a form of disposable diaper to keep babies dry and their skin protected. Some used the downy fibers of puff balls or CATTAILS. Others used dry rotted wood fibers or dried moss. Arapaho mothers used dried, powdered buffalo chips as an absorbent material. These were pounded and sifted several times to make a fine powder.

Before a baby was strapped into a CRADLEBOARD, he or she was rubbed with tallow and placed into a soft leather sack, sometimes called a moss bag. This was filled to waist-level with whatever soft material was traditionally used by his or her people. The baby was changed when needed, and the soiled filler was discarded. This practice was not only convenient, it kept American Indian infants comfortable and free from diaper rash. These disposable diapers were also biodegradable.

### Sources/Further Reading

"The Buffalo Culture of the Plains Indians." *The Wind River Rendezvous* 8, no. 2 (Spring 1983).

Capps, Benjamin. *The Indians.* New York: Time Life Books, 1973.

## dice games See GAMES, DICE.

## disability rights (social security) (ca. A.D. 600–A.D. 1400) *South American Andean cultures*

The Americans with Disabilities Act was lauded as a major piece of legislation that would allow citizens with physical or mental conditions that usually prevented them from equal access to opportunities others take for granted to participate in the American dream. Disabled persons had lobbied for this legislation for a long time in order to be recognized as valuable, productive individuals of society. Yet laws protecting the disabled and providing them with certain rights are not a new concept. Disability rights policies and laws originated among Indians of South America long before European contact. The Inca, whose empire was established about A.D. 1000 in what are now Peru and parts of Bolivia, created specific laws for the disabled. These ensured that people with disabilities had all of their basic needs met and, in many cases, that they were given jobs that would accommodate their handicaps. For example, in the mountainous region of Peru, the blind were able to work removing husks from CORN, while in western Peru they were allowed to clean COTTON, removing seeds and hulls from the fiber.

The Inca also had laws that allowed people with disabilities to marry (usually others with disabilities) and set up housekeeping. What they could not afford through work was provided to them by the government, which met all of their basic needs. They were encouraged to participate in the mainstream of their society to the greatest extent their handicaps would allow.

The Inca government also took care of the elderly and people whose chronic diseases prevented them from working. In contrast, European rulers generally ignored people with disabilities, many of whom were homeless and lived on the streets. During the Inquisition that swept Europe in the 1400s, many with disabilities were killed because they were thought to be possessed by demons. England later established debtor prisons for its poor and infirm, a concept that was translated into "poor farms," or county farms, in the United States.

Inca laws made certain that the gap between the ruling class and common people was not too large. They required that the wealthy were to feed the people in their districts three times a month, work in their own gardens, and not wear lavish jewelry or clothes too often. These laws were developed to prevent animosities between the upper and lower classes.

In North America the Indians did not have specific codified disability rights and laws, but people with disabilities were allowed to participate in society and often held special places in the tribe. Their contribution to society consisted of teaching, entertaining, and maintaining civic consciousness, since it was believed that disabled people were more empathetic and understanding. Many able-bodied people volunteered to assist and transport those with disabilities in the belief that they could learn much from the disabled.

Bartolomé de Las Casas, a Spanish priest who traveled to Hispaniola, wrote of the Arawak in *Historia de las Indias* in 1515: "Nobody had to watch other people eating who had nothing himself, because as I have said, nowhere in the world do they share so with those who have not, and they say that we Christians are bad people because we invite nobody. . . ."

## Sources/Further Reading
Bankes, George. *Peru before Pizarro.* Oxford, England: Phaidon, 1977.

Coe, Sophie. *America's First Cuisines.* Austin: University of Texas Press, 1994.

Hurst, David, Jay Miller, Richard White, Peter Nabokov, and Philip Deloria. *The Native Americans.* Atlanta: Turner Publishing, Inc., 1993.

## distillation (precontact) *Mesoamerican cultures*

Distillation is the process of evaporating liquid and collecting the condensation of vapors in order to extract certain substances. The Aztec, whose empire was established in about A.D. 1100 in Mesoamerica, had a fundamental knowledge of distillation. They were familiar with a crude form of the process that they used for extracting substances from bark, wood, liquids, roots, herbs, minerals, and plants. Ancient American Indian pharmacists used this process because the materials they needed in order to make medicines were not available in a pure form in their environment.

Samuel Fastlicht, an expert on Mesoamerica, writes in his book *Tooth Mutilations and Dentistry in Pre-Columbian Mexico,* "The Aztec knew and used alum for whitening teeth and knew how to obtain it in its purified and distilled form." He also gives a partial description of how the Aztec achieved distillation: "First they pulverize the aluminous earth and pour it into great earthenware vessels ending in a point. When it is perfectly condensed it is a solid, brilliant white, transparent, and having an acrid and astringent taste."

After conquest the Spaniards introduced the distillation process for making alcoholic beverages tequila and mescal, a brandy made from the AGAVE plant.

See also DENTISTRY; PHARMACOLOGY.

## Sources/Further Reading
Bancroft, Hubert Howe. *The Works of Hubert Howe Bancroft: Vol. II, The Native Races.* San Francisco: The History Company, 1886.

Bourke, John G. "Distillation by Early American Indians." *American Anthropologist O.S.* 8 (1894): 297.

Fastlicht, Samuel. *Tooth Mutilations and Dentistry in Pre-Columbian Mexico.* Mexico City: Quintessense Books, 1971.

Peredo, Guzman Miguel. *Medical Practices in Ancient America.* Mexico City: Ediciones Euroamericanas, 1985.

Vogel, Virgil. *American Indian Medicine.* Norman: University of Oklahoma Press, 1977.

## diuretics (precontact) *North American Northeast, Southeast, and Great Plains cultures*

Diuretics—medications that cause an increase in the output of urine—are routinely prescribed by modern physicians to treat water retention, which causes edema, or swelling. Hundreds of years ago, American Indian physicians were knowledgeable about the diuretic properties of various plants. Indigenous healers living in the Eastern Woodlands region relied on milkweed (*Asclepias syriaca*). They boiled the rootstock of this plant to make a tea that was administered orally to treat kidney and kidney-related problems that cause edema. Other tribes discovered local herbs that were just as effective. The Blackfeet, who lived in what is now Montana, used Rocky Mountain juniper and wild black currant. The Creek, who lived in the Southeast, used sarsaparilla, while the Ho-Chunk and Dakota of the northern plains used WINTERGREEN. The Natchez Indians, who lived in the southern Mississippi Valley, not only knew how to diagnose edema but were also aware of what caused the body to retain excess fluid. They therefore advised people with edema to avoid eating salty foods.

See also MEDICINE; PHARMACOLOGY.

## Sources/Further Reading
Hutchens, Alma R. *Indian Herbology of North America.* Boston: Shambhala, 1991.

Lust, John. *The Herb Book.* New York: Bantam Books, 1974.

Vogel, Virgil. *American Indian Medicine.* Norman: University of Oklahoma Press, 1977.

Weiner, Michael A. *Earth Medicine Earth Food: The Classic Guide to the Herbal Remedies and Wild Plants of the North American Indians.* New York: Fawcett Columbine, 1980.

## doctor bags See MEDICINE KITS.

## dogbane (*Apocynum androsaemifolium*) (precontact) *North American Northeast, Southeast, and Northwest Coast cultures*

Dogbane is a perennial plant that is native to North America. It is found along both coasts, growing best along the edges of wooded places in soil that is sandy and dry. American Indians used dogbane to treat dropsy, a condition characterized by a build-up of fluid in body tissue. This accumulation of fluid, also called edema, is caused by renal (kidney) and cardiac (heart) failure. The American Indians were the first to use dogbane to treat edema stemming from renal and cardiac failure. The Potawatomi of the Northeast boiled the green fruit of dogbane to produce an extract or tea to treat these problems. They also used dogbane as an oral contraceptive (see also CONTRACEPTION, ORAL) and as an antihypertensive to reduce high blood pressure.

The milky juice found in all parts of the plant is extracted by boiling it in water. Taken orally, it rids the body of excess fluid in several ways. It acts like digitalis (see also FOXGLOVE) by strengthening the action of the heart and by regulating its rhythm. Dogbane is also effective in decreasing excess body fluid by causing diaphoresis (profuse sweating), expectoration (the expulsion of mucous from the lungs), emesis (vomiting), and catharsis (emptying of the digestive system). Michael A. Weiner, author of *Earth Medicine, Earth Food,* states that "Since it has been shown that these plants act by regulating and strengthening the heart's action, it is easy to speculate that the Indian practitioner had a good understanding of the circulatory system, and selected those plants of his environment which would restore balance to a faltering unit."

Once they had encountered dogbane, American colonists quickly embraced its use to treat dropsy. Physicians followed suit, and by the 1800s it had become a popular remedy.

See also MEDICINE; PHARMACOLOGY.

**Sources/Further Reading**

Hutchens, Alma R. *Indian Herbology of North America.* Boston: Shambhala, 1991.
Lust, John. *The Herb Book.* New York: Bantam Books, 1974.
Weiner, Michael A. *Earth Medicine, Earth Food: Plant Remedies, Drugs, and Natural Foods of the North American Indians.* New York: Fawcett Columbine, 1990.

**dog breeds** (ca. 10,000 B.C.–5000 B.C.) *North American; Mesoamerican; South American cultures*

Dogs are mammals of the canine family. By the time Europeans arrived in the Americas, dogs had been domesticated from the Arctic to South America. Some scientists believe that dogs were domesticated in Asia and crossed the Bering Strait between 10,000 and 15,000 years ago, but there is also evidence that American Indians domesticated the indigenous North American plains wolf (*Canis lupus pallipes*). Bones of animals that closely resemble wolves, but are smaller than these animals, have been dated to 10,200 B.C. It is certain that American Indians had domesticated dogs in North America by 5,000 B.C., given remains found at the Koster site in what is now Illinois. Three breeds of dogs still raised today that are believed to have been bred by Native Americans are the xoloitzcuintlis, the Carolina dog, and the malamute.

Except for the Great Basin tribes, most dog owners in North and South America gave their dogs names and considered them pets to some extent. Rock art in Wyoming that has been dated to A.D. 400 shows a dog on a leash. Jesuit priest Bernardo de Sahagun provides clear evidence for the existence and the importance of dogs as companions in the Western Hemisphere in his writings, detailing six types of dogs kept by the Aztec, who established an empire in about A.D. 1100 in Mesoamerica. The Aztec dogs ranged in size from large to small and followed their masters, according to Sahagun. "They are joyous, and wag their tail in sign of peace," he wrote. "They growl and bark; they lower their ears toward their neck in sign of love. They eat bread and green CORN stalks, and raw meat and cooked as well."

In addition to being companions, dogs served utilitarian purposes. Throughout the Western Hemisphere, they were considered a food source and eaten ceremonially, and their fur and skin were used for clothing. In southern Greenland, dogskin was used for parkas, and in the Northwest of North America some tribes bred dogs for the fiber they produced in order to make belts and blankets. Flathead (Salish) women bred dogs with thick, white hair for this purpose and kept the animals on islands off the coast to prevent them from interbreeding with hunting dogs. (See also WEAVING TECHNIQUES.) The Inca, whose empire arose in what are now Peru and parts of Bolivia in about A.D. 1000, used dogs to guard their LLAMA herds. In North America, canines served as burden bearers. On the Plains, dogs carried packs and pulled travois for their Indian companions; in the Arctic they pulled sleds. Typically it was women who trained dogs used for transporting goods.

Some tribes used dogs for hunting. The Moche, who lived on the northern coast of Peru from about 200 B.C. to A.D. 600, and the Maya, whose culture arose in what are now Mexico in about 1500 B.C., used the animals to drive deer into nets. In North America the Tlingit of the Northwest Coast used hunting dogs. The Yurok, who lived in what is now California, used dogs to hunt rabbits and squirrels as well as larger game such as foxes, deer, and elk. The Penobscot in the Northeast hunted with dogs that some archaeologists believe were domesticated well before 700 B.C.

One of the distinct Aztec breeds encountered by the Spaniards in Mexico was the xochiocoyotl. That *xochiocoyotl* became transformed into the word *coyote* would tend to indicate that the breed did, in fact, resemble the wolflike carnivore *Canis latrans* common throughout much of North America.

*Xoloitzcuintlis* (also known as the xolo or Mexican hairless), the hairless dogs of the Aztec, are believed to be one of the oldest pure breeds of dog still in existence today; their archaeological remains date back at least 3,300 years. Their name in the Aztec language Nahuatl refers to Xotol, the god of the ball game, who was often depicted as a dog with deformed paws. The Aztec believed that the *xoloitzcuintlis* would guide the spirits of the dead to the next world. A number of red pottery statues dating from A.D. 200 to A.D. 900 have been found near burial sites in the state of Coloma in Mexico.

Although the Inca also bred hairless dogs, it was the hairless canines of the Aztec that were chronicled by de Sahagun: "They breed in this land some dogs with no hair at all, and if they had any hair strands they were few indeed. They raise other dogs that they call *xoloitzcuintli* with no hair at all, and by night they cover them with blankets to sleep." Chihuahuas, which are much smaller, are part of this family of dogs.

De Sahagun also mentioned short and round dogs bred by the Aztec "that are very good to eat." The dogs were reported to have been fed avocados as well as corn and meat. According to Sahagun, because canines were in such high demand, dog breeders were highly respected and became wealthy. Other Spaniards, including Hernán Cortés and his crew, found the dogs so tasty that they began butchering and salting them down as food supplies for naval vessels. They consequently killed and ate so many that the breed nearly became extinct.

The Carolina dog, which physically resembles a coyote, is often termed a "primitive dog" since even today it is in the rel-atively early stages of domestication. Some of these animals still live wild in the swamps and forests of the southeastern United States. Preliminary DNA testing by the University of South Carolina indicates that the Carolina dog may be related to the earliest domesticated hunting dogs on this continent. Their resemblance to coyotes made them the target of settlers' and soldiers' rifles until they reached near extinction. Only recently has the breed been recognized and revived, although its existence in the wild is still severely threatened.

According to some anthropologists, Alaskan malamutes, which resemble Siberian huskies and are used to pull sleds throughout the Arctic, may have migrated from Asia to what is now Alaska. This occurred as early as 8 million years ago and was a journey of thousands of years. Along the way their appearance took on slight variations. Malamutes in Greenland have longer coats and shorter legs than those that live in northern Canada.

An equally strong case can be made that about 10,000 to 15,000 years ago, indigenous northern hunters domesticated

The Inuit of northern North America bred malamute dogs for the purpose of pulling sleds. These dogs, which are a popular breed today, are more closely related to wolves than are other breeds of dogs. *(U.S. Bureau of Ethnography)*

wolves. Although all dogs are descended from wolves, malamute sled dogs are their closest genetic relatives. Like wolves, sled dogs do not bark but howl instead. They have sharp ears, and thick, bushy coats that may be black, white, or a range of shades and color mixtures. Unlike wolves, they carry their tails and heads high. No matter how the breed originated, early Russian and English explorers who encountered the tribes living in the Norton Sound area of Alaska were impressed by the work dogs that the people had bred to help them hunt seals and polar bears or to act as pack carriers and sled pullers. (See also DOGSLEDS.)

The number of dogs on a sled team depended on the driver's ability to feed them, but usually the largest teams numbered about seven dogs. A seven-dog team could carry a 900-pound load on a good trail, covering as much as 55 miles a day. Driving a team of dogs was no easy task. In theory, the lead dog was trained to respond to its master's commands, and the other dogs would follow—although sometimes they did not. When the team was too slow, a woman would run ahead of them, pretending to cut meat to encourage the dogs to lunge forward. Often a driver would have to run ahead of his team to look for rocks or other hazards in the sled's path.

Although children played with the puppies, these dogs were not considered pets. Dogs were a transportation necessity and as such they were well cared for. In winter the Inuit people built small snow houses for female malamutes carrying pups. In spring they often made boots for their dogs' paws to protect them from ice crystals.

The Malamute breed received its name from a northern tribe. Alaskan huskies, which resemble malamutes but contain other strains, are thought to have been bred by Johnny Allen, an Athapascan Indian, in the 1930s.

See also ANIMALS, DOMESTICATED.

## Sources/Further Reading

Coe, Sophie. *America's First Cuisines*. Austin: University of Texas Press, 1994.

Folsom, Franklin and Mary Elting Folsom. *America's Ancient Treasures*. 4th ed. Albuquerque: University of New Mexico Press, 1993.

Josephy, Jr., Alvin M., ed. *America in 1492: The World of the Indian People Before the Arrival of Columbus*. New York: Random House, 1991.

Oswalt, Wendell. *Eskimos and Explorers*. Novato, Calif.: Chandler & Sharp Publishers, 1979.

Schwartz, Marion. *A History of Dogs in the Early Americas*. New Haven: Yale University Press, 1997.

Tannahill, Rhea. *Food in History*. New York: Stein and Day, 1973.

## dogsleds (precontact) *North American Arctic and Subarctic cultures*

Dogsleds are conveyances designed to transport people and goods over ice and snow, using specially trained dogs to pull them. (See also DOG BREEDS.) The sleds were used to convey household goods from one camp to another or to bring meat home from a kill. Under good conditions a five-dog team with sled, driver, and cargo could cover about 60 miles a day, making this form of transportation extremely efficient. Indigenous people who lived in the northern third of North America looked forward to the winter months, because the snow-covered ground meant easier travel, enabling them to use their dogsleds for about nine months out of the year. Usually the sea ice stayed frozen longer, which added another month to dogsled travel.

The runners on the bottom of a typical dogsled ranged anywhere from four to 14 feet long. They were laid out parallel to each other and then connected at regular intervals across the top with pieces of antler, bone, or, when available, wood. Because wood was scarce and often nonexistent in the Arctic, sled runners were usually carved from whale jawbones. In the interior of the continent, where whales were unavailable, other materials were used. Sometimes strips of sealskin were molded to the proper form and filled with moss and earth over which water was poured to freeze and set the form. At other times fish were covered with rawhide, shaped into runners, and frozen. They served as runners as well as a source of food in emergencies.

These rails were tied to the runners with leather thongs passed through holes in both the rails and the runners so that the final arrangement looked like a ladder. The leather lashings made a flexible frame and served as a form of shock absorber. When uneven terrain forced the runners out of parallel, the flexible sled remained intact instead of breaking apart.

Inuit people who lived in the polar region traveled across ice and snow that was relatively flat and obstacle-free. They mortised the joints of their sleds, making them rigid. (Inserting pegs into holes that have been shaped to fit them forms a mortise joint.) In order to make sure the heavily loaded sled would glide over the snow, the Inuit fitted the runners with ivory lashed on with sinew threaded through countersunk holes. When the temperature became extremely cold and the snow grainy, additional measures were needed. A sled driver would commonly "grease" runners by melting snow in his mouth, spitting the water out, and rubbing it over the runners, where it would freeze and become slick.

Strategies for hitching dogs to their sleds varied from place to place and were adapted to the terrain that would be covered. In the far north, teams were hitched in a fan-shaped arrangement, with each dog hitched to the sled on an individual line. The lead dog, which responded to the driver's verbal commands, was connected to the sled with a 20-foot line. The other dogs' lines were about 10 feet long. Drivers hooked dogs who were new to the team and those that needed more discipline on shorter leashes, so that they would be closer to the driver, who controlled them with a flick of a whip to their ears. In an area of what is now known as Alaska, where dogsleds encountered more obstacles, the dogs were staggered on either side of a central trace. Sleds in northern Alaska,

Indigenous peoples of northern North America used dogsleds to travel and carry goods from place to place. Arctic explorers as well as the U.S. government, which used dogsleds to transport mail, later adapted this mode of transportation. *(Photograph No. PA-100614/National Archives of Canada Indian and Northern Affairs Collection)*

called carioles (see also SLEDS, CARIOLE), had built-up beds and stanchions topped with rails.

A large dog team consisted of about seven animals. Typically the malamute dogs, which had been specially bred for the purpose, would be broken to the harness at about two months. No matter how obedient the dogs were, steering a dogsled took great skill. When the sled stopped, the driver put each dog's front paw in the harness to keep the team from running away with the sled.

In the far north, snowmobiles have replaced dogsleds for much day-to-day work and travel. Consequently, dogsledding today has become a sport rather than a way of life. The Iditarod, the most well-known dogsled race, runs over 1,100 miles of rough terrain from Anchorage to Nome, Alaska. Every year 60 racing teams of up to 16 dogs each enter the race, which was first held in 1973. The Iditarod is based on a life-threatening crisis that occurred in February 1925, when a diphtheria epidemic swept through children living in Nome. The state's governor decided to transport the only antidiphtheria serum, which was in Anchorage, by train to Nenana and then the rest of the 674 miles to Nome by dogsled. Twenty drivers took part in the dogsled relay. Relying on the mode of travel honed to a fine art by indigenous people over centuries, they were able to transport the serum to Nome within a little over 127 hours after leaving Nenana.

## Sources/Further Reading

Josephy, Jr., Alvin M., ed. *America in 1492: The World of the Indian People Before the Arrival of Columbus.* New York: Random House, 1991.

Oswalt, Wendell. *Eskimos and Explorers.* Novato, Calif.: Chandler & Sharp Publishers, 1979.

Powell, J. W. *Ninth Annual Report of the Bureau of Ethnology to the Secretary of the Smithsonian Institution 1887–88.* Washington, D.C.: Government Printing Office, 1892.

**dome houses** See IGLOOS.

**domesticated animals** See ANIMALS, DOMESTICATED.

**double cropping (multiple cropping)** (precontact)
*North American Northeast, Southeast, and Great Plains cultures*
Double or multiple cropping consists of making a series of plantings of crops in the same plot of ground so that the seeds will mature at different times. This practice ensures a supply of produce during the growing season and provides a form of "crop insurance" against failure from bouts of bad weather or insect damage. Indians of North America routinely made two

and sometimes three successive plantings of crops. Colonial farmers soon adopted this practice.

The Creek and Cherokee Indians, who lived in what is now Georgia, and the Apalachee and Timucua Indians, who lived in what is now north Florida, practiced multiple cropping, as did the Hidatsa people, who lived along the northern Missouri River. Buffalo Bird Woman, a Hidatsa woman born in about 1839, told anthropologist Gilbert Wilson that her tribe made two plantings of CORN each year so that green corn could be eaten late in the season. The second planting was made when the June berries were ripe. "Nearly every garden owner made such a 'second planting' it was, indeed, a usual practice in the tribe," she reported.

See also AGRICULTURE; COMPANION PLANTING.

**Sources/Further Reading**
Hurt, R. Douglas. *Indian Agriculture in the Americas: Prehistory to Present.* Lawrence: University Press of Kansas, 1988.
Wilson, L. Gilbert. *Buffalo Bird Woman's Garden: Agriculture of the Hidatsa Indians.* Reprint. St. Paul: Minnesota Historical Society Press, 1987.

**drainage, surgical and wound** (precontact) *North American Southwest cultures*
A medical drain is an exit or tube for discharge of morbid matter from a wound or incision. One of the American Indian tribes that used surgical or wound drains was the Mescalero Apache of the Southwest. The Apache treated deep wounds caused by accidents or warfare with drains in order to speed up healing. The drains resembled wicks. Some were made from slippery elm and some were from cotton that had been twisted to the size of a kerosene lamp wick or a tongue depressor. The Apache placed one of these drains in the bottom of the wound and then sutured it in place. These drains would allow any discharge to exit the wound via the drain. Within about nine days they would remove the drain.

See also SURGERY.

**Sources/Further Reading**
Adams. "Aboriginal American Medicine and Surgery." *Proceedings of the Indiana Academy of Science* 60 (1951): 51–12.
Vogel, Virgil. *American Indian Medicine.* Norman: University of Oklahoma Press, 1977.

**drawing salve** See SALVE, DRAWING.

**dreamwork psychology** (precontact) *North American Northeast cultures*
Dream interpretation is an important technique some modern psychologists use as part of therapy or psychoanalysis. Analysts trained in Freudian psychology believe that dreams reveal a person's hidden desires. Those trained in Jungian psychology believe that dreams often offer important guidance for the

dreamer. Precontact Huron people held the same beliefs and made dream interpretation an integral part of their emotional, spiritual, and social lives. Beginning in 1612, Jesuit priests went among the Huron (Wyandot), meticulously detailing traditional belief systems so that an understanding of these so-called primitive beliefs would make them more effective in their religious mission to convert the Indians to Christianity.

The Huron held the sophisticated conviction that the soul had a dual nature, and unifying that duality was the main task during a person's life. Every soul was thought to have hidden but also very powerful desires. These desires were often revealed in dreams, when the soul was thought to travel to another reality. When the soul's desires were not met, it became angry. That anger caused the person, whose soul was upset, to become ill or suffer other misfortunes. When the soul's desire was satisfied, the person would recover. Some dreams expressed a desire for an object and others gave warnings or trouble that could be averted only if the soul's wishes were gratified. Others expressed the longing to act in ways that normally were not socially acceptable. These dreams sometimes had to do with sexual desires. The final category of dreams in Huron belief were those that contained a visit from a guardian spirit asking for offerings.

Huron who had these dreams were given community support in the fulfillment of their soul's desires. Sometimes dreamers received donations from their neighbors, and sometimes after such dreams they gave feasts, so that their soul would keep its part of the bargain. By identifying the dreamer's subconscious desires and then providing a structured way to address them, the Huron allowed troubled tribal members to act out repressed needs in a positive, socially acceptable manner, thus fostering emotional healing. Modern psychoanalysis is based on the theory that repressed desires, conflicts, and needs are often revealed in dreams and that, by consciously working with this dream material, clients can attain a higher level of mental health. Although the Huron belief about dreams is very similar to that of the Freudian concept of the subconscious and the Jungian concept of the collective consciousness, it predates those theories by hundreds of years.

The Iroquois were also frequently alluded to as having developed and practiced dream psychotherapy, which was well established by the time the Jesuits became aware of it during the 1600s. In his book *Man's Rise to Civilization,* Peter Farb cites an Iroquois describing that group's dream psychotherapy to a Jesuit priest: "In addition to the desires which we generally have that are free, or at least voluntary in us [and] which arise from a previous knowledge of some goodness that we imagine to exist in the thing desired, [we] believe that our souls have other desires, which are, as it were, inborn and concealed. These . . . come from the depths of the soul, not through any knowledge, but by means of a certain blind transporting of the soul to certain objects." Farb goes on to state, "The Iroquois recognized the existence of an unconscious, the force of unconscious desires, how the conscious mind attempts to repress unpleasant thoughts, how these unpleasant thoughts often emerge in dreams, and how the frustration of unconscious desires may cause mental and physical (psychosomatic) illnesses." (Psychosomatic illnesses have physical symptoms that are induced by mental processes.)

See also FREE ASSOCIATION.

### Sources/Further Reading

Borger, Irene. "Ritual Process of the Iroquois False Face Society." *Dreamworks* 2, no. 4 (Summer 1982): 301–309.

Farb, Peter. *Man's Rise to Civilization as Shown by the Indians of North America from Primeval Times to the Coming of the Industrial State.* New York: E. P. Dutton & Company, 1968.

Hurst, David, Jay Miller, Richard White, Peter Nabokov, and Philip Deloria. *The Native Americans.* Atlanta: Turner Publishing, Inc., 1993.

Trigger, Bruce G. *Case Studies in Anthropology: The Huron Farmers of the North.* New York: Holt Rinehart and Winston, 1969.

Wallace, A. F. "Dreams and the Wishes of the Soul: A Type of Psychoanalytic Theory among the Seventeenth-Century Iroquois." *American Anthropologist* 60, no. 2 (April 1958): 234–238.

**drill bits, metal** (ca. 5000–3000 B.C.)   *North American Northeast and Arctic, Mesoamerican, South American Andean cultures*

The prehistoric Indians of America made metal drill bits that they used with bow drills for boring holes. (See also DRILLS, BOW.) The oldest one that has been found is approximately 5,000–7,000 years old. It was produced by Paleo-Indians living in the present-day southern Great Lakes area. This drill bit was made of copper, and it resembled the drill bits of today.

The Maya, whose culture arose in Mesoamerica in about 1500 B.C., and South American Andean culture groups invented the second type of metal drill bit. It, too, was made of copper, but the similarity ended there. These drill bits resembled short pieces of copper tubing. Their length and diameter varied, depending on the job to be accomplished. These bits were used primarily for stone (see also STONEMASONRY TECHNIQUES) and dental work (see also DENTISTRY).

The end of this type of drill bit was placed against the material to be drilled. Unlike a solid bit, when the hollow drill bit was turned, it cut a donut-shaped circular hole. After the hole had been bored to a depth of about $\frac{1}{2}$ inch, the drill was removed. The person broke off the cylindrical piece left standing in the center of the hole, and then began the drilling process again. This was done until the desired depth was achieved.

### Sources/Further Reading

Benson, Elizabeth P. *The Maya World.* New York: Thomas Y. Crowell Company, 1967.

Driver, Harold E. *Indians of North America.* Chicago: University of Chicago Press, 1969.

Fastlicht, Samuel. *Tooth Mutilations and Dentistry in Pre-Columbian Mexico.* Mexico City: Quintessense Books, 1971.

Maxwell, James A. *America's Fascinating Indian Heritage.* Pleasantville, N.Y.: Reader's Digest Books, 1978.

**drills, bow** (A.D. 1000)   *North American Arctic, Mesoamerican cultures*

The Thule people, who lived in northern Alaska about A.D. 1000, invented a number of tools to help them adapt to the cold climate in which they lived. The most impressive of these inventions was the bow drill, which used the mechanical principle of converting the back-and-forth motion of a bow into the rotation of the shaft. They made drill bits from the leg bone of a seal then used the bits to make holes in wood, bone, and ivory. The bit was shaped so that it was concave on one side and convex on the other and had beveled edges. The Thule and later the Inuit placed it into a tapered wooden shaft. They then inserted this shaft into a stone socket that had itself been placed into a wooden mouthpiece. The mouthpiece allowed the person using the drill to put weight on the shaft while leaving both hands free to work the bow that was used to turn the shaft. This bow was usually made of ivory and averaged about 16 inches long.

A variation of the bow drill was also used to start fires. The friction of the wooden shaft (with no bit) on soft wood produced enough heat to light tinder and kindle a fire. Unlike bow drills, fire-starting drills were usually worked with a strap rather than a loose-thonged bow. In addition to drills, which were part of complex TOOL KITS, the Thule also invented, multiple-part, sinew-backed recurved bows (see also BOWS, LAMINATED) and detachable harpoon points (see also HARPOONS).

The Maya, whose culture arose in about A.D. 1500 in Mesoamerica, used a form of bow drill for dental procedures (see also DENTISTRY) and for finely detailed stonework (see also JADE). The bits they used were metal. (See also DRILL BITS, METAL.) Other Mesoamerican and South American culture groups also used the bow drill.

### Sources/Further Reading

Fastlicht, Samuel. *Tooth Mutilations and Dentistry in Pre-Columbian Mexico.* Mexico City: Quintessense Books, 1971.

Josephy, Jr., Alvin M., ed. *America in 1492: The World of the Indian People Before the Arrival of Columbus.* New York: Random House, 1991.

Murdoch, John. *Ethnological Results of the Point Barrow Expedition Annual Report of the U.S. Bureau of Ethnology 1887–1888.* Washington, D.C.: Government Printing Office, 1892.

Oswalt, Wendell. *Eskimos and Explorers.* Novato, Calif.: Chandler & Sharp Publishers, 1979.

**duck decoys**   See DECOYS, DUCK.

Bow drills such as this one were originally part of the tool kits of the Thule people who lived in northern Alaska in about A.D. 1000. Craftsmen used the drills to make holes in wood, bone, and ivory. *(Photograph No. NRIA-WME-PHOTOS-P898/National Archives and Records Administration—Pacific Alaska Region)*

## ducks, muscovy (*Cairina moschata*) (100 B.C.)

*Mesoamerican, South American Andean cultures*

The Maya and Aztec domesticated muscovy ducks as a source of food. The ducks, which are the largest breed in the world, are closely related to wood ducks and are the only domesticated duck that did not come from mallard stock. The Spaniards, who were more interested in domesticated turkeys (see also TURKEY BREEDING), left few records about Aztec duck raising. Muscovy duck bones have been found in what is now Ecuador in Maya archaeological sites dated from 100 B.C. to A.D. 800. The Maya culture arose in about 1500 B.C. in Mesoamerica. Although no duck bones have been found in Peru, an Inca ruler sent some ducks to Francisco Pizarro as he advanced on the empire's capitol. This would indicate that the Inca, who lived in what is now Peru starting in about A.D. 1000, had ducks.

Despite the fact that the Spaniards wrote little about the domestication of ducks by the indigenous people of Meso- and South America, they did take muscovy ducks to Europe, where they became the most popular duck raised there. More than 70 percent of ducks consumed in Europe today are muscovy. They are prized for their unique flavor and the fact that they are low in fat. (Because muscovy ducks originated in a warm climate, they did not develop the body fat northern ducks did in order to stay warm.)

Since muscovy ducks do not have highly developed oil glands, they rarely swim. They do fly, however, a fact that is amazing considering their size. Males grow from 10 to 15 pounds and females average five to seven pounds. The feet of muscovy ducks have sharp claws that enable them to grab tree limbs and roost. In addition to claws, a bright red crest around their eyes and above their beaks distinguishes muscovy ducks. Although wild muscovies are white or black, domestic muscovy ducks come in many colors, including blue, blue and white, brown, brown and white, black and white.

See also ANIMALS, DOMESTICATED.

### Sources/Further Reading

Coe, Sophie. *America's First Cuisines.* Austin: University of Texas Press, 1994.

Driver, Harold E. *Indians of North America.* Chicago: University of Chicago Press, 1969.

Stahl, P. W., and Presley Norton. "Precolumbian Animal Domestication from Salango, Ecuador." *American Antiquity* 52, no. 2 (1987): 382–391.

**dumplings** (precontact) *North American Northeast, Mesoamerican, South American Andean cultures*
Dumplings—lumps of dough boiled in water or broth until they are cooked—were a part of American Indian cuisine throughout North America. Typically, the dough was made from CORNMEAL and water. The Iroquois made dumplings or boiled corn bread from HOMINY flour mixed with boiling water to make a paste. To flavor the dough they added BLACKBERRIES, STRAWBERRIES, BLUEBERRIES, BLACK WALNUTS, or BEANS. The dough was shaped into a round disk about an inch and a half thick and then boiled for about an hour. It was sliced and eaten hot or cold, sometimes with maple syrup. Indians of the Eastern Woodlands sometimes used berry juice as the boiling liquid in order to produce a dessert.

The Aztec, whose empire was established about A.D. 1100 in what are now Mexico and parts of Mesoamerica, sometimes steamed tortillas in an *olla,* or clay cooking pot. The Inca, who established an empire in what is now Peru in about A.D. 1000, also made steamed dumplings from QUINOA. A plant that produces seeds that are high in nutritional value, quinoa was a staple in the Inca diet.

### Sources/Further Reading

Coe, Sophie. *America's First Cuisines.* Austin: University of Texas Press, 1994.

Nabhan, Gary. *Enduring Seeds: Native American Agriculture and Wild Plant Conservation.* San Francisco: North Point Press, 1989.

Oneida Tribe. *Three Sisters Cookbook.* URL: http://www.one-web.orgt/oneida/food-index.html. Downloaded on January 5, 1998.

**dyes** (precontact) *North American, Mesoamerican, Circum-Caribbean, South American cultures*
American Indians developed dyeing techniques, including the use of mordents (substances that prepare fiber to accept dye) and fixatives, a technology as equally advanced as those developed by other cultures at that time. The materials they used to impart pigments to textiles, baskets, feathers, and leather depended on what was available in the areas in which they lived. Not only did Indians use dyes for the above-mentioned items, they also developed edible FOOD COLORING. Many of the natural sources of American Indian pigments were adopted by Europeans who came to the New World, including a yellow dye made from the wood of a tree native to the West Indies and South America. At least one of these indigenous dyes, COCHINEAL, which imparted a brilliant crimson color, became an important trade item between the New World and the Old. The Maya, Aztec, and Inca all obtained a brilliant crimson from the cochineal, a tiny insect that lives on cactus. (The Maya culture arose in about 1500 B.C. in Mesoamerica. The Aztec established their empire in the same area about A.D. 1100. The Inca Empire was established in what are now Peru and parts of Bolivia in about A.D. 1000.)

The Maya are best known for their expert dyeing and WEAVING TECHNIQUES used to produce material that they used in TRADE. TIE-DYEING and batik were two sophisticated techniques the Maya used to color fabrics. (Batik uses wax to protect parts of the fabric from absorbing dye and is applied in patterns.) The Maya still use these techniques today as well as many of their original dyes. They and later the Aztec used genipa seeds to produce black. Dyers obtained lavender pigment from murex mollusks (*Purpura patula L.*) found along the seacoast. The Indians rubbed the mollusks against each other to extract the pigment from a gland in the gills. Textiles that had been dyed with the mollusk pigment found a ready market in Europe. Maya weavers also used INDIGO, Brazilwood, log wood, annatto or ACHIOTE, and genipa, in addition to mineral pigments. The Maya used an extract from crushed tempate (*Jatropha curcas L.*) leaves as a mordant to set the colors. They also used boiled rosemary for the same purpose. At the time of the Spanish invasion, observers noted that the dyes the indigenous people used in the area known today as Guatemala and El Salvador produced brilliant colors and were color-fast.

In the North American Southwest, American Indians used more than 20 species of plants to dye fabric. Mountain mahogany roots produced red dyes, and rabbit brush flowers and the entire Indian tea plant yielded yellows. The Hopi dyed with SUNFLOWERS. Three-leaf sumac twigs and leaves were mixed with pinion gum to produce a deep black. The three-leaf sumac served as a mordant to fix the color to the fiber. The Navajo (Dineh) used wild rhubarb roots to produce colors ranging from yellow, orange, and red to green and brown. They used ashes boiled in water to set dyes into fabric. Some western tribes used earth to obtain blues. Others made dyes from algae found in stagnant bodies of water.

In the North and Northwest, members of the Colville tribe, the Nez Perce, and the Flathead (Salish) dyed fabric yellow with the Oregon grape and used alder to produce a brown. Indians in the Columbia Plateau Region made dyes from red, orange, and yellow clay, as well as from algae scraped from river rocks, which produced a green color. Ground cedar was used in the northwest by the Blackfeet to set dyes.

On the plains, the Sioux (Dakota, Lakota, Nakota) used buffalo berries and currants to produce red. Prairie dock roots served as mordant. HICKORY nuts and BLACK WALNUTS produced blacks, as did wild GRAPES. They made yellow from sunflowers and yellow coneflowers. According to a modern informant, the Oglala Lakota living near the Badlands in what are now the Dakotas collected fine soil, possibly alum, from that area, mixed it with ground-up, pigment-containing plant materials, shaped it into balls, and burned it in a fire. When these dye balls were removed, they were pulverized and mixed with water to produce a fade-proof dye.

The Chippewa (Anishinabe) of the Upper Midwest obtained a light blue dye from larkspur flowers and a darker blue from BLUEBERRIES. Very old rotten maple wood and sandstone dust produced blue and purple. Their neighbors, the Potawatomi, used the inner bark from speckled alder and red oak for yellow, red, and brown. Sandbar willow roots yielded scarlet, as did wild strawberry fruits and scent wood. Blood root produced orange, and yellow came from the sap of the spotted touch-me-not and from black-eyed Susan flowers. They fixed these dyes with wild plum bark. The Iroquois of the Eastern Woodlands made red dye from the juice of CRANBERRIES. In addition to dyeing clothing, American Indians used vegetable dyes to color food. (See also FOOD COLORING.)

**Sources/Further Reading**

Bliss, Anne. *North American Dye Plants.* Boulder, Colo.: Juniper House, 1976.

Dunmire, William W. and Gail D. Tierney. *Wild Plants of the Pueblo Province: Exploring Ancient and Enduring Uses.* Santa Fe: Museum of New Mexico Press, 1995.

Forest Preserve District of Cook County Illinois. *Nature Bulletin No. 216-A,* 1966.

Grae, Ida. *Nature's Colors: Dyes from Plants.* New York: Macmillan Publishing Company, Inc., 1974.

Harris, Jennifer, ed. *Textiles, 5,000 Years.* New York: Harry N. Abrams, Inc. Publishers, 1993.

Osborne, Lilly de Jongh. *Indian Crafts of Guatemala and El Salvador.* Norman: University of Oklahoma Press, 1975.

von Hagen, Victor Wolfgang. *The Aztec Man and Tribe.* New York: New American Library, Inc., 1961.

**dyeing, tie**  See TIE-DYEING.

# E

**earache treatments** (precontact) *North American Northeastern, Mesoamerican cultures*

The Aztec Empire was established in about A.D. 1100 in Mesoamerica. Aztec physicians were experts at treating earaches. If the cause of the pain was an infection or abscess, these ancient doctors treated the problem in two steps. The first was to lance the infected gland or area, which drained the wound. Physicians then applied a poultice of datura (*Datura stramonium*), or jimson weed to the injured ear. The datura plaster provided anesthesia and relief to the patient. (See also ANESTHETICS.)

The Mohegan of the New England area used American hops (*Humulus Lupulus L.* and *H. Americanus*) for earache. They heated the leaves and applied them to the injured area. They also used sumac (*Rhus glabra L.*) both as a poultice for earaches and to successfully treat boils. Mohegan healers poured a sumac-based tea into the problem ear, much like modern ear drops are administered today.

Another treatment for earaches that was used by the Mesquaki of the Great Lakes area was wild ginger (*Asarum canadense L.*). The Indians ground or pounded the root of the wild ginger into a pulp and then boiled it. Once the mixture had cooled, they poured the liquid into the infected ear. Medical researchers have discovered that wild ginger contains two properties that are antibiotic in nature. According to James A. Duke, a botanist who studied medicinal plants for the United States Department of Agriculture, chemicals called *sesquiterpenes* that are present in ginger are effective against the common cold virus *rhinovirus*. Chemicals called gingerols and shogaols relieve pain.

See also ANTIBIOTIC MEDICATIONS; MEDICINES; PHARMACOLOGY.

## Sources/Further Reading

Duke, James A. *The Green Pharmacy.* New York: St. Martins Press, 1997.

Weiner, Michael A. *Earth Medicine Earth Food: The Classic Guide to the Herbal Remedies and Wild Plants of the North American Indians.* New York: Fawcett Columbine, 1980.

Vogel, Virgil. *American Indian Medicine.* Norman: University of Oklahoma Press, 1970.

**earth lodges** (A.D. 700) *North American Great Plains and Arctic cultures*

A number of North American Great Plains tribes used earth as a natural insulator to keep their homes warm in winter and for the storage of crops. Built into a hillside or made with earth-bermed walls and covered by a heavily thatched, earth-topped roof, such homes not only provided insulation, they also sheltered residents from drafts. Earth lodges also served as an excellent defense against enemy attack. (See also MILITARY TACTICS.)

The Mandan, Hidatsa, and Arikara began building earth lodges about A.D. 700 along streams that emptied into the Missouri River. The Pawnee, Omaha, Ponca, and Oto tribes also constructed these dwellings. The earliest earth lodges were rectangular; only later did they evolve into circular structures. Round homes were usually built by sinking four large central posts, often made of cottonwood, into the ground. Ancient builders then joined the posts with crossbeams and circled this frame with a wider ring of posts and crossbeams. Rafters radiated out from the central support to the outer ring. Mortised joints connected them, providing a solid support for the weight of the earth that would be heaped on the roof. (A mortised joint consists of a projection shaped to precisely fit into a hole.) They covered the frame with slanting posts of split planks called puncheons to support the earthen walls. An overlay of brush ensured that the layer of earth heaped over the house would not wash away.

French explorer Pierre de la Vérendrye was the first European to see an earth lodge. On his journeys near what is now

Earth lodges such as this one constructed by the Pawnee of the Great Plains not only provided protection from the elements but also served as an excellent defense. Modern architects have adapted the concept of the earth lodge to create energy-saving earth-bermed homes. *(Photograph No. NWDNS-106-INE-3/Smithsonian Institution Bureau of American Ethnology, ca. 1871–ca. 1907/National Archives and Records Administration at College Park)*

Bismarck, North Dakota, he visited a Mandan village that had 130 such structures. He later wrote: ". . . The streets and squares [are] very clean, the ramparts very level and broad; the palisade supported on cross-pieces mortised into posts of fifteen feet."

Inuit who lived in the McKenzie River region of Alaska also built earth-covered lodges. Constructed in the shape of a cross with a frame of driftwood, the home was topped with earth and snow. Water was then poured over it and left to freeze in place. A long underground tunnel served as the entryway and blocked cold air from entering through the doorway. A skylight made from a block of ice was positioned in the center of the roof, allowing for light. Separate families lived in each of the wings of the home, which was occupied only part of the year. (See also APARTMENT COMPLEXES.) The rest of the year the Inuit lived in dome houses that they built from snow and ice. (See also IGLOOS.) The Inuit living in the west of what is now Greenland built houses of turf and stones. They made windows that they framed with wood and covered with halibut stomachs or seal intestines to keep out the wind while letting in the light.

In modern times architects and housing "innovators" are taking another look at underground, or berm, housing as a low-cost alternative to conventional construction, as well as a way to cut heating and cooling costs.

See also CARPENTRY TECHNIQUES; INSULATION, HOME.

**Sources/Further Reading**

Josephy, Jr., Alvin M. ed. *America in 1492: The World of the Indian People Before the Arrival of Columbus.* New York: Random House, 1991.
Nabokov, Peter and Robert Easton. *Native American Architecture.* New York: Oxford University Press, 1989.
Oswalt, Wendell. *Eskimos and Explorers.* Novato, Calif.: Chandler & Sharp Publishers, 1979.

**ecology** (precontact) *North American, Mesoamerican, Circum-Caribbean, South American cultures*
Ecology is the science of the relationship between living organisms and their environment. It examines how everything in the world or ecosystem is interconnected and studies the impact of how each part of the environment affects the others. The modern science of ecology, which developed in the mid-1900s in response to concerns about air and water pollution and other damage to the environment, is built on principles known by American Indians for thousands of years.

Despite the differences among them, the indigenous peoples of North, Meso-, and South America shared a common thread of belief. Traditional Native American spirituality taught that all creatures—two-legged, four-legged, and winged—and plants were related. Many tribal religions taught that long ago people and animals shared the same language. Many indigenous people viewed the Earth as a mother or grandmother. In some tribes the Creator, later translated as the Great Spirit in North America, was seen as grandfather. American Indians therefore believed that individual people were a small part of a very large family, and for this reason they placed high value on cooperation. People, plants, animals, the rocks, the land, and natural forces like wind and water were all considered to be interconnected, like partners. Everything placed on Earth was a potential helper in this partnership. For instance, wild plants like sage were not considered weeds by Indian peoples as they were by Europeans. Instead, such plants were used as food or as medicines to heal people.

These beliefs affected the way American Indians lived their daily lives. In the upper Midwest of North America, for example, the Chippewa (Anishinabe), who harvested WILD RICE on the lakes of what are now Minnesota and Wisconsin, only took part of the rice, leaving the rest to go to seed. Northern Plains tribes, whose survival depended on BISON, typically used every part of the animal, wasting nothing. Tribes in the Northwest who fished for salmon did not try to snare all of them from the streams where the fish had come to spawn, although they had the fishing technology to do so. They understood that in order to ensure continuing harvests of fish, they had to conserve this renewable resource. Indigenous agriculturists throughout the Americas, such as the Maya of Mesoamerica, planted crops on a piece of land for two or three years and then allowed the land to rest in order to renew itself. (See also MILPA.) (Maya culture arose in what is now the Yucatán Peninsula of Mexico in about 1500 B.C.) North American Indians managed forests by cutting or burning underbrush, working in partnership with nature. (See also FOREST MANAGEMENT.)

In addition to the desire to remain in balance with their surroundings, American Indian ecologists were motivated by respect and gratitude. "The old people literally came to love the soil," wrote Luther Standing Bear of his Lakota people in *Land of the Spotted Eagle*. "They sat on the ground with the feeling of being close to a mothering power. It was good for the skin to touch the earth, and the old people liked to remove their MOCCASINS and walk with their bare feet on the sacred earth. The soil was soothing, strengthening, cleansing and healing."

The traditional Indian attitude that the earth is a good place filled with good things to feed, clothe, shelter, and heal the people ran counter to that of the European colonists who spent much of their time fighting to subdue natural forces rather than striving to live in harmony with them. The underlying European belief system taught that the material world—what can be touched, heard, seen, tasted, and smelled—was evil. Worldliness was considered sin.

For the most part, Christian colonizers thought themselves better than plants and animals, because they believed their God had ordained them to rule over the natural environment, much like the chain of emperors and kings that had ruled throughout Western history since Roman times. They justified this by quoting the Bible, Genesis 1, verse 24: "And God said, Let us make man in our image, after our likeness: and let them have dominion over the fish of the sea, and over the fowl of the air, and over the cattle, and over all the earth, and over every creeping thing that creepeth upon the earth."

American Indian belief systems were very focused on the places where important spiritual events took place. Most, if not all, American Indian tribes regarded certain natural places as especially sacred. Some of these were believed to be the site where the first people of the tribe were created. Others marked the location of other sacred events in the history of the tribe. Still other ground was considered sacred because it had been used for religious ceremonies for centuries. These beliefs continue today. Indigenous peoples of the Americas considered it their responsibility to care for these places.

Since conquest, many acres of private and public land, from the Amazon Basin to the frozen tundra of the North American subarctic, have been damaged as a result of logging, dam building, farming, ranching, road building, mining, development, and waste disposal. Many species of plants and animals are now extinct, either because of slaughter, or human-made changes to their natural habitat. Since the beginning of colonization, American Indians warned that the harm done to the environment would have dire consequences. For the most part, the colonizers ignored these warnings or regarded them as primitive superstitions.

Before the mid-20th century, only a few non-Indians spoke out about the need to protect the environment. One was Henry David Thoreau, a transcendentalist New England author who wrote *On Walden Pond* and *The Maine Woods*. Not until 1866 was the word *ecology* coined by German biologist Ernst Haeckel to describe looking at the environment as a system of interconnected parts. Even so, his "new" ideas were met with little popular support.

In 1962, with the publication of Rachel Carson's book *Silent Spring*, about the dangers of pesticides to humans, a number of people began to become alarmed about the consequences of environmental damage. Carson summarized her main argument in the book: "The 'control of nature' is a phrase conceived in arrogance, born of the Neanderthal age of biology and philosophy, when it was supposed that nature exists for the convenience of man." This idea supported American Indian beliefs that had been held for centuries, and it spurred concerned citizens into action. In 1969 the U.S. Congress passed the National Environmental Policy Act and created the Environmental Protection Agency.

In the 1970s James Lovelock created a theory called the Gaia hypothesis. He asserted that Earth is a self-sustaining system that modifies its surroundings to ensure its own survival—that is, it is a living organism. According to Lovelock, attention needed to be paid to the Earth's ecological subsystems, such as oceans, forests, and the atmosphere, since they were all dependent on one another. Although his notion that the Earth was a living thing seemed new to many non-Indians, it was the same philosophy that American Indians believed and lived by long before the coming of the colonists. "The earth is our mother," Bedagi, a Penobscot Indian told author Natalie Curtis in 1907. "She nourishes us; that which we put into the ground, she returns to us, and healing plants she gives us likewise."

The modern science of ecology owes a debt to the holistic thinking and practices of American Indians. In November 1995 President Bill Clinton gave credit where it was due in a proclamation declaring November as American Indian Heritage Month. "The gift of wisdom is one that our society has struggled with," he said. "Living in harmony with nature instead of seeking domination, American Indians have shown us how to be responsible for our environment, to treasure the beauty and resources of the land and water for which we are stewards, and to preserve them for the generations who will come after us."

Despite the extensive body of indigenous traditional ecological knowledge that still exists today, such as the uses and significance of plants and the migration patterns of animals and birds, much of it is often ignored by governments, policymakers, and business interests. In recent years, American Indians have formed organizations to ensure their voices are heard in environmental issues that affect not only tribal lands but also the planet as a whole, such as air and water pollution and toxic waste disposal.

See also AQUACULTURE; WHALING.

## Sources/Further Reading

Anderson, Kat. *Before the Wilderness: Environmental Management by Native Californians.* Menlo Park, Calif.: Ballena Publishers, 1993.

Anderson, Kat and Gary P. Nabhan. "Gardeners in Eden." *Wilderness* 55, no. 194: 27.

Booth, Annie L. and Harvey M. Jacobs. *Environmental Consciousness—Native American Worldviews and Sustainable Natural Resource Management: An Annotated Bibliography.* Chicago: Council of Planning Librarians, 1988.

Carmody, Delise Lardner and John Tully Carmody. *Native American Religions: An Introduction.* New York: Paulist Press, 1993.

Clinton, Bill. *Proclamation of American Indian Heritage Month 1995.* URL: http://www.publications-admin@whitehouse.gov. Posted November 2, 1995.

Cornell, George L. "The Influence of Native Americans on Modern Conservationists." *Environmental Review* 9: 2 (Summer 1985) 9: 104–117.

Curtis, Natalie. *The Indians' Book.* New York: Harper & Brothers, 1907.

Deloria, Vine, Jr. *God Is Red: A Native View of Religion.* Golden, Colo.: Fulcrum, 1994.

Durning, Alan. "Guardians of the Land: Indigenous Peoples and the Health of the Earth." *Paper Number 112.* Washington, D.C.: Worldwatch Institute, 1992.

Hirschfelder, Arlene and Paulette Molin. *Encyclopedia of Native American Religions.* New York: Facts On File, 1992.

Hughes, J. Donald. *American Indian Ecology.* El Paso: Texas Western Press, 1983.

Lovelock, James. *Gaia: A New Look at Life on Earth.* New York: Oxford University Press, 1987.

Michaelsen, Robert S. "We Also Have a Religion: The Free Exercise of Religion Among Native Americans." *American Indian Quarterly* (Summer 1983): 111–142.

Standing Bear, Luther. *Land of the Spotted Eagle.* Boston: Houghton Mifflin, 1933.

Vecsey, Christopher, ed. *Handbook of American Indian Religious Freedom.* New York: The Crossroad Publishing Company, 1993.

**education, compulsory** See COMPULSORY EDUCATION.

**elections** (ca. A.D. 1100) *Mesoamerican cultures*
Contrary to popular belief, the process of free elections, whereby people have the opportunity or right to choose their leaders freely, did not begin in the Americas with the U.S. Constitution. The Aztec, whose empire was established in Mesoamerica in about A.D. 1100, held free elections centuries before those held in the United States. Aztec lords could not inherit these leadership positions. They had to be nominated first, then elected by popular vote during the initial phase of the empire. Those nominated were honorable, wise, and capable. After election, district chiefs, or *calpulli,* were then confirmed by the emperor. Through the reign of these officials, heads of families were gathered in city plazas where they made their wishes known about the leader's proposals by voice vote. The *tecuhtli,* who governed cities and towns, appointed the officials who served beneath them. As time progressed and population increased, public assemblies and voice votes became impractical. Leaders were then chosen by a small group of people with high status in the community, who formed an electoral college. By the time of conquest only the emperor and his four top officials continued to be elected. Although Aztec emperors were chosen by the people they ruled, in theory, they were believed to have been divinely chosen.

## Sources/Further Reading

Peredo, Guizman Miguel. *Medical Practices in Ancient America.* Ediciones Euroamericanas: Mexico City, 1985.

Soustelle, Jacques. *Daily Life of the Aztecs on the Eve of Spanish Conquest.* Stanford: Stanford University Press, 1961.

**electricity** (ca. 200 B.C.–A.D. 600) *South American Andean cultures*
The most extraordinary and amazing invention of precontact American Indians was producing electricity through chemical means. Electricity is the physical phenomenon that arises from the interaction of electrical charges. The Moche, whose culture arose in what is now Peru in about 200 B.C., invented the electrochemical production of electricity. They produced electricity by using water and chemicals that they found naturally occur-

ring in their environment. The first step was to produce an acid solution to act as an acid bath. The next step was to produce an electric current. The Moche accomplished this by dipping copper into the acid solution. Copper is unique in that it can act as both an anode (a positively charged electrode) and cathode (a negatively charged electrode). Both are necessary to produce an electrical current. When the copper was dipped into the acid solution, an electrical current was produced. The Moche used the electricity only for electroplating.

See also ELECTROPLATING.

### Sources/Further Reading

Bynum, W. F., E. J. Browne, and Roy Porter, ed. *Dictionary of the History of Science.* Princeton, N.J.: Princeton University Press, 1981.

Donnan, Christopher B. "Masterworks of Art Reveal a Remarkable Pre-Inca World." *National Geographic* 177, no. 6 (June 1990): 17–29.

Morris, Craig and von Hagen, Adriana. *The Inka Empire and Its Andean Origins.* New York: Abbeville Press Publishers, 1993.

### electroplating (ca. 200 B.C.–A.D. 600) *South American Andean cultures*

Electroplating is the process of depositing a thin coat of one metal on the surface of another by using an electric current. It was one of many gold-plating techniques used by the Moche in South America to make items made of various metals appear as if they were actually gold. The Moche lived on the northern coast of what is now Peru from 200 B.C. to A.D. 600. Expert metalworkers, the Moche coaxed the power of ELECTRICITY from chemicals to gild copper and alloys they had made of silver, copper, and gold.

Electroplating requires a plating bath, a source of direct current, the object to be plated, and the metal that will serve as the plating. The positive terminal of the direct source is connected to the metal to be plated (the cathode), and the negative terminal is connected to the plating material (the anode). Positive charged metal ions from the plating metal migrate to the negatively charged cathode.

To invent electroplating the Moche first had to develop a corrosive liquid in which to dissolve gold for the gilding process. This was accomplished by mixing water with niter (potassium nitrate, a nitrate salt), salt (sodium chloride), and potash alum (a granular sulfur and oxygen compound). When combined, all of these chemicals, which are found in the natural environment, were able to produce a corrosive solution with a pH of nine, in other words, a strong acid. After this had occurred, the Moche dissolved gold in the solution, then they placed a copper object in it. (When dissolved in an acid solution, gold produces positively charged ions, which stay in the solution. The copper is negatively charged and will attract the positively charged gold ions.) The copper acted as both a cathode and an anode, creating the electricity. The Moche then allowed the solution to gently boil, causing a very thin coat of gold to adhere to the object that they were plating. After the metal was coated with gold, Moche metalworkers heated the object to 900-940° F in order to cause the gold to bond more permanently. (See also GOLD PLATING.)

The Moche, who also used this process for silver plating, preceded the Europeans in developing electrochemical plating by more than a thousand years. Sir Humphrey Davy (1778–1829) is credited with first isolating the alkali metals by electrolysis of fused salts. Yet American Indians, whom many Europeans of the time viewed as ignorant savages, not only had invented electricity hundreds of years before but were putting it to practical use on a regular basis. The invention of electroplating required an enormous amount of intelligence. The Moche had to have an understanding of science and, in particular, chemistry and the fundamentals of electricity and its properties. They had to experiment and organize all the resulting data to create electricity through chemical means. This was a monumental achievement of ancient American Indian chemists and metalworkers.

See also ANNEALING; METALLURGY; SOLDERING.

### Sources/Further Reading

Bynum, W. F., E. J. Browne, and Roy Porter, eds. *Dictionary of the History of Science.* Princeton, N.J.: Princeton University Press, 1981.

Donnan, Christoper B. "Masterworks of Art Reveal a Remarkable Pre-Inca World." *National Geographic* 177, no. 6 (June 1990): 2–33.

Mason, J. Alden. *The Ancient Civilizations of Peru,* Rev. ed. New York: Penguin Books, 1988.

Morris, Craig and Adriana von Hagen. *The Inka Empire and Its Andean Origins.* New York: Abbeville Press Publishers, 1993.

### embalming (ca. 5000 B.C.) *South American Andean cultures*

Embalming is the process of treating a corpse with preservatives in order to prevent decay. It is one of the main aspects of mortuary science and a part of mummification. (See also MUMMIES.) Egyptians, who are well known for their practice of embalming in conjunction with mummification, began the practice during the First Dynasty in about 2000 B.C. According to anthropologists, such embalming indicated a belief in an afterlife.

The Chinchoro, who lived in what is now Chile, were embalming as well as mummifying (wrapping) their dead, including embryos and fetuses, 7,000 years ago. Some experts believe the practice may have begun 1,000 years earlier, making the Chinchoro the world's earliest embalmers. Archaeologists have discovered that both sexes and people of all socioeconomic statuses were embalmed after death. The Chinchoro removed the internal organs of the body before treating them. They then skinned the body and disassembled it. Next they reinforced the spinal column, as well as legs and arms, with supports of wood and cane. Once they had treated the organs for preservation, the corpse was reassembled. They then filled the body cavity with fiber and feathers before coating it with clay. The clay was sculpted and painted so that it resembled faces and other features. Finally the embalmers placed a wig on the body.

Another group of South American Indians who embalmed their dead were the Paloma, whose culture arose north of where the Chinchoro lived and who were embalming by 4000 B.C. Salt was a major ingredient in the Paloma process, and the person was buried in the floor of the house he or she resided in. For a body's burial, the knees were drawn up toward the chin and against the chest.

The Inca of South America, whose empire was established in what is now Peru in about A.D. 1100, were embalming their dead at least by the 15th century. Precolonial Inca embalmers removed the viscera, or internal organs, from the body. Both the body and body cavity were then washed and allowed to dry. After this the body cavity was packed with cloth and allowed to air dry. Once the body was embalmed, it was later mummified.

Archaeologists have found traces of chemicals on the remains of Inca dead, but only powdered cinnabar (a form of MERCURY) has been positively identified. Cinnabar, which is reddish in color, is believed to have had religious significance. ALLSPICE was used by Mesoamerican tribes to embalm the dead.

**Sources/Further Reading**

Mason, J. Alden. *The Ancient Civilizations of Peru.* Rev. ed. New York: Penguin Books, 1988.
NOVA Online. "Ice Mummies of the Inca." *Mummies of the World (2).* URL: http://www.pbs.org/wgbh/nova/peru/mummies/mworld2.html. Downloaded on July 7, 1999.
von Hagen, Victor Wolfgang. *Realm of the Incas.* New York: New American Library, 1957.

**embroidery** (ca. 1800 B.C.) *Mesoamerican, South American Andean, North American Plateau cultures*
Embroidery—the technique of embellishing textiles with needlework—was developed by many ancient cultures throughout the world. In the Americas, the Maya, who lived in what are now Mexico, Guatemala, and Nicaragua starting in about 1500 B.C., are best known for their skill as embroiderers. They continue to practice the art today. Archaeologists believe that textiles (see also WEAVING TECHNIQUES), and textile embellishments began to flourish in Mesoamerica in about 1800 B.C., well before the Maya presence. Unfortunately, the region's heat and moisture have prevented few ancient textile samples from surviving to this day. Most evidence for the presence of ancient textile embellishments such as embroidery come from painted vessels, codices (see also BOOKS), and small figurines (see also POTTERY).

Textiles were an important TRADE commodity for the Maya and later the Aztec, whose empire was established in Mesoamerica in about A.D. 1100. Embroidered patterns of animals, birds, flowers, and geometric designs added value to textile goods. In addition to embroidery, ancient Mesoamericans decorated textiles with feathers, shells, BELLS, or paintings. Mesoamerican embroidery continues to be popular today and is sold throughout the world. Modern needleworkers continue to use many ancient techniques, such as sketching the design on the cloth with a bird quill dipped in INDIGO and then sewing the cloth onto a wooden frame or the top of a round basket that serves as an embroidery hoop.

The Nazca of Peru were expert embroiderers by about 400 B.C. (Nazca culture arose on the coast in about 600 B.C.) Their decorative stitches formed borders for huge cloths and were so close together that the background could not be seen through the designs. These embroiderers used a flat stitch called the stem stitch to produce their designs. By A.D. 700, they had begun to practice tapestry, a weaving technique using a weft-faced plain weave with discontinuous wefts (the vertical fibers on the loom) of different colors that are used to create patterns. Thanks to Peru's dry southern coast, fine examples of ancient Nazca embroidery and textiles exist today.

Nez Perce Indians who lived in the Columbia Plateau region of North America wove bags from bear grass and American hemp, which they then decorated with dyed plant fibers (see also DYES; HEMP, AMERICAN). Textile experts consider this weaving rather than embroidery because it was achieved by using a double weft. As the weaver worked, she twisted the weft so that the colored fiber would lie on top of the projects.

In addition to embroidery, North American Indians decorated garments and other items by sewing dyed porcupine quills to them with sinew. This technique, which is unique to the Americas, is called quillwork. North American needleworkers quickly adapted to the new materials after European contact, such as silk thread and beads, incorporating those items into their embroidery designs. The lazy stitch in beadwork is an example of the use of modern materials adapted to pre-Columbian embroidery technique.

See also TAPESTRY; TIE-DYEING.

**Sources/Further Reading**

Benson, Elizabeth P. *The Maya World.* New York: Thomas Y. Crowell Company, 1967.
Harris, Jennifer, ed. *Textiles, 5,000 Years.* New York: Harry N. Abrams, Inc. Publishers, 1993.
Osborne, Lilly de Jongh. *Indian Crafts of Guatemala and El Salvador.* Norman: University of Oklahoma Press, 1975.

**empyema treatment** See THORACENTESIS.

**enemas** (precontact) *Mesoamerican, North American Northeast cultures*
An enema is a procedure in which fluid is introduced into the colon and intestines through the rectum. It is used to treat diarrhea, hemorrhoids, constipation, and rectal bleeding not related to hemorrhoids. The Aztec, whose empire arose in about A.D. 1100 in what are now Mexico and parts of Mesoamerica,

were the first physicians in the world to use the enema administered with a rubber-bulbed syringe and rubber tubing.

North American Indians also administered enemas. Frenchman Pierre Charlevoix made one of the first reports documenting its use and describing its administration with a syringe in 1721. Virgil Vogel, author of *American Indian Medicine,* quotes Charlevoix: "They have a remedy for the bloody-flux which seldom or never fails; this is a juice expressed from the extremities of cedar branches after they have been boiled." The Menominee, a northeastern tribe of North America, used enemas to treat hemorrhoids.

See also ASTRINGENTS; LATEX; MEDICINE; SYRINGES.

## Sources/Further Reading
Hallowell, A. I. "The Bulbed Enema Syringe in North America." *American Anthropologist* 37 (1935).

Vogel, Virgil. *American Indian Medicine.* Norman: University of Oklahoma Press, 1970.

Weatherford, Jack. *Indian Givers: How the Indians of the Americas Transformed the World.* New York: Fawcett Columbine, 1988.

Wissler, Clark. *Indians of the United States.* Garden City, N.J.: Doubleday and Company, 1949.

## energy-efficient housing  See ADOBE; EARTH LODGES; INSULATION, HOME.

## ephedra (*Ephedra sinica*)  (precontact) *Mesoamerican, North American Great Basin and Southwest cultures*

Ephedrine, a chemical synthesized from the plant ephedra, is an ingredient that, until recently, was common in over-the-counter cold medicines. It is effective in causing the mucous membranes of the nose to contract and as a bronchodialator. The Aztec, whose empire was established in Mesoamerica starting in about A.D. 1100, treated symptoms of the common cold with ephedra, a plant that contains small amounts of ephedrine. In his book *Indians of North America,* anthropologist Harold Driver states ". . . a species of ephedra [was] used by the Aztec in the treatment of common colds . . ." Unlike Chinese ephedra, which is sometimes referred to as *ma huang* and contains high levels of ephedrine, ephedra that is indigenous to the New World, has a lower level of alkaloid.

Other tribes in the North American West, where ephedra also grew, used a tea boiled from its twigs as a cold medicine. These tribes included the Paiute and Shoshone people living in what is now Nevada. The Paiute also used ephedra tea to disguise the unpleasant taste of other medications. The Keres people, living in the Acoma and Laguna Pueblos and Navajo (Dineh) tribe of New Mexico, used tea made from ephedra as a cough medication. Tea made from ephedra was a common remedy for kidney ailments and was drunk as a tonic by tribes living throughout the West.

In recent years over-the-counter cold remedies and diet pills containing high levels of ephedrine, such as that found in *ma huang,* have come under scrutiny from the medical community because ephedrine raises blood pressure, increases heart rate, and stimulates the central nervous system, sometimes causing insomnia and nervousness. As a result, ephedrine has often been replaced by pseudoephedrine, which has reduced side effects.

See also MEDICINE; PHARMACOLOGY.

## Sources/Further Reading
Driver, Harold E. *Indians of North America.* Chicago: University of Chicago Press, 1969.

Lust, John. *The Herb Book.* New York: Bantam Books, 1974.

Moerman, Dan. *Native American Ethnobotany Database: Food, Drugs, Dyes and Fibers of Native North American Peoples.* URL: http://www.umd.umich.edu/cgibin/herb. Downloaded on May 11, 1999.

Taylor, Norman. *Plant Drugs that Changed the World.* New York: Dodd, Mead, and Company, 1965.

Train, Percy, James R. Henrichs, and W. Andrew Archer. *Medicinal Uses of Plants by Indian Tribes of Nevada.* Washington, D.C.: U.S. Department of Agriculture, 1941.

Vestal, Paul A. "The Ethnobotany of the Ramah Navaho." *Papers of the Peabody Museum of American Archaeology and Ethnology* 40, no. 4 (1952).

## epilepsy medicines  See ANTISPASMODIC MEDICATIONS.

## Erikson's developmental stages, American Indian influence on  (A.D. 1938) *North American Great Plains and Northwest Coast cultures*

Psychologist Erik Erikson's theory of human psychosocial development was a groundbreaking theory when it was completed in the 1950s because it broke with Sigmund Freud's idea that personality is set by the age of five. Erikson believed that development was an ongoing process. Unlike Freud, who studied the childhoods of his neurotic patients, Erikson sought to study normal childhood. His observations of indigenous child rearing practices during years that he spent among the Oglala Lakota of South Dakota and the Yurok of California, became the basis for eight developmental stages that are a cornerstone of child and developmental psychology today.

Erikson was born in Germany in 1902 of Danish parents. In 1927 he helped to establish a school in Vienna, where his interest in American Indians became evident. Part of the children's curriculum was to read about American Indians. In Vienna, Erikson was chosen by Sigmund Freud and his daughter Anna to be trained as a psychoanalyst. When Adolf Hitler rose to power, the young analyst chose to immigrate to the United States. By 1938 Erickson had become interested in the work of anthropologists, and he traveled to the Oglala Lakota reservation at Pine Ridge, South Dakota, where he spent several months. In his paper "Observations of a Sioux Education," he noted that Indian mothers were quieter and less nervous than their middle-class white counterparts and that the Indian children were breast-fed. He also observed that Indian toddlers were allowed greater freedom to explore the world around them. His work subsequently focused on the development of childhood as it unfolded in homes as well as schools.

In 1939, after moving to California, where he was affiliated with the Institute for Child Welfare, Erikson was asked to visit the Yurok tribe in the northern part of the state. There he began focusing on cultural differences in child-raising practices. It was this catalyst that caused him to break with Freud and to create his own theory of development. In its final form, the theory's stages are:

**Trust vs. Mistrust**  From birth through the first year of life, under ideal circumstances, a child learns that it is possible to grow and get his/her needs fulfilled by having physical needs met and comfort provided for by sensitive, responsive caregivers. Without this, the child cannot learn to trust.

**Autonomy vs. Shame and Doubt**  During a child's second year of life, he or she learns to become independent by asserting his or her own will in doing and exploring. When an infant is restricted too much or punished too harshly, he or she develops shame and doubt.

**Initiative vs. Guilt**  In early childhood a child learns to balance holding on and letting go as his or her social world widens. The child is also expected to assume more responsibility. When a child is made to feel too anxious, he or she feels guilt.

**Industry vs. Inferiority**  During middle and late childhood, a child learns to think logically and develop intellectual skills. Without reinforcement, the child feels incompetent.

**Identity vs. Identity Confusion**  In adolescence, young people need to find out who they are and what they want from their lives. This is a time of trying out many roles in order to find a clear sense of self. If a teenager is prevented from doing this, the result is identity confusion.

**Intimacy vs. Isolation**  The next developmental stage after adolescence is that of forming intimate relationships with others, including friends, family, and mates. If this is not learned, the person becomes isolated.

**Generativity vs. Stagnation**  During middle adulthood, the focus of development turns toward helping the younger generation in its development and in leading useful lives. When adults do not do this, they stagnate.

**Integrity vs. Despair**  Older adulthood is a time to look back over one's life and evaluate what has gone before. Depending on the person and how he or she has lived, this can lead to either integrity or despair.

See also DREAMWORK PSYCHOLOGY; PSYCHOTHERAPY.

## Sources/Further Reading

Coles, Robert. *Erik H. Erikson: The Growth of His Work.* Boston: Little, Brown, and Company, 1970.

Santrock, John W. *Life-Span Development,* 6th ed. Madison, Wisc.: Brown & Benchmark Publishers, 1997.

## etching, acid  (A.D. 100–A.D. 1100)  *North American Southwest cultures*

Etching is the process of using acid to eat into the surface of a material such as glass or metal. The earliest reference to etching in Europe that historians have discovered is that contained in a description of a coat of armor made in the 1400s. In contrast, the Hohokam, whose civilization flourished starting in about 300 B.C. and who lived in the desert of what is now Arizona, are believed to be the first people in the world to develop acid etching. The Hohokam used the etching process for artwork that they made from shells. These have been found at Snaketown, their principal village, which is near present-day Phoenix. Although archaeologists are uncertain exactly how the Hohokam achieved the etched designs, experiments conducted at Gila Pueblo have shown that fermented juice from the fruit of the saguaro cactus produces an acetic acid strong enough to eat away shell, which is nearly pure calcium carbonate. Researchers believe the Hohokam first covered shells with pitch to protect certain areas from the acid. Next the pitch was inscribed, creating a design. The acid dissolved the parts of the shell that were not coated with pitch. The shells were then immersed in an acid bath. Finally the shells were washed in order to remove both the acid and the pitch.

### Sources/Further Reading

Gladwin, Harold S., Emil W. Haury, E. B. Sayles, and Nora Gladwin. "Excavations at Snaketown: Revisions." Globe, AZ: *Medallion Papers No. 30, Gila Pueblo,* 1943.

The Hohokam, believed to be the first people in the world to invent acid etching, used it to create designs on shells. *(Arizona State Museum, University of Arizona)*

Waldman, Carl. *Atlas of the North American Indian.* New York: Facts On File, 1985.

Wormington, H. M. *Prehistoric Indians of the Southwest.* Denver: The Denver Museum of Natural History, 1978.

**etiquette classes**   See COMPULSORY EDUCATION.

**evaporative cooling**   (precontact) *North American Southeast cultures*

Many American Indian people who lived in hot, humid climates built ramadas or outdoor shades or arbors in the summer. Some of these were made of posts covered with boughs, but others were constructed with elaborate willow frames. Houses in the humid Southeast were often raised from the ground and open-sided to maximize airflow. The Seminole also had raised sleeping platforms to increase air circulation. On especially hot days, when mere air circulation was not enough, the outside walls of these homes' shades were splashed with water, so that when the water evaporated it lowered the temperature at least 10 degrees.

See also INSULATION, HOME.

**Source/Further Reading**

Nabokov, Peter and Robert Easton. *Native American Architecture.* New York: Oxford University Press, 1989.

**excision**   (A.D. 800) *Mesoamerican, South American Andean cultures*

Excision is a minor surgical procedure to remove surface growths on the skin (wens) and eyes (opthalmias) as well as similar growths. The Moche, whose civilization arose in what is now Peru in about 200 B.C., are known to have performed excisions by at least A.D. 800. The most common excisions were those of growths from the eyelid and the removal of surface tumors. The Aztec, whose empire was established in Mesoamerica in about A.D. 1100, were also known to excise cataracts from the eyes. In many cases, obsidian flint SCALPELS were used. (See also FLINTKNAPPING.) These scalpels were extremely sharp and were able to keep an edge for a long period of time when used on soft tissue.

See also CATARACT REMOVAL; SURGERY.

**Source/Further Reading**

Ortiz de Montellano, Bernard. *Aztec Medicine, Health and Nutrition.* New Brunswick, N.J.: Rutgers University Press, 1990.

**eyes, medical treatment of**   (precontact) *North American Northeast and Great Plains, Mesoamerican cultures*

American Indians used hundreds of herbs for the treatment of eye problems including infections and soreness. Their methods included eye drops, eyewashes, and eye poultices. The Illinois-Miami Indians boiled the bark of the white oak (*Quercus alba*), which grows from Canada to the Gulf of Mexico, and used it as an eyewash. After boiling the bark, the resulting mixture was an ASTRINGENT with ANTIBIOTIC properties that proved a very appropriate treatment for eye infections.

An excellent eyewash used by the American Indians who lived in what is now Minnesota and south and east of this area was goldenseal (*Hydrastis canadensis*). This herb has several common names, two of which are eye root and eye balm. The Indians steeped the roots in hot or cold water and used the result as an eye rinse. The choice of using goldenseal to treat eye infections was medically appropriate because, like white oak, the herb possesses antibiotic and astringent properties.

The Comanche, who lived on the southern plains of North America, used the prickly poppy (*Argemone intermedia*) as an eyewash. They extracted the sap and applied it to the problem eye. The Shoshone, who lived in what are now Nevada and Utah, pulverized the seeds of the prickly poppy and mixed them with water for an eye poultice. All of these were effective treatments.

The Aztec, whose empire arose in Mesoamerica in about A.D. 1100, used mesquite for eyewash. They made mesquite (*Psosopis sp.*) or *mizquitl*, in the Aztec language, into an eyewash by using the leaves for a tea. Mesquite contains vitamin A, a vitamin critical to eye health.

See also CATARACT REMOVAL; MEDICINE; PHARMACOLOGY.

**Sources/Further Reading**

Lust, John. *The Herb Book.* New York: Bantam Books, 1974.

Ortiz de Montellano, Bernard. *Aztec Medicine, Health, and Nutrition.* New Brunswick, N.J.: Rutgers University Press, 1990.

Weiner, Michael A. *Earth Medicine, Earth Food: Plant Remedies, Drugs, and Natural Foods of the North American Indians.* New York: Fawcett Columbine, 1990.

Vogel, Virgil. *American Indian Medicine.* Norman: University of Oklahoma Press, 1977.

# F

**fans** (ca. 1500 B.C.–A.D. 1500) *Mesoamerican cultures*
A fan is a large or small device that can be moved in order to produce a cooling breeze. The Maya, whose culture arose in what is now the Yucatán Peninsula in Mexico in about 1500 B.C., invented the fan independently from the Chinese. The ancient Maya fan was hand-held. It was used to produce a cooling breeze for the person holding it. In addition, because oxygen is an accelerant for flames, using a fan would help a fire burn better or hotter.

## Sources/Further Reading

Benson, Elizabeth P. *The Maya World.* New York: Thomas Y. Crowell Company, 1967.
Whitely, David S. *Reader in Archaeological Theory.* New York: Routledge, 1998.

**farina** (precontact) *Mesoamerican, Circum-Caribbean, and South American Tropical Forest cultures*
Farina, fine ground meal from cereal grains or vegetable matter, is usually served as a cooked cereal. Hundreds of years before contact with Europeans, American Indians in tropical regions ate farina they made from the MANIOC, or cassava, plants. Once they had extracted the moisture from the manioc roots, they slowly roasted them. Afterward they ground them into flour. In this state, the manioc remained edible for several years.

## Source/Further Reading

Coe, Sophie. *America's First Cuisines.* Austin: University of Texas Press, 1994.

**farming, terraced** (ca. 1700 B.C.) *North American Southwest, Mesoamerican, South American Andean cultures*
Terraced farming allows crops to be grown on hillsides. It makes use of small, flat plots of land held in place with stones to keep soil from washing away. American Indians of South America, Mesoamerica, and the North American Southwest relied on terraced farming so that they could make the most effective use of land and water in order to maximize crop yields. Terraced farming in the Americas was invented independently of that used by ancient farmers in Mesopotamia. The Olmec, whose culture arose in Mesoamerica in about 1700 B.C., were the first in the Americas to practice this way of farming. Although both the Maya, whose culture was established in Mesoamerica in about 1500 B.C., and the Aztec, whose empire was established in the same area in about A.D. 1100, practiced terraced farming, the Inca used it much more extensively.

The best-known use of terraced farming in the Americas occurred in what is now Peru between 300 B.C. and A.D. 200. Pre-Inca peoples planted BEANS, QUINOA, and POTATOES in plots on the steep slopes of protected valleys. These valleys obtained more moisture than the dry table land above them. Pre-Inca farmers used large blocks of Yucay limestone cut into polygons to hold back the soil. Terraced farming increased over time, so that by the start of the Inca Empire in about A.D. 1000, hundreds of acres of terraces surrounded the Inca capital city of Cuzco. (See also CITIES, AMERICA'S FIRST.) Archaeologists have found terraces surrounded by stone walls at Machu Picchu and terraces with walls cut from rock at Ollantaytambo. Often the Inca watered their terraced plots from reservoirs or streams that had been diverted to the fields in an elaborate IRRIGATION SYSTEM utilizing stone sluices.

Constructed in a manner resembling stairs on hillsides, this design slowed runoff from a stream, or rainfall runoff, until it could be absorbed by the soil. Many archaeologists believe that, given the necessity of understanding the properties of the soil, the contours of the land, and the characteristics of water-flow required to keep the system in order, terraces such as these must have been designed by specialists. Many of the terraces that were built over 500 years ago are still in use in Peru today.

Indigenous farmers of what is now Peru began using the technique of terraced farming between 300 B.C. and A.D. 200. By A.D. 1000, American Indian farmers had created hundreds of acres of terraced fields near Cuzco, the Inca capital city. *(Neg. No. 334768; Photo: Shippee-Johnson, Courtesy Department of Library Services, American Museum of Natural History)*

Some American Indian terraced fields were built across level, narrow valleys. Held by stone walls, they were designed to catch runoff from the slopes above while preventing soil from washing away when the heavy and sometimes infrequent rains came. Archaeologists believe that this type of terraced farming is the first type that the Inca used.

Terraces are one of several irrigation techniques used by indigenous farmers of North America. The Anasazi and Mogollon people, whose cultures arose in the North American Southwest in about 350 B.C., built stone dikes around fields. These dikes allowed silt to be deposited in layers about three to four feet deep each. As each field received moisture, the excess water would run down to the next terrace. (See also WATER CONSERVATION.) Fields of this design covered thousands of acres in what is now Arizona.

See also AGRICULTURE; AGRICULTURE, RAISED BED; WATER CONSERVATION; ZONED BIODIVERSITY.

## Sources/Further Reading

Donkin, R. A. *Agricultural Terracing in the Aboriginal New World.* Tucson: University of Arizona Press, 1979.

Hurt, R. Douglas. *American Indian Agriculture: Prehistory to Present.* Lawrence: University Press of Kansas, 1987.

Malpass, Michael A. *Daily Life in the Inca Empire.* Westport, Conn.: Greenwood Press, 1996.

von Hagen, Victor Wolfgang. *Realm of the Incas.* New York: New American Library, 1957.

Weatherford, Jack. *Indian Givers: How the Indians of the Americas Transformed the World.* New York: Fawcett Columbine, 1988.

**featherworking**   (ca. 1700 B.C.–400 B.C.)   *North American, South American, Circum-Caribbean, Mesoamerican cultures*

Featherworking is the production of utilitarian or asthetic items made wholly or in part with feathers. Even though the

Olmec, whose culture arose in the Yucatán Peninsula of what is now Mexico in about 1700 B.C., did extensive featherwork, trade in feathers began much earlier. Author and archaeology professor Brian M. Fagan, wrote that countless trade paths for carrying tropical foods, animal pelts, and feathers to the highlands existed centuries before the Olmec. The ancient craft of featherworking was such a specialized endeavor that many tribes had professional hunters who were responsible for obtaining feathers or capturing the birds possessing the desired feathers.

The most commonly used feathers in South and Mesoamerica were parrot, macaw, hummingbird, and quetzal feathers. The quetzal feathers were the most valued and prized because of their brilliant and iridescent green color. The color green was highly valued by all of the Mesoamerican tribes and some of the South American Indians. Feathers were so valued that TRADE was specifically developed to obtain them.

The Olmec are the first recorded Mesoamerican Indians to do featherwork, using feathers to make headdresses. The Maya, who followed the Olmec, continued the craft and produced many more items of feathers, including capes, stoles, tassels, belts, earrings, shields, and FANS, for both cooling and fires. (Maya culture arose on the Yucatán Peninsula in about 1500 B.C.) All of these tribes seemed to recognize the value of feathers in the production of fans in particular. Methods of attaching feathers to items varied: some were glued, some were sewed, and some were attached by crimping.

The Aztec, whose empire was established in Mexico in about A.D. 1100, were also expert at featherworking. In precontact North America the Indians used feathers for capes, fans, headdresses, arrows, and similar items. The Maya and Aztec produced a remarkable and intricate cloth of feathers. The featherworkers took feathers and spun them into wefts (crosswise threads in a fabric). They then wove the wefts into cloth. This type of work is very delicate, intricate, and tedious, and it requires very good vision. Featherwork is so delicate that today the career of a featherworker is over by the time a person reaches the age of 50 because of the toll the work takes on the eyes.

See also PARROT BREEDING.

## Sources/Further Reading

Benson, Elizabeth P. *The Maya World*. New York: Thomas Y. Crowell Company, 1967.

Daumas, Maurice, ed. *A History of Technology & Invention: Progress Through the Ages*. Translated by Eileen B. Hennessey. New York: Crown Publishers, Inc., 1962.

Fagan, Brian M. *Kingdoms of Gold, Kingdoms of Jade: The Americas Before Columbus*. London: Thames And Hudson, Ltd., 1991.

Townsend, Richard F. *The Aztecs*. London: Thames And Hudson, Ltd., 1992.

Morris, Craig and Adriana von Hagen. *The Inka Empire and Its Andean Origins*. New York: Abbeville Press Publishers, 1993.

Stuart, George E. and Gene S. Stuart. *The Mysterious Maya*. Washington, D.C.: National Geographic Society, 1977.

von Hagen, Victor W. *Realm of the Incas*. New York: New American Library, 1957.

**fertilizers** (ca. 5000 B.C.–3000 B.C.) *North American Northeastern and Great Plains, Mesoamerican, South American Andean cultures*

Fertilizer is organic matter added to the soil to enrich it, thus producing more abundant crop yields or healthier plants. Indigenous people in the Americas had been using a variety of fertilizers for thousands of years before European contact. The MILPA, or slash and burn, system of farming that had been practiced from the beginning of agriculture in South, Meso-, and North America added nutrients to the soil. Through experimentation over the years, various tribes developed other fertilizers.

By 3000 B.C. in what is now Peru, indigenous people were cultivating many types of crops. They fertilized these with LLAMA dung, anchovy heads, and guano, or bird droppings, from coastal islands. Mountains of these droppings had been deposited on certain coastal areas over the centuries. The Inca, whose empire was established in about A.D. 1000, regarded guano as a valuable resource. Believing it should be shared by all, they divided the deposits into districts, marking each area and allotting them to specific groups of farmers.

When the Spaniards arrived, they exploited the fertilizer deposits, selling them commercially. By the 1700s they were shipping guano throughout the world. In the 1800s the guano deposits had reached a depth of about 100 feet, but between 1840 and 1860 Peru exported an estimated 11 million tons of the fertilizer. Spurred by farmers, the U.S. government had plans to seize two of the guano islands from Peru, but the American Civil War broke out before the action could be carried out. Guano fertilizer from Peru was marketed in Europe. This import is credited with beginning modern agriculture in that area of the world. Interest in the nitrogen-rich guano spurred experiments to develop artificial fertilizers. Today dried anchovy heads are still being sold for fishmeal fertilizer, a major Peruvian export.

In about A.D. 1100, Aztec farmers in the Xochimilco-Chalco Basin of Mexico fertilized the raised fields they had created on swampland with compost made from aquatic plants. (See also AGRICULTURE, RAISED BED.) They also improved soil quality with muck from surrounding canals.

In the Eastern Woodlands of North America, Patuxet Indian, Squanto is famous for sharing the technique of using fish fertilizer with the Pilgrims, who established the Massachusetts Bay Colony in 1620. He had recently returned from captivity in Europe, where he had learned to speak English. In the spring of 1621, he taught the Pilgrims to plant CORN (maize), a grain they had never seen before, and to fertilize it with fish. The earliest Europeans on this continent were aware that fertilizer helped crops to grow, but Old World farmers relied on manure from domesticated animals, primarily cattle. Unfamiliar with the new soil and lacking herds of cattle, the colonists were at a loss about how to farm in their new environment.

Menhaden, the fish that Squanto used, were not eaten by the indigenous people who lived in the area. In fact, the name they given this fish, *munnoquohatean* or *munnawhatteauq*, meant "that which enriches the soil." The colonists quickly adopted the use of fish fertilizer, spelling it "munnawhatteang," a word that appears in written accounts as early as 1643. Fishmeal is still used extensively for fertilizer today.

North American Indian farmers viewed the European use of animal dung to boost soil nutrients with disgust. When U.S. government Indian agents insisted they use it on their gardens in the 1800s, many refused to comply with what they believed was a barbaric custom. Buffalo Bird Woman, a Hidatsa who lived on the Missouri River in what is now North Dakota, was interviewed by ethnologist Gordon Wilson at the start of the 20th century. She revealed that her people did not use dung, because not only did it contain worms, it also spread weeds. "I do not know that the worms in the manure did any harm to our gardens, but because we thought it bred worms and weeds, we did not like to have any dung on our garden lands; and we therefore removed it."

See also AGRICULTURE.

**Sources/Further Reading**

Armillas, Pedro. "Gardens on Swamps." *Science* 174 (November 12, 1971): 653–661.

Flexner, Stuart Berg. *I Hear America Talking: An Illustrated History of American Words and Phrases.* New York: Simon and Schuster, 1976.

Hurt, R. Douglas. *Indian Agriculture in the Americas: Prehistory to Present.* Lawrence: University Press of Kansas, 1988.

Weatherford, Jack. *Indian Givers: How the Indians of the Americas Transformed the World.* New York: Fawcett Columbine, 1988.

Wilson, L. Gilbert. *Buffalo Bird Woman's Garden: Agriculture of the Hidatsa Indians.* Reprint. St. Paul, Minn.: Minnesota Historical Society Press, 1987.

**fever medications** See SALICIN.

**field hockey** See HOCKEY, FIELD AND ICE.

**filé gumbo** (precontact) *North American Southeast cultures*
Filé gumbo is a dish flavored and thickened with dried, ground leaves from the SASSAFRAS tree, which are called *filé*. The Choctaw, a tribe that lived in what are now Mississippi and Alabama, introduced filé gumbo to southern settlers. The dish is made from vegetables cooked in a seafood stock to which the filé powder is added after about two hours. Shrimp and crab may then be added, and the stew is served over rice. Filé gumbo has become a famous part of Cajun cuisine.

**Sources/Further Reading**

Sokalow, Raymond. *Why We Eat What We Eat: How the Encounter Between the New World and the Old Changed the Way Everyone on the Planet Eats.* New York: Summit Books, 1991.

Weatherford, Jack. *Indian Givers: How the Indians of the Americas Transformed the World.* New York: Fawcett Columbine, 1988.

**fire starters, solar** See SOLAR FIRE STARTERS.

**fish decoys** See DECOYS, FISH.

**fishery management** See AQUACULTURE.

**fishhooks** (5000 B.C.–3000 B.C.) *North American, Mesoamerican, Circum-Caribbean, South American cultures*
Indians throughout the Americas constructed fishhooks, curved instruments affixed to a line and put into the water to catch fish. They made them out of several materials. Some were carved from bone, ivory, antler, and wood. A major technological breakthrough occurred around 5,000–4,000 B.C. when the ancient Paleo-Indians of the southern Great Lakes area produced a metal fishhook. This was certainly the oldest metal fishhook in the New World and probably the first metal fishhook in the entire world. The earliest fishhooks found in South America date between 4,000 and 3,000 B.C. These were made of shells and thorns and were used for freshwater fishing. These Paleo-Indians also made a unique fishhook called a stone sinker hook. The fishhooks were imbedded in the stone sinker. Archaeologists believe that most of the fishing that took place at this time was accomplished with cotton nets.

Indians were the first in North America to invent fishing with multiple hooks on a single line, and they were masters at this technology. Hundreds of years before Columbus arrived, they invented two methods of fishing in this highly efficient way. The first method is referred to today as "setlines," a technique that did not use a pole. Three or more fishhooks were attached to a line as well as a weight on the end of the line. After the fishermen baited the hooks, they cast them into the water. They accomplished this by loosely piling the string between the fisher and the water, then taking the end with the weight and hooks on it and twirling it overhead while letting it out a little at a time. When the appropriate length was reached, the fishermen released the line in the direction of the water. This method of casting was necessary because the extra hooks and bait required more line than a fishing rod could provide. They tied the end of the line to a branch, a rock, or a log. These lines could be checked at any time, even several days after they were set. Because this was not labor intensive, fishing with setlines freed the fisher to do other things.

The other method of multiple-hook fishing utilized a crossbar, a piece of wood about five feet long; a weight; and several lines with hooks on them. The American Indians attached the main line in the middle of a wooden crossbar. Then, using a short length of string, they connected a weight to this line at the bottom of the bar. They hung several lines with hooks along the length of the crossbar. The lines with the hooks on them were not the same length as the line with the weight on it. American Indians used this method for fishing in the ocean, in rivers, and lakes. Indigenous fishermen of the Northwest Coast favored this method of fishing over the others.

## Sources/Further Reading

Daumas, Maurice, ed. *A History of Technology and Invention: Progress Through the Ages.* New York: Crown Publishers, 1969.

Driver, Harold E. *Indians of North America.* Chicago: University of Chicago Press, 1969.

Josephy, Jr., Alvin M., ed. *America in 1492: The World of the Indian People Before the Arrival of Columbus.* New York: Random House, 1991.

Mason, J. Alden. *The Ancient Civilizations of Peru.* Rev. ed. New York: Penguin Books, 1988.

Maxwell, James A. *America's Fascinating Indian Heritage.* Pleasantville, N.Y.: Reader's Digest Books, 1978.

Weatherford, Jack. *Native Roots: How the Indians Enriched America.* New York: Fawcett Columbine, 1991.

**fishing, chemical** (precontact) *North American Plateau, California, Great Basin, and Southwest; Mesoamerican; Circum-Caribbean; South American Tropical Forest cultures*
Pre-Columbian American Indians throughout North and South America discovered several plants that produced chemicals that would poison and kill fish without tainting the meat. This innovative technique worked best in bodies of water where the water was pooled or slow moving, and thus the chemicals would not be diluted. The efficiency of this method of fishing was remarkable. Without expending a great deal of energy or time, one person could provide food for several families. The main areas where chemical fishing was used were the Plateau region, the Great Basin, the West Coast, and the Southwest of North America, as well as along the coast of what is now Mexico, the Amazon Basin, and Mesoamerica.

Indigenous people living in the tropics of Mesoamerica, the Amazon Basin, and the Caribbean used a variety of YAM (*Dioscorea*) to produce a fish poison known as *barbasco;* 80 to 90 types of yams grew in Mexico alone. American Indians knew which were safe for human consumption and which were not. Twelve types of yams were used to make *barbasco,* enabling fishermen to stun fish so that they could be easily scooped into nets. The yam roots were grated to release sapogenin, a chemical that acted on the nervous system of the fish. These shavings were spread over the surface of the water. When the fish came to the surface to investigate the yam scrapings, the chemical stunned them. The same types of yams responsible for fishing chemicals also produce a form of sapogenin called diosgenin,

which is the starting material the modern pharmaceutical industry uses to produce steroids and cortisone.

## Sources/Further Reading

Josephy, Jr., Alvin M. *The Indian Heritage of America.* Rev. ed. Boston: Houghton Mifflin Company, 1991.

Taylor, Norman. *Plant Drugs that Changed the World.* New York: Dodd, Mead, and Company, 1965.

Vogel, Virgil. *American Indian Medicine,* Norman: University of Oklahoma Press, 1970.

**fishing, ice** (precontact) *North American Northeast cultures*
Ice fishing is practiced in winter by dropping a line into the water through a hole in the ice and sitting in a small shelter while waiting for the fish to bite. What has become a popular sport today was practiced for centuries by the Great Lakes tribes who depended on it for their survival. Unlike modern fishermen, however, they speared the fish. They began by cutting a hole about 12 inches in diameter into the ice. Next they built a small shelter over the hole; this was just large enough to cover the fisher's head and chest when he was lying down on the ice to peer into the hole. The purpose of the shelter was not for protection against the elements, but rather to prevent the fish from seeing the human above and to allow the fisher to see into the water below. After the fisher dropped a lure into the water, he waited, and when a fish swam beneath the hole, he speared it. This fishing method allowed American Indians to obtain a valuable food source during the winter. The Inuit, who lived in the Arctic, used a somewhat similar technique in the wintertime to hunt for seals.

See also DECOYS, FISH.

## Sources/Further Reading

Josephy, Jr., Alvin M. *The Indian Heritage of America.* Rev. ed. Boston: Houghton Mifflin Company, 1991.

Oswalt, Wendell. *Eskimos and Explorers.* Novato, Calif.: Chandler & Sharp Publishers, 1979.

Weatherford, Jack. *Native Roots: How the Indians Enriched America.* New York: Fawcett Columbine, 1991.

**fishnet lures, olfactory** (precontact) *North American Northeast cultures*
Fishnet lures are substances rubbed on fishing nets in order to attract fish. People throughout the ancient world used the fishnet; however, only pre-Columbian American Indians increased their chances of netting a good catch by using scent to attract fish to the net. The innovation was a simple one, but it demonstrated a high level of scientific thinking as well as a knowledge of wildlife behavior—for instance, the fact that fish locate food by scent in addition to sight. An understanding of botany was also needed to find a plant that would work to attract fish.

The olfactory lures were used in precontact America primarily by the Menominee and Chippewa (Anishinabe) of the Great Lakes region of North America. They used sweet flag

(*Acorus calamus L.*) for this purpose. The Chippewa called this herb *'na'buguck,* which means "something flat." The Menominee and Chippewa also combined sweet flag and sarsaparilla (*Similex officinalis*) to produce another unique scent that was used as an olfactory decoy.

See also DECOYS, FISH (OLFACTORY).

## Sources/Further Reading

Kimball, Art and Brad Kimball. *Fish Decoys of the Lac Du Flambeau Ojibway.* Boulder Junction, Wisc.: Aardvark Publications, 1988.

Weatherford, Jack. *Native Roots: How the Indians Enriched America.* New York: Fawcett Columbine, 1991.

**fish trap** (weirs) (4000–2000 B.C.) *North American Northeast, Southeast, Northwest Coast, and California cultures*
Fish traps, or weirs, are devices constructed in shallow water in order to catch large numbers of fish or lobsters. The fish find it easy to swim into these traps but difficult to exit them. In effect, they are obstacle courses. Like ancient people throughout the world who depended on fish as mainstays of their diets, several American Indian tribes constructed traps. This was an efficient method of fishing that required little labor.

On the east coast of North America in what is now Boston, Massachusetts, Paleo-Indians constructed one weir made of about 65,000 wooden stakes that they had driven into clay where tidal waters were present. They wove small branches between the stakes so that water could pass through the wickerwork, but fish could not. Archaeologists have dated this fish weir to between 4000 and 2000 B.C. Archaeologists Franklin Folsom and Mary Elting Folsom wrote in *America's Ancient Treasures:* "The Archaic people who used this trap had obviously achieved a rather highly organized society; otherwise they could not have built and maintained such a large and complicated device for obtaining food."

Many tribes along the Atlantic coast continued to use fish traps until colonization pushed them from the shores. American Indians who lived in what are now the Florida Keys in about 100 B.C. used as shells, first to build up the islands on which they lived and then to build sea walls that some archaeologists speculate were fish traps. They believe the Indian people herded the fish into the traps with canoes. The French artist Hariot drew a picture of an elaborate wickerwork trap he observed in what is now Virginia when he visited the area in the 1600s. His drawing shows an ambitious construction that stretched across an inlet.

In the Pacific Northwest, American Indians trapped fish in large funnel-shaped nets. The Ahjumawi, Pit River Indians who lived in what is now California, constructed stone traps to catch fish that spawned in lake springs. In addition to serving as traps, these stone constructions aided the fish in their spawning and served as a way to manage a dietary resource that was important to these Indians.

See also AQUACULTURE; ECOLOGY.

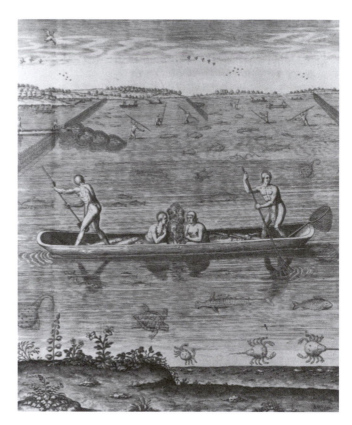

American Indians living on the east coast of North America made elaborate fish traps such as those in the background of this engraving made by Theodore De Bry in the 1590s. *(LC-USZ62-54016/Library of Congress)*

## Sources/Further Reading

Driver, Harold E. *Indians of North America.* Chicago: University of Chicago Press, 1969.

Folsom, Franklin and Mary Elting Folsom. *America's Ancient Treasures.* 4th ed. Albuquerque: University of New Mexico Press, 1993.

Foster, John W. *Ahjumawi Fish Traps.* URL: http://www.Indiana.edu/~maritime/caparks/fishtraphome.html. Downloaded on August 14, 1999.

**flintknapping** (ca. 11,000 B.C.) *North American, Mesoamerican, South American Paleo-Indians*
Flintknapping is the practice of shaping spear and arrow points and razor-sharp knife blades from flint, obsidian, chert, or quartzite—fine-grained, hard stones that can flake and produce a sharp edge. American Indians developed the technology of flintknapping independently of other ancient cultures throughout the world.

Paleo-Indians once mined flint from areas such as the one near what is now Brownsville, Ohio. They broke chunks from the stone by driving wooden wedges into naturally occurring cracks in the deposit with large rocks, called hammerstones. Flint miners shaped these chunks into cores. Next they used smaller hammerstones to chip smaller pieces, called blanks, from the core. These could be used as knives or scrapers and had edges sharper than steel. Often they shaped the stone into projectile points. The points were shaped by striking a blank with an antler in order to remove unwanted bits of flint or obsidian. Because flint was so useful, it was a valuable TRADE commodity.

The earliest points that were made in the Americas were Clovis-style points, named after the site where archaeologists found them near Clovis, New Mexico. These points, used for large game hunts, were about four to five inches long and shaped like the blade of a bayonet. They were lashed to shafts and used as spears. This style of point has been found throughout North America, Mesoamerica, and South America.

Folsom-style points, which have been dated to about 10,000 years ago, were an improvement on the simple, earlier points. Unlike Clovis points, Folsom points tended to be smaller and had grooves hollowed out from the surface on both sides. When points have these grooves, they are said to be fluted. This fluting allowed the points to be easily inserted into the split end of a wooden shaft. Folsom points were more elaborately worked than those made by the Clovis people and took more labor to prepare. They are named after the Folsom archaeological site in what is now New Mexico.

Plano points which were made by a culture named after an archaeological site in what is now Texas, later supplanted these points. Plano points are not grooved and tend to be smaller than Folsom points. They are also sturdier than Folsom points and less prone to fracture both during manufacture and hunting. With notched bases, they more closely resemble the arrow and spear points used by American Indians at the time of contact with Europeans.

The Maya who lived in Mesoamerica did the most elaborate flintknapping in the Americas during their classic period, which lasted from about A.D. 250 to 900. The flaked lance heads out of chert, giving them razor-sharp edges and shaping them into elaborate designs that included profiles of human heads on some pieces. Archaeologists believe that these lance heads, which took hundreds of hours to make, were ceremonial. Perhaps rulers used them as symbols of authority.

Ancient Mesoamerican surgeons, including the Aztec, relied on flint, chert, or obsidian blades to use as SCALPELS, despite the fact that they had the technology to produce metal knives. The reason obsidian flint was preferred by ancient American Indian physicians was that the cutting edge could be flaked to an extremely thin width, making it much sharper than metal scalpels of today. The only modern surgical process with the cutting capability of obsidian is laser technology.

## Sources/Further Reading

Folsom, Franklin and Mary Elting Folsom. *America's Ancient Treasures.* 4th ed. Albuquerque: University of New Mexico Press, 1993.

Hurst, David, Jay Miller, Richard White, Peter Nabokov, and Philip Deloria. *The Native Americans.* Atlanta: Turner Publishing, Inc., 1993.

Maxwell, James A. *America's Fascinating Indian Heritage.* Pleasantville, N.Y.: Reader's Digest Books, 1978.

Stuart, George. "Copan, City of Kings and Commoners." *National Geographic* 176, no. 4 (Oct. 1989): 488–504.

**floodplain farming** See FARMING, TERRACED; IRRIGATION SYSTEMS.

**flotation devices** (inflatable wet suits) (precontact)
*North American Arctic cultures*
Flotation devices keep people afloat in water. Life preservers are an example of modern flotation devices. The Inuit living in West Greenland devised a special garment made of dehaired sealskins worn to hunt whales from an *umiak,* or skin boat. This garment served as a flotation device. The suit had a head opening that could be tightened around the face with a

The Maya raised flintknapping to an art, creating intricate blades such as this one. Flintwork of this style was probably used for ceremonial purposes. *(bladelike head, Mexico, Chiapas, Coastal Lowlands style; ca. 300–900, greenstone, 25.3 x 4.5 x 18.6 cm. ® The Cleveland Museum of Art, 1999, Gift of Mrs. James C. Gruener, 1990.254)*

drawstring. Mittens and boots were sewn onto the shirt. The Inuit put on the garment by entering it through a large hole at the chest. They closed it with a drawstring after air had been trapped inside. If a hunter fell overboard during the hunt, the air inside the suit would keep him afloat for several hours. These suits allowed hunters to jump into the water to butcher a whale after it had been killed. Women who paddled boats for whale hunts also wore these flotation suits.

See also KAYAKS; PARKAS; WHALING.

**Source/Further Reading**

Oswalt, Wendell. *Eskimos and Explorers.* Novato, Calif.: Chandler & Sharp Publishers, 1979.

**foil, metal**   (1900 B.C.–1400 B.C.)   *South American Andean cultures*

In the Americas, the first foil, consisting of very thin sheets of metal, was made by the forerunners of the Chavin culture, which flourished in the northern highlands of what is now Peru from about 1000 B.C. to about 200 B.C. These Chavin ancestors were the first ancient American Indians to produce metal foil that was almost as thin as present-day metal foil wrap. The oldest pieces of gold foil were found along with a metal-working kit at Wawaka, the site of a small village, and were carbon-dated at 1900 to 1400 B.C. The technique used to make the foil did not spread for about a thousand years.

The Chavin, who lived on the northern coast of what is now Peru, were the next group of ancient American Indians to produce metal foil; they were followed by the Moche. These two cultures made copper, gold, and silver metal foils, developing this technology ca. 200 B.C. to A.D. 400. Ancient Peruvian metalworkers were able not only to make copper foil but also to plate it with gold. A piece of gold-plated copper foil was found in an area south of Lima, Peru, at a site called Mina Perdida.

South American Andean peoples used metal foils primarily for decorative purposes in ELECTROPLATING and GOLD PLATING. Copper was generally available to the common people, while the upper classes reserved the wearing or use of gold and silver for themselves.

See also METALLURGY; METALS, PRECIOUS.

**Sources/Further Reading**

Benson, Elizabeth P. *The Maya World.* New York: Thomas Y. Crowell Company, 1967.

Burger, Richard L. *Chavin and the Origins of Andean Civilization.* London: Thames and Hudson, 1992.

Donnan, Christopher B. "Masterworks of Art Reveal a Remarkable Pre-Inca World." *National Geographic* Vol. 177, no. 6 (June 1990): 17–33.

Rose, Mark. "Early Andean Metalworking." *Archaeology* 52 no. 1 (January/February 1999). URL: http://www.archaeology.org/9901/newsbriefs/andean.html.

von Hagen, Victor Wolfgang. *Realm of the Incas.* New York: New American Library, 1957.

**food coloring**   (precontact)   *North American Southwest, Mesoamerican, South American Andean cultures*

The practice of using vegetable DYES to impart color to food to make it more visually appealing is an old one in the Americas. The Pueblo peoples who lived in the North American desert Southwest used fourwing salt-brush ashes to color their wafer bread a greenish blue for centuries before contact with Europeans. The Zuni, who live in the same area, used ground AMARANTH seeds to give Zuni piki bread a reddish color. Throughout the Southwest, red tunas (fruits) of PRICKLY PEAR CACTI were used to tint CORNMEAL mush.

The Maya, whose culture arose in Mesoamerica in about 1500 B.C., used vegetable dyes such as *achol,* or ACHIOTE, to color foods as well as to produce a red color for textiles. Pigment from this plant is used to dye margarine today.

The Inca, who established an empire in what are now Peru and parts of Bolivia in about A.D. 1000, used a special variety of purple CORN for imparting color to beverages. The variety, called *Skcully Zea Mays,* has a high level of anthcyanin in its cob, a substance that is used today to make a natural red food coloring that is sold throughout the world. This corn grows only in Peru in the valleys near Lima, Ancash, and Arequipa.

**Sources/Further Reading**

Bliss, Anne. *North American Dye Plants.* Boulder, Colo.: Juniper House, 1976.

Dunmire, William W. and Gail D. Tierney. *Wild Plants of the Pueblo Province: Exploring Ancient and Enduring Uses.* Santa Fe: Museum of New Mexico Press, 1995.

Grae, Ida. *Nature's Colors: Dyes from Plants.* New York: Macmillan Publishing Company, Inc., 1974.

**food preservation**   (precontact)   *South American Andean, Mesoamerican, Circum-Caribbean, North American Great Plains and Northwest Coast cultures*

Storing food so that it would not spoil and could be used at a future date was the goal of several techniques devised by indigenous peoples throughout the Americas. Building secure pits against rodents and moisture for dried CORN and BEANS was one of the most frequently used methods. The Inca, whose empire was established about A.D. 1000 in what is now Peru, and the Maya, who lived in Mesoamerica starting about 1500 B.C., built stone warehouses that kept provisions dry. The Aztec, whose empire was established in the same region in about A.D. 1100, also built stone granaries. The Inca, Maya, and Aztec sometimes stored dried herbs with the food that served as an insect deterrent. (See also CROP STORAGE; INSECT REPELLENTS.)

North American Indians preserved meat by drying it to make JERKY and by making PEMMICAN, a mixture of pulverized jerky, fat, and dried fruit, usually berries. In climates where the humidity level was high, Indians often fire-dried, or smoked, meat to better preserve it. American Indian tribes of the Northwest Coast dried fish, including salmon. These were hung on racks, made from a number of poles tied together. Small fires beneath the racks kept insects away and imparted a smoked flavor to the salmon. Sometimes the dried fish was pounded, making it easier to store.

Vegetables, as well, were often dried after harvest and stored for future use. While the Inca who lived in the northern highlands of the Andes developed a unique FREEZE-DRYING process that was used mainly for potatoes, many other groups of indigenous people throughout the Americas developed their own drying techniques. For example, the Hidatsa, who farmed along the Missouri River in what is now North Dakota, built outdoor drying stages, or platforms, of timber in order to keep corn and SQUASH well above the reach of animals while allowing circulating air to remove moisture from the food. When it rained, they placed hides over the top of the stage to protect the food. In climates where rain was common, other tribes built fires beneath the platforms to hasten the vegetable-drying process.

Indians living on the Northwest Coast of North America dug roots from a number of varieties of plants, including biscuitroot, bitterroot, and camas. These they roasted in a large pit that was lined with rocks. A fire was built in the underground oven until the rocks were extremely hot. When the fire died down, the Indians placed leaves and grass on the rocks. After the roots were positioned atop leaves, they were covered with old mats and then with earth. Once the roots were roasted, women pounded them into flour. Sometimes they mixed this with dried elk or deer meat, berries, and animal fat or fish oil to make PEMMICAN.

Indians who lived along the northern and central Pacific coast also used fish oil as a preservative to cover berries stored in wooden boxes. The oil served as a barrier against mold, which needs oxygen in order to grow, and was an alternative to air-drying in a climate known for its dampness. The oil was often obtained from eulachon, a small fish that is rich in oil. After catching the fish in nets, the Indians stored them in pits until they began to decompose. Then they placed them in large wooden BOXES filled with water into which hot stones had been dropped. When the oil rose, they skimmed it from the surface.

**Sources/Further Reading**

Coe, Sophie. *America's First Cuisines.* Austin: University of Texas Press, 1994.

Driver, Harold E. *Indians of North America.* Chicago: University of Chicago Press, 1969.

Josephy, Jr., Alvin M., ed. *America in 1492: The World of the Indian People Before the Arrival of Columbus.* New York: Random House, 1991.

Wilson, L. Gilbert. *Buffalo Bird Woman's Garden: Agriculture of the Hidatsa Indians.* Reprint. St. Paul: Minnesota Historical Society Press, 1987.

**foods, snack**   See SNACK FOODS.

**foods, instant**   See INSTANT FOODS.

**footbag games**   See GAMES, FOOTBAG.

**foot plows**   (precontact) *South American Andean and Tropical Forest, Mesoamerican, North American cultures*
The foot plow, a device for tilling the soil, is prehistoric in origin and was used by ancient farmers throughout the world. In the Americas, indigenous peoples who lived in what is now Peru are believed to have been the first to employ this method of tilling the soil at the time AGRICULTURE arose in that area (ca. 8000 B.C.). These early Americans constructed the foot plow from a wooden pole that was about six feet long and had a two-inch diameter. The end that was used to till the soil was sharpened to a point, then heated over a fire to harden it. Finally, a footrest was attached about 12 inches from the bottom of the plow. This allowed the farmer to put her or his body

Indigenous farmers throughout the Americas used foot plows to till the soil, as illustrated in this drawing of potato planting after one made by Felipe Guamán Poma de Ayala that was published in 1615. (Nueva Coronica y Buen Gobierno)

weight on it and force the pointed end into the ground in order to break up the soil for planting.

American Indians continued farming with the foot plow until the Europeans introduced the modern, wedge-shaped plow. Historians have sometimes cited this fact as evidence that American agriculturists were less intelligent than their European counterparts. However, several reasons exist why American Indians continued to use the foot plow. First, there were no suitable animals in the New World that could be domesticated to pull a plow. Second, American Indian horticultural techniques, while highly efficient, did not include planting crops in rows. MILPA, COMPANION PLANTING, MULTIPLE CROPPING, intercropping, and raised bed horticulture made the wedge shaped plow impractical for indigenous American farmers.

See also AGRICULTURE, RAISED BED; DOUBLE CROPPING.

## Sources/Further Reading

Benson, Elizabeth P. *The Maya World.* New York: Thomas Y. Crowell Company, 1967.

Hurt, R. Douglas. *Indian Agriculture in the Americas: Prehistory to Present.* Lawrence: University Press of Kansas, 1988.

Mason, J. Alden. *The Ancient Civilizations of Peru.* Rev. ed. New York: Penguin Books, 1988.

Trigger, Bruce G., and Wilcomb E. Washburn, eds. *The Cambridge History of the Native Peoples of the Americas, Vol. I, Part I, North America.* New York: Cambridge University Press, 1996.

von Hagen, Victor Wolfgang. *Realm of the Incas.* New York: New American Library, 1957.

## forceps (ca. A.D. 1200) *South American Andean, Mesoamerican cultures*

Forceps are medical instruments used for grasping and manipulating or extracting objects or human tissue. The Inca, whose empire was established in what are now Peru and Bolivia in about A.D. 1000, made and used forceps for surgical purposes prior to contact with Europeans. Archaeologists speculate that the Inca used these medical tools to remove bone fragments from the head following traumas such as being hit on the head with a stone mace (club) or a stone from a sling. (The goal of much of the ancient warfare in South and Mesoamerica was not to kill enemies but to disable them and capture them live.)

Brain SURGERY, called TREPHINATION, was common in Meso- and South America. Doctors are depicted using forceps in some of the pictures on Mesoamerican pottery, murals, and pictographs, leading anthropologists to believe that Aztec physicians used these medical instruments as well. (The Aztec Empire was established in about A.D. 1100 in what is now Mexico.) One such portrayal shows an ancient dentist with forceps in hand, working in the mouth of a patient. (See also DENTISTRY.) The development and use of forceps and SCALPELS demonstrates a high level of American Indian medical knowledge and technology prior to contact with Europeans.

## Sources/Further Reading

Mason, J. Alden. *The Ancient Civilizations of Peru.* Rev. ed. New York: Penguin Books, 1988.

Ortiz de Montellano, Bernard. *Aztec Medicine, Health and Nutrition.* New Brunswick, N.J.: Rutgers University Press, 1990.

Peredo, Miguel Guzman. *Medical Practices in Ancient America.* Mexico City: Ediciones Euroamericanas, 1988.

Readers Digest Association, Inc. *Mysteries of the Ancient Americas.* Pleasantville, N.Y.: Reader's Digest Books, 1986.

von Hagen, Victor Wolfgang. *Realm of the Incas.* New York: New American Library, 1957.

## forest management (pre-2000 B.C.) *North American Northeast, Southeast, Subarctic, Great Plains, and California cultures*

American Indian peoples were well aware that forests and the wildlife that lived in them thrived best when they were managed wisely. Although the land the Europeans encountered when they set foot in North America was less "tamed" than that of Europe, it was not the vast, wild, and untended expanse many history books describe. American Indians had been deliberately shaping the character of the forests for centuries before they began the practice of AGRICULTURE, thousands of years before the arrival of non-Indians.

The large trees and parklike grassy areas that the colonists reported seeing in the New England forests of North America were a result of controlled burning practiced by American Indians to remove underbrush and allow trees such as pines and the hardwoods used for CANOES and roof beams of longhouses to grow unimpeded. These light burnings were carefully planned and executed to enhance rather than destroy the forest environment. The fact that the burns were planned and controlled is crucial to understanding their purpose. For example, Indians minimized the destruction of fires set by lightning strikes by removing easily combustible fuel for the flames; that is, because they used brush for fuel, they routinely cleared the forests of dead wood and undergrowth, which limited the effect of forest fires. They also knew how to use backfires to control larger fires. A backfire is a controlled burn behind the fire line and serves to destroy fuel the flames need to survive. American Indians taught settlers on the plains how to use this technique to protect their cabins and wagons during prairie wildfires.

The benefits of controlled burns were many. Perhaps most important, they encouraged new growth, which attracted deer and other animals because of increased browsing. Modern forest management research has shown that deer grazing in new-growth areas produce more and healthier offspring than do those in other areas. In addition to attracting and producing more game, the parklike character of the forests made hunting easier by providing easier travel through the trees and shrubs and a longer range of vision. Forests that had been cleared of underbrush also provided a measure of safety from enemy bands, for whom it was more difficult to hide for a sneak attack, given the lack of underbrush for cover.

Pest control was another motive for forest management. Gulf Coast Indians and American Indians living in the interior of what is now Alaska used the burns to reduce the number of insects that bred in dense underbrush. Explorer Alvar Nuñez Cabeza de Vaca noted that during the 1530s, American Indians in Texas set fire to underbrush to drive off mosquitoes. In the Southeast, controlled burns drove rattlesnakes from the woods and allowed travelers to see the ones that remained.

American Indians also found that light, controlled burns increased berry production in the areas where they gathered wild BLACKBERRIES, BLUEBERRIES, and huckleberries, by increasing new growth on the bushes and adding nutrients to the soil. This burning technique would eventually become the basis of MILPA, the Indians' method for clearing the land for farming.

On the prairies, where there were few trees, American Indians used controlled burns for the tall grass that grew there, promoting the growth of new grass. Burning was used for buffalo drives (see also BISON) and also, over the course of years shaped the animals' migratory patterns. In areas such as the Missouri and Mississippi Basin, carefully planned forest fires created more grazing area for the buffalo, moving them closer to Indian settlements. This became especially useful as agriculture increased and it became more difficult for Indians to take the time to travel long distances to hunt fresh meat. The buffalo's range was so influenced by controlled burning that by A.D. 1000 it extended east of the Mississippi, providing a new source of food for Eastern Woodland Indians.

California Indians used controlled burns to kill the mistletoe that grew on oak and mesquite trees. They also burned off areas of chaparral (low-growing piñyon, juniper, and scrub oak brush) that covered the Sierra foothills, a practice reported by a Spanish explorer in 1602. Because there was less dead underbrush to serve as fuel, wildfires such as those that plague the California foothills today were prevented.

Non-Indians in the eastern part of North America did not understand the technology of controlled burns. Once they had removed the Indians from the land, they routinely failed to clear or maintain the forests that were allowed to grow wild and dense until they became potential tinderboxes. In some areas, lumberjacks harvested all of the trees, leaving the soil to erode. In many others, they cleared the old growth and left the trees they did not want along with fallen dead trees. As railroads began to cross the United States, cinders from the boilers set off huge conflagrations, and in the early 1900s firestorms plagued parts of the country. Only after these disasters did the U.S. government realize the need to manage the forests as a renewable resource, as the indigenous people had done. The U.S. Forest Service was therefore established in 1905 to manage the newly created national forests and parks.

See also ECOLOGY.

## Sources/Further Reading

Barrett, Stephen W. *Ethnohistory of Indian Fires Practices in Western Montana.* Washington, D.C.: U.S. Forest Service and University of Montana School of Forestry, 1979.

Hughes, J. Donald. *North American Indian Ecology.* El Paso: University of Texas Press, 1983.

Josephy, Jr., Alvin M., ed. *America in 1492: The World of the Indian People Before the Arrival of Columbus.* New York: Random House, 1991.

Pyne, Stephen J. *Fire in America.* Princeton, N.J.: Princeton University Press, 1982.

Weatherford, Jack. *Native Roots: How the Indians Enriched America.* New York: Fawcett Columbine, 1991.

**forts**  See STOCKADES.

**foxglove  (Digitalis purpurea)** (precontact)  *North American Northeast cultures*

North American Indians used the American foxglove plant to treat heart disease. The American foxglove is also known as finger flower, fairy fingers, ladies glove, dead man's bells, purple foxglove, dog's finger, and folk's glove. The active ingredients in American foxglove that act upon the heart are glycosides. These glycosides diminish the volume of the heart by increasing the strength of the contraction. They also increase the output of blood that the heart pumps, thereby improving circulation; slow the pulse rate; and slow the conduction of nerve impulses in the heart that regulate that organ's rhythm. Additionally, foxglove is a DIURETIC that causes the body to rid itself of excess fluid. In modern times digitalis, a popular heart medication prescribed for congestive heart failure, has been synthesized from foxglove.

The American foxglove, like its European counterpart, is very toxic and has been known to cause nausea, rashes, and headaches when it comes into contact with bare skin. In order for foxglove to work effectively, it needs to be given in near-lethal doses. How the North American Indians discovered the cardiotonic effects of American foxglove and were able to determine the precise therapeutic dose is unclear. Non-Indian physicians reported that Indians were using it for heart disease in the 1700s much like digitalis is used today, but those sources do not mention specific tribes. In his book *American Indian Medicine,* Virgil Vogel cites a later source, writing: "Dr. Harlow Brooks praised the Indians for their knowledge of laxative, diuretic, emetic and febrifuge drugs, and added that the American variety of foxglove was correctly used by them for its cardiac stimulant properties for hundreds of years before Withering discovering digitalis in England." It is highly probable Indians had been using foxglove long before European contact.

See also DOGBANE; WAHOO.

## Sources/Further Reading

Brooks, Harlow. "The Medicine of the American Indian." *Bulletin of the New York Academy of Medicine* 5, no. 6 (June 1929): 509–37.

Lust, John. *The Herb Book.* New York: Bantam Books, 1974.

Vogel, Virgil. *American Indian Medicine.* Norman: University of Oklahoma Press, 1977.

## free association (precontact) *North American Northeast cultures*

Free association is the analytic technique of asking patients to relate the first thought that comes to their minds to the psychoanalyst who is treating them. The technique assumes that all memories are connected to other memories. By following this trail of free association wherever it leads, people may bring important and painful memories into awareness from the subconscious in order to work through the conflict that surrounds these memories. Prior to contact with Europeans, the Iroquois, who lived in the northeast of what is now the United States, practiced free association. The Iroquois encouraged the emotionally troubled tribal member to talk about whatever thoughts, ideas, or emotions came to mind, recognizing that if the person were allowed to free associate, eventually patterns would emerge and the source of the emotional distress would reveal itself. This technique was part of their sophisticated method of DREAMWORK PSYCHOLOGY and an integral piece of their religious beliefs and practices.

In the 1600s Jesuit priests serving as missionaries to the Iroquois recorded the details of their psychology techniques in an attempt to find the most effective way to convert them to Catholicism. These records describe a system that recognized both the conscious and unconscious part of the mind and showed an awareness that suppressed desires could cause both emotional and physical illness. Iroquois people believed that the deep desires of their souls were often hidden in the unconscious mind. When those "soul desires" expressed themselves in dreams, they could be acknowledged and interpreted by talking about them with a shaman, a more enlightened and experienced practitioner of indigenous medicine. When the unconscious longings were ignored, the Iroquois believed the soul reacted angrily, so members of the community helped in whatever way they could to provide support for meeting the needs that the troubled person's soul had expressed.

This technique was remarkably similar to the one devised hundreds of years later by the Viennese psychiatrist Sigmund Freud, who came to be known as the father of modern psychiatry. Freud, who was born in 1856, first began using free association as a psychoanalytic technique to reveal suppressed memories when he found that patients were too embarrassed to reveal their most significant memories and desires, or that those memories and longings were buried deeply in the subconscious mind. Yet the Iroquois had had this insight for centuries and had developed methods to accommodate suppressed desires. Free association is still used by psychiatrists today.

See also PSYCHOTHERAPY.

### Sources/Further Reading

Borger, Irene. "Ritual Process of the Iroquois False Face Society." *Dreamworks* 2 (Summer 1982): 301–309.

Farb, Peter. *Man's Rise to Civilization as Shown by the Indians of North America from Primeval Times to the Coming of the Industrial State.* New York: E.P. Dutton & Company, 1968.

Trigger, Bruce G. *Case Studies in Anthropology: The Huron Farmers of the North.* New York: Holt Rinehart and Winston, 1969.

Wallace, Anthony F. "Dreams and the Wishes of the Soul: A Type of Psychoanalytic Theory among the Seventeenth-Century Iroquois." *American Anthropologist* 60, no. 2 (April 1958): 234–248.

———. "Psychoanalysis Among the Iroquois of New York State." In *The Americas on the Eve of the Discovery,* edited by Harold E. Driver. Englewood Cliffs, N.J.: Prentice Hall, 1964.

Vogel, Virgil J. *America Indian Medicine.* Norman: University of Oklahoma Press, 1970.

## freeze-drying (A.D. 1000) *South American Andean cultures*

Freeze-drying, which gives food a shelf live of several years, works through a principle called *sublimation.* When solid material such as ice changes directly into a gas without first going through a liquid state, moisture is removed from food or whatever substance is being freeze dried. Freezing allows the object to retain its original shape. The absence of water makes it difficult for microorganisms to live in the food and stops chemical changes associated with spoilage. Freeze-drying helps food to retain much of its flavor.

Thousands of years ago the pre-Inca, living in what is now Peru, discovered the principle of freeze-drying, the underlying process that is used today for such foods as instant mashed POTATOES. (The Inca Empire was established in about A.D. 1000.) Although they utilized the technique with a number of vegetables, the Inca's main use of freeze-drying was to preserve their surplus potato crop and make it easier to transport and store. When the potatoes had been harvested, they were arranged on the ground and left overnight to freeze. After cold mountain temperatures froze the tubers, the water inside slowly vaporized under the low air pressure. The Inca hastened the process by walking over the potatoes to squeeze out the moisture, repeating the process several times. The finished product was either stored whole or ground into white potato flour that was used as the basis of a bread and could be stored for an indefinite period. When they were reconstituted, *ckaya* (freeze-dried SWEET POTATOES) and *ch'un~o* (freeze-dried "bitter" potatoes) were used in soups and stews as well as in bread. They remain a mainstay in the Andean diet today.

When Spanish explorers found the workers in the Andean silver mines eating freeze-dried potatoes, they recognized a chance to make money on this commodity. Within a short time speculators streamed across the Atlantic to purchase supplies from producers. They resold them at inflated prices to the Spaniards who now ran the mines and then returned home wealthy men. Despite the interest of speculators, for the most part non-Indians ignored the process of freeze-drying for hundreds of years. It gained acceptance outside of the Andes when scientists used it to preserve blood plasma during World War II.

In the 1960s commercial freeze-drying began to be used for foods, such as easily transported meals for campers. Instant potato flakes and freeze-dried coffee were the first products to be marketed on grocery store shelves. Today freeze-drying is used on about 400 foods, including vegetables, meat, and dairy products, such as cheese for macaroni and cheese dinners. It is also used to preserve flowers.

See also FOOD PRESERVATION.

## Sources/Further Reading

Aschkenasy, Herbert. "Freeze Drying." *Scientific American Working Knowledge.* URL: http://www.sciam.com/0996issue/0996working.html. Downloaded on August 15, 1999.

Coe, Sophie. *America's First Cuisines.* Austin: University of Texas Press, 1994.

Tannahill, Reay. *Food in History.* New York: Stein and Day, 1973.

Weatherford, Jack. *Indian Givers: How the Indians of the Americas Transformed the World.* New York: Fawcett Columbine, 1988.

**fringed clothing** (precontact) *North American Northeast, Great Plains, and California cultures*

Fringe, a decorative border of hanging strips, was often a feature of the hide clothing worn by Indians of many North American tribes. Because sewing tanned hides into garments was a time-consuming endeavor, American Indian clothing patterns were simple and came about as a compromise between the shape of the potential wearer's body and the shape of the hide being used for a particular garment. Often garment makers did not trim the hides when sewing seams, and the excess leather was cut into fringe instead. If there was not enough surplus hide for fringing, they might sew a band of fringe onto the garment after it was completed. Sometimes they tied thongs onto garments in pairs in order to stimulate long fringe. This form of edging was a popular ornamentation on the bottoms and shoulders of shirts and along the side seam of leggings. Sometimes the strands were decorated with seeds or shells. After contact with Europeans, American Indians decorated fringes with beads.

The style of fringe worn depended on the tribe. The Kiowa and Comanche who lived on the southern plains wore long twisted fringe, often gathered into bunches. The long heel fringes worn by southern plains dwellers were presumably to erase the tracks of the wearer as he walked. The Blackfeet, Cheyenne, and Crow of the northern plains also tended to wear long, twisted fringe on their garments. Other northern plains people tended to wear long, straight fringe. American Indians of the Eastern Woodlands generally wore garments with shorter fringes so they would not become tangled in underbrush. The buckskin aprons of males in some California tribes were partially fringed in order to provide ventilation in that warm climate.

European fur traders and early settlers quickly adopted fringed buckskin shirts, jackets, and leggings as their own. Mountain men and fur trappers dressed in hides of their own trapping, copying the traditional Indian style of dress they encountered on their travels. Typical mountain man attire in the early 1800s included a shirt and leggings that were worn over a breechcloth. Sometimes long fringes that decorated shirts and leggings consisted of individual thongs that had been pushed into the seams and knotted on the inside. The men believed that these fringes served to drain water from their garments in storms. They wore so much fringe that Indians of some tribes called them the "fringe people." Today modern fashion designers often decorate leather garments such as jackets with fringe. Although the popularity of this style of ornamentation waxes and wanes with fashion trends, it has endured for centuries.

See also MOCCASINS; TANNING, BRAIN; TROUSERS.

## Sources/Further Reading

Driver, Harold E. *Indians of North America.* Chicago: University of Chicago Press, 1969.

Koch, Ronald P. *Dress Clothing of the Plains Indians.* Norman: University of Oklahoma Press, 1977.

Paterek, Josephine, Ph.D. *Encyclopedia of American Indian Costume.* Denver, Colo.: ABC Clio, Inc., 1994.

Weatherford, Jack. *Indian Givers: How the Indians of the Americas Transformed the World.* New York: Fawcett Columbine, 1988.

Wilcox, R. Turner. *Five Centuries of American Costume.* New York: Charles Scribner's Sons, 1963.

# games, dice (precontact) *North American, Mesoamerican cultures*

Games of chance played by throwing dice, small objects with different markings on each side, were part of many ancient cultures throughout the world. American Indians were no exception. Nearly every indigenous American culture played dice games. The dice they used were made of many materials, including shells, peach or plum pits, grains of corn, beans, pottery disks, walnut shells, beaver or woodchuck teeth, bone staves, and wooden blocks, among others. In most cases the dice were marked on two sides. Indians tossed the dice by hand in some games and placed them into a bowl or basket in others. Dice games using baskets were usually played by women. Many of the American Indian dice games were ceremonial in nature and usually played by men. Some dice games were played by keeping count with sticks that passed from player to player, depending on the throw. Other games resembling modern BOARD GAMES were played with a counting board for keeping score. Gambling was frequently a part of dice games.

An example of an American Indian dice game is that of fox and geese, played for hundreds of years by Inuit in the North American Arctic. Inuit people living near the present-day community of Point Barrow, Alaska, fashioned ducks, geese, and a fox out of ivory. The ducks and geese were about $1\frac{3}{4}$ inch0es long, and the fox was about $2\frac{3}{4}$ inches long. The fox was made with four legs so that it could stand. The ducks and geese were shaped with flat bellies so that they could land upright without the aid of legs. The purpose of the game was to accumulate the most points by throwing the ivory ducks and geese in the air and then noting how they landed. The player who had the most ducks and geese in the upright position was awarded points. Another version of the game used carved figures in the shapes of men, women, and waterfowl. Those that landed in a standing position were awarded to the person they were fac-

ing. The game was played until one player had all of the dice and the other had none.

## Sources/Further Reading

Culin, Stewart. *Games of the North American Indians.* Reprint. Lincoln: University of Nebraska Press, 1992.

Gabriel, Kathryn. *Gambler Way: Indian Gaming in Mythology, History and Archaeology in North America.* Boulder, Colo.: Johnson Books, 1996.

Murdoch, John. *Ethnological Results of the Point Barrow Expedition. Ninth Annual Report of the Bureau of Ethnology, 1887–1888.* Washington, D.C.: Smithsonian Institution, 1892.

# games, footbag (hackey sack) (precontact) *North American Great Plains cultures*

Footbag games involve using the feet—or the feet, head and arms—to keep a softball in the air. Hackey sack is a modern version of a footbag game. Women and girls in a number of North American Indian tribes routinely played these games. The balls that they used were about six to seven inches in diameter and were stuffed with deer, antelope, or buffalo hair. They were covered with buckskin by the Inuit of the Arctic. The Cheyenne and Mandan of the plains sometimes decorated the buckskin covers with elaborate quillwork and, after European contact, beadwork. The Gros Ventre (Atsina) and Crow covered the animal fur with a bladder netted with sinew.

Maximillian, prince of Wied in Germany, who in 1832–34 observed Mandan women playing the sport, gave this description in *Travels in the Interior of North America:* "The women are expert in playing with a large leathern ball which they let fall alternately on their foot and knee, again throwing it up and catching it, and thus keeping it in motion for a length of time without letting it fall to the ground." Prizes were given for the winner.

Arapaho and Cheyenne women played the game somewhat differently. In this version of the game the balls had a thong attached to them. Among the Arapaho, a young woman would hold the thong in her hand while throwing and catching the ball. Cheyenne women held the 24-inch thong in their hands and kicked the ball. The game's goal was to kick the ball as many times as possible without missing. In the Cheyenne game, the ball had to be kicked without letting the ball or the foot touch the ground. A Ho-Chunk game was similar. Its goal was for the player to make 100 successful kicks. When young women missed, they had to pass their turn and the footbag to another person who would attempt to reach the set number of kicks.

## Sources/Further Reading

Culin, Stewart. *Games of the North American Indians.* Reprint. Lincoln: University of Nebraska Press, 1992.

Niethammer, Carolyn. *Daughters of the Earth: The Lives and Legends of American Indian Women.* New York: Macmillan Publishing Company, 1977.

**games, string** See CAT'S CRADLE.

**gardens, botanical** (ca. A.D. 1100) *Mesoamerican cultures*

The Aztec, whose empire was established in what is now Mexico in about A.D. 1100, planted lavish botanical gardens featuring enormous collections of plants both native to the area and imported from the tropical coast hundreds of miles distant. Botanist John Bartram is often credited with planting the first botanical garden in America. Although he started the first in the United States, the Aztec had botanical gardens long before Bartram's. These arboretums, containing varieties of medicinal, hallucinatory, and sweet-smelling plants, were for the amusement and education of those who visited these sites. Spanish historian Cervantes de Salizar described the gardens of the Emperor Montezuma as containing "medicinal and aromatic herbs, flowers, and trees with fragrant blossoms." (See also GARDENS, HERB.) Not only were plants collected so that they could be preserved and displayed, they were also actively used as the basis for an elaborate system of PLANT CLASSIFICATION and as laboratories for the discovery of medical breakthroughs. (See also PHARMACOLOGY; MEDICAL RESEARCH.) No vegetables were grown in these gardens.

The Tetzcotzinco garden of the poet-king Netzahualcoyotl, who reigned over the mountainous area of the Aztec Empire between 1426 and 1474, was legendary in its time. In 1530 one of his descendants described the experience of visiting it as being like falling into a garden raining with aromatic tropical flowers. Many of the plants there had been brought from remote places. Several botanical gardens were also a feature of the capital city of Tenochtitlan, which was the largest

metropolis in North America, and perhaps the world, serving as a residence for about a quarter of a million people. DAHLIAS and ZINNIAS were two of the flowers grown in Aztec gardens that still give gardeners pleasure today.

The Spaniards were astounded when they saw these Aztec gardens. Although some European monasteries had collections of plants in their herb gardens, they were small in comparison to the Aztec gardens. Some historians believe that the impetus for European botanical gardens came from a letter, first published in 1522, that Spanish explorer Hernán Cortés wrote to Emperor Charles V (King Charles I of Spain) describing Montezuma's gardens. The first private botanical garden in Europe belonged to Andrea Navagero, a Venetian statesman, who planted it the same year the Cortés letter was made public. The first public botanical gardens were in Pisa and Padua, Italy, and were not planted until the 1520s. The Cortés letter may not have directly inspired European botanical gardens, but certainly the exploration of the Western Hemisphere with its exotic flora sparked a European interest in botany, including the republication of several ancient works on plants.

## Sources/Further Reading

Coe, Sophie. *America's First Cuisines.* Austin: University of Texas Press, 1994.

Josephy, Jr., Alvin M., ed. *America in 1492: The World of the Indian People Before the Arrival of Columbus.* New York: Random House, 1991.

Nabhan, Gary. *Enduring Seeds: Native American Agriculture and Wild Plant Conservation.* San Francisco: North Point Press, 1989.

Ortiz de Montellano, Bernard. *Aztec Medicine, Health, and Nutrition.* New Brunswick, N.J.: Rutgers University Press, 1990.

**gardens, herb** (precontact) *North American Northeast and Southeast, Mesoamerican cultures*

American Indians not only cultivated food crops, they also planted herbs that were frequently used for medicinal purposes. Early European observers saw such gardens growing at Indian settlements that had been abandoned with the encroachment of colonists in the eastern part of North America. In his book *American Indian Medicine,* Virgil Vogel wrote that one colonial physician stated he was "persuaded that the reason why they took all these pains in planting these Simples was owing to their Doctor's Care, that upon all Occasions they might be provided with these Vegetables that were proper for the Indian Distempers, or any other use they might have occasion to make of them." (Simples were herbs used to cure disease.)

Anthropologist Harold Driver lists the following herbs as having been domesticated by Indians in the Americas: albahaca (*Ocimum micranthum*), aquau (*Bixa orellana*) (see also ACHIOTE), campana (*Datura candida*), chicasquil (*Jatropha acomitfolia*), flor de mechuda (*Caesalpina sp.*), physic nut (*Jatropha curcas*), and several types of maguey (see also AGAVE).

That the Aztec planted medicinal herbs in botanical gardens is well documented. The Aztec Empire was established in Mesoamerica in about A.D. 1100. According to Spanish historian Cervantes de Salizar, Montezuma I established a series of botanical gardens in 1467 that became a center for pharmacological experiments. The emperor ordered his physician to test the herbs on patients and to use his knowledge of them to treat members of the royal court. He recorded that plants were given free to patients in return for their promise to report on the results.

See also GARDENS, BOTANICAL; MEDICAL RESEARCH; PHARMACOLOGY.

### Sources/Further Reading

Hurt, R. Douglas. *Indian Agriculture in the Americas: Prehistory to Present.* Lawrence: University Press of Kansas, 1988.

Nabhan, Gary. *Enduring Seeds: Native American Agriculture and Wild Plant Conservation.* San Francisco: North Point Press, 1989.

Ortiz de Montellano, Bernard. *Aztec Medicine, Health and Nutrition.* New Brunswick, N.J.: Rutgers University Press, 1990.

Vogel, Virgil. *American Indian Medicine.* Norman: University of Oklahoma Press, 1970.

## gastroenteritis treatment (precontact)
*Mesoamerican; North American Northeastern, Great Plains, and Southwest cultures*

Gastroenteritis is an inflammation of the intestines and stomach, entailing several problems. This disorder is often caused by a bacteria, a virus, or other pathogens that are transmitted through food or water; symptoms are vomiting, diarrhea, abdominal cramps or pain, and nausea.

American Indians from a number of culture areas treated gastroenteritis successfully. The Aztec, whose empire was established in Mesoamerica in about A.D. 1100, took an approach to treatment that was very effective. As was usual in this culture, the first step was a steam bath. (See also STEAM ROOMS.) Aztec physicians then administered several possible medications from their pharmacy. (See also PHARMACOLOGY.) In the event the gastroenteritis was accompanied by fever, the patient would receive *achiotl* (*Bixa orellana*) (see also ACHIOTE), a medicinal plant cultivated in herb gardens that was effective in treating both. (See also GARDENS, HERB.) In cases where internal bleeding may have been present, the patient would receive *matlaliztic* (*Commelina pallida*) which was an effective HEMOSTAT and antidiarrheal medicine. For lower abdominal pain, the patient would be prescribed *macpalxochitl* (*Chiranthodendron*) also effective for both conditions. For diarrhea the patient would be given *capolin* (*Prunus capulli*), which was also effective in treating fevers. For indigestion *chichiualxochitl* (*Carica papaya*) was prescribed, because it was an effective digestive remedy. (See also PAPAYAS; PRESCRIPTIONS.) GUAVA was also used by indigenous Americans to treat gastroenteritis.

North American Indians used horsemint (*Monarda punctata*) as an antiemetic. (See also MINTS, BOTANICAL.) It was effective in treating nausea as well as vomiting. The Dakota and Ho-Chunk, who lived on the northern plains, used horsemint in treating cholera, a disease that causes vomiting and watery diarrhea. In 1882 horsemint was entered into the United States Pharmacopoeia (a list of drugs and dosages officially sanctioned by the medical community) and stayed there until 1950. The Catawba and Mesquaki tribes of North America used roots or vines or both to effectively treat diarrhea, vomiting, and internal bleeding. For difficult diarrhea the Menominee of the upper Midwest used the bark of the dogwood tree, a tree native to North America, prepared as a tea and administered into the rectum with a syringe. (See also ENEMAS.)

### Sources/Further Reading

Lust, John. *The Herb Book.* New York: Bantam Books, 1974.

Montellano, Bernard R. Ortiz. *Aztec Medicine, Health and Nutrition.* New Brunswick, N.J.: Rutgers University Press, 1990.

Vogel, Virgil J. *American Indian Medicine.* Norman: University of Oklahoma Press, 1970.

Weiner, Michael A. *Earth Medicine, Earth Food: Plant Remedies, Drugs, and Natural Foods of the North American Indian.* New York: Fawcett Columbine, 1990.

## geometry (ca. 1200 B.C.) *Mesoamerican, South American Andean, North American Southwest cultures*

The mathematics of the properties of measurement and relationships of points, lines, and angles, known as solid geometry, was developed by the Indians of North, Meso-, and South America independently of the systems devised by the ancient Greek, Chinese, or the people of the Middle East. Based on the circle, indigenous geometry has been practiced throughout the Americas for well over 2,000 years and probably longer. Archaeological evidence shows that ancient Americans applied their knowledge of the principles of geometry to architecture, city planning, and the ornamental designs they used in sculpture, painting, and textile patterns, such as those woven by the Maya of Mesoamerica for hundreds of years. (Maya culture arose in Mesoamerica and the southern part of Mexico in about 1500 B.C.)

Precise theoretical and working knowledge of geometry was needed to build the Mesoamerican PYRAMIDS that were constructed by pre-Peruvian people in El Aspero in about 3000 B.C. or by the Olmec in about 1200 B.C. in the Yucatán Peninsula of what is now Mexico. This knowledge was also needed to build the monumental stone works of the Moche, whose culture began to flourish in what is now Peru in about 200 B.C. Another example of geometrical theory and practice on a grand scale are the Nazca lines, huge geometrical designs scribed into the desert in what is now Peru. (The Nazca culture flourished from about 900 B.C. to A.D. 600.) These mysterious geometric figures and animal shapes, whose lines radiate from diverse centers, are organized by a set of principles. So vast in scope that they can only be viewed from the air, the designs would have been impossible to execute without careful prior planning and an understanding of geometry.

An analysis of the architectural structures throughout the Americas also shows evidence of a complex geometry. In the pueblos built by the Anasazi starting between A.D. 700 and A.D. 900 in Chaco Canyon in what is now New Mexico are kivas, or round ceremonial rooms, which show evidence of spatial planning, as do site plans of many ancient cities. The architectural and art works of Mesoamerica, offer similar proof.

In order to draw circles, which then could be bisected and turned into polygons, the Aztec, whose empire was established in Mesoamerica in about A.D. 1100, were known to have used a compass, consisting of a cord with a peg at each end. This was called a *tlayolloanaloni* in the Aztec language Nahuatl. The *temetzetepilolli*, a plumb made from a weight tied to a string, produced a vertical line. Aztec and Maya builders also used a level, called a *quamniztli*, and a square in order to be able to create right angles.

Western scientists were slow to recognize the American Indian command of geometrical principles. One reason for this is that the buildings they studied were often eroded, causing the angles, alignments, and circles to change somewhat over the hundreds of years since their construction. Second, all the world's geometries are essentially a grammar of space, based on certain principles. Although the "grammatical" rules of American Indian geometry are the same as those of Greek, Islamic, or Chinese geometrical systems, the message they were intended to convey differed. Often the angles and alignments of these buildings are not what one would expect operating from the perspective of Western geometry. In the past, they were written off as sloppy planning. Modern archaeologists, however, have identified several Mesoamerican sites that may have been used as astronomical OBSERVATORIES. (See also ASTRONOMY.) They also believe that the rising and setting of the planet Venus or stellar constellations often determined the positioning of buildings in sacred complexes.

According to Francine Vinette, a professor of applied mathematics writing in *Native American Mathematics,* Mesoamerican designers used patterns and templates, not only for the layout of their buildings but for sculpture and painting. In addition to the ability to create nearly perfect right angles and circles when desired, symmetry—the repetition of design elements on both sides of a central axis—is another feature of these works that proves an understanding of geometrical principles. Geometrical designs can be seen today in the POTTERY of the Zuni and Acoma Pueblo people, who are the descendants of the Anasazi, and those on the rugs woven (see also WEAVING TECHNIQUES) by the Navajo (Dineh) people of the desert Southwest of what is now the United States.

See also ARCHITECTS; STONEMASONRY TECHNIQUES; URBAN PLANNING.

## Sources/Further Reading

Aveni, Anthony. "The Nazca Lines: Patterns in the Desert." *Archaeology Magazine* 39, no. 4 (July–August 1986): 32–39.

Closs, Michael P., ed. *Native American Mathematics.* Austin: University of Texas Press, 1986.

Lawlor, Robert. *Sacred Geometry: Philosophy and Practice.* London: Thames and Hudson, 1992.

Nabokov, Peter and Robert Easton. *Native American Architecture.* New York: Oxford University Press, 1989.

Pinxten, Rik. *Towards a Navajo Indian Geometry.* Ghent, Belgium: Kultuur, Kennis en Intergratie, 1987.

Zazlow, Bert. "Pattern Dissemination in the Prehistoric Southwest and Mesoamerica: a Comparison of Hohokam Decorative Patterns with Patterns from the Upper Gila Area and from the Valley of Oaxaca." *Anthropological Research Paper: No. 25.* Tempe: Arizona State University, 1981.

**goggles, snow** See SNOW GOGGLES.

**goiter prevention (iodine)** (precontact) *North American Northwest Coast, Northeastern, Arctic, and Great Plains; Mesoamerican; South American Central and Southern Andes cultures*

A goiter is an enlargement of the thyroid gland that causes the neck to swell. Simple goiters are caused by a deficiency of iodine. Goiter affected the European immigrants to the New World but was rarely seen among American Indians. American Indians along the Pacific Coasts of North, Meso- and South America harvested iodine-rich kelp (*Macrocystis*) by the ton to prevent the disease. The Inca, whose empire was established about A.D. 1000 in what are Peru and parts of Bolivia, dried the kelp and distributed it as a food additive throughout the Andes.

American Indians who lived on both coasts of the Americas ate fish eggs, which are also high in iodine, to prevent goiter. Alaska natives of the frozen north ate fish eggs as well, adding goiter-preventing iodine to their diets. Precontact American Indians living inland from the coasts ate PUMPKIN seeds and SUNFLOWER seeds, two other good sources of iodine.

During the Middle Ages in Europe medicine consisted mainly of magic and alchemy. Even Renaissance medical practitioners had no idea what caused goiter, so Europeans were not able to prevent it. When it occurred, the wealthy wore neck ruffs in order to conceal the disfigurement. The element iodine was not isolated until 1863 by German chemists Ferdinand Reich and H. Richter. Only later would Western science discover the nutritional importance of iodine as a goiter preventative—something American Indians had known for centuries. Today in the United States iodine is added to table salt to prevent goiters.

## Sources/Further Reading

Bressani, R. and R. Arroyave. "Nutritive Value of Pumpkin Seed. Essential Amino Acid Content and Protein Value of Pumpkin Seed (Cucurbita Farinosa)." *Journal of Agricultural and Food Chemistry* 11, no. 29 (1963): 29–33.

Hutchens, Alma R. *Indian Herbology of North America.* Boston: Shambhala, 1991.

Vogel, Virgil. *American Indian Medicine.* Norman: University of Oklahoma Press, 1977.

Weatherford, Jack. *Indian Givers: How the Indians of the Americas Transformed the World.* New York: Fawcett Columbine, 1988.

Weiner, Michael A. *Earth Medicine Earth Food: The Classic Guide to the Herbal Remedies and Wild Plants of the North American Indians.* New York: Fawcett Columbine, 1980.

**gold**   See METALS, PRECIOUS.

**gold panning** (precontact) *Circum-Caribbean, South American Andean, Mesoamerican cultures*

Gold panning is the practice of scooping sediment from the bed of a stream, covering it with water in a slope-sided pan, and carefully rotating the pan or rocking it so that the water carries away the lighter particles and leaves behind heavier bits of gold. American Indians who lived in what are now the Caribbean, and Mesoamerica used this method to harvest gold that had been carried into streams by water runoff after storms. Content with the amount of gold they could take from streams and rivers or pick up from the ground, these metalworking tribes felt no need to go digging for it. Of all the indigenous Americans, only the Inca actually mined for gold, excavating underground shafts and pits to pull gold and silver ore from the earth, in mines located high in the Andes. They also employed placer mining (see also MINING, PLACER) and HYDRAULICS. (The Inca Empire was established in what are now Peru and parts of Bolivia in about A.D. 1000.)

When the Spaniards saw American Indians panning for gold, they were immediately fascinated by the practice. If gold was so easy to obtain that it could be scooped from the water with pans, then it was obvious that much more could be pulled from the earth by mining. Columbus brought back only a small amount of gold from his voyages, yet that was enough to spur a transatlantic gold rush. The Spaniards mounted expeditions to look for gold, including those of Hernán Cortés among the Aztec, Francisco Pizarro among the Inca in the Andes of what is now Peru, Hernando de Soto in what is now Florida and the Carolinas, Francisco Vásquez de Coronado in what is now New Mexico and Arizona, and Francisco de Orellana in the Amazon Basin.

In the mid-1800s, prospectors of European descent discovered nuggets in streams in what are now California, Colorado, and the Black Hills of western South Dakota. This led to a concerted migration westward to the gold fields, some on land ceded to the Indians by treaty to the United States before discovery of the ore and some on Indian land taken by the government after the gold strikes. Although mining operations were quickly established, the first gold seekers in the American West sought their fortunes by panning the streams to extract gold flakes and nuggets from them, relying on the same technology that Indians from what are now Mexico and the Caribbean had done for centuries.

See also GOLD PLATING; LOST WAX CASTING TECHNIQUE; METALS, PRECIOUS; METALLURGY.

**Sources/Further Reading**
Crow, John A. *The Epic of Latin America.* New York: Doubleday, 1946.

Driver, Harold E. *Indians of North America.* Chicago: University of Chicago Press, 1969.

Indians living in North America and the Caribbean panned for gold rather than mining it. The Spaniards who saw this practice adopted it. By the time of the California gold rush, which began in 1849, panning for gold in stream and rivers had become common among non-Indian prospectors. This drawing of Caribbean gold panners by Gonzalo Oviedo y Valdes was published in the early 1500s. *(Stock Montage/The Newberry Library)*

Josephy, Jr., Alvin M., ed. *America in 1492: The World of the Indian People Before the Arrival of Columbus.* New York: Random House, 1991.

Longhena, Maria. *Ancient Mexico: The History and Culture of the Maya, Aztecs, and Other Pre-Columbian Peoples.* New York: Stewart, Tabori & Chang, 1998.

Weatherford, Jack. *Native Roots: How the Indians Enriched America.* New York: Fawcett Columbine, 1991.

## gold plating (ca. 1000 B.C.) *South American Andean cultures*

Gold plating is one of several processes of using gold to covering other metals. The Chavin, who lived in what is now Peru starting in about 1000 B.C., devised several methods of gold plating. One involved hammering the metal into thin FOIL sheets that was then adhered to objects. Another used acid to dissolve copper contained in an alloy, leaving a thin layer of gold on the surface. ELECTROPLATING was yet another method the Moche used to give objects that were made from other metals the appearance of gold. The Moche, whose culture arose in what is now Peru in about 200 B.C., continued these metallurgical techniques, which they were the first people in the world to employ. (See also METALLURGY.) Goldworking began in the area of present-day Peru and spread toward present-day Mexico in the north.

The surface-fusion technique of gold plating invented by the pre-Inca cultures of Peru used gold foil or sheet metal that was hammered onto a copper object that was being plated. The metal workers then heated this until the gold melted, covering the copper. The same thing could be accomplished by pouring molten gold over the object.

The Moche achieved a remarkably high degree of sophistication compared to other world cultures at that time. An outstanding example of this is their development of an alloy called *tumbaga,* a mixture of gold and copper that can also contain other metals. By adding copper, metalworkers decreased the melting point of gold, making it much easier to work with. Once the Moche had formed a utensil or implement from *tumbaga,* the surface of that object contained some copper. Metalworkers immersed the object in an acid, which removed the copper, leaving a thin film of gold behind. They then heated and burnished this until it gave the appearance of pure gold.

The Inca, who established an empire in what are now Peru and parts of Bolivia in about A.D. 1000, learned metalworking from the Moche people, but they elaborated on their techniques, especially that for gold plating. First they smelted an alloy of gold, silver, and copper called *tumbaga,* as the Moche had done. Then they shaped it into an ingot that was annealed (heated) several times, and each time beaten into an ever-thinner sheet. With each ANNEALING a copper oxide was produced and removed with a saltwater rinse; as the copper was removed, the gold came to the surface. Finally, the Moche metalworkers used a paste of iron sulfate and salt to remove the silver from the sheet. The gold, which remained granular at the surface of the sheet, was heated and burnished to form the uniquely shiny surface of Andean goldwork.

### Sources/Further Reading

Kidwell, Clara Sue and Peter Nabokov. "Directions in Native American Science and Technology." In *Studying Native America: Problems and Prospects,* edited by Russell Thornton. Madison: University of Wisconsin Press, 1998.

Morris, Craig and Adriana von Hagen. *Inka Empire and its Andean Origins.* New York: Abbeville Press Publishers, 1993.

Reader's Digest Association, Inc. *Mysteries of the Ancient Americas: The New World before Columbus.* Pleasantville, N.Y.: Reader's Digest Books, 1986.

## gourds (8000 B.C.) *Mesoamerican, North American Northeast, Circum-Caribbean, South American Tropical Forest and Andean cultures*

Hard-shelled fruits that grow on vines are called gourds. Their sizes range from that of a marble to over seven feet long. The smaller gourds (*Cucurbita pepo,* var. *ovifera*) are a variety of the same family as PUMPKINS and SQUASH and are indigenous to the Americas. Bottle gourds (*Lagenaria siceraria*) are usually larger and are thought to be one of the first crops cultivated by American Indians. Bottle gourds were cultivated in what is now Mexico as early as 8000 B.C. and by agriculturists of the Eastern Woodlands of North America between 3000 and 2000 B.C. Bottle gourds are indigenous to Africa as well as North America.

Many gourds, unlike squash, are bitter and contain substances that are purgative at best and poisonous at worst. The buffalo gourd that grows in the North American Southwest is so pungent that it is used as an INSECT REPELLENT and DETERGENT by Pueblo peoples. Although gourds are grown today primarily for ornamental use, American Indians raised them for many purposes. These included their use as bowls, scoops, COLANDERS, ladles, and spoons, in addition to canteens and dippers. Larger gourds were used as cooking vessels that were filled with water into which hot stones were dropped. Gourds were also used as rattles, or MARACAS, and whistles. American Indians of the Eastern Woodlands sometimes hung clusters of gourds on a pole in their cornfields to serve as homes for insect-eating birds. Indians in what is now northern Peru used them for floats for their fishing nets. Some gourds were painted or engraved and used as decorative objects. Many of the uses for gourds were similar to those for CALABASHES.

European colonists to North America took up the practice of growing gourd vines on arbors to provide shade. They used the gourds that these vines produced in the same ways as the American Indians did. They also used them as darning eggs and homemade salt and pepper shakers.

### Sources/Further Reading

Bailey, L. H. *The Garden of Gourds.* Mt. Gilead, Ohio: American Gourd Society, Inc., 1956.

Decker-Walters, D. S., T. W. Walters, C. W. Cowan, and B. D. Smith. "Isozymic Characterization of Wild Populations of *Cucurbita pepo.*" *Journal of Ethnobiology* 13 (1993): 55–72.

Dunmire, William W. and Gail D. Tierney. *Wild Plants of the Pueblo Province: Exploring Ancient and Enduring Uses.* Santa Fe: Museum of New Mexico Press, 1995.

Heiser, C. B. *The Gourd Book.* Norman: University of Oklahoma Press, 1979.

Hurt, R. Douglas. *Indian Agriculture in the Americas: Prehistory to Present.* Lawrence: University Press of Kansas, 1988.

*Nature Bulletin No. 284-A.* Cook County, Ill.: Forest Preserve District of Cook County, 1967.

**grafts, skin**    See SKIN GRAFTS.

**granulation**    (ca. A.D. 1700) *North American Southwest, Great Plains, and Northeastern cultures*

When an open wound occurs on the body it begins to heal itself by supplying blood to the area. Granulation begins when the body starts growing capillary (small blood vessel) buds. These capillary buds look granular in appearance. Granulation is the process by which the body is able to heal itself by providing a large supply of blood to a wound that then granulates, or forms into grains. Granulation helps the body provide a surface where healing can be accomplished while keeping the risk of infection to a minimum. Capillaries (very small blood vessels) that have been damaged by a wound produce capillary buds. These buds then develop into capillaries that grow and come into contact with surrounding capillary buds and capillaries, which then turn into capillary loops after contact. Tissue cells near these capillaries begin to grow around these capillaries and granulate to establish a healing surface in the wound. All of this eventually becomes scar tissue when the healing process is complete.

Many North American Indian tribes understood that wounds, in particular large wounds, needed to heal from the inside out, and thus encouraged granulation. North American Indians stimulated it by the use of drains (see also DRAINAGE, SURGICAL AND WOUND) and HEMOSTATS (mechanical or chemical means of stopping or slowing bleeding). These drains were made of various materials depending on the tribe treating the wound. Some of the drains were made of plant fibers and some of wood or bark strips, which were placed in the wound at the bottom. Sutures were then placed around the drain. The stitches would be removed about nine days later. Eventually the drain would be removed when it appeared to be healing and there were no signs of infection. Some tribes used hemostats, in the form of fiber, to help blood clot more quickly and speed healing. In the event an infection started, Indian physicians would treat it with ANTIBIOTICS.

American Indians—including the Mescalero Apache of the Southwest, the Dakota and the Ho-Chunk of the Great Plains, and the Tuscarora of the Northeast—were using this type of medical knowledge and skills before the Europeans did.

Many European healers at the time of contact recommended treating wounds by pouring boiling oil on them and waiting for "laudable" pus, something they took as a sign of healing rather than infection.

**Sources/Further Reading**

Stone, Eric. *Medicine Among the American Indians.* Reprint. New York: Hafner Publishing Company, 1962. (Originally published in 1932.)

Vogel, Virgil. *American Indian Medicine.* Norman: University of Oklahoma Press, 1970.

**grapes**    (precontact) *North American Southeast and Northeast cultures*

Many varieties of grapes (*Vitis rotundifolia*) grew wild throughout the North American continent. American Indians who lived in the areas where these clusters of small, sweet fruits grew used them as a food source. Although grapes had been cultivated in the Old World for thousands of years, primarily for winemaking purposes, European explorers and later colonists were extremely impressed by the wild American grapes they found in their travels.

In 1524 Giovanni da Verazzano, the Italian navigator who explored the Cape Fear River Valley in what is now North Carolina, wrote in his logbook: "Grapes of such greatness, yet wild, as France, Spain, nor Italy hath no greater." Sixty years later two of Sir Walter Raleigh's captains, Philip Amadas and Arthur Barlowe, reported that grapes grew so profusely on the seacoast of what is now North Carolina that the waves washed over them. Raleigh said that they were "on the sand and on the green soil, on the hills as on the plains, as well as on every little shrub . . . also climbing towards the tops of tall cedars . . . in all the world the like abundance is not to be found." The grapes these explorers described are the variety now known as muscadine, native to the south and grown nowhere else. The SCUPPERNONG GRAPE, a sport (mutation) of the muscadine is perhaps the most well-known North American indigenous grape today.

In addition to muscadine and scuppernong, common types of indigenous grapes included the Arkansas grape, black grape, bull grape, bullace grape, bullet grape, bush grape, currant grape, flowers grape, Roanoke grape, southern fox grape, and the warty grape. They grew from southern Delaware to southern Illinois, through Arkansas, Missouri and Texas and east to the Atlantic. Because they need moisture, riverbanks, swamps, and sandy, well-drained bottomlands were and remain their favorite habitats.

Like the American Indians, the colonists ate wild grapes but made no attempts to cultivate them until the late 1700s. Abundant in the wild, muscadines became an ingredient of jellies and pies and were made into juice. Harkening to their European traditions, the settlers also made wine for their own consumption. Despite an abundance of grapes, commercial winemaking in the New World, at least in the French and Spanish territories, was frowned upon, ensuring that vintners in

France and Europe could continue to monopolize the wine market in the colonies.

Although many states, including California and New York, currently have flourishing wine industries, most of the commercially grown grapes come from imported European stock. Horticulturists, especially in the South, have begun to promote indigenous grapes as a cash crop, extolling the health benefits of the muscadine variety. According to studies conducted at Mississippi State University by horticulturist James B. Magee and nutritionist Betty Ector, muscadines contain high levels of reservatrol, a chemical compound, in their skins, pulp, and seeds. In a 1997 study reported in *Science,* University of Illinois researchers found reservatrol from grapes to be anticarcinogenic, inhibiting tumor promotion.

## Sources/Further Reading

Stanley, Doris. "America's First Grape, the Muscadine." *Agricultural Research Magazine* (November 1997). URL: http://www.usda.gor/lis/AR/archive/nov97/musc1197.htm.

The Winemaking Home Page/Napa Valley. "Native North American Grapes." URL: wysiwyg://16/http://www.geocities.com/Napa Valley/1172/rotundif.html. Downloaded on June 17, 1998.

## Great Law of Peace  See IROQUOIS CONSTITUTION.

## grits  See CORNMEAL.

## groundnuts  See PEANUTS.

## guacamole  (precontact) *Mesoamerican cultures*

The mixture of mashed AVOCADOS and sometimes TOMATOES that is used as a tortilla dip today was made and enjoyed by the Aztec. They called the dish a *huaca-mulli* in Nahautl, the Aztec language. Although precontact Aztec cooks used avocados and tomatoes, they did not include onions, a European plant. The Aztec Empire was established in Mesoamerica in about A.D. 1100.

## Source/Further Reading

Coe, Sophie. *America's First Cuisines.* Austin: University of Texas Press, 1994.

## guaiacum  (*Guaiac officinale*)  (precontact)  *South American, Circum-Caribbean cultures*

Guaiacum is a hardwood tree that is indigenous to the West Indies and the northern coast of South America. The wood of this tree, which grows from 20 to 30 feet tall, contains a resin that indigenous people used for a blood cleanser and a tonic. They obtained the resin from the bark, which they grated or pounded into a powder and then steeped in water. When swal-

lowed, the resin imparted a warm feeling to the throat and could serve as a stimulant, diaphoretic, antiseptic, diuretic, antitussive, and treatment for inflamed mucous membranes of the throat. The first Spaniards in the Americas believed that guaiac was a miracle cure for a multitude of European diseases. They called guaiac *lignum vitae,* or "wood of life." Many of them believed the resin was a panacea that could heal buboes, or syphilis sores.

Guaiacum was quickly adopted into the European pharmacopoeia, the official listing of drugs approved by the medical establishment and just as quickly became a common ingredient in cough syrups because of its expectorant properties. Guaifenesin, which is produced from guaiacum, is known commercially as Robitussin. Another modern drug made from guaiacum is guaiacol, an effective intestinal antiseptic, germicide, expectorant, and antiseptic. Today guaiacum is also commonly used as a valuable means of detecting unseen blood in stool samples, the guaiac-based fecal occult blood test.

See also MEDICINE; PHARMACOLOGY.

## Sources/Further Reading

Peredo, Miguel Guzman. *Medical Practices in Ancient America.* Mexico City: Ediciones Euroamericanas, 1988.

Vogel, Virgil. *American Indian Medicine.* Norman: University of Oklahoma Press, 1970.

## guava  (*Psidium,* various species)  (ca. A.D. 1)
*Mesoamerican, Circum-Caribbean, South American Andean and Tropical Forest cultures*

Guava is a sweet fruit indigenous to the tropics of the Americas from Mexico to Peru. Ranging in size from an egg to an apple, the oval fruits have orange flesh beneath skin that varies in color from purplish black to red. Indigenous people domesticated wild guava trees at least 2,000 years ago. Archaeologists have found guava seeds in food caches in Peru along with BEANS, CORN, and SQUASH. Today it remains a popular shade tree in the tropics and is part of many household gardens.

Indigenous Americans used guava primarily as a food source. They ate it raw and cooked it before it ripened. Higher in ascorbic acid (see also SCURVY CURE) than citrus fruits, guava also contains high amounts of vitamin A, calcium, phosphorus, iron, thiamin, and niacin. It is also high in dietary fiber and was considered to be a medicinal plant. American Indians boiled the leaves, roots, and bark as a tea and used it to treat diarrhea, dysentery, and GASTROENTERITIS. Chemical analysis has shown that guava fruits contain high levels of pectin, an enzyme that promotes digestion.

Early Spanish explorers enjoyed the distinctive taste of the fragrant fruit and began cultivating it commercially in 1526 in the West Indies. Because the fruits were too delicate to last on ocean voyages, and Europe did not have the proper climate for growing guava trees, the fruits remained relatively unknown there, but the Spaniards carried seeds to India, Malaya, the Philippines, and Africa. Cooks in India made it into a sauce called chutney, a form in which it made its way to Europe, eventually becoming popular in England.

### Sources/Further Reading

Duke, J. A. and R. Vasquez. *Amazonian Ethnobotanical Dictionary.* Boca Raton, Fla.: CRC Press, 1994.

Roman-Ramos, R. et al. "Anti-hyperglycemic effect of some edible plants." *Journal of Ethnopharmacology* (August 1995): 25–32.

Smith, Nigel, J. Williams, Donald Plucknett, Donald and Jennifer Talbot. *Tropical Forests and Their Crops.* New York: Comstock Publishing, 1992.

Yadav, Anand K. Commodity Sheets FVSU-003-Guava. URL: http://agschool.fvsc.peachnet.edu/html/Publications/ Commodity Sheets. Downloaded on May 12, 1999.

## guilds (A.D. 1100) *Mesoamerican cultures*

Guilds are professional associations organized to regulate the quality of their members' work and to set prices. Aztec craftspeople were so well organized that they were assigned their own living sections in their communities. Aztec craft guilds arose independently from those that were organized in Europe in the eleventh century. The Aztec ranked guilds according to a hierarchy. At the top were the jewelers, goldsmiths, and those who produced featherwork mosaics. (See also FEATHERWORKING.) The guilds at the bottom of the hierarchy were those of the salt makers and stone quarry workers.

One of the responsibilities of the Aztec guilds was to establish prices for their services and wares. This was accomplished by ranking the members within each guild, which allowed them to exert a certain amount of control over the quality of other guild members' services and products. Guilds identified the best craftspeople, who were in turn highly sought after by the wealthy and ruling class. The Aztec referred to the featherworkers, goldsmiths, and jewelers as *tolteca* (Toltec). Scholars believe that these trades had originated from the Toltec culture that flourished in the area from A.D. 950 to A.D. 1250. The Toltec, who were experts at LOST-WAX CASTING, are thought to have taught the Aztec the art of goldsmithing. The Aztec Empire officially recognized at least 30 different craft guilds.

### Sources/Further Reading

Brown, Dale, ed. *Aztecs: Reign of Blood & Splendor.* Alexandria, Virginia: Time-Life Books, 1992.

Soustelle, Jacques. *Daily Life of the Aztecs.* Stanford, Calif.: Stanford University Press, 1961.

## guinea pigs (cuy, *Cavia porcellus Linnaens*)

(precontact) *South American Andean cultures*

Guinea pigs—small, burrowing rodents that are popular as pets today—are indigenous to South America. American Indians domesticated these animals in about 9000 to 6000 B.C. For centuries the Inca, whose empire was established in what is now Peru in about A.D. 1000, raised the animals. They called them *qowi* or *cuy,* keeping them in their homes and often feeding them table scraps. The Inca kept cuy not as pets but as a food source. Guinea pigs are sexually mature at three months, have a short gestation period, and bear an average litter of two to four young. Ideally, 10 females and one male could produce about 77 pounds of high-protein, low-fat meat in a year.

Cuy raising was so much a part of Inca life that the animals were traded and given as gifts. Families without the animals in their households were considered poor and lazy. Those who raised cuy often devoted a special room in their homes to the enterprise. The Inca sometimes cooked the animals with seaweed and other times with POTATOES and CHILES. They also cooked cuy with mint. (See also MINTS, BOTANICAL.) Early Spanish explorers reported that the Indians removed the fur and left the skin on, then cooked whole cuy by placing heated rocks in their stomachs. One Spaniard compared cuy to a suckling pig and wrote that the Indians considered it a great delicacy.

The Inca considered the animals sacred. Those that died a natural death were buried with flowers. In addition to serving as food, the animals were used for divination and healing. For this reason, the Catholic Church began to forbid their possession. "They even have them in Rome," one priest grumbled, "where I saw them being sold in public, and asking as if I did not know what they were, they told me they were 'rabbits of the Indies.'" Spanish colonial administrators vetoed the notion of a ban on cuy, perhaps in part because they had developed a taste for it. A painting of the Last Supper in the cathedral in Quito depicts Jesus eating cuy with his disciples.

Today cuy continues to be a favorite dish in Peru. More than a quarter-million of the animals are killed commercially for meat each day. Agronomists are studying ways to improve breeding in order to step up production. Roasted whole and seasoned with mint, garlic, cumin, and salt, cuy is a popular dish for important celebrations. *Pepian de cuy,* or guinea pig stew, is a traditional dish prepared with pieces of fried guinea pig seasoned with PEANUTS, garlic, black pepper, and salt. It is served with potatoes.

Language historians believe that the name *guinea pig* is probably derived from Guyana, a French colony in South America.

See also ANIMALS, DOMESTICATED.

### Sources/Further Reading

Coe, Sophie. *America's First Cuisines.* Austin: University of Texas Press, 1994.

Morales, Edumundo. *The Guinea Pig: Healing, Food and Ritual in the Andes.* Tucson: University of Arizona Press, 1995.

## gum  See CHEWING GUM.

## gumbo  See FILÉ GUMBO.

**hackey sack**  See GAMES, FOOTBAG.

**hair conditioners**  (precontact) *Mesoamerican; North American Great Plains, Plateau, Northeast, California, and Southwest cultures*

A hair conditioner is a treatment placed on the hair after it has been washed. Pre-Columbian Indians used hair conditioners for the same reasons people use them today—to add shine to the hair, make it more manageable, and relieve dryness. They also used botanical hair conditioners to relieve scalp itch and as a dandruff treatment.

The Aztec, whose empire was established in about A.D. 1100 in what are now Mexico and parts of Mesoamerica, used the berries of the yiamolli (*Phytolacco octandra L.*) to make a conditioner. They also used SUNFLOWER (*Helianthus annus*) seeds, boiling them to extract the oil. This was then used as a rinse, much like a modern hot oil hair treatment.

North American Indian people from a number of tribes used rendered animal grease as a hair conditioner. To this they added herbs to provide fragrance. The Omaha, who lived on the southern plains, added prairie rose petals (*Rosa arkansana*) and wild bergamot leaves (*Monarda fistulosa L.*). The Blackfeet, a Plains tribe, and the Kootenai, who lived in the northern plateau region, used needles of the balsam fir (*Abies balsamea*). The Chippewa (Anishinabe), who lived in the upper Midwest, mixed balsam gum with bear grease. Balsam continues to be a popular ingredient in modern hair conditioners and shampoos.

The Cheyenne, who lived on the northern plains, made a tea of mint (*Mentha arvensis L.*) that they used as a hair rinse. (See also MINTS, BOTANICAL.) North American Indians who lived in areas where CATTAILS grew often used the plant's pollen as a conditioner. American Indians living in what are now southern Arizona, California, and Baja California in Mexico rinsed their hair with conditioners made from JOJOBA seeds

(*Simmondsia chinensis*). Jojoba is another ingredient found in many modern shampoos and hair conditioners.

See also DEODORANT; DETERGENT; HYGIENE, PERSONAL.

**Sources/Further Reading**
Hutchens, Alma R. *Indian Herbology of North America*. Boston: Shambhala, 1991.

Lust, John. *The Herb Book*. New York: Bantam Books, 1974.

Moerman, Dan. *Native American Ethnobotany Database: Foods, Drugs, Dyes and Fibers of Native North American Peoples*. URL: http://www.umd.umich.edu/cgi-bin/herb. Downloaded on August 7, 1999.

Prindle, Tara. *NativeTech: Cattails*. 1994–1998. URL: http://www.nativeweb.org/NativeTech/cattail/. Downloaded on August 7, 1999.

Vogel, Virgil. *American Indian Medicine*. Norman: University of Oklahoma Press, 1970.

**hairnets**  See KNITTING.

**hammocks**  (precontact) *Circum-Caribbean, South American Tropical Forest cultures*

The hammock, a swinging cot usually suspended between two trees or poles, was in use by indigenous peoples in the Caribbean when Columbus first arrived there. He was so impressed by this comfortable, cool, and clean way of sleeping that he wrote about it in his journals. The English word *hammock* comes from the Spanish *hamaca*, which was derived from a Taino word. The Taino were indigenous to the islands where Columbus landed.

In 1526 Gonzoalo Fernandez de Oviedo, the first European to draw a picture of a hammock, described the hammocks he observed on the island of Hispaniola (now Haiti and the

125

Dominican Republic) as a rug knitted from cotton with henequen ties. Henequen is a fiber made from the AGAVE, or century plant. Other tribes living on the east coast of what is now Brazil made their hammocks from a combination of COTTON fiber and vegetable fiber yarns. Later explorers to the Yucatán peninsula of what is now Mexico found indigenous people using hammocks as well. Throughout the tropics, hammocks were used by adults and also served as easily rocked cradles for infants. (See also CRADLEBOARDS.)

Because of its comfort and adaptability, the hammock became widely adopted by the Spaniards. Europeans used hammocks as the standard mode of sleeping on European naval and merchant ships. Today they are popular as outdoor furniture.

### Sources/Further Reading

Driver, Harold E. *Indians of North America.* Chicago: University of Chicago Press, 1969.

Harris, Jennifer, ed. *Textiles: 5,000 Years.* New York: Harry N. Abrams, Inc., Publishers, 1993.

Josephy, Jr., Alvin M., ed. *America in 1492: The World of the Indian People Before the Arrival of Columbus.* New York: Random House, 1991.

**harpoons** (precontact) *North American Arctic and Northwest Coast cultures*

A harpoon is a spearlike weapon that is used to hunt whales, seals, and walrus. Indigenous Americans from Alaska to Greenland hunted with sophisticated harpoon points that detached from the shaft while remaining fastened to a hand-held line. The shafts were made in sections that connected with a flexible joint, preventing them from breaking. This was an important consideration given the scarcity of wood in the Arctic. Although people from other parts of the world used harpoons, theirs did not have detachable points.

The Inuit of what is now West Greenland called harpoon hunting *maupok,* which means "waiting," because it required extensive knowledge of the habits of sea mammals as well as the ability to predict and imitate their behavior. Aware that seals would use their claws to scratch breathing holes in sea ice and revisit those holes often, a hunter would wait by one of these holes. When the seal came up to breathe, the hunter would harpoon it, let it thrash, and then pull it to the surface and kill it with a blow from his fist. To lure the seals closer, a hunter would sometimes place an ice pick into the ice and whistle along the shaft to imitate the sounds a seal makes, or he would drag an ice pick or special scratcher along the ice to arouse the seal's curiosity. (See also CALLS, ANIMAL AND BIRD.)

The Inuit also used harpoons for "peep sealing." This began by chopping a large hole in the winter ice. Hunters then chopped a smaller hole nearby and inserted a long-shafted harpoon into it. One man stood ready to thrust the harpoon, while another stretched out on a bench and covered his head so he could see beneath the water. When he viewed a seal swimming toward the smaller hole, he would signal the man with the harpoon to spear it. Even hunting seals on land with harpoons required great patience. Cautious animals, seals only sleep about a minute at a time. The hunter would wait silently, and when

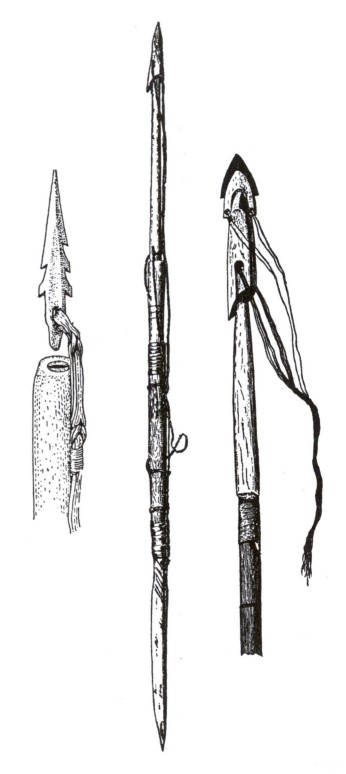

Detachable harpoon points such as that pictured above enabled hunters of the North American Arctic and Northwest Coast to spear whales and seals efficiently. The design is unique to American Indians. *(U.S. Bureau of Ethnography)*

the seal slept he would move closer until he was finally in thrusting range.

When the men hunted seals from boats, they attached seal bladder or sealskin floats to harpoon lines. The bladder marked the spot where the seal had been speared. It also exhausted the injured animal by providing resistance as it thrashed in the water. When the seal had given up the fight, hunters dealt the death blow and then used the harpoon line to tow it ashore. To make the latter task easier, they blew air into the animal's nostrils to inflate the lungs so that it would float better.

Hunters used a number of harpoons for whale hunting. (See also WHALING.) They attached several sealskin floats to each line, so that the huge sea mammal would encounter more resistance in its efforts to flee and would tire more quickly. The whale hunters also tied floats to their boats so that they would not capsize. The Makah and Nootka people of the Northwest Coast also hunted whales with detachable pointed harpoons and floats.

See also FISHING, ICE; FLOTATION DEVICES.

### Sources/Further Reading
Maxwell, James A., ed. *America's Fascinating Indian Heritage.* Pleasantville, N.Y.: Reader's Digest Books, 1978.

Murdoch, John. *Ethnological Results of the Point Barrow Expedition: Annual Report of the U.S. Bureau of Ethnology 1887–1888.* Washington, D.C.: Government Printing Office, 1892.

Oswalt, Wendell. *Eskimos and Explorers.* Novato, Calif.: Chandler & Sharp Publishers, 1979.

Trigger, Bruce G., and Wilcomb E. Washburn, eds. *The Cambridge History of the Native Peoples of the Americas, Vol. I, Part I, North America.* New York: Cambridge University Press, 1996.

## headache, knowledge of etiology (ca. A.D. 1100)
*Mesoamerican cultures*

Aztec physicians knew that many headaches were caused by an excess of blood in the arteries in the brain or on the surface of the head long before European doctors understood this. (The Aztec Empire was established in about A.D. 1100 in Mesoamerica.) Aztec physicians became expert at cranial anatomy and physiology as a result of warfare and the taking of prisoners. Many of the prisoners of war whom the Aztec captured to replenish their pool of slaves had suffered from head injuries. In order to restore the prisoner to health, the ancient Aztec physicians learned a great deal over the years about cranial anatomy and physiology, enabling them to perform brain surgery, or TREPHINATION. Their belief that excess blood in the head was a cause of headaches is supported by modern medicine. Aztec physicians advised their headache patients to rest and to avoid steam baths (see also STEAM ROOMS) as well as the sun, since heat is a vasodilator—that is, it would dilate the blood vessels and only make the headache worse.

See also ANATOMICAL KNOWLEDGE; HEADACHE MEDICATIONS.

### Sources/Further Reading
Ortiz de Montellano, Bernard. *Aztec Medicine, Health, and Nutrition.* New Brunswick, N.J.: Rutgers University Press, 1990.

Peredo, Miguel Guzman. *Medical Practices in Ancient America.* Mexico City: Ediciones Euroamericanas, 1985.

Soustelle, Jacques. *Daily Life of the Aztecs.* Stanford, Calif.: Stanford University Press, 1985.

## headache medications (precontact) *North American Southwest cultures*

A headache, or pain in the head, may be caused by a number of reasons. One common reason for headaches is the dilation of the blood vessels, either in the brain or on the surface of the head. (See also HEADACHE, KNOWLEDGE OF ETIOLOGY.) Migraine headaches are arterial in nature. Before contact with Europeans, the Zuni, who live in what is now New Mexico, routinely used a vasoconstrictor to shrink the diameter of the arteries and relieve vascular headaches. Modern physicians prescribe similar medications called vasoconstrictors for vascular headaches.

The Zuni used smut (*Ustilago zea*), a fungus that thrives on CORN, as a vasoconstrictor. After gathering it, they boiled the corn smut in water and drank the tea. The therapeutic value of the fungus for headaches is a substance called *ustilogine*. Scientists have found that ustilogine is an alkaloid and a very effective vasoconstricter, efficiently and significantly reducing the amount of blood in the cranium and scalp. This eliminates the throbbing pain accompanying many headaches.

See also MEDICINE; PHARMACOLOGY.

### Sources/Further Reading
Lust, John. *The Herb Book.* New York: Bantam Books, 1974.

Ortiz de Montellano, Bernard. *Aztec Medicine, Health, and Nutrition.* New Brunswick, N.J.: Rutgers University Press, 1990.

Vogel, Virgil. *American Indian Medicine.* Norman: University of Oklahoma Press, 1970.

## health, holistic  See HOLISTIC HEALTH.

## health, public  See PUBLIC HEALTH.

## heart medications  See DOGBANE; FOXGLOVE; HEMP, AMERICAN; WAHOO.

## helmets, sports (ca. 300 B.C.) *Mesoamerican cultures*

Helmets are head coverings designed to protect the wearer against injury. The people of Mesoamerica wore helmets when they played an ancient version of BASKETBALL. The Olmec, whose civilization arose in Mesoamerica in about 1700 B.C., invented this game. Players wore helmets in addition to protective padding that included gloves, a broad waist belt, knee and hip pads, and special footwear. The sports helmet and protective garb were made from wickerwork or leather. From statues of Mesoamerican ballplayers and depictions of them on pottery, it appears that these sports helmets resembled the leather football helmets worn by players during the early 20th century. They are an example of one of the first sports helmets used in history.

## Sources/Further Reading

Benson, Elizabeth P. *The Maya World.* New York: Thomas Y. Crowell Company, 1967.
Driver, Harold E. *Indians of North America.* Chicago: University of Chicago Press, 1969.
Stuart, George E. "New Light on the Olmec." *National Geographic* 184, no. 5 (November 1993): 88–114.

**hemostats** (ca. A.D. 1100) *Mesoamerican; North American Northwest Coast, Southeast, and Great Plains cultures*

Hemostats are devices or medicines that stem the flow of either internal or external bleeding. American Indians developed a number of hemostats that were very effective even by today's standards. Some of the first hemostats used in the precontact Americas were used by the Aztec of Mesoamerica. Their system of medicine was comprehensive, resembling the field of medicine in America today. The Aztec used many plants to treat open wounds, sores, dysentery, and diarrhea. Some of them were: *quahtzapotl (Annona cherimolia), ezquahuitl (Croton sanguifluum), quamochitl (Pithecellobium dulce), amamaxtha (Rumex mexicana), capolin (Prunus capulli), tequequetzal (Adiantum poiretti),* and *matlaliztic (Commenlina pallida).* The main therapeutic ingredient in each of these plants is tannin, a substance with hemostatic properties.

The Kwakiutl of the North American Pacific Northwest used spider webs to stem the flow of blood in the treatment of wounds. They packed the spider webs into wounds, causing the blood to thicken and clot. The Plains Indians used puffballs—fungi filled with spores that resemble dust. They placed the spores into the wounds, causing the blood to coagulate, and eventually the bleeding stopped. The Chickasaw used alum in the treatment of wound care. The alum caused tissue and vasoconstriction. (The first time Europeans saw alum in the New World was in 1588, according to Virgil Vogel in his book *American Indian Medicine.*)

During the late 1600s and early 1700s colonists in what is now North Carolina reported that the Catawba used powder made from dried, rotten CORN kernels to stanch bleeding. During the 20th century the Americans finally admitted corn smut into the official American pharmacopoeia, an official list of drugs and dosages that is sanctioned by the medicine community, as a vasoconstrictor (a substance that shrinks blood vessels) and a hemostat.

See also DRAINAGE, SURGICAL AND WOUND; HEADACHE MEDICATIONS; MEDICINE; PHARMACOLOGY.

## Sources/Further Reading

Brickell, John. *The Natural History of North-Carolina, With an Account of the Trade Manners, and Customs of the Christian and Indian Inhabitants.* Reprint. Dublin: James Carson, 1737.
Stone, Eric. *Medicine Among the American Indians.* Reprint. New York: Hafner Publishing Company, 1962.
Swanton, John R. "Social and Religious Beliefs and Practices of the Chickasaw Indians." *Forty-fourth Annual Report of the Bureau of American Ethnology, 1925–26.* Washington, D.C.: Government Printing Office, 1928.
Vogel, Virgil. *American Indian Medicine.* Norman: University of Oklahoma Press, 1970.

**hemp, American** (ca. A.D. 1600) *North American Northeast cultures*

American hemp (*Apocynum cannabinum*) is a plant that is indigenous to the eastern part of North America. The American hemp plant was a source of fiber that Indians used to make ropes, quilts, string, and twine. (This plant is not related to the marijuana plant, which American Indians did not utilize.) Indigenous Americans used the sap of the hemp plant as a CHEWING GUM and as a CHEWABLE DENTIFRICE. The Iroquois used it to stop internal bleeding (see also HEMOSTATS), while the Flambeau Chippewa (Anishinabe) used it as a kidney medicine and for pregnant women. The Penobscot used American hemp for intestinal worms; at one time American hemp was referred to as wormroot. (See also ANTIHELMINTICS.) When taken internally, American hemp contains a chemical that displays the same cardiotonic properties as digitalis. It affects the contraction of the heart and regulates the rhythm as well, and this was one of the primary reasons American Indians used American hemp. The prairie Potawatomi used American hemp as a cardiac medicine and as a kidney medicine. Doctor Harlow Brooks, as cited by Virgil Vogel in *American Indian Medicine,* credits American Indians with using herbs with digitalis properties for hundreds of years prior to the discovery of digitalis by the Scottish physician William Withering in 1775.

See also DOGBANE; FOXGLOVE; WAHOO.

## Sources/Further Reading

Vogel, Virgil. *American Indian Medicine.* Norman: University of Oklahoma Press, 1970.
Weiner, Michael A. *Earth Medicine Earth Food: The Classic Guide to the Herbal Remedies and Wild Plants of the North American Indians.* New York: Fawcett Columbine, 1980.

**henequen** See AGAVE.

**herb gardens** See GARDENS, HERB.

**hickory (*Carya juglandacae*)** (precontact) *North American Northeast and Southeast cultures*

The hickory is a deciduous hardwood tree, indigenous to the North American East Coast and Midwest. Many North American Indian tribes ate hickory nuts. The name *hickory* came into the English language in 1618 from *pawcohiccora,* the Algonquian word for a food made of pounded nuts and water. These nuts were also a large part of the diet of many southeastern tribes. Some Indians living in that area cultivated the trees; the Creek (Muskogee) grew 11 varieties. They used hickories for dye and valued them for their strong, hard wood.

European colonists quickly developed a taste for the nuts and found the wood useful—especially as a way to discipline children. References were made to the hickory stick or switch as early as 1734. Because hickory wood was so tough, hickory came to mean something or someone that was unyielding. Ironically, President Andrew Jackson was called "Old Hickory" because he was considered a tough fighter against the Creek, who were allied with the British in the War of 1812.

When hickory wood was imported to Europe, it was used for walking sticks and for golf clubs. In 1826 club manufacturer Robert Forgan of Scotland began to use hickory imported from America to manufacture shafts. It quickly became the wood of choice for golfers throughout the world. By 1900 baseball bat manufacturers were using hickory wood in the United States for bats that were sometimes called hickories.

**Sources/Further Reading**

Flexner, Stuart Berg. *I Hear America Talking: An Illustrated History of American Words and Phrases.* New York: Simon and Schuster, 1976.

Weatherford, Jack. *Indian Givers: How the Indians of the Americas Transformed the World.* New York: Fawcett Columbine, 1988.

**high john**   See JALAP.

**hockey, field and ice (shinny)** (precontact) *North American Great Plains, Plateau, Southwest, and Northeast cultures*

Hockey is a popular sport currently played throughout the world by teams of players who attempt to knock a ball into the opponents' goal by using curved sticks. While modern field hockey, whose players are usually women, is played on a grassy field, ice hockey is played on an ice-covered court. Both games are based on an American Indian stickball game called shinny, which was played by tribes throughout North America well before Europeans arrived on the continent. Frequently, Indians played shinny on ice. The players used a wooden ball or one made of buckskin that could only be touched with the stick or kicked with the feet.

It was primarily American Indian women who played shinny. Occasionally men and sometimes coed teams played shinny games. These original versions of field hockey were known by many names, depending on the tribe that played it, but they were given the universal name of shinny by early anthropologists. The modern name *hockey* came from the Jesuit missionaries who observed Indians living in what is now Canada playing the game. *Hoquet* is the French word for a shepherd's crook and referred to the curved sticks the players used to propel the ball down the field.

Although evidence exists that the Greeks and the Egyptians also played stickball games, historians have been unable to find a link between those games and the sport as it is played today.

See also LACROSSE.

**Sources/Further Reading**

Culin, Stewart. *Games of the North American Indians.* 1907. Reprint. Lincoln, Neb.: University of Nebraska Press, 1992.

Lowe, Warren. *Indian Giver.* Pencticton, British Columbia: Theytus Books, 1986.

Vennum, Jr. Thomas. *American Indian Lacrosse: Little Brother of War.* Washington, D.C.: Smithsonian Institution Press, 1994.

**holistic medicine** (precontact) *North American, South American, Circum-Caribbean, Mesoamerican cultures*

Holistic medicine seeks to address the social, psychological, spiritual, and economic needs of patients as well as the physical. It is based on the belief that illness is not always caused by pathogens or physical trauma alone. The patient's emotions or an environmental stressor might be the cause of the disorder or make an existing disorder more difficult to heal or bear. By the same token, the patient's thoughts and feelings can profoundly influence healing by exerting a positive effect on the immune system. Today this is often called the mind/body connection. Only in the latter part of the 20th century did the theory gain acceptance in the medical community after a number of scientific studies demonstrated the influence of mood on the human immune system.

American Indian physicians used holistic health practices for centuries before the arrival of Europeans. Psychosomatics, the influence of the mind and emotions on physical health and the understanding that emotions such as stress can cause disease was a basic tenet of American Indian healing. Some groups, including the Iroquois, were very explicit about this. Thomas Page, author of *The Civilization of the American Indians* calls certain Iroquois beliefs ". . . remarkably prescient, for the Iroquois were aware of psychosomatic illnesses and all the mechanics of repression of forbidden desires, or secret ambitions that appear in dreams."

Tribal healers in many American Indian culture groups looked at a number of things before making a diagnosis or prescribing treatment. A medicine man or woman might look to see if the patient had violated any taboos, which could be spiritual, dietary, or social. The precontact Indian physician could prescribe medications or invasive procedures, or he or she could have the patient discuss his or her dreams, personal problems, or unmet desires.

Songs, prayers, sacrifices, offerings, rituals, ceremonies, and the burning of incense addressed a patient's emotional needs. Sometimes a ceremony would be performed or sacrifices made so that the patient, his or her family, and the community could be treated at the same time. In some cases a steam bath (see also STEAM ROOMS) might be prescribed, or a massage might be given to the patient. (See also THERAPEUTIC TOUCH.) In cases of broken and fractured bones, the physician might pray or utter healing words while setting the broken bone. Some Indian healers might prescribe dietary changes until the crisis has passed.

When the patient was infirm, other tribal members met his or her survival needs. When necessary, the needs of the family were met as well until the patient recovered. In the event the patient died, the widow and orphans would still be taken care of until they were able to become self-sufficient. The elderly and the disabled were also cared for.

See also DREAMWORK PSYCHOLOGY; FREE ASSOCIATION.

## Sources/Further Reading

Benson, Elizabeth P. *The Maya World.* New York: Thomas Y. Crowell Company, 1967.

Coe, Michael D. *America's First Civilization: Discovering the Olmec.* Eau Claire, Wisc.: American Heritage Publishing Co. Inc., 1968.

Dossey, Larry, M.D. *Be Careful What You Pray for . . . You Just Might Get It.* San Francisco, Harper, 1996.

Fiedel, Stuart J. *Prehistory of the Americas.* New York: Cambridge University Press, 1987.

Ortiz de Montellano, Bernard R. *Aztec Medicine, Health, and Nutrition.* New Brunswick, N.J.: Rutgers University Press, 1990.

Soustelle, Jacques. *Daily Life of the Aztec: On the Eve of the Spanish Conquest.* Stanford, Calif.: Stanford University Press, 1961.

Vogel, Virgil. *American Indian Medicine.* Norman: University of Oklahoma Press, 1970.

Weiner, Michael D. *Earth Medicine Earth Food: The Classic Guide to the Herbal Remedies and Wild Plants of the North American Indians.* Rev. ed. New York: Fawcett Columbine, 1972.

**hominy** (precontact) *Mesoamerican; North American Southwest, Northeast; South American Andean cultures*
CORN that has been soaked and cooked in wood-ash water or lime water is called hominy. American Indians throughout North, Meso-, and South America invented this process, which they taught to the early colonists. Soaking corn in lye made from wood ashes or in a slaked lime solution (both of which are alkaline) removed the hulls and made the corn more easily ground. It also made the protein and niacin contained in corn more readily absorbed by the body. Niacin, a water-soluble vitamin also known as $B_3$, is rare in vegetable sources. In corn's

natural state most of the niacin is bound to carbohydrates and passes through the body without being utilized. The alkaline processing that is necessary to make hominy releases the niacin, which is necessary in order for the body to absorb calcium and potassium from other foods that are eaten.

The scientific name for this process is *nixtamalization.* The ancient Maya and the Aztec both used it. (The Maya culture arose in Mesoamerica about 1500 B.C.; the Aztec Empire was established in the same region in about A.D. 1100.) The Maya and Aztec used lime to make hominy and ate it in soups and stews. They also dried and ground the hominy kernels into flour for TORTILLAS and TAMALES. These two food items are still an essential part of southwestern and Mexican cuisine and continue to be made from a hominy flour called *masa harina.* It is the lime-water soaking and cooking that gives tortilla chips their distinctive taste.

Anthropologists believe that the technique of making hominy spread along with the cultivation of corn, since wherever the crop was grown in the Americas, Indian people ate it as hominy. American Indians in the Southwest made their version of hominy by cooking sun-dried corn kernels in water combined with ashes from corncobs and powdered lime (calcium-oxide).

The Northeast tribes of North America boiled oak, maple, or poplar wood ash in water and let the mixture stand overnight in order for the ash to settle out. Corn was then boiled in this lye-water until the hulls came off and the kernels turned a brilliant yellow. It was eaten fresh or dried and then cooked later or ground up. The CORNMEAL that North American Indians ate was actually ground hominy, or grits. When it was coarsely ground, it was called samp by some Eastern Woodlands tribes.

Non-Indian colonists quickly adopted corn, coming to depend on foods made of cornmeal for much of their caloric intake. They ignored the processing techniques American Indians had developed, however. As a consequence, many developed a disease called pellagra, which is caused by niacin deficiency. This name comes from Italy, where corn had become part of the diet in dishes such as polenta. As they came to rely on corn as a dietary staple, people throughout southern Europe, Africa, India, and the southern United States became afflicted with niacin deficiency. Pellagra causes scaly rashes, blisters, nausea, diarrhea, and a dementia resembling schizophrenia. It eventually leads to death. By the end of the 19th century, it had reached epidemic proportions.

Rather than drawing on the expertise of American Indians, whose dietary mainstay was corn and who were pellagra-free, Western physicians remained baffled by the cause of the disease. They feared it might be contagious and speculated that it might have been caused by a microorganism or from eating spoiled corn, but they could not find a way to prevent it or cure it. Not until 1914 did Joseph Goldberger, a member of the U.S. Public Health Service, discover the cause of pellagra. After noting that adults in insane asylums and prisons and children in orphanages developed pellagra while the staff did not, he concluded that differences in diet had something to do with the disease. While the staff ate a balanced diet, people who were institutionalized subsisted on cornbread, molasses, and pork fat. When people with pellagra ate fresh vegetables, milk, and meat (foods rich in vitamin B), their symptoms disappeared. The scientific community initially scoffed at Goldberger's work. The danger of subsisting mainly on unprocessed corn was not accepted by physicians and scientists until the late 1930s, as a result of the isolation of vitamins and the resulting concept of balanced nutrition—a concept American Indians had practiced for centuries.

## Sources/Further Reading

Coe, Sophie. *America's First Cuisines.* Austin: University of Texas Press, 1994.

*Health Answers Medical Reference Library.* URL: http://www.healthanswers.com/adam/top/vioew.asp?/filename=002409. htm. Downloaded on May 16, 1999.

*People and Discoveries: Pellagra shown to be dietary disease.* URL: http://www.pbs.org/wgbh/aso/databand/entries/dm15pa.html. Downloaded on May 26, 1999.

Sokalow, Raymond. *Why We Eat What We Eat: How the Encounter Between the New World and the Old Changed the Way Everyone on the Planet Eats.* New York: Summit Books, 1991.

Tannahill, Reay. *Food in History.* New York: Stein and Day, 1973.

Weatherford, Jack. *Native Roots: How the Indians Enriched America.* New York: Fawcett Columbine, 1991.

**hominy grits**   See CORNMEAL.

**honey**   See BEEKEEPING.

**hoses, rubber**   See ENEMAS; LATEX.

**hospitals**   (precontact)   *Mesoamerican culture*
Hospitals are centralized facilities for the diagnosis and treatment of medical disorders. The Aztec, whose empire was established in Mesoamerica in about A.D. 1100, founded the very first hospitals in the Americas. Like most hospitals today, these provided a wide range of services. They were staffed with doctors, surgeons, nurses, and an extensive pharmacy of medicines. (See also PHARMACOLOGY.) These ancient facilities were able to treat a wide range of pathologies and disorders. Aztec surgeons performed amputations (see also SURGERY), successful brain surgeries (see also TREPHINATION), and PLASTIC SURGERY. These hospitals also had dentists, obstetricians, eye doctors, and ear doctors among other specialists. The Aztec nursing staff included midwives, women who helped women giving birth.

The medical system of the Aztec was quite comprehensive and advanced beyond the medical system of Europe at the same time. In Europe, physicians and bloodletting surgeons did not

practice in hospitals, nor did apothecaries. A few hospitals were established by religious orders as asylums, or long-term residents, for the homeless, sick, disabled, lepers, and victims of disaster. Most provided a place to stay and little else. Not until the Renaissance in the 1500s did European hospitals become centers for medical treatment.

In contrast, the Aztec placed hospitals in all of their large cities and urban areas. These hospitals were well funded and supported by the government. Virgil Vogel writes in his book *American Indian Medicine,* "For severe cases, the expenses of treating which could not be borne except by the wealthy classes, hospitals were established by the government in all the larger cities, endowed with ample revenues, where patients from the surrounding country were cared for by experienced doctors, surgeons, and nurses well versed in all the native healing arts."

See also DENTISTRY; OBSTETRICS; MEDICINE.

## Sources/Further Reading

Bancroft, Hubert Howe. *The Works of Hubert Howe Bancroft, Vol. II, The Native Races.* San Francisco: The History Co., 1886.

Peredo, Miguel Guzman. *Medical Practices in Ancient America.* Mexico City: Ediciones Euroamericanas, 1985.

Vogel, Virgil. *American Indian Medicine.* Norman: University of Oklahoma Press, 1970.

**hot springs**   (precontact)   *North American cultures*
Hot springs are created when surface water nears the molten rock of the earth's crust. This heated water rises and returns to the surface through cracks in the rock. American Indians knew about hot springs in the areas where they lived and were using them for hundreds of years before European colonists and explorers discovered these geothermal features. Often the waters of these hot springs are rich in minerals.

Throughout North America, indigenous people used the springs for hygienic (see HYGIENE, PERSONAL) and medicinal purposes. Hot springs were used to treat gout, arthritis, and similar diseases. David Zeisberger, writing in the *Ohio Archaeological and Historical Quarterly,* stated, "In treating rheumatism, bathing and sweating plays a great part." Hot baths and steam baths were also used when pregnant women experienced difficult labor. (See also OBSTETRICS; STEAM ROOMS.) American Indian tribes near what is now the site of Hot Springs National Park in central Arkansas are said to have considered the spring there a neutral ground. Setting aside their differences, all bathed in the hot mineral water because they believed it to be a gift from their creator. Spanish explorer Hernando de Soto is thought to be the first European to have seen the spring in 1541. By the early 1700s Spanish and French health-seekers were making pilgrimages there.

As European colonists found and staked claims to the hot springs throughout the continent, entrepreneurs turned them into health resorts. They sold bottled water from some springs and charged people to bathe in the springs that were said to have health benefits. (See also SOFT DRINK INGREDIENTS.) Although the medical profession discounted them laypeople placed faith by them. In fact these spas were marketed with the fact that Indians had used them for centuries. Today, many health conscious people continue to enjoy hot springs for the same reasons American Indians used them. In some areas, tribes on whose reservations there are hot springs are trying to use this to boost tourism and therefore the local economy. This is being attempted on the Flathead Reservation in Hot Springs, Montana.

See also ARTHRITIS TREATMENTS.

### Sources/Further Reading

Shuman, John W., M.D. "Southern California Medicine." *Annals of Medical History* 10, no. 3 (May 1938): 215–36; 4 (July 1938): 336–68.

Vogel, Virgil. *American Indian Medicine.* Norman: University of Oklahoma Press, 1970.

Zeisberger, David. "History of the North American Indians." *Ohio Archaeological and Historical Quarterly* 19, nos. 1–2 (January and April 1910): 12–153.

### hydraulics (ca. 300 B.C.) *Mesoamerican, North American Southwest, South American Andean culture*

Hydraulics refers to the use of liquids, usually water, to perform a task or operate a device. Generally, hydraulics requires that the water be under some sort of pressure. According to Gregory Cajte, the author of *Native Science: Natural Laws of Interdependence,* hydraulic engineering began in the Americas about 300 B.C. in Mesoamerica, where it was used in conjunction with irrigation and terraced farming. Controlling water to use for agriculture was later also practiced extensively in South America and Southwest desert regions of North America. Mesoamerican farmers continued to be experts at diverting water, draining swamps, and diverting floodwater to refill them in order to build the chinampas garden plots near what is now Mexico City. South American Inca engineers also developed this technology and miners were using it to mine gold. The Inca Empire was established in what are now Peru and Bolivia in about A.D. 1000.

The Inca rechanneled rivers so that the water pressure was aimed against the specific areas at the bottom of cliffs where gold had been found. The resulting water pressure eroded the cliffs and exposed the underlying gold. The hydraulic mining practiced by Inca miners was more limited than the wholesale erosion of stream banks practiced during the North American California gold rush of the mid-1800s. In South America the use of hydraulic technology for mining, as opposed to enginering, began at least by the 14th century or earlier. The ancient American Indians were able to achieve monumental tasks with simple tools.

See also FARMING, TERRACED; GOLD PANNING; IRRIGATION SYSTEMS; MINING, PLACER; WATER CONSERVATION.

### Sources/Further Reading

Cajete, Gregory. *Native Science: Natural Laws of Interdependence.* Santa Fe: Clear Light Publishers, 2000.

Morris, Craig and Adriana von Hagen. *The Inca Empire And Its Andean Origin.* New York: Abbeville Press Publishers, 1993.

von Hagen, Victor Wolfgang. *The Royal Road of the Inca.* London: Gordon & Cremonesi, 1976.

### hygiene, personal (precontact) *North American, Mesoamerican, Circum-Caribbean, South American cultures*

Indians throughout the Americas bathed on a daily basis long before contact with Europeans. This practice included infants, children, and adults. Bathing was generally viewed as a good health practice, both to prevent illness and to help treat illnesses. Many tribes believed that bathing was a form of purifying oneself spiritually. Indians of the northern plains, for example, bathed on a daily basis, even in winter. This bathing took place in streams, rivers, HOT SPRINGS, and in STEAM ROOMS, or sweatlodges; the latter were used throughout the Americas. In Aztec cities, most homes or clusters of homes had their own sweatbaths. "Contrary to the assumptions of many whites, aboriginal Indians were a clean people and had a much higher regard for bathing than was common among their white neighbors," wrote Virgil Vogel in his book *American Indian Medicine.*

The Aztec, whose empire was established in Mesoamerica in about A.D. 1100, considered bathing a priority. When religious holidays required each person to sacrifice, or forego, something important, they would comply by not taking a bath. "But for all that a love of cleanliness seems to have been general throughout the population. No doubt the members of the ruling class gave up more of their time and attention to it than ordinary citizens," wrote Jacques Soustelle in *Daily Life of the Aztecs.* Andres de Tapia, who accompanied Hernán Cortés in the conquest of what is now Mexico, recorded that Montezuma "washed his body twice a day"—a practice that astonished the conquistadores.

The Aztec gave very specific instructions to their young regarding cleanliness. According to Soustelle, one such admonishment instructed women to wash their faces and hands and to clean their mouths in the morning: "If you want your husband to love you, dress well, wash yourself and wash your clothes," an Aztec father admonished his daughter.

This emphasis on cleanliness extended to food preparation. Fray Bernardino de Sahagun described the criteria for a good preparer of food: "The good cook is honest, discreet; [she is] one who likes good food—an epicure, a taster. [She] is clean, one who bathes herself, prudent; one who washes her hands, who washes herself; who has good drink, good food."

American Indians were bathing on a daily basis, as well as brushing their teeth (see also CHEWABLE DENTIFRICES; MOUTHWASH; TOOTHBRUSHES; TOOTHPASTES AND POWDERS), wearing DEODORANTS, shampooing, washing their clothing (see also DETERGENTS), and conditioning their hair (see also HAIR CONDITIONERS) when Europeans arrived. European hygiene habits at that time were much less involved and much less frequent. Although the Romans had established public baths throughout the European continent and England, the Christian Church began to forbid public bathing early in the Middle Ages. Under the edict, which held that any kind of bathing or cleaning of oneself was disgusting and abominable, Europeans generally stopped the practice. Because, in cities at least, clean water was rare, there was some basis in truth to the belief that bathing was unhealthy. Queen Isabella of Spain was proud of the fact that she had bathed only twice in her life. North American colonists carried beliefs about bathing with them when they came to the New World. They rarely bathed except for medical reasons.

This Western European attitude toward bathing persisted into the 19th and 20th centuries. They viewed bathing as something that would endanger their health, rather than improve it. A law passed in Boston as late as 1845 forbade bathing unless a doctor prescribed it. In the mid-1800s Daniel Drake, an American physician wrote: "An overwhelming majority of our population seldom bathe at all. Of the efficacy of daily bathing, in preservation of sound health and a hardy constitution, there can be no doubt; and it is much to be regretted, that the practice cannot be made more general." *Vitalogy,* a health book published in the early 1900s, offered its readers some advice on bathing: "Dr. Braithwait, a specialist on children, states that frequently diseases and deaths of children are due to improper and irregular bathing."

Despite the fact that American Indians were concerned with personal cleanliness for hundreds of years prior to contact, colonists, who rarely washed their hands even to perform surgery, frequently branded them with the epithet "dirty Indians." Although personal hygiene undoubtedly became a lower priority than survival for indigenous Americans after the European invasion brought waves of disease and near starvation, the notion of "filthy savages" is not based on historical truth.

See also HOT SPRINGS; INSECTICIDES.

## Sources/Further Reading

Coleman, Penny. *Toilets, Bathtubs, Sinks, and Sewers: A History of the Bathroom.* New York: Atheneum, 1994.

Drake, Daniel. *A Systematic Treatise, Historical, Etiological, and Practical, on the Principal Diseases of the Interior Valley of North America.* Cincinnati: Winthrop B. Smith & Co., 1850.

Soustelle, Jacques. *Daily Life of the Aztecs.* Stanford, Calif.: Stanford University Press, 1961.

Wood, George. P., M.D. and E. H. Ruddock. *Vitalogy or Encyclopedia of Health and Home.* Chicago: Vitalogy Association, 1913.

Vogel, Virgil. *American Indian Medicine.* Norman: University of Oklahoma Press, 1970.

**ice fishing**  See FISHING, ICE.

**ice hockey**  See HOCKEY, FIELD AND ICE.

**igloos** (precontact)  *North American Arctic cultures*
The Inuit people of the Arctic built dome-shaped houses of compacted snow. They called these structures *iglu,* a word written by English speakers as *igloo.* Coastal Inuit considered these houses temporary shelters and used them as hunting camps. The Inuit people living in the interior polar regions lived in these circular snow dwellings throughout the winter. They constructed larger igloos that were from 6 to 15 feet in diameter and six feet high. The Inuit entered them through a series of smaller entry domes. These igloos usually housed five to six people. Built from a spiral arrangement of vaulted snow blocks, a basic igloo could be finished by two men using a bone snow knife in less than an hour's time. Because of the diameter to height ratio and the use of a keystone block on top to lock the entire dome into place, the igloos were extremely sturdy. Since the snow served as insulation, they were remarkably warm inside as well, especially since small cooking fires were made inside them. (See also INSULATION, HOME; SPACE HEATERS, PORTABLE.)

Initially some anthropologists were reluctant to believe that indigenous peoples of North America were capable of engineering the vaulted roofs of these domed houses, so they developed a theory that Europeans had taught the Inuit to make igloos, contrary to oral Inuit history. Inuit summer homes had domed hide roofs as well, and the records of early explorers provided further proof that the Inuit were building snow houses long before European contact.

Before actual construction of an igloo began, the builder probed the drifts with a wooden rod to find snow of the right consistency. Compact snow that was neither too soft nor layered worked best. Next, one member of a two-man team cut the blocks from the snow with a bone knife, while the other fitted them together. The size of the blocks that were cut depended on the consistency of the snow as well as the size of the desired igloo. After the foundation had been laid, one man cut blocks from the inside while another one fitted them from the outside so that they would lean toward the interior. They deliberately cut the blocks larger than necessary so that they could trim the excess in order to make certain the spiral was even and the fit exact. They hammered the blocks into place, causing the snow to melt, but it quickly refroze, sealing the blocks in place. A keystone block capped the top and was twisted into place. The builders then chinked the cracks and covered the outside with a layer of snow, smoothing it with flat snow shovels. A window of fresh water ice was cut and put into place, as was a vent hole.

Next, the Inuit built a large snow sleeping platform, on top of which they placed whale baleen or willow mats covered with hides. Some igloos had sealskin ceilings to keep the snow from melting. If melting did occur, a new igloo could be built on the outside of the existing structure. The old one was dismantled and taken out through the door.

Dome houses became a popular form of alternative architecture during the 1960s. Although the framing for these homes was based on the geodesic dome designed by Buckminster Fuller, the concept of the dome house was invented by the Inuit people thousands of years before.

See also TOOLS.

### Sources/Further Reading

Josephy, Jr., Alvin M., ed. *America in 1492: The World of the Indian People Before the Arrival of Columbus.* New York: Random House, 1991.

Igloos, the domed-shaped snow houses made by Inuit people for centuries, incorporated such sophisticated architectural principles that early non-Indian explorers were reluctant to believe indigenous people were capable of such engineering. *(Photograph No. PA-055575/National Archives of Canada)*

Nabokov, Peter and Robert Easton. *Native American Architecture.* New York: Oxford University Press, 1989.

Oswalt, Wendell. *Eskimos and Explorers.* Novato, Calif.: Chandler & Sharp Publishers, 1979.

**ikat**  See TIE-DYEING.

**impeachment**  See U.S. CONSTITUTION, AMERICAN INDIAN INFLUENCE ON.

**Indian corn**  See CORN.

**indigestion medications**  (precontact) *Mesoamerican; South American Circum-Caribbean and Tropical Forest; North American Great Basin, Southeastern, Great Plains, and Northeast cultures*

Indigestion is a stomach discomfort resulting from the inability to digest certain foods. It is often accompanied by heartburn, a reflux of stomach acid that irritates the esophagus. American Indians had many medicines for common stomach upsets that remain in use as natural home remedies today. One of the most well known is the PAPAYA (*Carica*), a fruit-producing tree that is indigenous to the tropical areas of Meso- and South America. The Maya, whose culture began to flourish in Mesoamerica in about 1500 B.C., grew papaya trees in orchards. They used the juice of the papaya fruit as a digestive aid. Both papaya leaves and unripe papaya contain papain, an enzyme that breaks down protein, making it more easily digestible. Today papaya enzyme tablets are sold over the counter and are used to help digestion.

The Aztec, whose empire was established in Mesoamerica in about A.D. 1100, relied on CHILES to soothe their stomach upsets. Chiles contain a chemical substance called capsaicin that acts both as a digestive aid and a laxative by stimulating the production of gastric juices. Too much chile, however, can cause stomach pain, vomiting, and gastrointestinal distress.

The indigenous people of many North American tribes relied on mint teas to help alleviate indigestion. (See also MINTS, BOTANICAL.) The Paiute steeped mint (*Agastache urticifolia*) in cold water and drank the resulting tea for stomach pains. Other

Great Basin tribes, including the Shoshone, made a tea from the whole peppermint plant (*Mentha candensis*). The Shoshone also used this tea to treat colic in infants. The Cherokee, who lived in the Southeast of North America, drank a tea made of WINTERGREEN root (*Gaultheria procumbens L.*) for chronic indigestion. Northern plains tribes also drank mint tea. Although the U.S. Food and Drug Administration has ruled that mint is not an effective indigestion remedy, the German Commission E, an official body that advises the German government about natural remedies, has given its endorsement to mint as an indigestion cure. The common practice of eating after-dinner mints today originated as an indigestion cure.

The Menominee, who lived in the Upper Midwest, made a tea from the root of wild ginger (*Asarum caudatum L.*). Ginger contains chemicals called gingerols and shogaols that have been proven to soothe the stomach and increase the muscle contractions that move food from the stomach and through the intestine. Ginger also helps alleviate nausea. Other tribes prescribed a tea made from wild licorice (*Glycyrrhiza [Nutt.] Pursh*), which is also effective in digestive disorders.

Father Paul Le Jeune made one of the earliest recorded reports of successful treatment of digestive problems in North America. It took place in 1637 among the Huron of Northeast North America. The Huron used juice extracted from branches and leaves of a cedar. Although the report does not identify the cedar. In all probability it was red cedar (*Juniperus virginiana L.*). Many other tribes used the plant for the same condition.

Another commonly prescribed indigestion treatment among most North American tribes was a restricted diet. The patient was ordered to limit his or her food intake to gruels and broths until recovery from the digestive disorder was achieved.

See also GASTROENTERITIS TREATMENT; PHARMACOLOGY.

## Sources/Further Reading

Duke, James A. *The Green Pharmacy*. New York: St. Martins Press, 1997.

Gepts, Paul. *The Crop of the Day*. URL: http://agronomy. ucdavis.edu/GEPTS/pb143/crop/papaya/. Downloaded on August 11, 1999.

Hutchens, Alma R. *Indian Herbology of North America*. Boston: Shambhala, 1991.

Lust, John. *The Herb Book*. New York: Bantam Books, 1974.

Moerman, Dan. *Native American Ethnobotany Database: Food, Drugs, Dyes and Fibers of Native North American Peoples*. URL: http://www.umd.umich.edu/cgi-bin/herb. Downloaded on September 20, 1999.

Vogel, Virgil. *American Indian Medicine*. Norman: University of Oklahoma Press, 1970.

**indigo** (precontact) *North American Southwest, South American Circum-Caribbean cultures*
The name *indigo* is given to a number of shrubs of the genus *Indigofera*, a member of the pea family. A brilliant blue dye can be produced from these plants. Different varieties of indigo plants grow in warm climates throughout the world, including the West Indies and the desert Southwest of North America. The American species of indigo is called *Indigofera suffruticosa*. Independently of dyers in other parts of the world, American Indians discovered how to remove the colorless glucoside *Indican* from the leaves of the plants and separate it into a sugar and a yellow substance called *indoxyl*. First they soaked the plants in water and let them ferment for 10 to 15 hours. When a yellow liquid had formed, they stirred it to aerate it until it became oxidized and turned bright blue, forming indigo, a dye as permanent as it is vivid. (See also DYES.)

European colonists established large indigo plantations in North and South Carolina and in Georgia with *Indigofera suffruticosa* seeds they had obtained in the West Indies. With the invention of synthetic indigo in 1900, the industry declined. Today, however, the interest in natural fibers and dyes has revived the interest in plant-derived indigo, especially among weavers and quilters.

## Sources/Further Reading

Adrosko, Rita J. *Natural Dyes and Home Dying*. New York: Dover, 1976.

Grae, Ida. *Nature's Colors: Dyes from Plants*. New York: Macmillan Publishing Company, Inc., 1974.

**inflammation treatments**   See ARTHRITIS TREATMENTS.

**inflatable rafts**   See RAFTS, INFLATABLE.

**inflatable wet suits**   See FLOTATION DEVICES.

**inlays, dental**   See DENTAL INLAYS.

**insect bite and bee sting remedies** (precontact) *Mesoamerican; North American Subarctic, and Great Plains cultures*
American Indians used a number of botanical remedies for insect bites and bee stings, many of which continue to be used by herbalists today. Modern researchers have uncovered the scientific reasons why several of these remedies work.

The Maya, whose culture arose in Mesoamerica in about 1500 B.C., were known to apply PAPAYA leaves to insect bites and bee stings. Both papaya leaves and unripe papaya contain papain, an enzyme that breaks down protein in meat, making it tender. This enzyme is also thought to break down insect venom. Today fresh papaya is sometimes rubbed on insect bites.

The Inupiaq, who lived in the northwestern part of what is now Canada, used a poultice of wet willow leaves (*Salix sp.*) to take away the pain and remove the swelling of bee stings.

Willow contains SALICIN, a chemical compound proven to reduce swelling and block pain. Salicin is the basis for modern aspirin.

Plains Indians applied poultices made from purple coneflower (echinacea) to insect bites of all types. When taken internally, this plant provides antiviral properties. Externally, it serves as a mild antiseptic.

See also ANTIVIRAL MEDICINES; SNAKE BITE TREATMENTS.

## Sources/Further Reading

Duke, James A. *The Green Pharmacy.* New York: St. Martins Press, 1997.

Smith, Huron H. "Ethnobotany of the Ojibwe Indians." *Bulletin of the Public Museum of Milwaukee* 4 (1932): 327–525.

Weiner, Michael A. *Earth Medicine Earth Food: The Classic Guide to the Herbal Remedies and Wild Plants of the North American Indians.* New York: Fawcett Columbine, 1980.

Wilson, Michael R. "Notes on Ethnobotany in Inuktitut." *The Western Canadian Journal of Anthropology* 8 (1978): 180–196.

## insecticides (precontact) *North American Great Basin, Plateau, and Northwest Coast cultures*

Unlike repellents that simply drive insects away, insecticides are meant to kill insects. For the most part, the indigenous peoples of North America used INSECT REPELLENTS. The exception to this practice was their response to lice, tiny parasitic insects, generally found in the outdoors, which feed on animal and human blood. Once they have found a human host, they live on the hair-covered parts of the body and reproduce. Precontact American Indians did not tolerate such infestations and developed several herbal remedies to combat them. The Paiute and Shoshone of the Great Basin, for example, washed their hair in a hot infusion made from sweetroot (*Osmorhiza occidentalis*). The Bella Coola of what is now British Columbia rubbed mashed mountain ash berries (*Sorbus sitchensis)* on the scalp. The Tsimshian people, who lived in the same region, used mashed devil's club berries (see also DIABETES MEDICATION) to the same effect. The West Coast Karok used a decoction of the roots of the gum plant (*Grindelia robusta Nutt*). These are only a few of the preparations indigenous peoples used.

European colonists expressed disgust at what they perceived as lack of cleanliness among Indian people, despite the fact that Indians bathed more frequently than the newcomers did and also shampooed their hair more often. Settlers quickly formed a stereotype that not only did all Indians have lice, they considered the condition normal and did nothing about it. This image served to add credence to a belief held by many non-Indians—that indigenous people were more animal than human. In truth, from the 1400s through the American frontier period in the mid-1800s many Indians and non-Indians alike suffered from lice infestations. In the Old World, lice had been a daily fact of life for centuries and were responsible for spreading typhus epidemics that swept over the European continent in waves.

See also HYGIENE, PERSONAL; DETERGENTS.

## Sources/Further Reading

Moerman, Dan. *Native American Ethnobotany Database: Food, Drugs, Dyes and Fibers of Native North American Peoples.* URL: http://www.umd.umich.edu/cgi-bin/herb. Downloaded on September 11, 1999.

Train, Percy, James R. Henrichs, and W. Andrew Archer. *Medicinal Uses of Plants by Indian Tribes of Nevada.* Washington, D.C.: U.S. Department of Agriculture, 1941.

Turner, Nancy J., Laurence C. Thompson and M. Terry Thompson, et. al. *Thompson Ethnobotany: Knowledge and Usage of Plants of the Thompson Indians of British Columbia.* Victoria British Columbia: Royal British Columbia Museum, 1990.

## insect repellents (precontact) *Mesoamerican; North American Plateau, Southwest, Northwest Coast, Southeast, and Northeast; South American Tropical Forest and Andean cultures*

American Indians in South America, Mesoamerica, and North America had a variety of methods for discouraging insect pests. For example, pre-Columbian indigenous peoples in the tropics of South America built structures that were constructed of CASHEW wood, which contains a natural oil that repels termites. Sometimes they extracted it from the cashew trees and painted it on other wood as an insect-repelling varnish.

Indigenous people used plants to keep their possessions insect-free. In 1543, when four Maya lords traveled to the Spanish court, they presented gifts, including intricately woven textiles, to Prince Philip of Spain. These were packed in wooden boxes and layered with herbs that were then discarded. Anthropologists believed that the herbs were insect repellents. Some ancient Maya paper documents were also preserved in this manner in the area known today as Guatemala. The Maya culture arose in Mesoamerica in about 1500 B.C. In North America, the Kootenai of the Plateau Region sprinkled crushed, dried mint leaves on their possessions to keep them insect-free. (See also MINTS, BOTANICAL.) Other tribes did this as well.

American Indians were adept at insect control during both the storage and growing phases of crop production. The Maya stored a leaf of the linden family with CHILES in order to keep them free from attack by the chili moth. COMPANION PLANTING, the practice of growing several crops such as CORN, BEANS, and SQUASH in one space, was a method of insect control. Beans and squash tend to attract insects that eat the pests that can damage corn crops. The Akimel O'odham (Pima) in the North American Southwest kept squash bugs off their plants by sprinkling the plants with ashes.

In the North American Southwest, the Anasazi and later the Pueblo peoples relied on the softball-sized buffalo GOURD to repel insects. The plant is effective because it produces extremely bitter chemicals called cucurbitacins. Pueblo peoples crushed buffalo gourds and mixed them with water to sprinkle on squash plants to rid them of garden pests. They dried leaves and gourds and then hung them in the corners of their homes to keep insects at bay. Pueblo peoples used ground buffalo gourd roots to discourage bedbugs. Buffalo gourd is also an effective DETERGENT.

Inca COTTON farmers living in the Jequetpeque Valley of Peru in about A.D. 1250 planted a relative of the lemon verbena (*Lippia* sp.) near their cotton plants as a pesticide. When the verbena plants were burned they produced an INSECTICIDE smoke that repelled insects harmful to the plants. This practice is still continued by some indigenous cotton farmers in Peru. Throughout North, Meso-, and South America indigenous people burned herbs to discourage mosquitoes and flies. (See also FOREST MANAGEMENT.)

Personal insect repellents were just as numerous. The Flathead (Salish), who lived on the West Coast, rubbed wild onion bulbs on the skin to repel pests. A repellent used by the Cherokee, a tribe living in the Southeast of what is now the United States, pounded the root of the herb goldenseal (*Hydrastis canadensis*) in order to pulverize it and then mixed it with bear fat. They rubbed this on their bodies to discourage insects. The Iroquois mixed chestnut oil with bear grease for a similar purpose. A number of tribes used animal fat as protection from insects as well as the sun. (See also SUN SCREENS, MEDICINAL.)

### Sources/Further Reading

Coe, Sophie. *America's First Cuisines.* Austin: University of Texas Press, 1994.
Hurt, R. Douglas. *Indian Agriculture in the Americas: Prehistory to Present.* Lawrence: University Press of Kansas, 1988.
Schuster, Angela M.H. "Colorful Cotton! An Ethnoarchaeologist tries to revive a 5,000-year-old Peruvian Textile Tradition." *Archaeology* (July/August 1995): 40–45.
Weatherford, Jack. *Indian Givers: How the Indians of the Americas Transformed the World.* New York: Fawcett Columbine, 1988.

### instant foods (precontact) *Mesoamerican, North American Southwest, South American Andean cultures*

Instant foods are not a 20th-century invention. The Maya, whose culture arose in Mesoamerica in about 1500 B.C., parched BEANS and ground them into flour. These were reconstituted with water when they were needed. The Aztec, whose empire was established in Mesoamerica in about A.D. 1100, had a number of convenience foods that were used by travelers and required only the addition of water to make a meal. Pinolli, or ground toasted CORNMEAL, was one of these foods. It was carried by travelers in a small sack. CACAO or dried CHILES were added sometimes for flavor. Travelers mixed water with the pinolli and their dinner was ready.

Bernardo de Sahagun, the Spanish priest who accompanied Hernán Cortés, reported that the Aztec also dried TOR-TILLAS to carry on journeys or marches. Sometimes they carried CHIA seeds to sustain them on journeys, as did Indian peoples living in what is now California. The Inca, who established their empire in what are now Peru and Bolivia in about A.D. 1000, developed the process of FREEZE-DRYING. They used it for a number of vegetables, but primarily POTATOES, which they ground into a flour to which they added water, much like instant potato flakes today. They carried this flour, called *chuno*, on their journeys and used it to make a stew called *chupa*.

### Sources/Further Reading

Coe, Sophie. *America's First Cuisines.* Austin: University of Texas Press, 1994.
Nabokov, Peter. *Indian Running: Native American History and Tradition.* Santa Fe, New Mexico: Ancient City Press, 1981.

### instruments, musical   See MUSICAL INSTRUMENTS.

### insulation, home (precontact) *North American Northeast, Great Plains, Subartic, Artic, and Southwest; Mesoamerican; South American cultures*

Insulation provides protection against temperature variations. Even though weather conditions were sometimes extreme, American Indians used sophisticated home insulation techniques to keep themselves comfortable during cold winters or hot summers. For example, the Chippewa (Anishinabe), who lived in the upper Midwest of North America, built wigwams with double walls that enclosed a dead air space. They made the outer walls from tough reeds that the women sewed together with split spruce root or nettle fiber. The walls of the airspace were lined with plant material of finer filaments to prevent drafts. CATTAIL reed mats were tied in courses up to the smoke hole at the top of the wigwam; they were arranged in the same way as shingles are today. The reeds were aligned vertically so the rain would run off quickly. Wigwam builders used baked mud to fireproof the smoke holes.

Northern plains tribes used hide liners for their TIPIS in the wintertime in order to create dead air space. Sometimes they used double liners and stuffed grass between the layers of hide. In the winter they banked snow around the tipi to serve as insulation. On Alaska's Aleutian Islands, builders used the same double-wall technique, stuffing grass or moss between planked walls. They also stacked sod on the outside of the walls and on the roof for extra insulation.

Snow also worked as an insulating material for the Inuit of the northern regions of North America. They used loose snow to chink the winter houses, called IGLOOS, which they built from hard snow blocks. They built entryways that effectively blocked drafts in order to keep the cold wind outside when family members and visitors came and went. Other tribes who lived in cold climates used the same principal of building entryways.

Windbreaks were sometimes erected outside of doorways as well. These were made from snow blocks, ADOBE, or split planks, depending on the area and the materials at hand. Often

American Indians living in cool climates used woven mat partitions in their homes to stop drafts.

Houses built in cold climates tended to be compact, so less heat would radiate from the surface into the surrounding air. The Mandan, Arikara, Hidatsa, and Pawnee built semi-underground houses, or EARTH LODGES, using the soil itself as an extremely effective insulator. These round dwellings, which ranged from 15 to 30 feet across, consisted of radiating poles arranged over a six-foot-deep pit. Layers of cattail roofing mats covered the poles. Residents piled earth around the base of the roof to keep out drafts. During rain storms the mats would swell, becoming watertight and keeping out the drafts. In the winter they would become frozen and covered with snow, which served as added insulation. The floor was insulated with layers of mats as well.

Pueblo people used earth for their dwellings in the form of adobe. Although adobe is not properly an insulator, walls constructed of mud do soak up heat and radiate it into the rooms at night. The thickness of the walls provided ample protection against the elements. This style of construction was common in Mesoamerica and South America, as well.

Pioneers on the northern plains, where lumber was scarce and temperatures extreme, observed American Indian construction methods and adapted them when they built their own first dwellings. Cutting bricks of sod, they built sod houses, or soddies, to live in until they could erect a more permanent home of non-Indian design. Some of these early sod houses still stand today. In the Southwest, Mesoamerica, and South America, the Spaniards quickly adopted adobe construction methods.

See also EVAPORATIVE COOLING.

## Sources/Further Reading

Josephy, Jr., Alvin M., ed. *America in 1492: The World of the Indian People Before the Arrival of Columbus.* New York: Random House, 1991.

Nabokov, Peter and Robert Easton. *Native American Architecture.* New York: Oxford University Press, 1989.

**intercropping** See also COMPANION PLANTING.

**intestinal worm medications** See ANTIHELMINTIC.

**intramedullar nails** (ca. A.D. 1100–A.D. 1519)
*Mesoamerican culture*
Intramedullar nails are surgically implanted into a long bone when it has failed to callus (produce new bone growth) at the site of a fracture. If a break or fracture in a bone fails to heal, it is generally due to the callus (strands of bony material between the two ends of a break or fracture) failing to consolidate (harden). Ancient Aztec surgeons remedied the problem of fractures that refused to heal by using an intramedullar nail. In so doing, they performed one of the most spectacu-

lar orthopedic surgical techniques in precontact Mesoamerica. First, they scraped the tissue from around the break or fracture and inserted a small piece of sticky, resinous wood (the intramedullar nail) into it. When they had completed this procedure, they covered the entire area with a medicinal plant plaster. Usually the plants they chose had ANTIBIOTIC and ASTRINGENT properties that prevented infections and stopped any bleeding. The area was then rebandaged. This allowed the callus to consolidate and become true bone tissue. Western medicine did not use this technique until the 20th century.

## Sources/Further Reading

Ortiz de Montellano, Bernard R. *Aztec Medicine, Health, and Nutrition.* New Brunswick, N.J.: Rutgers University Press, 1990.

Sahagun, Fray Bernardino de. *Florentine Codex. General History of the Things of New Spain.* Edited and translated by C. E. Dibble and A. J. O. Anderson. Salt Lake City: University of Utah Press.

**iodine** See GOITER PREVENTION.

**ipecac** (precontact) *Mesoamerican, South American Tropical Forest cultures*
Ipecac, a drug made from the roots of a species of shrub (*Cephaelis*) indigenous to South America and parts of Mesoamerica, is one of the most important poison-control drugs ever to have been discovered. It works by causing vomiting, so that the stomach rids itself of its contents, including the poison that has been ingested. Indian peoples who lived in the Amazon region of Brazil dried the *Cephaelis* roots and rhizomes (rootlike, horizontal stems that grow underground). They powdered these and used the result as a powerful emetic and medicine against intestinal parasites that cause amebic dysentery. The active ingredients in ipecac are the alkaloids emetine, cephaelin, and psychotrine.

The ipecac plant was named by Portuguese colonists in Brazil after the name given it by the Indians, which meant "sick-making plant." Europeans did not take ipecac across the ocean until 1672, when a traveler carried some to Paris. A Paris merchant, who obtained about 150 pounds of the root, introduced it to a doctor, Jean Adrian Helvetier, who used it as a patent medicine to combat dysentery. Not until 1688 did the French government buy his patent and make the secret ingredient public. This disclosure did little to break his monopoly, since he kept the source of the roots a guarded secret. Finally, in 1800 a Portuguese navy physician brought ipecac roots back from what had become Brazil, solving the mystery.

See also ANTIHELMINTIC; PHARMACOLOGY.

## Sources/Further Reading

Duke, James A. *The Green Pharmacy.* New York: St. Martins Press, 1997.

Ipecacuanha. Botanical.com. URL: http://www.botanical.
com/mgmh/i/ipecac07.html. Downloaded on August 1,
1999.
Monographs: Cephaelis. HealthLink Online Resources. URL:
www.healthlink.com.au/nat_lib/htm-data/htm-
herv/bhp595.htm. Downloaded on August 1, 1999.

**ironwork** (precontact) *North American Arctic cultures*
Although Indians of the Americas devised sophisticated metallurgical techniques—including making alloys, ELECTROPLAT-
ING, and ANNEALING—unlike their European counterparts,
they did not, for the most part, work with iron. There is, however, an exception to this rule that rarely finds its way into history books. The Polar Inuit who lived near Baffin Bay exploited
a local source of iron in the form of meteorites, using this iron
to make blades. Unfortunately, they told early European explorers about the source of their metal, saying it had come from
"iron mountains." When the explorers analyzed the blades that
they collected from the Inuit and found it had come from a me-
teorite, they began searching for the source.

In 1894 Richard Peary found the source about 35 miles
east of Cape York and discovered that it consisted of three iron
chunks, which the Inuit had named "woman," "dog," and
"tent." The Inuit told him the large chunks of iron had been
hurled from the sky. By the time Peary saw the huge rocks,
many pieces had been chipped away. The Inuit told him that
after the sled carrying the woman's "head" had fallen through
the ice, they carried away only small pieces at a time. Peary rewarded the indigenous people for their openness by stealing the
meteorites. After a great deal of effort, the explorer and his crew
removed the 1,000-pound dog, the 6,000-pound woman, and
the 100-ton tent and took them back to New York. He justified
his actions with the rationale that, since the Inuit had now been
officially discovered, they could obtain iron for their blades
from ships' crews.

See also METALLURGY.

**Sources/Further Reading**
Driver, Harold E. *Indians of North America*. Chicago: University of Chicago Press, 1969.
Oswalt, Wendell. *Eskimos and Explorers*. Novato, Calif.: Chandler & Sharp Publishers, 1979.

**Iroquois Constitution  (Great Law of Peace)**
(ca. A.D. 1000–A.D. 1400) *North American Northeastern
cultures*
The Iroquois Constitution, or Great Law of Peace, was created
by the Iroquois to stop neighboring tribes from fighting. The
document, recorded on WAMPUM belts (now known as the Hiawatha belts after one of the founders), formed a confederacy
among the Iroquois nations: the Oneida, Mohawk, Cayuga,
and Seneca, (and later Tuscarora) who lived in the northeastern part of what is now the United States. The Iroquois place
the creation of this constitution at between A.D. 1000 and A.D.

1400. Contemporary historians date the document at about
A.D. 1450. In either case, the Great Law of Peace was pre-
Columbian.

The Iroquois Constitution included the principles of a bi-
cameral legislature and outlined procedure for passing laws. It
forbade the holding of dual office by leaders and provided an
orderly way to remove leaders of the Iroquois Confederacy. The
power to declare war was delineated as well as the balance of
power between individual tribes and the confederacy. Other
provisions detailed how new tribes would be admitted to the
confederacy and how new amendments would be made to the
constitution. It also forbade unauthorized entry into an individual's home and ensured that the citizens of each member
tribe would be able to practice their own, unique religious ceremonies. Some scholars believe it was the longest formal international constitution in the world until that time. The only
possible exception to this might be the oral English Constitution, which had its origins in the Magna Carta. The Iroquois
Constitution provided much of the inspiration for the Articles
of Confederation, and later the U.S. Constitution, which was
created after the 13 English colonies on the eastern seaboard
won independence from Britain.

See also UNITED STATES CONSTITUTION, AMERICAN IN-
DIAN INFLUENCE ON.

**Sources/Further Reading**
Farb, Peter. *Man's Rise to Civilization as Shown by the Indians
of North America from Primeval Times to the Coming of the
Industrial State*. New York: E.P. Dutton & Company,
1968.
Johansen, Bruce. *Forgotten Founders*. Boston: Harvard Common Press, 1987.
Weatherford, Jack. *Indian Givers: How the Indians of the Americas Transformed the World*. New York: Fawcett Columbine
1988.

**irrigation systems**  (ca. 8000 B.C.–7000 B.C.)
*Mesoamerican, South American Andean, North American
Southeastern and Southwestern cultures*
Irrigation is the practice of supplying dry land with water. In-
dians throughout the Americas began inventing methods of
irrigating crops soon after they first began cultivating them.
They achieved this by floodplain irrigation and canals. The
earliest floodplain farming occurred in Mesoamerica and pre-
Peruvian South America. In many areas, floodplain farming
evolved into terraced farming. (See also FARMING, TER-
RACED.) Some of the earliest irrigation canal systems are
those built by the Olmec, whose culture flourished in
Mesoamerica starting in about 1700 B.C. Although neither of
these agricultural techniques was unique, these independent
inventions rivaled those practiced in the Middle East and
China, the two other birthplaces of agriculture outside of the
Americas.

Floodplain irrigation—planting crops in areas where the
soil would be saturated by water that flooded the banks of

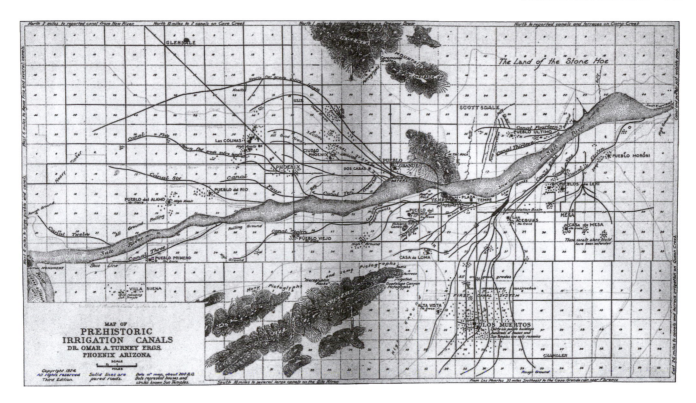

The Hohokam of the North American Southwest developed an extensive irrigation system of canals that would later be used by non-Indian farmers in the area that became Phoenix, Arizona. *(Arizona State Museum, University of Arizona)*

streams and rivers—was the earliest form of irrigation. It provided moisture for crops and added nutrients to the soil in the form of silt. In North America, floodplain farming was practiced by southeastern agriculturists from the Mississippian, Hopewell, and Adena cultures living along the valleys of the Mississippi and Ohio Rivers from ca. 1500 B.C. to 100 B.C. Although farming on flood plains took less initial effort than building extensive terraces with water courses or canal systems, it required a great deal of knowledge of the principles of runoff and stream flow in order to work successfully. Too little water, and the crops would not grow; too much, and they would wash away.

The Moche, who lived on the northern coast of what is now Peru from 200 B.C. to A.D. 600, were highly skilled water engineers. They built miles of irrigation ditches and flumes. Because the terrain where they lived was hilly, they built stone causeways, or AQUEDUCTS, to span the valleys. Later the Inca, who established their empire about A.D. 1100, controlled water in the same area by building narrow sluices controlled with stone slabs as gates. Their engineering included straightening streams and paving their beds. Not only did the Inca use water to irrigate their fields, they also channeled it into cities. In Cuzco they directed water into some buildings, including public baths. (See also HYGIENE, PERSONAL; PLUMBING.)

In the deserts of the North American Southwest, the Anasazi people began planting crops at the mouths of arroyos, as well as in river valleys. By between A.D. 1000 and A.D. 1200

they had created elaborate systems of terraces and small dams, called check dams, to ensure that their crops would be well-watered. In Mesa Verde, a large Anasazi settlement in the southwest of what is now Colorado, archaeologists discovered hundreds of such dams after a 1996 fire removed vegetation from the national park there. Master water engineers, the Anasazi living at Mesa Verde created reservoirs to store water for both household and agricultural use.

One of the best known irrigation systems developed in the New World is the complex organization of canals the Hohokam people began to build before A.D. 300 along the Salt and Gila River Valleys in what is now Arizona. After about 500 years of building, the Hohokam had engineered and constructed more than 150 miles of canals, some of them 30 feet wide and many over 10 feet deep in order to minimize surface evaporation. The longest of the canals stretched 14 miles. Brush and sand dikes or weirs channeled water from the rivers to the main canals.

With plastered trenches to minimize water seepage (see also WATER CONSERVATION), the system was built 30 miles into the desert east of the Gila River, using gravity flow to carry the water where it was needed so that the vegetable gardens of Hohokam communities such as Pueblo de los Muertos and Casa Grande were watered by sources six miles away. The entire project was accomplished with stone hoes, ironwood digging sticks, and cottonwood spades.

Because many communities used the canals as a way to irrigate their crops, archaeologists believe that the Hohokam had a system in place to administer this water and settle disputes over water rights, perhaps much like the water districts established by governments today. Once the canals had been built, they needed to be maintained by way of dredging for silt and replastering. This, too, was managed by water administrators.

The irrigation project continued for a period of 500 to 600 years until between A.D. 1200 and 1400, when the society declined for unknown reasons. Ethnobotanists believe this may have occurred because the soil became too alkaline as a result of irrigation buildup; drought is another possibility. Nevertheless, irrigation canal use continued on into the 18th century on a much smaller scale, carried on by the Akimel O'odham (Pima), who are considered by some to be descendants of the Hohokam. Flooding the fields to rid them of salt, the Akimel O'odham leveled the land to improve water flow, thus irrigating their crops, including COTTON, about five times during the growing season. During the 1800s they irrigated an estimated 13,000 to 16,000 acres. When necessary, they sent tribal members out to dig more ditches and allotted water to the members of the work crew.

Mormon settlers to the Salt River Valley of Arizona in the late 1800s cleared unused canals and irrigated their crops with the system. The Salt River Project, the water delivery system for Phoenix, uses many of the canals constructed by the Hohokam as part of its system today.

See also AGRICULTURE; AGRICULTURE, RAISED BED; PLUMBING.

**Sources/Further Reading**

Davico, Ana. "Scientists Optimistic about New Findings on Anasazi." Scripps Howard News Service. *Rapid City Journal.* July 29, 1999.

Doolittle, William E. *Canal Irrigation in Prehistoric Mexico: The Sequence of Technological Change.* Austin: University of Texas Press, 1990.

Hurt, R. Douglas. *American Indian Agriculture: Prehistory to Present.* Lawrence: University Press of Kansas, 1987.

Josephy, Jr., Alvin M., ed. *America in 1492: The World of the Indian People Before the Arrival of Columbus.* New York: Random House, 1991.

Mason, J. Alden. *The Ancient Civilizations of Peru.* Rev. ed. New York: Penguin Books, 1988.

Nabokov, Peter and Robert Easton. *Native American Architecture.* New York: Oxford University Press, 1989.

Trombold, Charles. *Ancient Road Networks and Settlement Hierarchies in the New World.* London: Cambridge University Press, 1991.

**isolation (quarantine)** (ca. 1700s) *North American Northeast cultures*

Isolation, or quarantine, is the practice of separating an individual or individuals infected with a contagious disease from other members of the population.

At the time of contact, most Europeans did not understand the concepts of germs or contagion. Europeans practiced isolation as well, basing the removal of lepers, and later those ill with plague, from the community at large on biblical injunctions to ostracize lepers because they were unclean in both a physical and spiritual sense. Until 1857 when Louis Pasteur theorized that germs caused illness, Western medicine believed contagious diseases were caused by miasma, an unpleasant vapor given off by the sick person. After contact, Europeans observed the practice of isolating patients with contagious diseases among the Huron (Wyandot). In the 18th century the first recorded incident of American Indians using isolation precautions was made by a French priest, Father Gabriel Sagard, who noted, "Sometimes the medicine-man orders one of the sick people to leave the town and encamp in the woods or in some other place apart, so that he may practice upon him there during the night his devilish contrivances. I do not know any other reason that he could have for removing the sick person, since usually this is only done for those who are infected with some unclean or dangerous disease, and such persons only, and no others, do they force to isolate themselves from the community until they are completely cured. This is a laudable and most excellent custom and ordinance, which indeed ought to be adopted in every country."

Although isolation is a routine hospital practice today, it did not become so until the 1900s—except among certain American Indian cultures. In his book *American Indian Medicine,* Virgil Vogel, an expert on North American indigenous medicine, wrote that the Indians ". . . understood the value of cleanliness in the treatment of wounds. They had a further advantage over their military opponents of the first part of the 19th century and earlier, in that they were treated individually in their own lodges and so were not subject to "hospital gangrene" which wreaked so much havoc in the military hospitals of the day."

See also ANTIBIOTIC MEDICATIONS; ASEPSIS.

**Sources/Further Reading**

Sagard, Father Gabriel. *The Long Journey to the Country of the Hurons.* Edited by George M. Wrong. Toronto: The Champlain Society, 1939.

Stone, Eric. *Medicine Among the American Indians.* Reprint. New York: Hafner Publishing Company, 1962.

Vogel, Virgil. *American Indian Medicine.* Norman: University of Oklahoma Press, 1970.

## jackstraws (pick-up sticks) (precontact) *North American Arctic and Northwest cultures*

Jackstraws is a game played with a number of small sticks. In the version still enjoyed by children today, players toss the sticks on a flat surface and then attempt to remove one at a time from the pile without moving any of the other sticks. The Haida, who lived on Prince of Wales Island in what is now Alaska, played a jackstraw game exactly like the one invented independently in Europe. The Inuit people of the western part of what is now Alaska also played this game. In their version of the game, players used a small wooden hook to remove the sticks from the pile where they had fallen. The Inuit also developed a different style of playing jackstraws. A player would place a bundle of 50 to 75 sticks on the back of his or her hand. After quickly removing the hand, the player would then try to grasp as many sticks as possible before they fell to the ground.

### Sources/Further Reading

Culin, Stewart. *Games of the North American Indians.* Reprint. Lincoln: University of Nebraska Press, 1992.

MacFarlan, Allan and Paulette MacFarlan. *Handbook of American Indian Games.* New York: Dover Books, 1958.

Prindle, Tara. "Native Tech Games." URL: http://www. nativeweb.org/NativeTech/games/ Posted 1994–1998. Downloaded on September 6, 1999.

## jade work (ca. 1200 B.C.) *Mesoamerican cultures*

Jade is a generic name that is used to describe a number of hard, fine-grained minerals. Mesoamerican jade ranges in color from a light, translucent green to a rich, transparent dark green resembling jade found in China. The minerals jadeite and nephrite were the jades of choice for Olmec, Maya, and Aztec lapidaries (gem cutters). Green serpentine or any green stone

was substituted when these were not available. Beginning with the Olmec, whose culture arose in Mesoamerica in about 1700 B.C., jade was valued for its beauty and its religious significance. Although the Chinese were fine jade carvers as well, the first jade carvings brought to Europe were from Mesoamerica by returning Spaniards.

The word *jade* originated with the Spaniards. When the conquistadores first saw the green mineral in the New World they called it *piedra de hijada,* meaning "stone of the kidneys." They chose the name because they believed these green stones were capable of healing kidney problems. Later, *hijada,* or kidney, was abbreviated to *jade.*

The Olmec are considered the first and greatest workers of jade in precontact America. Since jade is a very hard and dense mineral, great skill and sophisticated technology were required to fashion it into works of art and utilitarian objects. The Olmec were such excellent lapidaries that they could produce delicate items such as paper-thin ear ornaments from jade. These ear ornaments were created from several pieces so intricately made that they fit together perfectly. In addition to ear ornaments, the Olmec produced intricate figurines of various sizes, tools, masks (both life-sized and miniature), and some funerary objects of jade.

The Olmec also made axe heads, or celts, with amazing precision and quality. One axe head found by archaeologists was worked with the design of a footprint along its length. This impression was so well made and polished so precisely that it gave the appearance of a modern-day grinder having been used on it. The fact that the Olmec were able to practice sophisticated grinding technology is evidenced by their ability to produce surfaces on round, concave pieces of hematite with results resembling optical grinding technology of today. (See also OPTICAL TECHNOLOGY, BASICS OF.) Olmec jade workers, who were familiar with inlaying, also made ornaments of local shells inlaid with jade. Of the jade available to them, the Olmec valued the transparent, emerald green type most highly but were only able to acquire small amounts of it.

The Maya, whose culture arose in Mesoamerica in about 1500 B.C., also placed a high value on jade. They used the same hieroglyph for jade as for water because both were held in high esteem. When the Maya nobles buried their dead, they placed a round jade bead in the mouth of the corpse. This bead represented sustenance for the deceased's journey in the afterlife. Jade—like salt, cloth, shells, and CACAO beans—was used by the Maya as a form of currency in both local and long-distance TRADE.

In addition to making many of the same types of jade items, as the Olmec did, Maya lapidaries made miniature heads from pieces of jade. In addition they made rings, bracelets, ear spools (ear ornaments), necklaces, pendants, and pectorals (an ornament hung from the neck to cover a portion of the chest). These creations were intended for the ruling class. They cut and worked jade with a "string" saw made from a piece of cotton string or a strip of leather. Lapidaries first incised the jade with flint or another piece of jade. With this done, they placed wet sand over the mark and pulled the string back and forth across it. Sometimes they used crushed jade in place of sand. Once they had cut a groove into the jade, they placed a wedge of copper or wood into it and hit the wedge with a hammerstone, or similar tool, to break the jade apart. After the jade was cut to the desired size, it was ground and polished. Craftspeople used cane fibers or fibers from GOURD plants to accomplish this. Because these plants contain silica (sand) within their cells, they made excellent abrasives and polishes.

The Aztec, whose empire was established in Mesoamerica in about A.D. 1100, used jade in ways similar to those of the Olmec and Maya, producing sacred objects and jewelry for the ruling class and nobles. They also made jade embellishments for cloaks and other garments that were sewn onto the fabric, sometimes in combination with feathers (see also FEATHER-WORKING) and GOLD.

See also FLINTKNAPPING; STONEMASONRY TECHNIQUES.

## Sources/Further Reading

Brown, Dale, ed. *Aztecs: Reign of Blood & Splendor.* Alexandria, Va.: Time-Life Books, 1992.

Coe, Michael D. *America's First Civilization: Discovering the Olmec.* New York: American Heritage Publishing Co., Inc., 1968.

Schele, Linda and David Freidel. *A Forest Of Kings: The Untold Story of the Ancient Maya.* New York: William Morrow and Company, Inc., 1990.

Stuart, George E. "New Light on the Olmec." *National Geographic* 148, no. 5 (November 1993): 88–114.

## jalap (bindweed, high john, *Iponoea jalapa*)

(precontact) *North American; Mesoamerican cultures*

Jalap is an annual, twining plant that grows in warm areas of North America and in Mesoamerica. It is found in only one part of Mexico. The name *jalap* is derived from the town of Xalapa in Mexico, where the plant grows abundantly. Wild jalap (*Ipomoea pandurata*) is very similar to *Iponoea jalapa* and grows in an area between what are now Florida and Ontario and as far west as Texas. American Indians used both types of jalap as a powerful remedy for constipation. They steeped the root to release its resins in order to make a tea that was taken orally.

The Spaniards were so impressed by jalap's effectiveness as a cathartic that they introduced the medicine to Europe from Mexico in 1565. Jalap quickly became a popular constipation and indigestion remedy both in Europe and in the North American colonies, where people used it as a treatment for dropsy; jalap was administered with cream of tartar every two hours. It remained a standard part of the American pharmacology until the early 1900s. Because the action of jalap is so powerful that it can cause hypercardia (rapid heartbeat) if misused, the U.S. Food and Drug Administration has classified it as a dangerous remedy.

See also CASCARA SAGRADA; ENEMAS.

## Sources/Further Reading

Lust, John. *The Herb Book.* New York: Bantam Books, 1974.

Ortiz de Montellano, Bernard. *Aztec Medicine, Health, and Nutrition.* New Brunswick, N.J.: Rutgers University Press, 1990.

Vogel, Virgil. *American Indian Medicine.* Norman: University of Oklahoma Press, 1970.

**jar lids, twist-on**  See POTTERY.

**jerky** (precontact) *North American, Mesoamerican, Circum-Caribbean, South American Andean cultures*

Jerky, a popular snack in modern times, is dried meat that is often seasoned and cut into strips. American Indians throughout North America, Mesoamerica, and South America developed a variety of ways to dry meat, including the *barbecoa,* or BARBECUE, used in the West Indies. The word *jerky* comes from the Quecha language of the Inca, who called this food *charqui,* which meant dried meat. Experts at food preservation, the Inca sun-dried meat and also used a FREEZE-DRYING method to preserve the meat from llamas.

American Indians of the northern plains dehydrated buffalo meat, first cutting it into strips and sometimes smoking it over a fire before exposing it to air for several days. Meat that had been processed in this way would last up to three years and weighed about one-sixth as much as fresh meat. For the most part American Indians did not season jerky; however, some North American tribes did dry the meat with mint, which imparted a flavor to it. (See also MINTS, BOTANICAL.) Frequently the indigenous people of North America pounded jerky into powder, which they mixed with berries and fat. This was called PEMMICAN. Europeans explorers and travelers liked jerky for the same reasons American Indians did—its taste, long shelf life, and convenience. Today jerky is made from every-

Dried meat, or jerky, hangs on a drying rack in the camp of Comanche buffalo hunters captured on film in 1871. Turning meat into jerky not only helped to preserve it but also made it easier to transport. Jerky has become a popular snack food today. *(Photograph No. NWDNS-165-AI-15/National Archives and Records Administration at College Park)*

thing from turkey meat to ostrich meat, but it is beef jerky that has become a popular snack in the United States.

See also FOOD PRESERVATION.

### Sources/Further Reading

Weatherford, Jack. *Indian Givers: How the Indians of the Americas Transformed the World.* New York: Fawcett Columbine, 1988.

"The Buffalo Culture of the Plains Indians." *Wind River Rendezvous* 13, no. 2 (June 1983).

### Jerusalem artichokes (sunchokes, earth apples, breadroots, *Helianthus tuberosus*) (precontact) *North American Plains, Northeast, and Southeast cultures*

A species of SUNFLOWER, the Jerusalem artichoke grows from six to 10 feet tall and is topped with yellow daisylike flowers. It is native to the Great Plains and the eastern United States. Today, spread by cultivation, it grows throughout the United States. These plants, which modern farmers often consider weeds, produce roots, or tubers, about the size of a small to medium potato. Jerusalem artichoke roots were an important part of the diet of Indians throughout North America.

The nutritional value of Jerusalem artichokes is like that of POTATOES—with an important difference. Instead of starch, the Jerusalem artichoke's carbohydrate is in the form of inulin, a starchlike substance that is a major source of fructose, a simple sugar that is more easily digested by the body than other carbohydrates. Long before the Europeans came, members of many Indian groups, including the Iroquois, ate Jerusalem artichokes raw in addition to baking and boiling them. When Europeans arrived in southeastern North America in the 1600s, they found Indian people cultivating fields of these plants.

Jerusalem artichokes became popular once they were introduced to Europe, because they were easy to grow, tasted good, and could be used in many dishes. English gourmets favored cooking them in butter, wine, and spices. Jerusalem artichokes also made their way into British pies, where they were combined with dates, ginger, raisins, sack (a dry wine), and marrow. The English called them potatoes of Canada because they had been brought by the French to that country from Canada. The Italians called it *girasol aricocco,* or "turning toward the sun artichoke." In the mouths of American colonists, *girasol* became *Jerusalem*. Other names for the Jerusalem artichoke are sunchoke, earth apple, and bread-root.

Although people living in the southern United States sometimes pickle them or make relish from them, today Jerusalem artichokes are most popular in China and Europe. In the United States, they remain a specialty food, even though they can serve as a substitute for potatoes in most recipes except for French fries and can be eaten raw as a low-calorie snack. Most of the Jerusalem artichokes grown in the United States are used as animal feed. Since the early 1900s researchers have investigated using the artichokes to produce alcohol for fuel and fuel additives. Some believe that the tubers might be a superior source of commercial fructose. Even though both plans are viable, neither has been put into place.

## Sources/Further Reading

Carson, Dale. *New Native American Cooking.* New York: Random House, 1996.
Oregon State University College of Agricultural Sciences. URL: http://wwworst.edu/Dept/NWREC/artichje.html. Downloaded on May 14, 1999.
Weatherford, Jack. *Indian Givers: How the Indians of the Americas Transformed the World.* New York: Fawcett Columbine, 1988.
Weiner, Michael A. *Earth Medicine Earth Food: The Classic Guide to the Herbal Remedies and Wild Plants of the North American Indians.* New York: Fawcett Columbine, 1980.

## jewelry, metal (ca. 5000 B.C.–4000 B.C.) *North American Paleo-Indian culture*

The first metal jewelry in pre-Columbian America was made in about 5000 to 4000 B.C. The inventors of this jewelry were Paleo-Indians who lived in the southern Great Lakes region of North America. They are believed to be the first metalworkers in the world, so the jewelry they produced was perhaps the first of its kind. Archaelogists think that these people migrated from the north or northeastern part of North America to the Great Lakes region.

The copper jewelry these Paleo-Indians made included beads, rings, pendants, bracelets, and breastplates. In addition to copper jewelry, they produced many implements and utensils, including copper awls, gouges, picks, knives, wedges, and chisels. (See also TOOLS.) They made projectile points for spears, dart heads, and blades from copper as well. For reasons unknown today, these inventive and highly skilled artisans stopped producing these items about 3,000 years ago.

See also METALLURGY.

## Sources/Further Reading

Maxwell, James A. *America's Fascinating Indian Heritage.* Pleasantville, N.Y.: Reader's Digest Books, 1978.

## jewelry, turquoise and silver (200 B.C.–A.D. 1890) *Mesoamerican, North American Southwest cultures*

Turquoise is an opaque gemstone that is a complex phosphate of aluminum and copper. Deposits of this mineral are found throughout the world, usually in conjunction with deposits of copper. The coloring of turquoise ranges from blue to green. Blue turquoises contain more copper. Greenish turquoises contain more aluminum. Although turquoise from the Sinai peninsula in the Middle East was used by the Egyptians for jewelry about 4500 years ago, it is the relatively recent American Indian style of turquoise jewelry in the Southwest that is the best known and most popular throughout the world today.

Archaeological evidence shows that the Hohokam, pre-Anasazi, and Anasazi people mined turquoise at what are now Kingman and Morenci, Arizona; in the Conejhos area of Colorado; and at Cerillos, in the Burro mountains, and at Chaco Canyon in New Mexico. (Hohokam culture arose in what is now Arizona in about 300 B.C. Anasazi culture arose in the Southwest in about 350 B.C. and lasted until about A.D. 1450.) Pre-Anasazi turquoise miners began working in about 200 B.C. to provide artisans with gemstones. The artisans carved the stones and used them to make solid beads and as a material for MOSAIC inlays. They also mined turquoise as a TRADE commodity. Stones that the Anasazi mined in Chaco Canyon were traded as far as Chichén Itzá, the most influential Maya city in the Yucatán Peninsula. Turquoise stones from ancient mines at Cerillos, New Mexico, have also been found in Aztec archaeological sites in what is now Mexico. (The Aztec Empire arose in about A.D. 1100.)

Alta Vista, the center of the Chalchihuites culture, was the site of the first Mesoamerican turquoise mine. The Chalchihuites were the first Mesoamericans to work in turquoise. They made mosaic discs, rings, beads, and pendants. These were primarily used for burials. Archaeologists believe that these were traded with Teotihuacán. (See also CITIES, AMERICA'S FIRST.) MURAL painters at Teotihuacán ground turquoise to provide pigments for their frescoes. As demand for their turquoise products increased, the Chalchihuite prospected into the Southwest. In A.D. 700 they began importing turquoise from the Cerrillos mines several miles south of what is now Santa Fe, New Mexico.

Beginning in about A.D. 1000, the turquoise trade from the Southwest to Mesoamerica greatly increased. The ancient peoples of West Mexico, who had discovered METALLURGY and had begun making copper BELLS, sent traders up the coastline and across the Sierra Madre to purchase turquoise from the Hohokam and Anasazi in exchange for their bells. The Mesoamericans polished the stones they obtained and set them into mosaics. In addition to using turquoise in mosaics, the Mixtec, Aztec contemporaries who were excellent goldsmiths, began making turquoise jewelry with stones set in gold. Although Mixtec craftspeople obtained some turquoise from the area that is now Mexico, the finest came through trade with the Hohokam and Anasazi. After the decline of Chaco Canyon in about A.D. 1150, Casa Grande became the turquoise-trading center of the Southwest.

The Aztec continued the lapidary techniques of their ancestors and also imported Mixtec craftspeople. Although JADE was the most precious stone to the Aztec, jewelers also worked turquoise as well as rock crystal, agate, onyx, jasper, amber, and serpentine. Turquoise was the favored stone for mosaic work of the Aztec as it was of the Maya, who also incorporated it in objects denoting divine authority. (Maya civilization arose in Mesoamerica in 1500 B.C.)

Turquoise intended for personal adornment was called *xiutl* by the Aztec. They believed that the turquoise stones contained fire and had the ability to heal. From these stones they made rings, necklaces, lip plugs, masks, and chest ornaments, generally setting the stone into gold. The best turquoise, which was meant for the gods, was called *teuxiutl*. Most of the important Aztec gods were depicted wearing this gemstone. Pendants were made for the Turquoise Lord, the god of fire. The god of the traders, Quetzalcoatl, was depicted with turquoise mosaic earrings and a turquoise mask.

The Aztec obtained much of their turquoise from the Pacific coast of what is now Mexico, the northern part of Oaxaca, central Veracruz, and mines near Tula. The finest stones, however, could only be obtained through trade with the Indians of the desert Southwest. High demand for the turquoise sparked mining explorations by the Pueblo peoples, descendants of the Anasazi. In the 1100s they began new turquoise mining operations in the Mojave Desert, extending them to northern Nevada in the 1300s.

In modern times it is mainly the Navajo (Dineh) people who are known for making a unique style of turquoise jewelry that is set into silver. Combining silver with turquoise is a relatively new technique. Atsidi Sani is credited with becoming the first Navajo silversmith. He became friends with a Mexican blacksmith, who taught him the art of working with iron. By the mid-1800s the Navajo wore some silver jewelry, which they had purchased from Mexicans. The jewelry items they crafted themselves were from copper or brass. Atsidi Sani, whose name means Old Smith, learned to work with silver and taught his sons how to work it as well. Soon the craft spread. Navajo silversmiths began by making bells from quarters and creating small tobacco cases. Silver bridles were also popular projects. Some products of the earliest Navajo silversmithing were traded to the Ute for buckskin or hides.

In addition to working silver, the Navajo learned how to cast silver from Mexicans who made castings in clay. It is very likely that some of these teachers were descendants of the Aztec. Navajo silversmiths used fine-grained sandstone for their casting. (See also LOST WAX CASTING TECHNIQUE.) Atsidi Chom was the first Navajo silversmith to set turquoise into silver. His first attempt was a ring, which he made in the late 1870s. The piece gained much attention among the Navajo, and soon he began making more rings and creating bracelets. Young men who watched him started making jewelry as well. By the 1880s the art form flourished. Initially Navajo silversmiths obtained their turquoise from the Pueblo people of Santo Domingo who, in turn, obtained it from Cerrillios mine that had provided the Aztec with the blue gemstones hundreds of years be-

The Navajo, who began silversmithing in the mid-1800s, began incorporating turquoise into their work in the late 1870s. This 1870 photo of a Navajo silversmith shows the early stages of a jewelry design that would later include turquoise stones and become popular throughout the world. *(Photograph No. NWDNS-75-BAE-2421-b-6/Bureau of Indian Affairs/National Archives and Records Administration at College Park)*

fore. The Zuni, another tribe of the desert Southwest, traded turquoise to the Navajo as well, exchanging it for silver. Soon the Zuni and Hopi were making silver and turquoise jewelry too. Navajo women began making silver and turquoise jewelry soon after World War I.

In the late 1800s and early 1900s non-Indian miners rediscovered turquoise deposits in the Southwest that had long been forgotten, but they could not keep up with the demand from silversmiths who sold jewelry to tourists. Later stabilized turquoise—porous stones impregnated with acrylic—began to be used in some inexpensive pieces of jewelry. Today the work of Navajo and Zuni silver and turquoise artisans is known throughout the world.

See also JEWELRY, METAL; METAL, PRECIOUS.

## Sources/Further Reading

Adair, John. *The Navajo and Pueblo Silversmiths*. Norman: University of Oklahoma Press, 1994.

Karasic, Carol. *The Turquoise Trail: Native American Jewelry and Culture of the Southwest*. New York: Harry Abrams, 1993.

Northrop, Stuart A. *Turquoise and Spanish Mines in New Mexico.* Albuquerque: University of New Mexico Press, 1975.

## jicama (yam bean, Mexican potato, *Pachyrrhizua erosus*) (precontact) *Mesoamerican culture*

Jicama, also known as the yam bean and the Mexican potato, is a root crop. Jicama roots, which can weigh up to six pounds and are shaped like large radishes or turnips, grow in two colors—yellowish-gray and yellowish-brown. The raw flesh of the jicama is white, lightly sweet, cool, and crunchy. Jicama is native to Mesoamerica and was part of the diet of the Maya and other Mesoamerican Indians. Maya culture arose in about 1500 B.C.

The Spanish introduced jicama to the Philippines in the 1600s, and it spread throughout the world from there. When it is cooked it takes up the other flavors in the dish; most often it is eaten raw. Many people compare the texture to water chestnuts when they are raw or cooked. Jicama is a good source of potassium and vitamin C while being low in sodium. It is also cholesterol and fat free. One hundred grams of jicama contain 55 calories, 12.8 grams of carbohydrates, 1.4 grams of protein, and 85 percent water. In recent years, this "new" vegetable of precontact Maya chefs has found its way into many supermarkets and contemporary restaurants in the United States.

### Sources/Further Reading

Benson, Elizabeth P. *The Maya World.* New York: Thomas Y. Crowell Company, 1967.

Coe, Sophie D. *America's First Cuisines.* Austin: University of Texas Press, 1994.

*Jicama Nutritional Information.* URL: http://www.vegcountry.com/jicamainfo.html. Downloaded on August 10, 1999.

*Small Farm Center.* URL: http://www.sfc.ucdavis.edu/cgi-win/spec_crop.exe/show_crop&ID=6. Downloaded on August 10, 1999.

## jojoba (*Simmondsia chinesis*) (precontact) *North American Southwest cultures*

A native woody shrub of the Sonoran Desert in southern Arizona, California, and Baja California in Mexico, jojoba has small leaves and bears olive-sized fruits. Mature jojoba plants withstand high temperatures as well as cold to −10° C. They can be grown on almost any type of soil and do not require much water. They are believed to have a life span of at least 150 to 200 years. Jojoba was used for centuries by indigenous people in the areas in which it grew as a skin balm and a HAIR CONDITIONER. They also roasted the nuts to make a drink. By far the most significant uses were medicinal. In the 1700s Father Junípero Serra, founder of 21 California missions, wrote in his diary that Indians used jojoba to suppress their appetites when they could not find food and as a salve for bruises, sores, cuts, and burns.

The basis for jojoba's skin- and hair-protecting properties is a chemically unique "oil" in its seeds. In fact, this is not really an oil, but what scientists call a "long straight-chain liquid wax of non-glyceride esters." Unlike oils, liquid waxes do not break down under heat and pressure, nor do they turn rancid. Jojoba "oil" is also hypoallergenic and odorless. Its chemical structure is much like that of sperm whale oil, which has been banned in the United States since 1971 (prior to which it was used extensively in the cosmetics industry). For this reason, jojoba is used today in shampoos, conditioners, soaps, sunscreen, and as a base for body lotions and moisturizing creams.

In the past jojoba was hand-harvested from wild plants in Mexico, Arizona, and California. Because the supply was small, the price was high. During the last two decades of the 20th century, farmers began making commercial plantings in Arizona and California. Agricultural economists and researchers in the United States and in South American countries have begun laying the groundwork for large-scale commercial growing and harvesting operations.

In addition to being used in cosmetics, jojoba is used as a leather softener, engine lubricant, waterproofing agent, and automobile polish. Thus far, research scientists have derived 50 additional jojoba products that they believe have commercial possibilities. In the future jojoba may serve as a base for high-pressure lubricants, disinfectants, antifoaming agents, DETERGENTS, emulsifiers, protective coatings, resins, and surfactants. Some chemists believe that it may one day be used as a no-calorie vegetable oil, much like the one made from soybeans that is currently marketed.

See also SUNSCREENS, MEDICINAL.

### Sources/Further Reading

American Jojoba Association. URL: http:www.jojoba.org/history. Downloaded on May 12, 1999.

National Research Council (U.S.). *Jojoba: New Crop for Arid Lands, New Material for Industry.* Advisory Committee on Technology Innovation Ad Hoc Panel. Wash. D.C.: National Academy Press, 1985.

Thompson, Anson E. "Arid-land Industrial Crops." In *Advances in New Crops,* edited by J. Janick and J. E. Simon. Portland, Ore.: Timber Press, 1990.

# K

**kaolin** (ca. 1500 B.C.–A.D. 1500) *South American; Mesoamerican cultures*

Kaolin is a hydrated form of aluminum silicate that is found in South and Mesoamerica as a type of white clay. Because of its absorbency, it is used medicinally and also as a pigment. The first people to use kaolin in the precontact Americas were the Olmec of Mesoamerica, whose culture arose in about 1700 B.C. They used it widely in the production of their figurines and pottery. Other tribes used it to develop tints of white for their pottery as well.

The Quechua, contemporaries of the Inca, who established an empire in what is now Peru in about A.D. 1000, are known to have used kaolin medicinally. The Quechua lived near the area of Cuzco in what is now Peru. Quecha physicians discovered that because of kaolin's absorbency it was an effective remedy for "sour stomachs" and diarrhea. They administered this medicine orally, dipping potatoes in an aqueous solution of kaolin before eating them. The Inca, who conquered the Quecha, borrowed not only their language but their stomach remedy as well.

When modern researchers tested the same type of solution used by the Quecha and Inca, they found it contained a minute amount of coumarin, a blood thinner, or anticoagulant. Virgil Vogel, an expert in the field of American Indian medicine, wrote that the use of kaolin ". . . by a primitive people would appear rather remarkable in view of the comparatively recent introduction of kaolin into modern medicine as a protective agent for the gastric and intestinal mucosa and as a remedy for bacterial infections of the gut."

Kaolin is still used by modern Quechua people for the same reasons their ancestors took it. Many non-Indians also rely on this centuries-old cure. Today a commercial kaolin product is marketed widely as an upset stomach remedy in the United States.

See also INDIGESTION MEDICATIONS; IPECAC.

**Sources/Further Reading**

Engel, Frederic Andre. *An Ancient World Preserved.* New York: Crown Publishers, Inc., 1972.

Fagan, Brian M. *Kingdoms of Gold, Kingdoms of Jade: The Americas Before Columbus.* London: Thames and Hudson Ltd., 1991.

Spruce, Richard. *Notes of a Botanist on the Amazon and Andes.* London: MacMillan & Company, Ltd., 1908.

Vogel, Virgil. *American Indian Medicine.* Norman: University of Oklahoma Press, 1970.

**kayaks** (precontact) *North American Arctic and Subarctic cultures*

Kayaks–light boats similar to canoes—were used throughout the Arctic and subarctic region of what are now Canada and Greenland. Made from seal or walrus skin placed over a wooden frame with whalebone lashings, one-person kayaks were easily maneuverable and allowed those who used them to travel up to 70 miles a day under good conditions. Kayaks can also travel in very shallow water. The kayaker balanced the boat by sitting erect, often tightly braced inside a narrow boat. If stormy seas caused the kayak to be overturned, it could be quickly righted while remaining in the boat—an important feature in cold arctic waters.

Kayak craftsmanship was an art. Typically men constructed the frames, mortising U-shaped crosspieces into the gunwale and fastening them with wooden nails. Women sewed the skin coverings. Since pitch for waterproofing the seams was not available in the far north, they developed a special folded seam of the same type used for MUKLUKS, in order to keep the small vessels watertight. After completion, kayak makers further waterproofed the craft with seal oil. Sometimes they attached a hooded PARKA to the cockpit of the kayak, so that the boats became waterproof and, in effect, an item of clothing.

American Indians living in the northern regions of North America made kayaks by stretching walrus or sealskin over wooden frames. Kayaking has become a popular sport today. *(Photograph No. NRIA-WME-PHOTOS-P899/National Archives and Records Administration—Pacific Alaska Region)*

Men using a double paddle, which increased their speed, piloted the crafts, which averaged about 19 feet long. This double paddle and the special design of the kayak made it a highly efficient vehicle in terms of energy needed to move the boat. The double paddle was unique to the Inuit and the indigenous people of Siberia. So important was the kayak in Inuit culture that in Greenland a boy was given a kayak when he was 10 years old. By the time he was 20 years old, he was expected to build his own kayak. Throughout the north, kayaks were used for seal and walrus hunting. For WHALING the Inuit used *umiaks*. These were larger boats about 30 feet in length, five or six feet across, and two and a half feet deep. Today kayaks have become very popular sports boats, with different versions for use in surf and white water and for use on flat water. While most are now made from plastic or fiberglass, much of the original design and skill in paddling is based on what the Inuit developed long ago.

## Sources/Further Reading

Murdoch, John. *Ethnological Results of the Point Barrow Expedition Annual Report of the U.S. Bureau of Ethnology 1887–1888.* Washington, D.C.: Government Printing Office, 1892.

Oswalt, Wendell. *Eskimos and Explorers.* Novato, Calif.: Chandler & Sharp Publishers, 1979.

Weatherford, Jack. *Native Roots: How the Indians Enriched America.* New York: Fawcett Columbine, 1991.

**keros (beakers)** (ca. A.D. 850) *South American Andean cultures*

Beakers are vessels with wide openings, made for holding liquids. This commonplace equipment in laboratories around the world today was manufactured by the Sican culture of what is now Peru in about A.D. 850; they were called *keros.* Although the majority of the keros that have been found were made by the Sican, the Chimu, a culture group from the same area that arose in about A.D. 1000, made them as well. Unlike modern beakers made of glass, the Sican and Chimu keros were made of several different substances, including wood, ceramics, copper, gold, and silver; they were also made from alloys of these metals. The walls of the keros varied in thickness and in size, holding from about eight ounces to a gallon of liquid. Some were inlayed with precious and semiprecious stones. Chimu keros were more elaborate than those of the Sican.

See also METAL CASTING; METALLURGY; POTTERY.

## Sources/Further Reading

Bankes, George. *Peru Before Pizarro.* New York: E. P. Dutton, 1977.

Morris, Craig and Adriana von Hagen. *The Inka Empire and Its Andean Origins.* New York: Abbeville Press Publishers, 1993.

## knitting (needle knitting) (ca. 400 B.C.–A.D. 400)
*South American Andean cultures*

Indigenous textile workers who lived on the south and central coast of what is now Peru developed a needlework technique that is called needle knitting today. They used it to create decorative edgings for their textiles and garments. Although the appearance of items made with this technique resembles knitting, needle knitting uses a single needle instead of two. This technique, which uses cross-knit looping and the buttonhole stitch, closely approximates needle tatting or the needlepoint, or rosepoint, lacemaking techniques that were independently invented in Europe in the Middle Ages in about A.D. 1400. Unlike EMBROIDERY, needle-knitted edgings can be removed and resewn onto garments.

The Paracas and Nazca needle knitters, who began doing the work in about 400 B.C. in what is now Peru, often used very different design elements than those of European lacemakers. The edgings they produced, a kind of three-dimensional embroidery, sometimes portrayed tiny people that were, in many cases, less than an inch high. These people had detailed facial features and costumes and usually carried staffs or fans. Decorative borders also consisted of animals, birds, and more abstract designs. These were made from LLAMA or ALPACA fiber that had been dyed (see also DYES) and spun into fine thread.

Indigenous American needleworkers also produced gauzes using the same techniques. They were often intricate and contained elaborate designs. Made from COTTON thread, they took many hours of labor to produce and more closely resembled the European rosepoint laces.

Meshwork or netting is another single-needle technique that utilizes knotting and looping. This technique is called crochet today and is used to make laces with an open background, among other things. The Nazca, whose culture arose in what is now Peru in about 600 B.C., used it to make items ranging from fishing nets to hairnets. A number of hairnets, dated ca. A.D. 400, have been found in burial sites on the west central coast of what is now Peru. Each hairnet was made with five to six threads that were intertwined.

See also WEAVING TECHNIQUES.

## Sources/Further Reading

Harris, Jennifer, ed. *Textiles: 5,000 Years.* New York: Harry N. Abrams, Inc., 1993.

Mason, J. Alden. *The Ancient Civilizations of Peru.* New York: Penguin Books, 1988.

Weatherford, Jack. *Indian Givers: How the Indians of the Americas Transformed the World.* New York: Fawcett Columbine, 1988.

## labor laws (ca. A.D. 1000–A.D. 1519) *South American Andean cultures*

Laws designed to promote the safety and well-being of workers have come to be known as labor laws. The Inca, whose empire was established in what is now Peru in about A.D. 1000, taxed their citizens by having them perform services or pay tributes. To a certain extent, citizens could choose the type of tax they paid. (See also TAX SYSTEM.)

Gold mining was one way that some people paid taxes. In many cases the gold deposits existed in harsh areas at high altitudes. The nobility who demanded the tax in gold did, however, recognize the needs of their taxpayers. They therefore developed very specific labor laws to protect the miners, while also ensuring a constant supply of gold. These laws required that only married couples do the mining. The miner's wife cooked, washed clothes, and took care of the living quarters, but most of all she boosted her husband's morale. This was important for the miner, enabling him to work harder. Provisions and equipment were provided to each miner and his wife.

Sick miners were required by law to be removed and returned home. Most important, because of the difficult mining conditions, the miners were rotated so as to prevent damage to them. Another law required that miners only work during warm summer months. While in the mining camps they had designated rest periods, and the government would sponsor feasts and festivals for them. Yet another law required that the miner's job or farm be maintained by others through the tax system while he was in the mines.

See also GOLD PANNING; MINING, PLACER.

### Sources/Further Reading

Bankes, George. *Peru Before Pizarro.* Oxford, England: Phaidon Press Ltd., 1977.

von Hagen, Victor W. *Realm of the Inca.* New York: New American Library, 1957.

von Hagen, Victor Wolfgang. *The Royal Road of the Inca.* London: Gordon Cremonesi Ltd., 1976.

## lacemaking See KNITTING.

## lacrosse (precontact) *North American Northeast and Southeast cultures*

Sometimes called the fastest game on two feet, lacrosse is played by two teams on an open field with goals at each end. In the modern version of the game, 10 players on each team carry long-handled sticks with a triangular mesh pocket at the end. They attempt to put a five-ounce, hard rubber ball into the opponents' net while preventing them from scoring. They may not touch the ball with their hands.

The game of lacrosse was originally invented by American Indians and played in many parts of the North American continent. (Although some anthropologists have made attempts to relate the origins of lacrosse to the ancient BASKETBALL game played in Mesoamerica by the Aztec, Maya, and Olmec on elaborate stone courts, little evidence supports this.) However, the exact origins of lacrosse, the fastest growing sport in the United States today, remain uncertain. The first recorded instance of a non-Indian watching a lacrosse game was that of Jean de Brébeuf, a French missionary who described a Huron (Wyandot) game to his superiors in the 1600s. In his report he compared the curved playing sticks he had seen to a crosier, a staff with a cross or a crook at the end carried before Catholic officials to denote their office. Although legend has it that lacrosse derived its name from Brébeuf, more than likely the name lacrosse came from a type of French stickball called *jeu de la crosse*.

Other accounts from early missionaries indicated that lacrosse was played in the Great Lakes region, Lower Canada,

Upstate New York, and among the Cherokee of the Southeast. There were also a few scattered reports of a game similar to lacrosse played by some Pacific Coast tribes, but anthropologists do not believe the game was widespread in the West.

The game was a dangerous one, requiring players to have great skill to catch, carry, and pass the ball. According to some witnesses, the southeastern teams were so large that many players would never get near the ball. Instead, they used their sticks to injure other players in order to take them out of the game. The contests were typically played from dawn to sunset and lasted two to three days. The Cherokee, avid players, termed the sport "War's Little Brother." Not surprisingly, lacrosse was mainly played by young men who raced across the countryside to score points and block the other team from making goals. Although the game was mainly a man's sport, some tribes are said to have allowed women to play on teams with men. In a few instances women competed with other women.

The game had many variations. Among the Cherokee and other southeastern tribes, including the Choctaw, Chickasaw, Creek, Seminole, and Yuci, players often used two sticks to toss, catch, and pass a soft deerskin ball. These southeastern teams were composed of 100 to 1,000 players on each side. The goals, most often a big rock or a tree, were located from 500 yards to half a mile apart. Occasionally the goals were several miles from each other. Some tribes erected goal posts and threw the ball between them to score points. Tribes including the Chippewa (Anishinabe), Menominee, Potawatomi, Sac, Mesquaki, Miami, Ho-Chunk, and Santee Sioux (Nakota) played a version of the game that anthropologists call Great Lakes Lacrosse. These players used a three-foot stick with a small pocket and a wooden ball that was shaped into a sphere by charring the wood.

The Six Nations of the Iroquois, who lived in southern Canada and what is now New York State, called their version of the game *baggataway* or *twearaathon.* The Onondaga named it *dehuntshigwa'es,* or "men hit a rounded object." Iroquois players used a stick longer than three feet that ended in a large triangular pocket. Lacrosse sticks used in today's game are modeled after them.

Although requiring great skill, Iroquois matches were not as spectacular as those played by the southeastern tribes. In 1776 Ebenezer Elmer described an Iroquois game played by 15 to 20 players on each side. "The game is won by one's knocking the ball such a number of times beyond the lines fixed upon the side of his antagonists," he wrote. "The lines fixed were forty or fifty rods apart and in knocking the ball they showed the greatest dexterity and no less activity and ability of body in continuing to run with great fury over the field for at least two hours."

According to other accounts by European settlers at the time, the Iroquois had a reputation for good sportsmanship and fair play. Often the matches involved gambling, with women donating the goods and the ornaments wagered. During harvest season, a time when Iroquois men did not hunt, lacrosse contests were held nearly every day.

Throughout North America, lacrosse games were social events that also provided young men with combat training.

Sometimes matches were played between bands or tribes as a way to resolve disputes. Such was the case with a match between the Creek and Choctaw in the late 1700s that was held over rights to a beaver pond. Quite frequently the contests had a more religious nature and were held to prevent bad luck, stop epidemics, and affect the weather. Members of the Oneida Nation considered lacrosse a spiritual celebration that was carried out to please the Creator and to honor the Seven Thunders, whom they believed moved across the sky from west to east, purifying the earth with rain and wind. According to Oneida oral tradition, young men once held a game for one of the Iroquois Confederacy founders (Hiawatha, or Hayewat-ha), to comfort him after his children had died. (See also IROQUOIS CONSTITUTION.)

Canadians were the first non-Indians to adopt the Native sport. By the early 1800s Montreal's French settlers had begun playing lacrosse and changing the way the original Indian game had been played. They set dimensions for the field and limited the numbers of players on each team. When the Dominion of Canada was formed, lacrosse was designated the country's national sport. Lacrosse, along with ice hockey, which was patterned after the rules of lacrosse, remains popular in Canada today. (See also HOCKEY, FIELD AND ICE.) Montreal's Olympic Club organized a team in 1844 to play against an Indian team. Other matches with Indian teams were held in 1848 and 1851. In 1856 the new Montreal Lacrosse Club made the first set of written rules for the game.

At the same time that others were learning to play and love the game of lacrosse, by the mid-1800s, many Indians in the northern United States had stopped playing the sport. Often they turned away from the tradition at the direction of government officials and missionaries who took issue with the gambling that surrounded lacrosse games and believed that, because it was traditional, lacrosse would prevent Indian people from becoming "civilized."

From Canada, non-Indian interest in lacrosse spread to the United States, where by 1870 several New York City teams were started. Colleges including Boston University, Columbia, Cornell, Harvard, and Princeton soon played the game. Shortly afterward it acquired a reputation as a game for the sons of the rich. England, Ireland, Scotland, and even Australia began forming teams.

In 1867 a team of Indians traveled to England to play a match before Queen Victoria. Later non-native Canadian and Iroquois teams toured Europe putting on matches. The game was a hit there and the English Lacrosse Union was formed in 1892. Eventually the British would develop a version of the sport for women that was similar to field hockey. The modified game continues to be played by non-Indian women throughout the world. With its wooden stick, undefined sidelines, and mass attack, many sports historians say that women's lacrosse more closely resembles the traditional Indian game than does the modern men's version of the sport.

Eventually Indians began returning to the game that had traditionally been theirs. The Onondaga tribe started a team, and Glen "Pop" Warner, football coach at the Carlisle Indian

Artist George Catlin painted this Choctaw lacrosse game in the early 1800s. He wrote that as he watched, "an instant struggle ensued between the players, who were some six or seven hundred in number." The version of lacrosse played by Northeast tribes used fewer players on each side and more closely resembled the game that is played today. *(Rare Books Division, The New York Public Library Astor, Lennox and Tilden Foundations)*

School in Pennsylvania, substituted lacrosse for baseball at the boarding school. "Lacrosse is a developer of health and strength," he said. "It is a game that spectators rave over once they understand it."

The game continued to gain in popularity among non-Indians. It was played in Olympic competition, first in the 1904 Olympics in St. Louis and then at the London Games in 1908. Since that time lacrosse has occasionally been played at the Olympics as a demonstration sport. The International Lacrosse Federation has conducted tournaments since 1967. Although Indian lacrosse players toured in other countries, for nearly 100 years, they were banned from international amateur competition. Lacking the financial sponsorship that non-Indian teams could more easily attain, they had to charge money in order to pay transportation costs from match to match. As a result they were judged to be professionals and ineligible to compete. Only in the 1980s with the formation of the Iroquois Nationals did Indian lacrosse players overcome that barrier and become eligible to compete in the World Games.

Today lacrosse has attracted over a half milion players in the United States. More than 250 colleges and universities have men's teams as do more than 600 high schools. More than 100 colleges and universities and 150 high schools have women's teams. The Iroquois Lacrosse Association preserves the traditional game among the tribes that made up the Iroquois Confederacy.

### Sources/Further Reading

Oneida Indian Nation. *Lacrosse: An Iroquois Tradition.* URL: http://one-web.org/oneida/lacrosse.html. Downloaded on May 13, 1998.

Trigger, Bruce G. *The Huron Farmers of the North.* New York: Holt, Rinehart and Winston, Inc., 1969.

Vennum, Thomas, Jr. *American Indian Lacrosse: Little Brother of War.* Washington, D.C.: Smithsonian Institution Press, 1994.

**lady's slipper** (precontact) *North American Northeast and Southeast cultures*

Lady's slipper is the name given to many species of plants that belong to the genus *Cypripedium*. They are members of the orchid family and grow in the Americas, Asia, and Europe. Flourishing in damp places, lady's slipper grows from Canada to the

American South. American Indians discovered that the roots and rhizomes (root-like horizontal stems) of these plants contained substances that worked as a sedative, an ANTISPASMODIC for the treatment of epilepsy and seizures, and as a pain reliever. The varieties they used for these medicinal purposes include *Cypripedium acaule, C. humile, C. parvillaflorum,* and *C. pubescens.* They harvested and dried the plants, preparing them by boiling the entire root system in water or powdering the roots to mix with water.

According to Michael Weiner, author of the book *Earth Medicine Earth Food,* "The Lady's Slipper was first used by several tribes as a sedative and nerve medicine; it later became accepted in domestic American medicine as a cure for insomnia." Some of the tribes that used lady's slipper tea were the Chippewa (Anishinabe), Mohawk, Mesquaki, Menominee, and Penobscot of northeastern North America and the Cherokee of the Southeast. The Chippewa used *C. pubescens* as a sedative and antispasmodic for difficult labor. The Menominee used *C. parviflorum* for women's emotional and obstetric difficulties and *C. acaule* for men with nervous problems and or neuralgia. The Cherokee used *C. parviflorum* as an ANTIHELMINTIC, and the Penobscot used *C. acaule* to treat nervous problems. Many American Indian women used *C. humile* for difficult births. Although the Lakota people of the Plains were known to eat lady's slipper as a food, it is not known if they used it medicinally.

## Sources/Further Reading

Hutchens, Alma R. *Indian Herbology of North America.* Boston: Shambhala, 1991.

Lust, John. *The Herb Book.* New York: Bantam Books, 1974.

Moerman, Dan. *Native American Ethnobotany Database: Food, Drugs, Dyes and Fibers of Native North American Peoples.* URL: http://www.umd.umich.edu/cgi-bin/herb. Downloaded on December 25, 1999.

Rogers, Dilwyn J. *Lakota Names and Traditional Uses of Native Plants by Sicangu (Brule) People in the Rosebud Area, South Dakota.* St. Francis, South Dakota: Rosebud Educational Society, 1980.

Vogel, Virgil. *American Indian Medicine.* Norman: University of Oklahoma Press, 1970.

Weiner, Michael A. *Earth Medicine Earth Food: The Classic Guide to the Herbal Remedies and Wild Plants of the North American Indians.* New York: Fawcett Columbine, 1980.

**lamination**   See BOWS, LAMINATED.

## language, American Indian influence on

(contact) *North American, Mesoamerican, Circum-Caribbean, South American cultures*

Since contact with Europeans, American Indians have contributed hundreds of words from their indigenous languages to both English and Spanish, the predominant languages of the conquerors and colonizers. Often these adopted words were the names Indians had given to animals, plants, and places (see also PLACE-NAMES) that Europeans had never seen before. For example, the *manatee,* an aquatic mammal that is found in the coastal waters of both the tropical Americas and Africa, was named from the Carib Indian word *manati,* which meant "beast." The Spanish were the first to use it, and it entered the English language in 1672. *Chiggers*—tiny mites that burrow beneath the skin, causing intense irritation—derive their name from *chigoe,* a word used by Carib Indians for a small tropical flea (*Tunga penetrans*). The Carib were indigenous to islands in what is now the Caribbean, which is named after them.

In the Northeast, Algonquian speakers gave colonists a number of words. *Terrapin* is an Algonquian word meaning "little turtle," a source of food for indigenous people of the Eastern Woodlands. The European colonists added the freshwater turtles to their vocabulary by 1672 as well as to their diet, transforming the turtles into soup and stew as the American Indians did. The name of the nocturnal marsupials called *opossums* comes from the Powhatan word *aposoum,* meaning a "white animal." In 1610 it was shortened to *possum* by colonists.

*Chipmunk* (*Tamias striatus*) is derived from the Chippewa (Anishinabe) word *atchitamon,* which means "headfirst" and is a description of how chipmunks descend trees. The small squirrel-like rodents with characteristic stripes down their backs, are common to the eastern United States. In 1832 the word was spelled *chitmunk* in English and twenty-five years later was changed to its present spelling.

The first recorded English use of the word *coyote* appeared in 1759. It came from Mexican Spanish, who borrowed the term from the Nahuatl, or Aztec, word *coyotl.* The Aztec contributed a number of other words to Spanish and then English, including: *avocado, chile, chocolate, peyote, tamale,* and *tomato.*

The jaguar (*Felis jaguarundi*), a long-tailed grayish-brown wild cat native to tropical America, gets its name from the Guarani word for dog, *jaguarundi. Piranhas* are tropical freshwater fish that attack and kill other fish and animals. Their name came into the English language through the Portuguese from the Tupi words *pira,* meaning "fish," and *sainha,* meaning "tooth." The Guarani are indigenous to what is now Paraguay, and the Tupi are indigenous to what is now Brazil.

The Inca, a South American Andean culture group whose empire arose in about A.D. 1000, gave the Spanish, and eventually the English language many words from *Quecha,* their native language. In addition to the word *kuka* that became *coca* and *kuntur* from which *condor* is derived, English words adopted from Quecha include *guano, gaucho, llama, pampa, puma,* and *quinine.*

This linguistic borrowing of words continued well after colonization had been accomplished. For example, the word *mugwump* comes from the Algonquian *maquomp,* which meant "chief." The word became popularized in the 1884 U.S. presidential election after a prominent Republican left the party and refused to support James G. Blaine as a candidate for the U.S. presidency. The word has come to mean a person who acts independently, especially in politics. Sequoia trees, the giant redwoods of the Pacific Coast, were named in honor of the Cherokee Sequoia, who by himself developed a written alphabet for his native language. In the 20th century, auto manufacturers used the names of North American Indian chiefs Pontiac and Cadillac. Names of tribes, such as the Cherokee and the Dakota have been borrowed for vehicle models as well.

Some other English words that have American Indian roots are: *bayou, catalpa, Chinook, honk, hooch, hotchy-koochey, hub-bub, hurricane, mescal, moose, muskellunge, papoose, peewee, pep, piroque, podunk, potlatch, pow wow, punk, raccoon, sachem, savanna, scuppernong, shack, shark, skunk, tamarack, totem, tapir, tomahawk, wampum, wapiti, wood-chuck,* and *yankee.*

See also AVOCADO; BARBECUE; CANOE; CAUCUS, CIGARS; CHILES; CHOCOLATE; COCA; CURARE; GRAPES; GUACAMOLE; HAMMOCKS; HICKORY; IGLOOS; JERKY; KAYAK; LLAMAS; MARACAS; MUKLUKS; PERSIMMONS; PEYOTE; QUININE; SCUPPERNONG GRAPES; TAMALE; TOMATOES; WAMPUM.

### Sources/Further Reading

*American Heritage Dictionary, Second College Edition.* Boston: Houghton Mifflin Company, 1982.

Flexner, Stuart Berg. *I Hear America Talking: An Illustrated History of American Words and Phrases.* New York: Simon and Schuster, 1976.

Simpson, J. A. and Edmund S. Weiner, eds. *The Compact Oxford English Dictionary.* Oxford, England: Oxford University Press, 1991.

Weatherford, Jack. *Native Roots: How the Indians Enriched America.* New York: Fawcett Columbine, 1991.

**language, sign**   See SIGN LANGUAGE.

**latex (rubber)** (ca. 1000 B.C.) *Mesoamerican, South American cultures*

*Latex* is the term generally used to describe the milky fluid or juice that comes from the rubber tree (*Hevea brasiliensis*) that is native to parts of Mesoamerica and South America along the Amazon River. These trees are 30 to 60 feet tall. The sap produced by the trees is also called *caoutchouc* after the Quecha name for the tree. It is extremely sticky, and some consider its smell malodorous. The Olmec of Mesoamerica, whose culture flourished from about 1700 B.C. to about 400 B.C., are credited with first producing rubber products from this sap, including the rubber ball used for the game of BASKETBALL. The Olmec also produced other rubber and rubberized products that they used for trade goods. They became so identified with rubber in the ancient Americas that they were referred to as the "Rubber People" by other tribes. The Olmec also made rubber from the latex of the SAPODILLA tree.

The Maya learned to use latex to make rubber and waterproof materials as well. In her book *The Maya World,* Elizabeth

P. Benson states that rubber trees ". . . provided the Maya with rubber for their balls, rain-proofing for capes, and material to be traded with the non-rubber-producing Highlands." The Quecha, contemporaries of the Inca, whose empire was established in what is now Peru in about A.D. 1000, called this tree *caoutchouc* and produced many rubber and rubberized products, including ropes and bottles.

Indigenous people routinely harvested latex from what became known as the "weeping tree." Usually two collectors would open a trail between about 100 trees and harvest sap from these trees each day. They would make a slash in the bark with a small hatchet. These slanting cuts allowed latex to flow from ducts located on the exterior or the inner layer of bark (cambium) of the tree. Since the cambium controls the growth of the tree, growth stops if it is cut. Thus, rubber tapping demanded accuracy, so that the incisions would not be too many given the size of the tree, or too deep, which could stunt its growth or kill it. Harvesters would attach a clay cup to collect the latex. As the collectors moved back along the pathway, they emptied the cups into small gourd buckets. Usually one day's work would amount to only about one or two gallons. They then brought the latex back to camp, where they cleaned it of impurities.

Next, workers built a fire of palm nuts. The smoke from these nuts, most often from the uricuri palm, contained acetic acid and phenols that cured the rubber. A funnel-shaped "chimney" was built over the fire to concentrate the smoke. Objects such as waterproof shoes or bottles were made by holding a clay form in the smoke and carefully pouring latex over it until 20 to 25 thin coats had been applied. The process had to be done quickly so that the latex would not coagulate and become unusable. After allowing the object to dry for about five days, workers would wash the clay from the form and stuff the object with dried grass, then leave it to harden for several months, upon which it would be ready to use.

The earliest Spanish explorers brought reports of the "new" substance back to Europe. Pietro Martyre d' Anghiera, the chaplain to King Ferdinand and Queen Isabella of Spain, who had sponsored the voyages of Christopher Columbus, wrote in his report *De Orbo Novo* of a game played with BALLS "made of the juice of a certain herbe . . . [that] being stricken on the ground but softly [rebounded] incredibly into the ayer." Antonio de Herrera y Tordesillas, who served as a historian to Spanish king Philip II, reported that Christopher Columbus first encountered rubber on his second voyage to what is now Haiti from 1493 to 1496, and wrote that Columbus saw balls "made of the gum of a tree." In 1615 Father Juan de Torquemada reported that Indians made footwear (see also SANDALS) and bottles from this sap and that they brushed it onto clothing for WATERPROOFING. Rubber was given its present name in the English-speaking world when in the 1700s the gum was found to be an excellent eraser (which is called a rubber in England) for lead-pencil marks.

Frenchmen François Fresnau and Charles Marie de la Condamine were the first non-Indians to realize that rubber made from latex could have commercial uses for Europeans. They imported a small amount of this rubber to France in 1745, and in 1751, after traveling throughout South America for several years, they made a report on latex and its uses to the French Academy. Early scientists focused on the properties of the latex itself and ignored the processes that indigenous people had used to make it into useful objects. By the early 1800s Europeans were manufacturing small quantities of rubber syringes and galoshes. However, these were not in high demand since the untreated latex they were made from became hard and cracked in cold temperatures, and became sticky when temperatures rose. Even after Charles Goodyear accidentally dropped latex mixed with sulfur on a hot stove and reinvented the process of VULCANIZATION, which he patented in 1844, rubber remained mostly a curiosity for Europeans. With the bicycle craze of the 1890s and the discovery that tires made from the substance provided a smooth ride, rubber manufacturing began to boom.

In 1876 rubber tree seeds were sent to the Tropical Herbarium at Kew Gardens in London, then distributed to Ceylon (now Sri Lanka). From there rubber plants traveled throughout Southeast Asia, where tracts of land were cleared and plantations were established. Today rubber has become an integral part of modern life. Ironically, most of today's rubber comes from commercial plantations in Thailand, Indonesia, Malaysia, and Sri Lanka, rather than the Amazon Basin, where rubber tapping and manufacturing originated.

Today the term *rubber* generally refers to the substance that results when heat is applied to raw latex, causing proteins to be destroyed. Latex today has come to mean sap that is not subjected to heat and therefore contains proteins as well as water. After it has been chemically stabilized, it is used for the manufacture of items such as latex gloves. These are made by dipping forms into latex—essentially the same process American Indians invented hundreds of years earlier.

**Sources/Further Reading**

Benson, Elizabeth P. *The Maya World.* New York: Thomas Y. Crowell Company, 1967.
Coe, Michael D. *America's First Civilization: Discovering the Olmec.* Washington, D.C.: American Heritage Publishing Co., Inc., 1968.
Weinstein, Barbara. *The Amazon Rubber Boom 1850–1920.* Stanford, Calif.: Stanford University Press, 1983.

**laundry detergent** See DETERGENTS.

**laws** See CENSUS; DISABILITY RIGHTS; IROQUOIS CONSTITUTION; LABOR LAWS; PUBLIC DRUNKENNESS LAWS; TAX SYSTEMS; UNITED STATES CONSTITUTION, AMERICAN INDIAN INFLUENCE ON.

**laxatives** See CASCARA SAGRADA; JALAP.

**League of Nations, American Indian Influence on** (A.D. 19) *North American Northeast cultures*
The principles of the IROQUOIS CONSTITUTION were used in the Covenant of the League of Nations. This international peacekeeping assembly was organized in 1915 at the close of World War I and was the predecessor of today's United Nations. The democratic principles of the league are based upon those contained in the U.S. Constitution, many of which, in turn, were directly influenced by the Iroquois Constitution.

Several sections of the Iroquois Constitution are related to issues of peace and war among sovereign nations. The Iroquois Constitution was created sometime between A.D. 1000 and A.D. 1400 by Deganwidah, a political statesperson established a formal method for resolving disputes and bringing harmony to the warring Iroquoian nations. Although the ultimate goal of the Iroquois Constitution was to keep peace, it included provisions for war after all peace attempts had failed and one nation had begun hostilities. Signatories to the Covenant of the League of Nations agreed to "open, just, and honorable relations between nations" and to maintain justice and "scrupulous respect for all treaty obligations in the dealings of organized peoples with one another."

**Sources/Further Reading**

The Covenant of the League of Nations.URL:http://www.tufts.edu/departments/fletcher/multi/www/league-covenant.html. Downloaded April 14, 2001.
Johansen, Bruce E. *Forgotten Founders: Benjamin Franklin, the Iroquois and the Rationale for the American Revolution.* Ipswitch: Gambit Publishers, 1982.

**libraries** See BOOKS.

**lighthouses** (precontact) *Mesoamerican cultures*
A lighthouse is a tall structure with a bright light on the top to guide ships through treacherous waters filled with reefs and sharp rocks. The first lighthouse in precontact Mesoamerica was built by the ancient Maya. (Maya culture arose in the Yucatán Peninsula of what is now Mexico in about 1500 B.C.) This lighthouse is located in the ancient city of Tulum located on the Yucatán Peninsula—a city so imposing that the first Spaniards to see it called it Castillo (castle). The Maya lighthouse looked like a smaller version of the Maya PYRAMIDS and was built on a hill near the beach.

Researcher Michael Creamer, aided by a grant from the National Geographic Society, set out to discover how and why the lighthouse worked. On the face of the structure, facing the ocean, were several vertical, rectangular slots. Creamer placed lanterns in the slots and discovered that the light could only be seen from the ocean and, more specifically, only from a natural opening in the dangerous reefs offshore. The lighthouse at Tulum has the distinction of being the first Maya structure seen by the Spaniards.

**Sources/Further Reading**

Garrett, Wilbur E. "La Ruta Maya." *National Geographic* 176, no. 4 (October 1989): 424–479.

Tulum, Mexico—Mayan ruins, beautiful beaches and wonderful Maya People. URL: http://caribbeanmag.com/mayan-reviera-mexico/tulum.stm. Downloaded on January 24, 2000.

## llamas (*Camelidae lama*) (3500 B.C.) *South American Andean cultures*

Llamas are members of the camel family. Weighing from 250 to 400 pounds at maturity, they generally stand about 40 to 45 inches at the shoulder. Their coloring ranges from black to white along with many shades of brown. Their thick covering of "wool" protects them from the cold temperatures and rain that are common to their native environment. Like sheep and cattle, llamas are ruminants, or cud-chewing ani-

Indigenous people living in what is now Peru began domesticating llamas in about 5000 B.C. They used these animals for the fiber they produced, for meat, and as pack animals. *(After Felipe Guamán Poma de Ayala. Nueva Coronica y Buen Gobierno)*

mals, with a number of stomachs. Their ability to eat shrubs and trees as well as grass makes them highly adaptable. Under ideal conditions, they live from 15 to 20 years. The indigenous peoples who lived in the central Andes in what is now Peru began domesticating llamas between 6,000 and 7,000 years ago. At first they simply herded the animals. Later they bred them for specific uses such as wool, leather, food, and transporting of loads. By 3500 B.C. llamas were fully domesticated and had become an integral part of Andean civilization.

Although llamas do not produce a great deal of milk, they were a source of meat for the people of the Andes. Fresh llama meat is reported to contain a cholesterol level 10 times lower than that of beef. The Inca, who established an empire in about A.D. 1000 in what is now Peru, ate llama meat both fresh and dried. Early Spanish explorers wrote of seeing storehouses full of *charqui,* or dried llama meat. *Charqui* is the native word from which the modern word JERKY is derived.

As pack animals, llamas can carry loads of up to 88 pounds on long journeys and 133 pounds on short ones. They travel at a rate of about 26 kilometers (about 17 miles) a day in high elevations and over rugged mountain terrain. The Inca and their predecessors used llamas during trading expeditions.

Before the Spaniards arrived, the Inca held llama herders in high esteem, since the animals furnished many necessities of life. At first the conquerors butchered the animals indiscriminately for their own meat supply, but soon afterward they began spreading a rumor that llamas were the source of syphilis. As colonization progressed, Peruvians began to view the animals as inferior to cattle and sheep. Indigenous people continued to raise llamas, although not in the number they had before conquest.

In the late 1800s private animal collectors and zoos began importing the animals to North America as a curiosity. Llamas remained such until the 1970s when stock growers in the United States and Canada began raising them to be used as pack animals for wilderness hiking. Today spinners and weavers consider llama wool to be a luxury fiber. Llamas are also used today to guard sheep against predators. By the late 1990s more than 50,000 llamas were being raised in North America. Because of renewed interest in the animals, the llama population in South America has grown as well; the animals there now number about 7 million.

See also ALPACAS; VICUNAS.

**Sources/Further Reading**

Coe, Sophie. *America's First Cuisines.* Austin: University of Texas Press, 1994.

Llamaweb. URL: http://www.llamaweb.com. Downloaded on December 26, 1999.

von Hagen, Victor Wolfgang. *Realm of the Incas.* New York: New American Library, 1957.

Weatherford, Jack. *Indian Givers: How the Indians of the Americas Transformed the World.* New York: Fawcett Columbine, 1988.

**lobster traps** See FISH TRAPS.

**locker rooms** See BASKETBALL.

**looms** (ca. 2000 B.C.) *South American; Mesoamerican; North American Northeast, Plateau, and Southwest cultures*
Looms are devices used for weaving fabric. They allow a warp (the threads that lay lengthwise in the cloth) to be strung and kept under tension. Both complex and simple looms consist of the bars upon which the warp is strung; heddles (cords or wires) to pick, or raise, the desired number of warp threads so that a shuttle bearing threads (wefts) can pass through them crosswise; and a batten, reed, or beater, to firmly push the cross-thread, or woof, against those that were previously woven. American Indians invented looms, which they used to create beautiful and complex textiles, independently of those invented by other cultures. The most popular type of loom American Indian weavers used was the horizontal style, which includes the bow loom and the backstrap, or hip, loom. In a few instances indigenous weavers used the upright, or vertical, loom. (See also WEAVING TECHNIQUES.)

Although some anthropologists in the past termed the looms that were used by the first Americans "primitive," textile experts today prefer to call them simple looms. American Indians used these simple looms to weave complex fabrics, including gauzes, brocades, stripes, checks, twills, double cloth, and openwork. The traditional fabrics woven on American Indian looms remain popular today, as evidenced by the number of stores selling garments crafted by Guatemalan weavers who use the same type of backstrap looms that their ancestors did thousands of years ago.

The backstrap loom, which was used by Andean culture groups as well as by weavers in Mesoamerica and the North American Southwest, is about 20 inches wide. To create this type of loom, the weaver strings warp threads between two beams, or end sticks. One end of this loom is then tied to a tree or post to anchor it. The other is tied to a strap or to a hide TUMPLINE that fits around the weaver's waist or hips. By leaning forward or backward, the weaver, usually a woman, controls the tension on the warp threads. She frequently ties the far end of the loom higher than her waist so that she can see the work better.

The earliest American loom weavers, those who lived in the coastal region of what is now Peru, initially used only backstrap looms. Somewhere between 1400 B.C. to 400 B.C., they invented the heddle. After 1000 B.C. these weavers began weaving larger pieces of fabric on an upright or vertical loom. The vertical loom allowed them to keep uniform tension while weaving wide garments such as burial cloths. By 400 B.C. South American Andean weavers had independently invented sophisticated weaving techniques on their simple looms, including tapestry weaving.

Northeastern weavers of North America used the bow loom, a different version of the horizontal loom, to weave

Backstrap looms like this one originally drawn by Indian artist and historian Felipe Guamán Poma de Ayala in the early 1600s were used by precontact weavers in South America and Mesoamerica to produce textiles for their own use and for trade. (*Nueva Coronica y Buen Gobierno*)

WAMPUM belts. For the most part, however, they relied on finger weaving to produce headbands, belts, sashes, and bags for small objects. To make woven wampum belts, necklaces, and bracelets, they used a bow loom. This small, horizontal loom was constructed by stringing discontinuous warps through spreader bars. The ends of these warps were then tied to the ends of a stick that bent like a bow. The stick put tension on the warps, allowing beads to be strung on a weft and woven into the fabric that was created. This technique is one used for loom beadwork, an art form practiced by many North American Indian tribes today. The bow loom was also used by Subarctic tribes of North America.

Although the backstrap and bow looms worked well for narrow strips of cloth, North American weavers who made blankets needed another type of loom for their work. In the northern part of what is now Mexico, weavers worked on large horizontal looms that they built with four logs positioned close to the ground. Northwestern tribes developed weaving techniques for blankets by stringing wefts between two horizontal bars that were held in place with slats. The Nez Perce, a Plateau culture, wove mats and bags from corn husks and hung their wefts from a horizontal bar. Pre-Columbian weavers from California tribes had a slightly different approach to looms. In some instances they drove two vertical stakes into the ground and looped the continuous warp around them horizontally. The actual weaving took place vertically rather than from side to side.

In the desert Southwest, the forerunners of the Pueblo peoples began to practice fingerweaving (weaving without a loom) in about 1000 B.C. By A.D. 100 they were using the hip strap loom. Some anthropologists believe that this style of loom traveled northward from Mesoamerica with COTTON. The Anasazi weavers, whose culture arose about 350 B.C., also used a vertical blanket loom like that of northwestern textile artisans. Archaeologists believe that holes found in Pueblo kivas were for the insertion of beams that served as frames for these looms. Navajo (Dineh) weavers are believed to have learned the skill from Pueblo artisans in about 1700. The Navajo began working with wool from sheep introduced by the Spaniards. They, too, used vertical, or upright looms, to weave their blankets. These blankets, which continue to be made today, have become collectors' items and are considered by many to be works of art.

See also ALPACAS; DYES; LLAMAS; VICUNAS.

**Sources/Further Reading**

Driver, Harold E. *Indians of North America.* Chicago: University of Chicago Press, 1969.

Harris, Jennifer, ed. *Textiles: 5000 Years.* New York: Harry N. Abrams, Inc., 1993.

Osborne, Lilly deJongh. *Indian Crafts of Guatemala and El Salvador.* Norman: University of Oklahoma Press, 1975.

Prindle, Tara. *NativeTech: Wampum: History and Background.* URL: http://www.nativeweb.org/NativeTech/wampum/wamphist.htm. Downloaded on November 20, 1999.

Schevill, Margot Blum, Janet Catherine Berlo, and Edward B. Dwyer, eds. *Textile Traditions of Mesoamerica and the Andes: An Anthology.* Austin: University of Texas Press, 1996.

**lost-wax casting technique**  (ca. 100 B.C.–A.D. 100)
*South American Andean, Mesoamerican cultures*

A "lost-wax" technique for casting metal was developed by the Moche, a culture that arose in the area of present-day Peru in about 200 B.C. They discovered this method of casting independently of other cultures in the world and used it to make small, ritual objects from gold that were primarily used by the ruling class.

In his book *The Ancient Civilizations of Peru,* J. Alden Mason describes the lost wax method of casting metal: "The desired ornament was modeled in wax, either with or without a core of clay or of some similar substance. This was then covered with a thick envelope of clay through which an orifice was left. After the clay had hardened, the mass was heated and the melted wax allowed to run out through the hole." Once the Moche metalworker removed the wax from the mold, he poured molten metal into it and allowed it to cool. When the metal was cool, he broke the cast and removed the item. Another type of mold had two holes left in it before melting the wax; one hole was on the top and one was on the bottom. When the mold was heated, the wax ran out of the bottom. The metal worker then plugged this hole and poured molten metal in the top hole of the mold. When the metal had cooled, the metalworker broke the clay mold and extracted the ornament.

Pre-Columbian artisans throughout Mesoamerica would later practice lost wax casting. The Aztec, who established an empire in what is now Mexico in about A.D. 1100, were masters of the art of lost wax casting, which they are believed to have learned from the Toltec, a culture that flourished in the same region from about A.D. 950 to A.D. 1200. Aztec artisans used the technique to manufacture luxury items such as lip plugs, pendants, and BELLS. Aztec gold workers had their own GUILDS and lived in their own *calpolli,* or neighborhoods. Although much of their work was melted down by the Spanish conquistadores and shipped to Europe, many fine examples of indigenous American lost-wax casting exist in museums today.

See also BEEKEEPING; METAL CASTING; METALLURGY.

**Sources/Further Reading**

Bankes, George. *Peru Before Pizarro.* Oxford, England: Phaidon Press Limited, 1977.

Benson, Elizabeth P. *The Maya World.* New York: Thomas Y. Crowell, 1967.

Morris, Craig and Adriana von Hagen. *The Inka Empire and Its Andean Origins.* New York: Abbeville Press Publishers, 1993.

Smith, Michael E. *The Peoples of America: the Aztecs.* Cambridge, Mass.: Blackwell, 1996.

**lures, fishnet**  See FISHNET LURES.

# M

**macaws** See PARROT BREEDING.

**mahogany  (*Swietenia mahogani* and *S. macrophylla*)**
(precontact) *Mesoamerican, South American Tropical Forest cultures*

Mahogany is a hardwood-producing tree that grows in Meso- and South America, primarily in what are now Brazil, Bolivia, and southern Mexico. Although a variety of mahogany is indigenous to Africa (*Khaya ivorensis*), American big leaf mahogany (*Swietenia macrophylla*) is the most traded on the world market. Mahogany trees grow to heights of about 100 feet. The wood they produce has a reddish brown color, is easily worked, and can be polished to a high shine. Precontact Indians of both Meso- and South America utilized mahogany for making tools and utensils and as a building material because it was strong and waterproof; it resisted rotting; and it contained a natural INSECT REPELLENT, which helped to protect their homes against termites and other insects. The indigenous people of precontact South America were the first to make boats from mahogany. Since these trees were so large, only one was needed to make a canoe. They constructed these CANOES by hollowing out the huge logs.

Cuban mahogany (*Swietenia mahogani*) was the first encountered by Europeans. Spanish explorers quickly adapted mahogany for their purposes; Hernán Cortés began using mahogany wood for shipbuilding in 1521. Because the trees are so large, great distances could be spanned with a single length of timber, making mahogany planks very useful in the construction of ships. By the late 1600s mahogany was used to make furniture for the English upper class.

Mahogany wood is considered the most valuable Amazon timber on the world market today. It is used in furniture manufacturing, cabinetmaking, shipbuilding, and paneling. Auto manufacturers use it to produce full-size models of automobiles that serve as patterns for the final product. Brazil is the leading modern exporter of mahogany in the world. In the last two decades of the 20th century, the high demand for mahogany motivated loggers to cut trees deeper and deeper in the rainforest. Brazil legislated a two-year moratorium on the sale of mahogany in 1996 in an attempt to conserve a natural resource that is expected to be exhausted in two decades at current rates of logging. Other countries have attempted to regulate mahogany logging, but because it is so lucrative, illegal logging continues.

See also CARPENTRY TECHNIQUES.

## Sources/Further Reading

*An Amazon Adventure—Mahogany.* URL: http://168.216.238.53/amazon/mahogany.html. Downloaded on September 29, 1999.

Benson, Elizabeth P. *The Maya World.* New York: Thomas Y. Crowell Company, 1967.

*Bigleaf Mahogany.* URL:http://www.defenders.org/cfacmaho.html. Downloaded on September 29, 1999.

*Brazil Bans Mahogany Logging.* URL: http://www.csc.vsc.edu/com.web/echo/brazil.html. Downloaded on September 29, 1999.

*Forests Threatened by Mahogany Export.* URL: http://www.greanpeace.org/~thom/mahog.html. Downloaded on January 10, 1999.

**maize** See CORN.

**mandioca** See MANIOC.

## manioc (cassava, mandioca, yuca) (ca. 3000
B.C.–2000 B.C.) *Mesoamerican, Circum-Caribbean, South
American Tropical Forest cultures*

Manioc, or cassava (*Manihot esculenta* and *M. utilissima*), is a plant whose starch-filled root produces more calories per acre of land than any other food crop except sugarcane. For thousands of years it has been cultivated by indigenous people in what are now Mexico, Guatemala, northern Brazil, and the Caribbean. Some botanists believe it was being grown in the upper Amazon Valley as early as between 7000 and 5000 B.C. In addition to cultivating manioc, which is also called mandioca or yuca, indigenous Americans developed a complex technology for turning this naturally poisonous plant into an edible food. Manioc has consequently become a dietary staple for millions of people throughout the world today.

Manioc plants are propagated by stem cuttings that grow to bushy plants six to nine feet high within a few months of planting. They are covered with large leaves and green flowers, and their roots weigh from 10 to 30 pounds. Per acre, manioc produces six times the carbohydrate value of wheat. Since the unharvested roots remain edible for two or more years after maturity, cassava provides its own convenient storage.

Historically, cassava served as a dietary mainstay for indigenous people who lived in tropical areas in South America. Manioc roots are depicted on 4,000-year-old pottery uncovered in what is now Peru. Because the cassava that grew in that area was the nonpoisonous, or "sweet" variety, cooks prepared it by simply peeling and boiling the roots or cooking them over coals.

By about 3000 to 2000 B.C., indigenous people were cultivating manioc in the lowlands of Venezuela and Colombia. From South America, cultivation spread to Central America and the West Indian Islands. Many of the plants grown in this area were of the toxic variety, containing prussic, or hydrocyanic, acid in small sacs under the covering of the root. Because digestion breaks down the root's cyanogenic glucosides, releasing cyanide into the body, raw manioc of this type causes poisoning. American Indians were well aware of the differences between the two varieties of manioc and understood what scientists have only recently learned—that the difference between the two is not genetic but is determined by the environment in which the manioc plant is grown.

Columbus was the first European to observe and record American Indians raising manioc. Calling it *ajes,* he noted in his diary that the native people planted fields of the tubers.

This early drawing of manioc processing in the Caribbean depicts the centuries-old method of grating the starchy root on boards imbedded with stone chips. After the manioc was grated, indigenous people who cultivated the plants removed the toxic juice, making it edible. ("Histoire naturelle et morale des îles Antilles de L'Amerique"/*Stock Montage/The Newberry Library*)

The Portuguese observed American Indians growing manioc in what is now Brazil when they arrived there in the early 1500s. They watched Indians peeling raw manioc roots, then shredding them on graters made of stone chips set into wooden boards. Afterward, they squeezed the poisonous juice out with presses or filled woven fiber tubes called *tipitis* with the manioc pulp. Weights that hung from the bottom of these tubes narrowed their diameter and compressed the pulp so that the juice would drip out. Once the manioc pulp was detoxified, indigenous people washed, roasted, and ground or pounded it into meal called FARINA, then baked it into cakes or flat bread.

Manioc juice is normally highly poisonous because it contains hydrocyanic acid. Indigenous people discovered the process of detoxifying manioc: Linase, a natural enzyme in cassava, neutralizes the acid when the mixture is heated. They also knew that if the juice were to become too hot (above 167° F), then the linase would break down and the process would not work. Manioc juice that has been thus heated to remove the poison also acts as a meat tenderizer, and it was used by Indians as soup stock and in sauces. Once the poison was removed, the juice could also be boiled to become *cassareep,* used as both a flavoring and as a meat preservative even today, in British Guyana. Manioc juice continues to be used as a meat tenderizer in the United States.

In another process, Indians heated the starch that had settled from the bottom of the juice until the individual granules popped and clumped together to form tapioca. Today, in addition to serving as a base for the popular pudding, manioc starch is used for laundry starch and sizing. It is also sold as flour.

Indigenous people who lived in what is now Peru detoxified manioc in a different way. Understanding that fermentation will also break down the hydrocyanic acid, they put cassava roots in water, allowed them to ferment, and then placed them in sacks wedged between boards to squeeze the acid out. Afterward they dried pieces of root, toasted them, and pounded them into farina. In the Caribbean British Guyana and the northern part of Brazil, grated manioc was also fermented and the pulp was made into a beverage that is still popular today.

Because dried manioc bread keeps for up to three years and is more resistant to weevils than is hardtack, it was adopted by the Europeans as military and ships rations. Manioc first crossed the Atlantic Ocean in 1569 on Portuguese slave ships returning from Brazil to Africa. The Spaniards also introduced manioc to the Philippines and eventually to Southeast Asia. Because of its carbohydrate content and its ability to tolerate drought and poor soils, the spread of manioc has changed the course of world history. The gift of manioc and the technology to make it edible have provided a staple food in the diet of 500 million people worldwide who peel its roots and boil them or grind them into flour for bread. Farina remains as popular in parts of South America as it was thousands of years ago. In Africa even the tops of the manioc plants are eaten as vegetables. In Asia manioc strips are deep-fried and eaten like French fries. Most Americans and Europeans only encounter manioc in the form of meat tenderizer and tapioca, processed cassava starch used in pudding and fruit pies.

## Sources/Further Reading

Coe, Sophie. *America's First Cuisines.* Austin: University of Texas Press, 1994.

Heiser, Charles B. *Seed to Civilization: The Story of Food.* Cambridge, Mass.: Harvard University Press, 1990.

Josephy, Jr., Alvin M., ed. *America in 1492: The World of the Indian People Before the Arrival of Columbus.* New York: Random House, 1991.

Sokalow, Raymond. *Why We Eat What We Eat: How the Encounter Between the New World and the Old Changed the Way Everyone on the Planet Eats.* New York: Summit Books, 1991.

Tannahill, Reay. *Food in History.* New York: Stein and Day, 1973.

Weatherford, Jack. *Indian Givers: How the Indians of the Americas Transformed the World.* New York: Fawcett Columbine, 1988.

**maple syrup and sugar** (precontact)  *North American Northeast cultures*

Four varieties of maple trees (genus *Acer*) grow throughout what is now the eastern United States and Canada, as well as the upper Midwest. They were routinely harvested by American Indians for the sweet sap they yielded. Indian people drank the sap and also devised the technology to transform the watery liquid into thick syrup and sugar that they used to sweeten their food, especially dishes made from corn. Maple sugaring season, which lasted several weeks during the spring, was so important to the Chippewa (Anishinabe), a tribe of the upper Midwest that they named a month after it: *Slzhkigamisegi Geezis,* which means "moon of boiling." Algonquian speakers, who lived along the St. Lawrence River region, called maple syrup *sinzibuckwud,* which means "drawn from wood." Both the Iroquois and the Chippewa taught American colonists how to tap trees and make syrup and sugar. Unlike refined sugar, maple syrup, which is primarily sucrose, contains the minerals calcium, potassium, phosphorus, manganese, magnesium, and iron. It also contains riboflavin, pantothenic acid, pyridoxine, niacin, biotin, and folic acid.

Although silver, red, and ash leafed maple trees produce sap that can be boiled into syrup, it is less sweet than that of the sugar maples (*Acer saccharum*), whose colorless sap contains 3 percent sugar. Sugar maples must mature for about 40 years before they are ready for tapping. A renewable resource, these maple trees produce about 12 quarts of sap a day and continue to produce this amount for a century. During an entire sugaring season, one tree produces from 35 to 50 quarts of sap. When it is boiled, this amount makes 1 to 1 1/2 quarts of maple syrup.

The Iroquois cut V-shaped incisions in the trees and then inserted reeds or concave pieces of bark for taps. They collected the sap in birch-bark buckets. Next they concentrated

American Indians of the Northeast tapped maple trees each spring, collecting the sap in birch-bark buckets and boiling it into syrup. Colonists, who learned to tap the trees by observing Indians, quickly incorporated the sweetener into their diet. (LC-USZ62-105740/Library of Congress)

the sap into syrup either by dropping hot stones into wooden containers of sap or by freezing the sap and discarding the ice that formed at the top. (See also FREEZE-DRYING.)

When the Chippewa tapped maple trees, they used elderberry stem taps. Sugaring was a busy time, since on a warm day a birch-bark pail might take only an hour to fill. In sugar camps hundreds of trees might be tapped. The Chippewa word for the birch-bark pails the sap ran into was *nadoban,* a variation of "she goes and gets." To make sugar, they boiled sap until it was thick, then poured it onto snow to harden. The result was packed tightly in birch bark cones whose tops were sewn shut for storage.

The Chippewa made granulated sugar by dropping pieces of deer tallow into the syrup. Just before the sugar began to granulate, they poured it into wooden troughs and rubbed it with wooden ladles or with their hands to make grains. They then poured it into birch-bark containers or rawhide bags and used this sugar throughout the year to sea-

son fruit, vegetables, corn, meat, and fish. The granules were also used for sweetening herbal teas and added to water for a sweet drink.

Early colonial land speculators used maple syrup as one of several inducements to Europeans to settle in North America. Their advertising tracts promised immigrants that they could grow their own sugar if they settled on land that contained sugar maple trees. Colonists did just that, substituting iron kettles for birch buckets when they processed sap. Maple sugar sales soared during the Civil War when using this sweetener became a patriotic act of protest in the North—a way to boycott the cane sugar and molasses produced in the Confederate states. Maple syrup remains popular today—mainly for use on pancakes and waffles.

**Sources/Further Reading**

Densmore, Francis. *Chippewa Customs.* Washington, D.C.: Government Printing Office, 1929.

Eastman, Charles A. *Indian Boyhood.* New York: Dover Publications, 1971.

Geise, Paula. *Native American Indian Resources.* URL: http://indy4.fdl.cc.mn.us/~isk/food/maple. Downloaded on June 14, 1999.

Weatherford, Jack. *Indian Givers: How the Indians of the Americas Transformed the World.* New York: Fawcett Columbine, 1988.

**maps, first American** (precontact) *North American, Mesoamerican, South American cultures*
American Indians were the first in the Americas to create maps, graphic representations of the terrain of North, Meso-, and South America. On the whole, indigenous knowledge of geographical features, political systems, and trading economies was preserved and passed orally from individual to individual. Occasionally Indian peoples sketched maps on hides or birch bark, such as a directional message found by European explorers on a ridge between Ottawa in Ontario, Canada, and Lake Huron in May 1841. For American Indians, written maps were secondary to the mental maps that Indian cartographers had memorized. Directions in the form of a map might be drawn in the snow or scratched in the earth, but they did not survive past the snowmelt or the next rain. Archaeologists believe that some rock petroglyphs, such as Map Rock on the upper Snake River in the United States, may have represented hunting territories. (See also WRITING SYSTEMS.) The Codex Mendoza, one of four surviving pre-Columbian manuscripts (see also BOOKS), contains maps that the Aztec recordkeepers used to delineate land holdings of individual families. (The Aztec Empire arose to power in Mesoamerica in about A.D. 1100.) Because they served as an aid to communication, instead of being an end in themselves, maps were generally not preserved.

The oldest recorded North American map was made by an Indian named Miguel who was captured by the Spanish expedition headed by Don Juan de Oñate on the south central plains of what is now the United States. Oñate, who attempted to settle New Mexico in 1598 for the Spanish under a grant from the crown, had difficulties with this enterprise and decided in 1601 to travel northeast, following the Canadian River through Texas and Oklahoma to modern-day Kansas. He returned with Miguel to Mexico City, where the captive was asked to draw a map of his people's territory.

Miguel noted the American Indian villages he had actually visited and then continued to accurately map a large area of the south central plains, which he had only heard about. Hernando Esteban, the notary who annotated his map, wrote: "Miguel proceeded to mark on the paper some circles resembling the letter 'O' some larger than others; in a way easily understood he explained what each circle represented, and I by order of the factor, wrote in each one of the circles what the Indian said they represented, to make it clear. Then he drew lines, some snakelike and others straight, and indicated by signs that they were rivers and roads; they were also given names according to his explanation."

A birch-bark map that Ac ko mok ki, a Blackfeet chief, drew in 1801 for Peter Fiedler, an explorer for the Hudson's Bay Company, further demonstrates the depth of American Indians' extensive knowledge of the land. Stopped near what is now Alberta, Canada, Fiedler had no idea what lay ahead, so he asked Ac ko mok ki, to graphically describe the lay of the land. Ac ko mok ki first described the terrain to Fiedler orally and then drew a map on the snow outside of the trading post. His map started where the men were standing and expanded to encompass mountains and rivers extending to the Bighorn River in central Wyoming. Ac ko mok ki's map included tribal groups as well as their names and estimated populations. Fiedler copied the map onto paper. Meriwether Lewis and William Clark relied on the information contained in this map three years later as they sought a Northwest Passage to the Pacific Ocean.

See also ROAD SYSTEMS.

**Sources/Further Reading**
Driver, Harold E. *Indians of North America.* Chicago: University of Chicago Press, 1969.

Hurst, David, Jay Miller, Richard White, Peter Nabokov, and Philip Deloria. *The Native Americans.* Atlanta: Turner Publishing, Inc., 1993.

Warhus, Mark. *Another America: Native American Maps and the History of Our Land.* New York: St. Martin's Press, 1997.

**maracas** (precontact) *North American, Mesoamerican, Circum-Caribbean, South American cultures*
Hollow rattles made from dried GOURDS, containing dried beans or small rocks, were made by Indians in North America, Mesoamerica, and South America. The precontact version of this MUSICAL INSTRUMENT closely resembles the maracas of today. The name *maracas* came into the English language through the Portuguese from the Tupi word *maraca.* The Tupi are a South American culture from the Amazon Basin.

Culture groups living on the plains of North America made rattles that produced a sound similar to that of maracas by shaping two pieces of wet rawhide over a rock and allowing them to dry. As the hide dried, it took on the shape of the stone. Once the rawhide was stiff, the rattle maker sewed the two pieces together with sinew, inserting pebbles and attaching a handle.

**Sources/Further Reading**
*The American Heritage Dictionary Second College Edition.* Boston: Houghton Mifflin Company, 1985.

Driver, Harold E. *Indians of North America.* Chicago: University of Chicago Press, 1969.

Hassrick, Royal B. *The Sioux.* Norman: University of Oklahoma Press, 1964.

Salmoral, Manuel Lucena. *America 1492: Portrait of a Continent 500 Years Ago.* New York: Facts On File, 1990.

## marigolds (genus Tagetes) (ca. A.D. 1) *Mesoamerican cultures*

Marigolds *(genus Targetes)* are a popular bedding plant throughout the world. They are characterized by yellow, yellow-orange, or dark red flowers. Although marigolds grow wild from Arizona to Argentina, they were first cultivated by indigenous Americans in the western part of what is now Mexico about 2000 years ago. Marigolds were used by Mesoamericans for medicinal and ritual purposes and were grown as ornamentals.

The Aztec, who established an empire in what is now Mexico in about A.D. 1100, cultivated a number of flowers in botanical gardens (see also GARDENS, BOTANICAL). They called one variety of marigold *yauhtli* and used it to cure diseases that were thought to have been caused by an excess of phlegm. These conditions included kidney problems, swellings, and dropsy. Two substances (quercitagritin and kaempferitrin), called glycosides, that are contained in marigolds have been found by modern scientists to have diuretic and laxative properties, respectively.

Believed sacred to the god Tlaloc, marigolds were used as religious offerings. According to the Florentine Codex, an Aztec BOOK, this god was also called Yauhtli. The Aztec believed that marigolds offered a form of spiritual protection. Native spiritual healers in Mexico still use marigolds in curing ceremonies. Today marigold petals are used to line the route for the processions that are a part of Mexico's Day of the Dead. After conquest, Spanish priests grew them in mission gardens and used the plants medicinally as well as for landscaping. The Europeans gave their own name to the plant, calling it Mary's gold after the Virgin Mary.

See also DAHLIAS; NASTURTIUMS; POINSETTIAS.

### Sources/Further Reading
Nuttall, Z. "Los Jardines del Antiguo America." *Memoires de la Sociedad Ceientifica Antonio Alazate* 37 (1920): 193–213.
Ortiz de Montellano, Bernard. *Aztec Medicine, Health, and Nutrition.* New Brunswick, N.J.: Rutgers University Press, 1990.
Parsons, James A. "Southern Blooms: Latin America and the World of Flowers." *Queen's Quarterly* 99 no. 3 (1992): 542–561.
Soule, Jacques A. "Novel Annual and Perennial Tagetes." In *Progress in New Crops,* edited by J. Janeck. Arlington, Virginia: ASHS Press, 1996.

**marimbas** See MUSICAL INSTRUMENTS.

**massage** See THERAPEUTIC TOUCH.

## medical research (ca. A.D. 1100–A.D. 1519) *Mesoamerican cultures*

Medical research is the scientific study of diagnosis, treatment, and prevention of illnesses. It can be conducted in order to learn the cause of diseases or medical conditions, to develop a cure for a particular illness, or to modify existing treatment so that it will be more effective. Aztec physicians routinely engaged in medical research using the empirical method of scientific inquiry. Their botanical gardens served as research centers. (See also GARDENS, BOTANICAL.) In his book *Aztec Medicine, Health, and Nutrition,* Bernard Ortiz de Montellano writes, "Experience in the gardens was reflected in the Aztec's extensive and scientifically accurate botanical and zoological taxonomy. The gardens were also used for medical research, plants were given free to patients on the condition that they report the results, and doctors were encouraged to experiment with the various plants."

Since medical knowledge was passed orally from healer to healer in other North American Indian cultures, no direct evidence exists that medical research was conducted as systematically as that done by the Aztec. However, it is clear that American Indian healers possessed sophisticated knowledge of the properties and correct dosages of medicinal plants. North American Indians used botanical oral contraceptives (see also CONTRACEPTION, ORAL) and routinely used ANTISPASMODIC MEDICATIONS that could produce harm if not given in the correct dosages. The sophistication of their medical knowledge indicates that they were astute observers of the effects of botanicals against illnesses.

See also ANATOMICAL KNOWLEDGE; GARDENS, HERB; MEDICINE; PHARMACOLOGY; PLANT CLASSIFICATIONS.

### Sources/Further Reading
Frederiksen, Thomas H. "Aztec Medicine, Aztec Student Guide." Student Teachers Resource Center. URL: http://northcoast.com/~spdtom/a-med.html. Downloaded on October 14, 1999.
Ortiz de Montellano, Bernard R. *Aztec Medicine, Health, and Nutrition.* New Brunswick, N.J.: Rutgers University Press, 1990.
Vogel, Virgil. *American Indian Medicine.* Norman: University of Oklahoma Press, 1970.

## medicine (precontact) *North American, Mesoamerican, Circum-Caribbean, South American cultures*

Medicine is the science of diagnosing, treating, and preventing diseases. It is also concerned with maintaining health. American Indians were sophisticated healers, relying on a number of botanical drugs that remain in use today, including GUAIACUM, IPECAC, KAOLIN, and QUININE. Indians of both North and Mesoamerica routinely used ANTIBIOTIC MEDICATIONS. The Plains tribes of North America used ANTIVIRAL MEDICATIONS as well. The Aztec, whose empire was established in Mesoamerica in about A.D. 1100, performed MEDICAL RESEARCH, recording the medicinal uses for at least 1,200 plants. The precontact American Indians of Mesoamerica were the first people in the world to develop a public health care system and public health HOSPITALS, facilities which today are designed for people who cannot afford health care at regular medical facilities—as they were for precontact Aztec. Aztec physicians were specialists in areas such as obstetrics, the ears, and dentistry. Aztec eye specialists performed cataract surgery. (See also CATARACT REMOVAL.)

Indigenous physicians of the Americas demonstrated extensive ANATOMICAL KNOWLEDGE and understood how to set bones (see also ORTHOPEDIC TECHNIQUES), treat wounds, prevent infections (see also ASEPSIS), as well as perform complicated SURGERIES, such as ARTHROCENTESIS and the removal of cataracts from the eyes.

Father Bernardo Sahagun wrote of the duties of the Aztec physician in *Historia General de las Cosas de Nueva España* (General history of the things of New Spain): "The true doctor . . . is a wise man; he imparts life. A tried specialist, he has worked with herbs, stones, trees and roots. His remedies have been tested; he examines; he experiments, he alleviates sickness. . . ." The medical practices he described were well established before European contact and stand in sharp contrast to the limited understanding of Europeans who until the late 1700s were generally ignorant of the causes of disease. They held that illness was divine punishment for sins, and because of this view, the sick often went untreated in Europe. More advanced European physicians adhered to the teachings of Claudius Galen, an ancient Greek physician (ca. A.D. 130–200) who believed that illness was caused by an imbalance of bodily fluids, or humours, as these fluids were called. When doctors in Europe gave medical assistance, their treatments of choice most often were bleeding, vomiting, purging, and blistering. Although they used botanicals to treat illnesses, they often combined them with ingredients such as blood, dung, and urine. Beginning in the 1600s they added metals, such as lead and arsenic, to their medicines, doing their patients more harm than good. Bloodletting, harsh emetics, and blistering (burning the skin until it blistered), were also standard treatments in Europe.

Medicine was a specialized endeavor for the Aztec. Not only were there general practitioners, called *ticitl,* but also eye doctors (*teixpatli*), dentists (*tlanatonaniztli*), ear doctors (*tenacazpati*), interns (*tlana-tepati-ticitl*), surgeons (*texoxotla-ticitl*), and herbalist/pharmacists (*papiani-papamacani*).

The medical practices the conquistadores and colonists brought to the Americas from their homelands must have seemed barbaric to the Indian peoples they encountered. Susan Neiburg Terkel writes in *Colonial American Medicine.* "Ignorant of medicine, they [the colonists] failed to cure most ailments, and frequently inflicted harm on themselves when they tried. Unaware of germs they could not see, they spread infection."

Although infectious diseases were much rarer among Indians before the germs of the invaders decimated the indigenous population of America, evidence exists that American Indians understood how diseases were spread. (See also ISOLATION.)

In general, the health of indigenous Americans before contact was much better than that of Europeans at the time. Herman Viola and Carolyn Margolis, authors of the book *Seeds of Change: The Story of Cultural Exchange after 1492,* noted the comments of one Indian who lived before the European invasion: "There was then no sickness; they had no aching bones, they had no high fever, they had then no smallpox; they had then no burning chest; they had then no abdominal pain; they had no consumption; they had then no headache." Infectious diseases were rare, in part because people in North America lived primarily in small settlements and in part because, except for TRADE, they did not have extensive contacts with people outside of their groups. "The world's leading infections were the by-product of the rise of agricultural and pastoral peoples in the Eastern Hemisphere where humans began living in dense, often sedentary and usually unhygienic concentration . . ." according to Viola and Margolis.

Another factor that promoted lower rates of disease was an emphasis on personal hygiene (see also HYGIENE, PERSONAL) and sanitation (see also PLUMBING). Daily bathing was routine among indigenous people throughout the Americas, as was disposing of human waste far from villages and camps. The colonists, most of whom who rarely bathed or washed their hands, dumped their slop buckets into the streets, spreading disease among themselves as well as among American Indians.

Good NUTRITION also helped to keep American Indians relatively healthy before the European invasion. The indigenous people of North America ate foods high in vitamin C that guarded against scurvy. (See also SCURVY CURE.) Even inland culture groups included sources of iodine in their diet, preventing goiter, a condition that was epidemic among Europeans. (See also GOITER PREVENTION.)

European colonists quickly learned to rely on American Indian remedies. Many Indian botanical medicines were adopted into the U.S. Pharmacopoeia, a list of available drugs sanctioned by the medical community. By the beginning of the 1800s, non-Indian botanical or herb doctors began using herbal remedies learned from the American Indians to treat patients. As support for their practice, they pointed to the discovery of quinine as a treatment for malaria and digitalis, a heart medicine the Indians derived from FOXGLOVE. Non-Indian enthusiasm for Indian cures led to the creation of patent medicines. (See also MEDICINES, PATENT, AMERICAN INDIAN INFLUENCE ON; PHARMACOLOGY.) Nevertheless, Benjamin Rush, convinced that bloodletting worked, refused to believe that anything of benefit could be learned from American Indians. "We have no discoveries in the materia medica to hope for from the Indians in North-America," he wrote in 1774. "It would be a reproach to our schools of physic, if modern physicians were not more successful than the Indians even in the treatment of their own diseases." His opinion ran counter to reality.

Historian Fraser Symington, comparing non-Indian and Indian medical practices in the 1600s, wrote in *The Canadian Indian:* "The Iroquois excelled in their treatment of wounds, fractures and dislocations, and their herbalists provided a great fund of knowledge to Europe."

See also ANESTHETICS; ANTIASTHMATIC MEDICATIONS; ANTIHELMINTICS; ANTISPASMODIC MEDICATIONS; AROMATHERAPY; ARTHRITIS TREATMENTS; ASTRINGENTS; CASCARA SAGRADA; COCA; CURARE; DEBRIDEMENT; DIABETES

MEDICATION; DIURETICS; DOGBANE; DRAINAGE, SURGICAL AND WOUND; EARACHE TREATMENTS; ENEMAS; EPHEDRA; EXCISION; FORCEPS; GARDENS, BOTANICAL; GARDENS, HERB; GASTROENTERITIS TREATMENT; GRANULATION; HEADACHE, KNOWLEDGE OF ETIOLOGY; HEADACHE MEDICATIONS; HEMOSTATS; HOLISTIC HEALTH; HOSPITALS; HOT SPRINGS; INDIGESTION MEDICATIONS; JALAP; MEDICINE KITS; MINTS, BOTANICAL; OBSTETRICS; PETROLEUM; PEYOTE; PILLS; PLASTIC SURGERY; PRESCRIPTIONS; PULSE, RADIAL; SALICIN; SALVE, DRAWING; SKIN GRAFTS; SNAKEBITE TREATMENTS; STAPLES, SURGICAL; STRETCHERS; SUNSCREENS, MEDICINAL; SUPPOSITORIES; SYRINGES; THERAPEUTIC TOUCH; THORACENTESIS; TOURNIQUETS; TREPHINATION; WINTERGREEN; WITCH HAZEL.

## Sources/Further Reading

Hawke, Sharryl Davis and James E. Davis. *Seeds of Change: The Story of Cultural Exchange after 1492.* New York: Addison-Wesley Publishing Company, 1993.

National Library of Medicine. *United States 19th-Century Doctors' Thoughts about Native American Medicine.* URL: http://public.nml.gov/exhibition/if_yopu_knew_04.html. Downloaded on July 6, 1999.

National Museum of Natural History, Smithsonian Institution. *Seeds of Change: Readings on Cultural Exchange After 1492.* New York: Addison-Wesley Publishing Company, 1992.

Ortiz de Montellano, Bernard. *Aztec Medicine, Health, and Nutrition.* New Brunswick, N. J.: Rutgers University Press, 1990.

Rush, Benjamin. *An Inquiry into the Natural History of Medicine Among the Indians.* American Philosophical Society, 1789.

Symington, Fraser. *The Canadian Indian.* Toronto: McClelland and Stewart, 1969.

Turkel, Susan Neiburg. *Colonial American Medicine.* New York: Franklin Watts, 1993.

Viola, Herman and Carolyn Margolis. *Seeds of Change: 500 Years Since Columbus.* Washington, D.C. Smithsonian Institution Press, 1991.

Vogel, Virgil. *American Indian Medicine.* Norman: University of Oklahoma Press, 1970.

Weatherford, Jack. *Indian Givers: How the Indians of the Americas Transformed the World.* New York: Fawcett Columbine, 1988.

———. *Native Roots: How the Indians Enriched America.* New York: Fawcett Columbine, 1991.

Weiner, Michael A. *Earth Medicine Earth Food: The Classic Guide to the Herbal Remedies and Wild plants of the North American Indians.* New York: Fawcett Columbine, 1980.

## medicine kits (doctor bags) (ca. 1300 B.C.) *South American Andean, North American cultures*

A medicine kit is a collection of instruments intended for the treatment of illness. The doctor's bag was commonplace among the prehistoric American Indians. The first intact doctor's bag found by archaeologists in the Americas belonged to the ancient Paracas culture that arose in what is now Peru in about 1300 B.C. The bag contained several obsidian scalpel blades and spatulas that were made from sperm whale teeth. In addition, it contained COTTON balls, cloths, bandages, and thread and NEEDLES. The latter were presumably intended for suturing. (See also SURGERY.) Precontact American Indians used white cotton balls, bandages, gauze, and cloth for dressing wounds and sores and for surgery.

In precontact North America the doctor's bag was very similar among all culture groups. Some of the common supplies indigenous healers carried in kits or bundles included botanical medications (see also PHARMACOLOGY), SCALPELS, lancets, mortars, pestles, and SYRINGES. American Indians used syringes for irrigating wounds (see also DEBRIDEMENT; GRANULATION), injecting medications, cleaning ears, and for giving ENEMAS. Indigenous healers also often carried thin hollow tubes that were used for sucking substances from the patient's body.

See also MEDICINE.

## Sources/Further Reading

Fernandez, Omar. "Pre-Columbia Surgery." *Gramna Weekly Review.* URL: http://marauder.millersv.edu/~columbus/data/art/FERNAN01.AR T. Downloaded on January 12, 2000.

Vogel, Virgil J. *American Indian Medicine.* Norman: University of Oklahoma Press, 1970.

## medicines, patent, American Indian influence on (ca. 1793) *North American cultures*

Patent medicines are remedies registered with the U.S. Patent Office and sold over the counter without prescription. Today they are called over-the-counter drugs. Many of the makers of popular patent medicines sold in the United States in the 1800s and 1900s claimed that their recipes were the work of American Indian healers. Often these were false claims, but they helped to sell these tonics and cure-alls. By the mid-1880s an estimated 75 "Kickapoo" medicine shows traveled across the North American continent at the same time, selling potions the merchants claimed were made from genuine Kickapoo formulas. The Kickapoo are a western Great Lakes tribe. The largest of these entrepreneurial extravaganzas had as many as 100 performers and sold thousands of bottles of patent medicine a week.

Europeans who moved to the Americas quickly discovered the benefits of American Indian herbal cures. Spanish missionaries recorded and adopted indigenous methods of treating disease, and the conquistadores routinely put more faith in Native healers than in their own physicians. Europeans who settled the eastern colonies of North America trusted in Indian remedies so much that after federal regulations made provisions for the patenting of medicinal formulas in 1793, about 60 percent of the hundreds of tonics on the U.S. market bore Indian images. These eventually included such medicines as Dr. Kilmer's Indian

Cough Cure and Consumption Oil; Kickapoo Indian Cough Cure, Indian Oil, and Sagwa; Wigwam Tonic; Comanche War Paint Ointment; and Seminole Cough Balsam. Except for the presence of their images on labels or their participation as entertainers in medicine shows, Indian people had little to do with the creation of the hucksters' formulas that tended to be short on herbs and high in alcohol content and sugar.

In the early 1800s, non-Indian botanical or herb doctors began using herbal remedies learned from the American Indians to treat patients. As support for their practice, they pointed to the discovery of QUININE as a treatment for malaria; and digitalis, a heart medicine the Indians derived from FOXGLOVE. At first patent medicines were manufactured and consumed because many people lived far from cities and also may have wished to avoid contact with formally Western trained physicians. Heroic medicine, the standard of care at the time, viewed the sickroom as a battlefield where the doctor waged war on disease with an arsenal of techniques centering around bloodletting—a standard "cure" from the 1790s until after the Civil War—emetics, and blistering. (See also MEDICINE.)

In time, patent medicines, called nostrums, gained an enormous following, and unscrupulous entrepreneurs began cashing in on the market. Out of fear that their secret formulas would be revealed, medicine hucksters patented the bottles and labels rather than the formulas. By 1859, yearly sales of patent medicine topped $3.5 million, and later the U.S. government levied a special tax on them to help with the Civil War effort.

The medical community vehemently fought the patent-medicine makers. In 1864 Jonathan Kneeland presented a paper to the American Medical Association asserting, "The State of medical knowledge among these Indians (Onondagas) may be briefly told. Their knowledge of remedies and of diseases is so vague and limited that it is a marvel why any sane quack should think to add to his popularity by styling himself an Indian Doctor, or should hope to increase the sale of his nostrums, by giving them the christian name of some unpronounceable Indian tribe."

By 1904 the sale of patent medicines had risen to $75.5 million annually. The heyday of patent medicine ended in 1906 with the passage of the Pure Food and Drug Act by Congress. One of the strongest lobbying groups for the bill was that of the temperance supporters who objected to the high alcohol content of many of the medicines. Today patent, or over-the-counter remedies, undergo strict government regulation including extensive testing before they are marketed.

See also PHARMACOLOGY.

*Right:* Early colonists to North America were so impressed by indigenous medicines that they often preferred Indian remedies to those provided by their own physicians. In the 1800s entrepreneurs patented American Indian names and label designs for the medicines they sold. Red Jacket, a Seneca chief born in about 1756, had no connection to the Red Jacket Stomach Bitters that bore his name. *(LC-USZ62-55635/Library of Congress)*

## Sources/Further Reading

Kneeland, Jonathan. "On Some Causes Tending to Promote the Extinction of the Aborigines of America." *Transactions of the American Medical Association* 5 (1864): 257.

Lowen, James W. *Lies My Teacher Told Me: Everything Your American History Textbook Got Wrong.* New York: The New Press, 1995.

Lowes, Warren. *Indian Giver.* Penticton, B.C.: Theytus Books, 1986.

Stage, Safah. *Female Complaints: Lydia Pinkham and the Business of Women's Medicine.* New York: W.W. Norton & Company, 1979.

University of Toledo Library. *Patent Medicine.* URL: http://cl.utoledo.edu/canady/quackery/quack3c.html. Downloaded on July 7, 1999.

## megaphones (precontact) *North American Northeast cultures*

A megaphone is a conical or funnel-shaped device used to amplify a person's voice. The Chippewa (Anishinabe), a culture group living in the Great Lakes region, used small megaphones of birch bark rolled into a cone to call moose during hunts. (See also CALLS, ANIMAL AND BIRD.) The Iroquois also used birch-bark megaphones, called *speaking tubes,* so that everyone present could hear speakers during political meetings, or CAUCUSES.

## Sources/Further Reading

Driver, Harold E. *Indians of North America.* Chicago: University of Chicago Press, 1961.

Maxwell, James A. *America's Fascinating Indian Heritage.* Pleasantville, N.Y.: Reader's Digest Association, 1978.

## mercury (quicksilver, cinnabar) (ca. 1500 B.C.–A.D. 1500) *South American Andean, Mesoamerican cultures*

Mercury (Hg) is a metallic element that is silvery in color. Sometimes called quicksilver, it is a heavy element that is very poisonous and remains in a liquid state at room temperature. Mercury is occasionally found in a pure form. It can also be obtained by extraction from cinnabar, a red-colored, naturally occurring compound of mercury and sulfur. Ancient South American Indians found deposits of this element both as mercury and cinnabar. The Inca, whose empire was established in about A.D. 1000 in the Andean region of South America, mined mercury. One of the deposits they mined was located in an area called Huancavelica in the highlands of the present-day Andes. After the Spaniards conquered the Inca, they continued to use Indian miners to extract mercury from the same site.

The ancient Maya, whose civilization flourished in Mesoamerica starting in about 1500 B.C., were able to transform cinnabar into mercury. Both mercury and cinnabar have been found in Maya sites where religious rituals took place. According to author Robert J. Sharer, "Mercury, a liquid metal, apparently had powerful symbolic meaning for the Maya. As mercuric sulfide (cinnabar) it is a brilliant red, symbolizing the life essence, or blood. In rituals involving fire, the Maya priests would burn cinnabar, transforming it into metallic mercury with mysterious qualities."

Cinnabar was an important TRADE item in northern South America and in Mesoamerica. Archaeologists have found MUMMIES, skeletons, burial items, and tombs containing traces of cinnabar in both of those areas.

See also EMBALMING; METAL CASTING; METALLURGY.

## Sources/Further Reading

Morris, Craig and Adriana von Hagen. *The Inka Empire and Its Andean Origins.* New York: Abbeville Press Publishers, 1993.

Sharer, Robert J. *Daily Life in Maya Civilization.* Westport, Conn.: Greenwood Press, 1996.

von Hagen, Victor W. *Realm of the Incas.* New York: New American Library, 1957.

## mescal See DISTILLATION.

## metal casting (ca. 200 B.C.) *South American Andean cultures*

Casting is the shaping of objects from molten metal. It involves making a model slightly larger than the desired object to allow for shrinkage. This also allows the final product to be filed or further shaped. Once the metal worker has made the mold, it is placed in wet sand to make an impression. Melted metal is then poured in and is then allowed to cool and harden. When it is cool, the item is removed from the sand. Pre-Peruvian metalworkers, who had been working with gold since 1500 B.C., did not develop the process of casting until about 200 B.C. They casted with copper and used the process primarily to make weapons and tools for agricultural work. Later, metallurgists built upon this basic casting process to develop the technique of LOST-WAX CASTING, which they used to make golden objects.

Craig Morris and Adriana Von Hagen write in *The Inka Empire and Its Andean Origins,* "The Inka Treasure that so dazzled the gold-greedy Spanish invaders was created with techniques based on age-old Andean metal-working traditions. These traditions began some two millennia before Spanish ships began to prowl Peru's waters."

## Sources/Further Reading

Bankes, George. *Peru Before Pizarro.* Oxford, England: Phaidon Press Limited, 1977.

Benson, Elizabeth P. *The Maya World.* New York: Thomas Y. Crowell Company, 1967.

Morris, Craig and Adriana von Hagen. *The Inka Empire and Its Andean Origins.* New York: Abbeville Press Publishers, 1993.

**metallurgy** (ca. 5000 B.C.–4000 B.C.) *North American Northeast, Arctic, and Northwest; South American Andean; Mesoamerican cultures*

The term *metallurgy* refers to the science of extracting metals from ore, purifying them, and making objects from them. The Paleo-Indians of the southern Great Lakes area were the first American Indians known to have worked with metal, doing so approximately six to seven thousand years ago. According to Susan Hazen-Hammond, author of *Timelines of Native American History,* they are the first metalworkers in the world. Indigenous culture groups in South America, Mesoamerica, and the North American Arctic also practiced metallurgy. For the most part, American Indians did not work with iron, because deposits were not easily accessible. The Polar Inuit who lived near Baffin Bay, however, did make iron blades from a local source of iron in the form of meteorites. Precontact iron tools have also been found on the North American Northwest Coast. (See also IRONWORK.)

Paleo-Indian metalworkers of the southern Great Lakes region extracted copper from rock formations in that area, the largest and most accessible copper deposits north of what is now Mexico. To remove the metal from the ore, these earliest metallurgists built extremely hot fires into which was placed the ore containing copper nuggets. After the rocks became white-hot, they were immersed in cold water. This caused the copper-containing rock to crack and fall apart. Most of the rock in which the copper was encased came off, and the residue that remained was cleaned off with copper tools.

Paleo-Indian metallurgists produced copper jewelry and sheet metal. They also produced copper DRILL BITS, picks, projectile points, awls, FISHHOOKS, gouges, knives, pendants, AXES, beads, and wedges. (See also TOOLS; JEWELRY, METAL.) As they shaped these objects, the metalworkers again heated the copper, this time until it was red-hot, and then slowly allowed it to cool. This process, called ANNEALING, made it soft and malleable. Great Lakes Paleo-Indian, copper items were highly valued by other culture groups and became an important TRADE item for the southern Great Lakes Paleo-Indians. These copper items were so highly valued as trade goods that modern archaeologists have found them from the Gulf Coast to the Atlantic seaboard and from the Ohio Valley to the Great Plains.

Copper technology was developed by 1000 B.C. in the southern highlands of present-day Peru as well. The Chavin, who lived in the northern highlands of what is now Peru, were the first ancient Americans to create metal FOIL. The oldest piece of this copper foil has been dated to 1400 B.C. Approximately 2,000 years prior to the conquest by the early Spanish explorers, the Moche, whose culture arose in what is now Peru in about 200 B.C., made foil of gold and silver, as well as copper. They used these foils to plate objects.

The Moche excelled at metalsmithing. The intricate and delicate work of these remarkable smiths continues to astonish modern jewelers. They developed ELECTROPLATING by about A.D. 500. Electroplating is the process of depositing a thin coat of one metal upon the surface of another using an electric cur-

rent. Moche metalworkers used this process to electroplate copper with silver and gold. The work was so well done that the objects looked like they were made of solid silver or gold.

The Moche, who mined (see also MINING, PLACER) and smelted ore (see also SMELTING), developed a working knowledge of annealing and used it to make highly detailed objects such as jewelry, tweezers, BELLS, and SCALPELS. They developed alloys, including one called *tumbaga,* a mixture of gold, copper and other metals, which could be worked to resemble gold. (See also GOLD PLATING.) They also made bronze alloys (made of tin and copper). Other metals that they used for alloys were gold, silver, PLATINUM, and arsenic. (See also METALS, PRECIOUS.) They rarely used lead and mercury. These metallurgists were able to work with cinnabar and produce MERCURY besides having access to natural deposits of it. In addition, they discovered the techniques of SINTERING and SOLDERING to join pieces of metal together. The Moche were also able to make minute gold beads from gold sheet metal by soldering two pieces together. The resulting bead was so small that only a sewing needle could fit into the center. It is very difficult to see where the two pieces were soldered—a sign of the goldsmith's remarkable skill.

The Inca, who established an empire in what is now Peru in about A.D. 1000, carried on the Moche metalworking tradition in South America. Inca metalworkers worked with alloys in addition to creating objects of gold. Between A.D. 500 and 1000, knowledge of metalworking techniques, along with the metal objects themselves, traveled northward with traders over 2,400 miles of ocean to the west coast of what is now Mexico where, the indigenous people there learned to work with silver, copper, arsenic, and gold and made a number of alloys, including tin and bronze. The Mixtec, whose culture flourished in Mesoamerica before that of the Aztec, and the Toltec, whose culture flourished in Mesoamerica from about A.D. 950 to 1200, became famous for their metalwork. That skill passed to the Aztec, whose empire was established in about 1100 A.D. At first the Aztec employed Toltec metalworkers and then learned the techniques themselves. The gold and gold-plated objects they made, as well as those crafted by Inca metalworkers, overwhelmed the Spanish conquistadores because of their number and sophistication. The Spaniards' shock quickly turned to greed as they sought cities of gold and melted many of the objects they found, shipping them back to European treasuries and maintaining a portion for their efforts.

See also GOLD PANNING; HYDRAULICS; LOST-WAX CASTING TECHNIQUE; MINING, PLACER; NEEDLES; PINS, STRAIGHT; TUBING, COPPER; WELDING, SWEAT.

**Sources/Further Reading**

Anawalt, Patricia Rieff. "Traders of the Ecuadorian Littoral." *Archaeology* (November/December 1997): 48–52.

Benson, Elizabeth P. *The Maya World.* New York: Thomas Y. Crowell Company, 1967.

Driver, Harold E. *Indians of North America.* Chicago: University of Chicago Press, 1969.

Hazen-Hammond, Susan. *Timelines of Native American History: Through the Centuries with Mother Earth and Father Sky.* New York: Berkeley Publishing Company, 1997.

Mason, J. Alden. *The Ancient Civilizations of Peru.* Rev. ed. New York: Penguin Books, 1988.

Maxwell, James A. *America's Fascinating Indian Heritage.* Pleasantville, N.Y.: Reader's Digest Books, 1978.

Oswalt, Wendell. *Eskimos and Explorers.* Novato, Calif.: Chandler & Sharp Publishers, 1979.

**metals, precious**  (ca. 1900 B.C.–300 B.C.)  *North American, Mesoamerican, South American cultures*

Metals are considered to be precious when they are scarce. Gold (Au), silver (Ag), and PLATINUM (Pt) are considered to be precious metals. Gold is considered by many researchers to have been the first metal worked by prehistoric Indians in precontact South America. Gold and copper objects appeared in the present-day area of Bolivia and Ecuador by 1900 B.C. Platinum was worked in the present-day areas of Ecuador and the southern area of Columbia, but to Europeans, who did not have the technology to work with it, platinum was not considered precious. In North America indigenous peoples generally did not make use of the gold that lay on and beneath their land, neither panning for it nor working it into shapes.

Many Mesoamerican and South American cultures shaped gold into jewelry and ornamental objects but did not place a high value on the metal itself. Gold was not seen as a measure of wealth but rather as a status symbol. These cultures valued the transformative process of the craftsperson who turned the raw material into a work of art. The Mixtec, whose culture existed from A.D. 800 to A.D. 1500 in what is now Mexico, created beautiful artworks in gold. They used the metal for masks, breastplates, and vessels as well as jewelry, forming these objects using the LOST-WAX CASTING TECHNIQUE, filigree, and repoussé (producing raised patterns by hammering on the back of a piece).

The Aztec, who established an empire in what is now Mexico in about A.D. 1100, believed that gold was the tears of the sun. JADE and quetzal feathers were worth more than gold in their economy, despite the fact that they employed Mixtec and Toltec goldsmiths to create the lavish golden objects. These so impressed the Spanish conquistadores that they became the primary object of their looting.

Explorations were mounted to look for gold, including those of Hernán Cortés among the Aztec; Francisco Pizarro among the Inca, who had established an empire in about A.D. 1000 in what is now Peru; Hernando de Soto in what is now Florida and the Carolinas; Francisco Vásquez de Coronado in what is now New Mexico and Arizona; and Francisco de Orellana in the Amazon Basin. Whenever they found gold, they enslaved American Indians and set them to mine it.

They did the same when they found silver. One of the largest, single sources of silver was found in the mountains of Potosí in what is now Bolivia. It was accidentally discovered in 1545 by an Indian walking in the mountains. He reported the find to a Spaniard, and consequently the Spaniards started a large-scale mining operation. Potosí became the largest supplier of silver in the world by 1600. The Spanish also found silver in 11 other places in the present-day area of Mexico. Eventually, Mexico became the richest silver-bearing site in the world. At one point, Spanish silver pesos and pieces-of-eight were used as currency by half of the world.

Historians estimate that in 1492 about $200 million worth of gold and silver, or about $2 a person, was either stored in the coffers of Europe or circulated there in the form of money. Ships bearing gold from the New World caused that amount to triple within 50 years. By 1600 the amount of gold and silver in Europe had increased eightfold. The rapid increase in assets caused the economy to boom at first, but then sparked soaring inflation, a condition in which prices for goods rise sharply as the value of money declines. This economic unbalance lasted about a century.

**Sources/Further Reading**

Bankes, George. *Peru Before Pizarro.* Oxford, England: Phaidon Press Limited, 1977.

Burger, Richard L. *Chavin and the Origins of Andean Civilization.* London: Thames and Hudson, 1992.

Engel, Frederic Andre. *An Ancient World Preserved: Relics and Records of Prehistory in the Andes.* New York: Crown Publishers, Inc., 1976.

Fagan, Brian M. *Kingdoms of Gold, Kingdoms of Jade: The Americas Before Columbus.* New York: Thames and Hudson, 1991.

Fehrenbach, T. R. *Fire and Blood: A History of Mexico.* New York: Macmillan Publishing Co., Inc., 1973.

Fiedel, Stuart J. *Prehistory of the Americas.* Cambridge, England: Cambridge University Press, 1987.

Hazen-Hammond, Susan. *Timelines of Native American History.* New York: The Berkley Publishing Group, 1997.

Josephy, Jr., Alvin M., ed. *The American Heritage Book of Indians.* New York: Bantam Books, 1968.

Mason, J. Alden. *The Ancient Civilizations of Peru.* New York: Penguin Books, 1968.

Morris, Craig and Adriana von Hagen. *The Inka Empire and Its Andean Origins.* New York: Abbeville Press, 1993.

Weatherford, Jack. *Indian Givers: How The Indians of the Americas Transformed the World.* New York: Fawcett Columbine, 1988.

**midwives**  See NURSES, NURSING.

**military tactics**  (precontact)  *North American Northeast, Northwest, and Plains; Mesoamerican; South American cultures*

Because the armies of the conquistadores and colonists ultimately defeated the indigenous people of the Americas, many people mistakenly assume that American Indian military tactics were less effective than those of the Europeans. The opposite is true. American Indians were highly skilled in guerrilla warfare. In addition to their intimate knowledge of the land, they excelled at the techniques of ambush and stalking the enemy, which they had devised during the hunt. Indigenous fighters were also expert in the tactic of raiding. They sent scouts to gather information on both the lay of the land and the enemy, something Europeans often did not do.

At first the European armies, marching in close columns into unknown territory and fighting in formation, were highly critical of the indigenous style of fighting. They believed it was disorganized, despite the fact that lightning-fast strikes followed by quick retreats into the woods enabled Indians to win skirmishes and even early battles. Generals labeled North American Indians "skulking Indians" and termed their style of fighting "ignoble." At the same time they criticized Indians for not killing enough people during battle. They derided indigenous weapons, war axes, and arrows as primitive. When it became obvious, however, that what worked in war in the New World differed from that in the Old World, French and British commanders enlisted Indian aid in fighting the French and Indian Wars. Not until the British and French adopted American Indian military techniques were they able to defeat the Indian people of North America in battle.

Indigenous armies in Mesoamerica, South America, and North America used guerilla tactics to resist the Spanish conquistadores. Popé's Rebellion in August 1680 is an outstanding example of this. Popé, a Tewa, operating from Taos Pueblo, organized a brilliant and successful rout of the Spaniards from what is now New Mexico. He planned the campaign in secret, a feat in itself since he was able to gain the help of all of the pueblos, except for Pueblo Grande. Before the pueblos would agree to join with him, they had to reach consensus in their councils. Popé used messengers, or runners, to carry information from pueblo to pueblo. They carried knotted strings to use as CALENDARS so that the timing would be coordinated. (See also QUIPUS.) When information about the surprise attacks was leaked, Popé moved the date ahead. On August 10, 1680, his men burned missions at both Taos and Acoma pueblos. Five days later, 500 indigenous soldiers marched on Santa Fe, the Spanish headquarters, driving the enemy away. Although Popé's campaign was successful, the Spaniards returned to reestablish their rule several years later. However, when they did they toned down some of their most oppressive measures for a number of years; historians believe this was in direct response to Popé's revolt.

The English colonizers of New England faced heavy resistance from Metacom, a Wampanoag chief whom they called King Philip. He was able to successfully pull off a number of raids and ambushes by hiding in the Rhode Island wilderness. The Rhode Island militia, who had learned the usefulness of this tactic, tried it but failed in the summer of 1675 when one of their troops lit a PIPE of TOBACCO, giving away their position and making them the target of attack from Metacom's troops. An observer wrote that the defeat had come because of the militia members "being troubled with the Epidemical plague of lust after tobacco."

At the battle of Pocaset Swamp a few days later, between seven and 15 Englishmen died because of their ineptitude in guerrilla warfare, at which Indians were so expert. Increase Mather wrote of that encounter: "The Swamp was so Boggy and thick of Bushes, as that it was judged to proceed further therein would be but to throw away Men's lives. It could not there be discerned who were *English* and who the *Indians*. Our Men when in that hideous place if they did but see a Bush stir would fire presently, whereby 'tis verily feared that they did sometimes unhappily shoot *Englishmen* instead of *Indians*."

When moving across the land, American Indian soldiers spaced themselves out, so that they would not be an easy target for enemy fire. This indigenous tactic also made it extremely difficult for the colonizers to know how many Indians they were up against in a military encounter. English troops did the opposite. Benjamin Church, a British officer who recruited Indian soldiers for the British army, commented, ". . . the English always kept in a heap together, that it was as easy to hit them as to hit an House. . . ." Recognizing that Metacom could not possibly be defeated by European military strategy, Church finally convinced 140 "friendly" Indians to join 60 British soldiers to pursue the war chief in 1676.

American Indians who advised British troops on guerrilla military strategy quickly became frustrated by the British's unwillingness to listen to the advice they had solicited. During the French and Indian War (1689–1763), Tanaghrisson, a Seneca chief, watched then-Lieutenant Colonel George Washington's troops throw together a stockade in a meadow after retreating from French-occupied Fort Duquesne, which was located on the site of what is Pittsburgh today. Washington termed the stockade "Fort Necessity." Tanaghrisson later wrote of Washington that he ". . . would by no means take Advice from the Indians. . . . he lay at one Place from one full Moon to the other and made no Fortifications at all, but that one little thing upon the meadow . . ." Tanaghrisson called the English fools for their carelessness and the French cowards for not attacking them. General Washington later ignored American Indian military intelligence about the interior of the French fort and about its inhabitants, information modern military historians believe would have given him a decided advantage. Washington was not an exception in this regard. The British generally held Indian war chiefs in contempt during the French and Indian War; however, French commanders actively courted Indian allies and listened to their advice.

After the Civil War (1861–65), the U.S. Army attempted to push American Indians living on the Great Plains onto reservations in order to free the land for non-Indian settlement. Once again they faced guerrilla warfare and, as they had two hundred years before, non-Indian commanders clung to tactics that had been used in Europe. The most crushing defeat they suffered was at the Battle of Little Bighorn, where George Armstrong Custer, overly confident of his military superiority and unfamiliar with the land, commanded an attack against a group of Indians led by Lakota chief Crazy Horse, even though the U.S. troops were outnumbered at least two to one. Many modern military historians credit American Indian warriors on

Stand Watie, a Cherokee, was the only Indian to attain the rank of general in the Confederate army during the U.S. Civil War. He was also the last Confederate general to surrender to the Union. This portrait of him was taken at the Mathew Brady Studio between 1860 and 1865. *(Photograph No. NWDNS-111-B-4914/National Archives and Records Administration at College Park)*

the plains as being more expert horsemen than the U.S. Army cavalry troops and as being excellent military tacticians as well. They believe that American Indian war chiefs lost the protracted Indian Wars on the plains because they led their fighters rather than commanded them as did U.S. Army generals. Following Indian leaders was always voluntary. Indian leaders did not issue orders to the soldiers who fought with them. Another important factor in the loss was that while the U.S. Army was unified under the ultimate command of the president of the United States, Plains Indians fought using loose-knit coalitions of bands or tribes. Disease combined with waves of European immigration meant that by the last half of 1800s, at the start of the Sioux Wars (1854–90), non-Indians already outnumbered Indians in the American West by 10 to one.

Another example of the effectiveness of American Indian military tactics is that of Chief Joseph of the Nez Perce. He is known for his strategies of field fortifications, skirmish lines, and rear and advance guards while retreating from the U.S. Army for 1,600 miles in 1877. The Nez Perce were ordered to move from a government-imposed reservation on their ancestral homeland in what is now Washington state to the Lapwai Reservation in Idaho. Before the move could be accomplished,

young men from one of the Nez Perce bands killed four white men. The U.S. Army retaliated with disproportionate force. Chief Joseph consequently moved his people (mostly old men, women, and children) on the tribe's APPALOOSA HORSES in an attempt to seek sanctuary first with the Crow and then with Sitting Bull in Canada. During this time, Nez Perce warriors under his command fought the U.S. Army in 13 battles and skirmishes with 10 different army commands, defeating nearly all of them. U.S. general William Tecumseh Sherman commented it was ". . . one of the most extraordinary Indian Wars of which there is any record." Some of the strategies and battle plans devised by Chief Joseph are still taught at West Point, a U.S. military academy, today.

According to modern military historians, American Indians ultimately lost the battle with non-Indians to keep their land, despite their excellence as military strategists, because the colonizers arrived with both firearms and disease. Although North American Indians, who obtained guns first from the fur trade and later in raids, quickly learned how to use them effectively, they were never as adequately armed as the colonizers, who possessed cannons in addition to guns. The numbers of indigenous peoples available to fight to defend their homelands was also decreased by diseases such as smallpox, measles, cholera, and tuberculosis, which Europeans introduced inadvertently at first but then later used intentionally as a military tactic by giving the Indians smallpox-infected blankets during the French and Indian Wars.

## Sources/Further Reading

Axelrod, Alan. *Chronicle of the Indian Wars from Colonial Times to Wounded Knee.* New York: Prentice Hall, 1993.

Beal, Merrill D. *I Will Fight No More Forever: Chief Joseph and the Nez Perce War.* Seattle: University of Washington Press, 1991.

Hook, Jason. *American Indian Warrior Chiefs.* Dorset, England: Firebird Books, 1989.

Malone, Patrick M. *The Skulking Way of War: Technology and Tactics among the New England Indians.* New York: Madison Books, 1991.

## milkweed (Asclepiadaceae) (precontact) *North American Northeast cultures*

The term *milkweed* refers to a family of flowering plants (Asclepiadaceae), all of which contain latex. Most of the approximately 100 known species of this plant are native to the Americas. American Indians used milkweed for food and to poison fish. (See also FISHING, CHEMICAL.) Many tribes of present-day Canada and the United States ate the young seed pods, shoots, and flowers as a source of nutrition. They also used milkweed fibers for making fishing nets and ropes. The fluff from milkweed served as a disposable diaper (see also DIAPERS, DISPOSABLE) when it was used to line CRADLEBOARDS. Some culture groups used the latex, which turns dark upon exposure to air, as a DYE. North American Indians used the milky white sap of the milkweed plant as CHEWING GUM and a breath freshener. European colonists eventually picked up this habit. Medicine was an important use for this plant—one that was also adopted by European colonists.

American Indians who lived in the eastern half of what is now the United States used swamp milkweed (*Asclepias incarnata*) as a diaphoretic to produce perspiration and as an expectorant. Larger doses produced a laxative effect. Indians used common milkweed (*Asclepias cornuit* or *A. syriaca L.*) as an expectorant and pain reliever. A number of tribes used *Asclepias syriaca,* which was found all over the United States and Canada, to treat dysentery and dropsy (generalized swelling due to fluid buildup). Other medicinal uses for milkweed include a treatment for wart removal invented by the Catawba, a southeastern tribe, and a treatment for tapeworms created by the Mesquaki, a Northeast tribe. (See also ANTIHELMINTICS.)

At least one southeastern North American culture, the Natchez, made a tea from various milkweed species and used it to treat kidney problems. This remedy was effective because of the plant's diuretic properties. Natchez healers advised patients undergoing this treatment to avoid consuming salt. Since salt intake causes water retention that contraindicated edema and kidney problems, the advice was sound. Navajo (Dineh) women made a tea of *Asclepias halli,* taking it after giving birth to provide temporary sterility. (See also CONTRACEPTION, ORAL.) Some tribes used *Asclepias syriaca* for the same reason.

Milkweed varieties *Asclepias tuberosa, A. incarnata,* and *A. syriaca* were listed in the official United States Pharmacopoeia from 1820 to 1863 and from 1873 to 1882. A pharmacopoeia is an official list of standards for medicinal drugs and instructions on how to prepare them. The first U.S. Pharmacopoeia, created in 1820s, was written and sanctioned by the medical profession. This reference advised physicians to use milkweed as an expectorant and diaphoretic in small doses and as a purgative and emetic in larger doses—the same purposes for which American Indians had used the plant.

### Sources/Further Reading

Hutchens, Alma R. *Indian Herbology of North America.* Boston: Shambhala Publications, Inc., 1973.

Lust, John. *The Herb Book.* New York: Bantam Books, 1974.

NativeTech: Native American Technology and Art. "Milkweed." URL: http://www.nativetech.org/plantgath/milkweed.htm. Downloaded April 11, 2001.

Vogel, Virgil J. *American Indian Medicine.* Norman: University of Oklahoma Press, 1970.

Weiner, Michael A. *Earth Medicine, Earth Food: Plant Remedies, Drugs, and Natural Foods of the North American Indians.* New York: Fawcett Columbine, 1990.

## milpa (slash-and-burn agriculture, swidden agriculture) (ca. 8000 B.C.–7000 B.C.) *North American, Mesoamerican, South American cultures*

Milpa, also called slash-and-burn or swidden agriculture, is characterized by cutting and burning unwanted trees and brush in order to clear the land. It is a form of AGRICULTURE practiced extensively throughout North America, Mesoamerica, and South America for thousands of years, and it differs from the types of farming developed in Europe. Usually field rotation and intercropping, or COMPANION PLANTING (growing different plants in the same plot), accompanies milpa. This method of agriculture is an ecologically sound way of farming in areas with relatively low population density. It is still practiced by farmers in parts of Mexico and South America, where the word *milpa* has come to mean not only the technique but also the actual field in which the crops are grown. Milpa then and now requires farmers to possess a deep understanding of the interaction of soil, seeds, climate, and moisture. It also necessitates a clear understanding of the specific nutrients plants remove from the soil and which nutrients they add.

Typically American Indians cut trees and clear brush on a piece of land in the spring. They then evenly spread the trunks and limbs across the land and burned them. The resulting ash reduced soil acidity and spurred bacterial activity in the soil. Burning also added magnesium, calcium, potash, and phosphorous to the soil and helped to form nitrogen. Indians tilled the new fields with a FOOT PLOW, planting crops in the holes they had made. Mohawk farmers of northeastern North America waited two years to plant after burning the brush from an area they had cleared with fire.

Milpa is believed to have originated in the lowland area of the Tehuacan Valley and Oaxaca, Mexico, as early as 10,000 years ago, but it was also used by groups as diverse as the Huron and Mohawk of northeastern North America, the Hidatsa of the Missouri River Valley, and the Apalachee and Timucua Indians of north Florida.

By using milpa, indigenous farmers throughout the Americas practiced a form of soil rotation, creating new fields and abandoning old ones. This was possible because of the large amount of land available to them. European farmers, on the other hand, rotated the crops they planted on one piece of ground because land available for farming in Europe was scarce. American Indians understood that the nutrients in the earth would be depleted by constant planting, so after a growing season or two they would allow fields to lie fallow. For example, Huron farmers' fields typically yielded about 25 to 30 bushels of corn an acre. When yields dropped to a third of that, they cleared new plots. Every 10 to 12 years they relocated their villages. The Maya, who lived in Mesoamerica and whose culture arose in about 1500 B.C., cleared new crop lands, then used the new fields for two or three years before abandoning them from 15 to as long as 40 years. New growth on the resting fields prevented erosion.

After European contact, the North American Indian tribes who had farmed extensively lost their agricultural landbase quickly and could no longer clear and plant the land in the ways that had served them so well. The practice of milpa has continued in Central and South America to some extent. Huastec Indians in Mexico today manage a number of fields, home gardens, and forest plots that are planted with about 300 species of crops. In other areas, such as the Amazon Basin, population growth and economic pressure forced Native farmers to shorten fallow periods, sometimes dispensing with them altogether. Under the direction of multinational business interests, indigenous farmers have been encouraged to clear huge tracts of land in order to raise cattle, disturbing the delicate ecological balance that subsistence farming using milpa once provided.

## Sources/Further Reading

Altieri, Miguel. *Agro-ecology: The Science of Sustainable Agriculture.* Boulder, Colo.: Westview Press, Inc., 1995.

Hurt, R. Douglas. *American Indian Agriculture: Prehistory to Present.* Lawrence: University Press of Kansas, 1987.

Matyas, James. "Reclamation of Lowland Tropical Forests after Shifting Agriculture." *Restoration and Reclamation Review* 1 (Spring 1996). URL:http://www.hortiagri.umn.edu/h5015/96papers/matyas.htm.

**mining, placer**  (ca. A.D. 1000)  *South American Andean cultures*

Placer mining is the process of recovering precious metals from sand or gravel deposits that are left by glaciers or rivers. (See also METALS, PRECIOUS.) The Inca, who established an empire in the Andean region of South America in about A.D. 1000, used sophisticated placer mining techniques to sort gold from the sand and gravel in stream and river beds. Inca engineers built slats and grooves of stone and placed them across streams. They chose to place them where very little water ran normally, but where there would be heavy runoff after a rain. The runoff brought gold-bearing sand and gravel from upstream. As swift-moving water passed over the structures, sand and gravel was carried downstream while the gold, which was heavier, remained trapped by the stone structures. When the rains stopped and the water level dropped, the Inca miners walked along the stream, picking the gold out of the stone. Ancient Inca gold miners also panned for gold in much the same way the '49ers later would during the California gold rush that peaked in 1849. Tribes in the North American Southeast occasionally panned for gold as well. The Inca also dug underground mines, excavating shafts and pits for gold and silver ore in mines high in the Andes. Because their work was so difficult, LABOR LAWS protected miners.

See also GOLD PANNING; HYDRAULICS; METALLURGY.

## References/Further Reading

Benson, Elizabeth P. *The Maya World.* New York: Thomas Y. Crowell Company, 1967.

Morris, Craig and Adriana von Hagen. *The Inka Empire and its Andean Origins.* New York: Abbeville Press Publishers, 1993.

Soustelle, Jacques. *Daily Life of the Aztecs.* Stanford, Calif.: Stanford University Press, 1955.

**mints, botanical**  (precontact)  *North American Northeast, Plateau, Great Basin, Great Plains, Southwest, and Southeast cultures*

Plants that belong to the mint family (Lamiaceae) contain a volatile oil in their stems and leaves. It is this oil that gives them their distinctive aroma and taste. A number of wild mint plants are indigenous to the temperate zones of North America. These include elk mint, wild mint, pennyroyal, horse mint, bergamot, and marsh mint. American Indians developed a number of uses for these plants, including cold remedies, sore muscle balms, upset stomach remedies, seasonings for food, insect repellents, and air fresheners.

The Cheyenne of the northern plains used mint tea to ease chest pains caused by coughing. A number of tribes indigenous to what is now Nevada, including the Shoshone, used mint tea to treat symptoms of the common cold, as did the Navajo (Dineh) of the Southwest and the Cree of the upper Midwest. The Kootenai, who lived in what is now Montana, drank mint tea for coughs and chewed the leaves to prevent coughing as well. The Paiute of the Great Basin and the Kiowa of the plains chewed the leaves to soothe sore throats. Mint in the form of menthol is a common ingredient in today's cough drops. The Menominee of the Midwest drank mint tea and applied a mint poultice to the chest to treat pneumonia, much like the menthol chest rubs used today.

The Thompson tribe of what is now British Columbia placed leaves in sweatbaths (see also STEAM ROOMS) to treat severe colds and for rheumatism. Great Basin tribes applied poultices of mint leaves to aching and swollen joints as a rheumatism or arthritis treatment. The Gros Ventre (Atsina) also used mint as an analgesic, or painkiller. The Kootenai recognized the analgesic properties contained in mint's volatile oils contained in mint as well and chewed mint leaves to ease the pain of toothache.

The Paiute drank cold mint tea for indigestion and stomach pains. Mint was used for this purpose by the Dakota of the plains, the Mohegan and Chippewa (Anishinabe) of the Northeast and the Washo of Nevada and eastern California. Members of the Colville tribe in the Plateau region used mint tea to treat colic in infants and children.

Sometimes American Indians chewed mint leaves simply for the taste they provided. The Pueblo peoples of the desert Southwest did this. Most of the time, however, American Indians brewed the leaves to make a refreshing herbal tea. The Cheyenne, Lakota, Dakota, Pawnee, Ponca, and Ho-Chunk of the northern plains were all reported to drink mint tea, as were the Kawaiisu, Colville, Paiute, Flathead (Salish), Shuswap, and Shoshone of the Plateau and Basin area. The Chippewa of the Northeast drank mint tea, as did the Cherokee of the Southeast.

People of several culture groups used dried, pulverized mint leaves as a seasoning for food, especially meat. American Indians who used mint as a flavoring included the Kootenai, who packed dried meat and berries with mint, not only to flavor them but also to repel insects (see also INSECT REPELLENTS). The Blackfeet, Chippewa, and Dakota also did this.

The Pueblo peoples of the Southwest used mint as a flavoring, as did the Apache and the Hopi of the Southwest.

Sometimes American Indians used mint as a perfume because of its pleasant aroma. Members of the Thompson tribe from what is now British Columbia lined fish platters with mint leaves to neutralize the strong smell of the food. The Cheyenne mixed horse mint with sweet grass, sweet pine, and dried flowers to make a perfume. At times this mixture was used as a dwelling deodorizer. They also combined mint with animal fat to make a hair pomade.

The odor-neutralizing properties of mint came in handy for hunting purposes. The Colville tribe of the Northwest wiped fishing hooks, lines, and harpoons with mint to remove the smell of blood. The Lakota, Dakota, Nakota, Ho-Chunk, and Blackfeet boiled their traps in a mint solution in order to conceal their human scent from the animals they hoped to catch.

See also DECOYS, FISH (OLFACTORY); HYGIENE, PERSONAL; INDIGESTION MEDICATIONS.

## Sources/Further Reading

Duke, James A. *The Green Pharmacy.* New York: St. Martins Press, 1997.

Lust, John. *The Herb Book.* New York: Bantam Books, 1974.

Moerman, Dan. *Native American Ethnobotany Database: Food, Drugs, Dyes and Fibers of Native North American Peoples.* URL: http://www.umd.umich.edu/cgi-bin/herb. Downloaded on September 24, 1999.

**mirrors** (ca. 1700 B.C.) *Mesoamerican cultures*
Mirrors are implements used for reflecting images. The Olmec invented the oldest mirror in pre-Columbian Mesoamerica. Olmec culture flourished in the Yucatán Peninsula from about 1700 B.C. until about 400 B.C. Many experts consider the Olmec the first true civilization in the precontact Americas. They are also considered the "mother" of the civilizations that followed.

The most common material that the Olmec used to produce mirrors was polished hematite. Hematite ($Fe_2O_3$) is a black to reddish mineral that is the most common source of iron. The Olmec developed a technology for grinding and polishing their mirrors, but this technology remains a mystery today according to archaeologist Michael Coe. (See also OPTICAL TECHNOLOGY, BASICS OF.) Two holes were drilled along the edges of Olmec mirrors so that string could be attached; the mirrors could then be hung on a wall or around the neck.

The Maya, whose culture arose in Mesoamerica in about 1500 B.C., used iron pyrite for their mirrors. Maya mirrors were the symbol for kings and royalty. Other Mesoamerican culture groups used gold, silver, copper, anthracite (hard coal), and obsidian for the mirrors that they made.

## Sources/Further Reading

Coe, Michael D. *America's First Civilization: Discovering the Olmec.* Eau Claire, Wis.: American Heritage Publishing Co., Inc., 1968.

Schele, Linda and Freidel, David. *A Forest of Kings: The Untold Story of the Ancient Maya.* New York: William Morrow and Company, Inc., 1990.

**mit'a**   See TAX SYSTEMS.

**moccasins** (precontact) *North American cultures*
A number of Indian cultures in North America designed and wore a distinctive style of leather footwear called moccasins. These shoes were made in both hard- and soft-soled versions. Their name comes from at least three tribes. The Narragansett, a northeastern tribe, called the footwear *mockussinchass* or *mocussinass*. The Micmac of the upper Midwest called them *mkussin*. The Powhatan of what is now Virginia called them *mockasin*. Comfortable and tailored moccasins have become a popular style that is worn by people throughout the world today.

Like people of other world cultures, American Indians invented shoes to protect their feet from cold temperatures and sharp objects. Indigenous Americans constructed moccasins from leather made from BISON, moose, elk, or deer skins. (See also TANNING, BRAIN.) Although most moccasins were low-topped, they could quickly and easily be made into a boot by attaching leggings to them. Moccasins intended for use in winter were lined with fur or grass to provide insulation. Women of some Plains tribes wore stockings made of thin leather in addition to their moccasins.

The style of moccasins that American Indians made varied from culture to culture. For example, the Navajo (Dineh) of the Southwest; the Comanche of the southern plains; the Flathead (Salish) and Kootenai of the Plateau region; and the Inuit and Yup'ik of the Arctic, where temperatures reached extremes, made high-topped moccasins, or boots. Those made by Arctic cultures are called MUKLUKS. It was primarily people of the Arctic, the Great Basin, the Southwest, and the Great Plains who wore moccasins with hard soles made from shaped rawhide.

Northeastern Indians, including the Narragansett, made soft-soled moccasins with a puckered U-shaped vamp sewn over the instep. The size of the vamp varied from tribe to tribe. Other northeastern tribes, such as the Iroquois, made moccasin tops from one piece of leather. These had a center seam along the top of the instep. The Apache of the Southwest used a similar design, but one with slightly turned-up toes. Moccasin uppers made by Plains and Northwest Coast cultures were also constructed from one piece of leather. Unlike the moccasins of the Northeast, these were sewn along the side of the foot instead of the center. Many styles of northeastern and plains moccasins were constructed with a cuff. Sometimes leather or fur was added to make a cuff. In other instances the leather was simply folded over. Some northeastern moccasins were made with a heel tab.

Moccasin styles were so unique that trackers could deduce what tribe the person wearing them belonged to by his or her

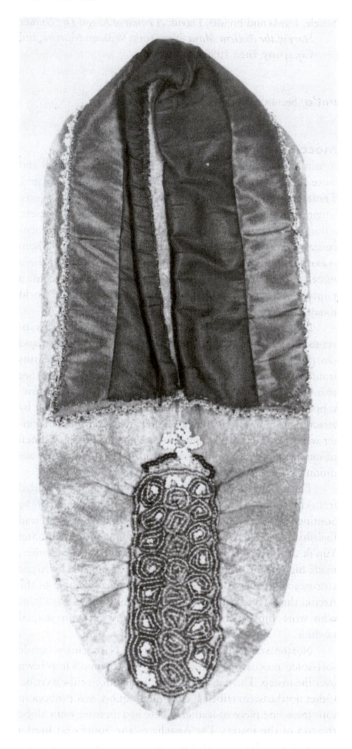

Members of tribes in the Northeast wore cuffed moccasins. The Huron moccasin shown in the photograph detail above is decorated with beads and ribbon. Before contact, American Indians used porcupine quills to decorate moccasins. Afterward, they began using glass beads as decoration. *(Marius Barbeau/National Archives of Canada/PA-175385, National Museums of Canada Collection)*

footprints alone. Moccasins made by some Great Plains tribes had fringes at the heels. (See also FRINGED CLOTHING.) These probably served to brush out the wearer's tracks. Sometimes

American Indians tied animal tails to the heels of moccasins for the same purpose. Tribes that lived in the northeastern North America, such as the Chippewa (Anishinabe), occasionally tied fur strips to the bottom of their moccasins to provide traction on ice. (See also CRAMPONS.)

Throughout North America, moccasin makers decorated their creations. Before contact, they embroidered the insteps and tongues of these shoes with dyed porcupine quills, a technique called quillwork. Northeastern and southeastern tribes used floral designs. Those who lived on the plains and in the Southwest decorated their moccasins with geometric designs. (See also GEOMETRY.) After contact with Europeans, moccasin makers often substituted glass beads for quills.

### Sources/Further Reading

Driver, Harold E. *Indians of North America.* Chicago: University of Chicago Press, 1969.
Koch, Ronald P. *Dress Clothing of the Plains Indians.* Norman: University of Oklahoma Press, 1977.
Paterek, Josephine, Ph.D. *Encyclopedia of American Indian Costume.* Denver: ABC Clio, 1994.
Prindle, Tara. *NativeTech: Moccasins.* 1994–1998. URL: http://www.nativeweb.org/NativeTech. Downloaded on September 14, 1999.

**money** (ca. A.D. 800) *South American; Mesoamerican cultures*
Money is a standard medium of exchange. It is used to set prices, pay for services and goods, and discharge debts. Although not widespread, copper coins were used by some precontact South and Mesoamerican cultures. The ancient pre-Peruvian Sican people, whose culture arose in what is now Peru in about A.D. 800, called their money *naipes*. These copper coins, which were shaped like capital *Is*, were used in TRADE and held a set, common standard of value. The metal coins made economic transactions less cumbersome for traders than exchanging bulky goods for goods.

Some coins were T- or axe-shaped and were used in international trade. Archaeologists have found some of these copper money axes in the west of Mexico. According to author Stuart J. Fiedel, "Copper money axes were even more common in the Milago culture of the Guayas River Basin, a neighbor and contemporary of the Montego." He believes that precontact traders of Ecuadorian Littoral used this copper money as a medium of exchange with the people of western Mexico. Many archaeologists speculate that trade between the two areas, separated by 2,400 miles of open sea was extensive. The traders are believed to have used balsa rafts. (See also RAFTS, BALSA.) The evidence they cite for this trade consists of similarities in METALLURGY techniques and funeral practices between the two cultures, as well as similarities in clothing. The Mexican hairless dog, *the Xochiocoyotl,* also exists in these two areas. (See also DOG BREEDS.) Although they did not use coins, Maya traders, relied on CACAO beans as a convenient medium of exchange.

## Sources/Further Reading

Engel, Frederic Andre. *An Ancient World Preserved: Relics and Records of Prehistory in the Andes.* New York: Crown Publishers, Inc., 1976.

Fiedel, Stuart J. *Prehistory of the Americas.* Cambridge, England: Cambridge University Press, 1987.

Morris, Craig and Adriana von Hagen. *The Inka Empire and its Andean Origins.* New York: Abbeville Publishers, 1993.

Thompson, J. Eric S. *Maya History and Religion.* Norman: University of Oklahoma Press, 1972.

**moose calls** See CALLS, ANIMAL AND BIRD.

**morning glories** (precontact) *Mesoamerican, South American Tropical Forest cultures*

Morning glories are climbing vines that produce trumpet-shaped flowers. The flowers produced by these plants bloom in a variety of colors, including blue, white, red, purple, and yellow. They belong to the same family (*Convolvulaceae*) as do JICAMA and SWEET POTATOES do. Bindweed is another relative of cultivated morning glories. The morning glories grown in gardens throughout the world today were developed from plants indigenous to Mesoamerica and the tropical forests of South America. The Aztec, who established an empire in Mesoamerica in about A.D. 1100, were among those cultures who cultivated morning glories.

The two most interesting Mexican varieties of the plant are *Ipomoea tricolor (I. violacea)* and the white-flowered *Turbina corymbosa.* The Aztec called the seeds of these *ololiuhqui* in Nahuatl, the Aztec language. Aztec physicians applied a poultice of *ololiuhqui* externally as a treatment for gout and had patients ingest the seeds as a fever treatment. In ceremonies, Aztec priests drank a tea made from morning glory seeds to communicate with the gods. The seeds of both varieties of morning glories contain a lysergic acid alkaloid called *ergine* (d-lysergic acid amide), which is better known as natural LSD. Although this compound is not as potent as manufactured LSD, overdoses could be deadly. Anthropologists speculate this is why the Aztec limited the potion to priests.

One of the first Europeans to write about the religious use of morning glory seeds was Father Bernardo de Sahagun, who wrote in the 1500s in *Historia General de las Cosas de Nueva Espana:* "There is an herb called *coatl xoxouhqui* (green snake), which produces seeds that are called *ololiuhqui.* These seeds stupefy and deprive one of reason: they are taken as a potion." Francisco Hernando, the physician sent to study Aztec medicine by King Philip II of Spain in 1570, called the morning glory a "snake plant" and described it as a climber that had green, heart-shaped leaves. Because the Spaniards wanted to convert the Aztec to Christianity and *ololiuhqui* ingestion was a part of the indigenous religion, they forbade the practice after conquest. Despite the ban, some indigenous people living in remote regions of modern-day Mexico—the Zapotec, Chinantec, Maztec, and Mixtec tribes—continue to use *ololiuhqui* for religious purposes.

## Sources/Further Reading

Hoffman, Albert. *LSD My Problem Child: The Mexican Relatives of LSD.* Schaffer Library of Drug Policy. URL: http://www.druglibrary.oprg/schaffer/lsd/child6.htm. Downloaded on September 25, 1999.

Ortiz de Montellano, Bernard. *Aztec Medicine, Health, and Nutrition.* New Brunswick, N.J.: Rutgers University Press, 1990.

Parsons, James A. "Southern Blooms: Latin America and the World of Flowers," *Queen's Quarterly* 99 no. 3 (1992): 542–561.

Wasson, R. Gordon. "A Contribution to Our Knowledge of Rivea Coryembosa the Narcotic Ololiuqui of the Aztecs." *Botanical Museum Leaflets,* Harvard University. 20, no. 6 (1963): 161–212.

**mosaics** (ca. 1700 B.C.–400 B.C.) *Mesoamerican, South American Andean, North American Southwest cultures*

Mosaics are a surface decoration made by inlaying pieces of different materials, such as glass, tiles, or colored stones. The Olmec, whose culture flourished in Mesoamerica from about 1700 B.C. to about 400 B.C., made mosaics on an enormous scale from green serpentine tiles about the size of present-day cinder blocks. They constructed these mosaics in deep pits and, for unknown reasons, would bury them immediately. One such pit found by archaeologists was 16 feet deep and contained a mosaic depicting an Olmec God. Another pit, called "Massive Offerings," was 24 feet deep. The mosaic in this pit contained over 1,000 tons of green serpentine blocks.

In the Andes of South America, ancient Peruvian goldsmiths made mosaic pieces out of shells, turquoise, and other precious and semiprecious gems. The setting they used for these pieces was gold. (See also METALLURGY; METALS, PRECIOUS.) They made such things as hand MIRRORS with mosaics on the back sides. In design, these mirrors resemble the hand mirrors of today. Goldsmiths also placed their mosaic works on beakers (see also KEROS), breastplates, and smaller objects such as ear plugs, a type of earring. Moche metallurgists of South America, whose culture flourished from 200 B.C. to A.D. 600, made very intricate pieces of jewelry with mosaics on them.

In North America the Hohokam of the present-day Southwest also made mosaics, inlaying turquoise on shells. The nobility of their culture wore these shells as necklaces.

In Mesoamerica, Alta Vista, the center of the Chalchihuites culture, was the site of the first Mesoamerican turquoise mine. These artisans made mosaic discs from turquoise, in addition to rings, beads, and pendants, which were primarily used for burials. Archaeologists believe that these items were traded with Teotihuacán, a large city in the central part of what is now Mexico. (See also CITIES, AMERICA'S FIRST.) The Toltec, whose culture arose in Mesoamerica in about A.D. 950, and the

Aztec, who established an empire in the same region in about A.D. 1100, also used mosaics to decorate objects. They set small pieces of turquoise, jade, and shell into stone or wood. The Maya, whose culture flourished in Mesoamerica from about 1500 B.C. until about A.D. 1500, were experts at making mosaics. One such work of art found by archaeologists in the Yucatán Peninsula at Chichén Itzá was made up of over 3,000 small stone pieces.

See also JEWELRY, TURQUOISE AND SILVER.

## Sources/Further Reading

Donnan, Christopher B. "Masterworks of Art Reveal a Remarkable Pre-Inca World." *National Geographic* 177 (June 1990): 17–33.

Driver, Harold E. *Indians of North America.* Chicago: University of Chicago Press, 1969.

Fagan, Brian M. *Kingdoms of Gold, Kingdoms of Jade: The Americas Before Columbus.* London: Thames & Hudson Ltd., 1991.

## mouthwash (precontact) *North American, Mesoamerican cultures*

Mouthwash is a liquid used as a breath freshener as well as a treatment for problems of the gums and the interior of the mouth. Precontact American Indians placed an emphasis on oral hygiene. This extended to all aspects of dental care and included using mouthwash.

Many tribes in northeastern North America used gold thread (*Coptis trifolia*) as a mouthwash. The therapeutic value of this plant comes from the alkaloid berberine, which it contains. This alkaloid, similar in nature to nicotine and morphine, eases pain. Indigenous people collected gold thread in the fall and used the roots to prepare mouthwash. The Pillager Chippewa (Anishinabe), Mohegan, Potawatomi, and Menominee people used it as a mouthwash for babies, rubbing it on their gums while they were teething, to ease the pain. People of the Menominee and Penobscot tribes also used gold thread as an astringent mouthwash and as a canker sore cure for both adults and children. The Penobscot chewed the stems of gold thread once such a sore began in order to retard its further growth and minimize its effect. Wherever this plant grew, the American Indians used it for the same purposes. Gold thread was so effective that early colonists in North America adopted it. WITCH HAZEL was also used as a mouthwash.

The Aztec of Mesoamerica used salt as a mouthwash and as a rinse for sore throats. The Aztec, whose knowledge and practice of DENTISTRY surpassed that of their European contemporaries, established their empire in about A.D. 1100.

See also HYGIENE, PERSONAL.

## Sources/Further Reading

Lust, John. *The Herb Book.* New York: Bantam Books, 1974.

Moerman, Dan. Native American Ethnobotany Database. URL: http://www.umd.edu/cgi-bin/herb.

Vogel, Virgil J. *American Indian Medicine.* Norman: University of Oklahoma Press, 1970.

Weiner, Michael A. *Earth Medicine, Earth Food: Plant Remedies, Drugs, and Natural Foods of the North American Indians.* New York: Fawcett Columbine, 1980.

## mukluks (precontact) *North American Arctic cultures*

Mukluks are soft boots made of reindeer or seal skin. This word was taken from the Inuit word *muklok,* which means "large seal." Indigenous people living in the Arctic regions employed a number of innovative strategies for keeping their feet warm. Many of these have been copied by modern footwear manufacturers and made from modern materials for today's outdoorspeople.

Mukluks were constructed not only of animal hides but of fish skin as well. The Alaskan Yuit sometimes made boots from chinook, or king salmon, skins. These were both lightweight and waterproof. When worn with woven grass socks or wadded grass liners, they kept the feet warm in sub zero temperatures. Hudson Strait Inuit men wore short boots over skin socks, but the women's boots were tall, resembling hip waders. According to early European explorers, women's mukluks were designed with tops large enough to carry a baby.

See also CRADLEBOARDS; CRAMPONS; MOCCASINS.

## Sources/Further Reading

Oswalt, Wendell. *Eskimos and Explorers.* Novato, Calif.: Chandler & Sharp Publishers, 1979.

Paterek, Josephine. *Encyclopedia of American Indian Costume.* Denver, Colo.: ABC Clio, Inc., 1994.

Powell, J. W. *Ninth Annual Report of the Bureau of Ethnology to the Secretary of the Smithsonian Institution 1887–88.* Washington, D.C.: Government Printing Office, 1892.

## multiple cropping See DOUBLE CROPPING.

## multiple family dwellings See APARTMENT COMPLEXES.

## mummies (ca. 5000 B.C.) *South American Andean, Mesoamerican cultures*

Mummies are dead bodies that have been embalmed (see also EMBALMING) and wrapped with layers of fabric in order to preserve them. Although the ancient Egyptians are the best-known mummy makers, the ancient Chinchoro, who lived in what is now Chile, made mummies in around 5000 B.C. (The Egyptians are believed to have begun mummifying bodies about the time of the First Dynasty in about 3100 B.C.) In addition to mummifying adults and children, the Chinchoro also mummified fetuses and embryos. The Moche, whose culture flourished in the Andean region of South America from about 200 B.C. to A.D. 600, made mummies as well, wrapping them in exquisitely woven burial cloths. (See also WEAVING TECHNIQUES.)

The Maya, whose culture flourished in Mesoamerica from about 1500 B.C. to about A.D. 1500, also mummified human remains, a practice that was closely tied to their religious beliefs. Although the Maya had no contact with the people of Egypt, their burial practices were remarkably similar. The mummies of Maya rulers were entombed in PYRAMIDS, which contained false chambers, similar to those of the Egyptian pyramids. Goods and servants were buried with them for their trip to the spirit world.

## Sources/Further Reading

Alva, Walter. "The Moche of Ancient Peru: New Tomb of Royal Splendor." *National Geographic* 177, no. 6 (June 1990): 2–15.

Mason, J. Alden. *The Ancient Civilizations of Peru.* New York: Penguin Books, 1988.

NOVA Online. *Ice Mummies of the Inca. Mummies of the World (2).* URL: http://www.pbs.org/wgbh/nova/peru/mumies/mworld2.html. Downloaded on January 17, 2000.

**murals** (ca. 1500 B.C.–A.D. 1500) *Mesoamerican cultures*
Murals are very large pictures that are painted on walls and sometimes ceilings. Mesoamerican artists developed mural painting independently of techniques created by other world cultures. The Chalchihuites, who lived in what is now the state of Durango, Mexico; the Aztec, whose empire arose in about A.D. 1100 in the Valley of Mexico; and other culture groups in Mesoamerica all painted murals. The Maya, however, are regarded as the most prolific and sophisticated Mesoamerican mural painters. (Maya culture arose in what is now Mexico in about 1500 B.C.) Some exquisite examples of their murals have survived into the present time.

One of the best-known archaeological sites with well-preserved murals is that of Bonampak in what is now Chiapas, Mexico. The murals at Bonampak were painted during the Late Classic Perid of Maya culture (A.D. 600 to A.D. 900). These vividly colored drawings depict the history and culture of the Maya people of Bonampak, including coronations and battles. Mural painters stopped their work in about A.D. 792, leaving the paintings unfinished. At about this time the death rate in the region overtook the birth rate, and following an unknown catastrophe, the city ceased to flourish. Another example of Maya murals are the battle scenes painted on the interior walls of the Upper Temple of the Jaguar at Chichen Itza. The Toltec, whose culture shortly thereafter fused with that of the Maya, founded Chichén Itzá in about A.D. 987.

Maya painters used five basic colors—black, blue, red, white, and yellow—for their murals. To obtain these colors, they used several minerals for paints. These included crushed hematite (iron-containing minerals), carbon (coal or ashes), and yellow ocher (mineral iron oxide). They used nopal cactus juice as a medium for mixing the pigments. The formula made an enduring paint that has lasted for more than a thousand years.

The important people portrayed in ancient Mesoamerican murals are often labeled, both by the insignia they are depicted wearing and by glyphs, or symbols, painted nearby. Many Mesoamerican murals contain speech scrolls, spiral designs emanating from the characters' mouths. Some anthropologists believe that these scrolls depict language. In the Aztec language Nahuatl, the word for "speech" is *tlenenepilli,* or "fire tongue." Murals, along with BOOKS, served as a way to record and preserve Mesoamerican history.

The Aztec covered both interior and exterior walls in their capital city of Teotihuacan with murals. Where murals had not been painted, surfaces were whitewashed. Father Juan de Torquemada, who traveled with Hernán Cortés, reported that the whitewash was polished "with pebbles and very smooth stones, and they looked as well finished and shone beautifully as silver plate . . . so smooth and clean that one could eat any morsel off them without a tablecloth and feel no disgust."

See also AMERICAN HISTORY, RECORDED; DYES; WRITING SYSTEMS.

## Sources/Further Reading

DeTorquemada, Juan. *Monarquia Indiana.* Madrid: 1616.

Fagan, Brian M. *Kingdoms of Gold, Kingdoms of Jade: The Americas Before Columbus.* New York: Thames and Hudson, Inc., 1991.

*Mesoamerican Encyclopedia.* URL: http://www.mesoweb.com. Downloaded on January 17, 2000.

*Mesoamerican Photo Archives: Bonampak.* URL: http://studentweb.tulane.edu/~dhixson/bonampak/bonampak.htm l. Downloaded on January 17, 2000.

Sharer, Robert J. *Daily Life in Maya Civilization.* Westport, Conn.: Greenwood Press, 1996.

Stuart, George E. "Mural Masterpieces of Ancient Cacaxtla." *National Geographic* 182, no. 3 (September 1992): 120–136.

Stuart, George E. and Gene S. Stuart. *The Mysterious Maya.* Washington, D.C.: National Geographic Society, 1977.

**muscle relaxants** See ANTISPASMODIC MEDICATIONS; CURARE.

**muscovy ducks** See DUCKS, MUSCOVY.

**musical instruments** (precontact) *North American, Mesoamerican, Circum-Caribbean, South American cultures*
Music was an important part of the lives of indigenous people throughout the Americas. For the most part they used instruments to accompany singing, but some precontact Americans played the flute and the hunting bow, a stringed

instrument, without vocal accompaniment. American Indians devised a number of percussion and wind instruments. Some of these, such as the drum and the PAN PIPES, were also invented independently by people in many parts of the world. For example, the Aztec tongue drum, the precursor of the modern marimba, is similar to the tone drum developed by indigenous Africans.

In North America, Indians of the Northwest Coast made drums by placing a plank over a pit in the floor. They used drums made from wooden boxes and rattles also made from wood. (See also CARPENTRY TECHNIQUES.) Some Northwest tribes played reed instruments that were shaped like tubes and contained one or more reeds. These instruments did not have finger holes. Indians of the Northwest Coast also used rattles that were made from rawhide that had been shaped and filled with pebbles. California tribes used foot drums in order to make music, as well as split-stick clappers and rattles made from turtle shells, gourds, large cocoons filled with pebbles, or deer hooves.

Indians of the Plateau Region and the Great Basin played music on the hunting bow. The bow player held the string of the bow in his teeth and struck it with a stick, changing the shape of his mouth to vary the tone. Archaeologists believe that the hunting bow is the only stringed instrument of the Americas.

Culture groups living in the North American Southwest played double-headed drums and foot drums and made rattles from gourds, turtle shells, and hollow horns. The Anasazi made hollow pottery shaped like sleigh BELLS that contained clay pellets. It is believed that the pattern for these POTTERY bells were the metal bells obtained through trade from Mesoamerican metalworkers. Anasazi culture flourished from about 350 B.C. to about A.D. 1450.

Indians of the Northeast made music with wooden kettle drums and cane flutes. Plains Indians used drums and wind instruments. They made whistles from eagle bones and flutes from cedar, as well as rawhide rattles.

In South America, musicians played pan pipes. They also made music with pottery ocarinas that were often double, triple, or quadruple barreled. Many of these ocarinas and whistles were shaped in the form of animals. In addition, early South American potters made clay pots that when filled with water and moved, produced whistling sounds. The Moche, whose culture arose in what is now Peru in about 200 B.C., made tambourines and gongs.

Inca musicians had flutes called *quenas*. (The Inca Empire was established in the Andean region of what is now Peru in about A.D. 1000.) These flutes were made of reed or bone and could produce up to five notes. The Inca also developed another unique musical instrument—a short, ceramic trumpet. It had no finger holes, but they could control the tones they made by an innovative piece of musical technology that demonstrated a knowledge of ACOUSTICS. The hole through the center of the trumpet doubled back on itself, making an S-shape. This allowed the short trumpet to produce deeper tones than one with a straight hole. Another instrument of the Inca was the *chilchil,* a copper disk that was hit with two sticks. This resembled the cymbals of modern musicians.

More is known today about Aztec and Maya music than that of any other Mesoamerican culture group because they portrayed musicians on MURALS, which they painted on the walls of their major cities, such as the murals at Bonampak, a Maya city in what is now the state of Chiapas, Mexico. (Maya culture flourished in Mesoamerica from about 1500 B.C. to about A.D. 1500. The Aztec Empire was established in what is now Mexico in about A.D. 1100.) The Maya and Aztec played trumpets shaped like tubes. These were often more than two feet long and were made of clay, wood, or cane. Sometimes they added a gourd to the tube to serve as a resonator. (This is known as a mute today.) Mesoamerican musicians also made trumpets from conch shells, which were used for both military and religious purposes. The Aztec made flutes of reed, bone, or clay. These flutes had mouthpieces and up to five holes. Aztec musicians played pan pipes as well as ocarinas and whistles made from baked clay. They also played rasps made of notched bone. They produced and played metal timbrels and bells. The tone of instruments and bells were very important to the peoples of precontact Mesoamerica, who devoted much time developing alloys to produce bells with different tones. They also understood that tone depended on the size of bells.

The Aztec considered drums sacred. Perhaps the most well-known Aztec instrument today is the *teponaztli,* a drum that was shaped like a barrel and made with five tongues. When struck with rubber-tipped mallets, produced different tones. (See also LATEX.) This instrument served as the inspiration for the modern marimba. In addition to *teponaztli,* the Aztec made drums with hide heads that could be tuned. These were both single- and double-headed. Aztec musicians also used small kettle drums that they beat with their hands.

After conquest, Spanish priests in Mesoamerica and South America banned traditional music in an attempt to eradicate religious practices. Within a short time, indigenous people were singing in Latin. Except for some ethnographic recordings of North American Indian Plains and southwestern music, the musical tradition of indigenous Americans was not an object of extensive study by ethnographers for many years. One reason for this is that they assumed that all music produced by American Indians was similar and that the Plains and southwestern music represented all North American tribes. Another reason was that the musical compositions created by indigenous Americans were very different from those of the European music traditions. Most songs are pentatonic (consisting of five tones) melodies consisting of chains of major and/or minor thirds. Ethnologists, who judged the music throughout the Americas as being "off key" and offensive according to their own tastes, refused to give it serious study.

Despite the harsh judgments of ethnographers, the indigenous people of North America, Mesoamerica, and South America continued using their instruments to make music. Today, with the popularity of world music, people throughout the world are finally having the opportunity to enjoy native music of the Americas.

See also MARACAS; METALLURGY.

## Sources/Further Reading

Driver, Harold E. *Indians of North America.* Chicago: University of Chicago Press, 1969.

Hassrick, Royal B. *The Sioux.* Norman: University of Oklahoma Press, 1964.

Mason, J. Alden. *The Ancient Civilizations of Peru.* Rev. ed. New York: Penguin Books, 1988.

Morris, Craig and Adriana von Hagen. *The Inka Empire and Its Andean Origins.* New York: Abbeville Press Publishers, New York, 1993.

Salmoral, Manuel Lucena. *America 1492: Portrait of a Continent 500 Years Ago.* New York: Facts On File, 1990.

Whitley, David S., ed. *Reader in Archaeological Theory: Post-Processual and Cognitive Approaches.* New York: Routledge, 1998.

## names, place   See PLACE-NAMES.

## nasturtiums  (*Tropaeolum tuberosum*)  (precontact)
*South American Andean cultures*

Nasturtiums are commonly grown as decorative plants in gardens throughout the world today. They are indigenous to South America. These short, soft-stemmed, climbing plants produce flowers that are yellow, orange, or scarlet in color. The plants are called *mashua* or *anu* in Quecha, the language of both the Quecha, who were contemporaries of the Inca, and the Inca, whose empire was established in about A.D. 1000 in the Andean region of what is now Peru.

The Quecha cultivated the plants, which are high in vitamin C, for food. They and other South American culture groups ate the roots as a vegetable after boiling them. Often they used freeze-drying to preserve nasturtium blossoms. South American Indians also used peppery-flavored nasturtium leaves in salads. This practice spread to Europe, where the flowers were grown in royal gardens. U.S. president Thomas Jefferson grew nasturtiums in the garden at his home, Monticello. By the late 1700s cooks were using nasturtium blossoms to flavor butter, cream cheese, or vinegar. Today nasturtiums are grown by gardeners primarily as ornamentals and as a form of natural pest control, since the plants contain a substance that repels aphids.

See also FREEZE-DRYING; DAHLIAS; MARIGOLDS; POINSETTIAS.

### Sources/Further Reading
Coe, Sophie. *America's First Cuisines.* Austin: University of Texas Press, 1994.
Glimmer, Maureen. "New World Nasturtiums." *Plants Profiles.* URL: www.gardenforum.com/nasturtiums.html. Downloaded on January 17, 2000.

Parsons, James A. "Southern Blooms: Latin America and the World of Flowers." *Queen's Quarterly* 99, no. 3 (1992): 542–561.

## needle knitting   See KNITTING, NEEDLE.

## needles  (ca. 8000 B.C.)   *North American Northwest, South American Andean cultures*

Needles that are used for sewing are slender in order to pierce fabric or leather. They have an opening in one end, called an eye, to carry thread or sinew. In the Americas, the oldest sewing needle with an eye was invented by Paleo-Indians, the first American Indians in the New World. Archaeologists found this needle in the area that is now Washington state. When it was carbon dated, this bone needle was discovered to be 10,000 years old.

South American Andean Indians, expert metalworkers, developed a copper sewing needle with an eye for thread between A.D. 800 to A.D. 1100. This was invented independently of similar needles used in Europe. Before creating the copper needles, they had used needles made from other materials. One of their primary uses of needles was for a technique called needle knitting that resembled what is called the buttonhole stitch today.

See also KNITTING; PINS, STRAIGHT.

### Sources/Further Reading
Benson, Elizabeth P. *The Maya World.* New York: Thomas Y. Crowell Company, 1967.
Canby, Thomas Y. "The Search for the First Americans." *National Geographic* 156, no. 3 (September 1979): 330–363.
Driver, Harold E. *Indians of North America.* Chicago: University of Chicago Press, 1969.

Mason, J. Alden. *The Ancient Civilizations of Peru*. Rev. ed. New York: Penguin Books, 1988.

**nixtamalization** See HOMINY.

**nurses, nursing** (ca. A.D. 1100–A.D. 1519)
*Mesoamerican cultures*
A nurse is an individual who is trained to care for the ill and who works under the supervision of a physician. The Aztec, whose empire was established in what is now Mexico in about A.D. 1100, built HOSPITALS. Maintained by the government, these medical centers were staffed by both doctors and nurses. Then, as now, the nurse was a vital component of the medical team.

In the Aztec world the field of nursing was highly organized and well defined. Several categories of nurses existed, depending on their level of training and field of specialization. One group of nurses tended patients in the hospitals, working with the surgeons, physicians, herbalists (the equivalent of today's pharmacists), and a type of doctor that would be considered an internist today. These nurses administered medications and provided various treatments prescribed by the doctors.

Midwives, who were responsible for working with pregnant women, were called *tepalehuiani*, which meant to "help some one" in Nahuatl, the Aztec language. The first line of treatment provided by the midwife was usually therapeutic massage (see also THERAPEUTIC TOUCH) or a steambath before administering medications (see also STEAM ROOMS). Once the baby had been born, the mother would undergo a steam bath.

Another type of nurse/midwife had more advanced training but was not as well trained as a physician. This nurse was called *temixihuitiani*, which means "to give birth *or* to cause someone to give birth" in Nahuatl. This nurse was the equivalent of the nurse practitioner today. When the *temixihuitiani* encountered complications with a pregnancy that were beyond her range of knowledge and training, she would call in the *tic-itl*, or physician, to help her.

See also MEDICINE; OBSTETRICS; HYGIENE, PERSONAL.

**Sources/Further Reading**
Frederiksen, Thomas H. *Aztec Student Research Guide, Aztec Medicine-Aztecs of Mexico, History.* http://northcoast.com/~spdtom/a-med.html. Downloaded on January 30, 2000.
North Seattle Community College. *Surgery and Related Techniques.* URL: http://nsccux.sccd.ctc.edu/~continued/distance/nacescience/ surg.html revised. Copyright January 14, 1997.
Vogel, Virgil J. *American Indian Medicine*. Norman: University of Oklahoma Press, 1970.

**nutrition** (precontact) *North American, Mesoamerican, Circum-Caribbean, South American cultures*
Nutrition is the science of food and nutrients and the relationship of these two elements to health. Nutrition affects not only health per se but also stature, lifespan, and the ability to reproduce. American Indians—both the culture groups that practiced AGRICULTURE and those that practiced hunting and gathering—tended to be more adequately nourished than the average European peasant of the era. Anthropologist Harold Driver noted, "The meat and fish eaten by Indians contained an abundance of protein, fat, mineral salts, and vitamins, including ascorbic acid [vitamin C] in raw meat and blood." Although American Indians who practiced agriculture did not ingest as much protein as the hunters and gatherers did, they compensated by combining CORN and BEANS in their diets, two foods that when eaten together provide a complete protein. The result impressed a 16th century conquistador who wrote of the Aztec: "The people of this land are well made, rather tall than short. They are swarthy as leopards . . . skillful, robust, and tireless, and at the same time the most moderate men known." When the foods American Indians ate were introduced to other parts of the world—including Europe, Asia, and Africa—health improved and population increased in those areas.

One reason for the high quality of American Indian nutrition was the sheer variety of foods available. Although diets varied from tribe to tribe, Indians of North America ate BISON and game, including turkeys (see also TURKEY BREEDING); berries, including CRANBERRIES, BLUEBERRIES, and STRAWBERRIES; chenopod, or goosefoot; marsh elder, or sumpweed; SUNFLOWER seeds, PUMPKINS, HICKORY nuts, PECANS, JERUSALEM ARTICHOKES, PAWPAWS, PEANUTS, corn, beans, and SQUASH.

In addition to corn, beans, and squash, the Mesoamerican and South American diet consisted of white POTATOES, SWEET POTATOES, TOMATOES, CHILE peppers, sweet peppers, JICAMA, MANIOC, PAPAYAS, PASSION FRUIT, PINEAPPLES, AVOCADOS, BRAZIL NUTS, CASHEWS, CHOCOLATE, and the super grains AMARANTH and QUINOA. The Aztec, whose empire was established in about A.D. 1100 in what is now Mexico, ate BLUE-GREEN ALGAE, or spirulina, a nutrition-packed substance sold in health food stores today as a food supplement.

In contrast, under the best of conditions European diets were limited to asparagus, beets, Brussels sprouts, cabbage, carrots, celery, chard, watercress, cucumbers, garlic, onions, leeks, lettuce, parsnips, peas, radishes, spinach, turnips, barley, wheat, and rye. Except for root vegetables, which were stored underground, most European commoners subsisted on bread and pease porridge, a gruel made from dried peas, throughout the winter. Some families were able to keep a cow that furnished milk, but meat was not generally eaten. With the advent of the feudal system, European royalty established huge game parks or preserves in order to furnish game for their consumption and for sport hunting. These preserves were off-limits to peasant hunters, who were severely punished for poaching.

In Europe diseases such as goiter, an iodine deficiency (see also GOITER PREVENTION), and scurvy, a vitamin C deficiency (see also SCURVY CURE) were common. Among American Indians these diseases were rare. Coastal Indians ate seaweed, which is high in iodine. Culture groups living inland ate sunflower seeds, which also contain significant amounts of iodine.

In Mesoamerica, sea salt, an important TRADE item, provided iodine in the diet. When fresh sources of vitamin C were not available, American Indians made teas of bark, leaves, and dried herbs that provided this important nutrient.

TOMATOES, which are indigenous to the Americas and were cultivated by American Indians in South America and Mesoamerica, are only one of the American Indian food gifts to the world that serve as preventative medicines. In the late 1990s a Cornell University researchers identified two cancer-fighting substances in tomatoes—P-courmaric and chlorogenis acids. Both inhibit the body's production of cancer-causing compounds formed in the body from nitrates, a common ingredient in cured meats. Tomatoes are also high in lycopene, an antioxidant related to beta carotene, another cancer-fighting compound. According to one recent study, people who ate seven or more servings of tomatoes a week reduced their chances of developing colon or rectal cancer by 69 percent.

Even when the nutritional value of certain foods was not readily apparent, American Indians found technologies to make them edible. Manioc, a dietary staple of Circum-Caribbean and South American Tropical Forest culture groups, is an example of this food-processing sophistication. In its raw state, manioc, a root crop that is indigenous to the South American tropics, is poisonous. Only when it has been heated or fermented is it safe to eat. By devising the process to detoxify manioc, indigenous people of the Americas were able to add an important nutritional resource to their diets, and eventually to the diets of people living in many parts of the world.

The acorn processing practiced by California culture groups is another example of this ingenuity. American Indians ate the acorns of 27 out of the 60 varieties of oak trees in North America. In their natural state, acorns, although high in starch and fat, are also high in tannic acid, which has a bitter taste and in large quantities is toxic. Indians devised ways to process acorn meal to remove the tannic acid. California Indians, for example, processed acorns by cracking them open and grinding the nutmeats. Next, they placed this meal in a depression made in a sandy stream bank. They would pour water dipped from the stream onto the meal. As the water drained away, it leached out the tannic acid. Acorn meal that had been treated in this manner made up more than half of their caloric intake.

Differences in the social systems between Europe and the Americas before contact also contributed to the disparity in nutrition between American Indians and the people who eventually conquered them. In Europe at the time of conquest, the peasantry made up 85 percent of the population. When food shortages occurred, starvation was a fact of life for the lower class. This stands in direct contrast to the social welfare system that operated informally in North and Mesoamerica and formally in the Inca Empire that was established in what is now Peru in about A.D. 1000. The indigenous people of the Americas made certain that everyone in their tribe or band had food when it was available, even those who were too old or disabled to work. (See also DISABILITY RIGHTS.)

In addition to sharing what food they had, American Indians devised strategies to guard against famine. One of these,

intercropping, or COMPANION PLANTING, involved planting a number of food crops in the same plot. Often several plantings were made of the same crop, such as corn, to maximize the chances of a successful harvest. This practice was called DOUBLE CROPPING, or multiple cropping. American Indian farmers also practiced ZONED BIODIVERSITY, planting crops in several fields that would provide a variety of growing conditions. Surplus crops were stored as famine insurance. (See also CROP STORAGE.) They taught these strategies to the early colonists in the Americas, who had little idea about how to farm in their new environment.

Early conquistadores and explorers returned to Europe with samples of indigenous American foods ranging from tomatoes and potatoes to the muscovy duck. (See also DUCK, MUSCOVY.) The population of Europe increased sharply after the introduction of foodstuffs that were part of the American Indian diet. One of the most dramatic instances of this occurred in Ireland, where the population increased from 1.5 million to 9 million between 1760 and 1840 with the introduction of the potato, a crop that grew even in poor soil and had high caloric value. A 500- to 800-yard-long strip of potato plants could feed a family for a year. Because the Irish peasantry came to rely solely on potatoes, a series of crop failures caused by plant disease led to widespread famine in the mid-1800s. Potatoes, spread by Spanish and Portuguese explorers, also became a staple food in Asia, although not to the extent they had become in Ireland.

After corn, or maize, was introduced to Europe, it became a dietary staple there. As the Irish peasantry had relied on the potato, Italian peasants and workers soon relied on corn for a major part of their caloric intake. Italy was one of the few places in Europe where corn was seen as fit for human consumption. Polenta became a popular dish. Because they did not use nixtamalization, an American Indian process for treating corn so that amino acids would be more readily absorbed by the body, many developed the vitamin deficiency known as pellegra—a disease American Indians did not suffer. (See also HOMINY.)

Europeans not only grew in number because of improved nutrition, but those who migrated to North America grew in stature as well. In Medieval England, the average height for males was between 5'6" and 5'7". This was also the average height of early American colonists in North America. "By the time of the American Revolution, native-born whites appear to have achieved nearly modern heights," writes historian Carolyn Freeman Travers. This conclusion is based on Revolutionary military records. Although the increase in height may to some extent have occurred because of an expanded gene pool, it may have happened because of an increase in caloric intake and better nutrition, conditions that would not have been possible without the food contributions from indigenous peoples of the Americas.

The contribution of American Indians to the world's nutrition is a legacy that is ongoing. Today three-fifths of the food crops currently in cultivation in the world are indigenous to the Americas. Most were cultivated by American Indians.

See also ACHIOTE; ALLSPICE; AQUACULTURE; BARBECUES; BEEKEEPING; BISON; BLACK WALNUTS; BLACKBERRIES; CACAO; CARAMEL CORN; CASSEROLES; CATTAILS; CHIA; CLAMBAKES; CORNBREAD; CORNMEAL; CORN, PARCHED; CORN SYRUP; DUMPLINGS; FARINA; FARMING, TERRACED; FOOD COLORING; FOOD PRESERVATION; FREEZE DRYING; GUAVA; GUINEA PIGS; INSTANT FOODS; JERKY; MAPLE SYRUP AND SUGAR; OR-CHARDS; PAPRIKA; PEMMICAN; PEPPERS, SWEET OR BELL; PER-SIMMONS; POPCORN; PRICKLY PEAR CACTI; SAPODILLA; SNACK FOODS; SUCCOTASH; TAMALES; TORTILLAS; VANILLA; YAMS.

## Sources/Further Reading

California Tomato Growers Association. *Tomatoes are Healthy, Versatile and Delicious.* URL: http://www.tomato.org. Downloaded on July 6, 1998.

Coe, Sophie. *America's First Cuisines.* Austin: University of Texas Press, 1994.

Driver, Harold E. *Indians of North America.* Chicago: University of Chicago Press, 1969.

Hobhouse, Henry. *Seeds of Change: Five Plants that Transformed Mankind.* New York: Harper & Row, 1986.

Hurt, R. Douglas. *Indian Agriculture in the Americas: Prehistory to Present.* Lawrence: University Press of Kansas, 1988.

National Museum of Natural History, Smithsonian Institution. *Seeds of Change: Readings on Cultural Exchange After 1492.* New York: Addison-Wesley, 1992.

Travers, Carolyn Freeman. *Were They Shorter Back Then? Plymouth Plantation.* URL: http://www.plimoth.org/Library/l-short.htm. May 29, 1998.

Weatherford, Jack. *Indian Givers: How the Indians of the Americas Transformed the World.* New York: Fawcett Columbine, 1988.

## observatories, astronomical (ca. A.D. 800)

*Mesoamerican, South American Andean, North American*
*Southwest and Plains cultures*

Observatories are structures that are designed and equipped for the purpose of observing astronomical events. Mesoamerican and South American Andean astronomers constructed towers from which they could watch the movements of the planets as well as observe other astronomical features and events. Although culture groups throughout the world observed the planets and stars and recorded their movements, the stone structures of the Mesoamerican and South American Andean culture groups are significant because they show the emphasis these early astronomers placed on making clear and accurate observations. In North America, as well, the Anasazi, whose culture flourished in the Southwest of North America from about 350 B.C. to about A.D. 1450, built structures with windows aligned for the observation of celestial events. The Pawnee, a North American Plains culture group, used their EARTH LODGES as observatories.

Maya astronomers used fixed locations, such as temples, to observe the sun, moon, planets, and stars at the horizon by placing crossed sticks along the line of sight. (The Maya culture arose in Mesoamerica in about 1500 B.C.) The constellation Sirius was an important part of the Mesoamerican cosmology, as was Venus, a planet whose movements the Maya both recorded and predicted in CALENDARS and ALMANACS. The Maya also used astronomical observations to plan buildings (see also ARCHITECTS) as well as cities (see also URBAN PLANNING).

The Caracol in Chichén Itzá is an example of a Maya building with astronomically aligned windows. Chichen Itza, an important Maya culture center, was built during the Maya Post Classic period during the early 10th century A.D. The tower structure of the Caracol reminds modern observers of a domed observatory, because crumbling walls have given a domelike shape to what once was a cylindrical upper tower. The building originally consisted of a lower and an upper tower situated on a high stone platform. The roof of the upper tower has a large opening that could have been used for making astronomical observations. In 1975 archaeoastronomers Anthony F. Aveni and Horst Hartung surveyed the site and suggested that ancient astronomers used the structure to observe the planet Venus. The Maya, as well as other Mesoamerican culture groups, used Venus to set times for ceremonies and as a divination tool.

Another Maya site that has been suggested as an observatory is one at Uaxactun consisting of temples and a pyramid that were built during the early Maya Classic period in what is now the Guatemalan jungle. Many archaeoastronomers also believe that a Maya tower at Palenque in the modern-day state of Chiapas in Mexico was an observatory because of astronomical glyphs (see also WRITING SYSTEMS) on the inside walls. Structures at Uxmal, a Maya city in the Yucatán Peninsula of what is now Mexico that was built between A.D. 800 and A.D. 1400, have also been found to be aligned to form site lines to the rising and setting of celestial features important to Maya cosmology.

Some archeoastronomers believe that a stone structure in South America called the Torreon, which was built at Machu Picchu, is also an astronomical observatory. Machu Picchu served as a main city of the Inca Empire. (The Inca established an empire in what is now Peru in about A.D. 1000.) Part of this structure, which is built on a natural rock outcropping 2,000 feet above a river, is rectangular and has straight walls. The east wall, however, is curved in such a way that it separates the structure into an outer hall and an inner chamber. In 1980, when astronomers Ray White and David Dearborn from the Steward Observatory in Tucson, Arizona, measured the windows and studied the building's orientations, they found that one of the windows centered on the sunrise that would occur during the summer solstice. A stone structure in the room had been carved to make a vertical surface perpendicular to the window. Some archaeologists now believe that this stone may have served as some sort of astronomical equipment that enabled ancient Inca astronomers to make their observations.

Other astronomers are skeptical about the function of the Torreon as well as the Maya structures to the North, despite extensive surveys showing the alignment of windows toward the rising and setting of planets. They argue that such surveys are circumstantial, and because the Maya and Inca recorded their history in glyphs, which are open to various interpretations, no certain conclusions can ever be drawn about the function of the Mesoamerican and South American stone towers.

In North America the Anasazi built a kiva called Casa Rinaconda in the Chaco Canyon area of what is now New Mexico. This kiva, built in about A.D. 1100, has windows and niches that, when surveyed, have been found to align with the summer solstice. Pawnee earth lodges built on the North American plains also served as observatories. The lodges were built to represent the cosmos, with the domed roof symbolizing the sky and the four main posts symbolizing the stars. The fireplace was said to be the sun. Pawnee astronomers watched the changing planets and constellations through the smoke holes in the roofs of their earth lodges.

See also ASTRONOMY; STONEMASONRY TECHNIQUES.

## Sources/Further Reading

Aveni, A. F., ed. *Archaeoastronomy in the New World: American Primitive Astronomy.* London: Cambridge University Press, 1982.

Beecher, Kenneth and Michael Feirtag, eds. *Astronomy of the Ancients.* Cambridge, Mass.: Massachusetts Institute of Technology Press, 1980.

Hoskin, Michael, ed. *Cambridge Illustrated History of Astronomy.* New York: Cambridge University Press, 1997.

Krupp, E. C. *Echoes of the Ancient Skies: The Astronomy of Lost Civilizations.* New York: Harper and Row, 1983.

———, ed. *In Search of Ancient Skies.* New York: Doubleday & Company, 1978.

**obstetrics** (precontact) *Mesoamerican, North American Northeast and Northwest cultures*
Obstetrics is a branch of medicine concerned with pregnancy and birth. American Indians developed many techniques to help with the birth process. These included prenatal care, labor induction, remedies for stopping uterine bleeding, pain relief, and a massage technique for expelling the placenta that is used by doctors throughout the world today. Mesoamerican physicians are known to have performed cesarean sections, the extraction or birth of a fetus by surgical means. Precontact Mesoamerican POTTERY depicts physicians performing cesarean sections, a technique invented independently from that practiced earlier by the Romans. In general, New World obstetric practices were much more advanced than those of Europe during the Middle Ages, when earlier medical knowledge was ignored. Dr. Ian Carr, a professor of pathology wrote,

"These skills largely disappeared during the Dark Ages; there is little record of obstetric practice after this until early modern times."

The Aztec, whose empire was established in about A.D. 1100 in what is now Mexico, viewed prenatal care as extremely important. A trained midwife (see also NURSES, NURSING) visited the expectant mother during the sixth month of pregnancy. The midwife provided instructions to the mother-to-be about how to care for herself and the child she carried. Aztec midwives also gave their clients a steam bath and washed them. (See also STEAM ROOMS.) Pregnant women lay on their backs in the steam bath while being massaged. If the midwife learned that the fetus was in a breech position (the reverse position for a normal birth), she repositioned it by manipulating it externally. Before delivery, the midwife would again take the mother into the steam bath for washing and massaging. If the mother experienced difficulty with labor, the midwife administered an herbal oxytocic to hasten the birth. The oxytocic used by the Aztec was *Montanoa tomentosa,* which not only strengthened the mother's contractions but also helped to prevent excessive postpartum bleeding. (The Cherokee of the North American Southeast used *Cicutamaculata* for these purposes; the Quinault of the North American Northwest used *Cnicus benedictus.*)

North American Indians who lived in the Northeast used the plant blue cohosh (*Caulophyllum thalictroides*) as an obstetric aid. Some of these tribes were the Mesquaki, Chippewa (Anishinabe), Potawatami, and the Menominee. Blue cohosh is indigenous to North America and generally found in the eastern half of what is now the United States. American Indian healers dried and then powdered roots and rhizomes (horizontal stems growing beneath the ground) of this plant. When needed, the powder was steeped in water to make a tea. This tea was analgesic and relieved the pain of labor. It also acted as a sedative (muscle relaxant) and as an antiseptic. (See also ASEPSIS.) In addition, American Indians used blue cohosh as an ANTISPASMODIC MEDICATION to relieve menstrual cramps. Blue cohosh was so effective and valued that colonists began using it as a remedy for "female troubles." Blue cohosh remained a popular herbal remedy among non-Indians into the 20th century and is still sold in health food stores.

In modern medicine the use of massage in order to aid the expulsion of the placenta from the mother's uterus after giving birth is called Crede's method. Although the procedure is credited to Karl Crede, a Frenchman who lived in Germany in the 1800s, it was first used by American Indians hundreds of years before Crede discovered it. In *American Indian Medicine,* medical historian Virgil Vogel cites evidence for this: "Dr. George Engelmann, whose study of labor among primitive peoples was first published in 1883, regarded the obstetrical methods of primitive tribes as more reasonable than those used among civilized people. He described massage and manipulation techniques used in various tribes for the expulsion of the fetus and afterbirth which were in his own time just beginning to be adopted in white medicine." Engelmann asserted that many of these techniques had "been recently rediscovered by learned men, clothed in scientific principle and given to the world as new."

See also MEDICINE; PHARMACOLOGY.

## Sources/Further Reading

Carr, Ian. *Some Obstetrical History. Dying to Have a Baby: The History of Childbirth.* URL: http://www.umanitobe.ca/outreach/manitoba_womens_health/hist1a.ht m. Downloaded on February 1, 2000.

Hutchens, Alma R. *Indian Herbology of North America.* Boston: Shambhala, 1991.

North Seattle Community College. *Surgery and Related Techniques.* URL: http://nsccux.sccd.ctc.edu/~continued/distance/nacescience/ surg.html revised. Copyright January 14, 1997.

Vogel, Virgil. *American Indian Medicine.* Norman: University of Oklahoma Press, 1970.

Weiner, Michael A. *Earth Medicine, Earth Food: Plant Remedies, Drugs, and Natural Foods of the North American Indians.* New York: Fawcett Columbine, 1990.

**ocarinas**  See MUSICAL INSTRUMENTS.

## optical technology, basics of  (ca. 1700 B.C.–400 B.C.)  *Mesoamerican cultures*

Optics is the science of light refraction and reflection. The Olmec, whose culture arose in the Yucatán Peninsula of what is now Mexico in about 1700 B.C., produced a SOLAR FIRE STARTER that utilized optics to concentrate reflected sunlight. An even more fascinating aspect of this device was its capability of projecting images onto another surface. In his book *America's First Civilization,* archaeologist Michael Coe discusses the construction of this optical device. "The reflecting surfaces are concave, and it has been found that they had been ground, by a totally unknown process, to optical specifications, being just slightly parabolizing in curvature (the radius of curvature grows progressively greater as the edge is approached)," he writes. Coe, who discusses the ability of the solar firestarter to project images onto a surface several feet from it, also speculates that this optical device may have been used to project an image into a cave from an outside position. The ability to grind such a surface shows an extremely high level of sophistication, considering the TOOLS that were available to the Olmec. The ability to make the device symmetrical is astounding.

## Sources/Further Reading

Coe, Michael D. *America's First Civilization: Discovering the Olmec.* Eau Claire, Wisc.: E.M. Hale And Company, 1968.

Fiedel, Stuart J. *Prehistory of the Americas.* Cambridge England: Cambridge University Press, 1987.

Hurst, David, Jay Miller, Richard White, Peter Nabokov, and Philip Deloria. *The Native Americans.* Atlanta: Turner Publishing, Inc., 1993.

**oral contraception**  See CONTRACEPTION, ORAL.

## orchards  (precontact)  *North American Northeast and Southeast, South American, Mesoamerican cultures*

Orchards are fields devoted to the cultivation of fruit or nut trees. Indians throughout the Americas cultivated fruit and nut trees. For example North American Indians cultivated HICKORY and PECAN trees, in addition to PAWPAW trees. American Indians living in Mesoamerica and South America grew more extensive orchards that included a number of varieties of trees.

The Inca, whose culture arose in what is now Peru in about A.D. 1000, cultivated a number of fruit trees. Except for PASSION FRUIT, many of the fruits they grew are not widely known outside of Peru and Bolivia today. One of these fruits, the pepino, is now marketed in the exotic foods section of large grocery stores. It is similar in shape and size to an eggplant, is reddish in color, and has a tough skin. The flesh inside is yellow-colored and sweet.

Mesoamerican farmers cultivated CASHEWS as well as GUAVA, PAPAYA, SAPODILLA, and sapote trees. The sapote (*Casimiroa edulis*), is a sweet football-shaped fruit that weighs one to three pounds.

Besides planting formal orchards, the Maya, whose culture arose in what is now Mexico in about 1500 B.C., surrounded their homes with fruit trees. Spanish explorers, including Hernandez de Cordoba, described their extensive orchards. The Maya grew CACAO in areas where it was not native, planting the trees in limestone sinkholes so they could have the moisture and nutrients they needed. In addition to growing fruits commonly eaten today, such as papayas and AVOCADOS, the Maya grew a number of other types of fruits in their orchards. Although these fruits are still eaten in Mexico, they did not cross the Atlantic. The Aztec, who established an empire in what is now Mexico in about A.D. 1100, also planted orchards.

When the Spaniards colonized the Yucatán Peninsula, they forced the Maya to move near the towns they had built around churches. To encourage them to relocate, they not only burned their old towns but also cut down the fruit trees. The justification they gave for destroying the orchards was that sometimes the fruit produced there was fermented to make intoxicating drinks. Spanish priests reportedly believed that the devil, in the form of worms and snakes, lived in the drinks and that these creatures ate the souls of the Maya.

See also AGRICULTURE; PINEAPPLES.

## Sources/Further Reading

Coe, Sophie. *America's First Cuisines.* Austin: University of Texas Press, 1994.

Driver, Harold E. *Indians of North America.* Chicago: University of Chicago Press, 1969.

Hurt, R. Douglas. *Indian Agriculture in the Americas: Prehistory to Present.* Lawrence: University Press of Kansas, 1988.

**orthopedic techniques** (ca. 1000 B.C.) *North American Great Plains and Great Basin, Mesoamerican, South American Andean cultures*

Orthopedics is the branch of medicine that deals with diseased or injured bones. American Indians in North America, Mesoamerica, and South America reduced, or set, bone fractures, breaks, and dislocations long before contact with Europeans. They were skilled not only in using traction but also in using open reduction, performing SURGERY to set bones. North American Indians were among many who reduced fractures and used posterior splints to keep the injured limb immobilized.

The oldest American culture group known to have practiced orthopedic medicine are the ancient surgeons who lived in what is now Peru and performed TREPHINATION, a form of brain surgery, in about 1000 B.C. This procedure involved drilling a hole into the skull, then covering the resulting opening with specially made plates. The surgeons hammered gold into thin sheets and cut it to the size that they needed, then placed the plate under the scalp and over the opening to protect the wound while it healed. The Moche, who lived in what is now Peru from about 200 B.C. to A.D. 900, made POTTERY showing people with amputated limbs.

The Aztec of Mesoamerica, whose empire was established in about A.D. 1100, also performed amputations and made prosthetic devices. Perhaps the most sophisticated orthopedic technique they invented was the use of INTERMEDULLAR NAILS, or surgical pins, a technique Western physicians neither understood nor used until the 20th century. The Aztec used simple PULLEYS to perform TRACTION AND COUNTERTRACTION, a technique of applying tension or pressure to each end of a bone in order to reduce bone breaks and fractures. The first Spaniard conquistadores to witness this technique recorded it. According to Bernard Ortiz de Montellano, an expert on Aztec medicine, the Aztec physicians' treatment of broken bones was ". . . possibly the most advanced aspect . . ." of their medicine.

North American Indians also used traction and countertraction and made posterior splints, a technique the Shoshone, Dakota, Lakota, and Nakota all used. These splints were half-casts that were placed on the posterior of the leg after the bone had been set. They were made of rawhide that had been soaked in water to make it very pliable. The patient would place his or her leg on top of the wet rawhide, and the healer would then make a cast that fit the shape of the leg being reset. After the rawhide dried, the healer placed this support on the posterior of the injured leg, then attached it to the leg with sinew or strips of leather. When the leg had healed, the partial cast was removed.

Other tribes used splints as well. Sometimes they used splints to immobilize the back, making partial casts for the back from bark and cutting holes into it so that the Indian surgeon could watch the progress of the healing. These back splints covered the body between the armpits and the hips and were wrapped with sinew or leather strips. American Indians also used wet clay and poultices, as well as plasters made of down, resin, rubber, and gum. These casts dissolved naturally by the time the bones had healed. The American Indians' expertise moved one non-Indian medical observer to write, "Their skill in the care of wounds, fractures and dislocations equaled and in some respects exceeded that of their white contemporary."

## Sources/Further Reading

Ortiz de Montellano, Bernard R. *Aztec Medicine, Health, and Nutrition.* New Brunswick, N.J.: Rutgers University Press, 1990.

Peredo, Miguel Guzman. *Medical Practices in Ancient America.* Mexico City: Ediciones Euroamericanas, 1985.

Soustelle, Jacques. *Daily Life of the Aztecs on the Eve of the Spanish Conquest.* Stanford, Calif.: Stanford University Press, 1961.

Vogel, Virgil. *American Indian Medicine.* Norman: University of Oklahoma Press, 1970.

Weatherford, Jack. *Indian Givers: How the Indians of the Americas Transformed the World.* New York: Fawcett Columbine, 1988.

# P

**pain medications** See ANESTHETICS.

**pan pipes** (ca. 1000 B.C.–200 B.C.) *South American Andean, North American Southeast cultures*
Pan pipes are hand-held wind instruments that consist of a series of graduated pipes bound together side by side. The different lengths of the pipes produce different tones or pitches. The number of pipes a pan pipe had would vary. The more pipes it contained, the more tones it could produce. American Indians invented pan pipes independently from those made by the Asians or Greeks. Indians made pan pipes in different sizes and of various materials, including ceramic, wood, reed, cane, and copper. They also used gold and silver, but these instruments were reserved for the nobility. Pan pipes were most prevalent in pre-Peruvian South American cultures. The invention of this instrument demonstrates a working knowledge of musicology and of a pitch scale.

The Chavin people of South America made pan pipes. Chavin culture arose in what is now Peru in about 900 B.C. Archaeologists found a 15-pipe ceramic Nazca pan pipe that was made in one solid piece. (The Nazca culture existed in what is now Peru from 600 B.C. to A.D. 900.) Most pipes were laced together. The Inca, who established their empire in what is now Peru in about A.D. 1000, also made pan pipes.

Ancient American Indians of the southeast area of what is now Florida possessed copper pan pipes between 500 B.C. and A.D. 350. They obtained their copper products through TRADE with the southern area of present-day Great Lakes region. (See also METALLURGY.) Today the Andean people continue to create music with pan pipes that is enjoyed throughout the world.

See also MUSICAL INSTRUMENTS; TRADE.

## Sources/Further Reading

Melanich, Jerald T. *Florida's Indians from Ancient Times to the Present: 12,000 Years of Florida's Indian Heritage.* Gainesville: University Press of Florida, 1998.

Morris, Craig and Adriana von Hagen. *The Inka Empire and Its Andean Origins.* New York: Abbeville Press Publishers, 1993.

von Hagen, Victor W. *Realm of the Incas.* New York: New American Library, 1957.

**papayas (*Carica papaya*)** (precontact) *Mesoamerican, Circum-Carribean cultures*
Papayas are fleshy, succulent fruits that grow on large plants indigenous to the tropics of South and Mesoamerica. Although these plants resemble trees, they are technically classified as herbs because their stems are not as woody as those of true trees. Of the 22 species of papaya that exist, five are edible. Indigenous people in the Circum-Caribbean region cultivated papayas for hundreds of years before Columbus landed. The Maya, whose culture arose in what is now Mexico in about 1500 B.C. planted the trees in their extensive OR-CHARDS. High in vitamin C, the pear-shaped fruits, which are botanically classified as berries, were eaten both fresh and cooked.

Both papaya leaves and unripe papaya contain papain, an enzyme that breaks down protein in meat, making it more tender. It is not known whether American Indians used papaya as a marinade, as is done today. In addition to eating papayas for the nutrition they provided, American Indians used them for MEDICINE. The fresh leaves sometimes served as a wound dressing, and indigenous peoples drank papaya juice as a digestive aid. (See also INDIGESTION MEDICATIONS.) Papain, the enzyme that breaks down meat, is reported to have a similar effect on venom, so sometimes even today fresh papaya is rubbed on insect bites. (See also INSECT BITE AND BEE STING REMEDIES.)

In the mid 1500s Spaniards and Portuguese took papaya seeds to what are now Panama and the Dominican Republic. Soon afterward, sailors carried them throughout the world, including to India, Malaysia, and the Philippines. From India papaya seeds were carried to Florida. In English-speaking Europe the fruits were called pawpaws. This causes them to sometimes be confused with the North American PAWPAW (*Asimina triloba*). By the 1900s, papayas were grown commercially in Florida and Hawaii. Today the fruits are enjoyed throughout the world. Commercially, papain is used as a meat tenderizer and as an additive to beer to keep it clear when it is chilled. Papaya extract is also used for exfoliative cytology in the treatment of stomach and colon cancer. Papaya enzyme tablets are sold in health food stores as a digestive aid.

## Sources/Further Reading

Coe, Sophie. *America's First Cuisines.* Austin: University of Texas Press, 1994.

Gepts, Paul. *The Crop of the Day.* URL: http://agronomy. ucdavis.edu/GEPTS/pb143/crop/papaya/. Downloaded on September 4, 1999.

*Papayas.* URL: http://eddie.mannlib.cornell.edu/instruction/ horticulture/H415/ species/papaya/overview/papaya.html. Downloaded on September 4, 1999.

## paper (ca. 1000 B.C.) *Mesoamerican cultures*

*Paper* is a term for thin sheets of a substance made of fiber. It is usually intended to be written or drawn upon. The Maya and later the Aztec of Mesoamerica wrote on cloth and deerskin and carved hieroglyphs into stone, but more commonly they used paper. (Maya culture arose in about 1500 B.C.; the Aztec Empire was established in about A.D. 1100.) Mesoamericans used paper not only for writing but for religious ceremonial purposes as well.

Mesoamerican paper was invented independently of that which comes from other parts of the world. Most of the paper manufactured by the Maya and Aztec was made from the inner bark of the wild fig tree (*Ficus*) or the amate tree. The Aztec called this paper *amate.* In Mesoamerican cultures paper was in such high demand that communities devoted to the art of making it sprung up in the areas where these trees were prevalent. Different towns manufactured different types of paper, including sheets of paper and yellow paper that was made in rolls. Much of the paper that was produced ended up as BOOKS.

In the mid-1500s botanist Francisco Hernandez observed various papers being made in the town of Tepoztlán and recorded his observations. Archaeologists believe that the process he described is the same one that Mesoamericans had used as early as 1000 B.C. According to Hernandez, papermakers first stripped bark from trees with stone knives and then soaked it in running water so that the sap would coagulate. After scraping off the sap, they boiled the bark in an alkaline solution so that the fibers separated. When this had been done, papermakers arranged the fibers on a wooden drying board, where they were pounded with a beater, a grooved basalt stone attached to a handle. Beating the fibers made them pliable and fused them together into sheets.

When the sheets of paper had dried, they were trimmed and polished with a heated stone to close the pores and burnish the surface. Next, papermakers applied white lime sizing (a starch or stiffener) to both sides of the paper. Because Mesoamerican paper is not made from pulp, as Asian and European paper was, it is sometimes classified as something other than "true" paper. Technical distinctions aside, Mesoamerican paper was of high quality. Hernandez commented that the Aztec paper he saw being made was whiter and thicker than that being made in Europe at the time. The basic method for making *amate* is still used in parts of Mexico today.

## Sources/Further Reading

Smith, Michael E. *The Peoples of America: The Aztecs.* Cambridge, Mass.: Blackwell, 1996.

von Hagen, Victor Wolfgang. *The Aztec: Man and Tribe.* New York: The New American Library, Inc., 1961.

## paprika, American Indian influence on (ca. A.D. 1513) *Mesoamerican, South American Andean cultures*

Paprika is a spice that is an essential ingredient in Hungarian and Yugoslavian cuisine. It is also used to color and flavor food in other countries. Paprika is made from a number of varieties of pepper pods; its color depends on the types of pepper used. The mild, and even sweet, paprika manufactured or sold outside of Eastern Europe is the most popular. Hungarian paprika for domestic consumption is made in several grades, from mild to hot. This spice owes its existence to sweet and chile peppers that were originally cultivated by American Indians in South America and Mesoamerica. (See also CHILES; PEPPERS, SWEET OR BELL.)

After conquest, both the Spanish and Portuguese colonizers spread pepper cultivation throughout the world. Ottoman Turks, who had obtained red chiles as early as 1513 during the siege of the Portuguese colony at Hormuz in the Persian Gulf, carried them to Eastern Europe from the Balkans. Hungarians, who began grinding dried peppers as a seasoning for food, called the spice *paprika,* a variation on a slavic term for "pepper." Today paprika is manufactured in California, Spain, Morocco, Bulgaria, and in other parts of Europe in addition to Hungary.

## Sources/Further Reading

American Spice Trade Association. *Capsicum Spices and Oleoresins.* URL: http://astaspice.org/sp_cap.htm. Downloaded on August 6, 1999.

Sokalow, Raymond. *Why We Eat What We Eat: How the Encounter Between the New World and the Old Changed the Way Everyone on the Planet Eats.* New York: Summit Books, 1991.

Weatherford, Jack. *Indian Givers: How the Indians of the Americas Transformed the World.* New York: Fawcett Columbine, 1988.

## parched corn See CORN, PARCHED.

**parkas** (precontact) *North American Arctic and Subarctic cultures*

Parkas—loose-fitting, hooded jackets—were invented by the Inuit people who lived near the Arctic Circle. The parka has been adopted by non-Indians and has become a popular and fashionable winter-wear design throughout the world. Although the design is an American Indian invention, the word *parka* is of Russian origin given to this unique style of jacket. *Parka* in Russian means "reindeer fur coat." The Inuit call a parka an *anorak*. Caribou and seal skins provided the most common material used to make Inuit parkas, but polar bear and fox furs, ground squirrel pelts, and even the skins of birds were also used to make them.

Worn by native people from Greenland to Alaska long before contact with Europeans, parkas varied in length from mid-thigh to ankle length. The main purpose of parka construction and design was to provide warmth for the wearer. To that end, in winter two parkas were usually worn, one with the fur facing in and the other with the fur facing out. The layering allowed for air circulation and also provided better insulation. The Inuit often made the inner garment of young caribou or sealskin to provide softness for the wearer. Caribou fur, one of the most popular liners, has hollow hairs, providing high thermal efficiency, even in the coldest of temperatures. Parka makers sometimes lined the garments with cormorant or puffin skins with the feathers left on, a technique that produced the same effect as today's duck, goose, or eider down jackets. When entire parkas were made from bird skins, the seams were insulated with ermine, caribou, or mountain goat fur that served as a barrier against the wind.

A garment's ability to conserve body heat means nothing if the article of clothing becomes wet and evaporation quickly lowers the wearer's body temperature. Sealskin by itself is relatively water-repellent, but Inuit hunters improved on it further by making parka covers from Chinook salmon skins and wearing these over parkas during snow or rain. (See also WATERPROOFING.) Inuit living in some areas pieced together parka covers from whale bladders or intestines, or from the skin of a whale's tongue. Although European contact brought many changes to Inuit life, hunters kept their parkas and parka covers, long after the introduction of trade cloth because they worked better at keeping out cold and dampness than factory-made imports.

The parka's hood made this style of jacket ideal hunting attire. Because the hood was close-fitting, it left vision unobstructed. Since it was attached to the jacket, it did not blow away in the wind the way a hat would have done. The parka's construction featured broad shoulders, enabling a full range of arm movement and allowing a hunter to pull his arms into the body of the garment for added warmth. Often hunters dressed in caribou fur parkas, not only to keep warm but also to pursue caribou. By the same token, a seal hunter might wear a sealskin parka while seal hunting—a strategy that Inuit hunters used for CAMOUFLAGE and to help themselves identify with their prey. George Best, who served as an officer on Englishman Martin Frobisher's expeditions to

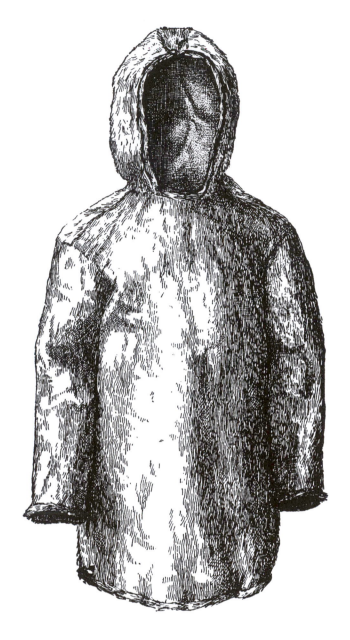

The Inuit of the North American Arctic invented the parka, a style of jacket worn today. They often made these jackets from caribou or seal skin but used other materials as well, including bird skins. *(U.S. Bureau of Ethnography)*

locate a Northwest Passage in the late 16th century, wrote of the Inuit, "They are good fishermen, and in their small boats, and disguised with their sealskin coats, they deceive the fish, who take them for fellow seals rather than deceiving men."

The Inuit designed women's parkas slightly differently than those made for men. Women's parkas were made with a pouchlike recess on the back in the inside for carrying an infant, who was supported by a strap around the mother's chest. This pouch was called an *amaut*. Mothers carried their infants in this baby carrier for the first two to three years of their lives.

(See also CRADLEBOARDS.) The larger hoods on women's parkas allowed air to circulate, and the broader shoulders allowed a mother to move the child to breastfeed it without exposing it to the cold.

See also MUKLUKS.

## Sources/Further Reading

Driscoll, Bernadette. *The Spirit Sings: Artistic Traditions of Canada's First Peoples.* Toronto: McClelland and Stewart, 1987.

Josephy, Jr., Alvin M., ed. *America in 1492: The World of the Indian People Before the Arrival of Columbus.* New York: Random House, 1991.

Oswalt, Wendell. *Eskimos and Explorers.* Novato, Calif.: Chandler & Sharp Publishers, 1979.

Paterek, Josephine, Ph.D. *Encyclopedia of American Indian Costume.* Denver: Colo.: ABC Clio, Inc., 1994.

## parrot breeding  (macaw breeding)  (A.D. 850)
*Mesoamerican, North American Southwest, South American Tropical Forest cultures*

Parrots are brightly feathered birds that belong to the Psttacidae family. In addition to brilliant plumage, they have large heads and strong bills. Over 300 species of parrots are native to the tropical zones throughout the world, including South and Mesoamerica, Africa, Malaysia, Australia, and New Zealand. The macaw, a very large species of parrot indigenous to South America, can grow as large as three feet long. Macaws have brilliant feathers that are colored red, yellow, blue, or green. Other types of parrots once lived on Caribbean islands, but these birds are now extinct. American Indians in South America, Mesoamerica, and North America valued parrot feathers, especially those of the macaw, and used them in their FEATHERWORK. Both the Maya and the Aztec are believed to have bred macaws. (Maya culture flourished in the Yucatán Peninsula in what is now Mexico from about 1500 B.C. to A.D. 1500. The Aztec established their empire in what is now Mexico in about A.D. 1100.)

Macaw feathers were an important TRADE item. Archaeologists have found a macaw breeding area as far north as a large Anasazi-style settlement in Chihauhua, Mexico. (The Anasazi culture arose in the North American Southwest in about 350 B.C. and flourished until about A.D. 1450.) Archaeologists believe that this breeding area was either designed to produce macaws for local use or for trade with people living further north. Although both macaw feathers and bones have been found in Anasazi sites in the American Southwest, including Pueblo Bonito at Chaco Canyon in what is now New Mexico, no immature macaw bones have been uncovered there. This absence leads archaeologists to theorize that, although both birds and feathers were traded, the Anasazi living at Chaco Canyon and other sites throughout the North American Southwest did not breed macaws. Many speculate that these feathers and birds were traded sometime in the 11th century by southern merchants for turquoise (see also JEWELRY, TURQUOISE

AND SILVER) and BISON robes. Because depictions of macaws have been found on POTTERY dated to A.D. 850, they believe that intermittent trade must have taken place at least shortly before that time.

The Maya and Aztec also valued the quetzal (*Pharomachrus mocinno costaricensis*), a bird that, although not a parrot, has brilliantly colored iridescent blue and green plumage. The quetzal received its name from the Aztec. In Nahuatl, the Aztec language, this name means "feathers, precious and beautiful." The Maya considered the quetzal a sacred symbol and traded its feathers to the Inca, who lived in the Andes of what is now Peru, 3,000 miles to the south. Inca civilization arose in about A.D. 1000.

Christopher Columbus brought back stories of the bird long before the birds themselves were brought to Europe. Today macaws and quetzals have become popular as exotic pets in many parts of the world. Eight of the 18 species of macaws are endangered as a result of both capture for the commercial trade and the loss of habitat that has come from the destruction of the tropical rain forest. The quetzal is also endangered.

See also FANS.

## Sources/Further Reading

Mathien, F. J. *Mesoamerican Themes and Chaco Canyon.* URL: www.colorado.edu/Conferences/chaco/mesomod.htm. Downloaded on January 21, 2000.

Minnis, P. A., M. E. Whalen, J. H. Kelley, and J. D. Stewart. "Prehistoric Macaw Breeding In The North American Southwest." *American Antiquity* 58, no. 2 (1993): 270–276.

Trigger, Bruce. *The Cambridge History of the Native Peoples of the Americas: North America (Vol. 1, Part 1).* Cambridge, England: Cambridge University Press, 1996.

## passion fruit  (precontact)  *South American Andean and Tropical Forest cultures*

Passion fruit (*Passaflora*) are fruit-bearing, climbing vines that are native to the tropical regions of what are now Brazil and Ecuador. Their fruit is orange and green or purplish and similar in size and shape to a chicken egg. It contains a sweet, gray pulp and thousands of tiny seeds. Food for both people and animals in the tropical rainforest for years before European contact, passion fruit was also used as a medicine. Indigenous people used it as a heart tonic, an asthma treatment, and as a calmative. The Inca, whose culture arose in about A.D. 1000 in the Andean region of South America and expanded to the tropics in the 1400s, cultivated passion fruit vines. More than 200 types of passion fruit have been classified. Today *Passiflora quadrangularis* is the variety most commonly sold in grocery stores. Passion fruit juice has also become a popular tart/sweet ingredient in fruit juice blends.

Many people mistakenly assume that passion fruit received its name because it is an aphrodisiac. Actually Portuguese explorers, who were Catholic, named the plant because they thought that parts of the flower resembled the crown of thorns, the five wounds, three nails, and the lashes—all symbols of Christ's crucifixion, or passion.

Today passion fruit is grown in warm climates worldwide, including Australia, New Zealand, California, Florida, and Hawaii, as well as in Brazil, Ecuador, Colombia, and Peru. The market for the fruit is growing as it becomes an ever more popular component in juice drinks because of its high acid content, distinct flavor, and pleasing aroma. In the mid-1990s the demand for passion fruit drove prices to double and even triple those previously paid.

## Sources/Further Reading

Coe, Sophie. *America's First Cuisines.* Austin: University of Texas Press, 1994.

Herbst, Sharon Tyler. *The Food Lover's Companion.* 2nd ed. New York: Barron's Educational Services, Inc., 1995.

Smith, Nigel, et. al. *Tropical Forests and Their Crops.* New York: Comstock Publishing, 1992.

**patent medicines** See MEDICINES, PATENT, AMERICAN INDIAN INFLUENCE ON.

**pawpaws (*Asimina triloba*)** (precontact) *North American Northeast and Southeast cultures*

The pawpaw is the only tropical tree that grows in temperate zones. Sometimes called the Indiana, or poor man's, banana, this deciduous tree is native to the hardwood forests of the eastern part of North America, ranging from what is now Florida to the southern part of Ontario. It grows as far west as Nebraska. Pawpaw trees produce flowers of up to two inches across. In the fall these flowers produce oblong fruit with a flavor that some have compared to a cross between bananas and VANILLA custard. Others describe the taste as a blend of mango, PAPAYA, and banana flavors. Although the pawpaw fruits are small—from 1 1/4 to 6 inches long and 1 1/4 to 4 inches wide—they are the largest fruits produced by a tree native to what is now the continental Unted States.

American Indians from a number of tribes cultivated pawpaw trees for their fruit, in addition to gathering wild pawpaws from river bottoms, where the trees flourished. When cultivated, pawpaw trees produce many more fruits than wild trees do. The name *pawpaw* is derived from the Spanish word *papaya,* another tropical fruit indigenous to the Americas. Spanish explorer Hernando de Soto was the first European to encounter pawpaws. On his 1540 exploration of the Southeast, he observed that American Indians cultivated the trees. About 200 years later John Bartram, an American botanist, sent pawpaw specimens to England. Europeans and North American colonists showed little interest in the trees and the fruit they produced until about 1800. Although pawpaws were not grown commercially, probably due to the relatively short shelf life of the fruit without refrigeration, eventually the pawpaw became a popular garden tree. In the mid-1900s, however, interest in the tree again diminished because of the availability of many varieties of fruit in supermarkets. Today agronomists are taking another look at the pawpaw, not only for its potential as a fruit-producing tree, but because of substances in the tree's twigs called *annonaceous acetogenins,* which are currently used to develop cancer-preventing drugs and pesticides.

See also GARDENS, BOTANICAL; ORCHARDS.

## Sources/Further Reading

Glick, Barry. *Pawpaw: A Tropical Tree for the Temperate Zone.* URL: http://www.au.gardenweb.com/cyberplt/plants/pawpaw.html. Downloaded on November 5, 1999.

Layne, Desmond. *New Crop FactSheet. Purdue University Center for New Crops and Plant Products.* URL: http://www.hort.purdue.edu/newcrop/cropfactsheets/pawpaw.html. Downloaded on November 5, 1999.

Reich, Lee. "Uncommon Fruits." *Mother Earth News* (February/March 1998).

Weatherford, Jack. *Indian Givers: How the Indians of the Americas Transformed the World.* New York: Fawcett Columbine, 1988.

**peanuts (ground nuts, *Atachis hypgea*)** (ca. 3900 B.C.) *South American Tropical Forest, Circum-Caribbean, North American Southeast cultures*

Not true nuts, peanuts are classified as legumes and are part of the same family as beans and peas. When the blossoms drop from low-growing peanut bushes, stems that will eventually bear pods droop to the ground. Penetrating the soil, these stems, or pegs, remain there until the pods form and ripen. Botanists believe that peanuts originated in the South American semiarid region in what is now Brazil. No wild peanut varieties have been found any place outside of South America. The ancestors of the Arawak people cultivated peanut plants on Caribbean Islands as early as 5,000 years ago. Indigenous peoples in South America grew peanuts as well. Pre-Inca people living in the Andean region of what is now Peru are believed to have obtained the plant from what is now Brazil and were growing them as early as 3,900 to 2,500 B.C. Archaeologists have uncovered plazas covered with peanut shells. Peanuts are depicted on ancient Peruvian POTTERY dating back 3,500 years; some of these pots are shaped like peanuts. Along the semiarid western coast of Peru, jars of peanuts have been found buried with pre-Inca MUMMIES.

Spanish explorers observed peanuts being cultivated by American Indians as far north as what is now Mexico. (They are believed to have been grown in Tehuacan in about A.D. 500.) Initially, the Spaniards did not like the taste of this new food. Fernandez de Oviedo y Valdez, who wrote *La Historia general y natural de las Indias,* published in Seville in 1535, said peanuts were mediocre. Other early European explorers claimed they gave people headaches.

In the 1500s Portuguese explorers took peanuts to Asia and West Africa, along with CORN and SWEET POTATOES. They began cultivating these foods in Africa in order to produce crops that would feed the African slaves they had begun to ship throughout the world. From this beginning, peanuts became an important part of the diet of indigenous West Africa people. The peanuts grown in the North American South today were reintroduced to the continent from Africa.

After their introduction to the American South, peanuts did not immediately become an important crop. Generally considered fit for only hogs and slaves to eat, they were not eaten in any great amounts until the Civil War, when food shortages abounded. By the late 1800s peanuts were on their way to becoming the popular snack food they are today. In the early 1900s black chemist George Washington Carver encouraged farmers to plant them, in addition to sweet potatoes—another American Indian crop—in order to diversify from cotton and to revitalize the South's economy, which had not rebounded from the Civil War. Repeated plantings of TOBACCO had also depleted the soil, whereas peanuts improved soil quality due to the nitrogen-fixing nodules in their roots. Carver found more than 300 uses for peanuts, including a coffee-like beverage, ink, dyes, wood stains, insulation, and the most famous—peanut butter.

Per ounce, peanuts contain more protein than steak. Their high fat and carbohydrate content provides energy; four-fifths of the fats contained in them are unsaturated. Peanuts contain niacin and vitamin E as well as a bioflavonoid called *reservatrol*, which is believed to lower cholesterol. In some countries today they are eaten as a fresh vegetable. Although peanuts became an integral part of the cuisines of Africa and Asia, they never became popular in Europe except as a source of oil and animal food.

Today people in North America prefer their peanuts roasted, or roasted and ground to make peanut butter. Peanut oil is also used in salad dressings and for cooking. The parts of the peanuts that remain after processing are used as animal feed. Various parts of peanut plants are used to make other nonfood products as well, including products such as metal polish, bleach, detergent, axle grease, face creams, shaving cream, rubber, cosmetics, paint, shampoo, and medicine. Shells are used for fireplace logs, wallboard, and kitty litter. The peanut industry contributes about $4 billion annually to the U.S. economy.

## Sources/Further Reading

Coe, Sophie. *America's First Cuisines.* Austin: University of Texas Press, 1994.

Forest Preserve District of Cook County, Illinois. *Nature Bulletin* No. 254 A. January 28, 1967.

*The Natural Food Guide to Common Nuts.* URL: http://www.naturalhub.com/natural_food_guide_nuts_common.htm. Downloaded on September 26, 1999.

Weatherford, Jack. *Indian Givers: How the Indians of the Americas Transformed the World.* New York: Fawcett Columbine, 1988.

## pecans (precontact) *North American Southeast cultures*

Pecan trees (*Carya pecan*) are native to the southern United States and northern Mexico. They produce nuts with a thin shell and large meats. The word *pecan* comes from the Algonquian word *pakan*, or *pagan*, which translates as "bone shell." These nuts were a staple in the diet of southeastern American Indian people who used them to season HOMINY and corn cakes as well as for the basis for a drink. Indian people also extracted the oil from pecans and used it as a thickener for venison soups and stews.

American Indians first gathered the nuts from wild trees and later planted pecan trees to ensure a steady harvest. Spanish explorer Alvar Núñez Cabeza de Vaca, who was shipwrecked on the gulf coast and remained with the Indians in the area of what is now Texas from 1528 to 1535, reported that the indigenous people camped and harvested nuts along the rivers where pecan trees grew every fall. According to Cabeza de Vaca, pecans were a major source of food for them for at least four months of the year. (Shelled, pecans can be stored for about three months. Left whole, they remain fresh for about six months.) A member of Hernando de Soto's crew later reported that Indians living in the Mississippi River Valley also relied on pecans for food.

Pecans are a high-quality food source. They provide vitamin E, unsaturated fats, and an omega-3 fatty acid. They are also high in potassium, thiamin, zinc, copper, magnesium, phosphorous, niacin, folic acid, iron, and vitamin $B_6$. Today pecans are used in cooking and baking. They are an important part of U.S. southern cuisine, including pecan pie.

See also AGRICULTURE, HICKORY.

## Sources/Further Reading

Flexner, Stuart Berg. *I Hear America Talking: An Illustrated History of American Words and Phrases.* New York: Simon and Schuster, 1976.

*Pecan History.* URL: http://www.texaspecans.com/history.htm. Downloaded on September 26, 1996.

Trager, James. *The Food Chronology: The Food Lover's Compendium of Events and Anecdotes from Prehistory to Present.* New York: Henry Holt, 1995.

## pemmican (precontact) *North American Great Plains and Northeast cultures*

Pemmican, a combination of dried meat and animal fat, was used as a high-energy trail food for American Indian travelers in many parts of North America. It was an important source of calories, iron, and vitamin C during the wintertime, especially on the North American plains. Made from pounded dried meat, or JERKY, and tallow, pemmican was sometimes flavored by the addition of dried berries and nuts. The word *pemmican* comes from the Cree word *pimikkan*, derived from *pimmi*, which means "fat" or "grease." It came into the English language in the late 1700s. Each Great Plains tribe had a slightly different recipe and called the food by a different name.

Once Indians had dried the meat and pulverized it, they mixed it with dried fruit and put it into rawhide bags. Next they poured enough fat over the dried meat to thoroughly coat it. They sewed the bags shut, and before the fat congealed they walked on the bags to compress the pemmican, squeezing out the air and making the packages more convenient to store. Prepared and packaged in this way, pemmican could last for years. Frontier reports exist of 30-year-old pemmican that had not spoiled.

Although not all Europeans who ate pemmican, which they named "Indian bread," liked it, many did enjoy it and recognized its usefulness. When carrying pemmican it was not necessary to stop and hunt to fill one's stomach. European trappers, traders, and soldiers called pemmican bags "pieces" and traded with the Indians for them at forts and posts. In the early 1800s a trader at a post on the Saskatchewan river in what is now Canada said that even men used to eating eight pounds of meat a day could be satisfied with a pound and a half of pemmican. He recommended it as a provision for the army or navy.

In time pemmican making became a booming business for American Indians and non-Indians alike. In 1845 the Saskatchewan District in Canada alone supplied 1,100 bags of pemmican weighing 90 pounds each to provision brigades throughout the Hudson Bay Company's territories as well as supply hunters and travelers. The Plains Indians provided much of this pemmican, but workers at Fort Edmondton in the Saskatchewan District manufactured it as well, melting grease on kitchen wood stoves and mixing it with meat in large wooden troughs. Pemmican has been termed one of the most effective ways of food processing ever devised.

See also FOOD PRESERVATION, SNACK FOODS.

## Sources/Further Reading

"The Buffalo Culture of the Plains Indians." *The Wind River Rendezvous* 13, no. 2 (Spring 1983).

Bell, Selden. Cornell University, Wilson Lab. "Pemmican: Recipes, Stories & Stores." Updated October 14, 2000. URL: http://www.ins.cornell.edu/~seb/pemmican.html.

Flexner, Stuart Berg. *I Hear America Talking: An Illustrated History of American Words and Phrases.* New York: Simon and Schuster, 1976.

## peppers, chile See CHILES.

## peppers, sweet or bell (7000 B.C.) *Mesoamerican, South American, Circum-Caribbean cultures*

Sweet peppers, like CHILES, are indigenous to tropical areas of the Americas. They belong to the capsicum family but lack the gene that produces capsaicin, the substance that causes the hot taste in chile peppers. American Indians began cultivating peppers about 7000 B.C. The sweet peppers that Christopher Columbus brought back from his voyages to the Caribbean Islands were incorporated quickly into Spanish and then Italian cuisine.

Some varieties of sweet peppers include the yellow banana pepper and the Cubanelle. The best known type of sweet pepper is the green bell pepper, which turns red if left on the vine to full maturity, becoming sweeter than when it was green. Sweet peppers grow in many colors from green to orange, yellow, and purple. The pimento, a large, heart-shaped variety of sweet pepper, is often cut into strips and canned or bottled. It is also used to stuff olives.

As chiles do, sweet peppers contain high amounts of vitamin C and fair amounts of vitamin A as well as smaller amounts of calcium, phosphorus, iron, thiamin, riboflavin, and niacin.

See also PAPRIKA.

## Sources/Further Reading

Coe, Sophie. *America's First Cuisines.* Austin: University of Texas Press, 1994.

Herbst, Sharon Tyler. *The Food Lover's Companion.* 2nd ed. New York: Barron's Educational Services, Inc., 1995.

## persimmons (precontact) *North American Northeast and Southeast cultures*

American persimmon trees (*Diospyros virginiana*) produce a small, round fruit that is sweet to the taste when ripe and is burnt-orange in color. Some people have described the jelly-like pulp of the persimmon as being similar to the flavor of honey. Growing up to 40 feet tall, these trees are indigenous to what is now the United States from the Gulf Coast to Pennsylvania. They grow as far west as Illinois. American Indians gathered and ate wild persimmon fruits. Often they dried them in order to preserve them throughout the winter. (See also FOOD PRESERVATION.) American colonists borrowed the name for these fruits from the Cree word *pasimian,* which means "dried fruit."

High in vitamin C and containing 70 percent of the required daily dosage of vitamin A, persimmons were a valuable addition to the diet of indigenous Americans. (See also NUTRITION; SCURVY CURE.) American Indians ate persimmons fresh and made them into drinks, in addition to drying them. Persimmons did not become very popular with American colonists, perhaps because the fruit has an extremely sour taste until it is completely ripe. The persimmons that are grown commercially today originated in Asia and have larger fruits than American persimmons. The fruits of the variety indigenous to the Americas, although smaller than the Asian variety, are said to have a richer taste. Because ripe persimmons are soft and do not ship well, they continue to be a specialty item in grocery stores.

## Sources/Further Reading

Flexner, Stuart Berg. *I Hear America Talking: An Illustrated History of American Words and Phrases.* New York: Simon and Schuster, 1976.

The Food Museum. "Persimmon." URL: http://www.swcp.com/hughes/persim.htm. Downloaded on February 23, 1999.

Reich, Lee. "Uncommon Fruits." *Mother Earth News* (February/March 1988).

**personal hygiene** See HYGIENE, PERSONAL.

**petroleum** (A.D. 1415) *North American Northeast cultures*
Petroleum is a naturally occurring liquid that is made up of organic chemicals called hydrocarbons. It is formed beneath the ground when plant and animal sediments come under pressure. The mineral parts of these sediments harden into rocks, while the organic portion becomes the substance known as petroleum. One of the forms that petroleum in its natural state can take is crude oil. Credit for the first discovery of oil in the United States is usually given to Edwin L. Drake, who drilled an oil well in Titusville, Pennsylvania, in 1859. Although Drake is given the credit, he was not the first to dig for oil. American Indians had sunk pits in the ground in that area to collect oil seepage over 400 years earlier.

American Indians also dug oil pits in other parts of the region, but the Pennsylvania excavations are the ones that have been most studied by archaeologists. The pits that Indians dug in the Oil Creek flats of Pennsylvania's Allegheny region show evidence of a sophisticated oil-collecting endeavor. These pits are from 15 to 20 feet deep and are circular, square, and oblong in shape. American Indians walled the collection pits that they dug with vertical timbers that had been cut with stone axes. This reinforced the walls in order to prevent them from collapsing. In 1998 one of these timbers was carbon dated to A.D. 1415–40; however, researchers believe it is possible that excavating for oil began much earlier. Ladders made by carving notches into pine tree trunks have also been found in the pits, as well as collecting devices made from tree twigs and branches. Leaves and clay probably served as filters.

J. A. Caldwell reported in his *Caldwell's Illustrated Combination Atlas of Clarion Co., Pennsylvania,* published in 1877: "From the number of pits and their systematic arrangement, petroleum was doubtless obtained in considerable quantities." Unable to admit that American Indians were capable of such advanced technology, he said the pits were the work of "a race of people who occupied the country prior to the advance of the Indian tribes."

The first European to mention the presence of oil in Pennsylvania was the British General Montcalm, who passed through the area on his way to Fort Duquesne in 1750. He observed Seneca Indians performing a ceremony on Oil Creek and noted that they had set fire to the oil that seeped from the ground. The Seneca and other Iroquois used oil to fuel ceremonial fires and as a protective lotion for the body, much like today's petroleum jelly. (See also SUNSCREENS, MEDICINAL.)

American Indians were also reported to have believed that oil had medicinal benefits. The first American oil that was exported by the conquistadores from Venezuela in 1539 was a gift to the Holy Roman Emperor Charles V to treat his gout. The rumored medicinal powers of petroleum attracted the interest of Europeans. What came to be called "Seneca oil" was sold primarily by pharmacists, or chemists, and used for flesh wounds and rheumatism. Enterprising non-Indians also sold oil, which they called snake oil, as a patent medicine. (See also MEDICINES, PATENT, AMERICAN INDIAN INFLUENCE ON.)

In addition to collecting oil in pits, American Indians "panned" for oil on the creek, skimming it off the surface. In 1772 a frontier trader had reported that they also used feathers to skim oil from the surface of the water. While this may seem like a primitive method of oil collection by today's standards, it was advanced for its time. Non-Indians used a similar method for collecting oil, which they called *naptha,* from Oil Creek by dipping blankets in the water and wringing them out. The price for oil, which was still used primarily for medicinal purposes, was between $4 to $5 a gallon by 1790.

It is interesting to note that Edwin Drake, who began drilling after the invention of the kerosene lamp in 1854 had created a huge demand for "black gold," first tried a similar method to that of the Seneca and other Iroquois. Although he dug a shaft, the walls kept caving in—the same problem the American Indians had faced with their pits. The next year he began drilling a well, yet he still experienced cave-ins. His invention of pounding a drive pipe into the ground to keep the shaft walls from collapsing led to his success.

Precontact California Indians also collected petroleum in the form of ASPHALT from tar pits near what is now Los Angeles. They used it as waterproofing and caulking.

**Sources/Further Reading**

Chevron. *What Is Crude Oil?* URL: http://www.chevroncars.com/know/crude/index.html. Downloaded on November 6, 1999.

*Geological Survey and History of Petroleum in Clarion and Adjoining Counties.* URL: http://www.public.usit.net/mcnamara/clarion/oil1.htm. Downloaded on March 3, 1999.

Pees, Samuel T. *Oil History: Precolumbian Mining.* URL: http://oilhistoryu.com/gathering/precolumbian/precolumbian.html. Downloaded on November 6, 1999.

Weatherford, Jack. *Indian Givers: How the Indians of the Americas Transformed the World.* New York: Fawcett Columbine, 1988.

**petroleum jelly** See PETROLEUM; SUNSCREENS, MEDICINAL.

**peyote** (*Lophophora williamsii*) (ca. 8000 B.C.)
*Mesoamerican, North American Southwest cultures*
Called *peyotl* in Nahuatl, the language of the Aztec, peyote is a small, flowering cactus that is native to the Chihauhuan Desert region of what is now Mexico and the extreme southern part of what is now Texas. Some of the alkaloids contained in this plant have psychoactive properties. A number of culture groups indigenous to the areas near where peyote grew used it before contact with Europeans. Research associate Nkechi Taifa and legislative counsel research associate Sam Mistrano writing in support of H.R. 4230, A Bill Pro-

viding the Native American Use of Peyote in 1996, reported that anthropologists date the religious use of peyote back 10,000 years. The Olmec, whose culture arose in the Yucatán Peninsula in what is now Mexico in about 1700 B.C., carved images of the peyote cactus on large stone items, which would indicate that they valued the plant. Succeeding tribes of Mesoamerican and precontact Southwest culture peoples continued the use of peyote.

The use of peyote was widespread. Archaeologists have found a cache of peyote in a cave in what is now Texas. This dried peyote was dated at 5000 B.C. Thousand-year-old human remains in a cave in Coahuila, Mexico, were buried wearing a necklace of peyote buttons. The Aztec, who established an empire in what is now Mexico in about A.D. 1100; the Tarahumara and Huichol, mountain tribes along the western coast of Mexico; and the Lipan Apache and the Caddo, who lived in what is now Texas, all were known to utilize peyote.

American Indians valued the small cactus for medicinal purposes, including its anesthetic properties. (See also ANESTHETICS.) Two alkaloids contained in peyote also have antibiotic properties. (See also ANTIBIOTIC MEDICATIONS.) The Huichol people took advantage of this property by rubbing cut peyote plants on open wounds in order to prevent infections. American Indians also used peyote in religious ceremonies.

The Spaniards, who had not seen cacti before their arrival in the Americas, believed that peyote was a mushroom. This misidentification has persisted to this day among the uninformed, who continue to mistakenly believe that psilocybin, a drug that is synthesized from a type of mushroom, and peyote are the same. Initially Western scientists confused peyote with other plants as did bureaucrats, further adding to the confusion. For example, the U.S. Bureau of Indian Affairs, when it first attempted to outlaw peyote, referred to it as mescal, which is actually a distilled beverage made from the AGAVE. (See also DISTILLATION.)

In 1561 Father Bernardo de Sahagun became the first Spaniard to describe the plant he called *peyotl*. His statement that *peyotl* was a bad influence was based on his belief that if Indian people were allowed to use it or to practice any of their own traditional beliefs, then converting them to Catholicism would be more difficult. Fernando Hernandez, a physician whom Spanish king Charles II sent to the New World to study plants and record their medicinal benefits, reported in 1577 on the use of peyote by the Chichimeca Indians of what is now Mexico: "It is a common food of the Chichimecas, for it stimulates them and gives them sufficient spirit to fight and have neither fear, thirst, nor hunger, and they say it guards them from all danger." Despite Hernandez's endorsements, by 1620 the Spanish Inquisition in the Americas had passed an edict that forbade the use of peyote. The Spaniards also banned AMARANTH and GUINEA PIGS because of their religious use by indigenous people.

U.S. Civil War physicians used peyote as an anesthetic. By the early 1900s states began passing laws to make peyote use illegal. Although it was driven underground, ceremonial peyote use continued. After the Civil War, this form of religion spread to many parts of the United States. American Indians living in the United States chartered the Native American Church in 1918 and began a campaign to ensure their right to worship freely. (In 1955 the charter was amended to include Canada, and the organization became Native American Church of North America.) At that time anthropologist Francis La Flesche said: "In connection with this new religion they used a plant called Peyote as a sort of sacrament. This Peyote, they said, helped them not only to stop drinking, but it also helped to think intelligently of God and their relations to Him." In his book *American Indian Medicine,* Dr. Virgil Vogel, cites a scientific study: ". . . hospital tests showed that the alkaloidal principal contained in the cactus furnishes a valuable remedy for certain troubles of the nervous system."

Today, the U.S. Drug Enforcement Administration has classified peyote as a controlled substance. However, American Indians lobbied Congress and in 1994 the U.S. Congress enacted the American Indian Religious Freedom Act Amendments (Public Law 103–344). This law makes legal the use, possession, and transportation of peyote by American Indians for "bona fide traditional ceremonial purposes." Currently an estimated 250,000 American Indians consider themselves Native American Church members. The U.S. government grants them religious freedom on an individual basis to legally use peyote in their religious services.

See also COCA, MORNING GLORIES.

## Sources/Further Reading

American Indian Religious Freedom Act Amendments of 1994. Public Law 103–344.

Anderson, Edward F. *Peyote, the Divine Cactus.* Tucson: University of Arizona Press, 1980.

Coe, Michael D. *America's First Civilization: Discovering the Olmec.* Eau Claire, Wisc.: E. M. Hale and Company, American Heritage Publishing Co. Inc., 1968.

Schaeffer, Stacy B. and Peter T. Furst, eds. *People of the Peyote: Huichol Indian History, Religion, & Survival.* Albuquerque: University of New Mexico, 1996.

Mercado, Leo. *The Peyote Foundation.* URL: http://www.erowid.org/plants/peyote/peyote_faq.shtml. Downloaded on February 3, 2000.

Nkechi, Taifa and Sam Mistrano. *The Need for H.R. 4230, A Bill Providing for the Native American Religious Use of Peyote.* URL: http://www.aclu.org/congress/peyote.html. Downloaded on February 3, 2000.

Ortiz de Montellano, Bernard. *Aztec Medicine, Health, and Nutrition.* New Brunswick, N.J.: Rutgers University Press, 1990.

Stewart, Omer. *Peyote Religion: A History.* Norman: University of Oklahoma Press, 1987.

Vogel, Virgil. *American Indian Medicine.* Norman: University of Oklahoma Press, 1970.

**pharmacology** (precontact to present) *North American, South American, Circum-Caribbean, Mesoamerican cultures*
Pharmacology is the science of drugs. It includes their composition, the way they are used, and the effects they have on the human body. The indigenous people of the Americas effectively utilized a great number of plant-based drugs to treat illnesses. Modern physicians rely on many of these drugs today, including CURARE, which is used as a muscle relaxant. In order to develop such plant-based drugs, American Indians needed to understand the properties of plants as well as what dosage of a particular plant substance would produce the desired result. Additionally, since chemical compounds in many medicinal plants can be toxic if too much is ingested, indigenous healers had to know the exact amount of the substance to administer so that the patient would not be harmed.

According to a report by the National Institute of General Medical Studies (NIGMS), a part of the U.S. National Institutes of Health, the pharmaceutical wisdom of ancient cultures was impressive. "Based on the observations of countless generations, ancient cultures throughout the world developed extensive, and often effective, stocks of medicines that exploited the soothing properties of many natural substances, particularly those from plants," the report stated. "The natives of North and South America, for example, cultivated vast gardens of medicinal herbs." (See also GARDENS, HERB; MEDICAL RESEARCH.) According to Daniel Moerman, the foremost expert on North American Indian ethnobotany in the United States, North American Indians had medicinal uses for 2,564 species of plants. They used more than 10 percent of the flora available to them as medicine. The Aztec, for example, could buy over-the-counter remedies for problems such as indigestion (see also INDIGESTION MEDICATIONS), coughs, and fevers in the marketplaces that served as a focal point of their CITIES.

American Indian pharmacological practices were quite dissimilar to those that evolved in Europe during the Middle Ages and the Rennaissance. One of the most significant differences was that indigenous physicians of the Americas generally prescribed one specific plant-based medication in order to treat a particular condition. European pharmacists, or apothecaries as they were called, used medications made from a number of ingredients. The most popular of these medications was called theriac and was based on a recipe by Galen, the ancient Greek physician. A late Renaissance medicine, theriac contained 64 ingredients, including the skin of roasted vipers. It took 40 days to concoct and 12 years to age. This remedy was touted to cure nearly every known illness, including insomnia and plague, but it was available only to the wealthy. American Indians who gathered and distributed herbal remedies did not make such class distinctions. When theriac or similar medicines failed, ill Europeans were often told that their sickness was divine punishment for sin and were blamed for their suffering and deaths.

Both conquistadores and colonists were impressed by the pharmacological sophistication of indigenous Americans. Spanish explorers took samples of medicinal plants to Europe where they became part of the pharmacopoeia, a reference book for physicians listing botanical cures. Spanish priests extolled the virtues of CASCARA SAGRADA as a laxative and GUIACUM as a cold remedy. British colonists in North America quickly came to rely on WAHOO, DOGBANE, and FOXGLOVE as heart medications and began to use LADY'S SLIPPER as a sedative as they had observed American Indians doing. Over 200 plants that had served as American Indian remedies became part of the U.S. Pharmacopoeia. (The first official U.S. Pharmacopoeia was written and authorized by the professional medical community in 1837.)

Ill colonists' alternative to borrowing medical treatments from the Indians was to visit an apothecary. These purveyors of medicine stocked over 200 remedies ranging from plants to metals, including lead, arsenic, and mercury chloride, as well as dung and urine. Plant medications were prescribed, based not on research or observation of their effects on humans, but on their appearance according to the doctrine of signatures invented by Galen. An example of this would be prescribing walnuts for brain damage because the meats in a walnut resembled the brain in appearance. A growing distrust of their own medical traditions led colonists not only to try actual herbal remedies but to rely on patent medicines (see also MEDICINES, PATENT, AMERICAN INDIAN INFLUENCE ON), many of which were sold with the claim that they were made from American Indian formulas.

In the 1700s heroic medicine, the medical philosophy that "heroic" measures such as bloodletting and surgery were necessary to cure disease, became the norm in the Western medical establishment. By the 1900s herbal medications were thought unscientific and called folk cures. Consequently, physicians and medical researchers tended to ignore them. Although there are approximately 3 million plant species in the world today, only about 5,000 of them have been studied by scientists for their medicinal usefulness, according to Norman Farnsworth of the University of Illinois College of Pharmacy.

Today that is changing. According to the NIGMS report, ". . . green plants, a source of drugs for millennia, continue to be the major storehouse of potential therapeutics." Over 120 drugs that are prescribed by doctors today were first made from plant extracts; 75 percent of these were derived from examining plant use in traditional indigenous medicine. In 1989, the National Cancer Institute, a division of the National Institutes of Health, set up a plant screening system to test as many as 10,000 plants from the Amazonian tropical rainforest to determine if any of them can slow cell growth in any of the more than 100 types of human cancer. A similar research project has been put into operation in order to screen for botanical cures for the AIDS virus.

At first the scientific basis of some American Indian cures often does not make sense to the Western "scientific" mind. For instance, scientists once scoffed at the practice of some Argentinean Indians of tying a certain species of live frog, called the African clawed frog, onto a wound in order to cause it to heal. When NIH researcher Michael Zasloff studied the frog, he discovered that it produced two peptides in its skin that were able to kill many types of bacteria, yeast, amoebae, and protozoa. Researchers believe this rediscovery of a cure that indigenous people knew about for hundreds of years will lead to a totally new type of infection-fighting drug.

Another example of an ancient remedy being incorporated into modern medicine is that of the jaborandi tree (*Pilocarpus jaborandi*). The leaves of this plant have been used for centuries by the people of the Amazon basin in South America as an expectorant, diuretic, and stimulant, as well as to induce sweating. Chemists have discovered that the jaborandi contains a substance called pilocarpine that aids in the transmission of impulses from the ends of the autonomic nerves to the muscles. Pilocarpine is used in modern medicine as a treatment for glaucoma. When it is applied to the eye, it stimulates the muscle that contracts the pupil of the eye. This relieves the pressure that produces glaucoma.

Physicians also administer pilocarpine today in pill form to treat a condition known as dry-mouth syndrome. The Tupi Indians of Brazil, whose name for the jaborandi tree translates as "slobber mouth plant," used it for the same purpose long before modern doctors discovered it. Botanist Steven R. King, senior vice-president for ethnobotany and conservation for a San Francisco-based pharmaceutical company, pointed out the irony of the situation: "Had we listened more closely to what the indigenous people of Brazil called their folk remedy and questioned its purposes in their medicinal storehouse of knowledge, the development of our dry-mouth syndrome product might have come years earlier."

See also AGAVE; ANESTHETICS; ANTI-ASTHMATIC MEDICATIONS; ANTIBIOTIC MEDICATIONS; ANTIHELMINTIC; ANTIVIRAL MEDICATIONS; ASTRINGENTS; CHILE; COCA; CONTRACEPTION, ORAL; DIABETES MEDICATIONS; DIURETICS; EARACHE TREATMENTS; EPHEDRA; GASTROENTERITIS MEDICATIONS; HEADACHE MEDICATIONS; HEMP, AMERICAN; JALAP; KAOLIN; MINTS, BOTANICAL; PAPAYAS; PILLS; WITCH HAZEL; YAMS.

**Sources/Further Reading**

Farnsworth, N. R. "Screening Plants for New Medicines." In *Biodiversity,* edited by E. O. Wilson. Washington, D.C.: National Academy Press, 1988.

King, Steven. "Medicines that Changed the World." *Pacific Discovery* 45, no. 1 (Winter 1992): 23–31.

Laing, Lloyd and Jennifer Laing. *Medieval Britain: The Age of Chivalry.* New York: St. Martin's Press, 1996.

Moerman, D. E. "An Analysis of the Food Plants and Drug Plants of Native North America" *Journal of Ethnopharmacology* 52 (1996): 1–22.

National Institute of General Medical Science. *Medicines by Design: The Biological Revolution in Pharmacology.* Washington, D.C.: National Institutes of Health, 1997.

Turkel, Susan Neiburg. *Colonial American Medicine.* New York: Franklin Watts, 1993.

Viola, Herman J. and Carolyn Margolis. *Seeds of Change: 500 Years Since Columbus.* Washington, D.C. Smithsonian Institution Press, 1991.

**phlebotomy** (ca. A.D. 1100–A.D. 1519) *Mesoamerican cultures*

Phlebotomy is the medical procedure of surgically removing blood from a blood vessel. It is used to draw blood from a patient for testing, for infusing blood to another person, and for removing blood that has built up inside an enclosed space in the body due to hemorrhage. In modern medicine, phlebotomy has become a specialty. It was a specialty as well in Aztec medicine before contact with Europeans. (The Aztec Empire was established in what is now Mexico in about A.D. 1100.) The Aztec phlebotomist was responsible for drawing blood from vessels and for treating a number of health problems. (See also SURGERY.) The Nahuatl, or Aztec, word for phlebotomist was *texoxotla-ticitl,* and the word used for the lancet was *itztli.* Aztec phlebotomists knew the difference between arteries and veins, and they always drew blood from the veins.

The early Spanish conquistadores were accompanied by doctors trained in the Galenic school of medicine, which was pervasive at that time. Galen was an ancient Greek, and his theory dealt with four humours, the bodily fluids said to represent the four elements—fire, air, water, and earth. Too much or too little would cause disease. Galenic medicine taught that bleeding would remedy these imbalances. New World physicians and their phlebotomy techniques fascinated the Spaniards. As a result, they wrote many reports about their techniques. These reports documented that the Aztec were familiar with the circulatory system and beating of the heart. (See also ANATOMICAL KNOWLEDGE.) American Indian physicians were also familiar with taking the radial pulse. (See also PULSE, RADIAL.)

**Sources/Further Reading**

Ortiz de Montellano, Bernard R. *Aztec Medicine, Health, and Nutrition.* New Brunswick, N.J.: Rutgers University Press, 1990.

Peredo, Miguel Guizman. *Medical Practice in Ancient America.* Mexico City: Ediciones Euroamericanas, 1985.

Vogel, Virgil. *American Indian Medicine.* Norman: University of Oklahoma Press, 1970.

**picks** See TOOLS.

**pick-up sticks** See JACKSTRAWS.

**pills** (ca. A.D 1100–A.D. 1519) *Mesoamerican; North American Northeast cultures*

A pill is a pellet or tablet of medicine that is small enough to be swallowed. Prior to contact with Europeans, the Aztec made pills out of their medicine in order to make it easier to ingest. (The Aztec established an empire in what is now Mexico in about A.D. 1100.) Aztec physicians recognized that some people had difficulty taking certain medicines. When this was the case, the Aztec physician wrapped the medicine to be administered in flower petals so that the medicine would be easier to swallow.

In North America the Eastern Woodland Indians also used pills. Indians made them from high-bush CRANBERRY (*Viburnum opulus L.*) bark, grinding it while it was moist and compressing it into pills. American colonists, who borrowed the remedy, called this bark "cramp bark"—an appropriate name, since American Indians used its antispasmodic properties to treat menstrual cramps. Modern herbalists recommend it for the same treatment today. The Maliseet and Penobscot Indians also administered cramp bark pills to treat mumps because of its diuretic properties. The elimination of fluids when one has the mumps is desirable.

See also PHARMACOLOGY.

**Sources/Further Reading**

Frederiksen, Thomas H. *Aztec Medicine, Aztec Student Research Guide.* URL: http://northeast.com/~spdtom/a-med.html. Downloaded on December 14, 1999.

Vogel, Virgil. *American Indian Medicine.* Norman: University of Oklahoma Press, 1970.

Weiner, Michael A. *Earth Medicine, Earth Food: Plant Remedies, Drugs, and Natural Foods of the North American Indians.* New York: Fawcett Columbine, New York, 1990.

**pimentos** See PEPPERS, SWEET AND BELL.

**pineapples** (*Ananas cosmosus*) (precontact) *South America Tropical Forest, Circum-Caribbean, Mesoamerican cultures*

The pineapple is a bromeliad that somewhat resembles an AGAVE or YUCCA with spike-shaped leaves. Noted for its fruit, the pineapple is indigenous to the tropics and subtropics of the Americas. Pineapple cultivation is thought to have originated in the Orinoco valley of what is now Brazil and the Parana valley of what is now Paraguay. From there pineapple cultivation spread throughout Mexico, to Central and South America and the West Indies. American Indians used the pineapple for food.

In 1493, when Christopher Columbus and his crew landed on what is now the island of Guadeloupe, a party of men returned to the ship with pineapples. Only one of the fruits survived the voyage back to Spain, where Columbus presented it to King Ferdinand.

Gonzalo Fernandez de Oviedo y Valdez, whose book *Historia General y Natural de las Indias* was published in Seville in 1535, called the pineapple the most beautiful fruit he had ever seen. According to Oviedo, since other food and even wine dimmed in comparison to the pineapple, it would be a good cure for drunkenness. In 1559 André Thévet, a French traveler who wrote about his journey to the Americas mentioned pineapples in his work, calling them *nana,* their Indian name. The plant's botanical name, *Ananas,* comes from the Tupi-

Guarani Indian language and means "fragrant delicious fruit." (The Tupi are a tribe of the Amazon basin.) The pineapple's common name comes from the Spanish explorers who named it *pina* because it looked like a pine cone. The English added *apple.*

The Portuguese took the fruits from Brazil to their other colonies. The pineapple could be found in China as early as 1518 and Madagascar in 1548, and they were being grown in India by 1550. An excellent source of vitamins C and A, pineapple was an excellent scurvy preventative. (See also SCURVY CURE.)

Pineapples were initially a curiosity in Europe, but before long they became popular with the nobility. By the 1700s the plants were being grown in greenhouses called pineries and sold on a limited basis in European marketplaces. Difficult to import because they would rot before their voyage ended, they remained scarce. In England they became such conversation pieces that they were rented out as centerpieces. As transportation improved, pineapples were imported in greater numbers. Large pineapple plantations were eventually established not only in South America but also Hawaii, Formosa, the Philippines, and Australia.

**Sources/Further Reading**

Coe, Sophie. *America's First Cuisines.* Austin: University of Texas Press, 1994.

Trager, James. *The Food Chronology: The Food Lover's Compendium of Events and Anecdotes from Prehistory to Present.* New York: Henry Holt, 1995.

**pine, white** See WHITE PINE.

**pins, straight** (ca. 5000 B.C.–3000 B.C.) *North American Southeast, South American Andean cultures*

Straight pins today are stiff pieces of wire that have a sharp point on one end and a blunted head on the other. Typically they are used as fasteners. American Indians invented pins independently from those made by other cultures. Some of the oldest pins found in precontact North America were produced by the Middle Archaic Culture Indians, who lived in what is now Florida from about 5000 B.C. to 3000 B.C. The Middle Archaic Culture pins were made of bone, and they produced bone sewing needles as well. (See also NEEDLES.) Peoples of the Chavin culture, which existed in what is now Peru from about 900 B.C. to 200 B.C., were so adept at metalsmithing that they made pins of silver and gold. The shafts of these pins were made of silver and the heads were made of gold. Chavin metallurgists were able to bond different metals by SOLDERING and WELDING.

See also METALLURGY.

**Sources/Further Reading**

Alden, Mason J. *The Ancient Civilizations of Peru.* New York: Penguin Books, 1957.

Melanich, Jerald T. *Florida's Indians from Ancient Times to the Present: 12,000 Years of Florida's Indian Heritage.* Gainesville: University Press of Florida, 1998.

**pins, surgical**  See INTRAMEDULLAR NAILS.

**pipes, pan**  See PAN PIPES.

**pipes, tobacco**  (ca. 2000 B.C.–present) *Mesoamerican; North American Southwest, Southeast, Northeast, and Great Plains cultures*

Pipes are devices used for smoking TOBACCO, a plant cultivated by indigenous peoples throughout the Americas. Archaeologists use the presence of pipes to date tobacco cultivation. The first pipes, used by Mesoamerican cultures and those in the North American Southwest, were tubes that were filled with tobacco. Stone carvings show the Maya priests used a ceramic pipe shaped like a tube in religious ceremonies. (Maya culture arose in Mesoamerica in about 1500 B.C.) Later, the Aztec, whose empire was established in about A.D. 1100, used smoking tubes of reed or cane.

Effigy pipes carved by Algonkin pipemakers were made to resemble birds and animals. These were made by indigenous people in Ontario. *(Canadian Museum of Civilization/Image number K-71-3)*

In the North American Southwest, filling short pieces of cane with tobacco dates from the first stages of the Anasazi culture in about 350 B.C. The earliest tobacco pipes found in North America were a product of a Mound Builder culture in the southeastern part of what is now the United States. These pipes, with a bowl and a stem, are forerunners of the pipes that are smoked today. Stealite, or soapstone, pipes were being made in this area by 2000 B.C. Later, the Hopewell culture, which flourished from about 300 B.C. to A.D. 700 in the river valleys in the center of North America, produced effigy pipes. These were pipes carved with images of birds and animals. These figures served as bowls, and they sat on a slender platform that had been drilled to serve as a stem.

In the Northeast, Algonkin pipemakers also carved birds and animals on stone pipes in addition to making simpler pipes with curved or flaring bowls. In addition to making stone pipes, the Huron and other tribes also made them from clay that was formed around a grass core. When these clay pipes were hardened in a fire, the grass burned away. Archaeologists have found that the Huron used finer clay to make pipes than they did for other POTTERY and that the pipes were more carefully fired. They darkened the surface of their clay pipes by covering them with animal grease and letting it burn away. This also provided a polished surface. Pipemaking was a specialized trade for peoples of the Northeast, with one or two pipemakers providing tobacco pipes for an entire village.

Perhaps the best-known tobacco pipes made by North American Indians are the calumets of the Great Plains tribes, which later came to be known as *peace pipes*. *Calumet* is a French word for "reed" or "tube" and describes the long stems to which pipemakers attached bowls. Often the stems were decorated with carving, quillwork, and feathers. The bowls were elbow and T-shaped. Many had decorative carvings that varied with each pipemaker. The Dakota, Lakota, Nakota, and Pawnee pipe makers were known for making effigy pipes whose bowls were shaped in the likeness of people, birds, or animals.

Great Plains pipemakers carved the bowls of their pipes from pipestone that they quarried from a deposit in the southwestern part of what is now Minnesota. American Indians, who first began to quarry the stone about 2,300 years ago, traded it throughout the great Plains and Midwest. This soft red stone is called catlinite today after the artist George Caitlin, the first non-Indian to describe it after seeing the quarry in 1836. Because settlers saw Indians smoking these pipes at treaty signings, they named the pipes "peace pipes." In addition to using pipe smoking as a way to ratify alliances and make treaties binding, Great Plains Indians used the pipes as guarantees of safe passage and in ceremonies.

According to anthropologists, pipe smoking and tobacco use in Mesoamerica and North America was used primarily for ceremonial and circumscribed political purposes. The Maya, for example, smoked tobacco pipes at special events such as feasts. The Aztec of Mesoamerica and the Akimel O'odham (Pima) of the North American Southwest forbade the use of tobacco by children because they correctly believed that smoking would create breathing problems. (The Aztec established an empire in what is now Mexico in about A.D. 1100.)

North American colonists took up tobacco use soon after their arrival. Unlike the American Indians, they smoked socially. They used both corn cob pipes and clay pipes for this purpose. Pipes were exported to Europe with tobacco. The English began making pipes as early as 1575.

See also CIGARETTES; CIGARS.

## Sources/Further Reading

Deuel, Leo. *Conquistadors Without Swords: Archaeologists In The Americas.* New York: St. Martin's Press, Inc., 1967.

Driver, Harold E. *Indians of North America.* Chicago: University of Chicago Press, 1969.

Folsom, Franklin and Mary Elting Folsom. *America's Ancient Treasures.* 4th ed. Albuquerque: University of New Mexico Press, 1993.

Hassrick, Royal B. *The Sioux.* Norman: University of Oklahoma Press, 1964.

Hazen-Hammond, Susan. *Timelines of Native American History.* New York: The Berkley Press Publishing Group, 1997.

Sharer, Robert J. *Daily Life In The Maya Civilization.* Westport, Conn.: Greenwood Press, 1996.

Trigger, Bruce G. *The Huron Farmers of the North.* New York: Holt, Rinehart and Winston, Inc., 1969.

**place-names** (precontact/contact) *North American, Mesoamerican, Circum-Caribbean, South American cultures*
Thousands of geographical names in North America, Mesoamerica, and South America are derived from Indian words. American Indians gave many of these names to locations and geographic features long before Europeans arrived in the Americas. Others were borrowed from Native languages by the conquerors and colonizers. Mountains, rivers, lakes, cities, counties, states, and even countries bear Native names today. For example, the name Mexico comes from the Aztec, or Nahuatl, word *mexihco,* meaning "place of the war god." The name Canada is derived from the indigenous word *kanata,* which means "settlement" or "village." The Canadian provinces Manitoba and Saskatchewan also bear Indian names. The name of another Canadian province and the smallest of the Great Lakes, Ontario, comes from the Iroquoian *oniatario,* which means "fine lake."

The Adirondack Mountains of upstate New York were named for the Native people who originally lived in the area. The word comes from the Iroquoian *ratirontacks,* meaning "bark eaters." Iroquois in the North and Cherokee in the South inhabited the mountainous area known today as Appalachia, but Europeans named it after the Appalachee, a tribe that lived in what is now the Florida panhandle.

The city of Miami in Florida is named after the Muskogean tribal name Mayaimi. However, in the Midwest the name of Miami, Ohio, is derived from the Chippewa (Anishinabe) word for "tribe." Chicago, Illinois, was named from the Algonquian word meaning "onion place," probably because of the wild onions that grew in the marshy area before the present city was built.

Twenty-six of the contiguous United States, as well as Alaska, were given names derived from American Indian languages.

**Alabama:** a Choctaw word for the name of a tribe that was part of the Creek Confederacy and whose members lived in what is now the central part of the state. Alabama comes from the Choctaw word *alba,* which means "vegetation or thicket," and *amo,* which means "gatherers or clearers." Some historians think that the name referred to the tribe's land clearing endeavors for agricultural purposes, sometimes called MILPA. The word Alabama was used in the first accounts of the 1540 journey through the area by Spanish conquistador Hernando De Soto.

**Alaska:** according to some historians, the Russian derivation of the Aleut word alyeska, which means "mainland" or "great lands". Others believe the name came from another native word, alaxsxaq, a Yup'ik word that means "object toward which the action of the sea is directed" or the "mainland."

**Arizona:** the Spanish version of *aleh-zon,* Akimel O'odham (Pima) words that mean "small spring." As early as 1736, Spaniards used the term to refer to springs located near a large silver find that had been made the year before.

**Arkansas:** perhaps a phonetic spelling of the name that people of the Illinois tribe had for American Indians who lived along what is known as the Arkansas River, which means "down river" or "downstream people." Another explanation is that the state is named after the Kansas, a Siouian-speaking tribe.

**Connecticut:** from the Mohegan word *guonehtacut,* which can be translated as "long river place" or "the long river." The original inhabitants of Connecticut were the Mohegan, Pequot, and Narraganset tribes.

**Dakota (North and South):** refers to the people who lived in the area. Both states were carved from Dakota Territory in 1889, which was established by the United States government in 1861, from land that was inhabited by the Dakota. The word means "friends" or "allies" in the Dakota language.

**Illinois:** the French spelling for the Ilini, a tribe of American Indians living along the bank of the river Cavalier de La Salle traveled in 1679. The word meant "man" or "warrior."

**Iowa:** named for the tribe of Indians that lived in the region, the Ayuxwa, whose name means "one who puts to sleep." The French spelled the word Ayoua and it became Ioway in English.

**Kansas:** the French spelling of the name of the tribe who lived in the area of the present state. According to some scholars, the word means "south wind" in the Kansas, Omaha, Kaw, Osage, and Dakota languages, which are all part of the Siouan linguistic family. It was first applied to the river, then to the territory, and finally to the state.

**Kentucky:** a Wyandot word for "plain," referring to the central plains of the state. It was first used in 1753.

**Massachusetts:** named for the Massachusetts Bay Colony, established by the Puritans who landed in 1620. In Algonquian the word means "large hill place" or "at the hill." This probably refers to Blue Hill near what is now Boston.

**Michigan:** possibly derived from the Chippewa (Anishinabe) words *mici* and *gami,* which mean "big water." Some believe the state was named after a clearing in the western lower peninsula that the Chippewa called *majigan,* or "clearing." The word was first written in 1672 in reference to that clearing.

**Minnesota:** named after the Minnesota river that the Dakota called *mni shota,* meaning cloudy or milky water. At the time of European contact, the Santee Sioux (Nakota) were the primary inhabitants of what is now the state.

**Mississippi:** after the river's name, which comes from the Algonquian language's *mici sibi,* meaning "big river." Cavalier de La Salle's map of 1695 assigns the Mississippi River its current name.

**Missouri:** derived from the Algonquian word that means "muddy water." This was also the name of a small tribe in the area that lived along the river. Some historians believe Missouri comes from an Algonquian word meaning "river of the big canoes." (After removal to Indian Territory, members of the Missouri tribe were classified as Oto.)

**Ohio:** named after the Ohio River. French explorer Cavalier de La Salle noted as early as 1680 that the Iroquois called the river Ohio, meaning "large or beautiful river."

**Oklahoma:** made up of the Choctaw words *ukla* and *huma',* which together mean "red person." The Choctaw did not refer to themselves in this manner. Allen Wright, an American Indian missionary, made up the name, which was used for the first time in the 1866 Choctaw-Chickasaw Treaty. What is now the state of Oklahoma was originally known as Indian Territory, an area set aside in 1825 under the order of Andrew Jackson for the Indian peoples who were forcibly removed from areas in the east containing fertile lands, which non-Indian settlers desired. Later, when the U.S. government took the land from the Indians and gave it to settlers, the area became the state of Oklahoma.

**Oregon:** origin of the name unclear. Possibly it was derived from *oyer-un-gon,* a Shoshonean word for "place of plenty" or the Siouan word *ourigan,* which means "great river to the west." Some scholars believe the name was derived from the Spanish *orejon,* a name they used for some American Indian tribes in the region.

**Tennessee:** comes from *Tanasi,* the Cherokee name for two villages on the Little Tennessee River, which they named for the villages. The name was also spelled *Tanase, Tennessee,* and *Tinasse.* As early as 1567, the Spanish referred to the Indian settlement Tenaqui. Historians are uncertain what Tanasi means.

**Texas:** named after *teysha* in the Caddo language, which means "hello friend." Spaniards adopted the term to mean any friendly tribe in the Louisiana Territory. They called the tribes that belonged to the Caddo confederacy in the western part of Louisiana and the eastern part of Texas "the kingdom of the Tejas," or allies, beginning in 1541.

**Utah:** a name given to the Navajo (Dineh) by the White Mountain Apache, who called them *uttahih,* or "one that is higher up." Europeans understood the Apache term to refer to the Ute who lived even further north.

**Wisconsin:** named after the Wisconsin river. In Chippewa (Anishinabe), Wisconsin means "gathering of waters" or "grassy place." Some historians believe it meant "the place where we live." The French first used it in 1695. They spelled it both *Ouisconsin* and *Mesconsing.*

**Wyoming:** derived from two (Lenni Lenape Delaware) words, *meche weamiing,* which mean "at the big flats." It was translated to mean "large plains." The Lenni Lenape people lived on the Atlantic coast, far from the area known today as Wyoming. (The tribe was given the name Delaware by the British after Lord de la Warr, an early Virginia governor. These people call themselves the Lenni Lenape or Lenape.) A Kearney, Nebraska, newspaper publisher for the southwest part of the Dakota Territory suggested the name Wyoming.

See also LANGUAGE, AMERICAN INDIAN INFLUENCE ON; SETTLEMENT PATTERNS.

## Sources/Further Reading

*Alabama Archives and History Department.* URL: http://www.asc.edu/archives/statenam.html. Downloaded on 1/24/1999.

*Alaska Blue Book 1993–1994.* 11th ed. Juneau: Department of Education, Division of State Libraries, Archives and Museums, 1993.

Chicago Historical Society. URL: http://www.Chicago's. org/history/. Downloaded on January 24, 1999.

Flexner, Stuart Berg. *I Hear America Talking: An Illustrated History of American Words and Phrases.* New York: Simon and Schuster, 1976.

Shearer, Benjamin F. and Barbara Shearer. *State Names, Seals, Flags, and Symbols: A Historical Guide.* Westport, Conn.: Greenwood Press, 1994.

Waldman, Carl. *Atlas of the North American Indian, Revised Edition.* New York: Facts On File, 2000.

**placer mining**  See MINING, PLACER.

**plant breeding**  See AGRICULTURE; SEED SELECTION.

**plant classifications**  (ca. A.D. 1100) *Mesoamerican cultures*
Classification systems are ways of ordering knowledge. American Indians developed their own system of plant, or botanical, classification long before the Swedish botanist Carolus Linneaus devised the European binomial system for naming plants in the mid-1700s. Linneaus' system for flowering plants was based on how many pistils and stamens a plant possessed and the way in which they were joined together. Aztec horticulturists classified plants according to their form, their use, and their economic value. The form categories were trees, bushes, and herbs. The use categories included "medicinal," "food," and "ornamental." The economic category divided plants according to whether they were used to make clothing, for building, or for other economic uses. This sophisticated system predated the work of Linneaus by at least 400 years.

Nearly every American Indian cultural group throughout the Americas organized the plants they encountered in their environment into categories. For example, the Thompson Indians who lived in British Columbia named medicinal plants according to their specific uses. They grouped some plants with others that tended to grow in the same locations. Ethnographers, working from an ethnocentric viewpoint, tended to dismiss the validity of any system not based on the Linnean model. Only recently have American Indian plant classification systems been the subject of serious study by non-Indian scientists who realize that they are both sophisticated and workable.

See also PHARMACOLOGY.

**Sources/Further Reading**

Kidwell, Clara Sue and Peter Nabokov. "Directions in Native American Science and Technology." In *Studying Native America: Problems and Prospects,* edited by Russell Thornton. Madison: University of Wisconsin Press, 1998.

Ortiz de Montellano, Bernard. *Aztec Medicine, Health, and Nutrition.* New Brunswick, N.J.: Rutgers University Press, 1990.

**plastic surgery**  (ca. A.D. 1100–A.D. 1519)
*Mesoamerican, North American Northeast cultures*
Plastic surgery is the field of medicine that involves restoring or repairing defective or missing tissue or structures on the human body. The Aztec, whose empire was established in about A.D. 1100, were experts at SURGERY. Aztec surgeons were able to perform complex and delicate procedures unknown to European physicians practicing during the Middle Ages. Plastic surgery was only one of these techniques.

In his book *Medical Practices in Ancient America,* author Miguel Peredo provides information about the writings of Fray Bernardino de Sahagun on Aztec plastic surgery: "Sahagun tells us that Doctors endeavored to treat face wounds with such care that no pronounced scars would remain. . . . cuts and wounds on the nose after an accident had to be treated by suturing with hair from the head and by applying to the stitches and the wound white honey and salt. After this, if the nose fell off or if the treatment was a failure, an artificial nose took the place of the real one." In cases where lips were cut open the Aztec physician would suture them with human hair. After the suturing was completed the doctor would pour maguey juice on the wound. (See also AGAVE.) The maguey juice had antibiotic and healing properties. (See also ANTIBIOTICS.) If the wound area became an unsightly blemish for some reason, the physician performed the whole procedure again until the wound healed normally.

The Chippewa (Anishinabe) of northeastern North America performed surgery to repair torn ears. They trimmed the ear tissue so that both sides of the tear matched up evenly and then they sutured them together.

See also DEBRIDEMENT; GRANULATION.

**Sources/Further Reading**

Driver, Harold E. *Indians of North America.* Chicago: University of Chicago Press, 1969.

Ortiz de Montellano, Bernard R. *Aztec Medicine, Health, and Nutrition.* New Brunswick, N.J.: Rutgers University Press, 1990.

Peredo, Miguel Guzman. *Medical Practices in Ancient America.* Mexico City: Ediciones Euroamericanas, 1985.

Vogel, Virgil. *American Indian Medicine.* Norman: University of Oklahoma Press, 1970.

**platinum (Pt)**  (ca. 300 B.C.)  *South American Andean cultures*
Platinum is a precious metal that is more valuable than gold. (See also METALS, PRECIOUS.) One of the main reasons for this is that less platinum exists in the world than any other precious metal. According to some experts, if all the platinum in the earth were mined, it could fit into an average-sized room. Platinum is also the strongest precious metal and has tremendous durability. American Indians who lived in northwest South America in the areas that are now Colombia and Ecuador found platinum along with silver on the banks of streams and rivers. Excellent metallurgists, they managed to

work the platinum, a feat today's scientists believe was nearly impossible. (See also METALLURGY.)

J. Alden Mason, author of *Ancient Civilizations of Peru*, states: "The discovery of ornaments of platinum on the coast of Ecuador has astounded and intrigued modern metallurgists for its melting point (about 1770° C or 3218° F) is beyond the capabilities of primitive furnaces." Although precontact American Indians did not possess a furnace or kiln capable of producing this kind of heat, they were able to develop a brilliant solution in the form of a process called SINTERING to make an alloy of platinum and gold—using only stone-age tools. Once the platinum-gold alloy was produced, it lowered the melting point of the platinum, making it more malleable. European metalworkers did not make objects from platinum until the 19th century.

**Sources/Further Reading**

Bergsoe, Paul. *The Metallurgy and Technology of Gold and Platinum among the Pre-Columbian Indians. A, Ingeniorvidenska-beliege Skrifter* A, no. 44 1937.

Daumas, Maurice, ed. *The Origins of Technological Civilization.* New York: Crown Publishers, Inc., 1962.

Engel, Frederic Andre. *An Ancient World Preserved: Relics and Records of Prehistory in the Andes.* New York: Crown Publishers, Inc., 1976.

Mason, J. Alden. *The Ancient Civilizations of Peru.* New York: Penguin Books, 1964.

*Renaissance Platinum.* URL: http://www.renaissanceplatinum.com/learnmore.html. Downloaded on February 9, 2000.

**plazas**  See CIVIC CENTERS.

**plumbing**  (ca. 1700 B.C.–400 B.C.)  *Mesoamerican, South American Andean cultures*

Plumbing refers to pipes and fixtures used to conduct water into a building or to remove wastewater. The Olmec, whose culture arose in the Yucatán Peninsula of what is now Mexico in about 1700 B.C., were the first known American Indians to use plumbing. They developed it independently of plumbing systems invented in the Middle East and Mediterranean and long before the Romans built AQUEDUCTS to deliver fresh drinking water to the cities they established throughout Europe. The Olmec made their water conduits of carved, rectangular U-shaped blocks about three to five feet long. They covered them with capstones to keep the water from evaporating or becoming polluted. (See also WATER CONSERVATION.) These conduits were built to provide water to individual buildings in a community. Later Mesoamerican cultures such as the Aztec whose empire was established in what is now Mexico in about A.D. 1100 followed suit.

The Aztec were concerned about sanitation. Many residences had personal restrooms, and there were public restrooms as well. There were canals for conveying urine out of the community and for bringing fresh water into it; human waste was transported out of the community manually as well. These canal systems each consisted of dual, plaster-lined canals, allowing one to be cleaned or repaired while the other continued to bring in fresh water in.

South American culture groups also developed plumbing. The Chavin, whose culture flourished in what is now Peru from about 900 B.C. to 200 B.C., were one of them. (They also produced intricate VENTILATION SYSTEMS.). The Inca, who established an empire in what is now Peru in about A.D. 1000, made stone water conduits. In addition to these, they also used copper pipes to transport hot and cold water to the sunken bathtubs in their bath houses. When the conquistadores saw the plumbing of the Inca, they were impressed.

In contrast to the sanitation practices of indigenous Americans, Europeans had made minimal improvements on the plumbing conduits the Romans had built throughout the continent hundreds of years before. (These aqueducts would not be improved until the 1800s.) In North America colonists relieved themselves in forests and in chamber pots that they emptied in the streets. Outhouses either had a bucket or a pit to hold waste. Often they were constructed dangerously close to wells. The colonists disposed of their garbage by tossing it in the streets along with the contents of their chamber pots. Even large cities lacked plumbing. Boston, one of the first cities to provide water for its dwellings, did so in the mid-1800s and made pipes out of wood.

See also HYGIENE, PERSONAL; IRRIGATION.

**Sources/Further Reading**

*Andes 2: Emergence of State Society.* URL: http://www.cc.columbia.edu/cu/arthistory/andes2.htm. Downloaded on October 30, 1999.

Coe, Michael D. *America's First Civilization: Discovering The Olmec.* New York: American Heritage Publishing Co., 1968.

Coleman, Penny. *Toilets, Bathtubs, Sinks, and Showers: A History of the Bathroom.* New York: Atheneum Books, 1994.

Ortiz de Montellano, Bernard R. *Aztec Medicine, Health, and Nutrition.* New Brunswick. N.J.: Rutgers University Press, 1990.

Sabloff, Jeremy A. *The Cities Of Ancient Mexico: Reconstructing a Lost World.* New York: Thames And Hudson, 1989.

Soustelle, Jacques. *Daily Life of the Aztecs on the Eve of the Spanish Conquest.* Stanford, Calif.: Stanford University Press, 1961.

**poinsettias**  (*Euphorbia pulcherrima*)  (precontact)  *Mesoamerican cultures*

Poinsettias are perennial shrubs that are known for their distinctive red, white, yellow, or pink blooms. They are not really flowers but colored bracts, or leaves, that encircle a tiny yellow cluster of true flowers. The bracts turn from green to their characteristic colors in the fall. Known as the Christmas flower and grown primarily as houseplants today, poinsettias are native to what is now Mexico where the Aztec cultivated them for centuries before the arrival of the Europeans. In their natural state in warm climates, poinsettias grow to be about eight feet tall.

The Aztec used the colored bracts of the poinsettia to make a red-purple DYE. They also used the plants medicinally, treating fever with the LATEX found in their stems. Midwives (see also NURSES, NURSING) applied poultices to nursing mothers in order to help them produce more breast milk.

Poinsettia plants were not imported to North America until 1925, when botanist Joel R. Poinsett, the first U.S. ambassador to Mexico, sent seeds and plants to his home in South Carolina. The plants are named after Poinsett. They have become very popular in the United States as Christmas decorations.

See also DAHLIAS; MARIGOLDS; NASTURTIUMS; ZINNIAS.

## Sources/Further Reading

Anderson, Christine and Terry Tisher. *Poinsettias: Myth and Legend—History and Botanical Fact.* Tiburon, Calif.: Waters Edge Press, 1997.

Kansas State University. "KSU Professor Researches Poinsettias." *K State News.* URL: http://www.newww.ksu.edu/WEB/NewsReleases/listpoinsettias.html. Downloaded on September 27, 1999.

Ortiz de Montellano, Bernard. *Aztec Medicine, Health, and Nutrition.* New Brunswick, N.J.: Rutgers University Press, 1990.

Parsons, James A. "Southern Blooms: Latin America and the World of Flowers," *Queen's Quarterly* 99, no. 3 (1992): 542–561.

## ponchos (precontact) *South American, Mesoamerican cultures*

Ponchos are simple garments with unsewn sides. They are constructed by making a slit for the neck in a length of fabric that is then folded over the wearer's shoulders. The Mapuche, whose culture was established before European contact and who lived in what are now Chile and Argentina, are believed to have been the first to invent this garment. Some anthropologists believe that the Mapuche, who quickly adapted an equestrian lifestyle after Spaniards introduced the horse, modified the garment from a shirt with sewn sides that was worn by the Inca, whose empire was established in what is now Peru in about A.D. 1000.

An equally strong argument can be made that the poncho was developed from the Aztec *xicolli*, or sleeveless jacket, worn in pre-Columbian times. (The Aztec established an empire in what is now Mexico in about A.D. 1100.) These jackets were tied together in the front and fringed at the bottom. Their wear was limited to the priests and merchant class. The feminine counterpart to this garment was called a *huipilli* in Nahuatl, the Aztec language. A women's outergarment, called a *quesquemetl*, did not have sewn sides.

Ponchos worn by the Mapuche spread throughout Latin America and Spain. A modified version of the poncho became the standard-issue raincoat for U.S. troops in World War I. This was not the first use of the poncho as rainwear. In addition to being worn in Meso- and South America, sleeveless garments with unsewn sides were also worn by North American northeastern culture groups. They made ponchos from mats woven so tightly that they were waterproofed as a protection against the rain. The poncho design became a popular style in North America in the 1970s.

See also WEAVING TECHNIQUES.

## Sources/Further Reading

Anawalt, Patricia Rieff. *Indian Clothing Before Cortes: Mesoamerican Costumes from the Codices.* Norman: University of Oklahoma Press, 1981.

Driver, Harold. *Indians of North America.* Chicago: University of Chicago Press, 1969.

Harris, Jennifer. *Textiles: 5,000 Years.* New York: Harry Abrams, 1993.

## pontoon bridges  See BRIDGES.

## popcorn (ca. 2500 B.C.) *Mesoamerican, South American Andean, North American Southwest cultures*

Popcorn is a variety of CORN that, when dried, contains some moisture in the starchy interior of the kernel. When the popcorn kernel is heated, this moisture expands, creating enough pressure to cause the starch to explode literally, bursting the hard hull. American Indians developed popcorn by using SEED SELECTION from four to five thousand years ago. Some archaeologists believe that popcorn may have been the first variety of corn they developed. Its cultivation, which began in what is now Mexico, spread from there to both North and South America. Evidence for popcorn's long-term popularity and widespread use includes a 1,000-year-old popped kernel found in a Utah cave that had been inhabited by the Anasazi. (Anasazi culture arose in the North American Southwest in about 350 B.C.) Popcorn kernels dated from the same period also have been found in tombs on Peru's western coast. Archaeologists have found a funeral urn in Mexico, dated at A.D. 300, that depicts a Zapotec god wearing a headdress containing popcorn.

Popcorn was one of the first "new" foods that Spaniards experienced in the Americas. When Columbus landed in Hispaniola, the Arawak traded popcorn corsages with his crew as a form of exchange. Hernán Cortés and his men observed the Aztec using popcorn, not only as food but also as a part of ceremonial headdresses. (The Aztec established an empire in what is now Mexico in about A.D. 1100.) They called popcorn *momochitl* in Nahuatl, their native language, and believed that it had religious significance. The Aztec made necklaces from popped kernels and decorated religious statues with popcorn. Popcorn that they made by placing whole ears of corn into a fire was also used as an offering to the gods. An account of a one such ceremony reports that the Aztec referred to the kernels as "hailstones." The Inca, whose culture arose in the Andean region of South America in about A.D. 1000, made popcorn as well. They called it *pisancalla* in Quecha, their language. The

Spaniard Bernardo Cobo reported in 1650 that the Inca considered popcorn a confection, implying that it was sweetened. (See also CARAMEL CORN.)

French explorers in the North American Northeast found the Iroquois making popcorn in poppers filled with sand in the early 1600s. (See also POPCORN POPPERS.) Not only did Northeast culture groups eat popcorn by the handful, they also made it into soup. On occasion, Indians from various tribes brought popcorn for British colonists during peace negotiations as a goodwill offering. European settlers to the continent quickly adopted popcorn, eating it both as a snack and with milk and sugar as the first puffed cereal.

According to the Popcorn Board, a nonprofit trade organization of producers, popcorn is the top-selling snack food in the world today. People in the United States eat 18 billion quarts of popcorn a year, an average of 73 quarts per person. Consumption of the popular snack doubles about every 10 years. No doubt a great deal of popcorn's popularity can be attributed to its taste, but some of the industry's growth is because of popcorn's nutritional value. Low in fat, ounce for ounce, the kernels provide more protein and dietary fiber than does whole wheat bread. The iron content of popcorn is higher than that of spinach. Weighing only 3 1/2 ounces, a gallon of unbuttered popcorn contains 390 calories.

## Sources/Further Reading

Popcorn Board. *Popcorn!* http://www.popcorn.org/mpmain. htm. Downloaded on July 16, 1999.

Hauser, Nan and Sue Spitler. *The Popcorn Lover's Book.* Chicago: Contemporary Books, 1983.

Hurt, R. Douglas. *Indian Agriculture in the Americas: Prehistory to Present.* Lawrence: University Press of Kansas, 1988.

**popcorn poppers** (ca. A.D. 300) *Mesoamerican, South American Andean, North American Southwest cultures*

Popcorn poppers are containers specifically designed for making POPCORN. The first methods of popping corn that American Indians used was to throw kernels onto hot coals and collect them after they had popped. Another way was to push a stick through the cob and toast the whole ear in the flames. Sometimes they spread animal fat on the ear before heating it. Heating sand in a fire and then stirring the kernels and hot sand together until the kernels popped was yet another method of popping corn. American Indians invented clay pots to hold the sand and make this task easier. (See also POTTERY.) These pots evolved into poppers made from metal, clay, or soapstone to hold the melted animal fat and kernels. Some of these poppers had lids and others did not.

Shallow, decorated clay poppers with a hole on the top and a single handle made by the Moche about 300 A.D. have been found on the north coast of Peru. The pots spread to North America, where Northeast culture groups used the technique. In the North American Southwest the Tohono O'odham (Papago) continue to make popcorn today in large clay pots, or *ollas,* that are sometimes as large as eight feet in diameter.

Although American Indians sometimes popped corn by placing ears directly into the fire, a more convenient method was to use a pottery popcorn popper. They filled the popper with heated sand, added kernels, and then stirred them into the sand to heat them. *(A96664/Field Museum)*

European colonists, who adopted popcorn into their diet, also borrowed the concept of popcorn poppers from Indians.

In the 20th century it was the American Indian contribution of popcorn that indirectly led to the invention of the microwave oven. After the end of World War II, American inventor Percy Spencer noticed that a CHOCOLATE bar in his pocket had melted as he stood in front of a magnetron power tube that produced radar waves. On a hunch, he set a bag of unpopped popcorn kernels beside the tube. The corn popped, spurring him to experiment further and finally come up with the microwave oven.

## Sources/Further Reading

Hauser, Nan and Sue Spitler. *The Popcorn Lover's Book.* Chicago: Contemporary Books, 1983.

Josephy, Jr., Alvin M., ed. *America in 1492: The World of the Indian People Before the Arrival of Columbus.* New York: Random House, 1991.

*Lemelson-MIT Awards Program's Invention Dimension.* URL: http://web.mit.edu/investorsR-Z/spencer.html. Downloaded on July 16, 1999.

Popcorn Board. *Popcorn!* URL: http://www.popcorn.org/mpmain.htm. Downloaded on July 16, 1999.

## pop guns  See TOYS.

## potato chips  (A.D. 1853)  *North American cultures*

Potato chips are thinly sliced POTATOES that have been deep-fried in oil until they are crisp. Although American Indians had cultivated potatoes for thousands of years, the potato chip is a modern invention devised by George Crum, a Mohawk cook at an elegant resort in Saratoga Springs, New York.

During the summer of 1853, wealthy railroad baron Cornelius Vanderbilt, a diner at Moon Lake Lodge, sent a plate of french fries back to the kitchen, complaining they were too thick. Chef Crum made another order, this time slicing the potatoes thinner; that too was rejected. Angry, Crum decided to shave the potatoes into paper-thin slices with a peeler so they would be too crisp to eat with a fork once they were fried.

Vanderbilt and his friends were delighted with Crum's culinary invention and soon other diners wanted to sample the chips. Before long "Saratoga Chips" were not only part of the Moon Lake Lodge menu, they were being packaged and sold throughout New England. Crum opened his own restaurant that featured his gourmet treat. In the 1920s the invention of the automatic potato peeler and the waxed paper bag allowed mass production and distribution. By 1990 snackers throughout the world were eating a billion and a half pounds of potato chips each year. As of 1999 about 8 percent of the potatoes grown in the United States are made into chips.

## Sources/Further Reading

Carson, Dale. *New Native American Cooking.* New York: Random House, 1996.

Panati, Charles. *Panati's Extraordinary Origins of Everyday Things.* New York: Harper and Row, 1987.

Snack Food Association. URL: http://www.snackfood.com. Downloaded on September 6, 1999.

## potatoes  (white potatoes, *Solanum tuberosum*)

(8000 B.C.)  *South American Andean cultures*

Potatoes are a tuber-producing crop indigenous to the Americas. (Tubers are the swollen ends of underground stems.) Potato plants belong to the Solanacea family, to which TOBACCO, TOMATOES, and CHILES, also belong. Over 200 varieties of wild potatoes grow from what is now Colorado to what are now Chile and Argentina. The indigenous peoples of the Andean region of South America were the first to domesticate potatoes and to cultivate them as a food crop. The earliest potato, found in an archaeological site in central Peru, has been dated to about 8000 B.C. Scientists believe that American Indians began domesticating potatoes at the end of the ice age. Four thousand years later, indigenous people living in the Andean highlands had begun to rely on potatoes as a major part of their diet. By about 2000 B.C. Indians in the coastal region of what is now Peru were also cultivating this crop extensively.

During the reign of the Inca, who established their empire in what is now Peru in about A.D. 1000, American Indian farmers were growing not only white potatoes but red, yellow, black, blue, green, and brown ones as well. They were deliberately developing potatoes of varying sizes and shapes that would do well under a number of growing conditions. (See also SEED SELECTION; ZONED BIODIVERSITY.) Because potatoes are easily grown, flourish in a number of climates, and are high in both vitamin C and starch, they were an efficient way of meeting dietary needs for a number of people.

In 1531, when Spanish conquistador Francisco Pizarro landed in what is now Peru, the indigenous Andean people had developed about 3,000 types of potatoes and had also invented a method to FREEZE DRY them for storage. The Inca, who called potatoes *papas* in Quecha, their language, ate boiled potatoes as a vegetable and also made a kind of unleavened potato bread made from flour that had been ground from freeze-dried potatoes. They also added this potato flour to soups and stews and made a gruel, or porridge, from it.

Pedro de Cieza, who traveled with Francisco Pizarro's expedition, compared potatoes to chestnuts. Because the tubers grew underground and were small, the Spaniards believe potatoes were truffles and began calling them *tartuffo*. When English explorer Sir Francis Drake crossed the Strait of Magellan, he ate potatoes on the coast of what is now Chile that same year. Historians are uncertain exactly whether the Spaniards or the English brought potatoes to Europe. It is clear, however, that for the first 200 years, Europeans gave potatoes mixed reviews.

On one hand, many self-appointed experts claimed that the potato was not fit for human consumption because it had not been mentioned in the Bible. In 1618 potatoes were banned in the Burgundy region of France because people were convinced that eating then caused leprosy. In Switzerland experts blamed potatoes for causing scrofula, a disease characterized by swollen glands and coughing. Some European Orthodox religious sects declared the potato the devil's plant and made it a sin for their members to eat it. German peasants refused to eat potatoes, but an English author of the day, William Salmon, told his readers that potatoes could cure consumption and diarrhea. However, he warned, "They increase seed and provoke lust causing fruitfulness in both sexes." Until the late 1700s, the French believed potatoes were an aphrodisiac as well.

Despite the debate, the Spanish adopted potatoes as part of basic ships stores in addition to feeding them to the indigenous miners that they forced to work in Andean silver mines after conquest. (See also METALS, PRECIOUS.) Spanish speculators who bought dried potatoes and sold them to the mine administrators made fortunes in the freeze-dried potato trade. In Europe, peasant farmers in northern Spain began growing potatoes, and by 1601 the crop was being cultivated by peasants in Italy, who added potatoes to stews along with the traditional turnips and carrots.

After a number of severe famines swept across Europe in the 1700s, monarchies made laws ordering peasants to plant potatoes. (Two and a half acres of land planted in potatoes produced over 7.5 million calories, about twice as much as the same area of land planted with wheat.) Chronic malnutrition among mothers and infants, a problem that had been a constant for European peasantry, was suddenly and dramatically alleviated. Within 200 years after the introduction of the potato, European population tripled. Potatoes became the basis of subsistence in Ireland, Russia, and Germany. Potatoes had the added benefit of being less likely to be stolen by passing armies, who often took crops from fields to feed their men. Potatoes had to be dug from underground and this work discouraged their pillage. Because an acre and a half of potatoes could feed an average family for a year, less labor was required. As a result, many farmers resettled in cities. Some European historians credit the potato for making the Industrial Revolution possible. (The Portuguese introduced potatoes and SWEET POTATOES to China, providing alternative NUTRITION against rice failures.)

Irish tenant farmers became so dependent on the potato for their subsistence that a series of blights in the mid-1800s caused widespread starvation. Unlike South American Indian farmers, who planted a number of varieties of potatoes as an insurance against crop failure, Europeans had become dependent on one variety—the "Irish" potato. Within the space of a few years, the population of Ireland decreased from 9 million to about 4 million because of deaths as a result of the famine, emigration, and other causes.

Today about 250 varieties of potatoes are grown in the United States, with 20 of these varieties constituting three-fourths of the total harvest. According to the U.S. Department of Agriculture, the 1995 potato crop totaled 25 million tons.

See also AGRICULTURE.

## Sources/Further Reading

Coe, Sophie. *America's First Cuisines.* Austin: University of Texas Press, 1994.

Heiser, Charles B. *Seed to Civilization: The Story of Food.* Cambridge, Mass.: Harvard University Press, 1990.

Hobhouse, Henry. *Seeds of Change: Five Plants that Transformed Mankind.* New York: Harper & Row, 1986.

Salaman, Redcliffe N. *The History and Social Influence of the Potato.* Cambridge, England: Cambridge University Press, 1949.

Smith, Bruce D. *The Emergence of Agriculture.* New York: Scientific American Library, 1995.

Tannahill, Reay. *Food in History.* New York: Stein and Day, 1973.

Trager, James. *The Food Chronology: The Food Lover's Compendium of Events and Anecdotes from Prehistory to Present.* New York: Henry Holt, 1995.

Ugent, Donald and Linda W. Peterson. "Archaeological Remains of Potato and Sweet Potato in Peru." *The Circular of the International Potato Center* 16, no. 3 (1988): 1–10.

Weatherford, Jack. *Indian Givers: How the Indians of the Americas Transformed the World.* New York: Fawcett Columbine, 1988.

**potatoes, sweet** See SWEET POTATOES.

**pottery (ceramics)** (ca. 3000 B.C.) *North American Northeast, Southeast, Southwest; Mesoamerican; Circum-Caribbean, South American Andean cultures*
Pottery objects are made from clay that is heated so it will not absorb water and soften. This fired pottery is also called ceramics. Indians throughout the Americas produced a number of pottery items, inventing the process of shaping and firing clay independently of techniques used by other world cultures. The oldest piece of pottery in the Americas was discovered in the area of what is now Puerto Hormigas in Colombia, South America. It was dated at 3000 B.C.

Archaeologists believe that BASKET WEAVING TECHNIQUES influenced the form of pottery in America. Indigenous American potters constructed pottery objects using three techniques, called coiling, molding, and modeling. Sometimes these were used alone and sometimes they were used in combinations. Because American Indians did not use the wheel to throw pottery and shape it, they were not limited to producing symmetrical pots.

Generally, American Indians made two types of pottery: figurines and utilitarian items, such as storage and cooking vessels. Figurines were hollow or solid. They ranged in size from life-sized to several inches high, depending on the culture that made them. Frequently they were used for funerary or ritual purposes.

Utilitarian items varied widely throughout the Americas. They included: plates—plain, tripod, and with pedestals; bowls, with or without legs; bottles, with or without stoppers;

By 1916, when this photograph of potters at Santa Clara Pueblo in New Mexico was taken, pottery made by Southwest tribes had begun to be highly valued by collectors. Santa Clara pottery is distinguished from that made by other Southwest pottery makers by the use of impressing and carving as a means of decoration. Photographer H. T. Corey *(Photograph No. NWDNS-75-N-PU-40/ National Archives and Records Administration at College Park)*

palettes; incense burners; beakers, with or without ears (see also KEROS); urns, with or without lids or legs; and TOBACCO or SNUFF boxes. American Indians made a variety of jars. Some of these had handles and some did not; some were double, with two jars attached to each; and some had two spouts. The styles of these everyday objects varied from culture to culture.

Precontact people of the Americas also made MUSICAL INSTRUMENTS from fired clay. The oldest instruments were whistles. The earliest clay whistle found so far is one that is 1500 years old, made by the Maya of Mesoamerica. (Maya culture arose in about 1500 B.C.) Other instruments created by American Indian potters included flutes, drums, ocarinas, PAN PIPES, and horns. South American potters made long ceramic tubes used for blowing on the fires used for SMELTING ore.

South American cultures began making pottery as early as 3000 B.C. in what are now Ecuador, Colombia, and the Amazon lowlands. They made shallow bowls and neckless cooking pots that were used to boil food. The first decorations these South Americans made on pottery consisted of strips of clay that were appliquéd to the pot or bowl. Pottery making had

spread to what is now Peru by about 1000 years later. In about 1500 B.C. the Chavin culture that arose in Peru began making stirrup jars, two jars that are joined with a connecting bridge, or stirrup. By 900 B.C. Chavin potters had made great technological strides. They exercised control in their selection of clay and of the atmosphere and temperature at which they fired their pots. Although they had initially fired pottery in the open, starting in 900 B.C., Chavin potters began using updraft kilns built in pits lined with refractory, heat-resistant, clay. Archaeologists have found dozens of these pits in the same area, indicating that making pottery was a specialization and that one large production facility supplied the needs for a region.

Many ceramics experts agree that the Moche, whose culture flourished in what is now Peru from about 200 B.C. to about A.D. 800, were the finest potters in the world. Like the Chavin, they made stirrup jars, refining the technique. Their most well-known pottery items consisted of life-sized and life-like portraits. The Moche transformed the craft of pottery into an art form by making pottery vessels that reflected the natural world and culture around them. In doing so, they left a historical record of their lives in clay. (See also AMERICAN HISTORY, RECORDED.) Some of the Moche jars resembled agricultural products, including potatoes, beans, peanuts, cotton, fruit, and cacao. Others depicted people with illnesses and deformities, while others had small figures atop them going about the business of everyday life.

Moche potters often used molds in order to create these jars, which seemed to combine sculpture and pottery. They were among the first potters in South America to use molds. In addition to leaving a cultural record of molded vessels, Moche potters also painted scenes on the sides of jars that were symmetrically shaped and had smooth surfaces. These scenes depicted every aspect of Moche life from medicine to war to women giving birth.

Moche potters also made musical jars in the shape of birds. These were constructed so that when water was poured out, it forced air through a whistle. Potters made other jars that were double-walled and had a pellet in the space between the walls. When the jar was moved, the pellet rattled. They created stirrup jars with two spouts on opposite sides at the neck. These curved outward and then came together to form one spout. This made the jar look like it had a stirrup on top.

The Inca, who established an empire in about A.D. 1000, carried forward some of the Moche traditions, but their work did not attain such artistic heights. Their most unique pottery items were rectangular clay stoves that resembled wood cooking stoves of the 1800s. The clay stoves that the Inca made had openings at the top where the cooking took place and an opening in the front for inserting fuel into a compartment where the fire was built.

Mesoamerican pottery is usually divided into three periods. In the Formative period that began in 2000 B.C., most of the pottery that was produced consisted of jars and bowls made for domestic use. Mesoamerican Formative potters used black, brown, red, or white slip (a thin clay finish coating) and burnished it with a smooth pebble. They also decorated pots by incising designs into them and using wax resist, a method of painting a design onto a pot with hot wax and dipping the pot into a pigment of a different color.

During the Classic period, which began in about A.D. 300 and lasted 600 years, Teotihuacan and Maya potters produced a number of distinctive items. The Teotihuacán culture, which arose in the Valley of Mexico in about 150 B.C. and lasted to about A.D. 650, produced dolls with movable legs and arms that could swivel 360 degrees. These dolls could be posed in many positions. Teotihuacán potters covered their utilitarian vessels with dark brown or black slip and then incised designs into them. Sometimes they painted these incised designs with cinnabar. (See also MERCURY.)

The Maya, who inhabited the Yucatán Peninsula of what is now Mexico at this time, also made an unusual doll. These Maya figurines had clothing and trappings that could be put on or removed. One of the most unique pottery items the Maya made was a jar with a twist-off lid in about A.D. 400. These flat-bottomed jars were large enough to hold about a gallon of liquid, and the mouth openings were about six inches across. The lids fit onto the jars like lids fit on jars today. They were twisted open by turning them clockwise. The jars could be carried with one hand without spilling their contents when the lid was snugly tightened. Many historians claim that the precontact people of the Americas did not have knowledge of the screw, a simple machine. The Mayan locking jar lids provide evidence of a basic understanding of a simple concept of the screw, even though they did not apply it to areas other than pottery.

The Post Classic period of Mesoamerican pottery making began in about A.D. 900. During this time the Maya began using colored pigments. (See also DYES.) These produced a more decorative effect but had to be fired at a lower temperature, resulting in more fragile pottery. Decorative designs became more abstract. Maya potters began making orange ware as well as black pottery that is called plumbate ware today. They achieved the black color by careful control of the kiln. They also developed paint rollers and stamps in order to decorate their clay vessels.

The Aztec, who established an empire in what is now Mexico in about A.D. 1100, made pottery as well and sold their pots in the marketplaces of large cities. Bernard Diaz, a Spaniard who recorded Aztec life shortly after the arrival of Cortés, wrote that he saw ". . . every sort of pottery, made in a thousand forms from great water jars to little jugs" at the market in Tiateloco, near what would become Mexico City.

Potters made ceramic vessels throughout North America. For the most part they made utilitarian objects such as bowls and pots. These were usually decorated with geometric designs, or they were embellished by pressing objects, such as a CORN cob, into the wet clay to produce texture. Southwestern potters are the most well-known, both for their technique and design.

Potters of the North American Southwest began making plain gray clay cooking vessels. In time they began using colored slips. Later they made pitchers and mugs out of pink or red clay. The Anasazi, whose culture flourished in the North

Anasazi potters, who lived in the four corners area of the Southwest, created drinking vessels remarkably similar to modern coffee mugs in design. *(U.S. Bureau of Ethnography)*

American Southwest from about 350 B.C. to A.D. 1250, produced pottery mugs that were more similar in design to modern coffee mugs than drinking vessels of European design, including tankards.

Different tribes evolved unique styles of pottery decoration. During the Developmental Pueblo period, which lasted from about A.D. 700 to A.D. 1100, potters began using finer grades of clay for their pots. Although potters continued to make plain grayware, they also made black-on-white pottery and a lustrous black on red ware. Potters painted designs onto the pots with vegetable dyes at this time, and they begin using slips to give their work a smoother finish. Mimbres ware that was produced in about A.D. 950 in the southwestern part of what is now New Mexico featured stylized representations of birds, animals, and insects. Many southwestern art historians believe that the Mimbres style is the high point of precontact southwestern pottery. "These designs are not only beautifully drawn but spaced in such a way as to imply tension and a concern for the finer aspects of art," wrote art historian Emmanuel Cooper. Today the pueblos of the Southwest continue to produce pottery. Each pueblo is known for its distinctive pottery designs. These pots are recognized as art and have become collectors' items. One of the most highly regarded styles is the black pottery decorated with matte black designs first made at San Ildefonso Pueblo by Julian and Maria Martínez in 1919.

## Sources/Further Reading

Adams, R. E. W., ed. *The Origins of Maya Civilization*. Albuquerque: University of New Mexico Press, 1977.

Adams, Richard E. W. "Rio Azul: Lost City of the Maya." *National Geographic* 169, no. 4 (April 1986): 420–451.

Benson, Elizabeth P. *The Maya World.* New York: Thomas Y. Crowell Company, 1967.

Cooper, Emmanuel. *A History of Pottery.* New York: St. Martin's Press, 1972.

Deuel, Leo. *Conquistadors Without Swords: Archaeologists in the Americas.* New York: St. Martin's Press, Inc., 1967.

Engel, Frederic Andre. *An Ancient World Preserved: Relics and Records of Prehistory in the Andes.* Translated by Rachel Kendall Gordon. New York: Crown Publishers, Inc., 1972.

Fehrenbach, T. R. *Fire and Blood: A History of Mexico.* New York: Macmillan Publishing Co., Inc., New York, 1973.

Fiedel, Stuart J. *Prehistory of The Americas.* Cambridge, England: Cambridge University Press, 1987.

Gorenstein, Shirley. *Not Forever on Earth: Prehistory of Mexico.* New York: Charles Scribner's Sons, 1975.

Hazen-Hammond, Susan. *Timelines of Native American History.* New York: The Berkley Publishing Group, 1997.

Stuart, George E. "The Timeless Vision Of Teotihuacan." *National Geographic* 188, no. 6 (December 1995): 2–35.

Willey, Gordon R. *An Introduction to American Archaeology: Volume Two. South America.* Englewood Cliffs, N.J.: Prentice-Hall, Inc., 1971.

Wormington, H. M. *Prehistoric Indians of the Southwest.* Denver, Colo.: The Denver Museum of Natural History, 1947.

**potting soil**   See TRANSPLANTING, AGRICULTURAL.

**prescriptions**   (ca. 1000 B.C.)   *South American, Mesoamerican, North American cultures*

A prescription is an order or recommendation to administer a medication or treatment. The practice of ordering an established remedy or procedure for curing a particular disease is one that occurred many centuries ago in a number of cultures throughout the world. American Indians developed standard treatment protocols for illnesses and injuries that were based on close observations of which treatments worked for specific medical conditions. These prescriptions varied from culture to culture. Because American Indians relied primarily on oral tradition to preserve the body of their medical knowledge, European observers tended to assume that Native American healers selected treatments and medications in a random manner. This was not the case.

The sophisticated and extensive medical knowledge that American Indian physicians possessed was gained through experience. When ancient people living on what is now coastal Peru began the practice of TREPHINATION (brain SURGERY) sometime before 1000 B.C., they no doubt tried and failed many times before finding which herb made the best ANESTHETIC—much like modern pharmaceutical companies put drugs through trials. After they discovered that COCA worked best for their purposes, it became the anesthetic of choice for surgeons in that culture area. By the time of European contact, Indians throughout the Americas used ANTIBIOTIC MEDICATIONS and ORTHOPEDIC TECHNIQUES, prescribing them in a systematic and consistent manner.

Mesoamerican medical knowledge was the most codified in the Americas. (See also MEDICINE; MEDICAL RESEARCH.) For example, the Maya, whose culture arose in the Yucatán Peninsula of what is now Mexico in about 1500 B.C., and the Aztec, who established an empire in the central part of what is now Mexico in about A.D. 1100, prescribed specific treatments for dental problems (see also DENTISTRY), including the drilling and filling of cavities for toothaches. The Aztec had prescriptions for other dental problems as well, such as very specific treatments for halitosis (bad breath). When patients' teeth had too much plaque on them, they were cleaned with a metal instrument and polished with specific substances. (See also TARTAR REMOVAL.) Aztec medicine expert Bernard Ortiz de Montellano, relates other prescriptions: "For example, people with headaches were told not to sit in the sun, work, or enter hot steam baths. . . . Hot and irritated eyes were to be shielded from the heat of the sun, the glare of white things, and the irritation of smoke and wind." (See also HEADACHE MEDICATIONS.) The Aztec prescribed a standard and specific treatment for sore throat in the form of a saltwater gargle, and they also recognized the value of AROMATHERAPY, prescribing it for patients experiencing fatigue or depression. After conquest, Spanish priests recorded many of the Aztec treatment protocols. Consequently, knowledge of them has survived through time.

Modern understanding of treatment protocols, or prescriptions, in North America is sketchier. Although colonists borrowed many American Indian treatments, especially botanical drugs (see also PHARMACOLOGY), for the most part they did not observe or record American Indian medical practices as early or as extensively as the Spaniards did in Mexico and Peru. Despite this, some knowledge of North American Indian treatment protocols has survived. Anthropologists know that in precontact North America, many tribes prescribed lancing of the bite area and sucking out the poison for snake bites. (See also SNAKEBITE TREATMENTS.) This is known as cupping and suction today. Physicians from most North American culture groups understood the use of the TOURNIQUET and prescribed it for bleeding problems when appropriate, placing a ligature between the open wound and the heart. They also prescribed the sweat bath or lodge for rheumatism and arthritis. (See also ARTHRITIS TREATMENTS; STEAM ROOMS.)

**Sources/Further Reading**

Fernandez, Omar. "Pre-Columbian Surgery." *Gramna Weekly Review.* URL: http://www.marauder.millersv.edu/~columbus/data/art/FERNAN01.ART. Downloaded on November 6, 1999.

La Vega, Garcilaso de. *The Royal Commentaries of the Inca Garcilaso de la Vega, 1539–1616,* edited by Alain Gheerbrant. New York: The Orion Press, 1962.

Ortiz de Montellano, Bernard R. *Aztec Medicine, Health, and Nutrition.* New Brunswick, N.J.: Rutgers University Press, 1990.

Vogel, Virgil. *American Indian Medicine.* Norman: University of Oklahoma Press, 1970.

## prickly pear cacti (*Opuntia phaecantha*)

(precontact) *Mesoamerican, North American Southwest cultures*
The prickly pear is a variety of cactus that grows in the desert of the U.S. Southwest and northern Mexico. Flat stems, called pads, that are topped with flowers in the spring characterize the prickly pear. The flowers become fruits, or tunas, in the summer. Even in especially dry summers this cactus produces sweet fruits that are high in water content. Left on the cactus, they remain edible and can be picked and eaten well into the winter. In addition to using the prickly pear cactus for food, indigenous Americans also used it for medicine and as a DYE.

The Aztec, who established their empire in what is now Mexico in about A.D. 1100, also ate prickly pear tunas. The Spaniard Bernardo de Sahagun described seeing 13 types of tunas sold in the Aztec marketplace. He noted that some were sour and others were sweet. The Aztec boiled the juice of sweet tuna to make sugar. After removing the spines, the Aztec ate cactus pads raw in addition to boiling them as greens. The Maya, whose culture arose in what is now Mexico in about 1500 B.C., sometimes added prickly pear tunas to a fermented drink called *balche.*

The fruits as well as the pads of the prickly pear cactus were an important part of the Anasazi diet. (Anasazi culture arose in the North American Southwest in about 350 B.C. and flourished until A.D. 1250.) When archaeologists tried to replicate the harvest of *tunas* near a prehistoric Anasazi pit house, they found that one person wearing a glove could gather 19 pounds of fruit in 20 minutes, making the cacti an easily obtainable source of nutrition.

American Indians in the desert Southwest used prickly pear cactus pads as a kind of heating pad. After breaking off a cactus pad and burning off the spines, they would warm it over a fire. When it was hot, they would split it in half and apply it to aching joints. They used the same treatment for earaches and hemorrhoids. (See also EARACHE TREATMENTS.) Prickly pear cactus juice, like the juice of the AGAVE, was applied to the skin to treat rashes, sunburn, and chapped skin.

The Zuni, a Southwest desert tribe, used prickly pear tunas to make a reddish shoe polish for their MOCCASINS and to dye fibers for weaving. They dried and ground the tunas and then dissolved the powder in water with beeplant (*Cleome serralata*).

Today prickly pear tunas and pads remain a part of southwestern cuisine and are sold fresh in many grocery stores. Pads are also pickled, and canned juice from the tunas is made into candy.

### Sources/Further Reading

*Arizona Cactus & Succulent Research.* URL: http://www.primenet.com/~azcacus/medicine.htm. Downloaded on January 27, 1999.

Coe, Sophie. *America's First Cuisines.* Austin: University of Texas Press, 1994.

Dunmire, William W. and Gail D. Tierney. *Wild Plants of the Pueblo Province: Exploring Ancient and Enduring Uses.* Santa Fe: Museum of New Mexico Press, 1995.

## psychosomatics  See HOLISTIC HEALTH; PSYCHOTHERAPY.

## psychotherapy (talk therapy) (ca. A.D. 1100–A.D. 1519) *Mesoamerican, North American Northeast cultures*

Psychotherapy is the psychological treatment of mental or emotional disorders. The goal of most modern psychotherapeutic approaches is to help the client gain insight in order to resolve the problem or to help make the problem more bearable. Although Sigmund Freud, a Viennese physician, is credited with inventing the technique that he called psychoanalysis in the 1890s, a precursor to many modern schools of psychotherapy, American Indians had been practicing remarkably similar techniques for hundreds of years before this time. The Aztec, who established an empire in what is now Mexico in about A.D. 1100, and the Iroquois and Huron, North American northeastern tribes, developed and practiced psychotherapy well before contact with Europeans.

When medications were not working and SURGERY was not required, or when a patient's illness was very serious or chronic, Aztec physicians urged the patient to talk about what might be the cause of the disorder. They believed that if, for example, the trauma or pain of a sexual indiscretion had caused the illness, the patient would need to talk about the incident. Modern therapists who use this technique call it abreaction. After allowing the patient to talk the problem out, the physician advised that person to bathe immediately. The bathing was a symbol of the emotional cleansing that had come about from talking. Sometimes the physician suggested other rites or gave instructions that would allow the patient to atone for the problem. When modern psychotherapist do this, it is called suggestion. By using the psychological tools of abreaction and suggestion, Aztec physicians were able to treat many psychosomatic illnesses effectively.

In the North American Northeast the Iroquois and Huron also practiced psychotherapy. Jesuit priests writing in the 1600s described their techniques, which anthropologists believe were practiced long before contact with Europeans. The precontact American Indian method of psychotherapy was based on FREE ASSOCIATION and dream analysis (see also DREAMWORK PSYCHOLOGY), two key elements of modern psychotherapy. When standard medications did not relieve a patient's illness, Iroquois and Huron healers believed that the illness was psychogenic, stemming from the patient's unmet or unspoken needs. The Iroquois and Huron thought that if these unmet needs continued, further psychosomatic problems might ensue. They also recognized that dreams were important and needed to be talked about, just as Freud discovered hundreds of years later. If this did not work, the Indian physician encouraged patients to talk about anything that came to mind—a technique called free association that is also practiced in modern psychoanalysis.

North American Indian psychotherapy was advanced in yet another respect. It encouraged the family and community to become involved in the patient's recovery. In a 1946 article, Erwin H. Ackerknecht compared Iroquois psychotherapy to medical practice in the mid-20th century: "The participation of the community in the healing rites, and the strong connection between these rites and the whole religion and tradition of the tribe, produce certain psychotherapeutic advantages for the medicine man which the modern physician lacks." Starting in the 1970s, the tool of involving a patient's family and friends in the healing process has been adopted by many modern therapists.

See also MEDICINE.

## Sources/Further Reading

Ackerknecht, Erwin H. "Primitive Medicine: A Contrast with Modern Practice." *The Merck Report* (July 1946): 4–8.
Ortiz de Montellano, Bernard R. *Aztec Medicine, Health, and Nutrition.* New Brunswick, N.J.: Rutgers University Press, 1990.
Vogel, Virgil. *American Indian Medicine.* Norman: University of Oklahoma Press, 1970.

## public drunkenness laws   (ca. A.D. 1100–A.D. 1519) *Mesoamerican cultures*

Although the Aztec, who established an empire in what is now Mexico in about A.D. 1100, fermented an alcoholic beverage called *pulque* from the AGAVE plant, they had very strict laws regulating its use. In the Aztec world, alcohol consumption for most people was limited to feasts and holidays. The exception to this was the elderly, who could drink at any time by virtue of their age. When intoxicated priests or nobles were caught, they were severely punished, since they were expected to be role models for others in society. In many cases they were put to death. Alcohol was prohibited to the young, and commoners who were found intoxicated were punished by having their heads shaved. If they were caught again, they could be put to death as well.

The Aztec also had an alcoholic drink called *octli*. In his book *Daily Life of the Aztecs on the Eve of the Spanish Conquest,* author Jacques Soustelle cites a speech given by an Aztec noble who called the drink, "the root and the origin of all evil and of all perdition; for *octli* and drunkenness are the cause of all the discord and of all dissensions, of all revolt and of all troubles in cities and in realms. It is like the whirlwind that destroys and tears down everything. It is like a malignant storm that brings all evil with it. Before adultery, rapes, debauching of girls, incest, theft, crime, cursing and bearing false-witness, murmuring, calumny, riots and brawling, there is drunkenness. All those things are caused by *octli* and by drunkenness." These ancient American Indians thus recognized and knew the dangers

of alcohol but were able to control it by establishing very strict regulations for its use.

See also DISTILLATION.

## Sources/Further Reading

Coe, Sophie. *America's First Cuisines.* Austin: University of Texas Press, 1994.
Ortiz de Montellano, Bernard R. *Aztec Medicine, Health, and Nutrition.* New Brunswick. N.J.: Rutgers University Press, 1990.
Soustelle, Jacques. *Daily Life of the Aztecs on the Eve of the Spanish Conquest.* Translated by Patrick O'Brian. Stanford, Calif.: Stanford University Press, 1961.

## public health   (ca. A.D. 1100–A.D. 1519) *Mesoamerican cultures*

Public health, a relatively new area of Western MEDICINE, concerns itself with improving the health of an entire community. The discipline of public health focuses on wellness, personal HYGIENE, sanitation, public health institutions, health education, population issues, and social welfare.

The Aztec, who established an empire in what is now Mexico in about A.D. 1100, practiced public health measures long before contact with Europeans. The Aztec made both personal hygiene and community cleanliness high priorities. City residents had access to clean running water through plaster-lined canals built throughout the communities. Water for personal use was conveyed through communities by a dual canal system. Human waste products were conveyed out of the community manually or by canals. (See also PLUMBING.) Empire administrators employed street cleaners to keep the streets and walkways spotless. After they had swept the streets, they washed them to keep the dust down. Spanish conquistadores were extremely impressed by the cleanliness of Aztec cities compared to those in Europe. (See also CITIES, AMERICA'S FIRST.)

The Aztec Empire built public health HOSPITALS for the poor—the first public health hospitals in the world. These institutions were staffed by doctors who were specialists, as well as by midwives and NURSES. The Aztec health system made prenatal care available to expectant mothers.

Aztec parents provided sex education for their young people, warning them of the dangers of premarital sex. Aztec medicine expert Bernard Ortiz de Montellano gives an example of this education in his book *Aztec Medicine, Health, and Nutrition.* According to Ortiz de Montellano, typical instructions a young man might receive were: "Do not throw yourself upon women like the dog which throws itself upon food. Be not like the dog when he is given food or drink, giving yourself to women before the time comes. Even though you may long for women, hold back, hold back your heart until you are a grown man, strong and robust. . . . before you know woman you must grow and be a complete man. And then you will be ready for marriage; you will beget children of good stature, health, agile and comely."

The Aztec made certain that all people, even the young, were productive citizens and worked at some job. They recognized that dependency could hurt others and become a community problem because the dependent or lazy person would become a poor worker and eventually become a burden to others. The Nahuatl, or Aztec, word for this condition was *netepalhuilztli*, which meant "harm due to dependence on another." When Aztec administrators noticed that a person had become too dependent on others, they referred the person, who was considered to be ill, to a physician who specialized in mental health. (See also PSYCHOTHERAPY.)

**Sources/Further Reading**
Coe, Sophie. *America's First Cuisines.* Austin: University of Texas Press, 1994.
Ortiz de Montellano, Bernard R. *Aztec Medicine, Health, and Nutrition.* New Brunswick, N.J.: Rutgers University Press, 1990.
Soustelle, Jacques. *Daily Life of the Aztecs on the Eve of the Spanish Conquest.* Translated by Patrick O'Brian. Stanford, Calif.: Stanford University Press, 1961.
Vogel, Virgil. *American Indian Medicine.* Norman: University of Oklahoma Press, 1970.

**pulleys**  (precontact)  *North American, Mesoamerican cultures*
The pulley is a simple machine that is used to change the direction of a pulling force. It is one of the five basic machines invented by the ancient Greeks—the pulley, the wedge, the inclined plane, the lever, and the screw. Ancient Mesoamerican Indians also understood the concept of the pulley. Unlike the Greeks, who used the principle for architecture and engineering, the Maya and Aztec of Mesoamerica used the pulley for MEDICINE, specifically for setting broken and dislocated bones. (Maya culture arose in what is now Mexico in about 1500 B.C. The Aztec established their empire in what is now Mexico in about A.D. 1100.) Maya and Aztec physicians would attach a line to the limb that needed to be set, run the free end over a beam, and pull on it. The American Indians of North America also used the pulley to set broken bones. Clara Sue Kidwell and Peter Nabokov, writing in *Studying Native America,* cite this method as one example of American Indian technology. ". . . a simple pulley was used in a plains medical technique. To reset a dislocated joint, a man would tie a rawhide rope around the affected limb, throw the rope over a tree branch, and pull on it. This was a simple, but generally effective method of exerting sufficient force to pop the joint back into place."

See also TRACTION/COUNTERTRACTION; ORTHOPEDIC TECHNIQUES.

**Sources/Further Reading**
Adams, William R. "Aboriginal American Medicine and Surgery." *Proceedings of the Indiana Academy of Science* 61 (1951): 15–36.
Kidwell, Clara Sue and Peter Nabokov. "Directions in Science and Technology." In *Studying Native America,* edited by Russell Thornton. Madison: The University of Wisconsin Press, 1998.
Vogel, Virgil. *American Indian Medicine.* Norman: University of Oklahoma Press, 1970.
Zeisberger, David. "History of the North American Indians." *Ohio Archaeological and Historical Quarterly* 19, nos. 1–2 (January and April 1910): 12–153.

**pulse, radial**  (ca. A.D. 1100)  *Mesoamerican cultures*
The radial pulse is the spot on the wrist at the base of the thumb that medical practitioners use to count the heart's beats in order to determine heart rate. In pre-Columbian times, the Aztec of Central America were well aware of the radial pulse, because they had a word for it: *tlahuatl.* (The Aztec established an empire in what is now Mexico in about A.D. 1100.) In his book *American Indian Medicine,* Virgil Vogel states, "Indian doctors sometimes felt the patient's pulse." Several other sources also make reference to this practice of American Indian healers.
See also ANATOMICAL KNOWLEDGE; MEDICINE.

**Sources/Further Reading**
Peredo, Miguel Guizman. *Medical Practice in Ancient America.* Mexico City: Ediciones Euroamericanas, 1985.
Vogel, Virgil. *American Indian Medicine.* Norman: University of Oklahoma Press, 1970.

**pumpkins**  (ca. 8000 B.C.)  *Mesoamerican, North American cultures*
Pumpkins are a variety of the *Cucurbita pepo* genus, commonly known as summer SQUASH. Pumpkin plants produce fruits that are large, round, and orange, and their flesh is mild and sweet. American Indians in both Mesoamerica and North America independently domesticated pumpkins. Indian farmers of North America grew them for thousands of years before the arrival of the Europeans and the first THANKSGIVING. They roasted or boiled pumpkins and served them as vegetables. As they did with squash seeds, American Indians roasted and ate pumpkin seeds. These are called *pepitas* in Mesoamerica and South America today.

English colonists quickly incorporated pumpkins into their diet. Historians believe it was probably a dish resembling pumpkin pudding, rather than pumpkin pie, that might have been served at the feast that was immortalized as the first Thanksgiving. Colonial women in North America made pumpkin pies in the years afterward. The dessert became such a standard part of the Thanksgiving menu that one Connecticut settlement is reported to have postponed their Thanksgiving feast because a shortage of molasses made it impossible to prepare the pies. Colonists also used pumpkins as the basis for beer when they found that the New England soil did not produce barley and hops in the amounts they required.

**Sources/Further Reading**
Herbst, Sharon Tyler. *The New Food Lover's Companion: Comprehensive Definitions of Over 4,000 Food, Wine, and Culinary Terms.* New York: Barrons Educational Services, Inc., 1995.

Matthews, Todd. "Thanksgiving with Reader's Digest: Gorgeous Gourds, Squash, and Pumpkins." *Reader's Digest Association.* URL: http://www.rdthanksgiving.com/tasty-traditions/gourd.html. Downloaded on July 7, 1998.

Weatherford, Jack. *Indian Givers: How the Indians of the Americas Transformed the World.* New York: Fawcett Columbine, 1988.

**pyramids**  (ca. 3000 B.C.)  *North American, South American, Mesoamerican cultures*

Pyramids are massive structures that are broad at the bottom and taper to a point, or apex, at the top. American Indians in Mesoamerica and South America built pyramids of ADOBE and stone. (See also STONEMASONRY TECHNIQUES.) North American Indians built huge, somewhat pyramid-shaped mounds of earth.

The Pyramid of the Magician built by the Maya during the late Classic period at Uxmal in the Yucatán Peninsula is 100 feet tall. It was built in five stages, one superimposed on the other. The stairway of the pyramid faces the setting sun at the summer solstice. *(Abbye A. Gorin Collection from the Latin American Library Photographic Archive, Tulane University)*

Some of the pyramids built in the Americas were equal in size to the Egyptian pyramids. The first American pyramid builders were the indigenous inhabitants of what is now Peru who began building their first pyramids of adobe in about 3000 B.C. Two of the first of these were at El Aspero, located in the central coastal area of present-day Peru, and Caral, 120 miles north of what is Lima. This settlement covered 33 acres and had terraces, underground storage niches, and residential areas as well as a ritual center. South American pyramid builders began constructing these structures several hundred years before the pyramids of Egypt. (Archaeologists believe that the Egyptians built their first pyramid at Sakkara between 2886 and 2613 B.C. and constructed the famous Giza pyramids between 2589 and 2504 B.C.) In about 1800 B.C., South American ceremonial centers and pyramids took on a different look. Ancient engineers and architects started building them in a U shape that faced the plazas. (See also URBAN PLANNING.) Archaeological writer and professor Brian M. Fagan has written that these South American pyramids ". . . rank among the most ambitious of all public works undertaken by the prehistoric Americans."

The Huaca del Sol, built by the Moche, is known as the largest adobe structure in the precontact Americas. Moche culture arose in what is now Peru in about 200 B.C. *Huaca*, which means "sacred structure," is the term used for pyramids in Peru. The base of the Huaca del Sol pyramid is 1132 feet by 525 feet, and it is 98 feet tall. Archaeologists estimate that about 140 million adobe bricks were molded and arranged in columns in order to construct it, making it the largest adobe structure in the Americas. Huaca del Sol is paired with a smaller pyramid, Huaca del Luna. Together they served as a ritual and administrative center. Although early pre-Peruvian cultures mummified (see also MUMMIES) their dead and also used EMBALMING, they buried them in caves rather than in *huacas*.

In Mesoamerica, the Olmec began building pyramids between 2000 and 1500 B.C. The pyramid they built at La Venta was one of the tallest ones their culture produced; it stood 112 feet high. Olmec engineers constructed these pyramids in a unique way. They built rooms on each level, or tier, and then filled them in with rock, sand, and gravel. When all the rooms were full, they built another level, filled it, and repeated the process until the pyramid was completed. The ancient engineers then built an outer surface, called a facing, on the pyramids. These facings were often made of basalt or granite. The Olmec, like the Egyptians, built sarcophagi (sandstone coffins) and interred their dead royalty within the pyramids.

The Maya built the largest pyramid in Mesoamerica. (Maya culture arose in what is now the Yucatán Peninsula of Mexico in about 1500 B.C.) This pyramid is located at Cholula, Mexico in the Mexican highlands near Popocatepetl and Iztaccihuatl, twin volcanic peaks. Standing 181 feet high, it was part of a complex that covered an area of at least 25 acres. The Aztec, whose empire was established in what is now Mexico in about A.D. 1100, continued to build pyramids in the Mesoamerican tradition begun by the Olmec.

In precontact North America around A.D. 1000, the Mississippian culture built a city—called Cahokia today—near the confluence of the Mississippi and Illinois Rivers. When this culture was at its height more than 30,000 people lived in Cahokia. The largest structure in the complex was Monk's Mound, standing 100 feet high. Although Monk's Mound was small in comparison to many South American and Mesoamerican pyramids, it was the largest structure in North America during prehistoric times. The builders of Cahokia also built 68 smaller mounds in their city. Southeastern people built earthen pyramids throughout the Southeast, including locations in what are now Florida, Georgia, and Alabama. The Mound Builders also built smaller constructions as far north as what are now Minnesota and Michigan. Most of these mounds were used for burials.

## Sources/Further Reading

Coe, Michael D. *America's First Civilization: Discovering the Olmec.* Eau Claire, Wisc.: E. M. Hale And Company, 1968.

Fagan, Brian M. *Kingdoms of Gold, Kingdoms of Jade: The Americas Before Columbus.* London: Thames and Hudson, Ltd., 1991.

*Olmec.* URL: http://library.advanced.org/18778/olmec.htm. Downloaded on November 23, 1999.

*Olmec Advanced Materials Ltd.—Olmec Civilization.* URL: http://www.olmec.co.uk/olmec.html. Downloaded on November 23, 1999.

*Mexico History—The Classic Period (300–900 A.D.): Cholula, Monte Alban.* URL: http://www.mexconnect.com/mex_/hclassic2.html. Downloaded on November 23, 1999.

Stuart, Gene S. *The Mighty Aztecs.* Washington, DC: Special Publications Division, National Geographic Society, 1981.

Thompson, J. Eric S. *Maya History and Religion.* Norman: University of Oklahoma Press, 1970.

**quarantines** See ISOLATION.


**quicksilver** See MERCURY.


**quinine** (precontact)  *South American Andean cultures*
Quinine is a medicine once widely used to cure malaria, a serious, chronic disease contracted from pathogens that are carried from human to human by mosquitoes. The symptoms of this disease include chills, fever, anemia, and enlargement of the spleen, and it often has fatal complications. The drug quinine comes from the bark of a tree that grows in the mountains of Peru. The Inca, who established an empire in what is now Peru in about A.D. 1000, and the Quecha before them called the tree *quina,* or *quinquina,* a native word that means "bark of barks;" quinine derived its name from this word. The active ingredient in *quinquina* is an alkaloid called cholorquine, which acts by inhibiting the growth of malaria parasites in the infected person's red blood cells.

In addition to being used to treat malaria, quinine was also prescribed for fevers. It works to lower the body temperature by dilating the small blood vessels and alleviate pain by acting on the central nervous system. American Indians living in the area where the quina tree grew used it for fevers, childbirth, and postnatal therapy. (See also OBSTETRICS.)

Malaria did not exist in the Americas until Europeans introduced it. In Europe the disease had been known for centuries. In *Plant Drugs That Changed the World,* author Norman Taylor wrote, "It is next to impossible to exaggerate the curse that malaria has been for countless centuries. It has killed more people than all the wars, more than all the plagues, even the Black Death. And the millions it does not kill it leaves a legacy of fever, chills, weakness and such a lack of ambition that the poor and destitute victims are usually left to swelter 'in their own stench.'"

In 1638 the countess of Cinchon—wife of a Spanish colonial count who lived in Lima, Peru—fell ill with malaria. The court physician, Juan de Vega, who obviously relied on native healing practices, recommended she be given a preparation made from the bark of the quinquina tree that could be found growing 500 miles away in what is now Ecuador. Conquistadores and colonists alike frequently relied on American Indian medicines in preference to the blood-letting that played a key role in their own medical traditions. More than likely de Vega hoped to lower the countess's fever with this indigenous botanical drug. After she took the quinquina bark medicine, she became the first European on record to be cured with quinine. Botanists renamed Cinchona in her honor. Eager to seek his fortune from his "discovery," Dr. de Vega returned to Spain in 1648 and began to sell the South American bark in Seville for $75 an ounce.

Many historians subsequently edited American Indians from the story of quinine's discovery. According to Virgil J. Vogel, an expert on American Indian medicine, "Because some of the early history of cinchona has been wrapped in myth and mystery, some writers have hesitated to grant the Indians credit for the discovery of it, but several authorities have marshaled imposing evidence of aboriginal use of this remedy for fevers." He cites as an example a Jesuit missionary in what had become Peru who was cured of an intermittent fever in 1600 by the cinchona bark that he had received from an American Indian healer. TONIC WATER containing quinine was drunk in the British colonies as a medicine. Quinine was commercially produced in 1827 and was used to treat malaria until WWI, when researchers made a synthetic drug that replaced it.

See also MEDICINE; PHARMACOLOGY; TONIC WATER.

### Sources/Further Reading
Haggis, A.W. "Fundamental Errors in the Early History of Cinchona," *Bulletin of the History of Medicine* 10, no. 3

(October 1941): 417–59; no. 4 (November 1941): 568–92.

Hobhouse, Henry. *Seeds of Change: Five Plants that Transformed Mankind.* New York: Harper & Row, 1986.

Lust, John. *The Herb Book.* New York: Bantam Books, 1974.

Taylor, Norman. *Plant Drugs that Changed the World.* New York: Dodd, Mead, and Company, 1965.

University of Iowa Medical Museum. "Nature's Pharmacy: Ancient Knowledge: Modern Medicine." URL: www.uihealthcare.com/depts/medmuseum/naturespharmacy/cinchonaplant/cinchona.html Downloaded April 11, 2001.

Vogel, Virgil. *American Indian Medicine,* Norman: University of Oklahoma Press, 1970.

Weatherford, Jack. *Indian Givers: How the Indians of the Americas Transformed the World.* New York: Fawcett Columbine, 1988.

## quinoa *(Chenopodium quinoa, chesiya mama)*

(ca. 3000 B.C.)   *South American Andean cultures*

Quinoa, pronounced "keenwa," is a seed-bearing plant that is related to the common weed called lamb's quarters. Quinoa plants produce thousands of small seeds clustered like plumes at the ends of their stalks. These resemble a cross between sesame seeds and millet—a fact that led early Spanish explorers to mistakenly called the broad-leafed plants millet. Quinoa is an annual plant that grows from three to six feet high. The seeds, as well as the plant itself, were a staple in the diet of South American Indians, who had cultivated it for at least 5,000 years in the cold, dry climate of the Andes. Quinoa seeds, which are not considered a true grain, contain twice as much protein as barley, corn, or rice. They are high in the amino acid lysine. The protein they contain is nearly complete, making it easily used by the body. Quinoa seeds are also relatively high in fat. The carbohydrates in quinoa are more easily digested than those of sorghum, wheat, corn, rye, or millet. In addition, quinoa contains phosphorous, calcium, iron, vitamin E, and B vitamins.

The Inca, who established an empire in what is now Peru in about A.D. 1000, recognized quinoa's nutritional value and fed it to their armies. They marched for days while sustaining themselves with a mixture of quinoa and fat that they called "war balls." (See also FAST FOOD; PEMMICAN.) South American Andean cultures called the crop *chesiya mama,* which means "the mother of grains" in Quecha, the Inca language. Every year the Inca ruler planted the first quinoa seeds with a golden spade. During the solstice, priests made offerings of the grain to the sun god Inti.

The Inca ground quinoa into flour and used it to make TAMALES. Combined with water, ground quinoa also served as a high-energy drink. The Inca used ground quinoa to make bread that could be dried for storage as well as a type of DUMPLINGS—steamed balls of flour that had been mixed with fat, salt, and seasonings. A Spanish observer recorded that the Inca made cakes from quinoa flour. Quinoa flour also served as the basis for a sweet gruel. The Inca used the leaves in stews and cooked whole quinoa seeds in soups and stews in combination with POTATOES and CHILE. Andean Indians also ate the entire plant as a salad or vegetable. The Inca made *chicha,* or beer, from quinoa by chewing on it to help begin the fermentation process and then spitting it out.

Andean Indians also used quinoa for medicinal purposes—for instance, as an antiinflammatory, a toothache remedy, and a disinfectant. The Inca used quinoa to stop internal bleeding and as an INSECT REPELLENT.

Since quinoa seeds are coated with a naturally occurring bitter chemical, a toxic glycoside called saponin that discourages birds from eating it, indigenous farmers carefully washed the seeds after harvest in order to remove the chemical. When ingested, saponins not only taste bitter but also decrease the body's absorption of the seeds' nutrients and can cause damage to the small intestines. Andean Indians used the by-product of saponin from quinoa processing as a laundry DETERGENT and as an ANTISEPTIC that was used on injuries to the skin.

Quinoa cultivation began to decline after the Spaniards introduced crops such as barley and wheat to what would become Bolivia and Peru. Because quinoa took longer to harvest and thresh, and because it required processing in order to remove the saponins, it was a labor-intensive crop. The Spaniards did not introduce quinoa to Europe as they had potatoes and CORN. Some historians believe that omission occurred because they had tasted unwashed seeds that were still coated with saponin and thought the crop useless because of its bitter taste. Some farmers living in the Andes did continue to cultivate this crop. In 1984 a Colorado entrepreneur introduced quinoa to the U.S. market. Production in South America has expanded from Peru and Bolivia to Columbia, Ecuador, and Chile. In the United States it is grown primarily in Colorado. Modern processors remove saponins from the seeds by washing or abrasion.

Quinoa seeds are sold primarily in health food stores. The saponins that are removed from quinoa have a number of uses. Those removed from the variety of the plant that produces white seeds are being explored by the pharmaceutical industry for the production of steroids. (See also YAMS). Saponins from yellow quinoa seeds are used in the manufacturing of detergents, soaps, shampoos, cosmetics, beer, photographic chemicals, fire extinguishers, and synthetic hormones. The entire plant is used as animal food.

See also AGRICULTURE; AMARANTH; CHIA; MANIOC

### Sources/Further Reading

Bermejo, J. E. Hernando, and J. Leon, eds. *Neglected Crops: 1492 From a Different Perspective.* Rome, Italy: FAO, 1994.

Coe, Sophie. *America's First Cuisines.* Austin: University of Texas Press, 1994.

Cox, Beverly and Martin Jacobs. "Quinoa—Mother Grain of the Incas." *Native Peoples Magazine* (Spring 1997).

Johnson, Duane L. and Sarah M. Ward. "Quinoa." In *New Crops,* edited by J. Janick and J.E. Simon. New York: Wiley, 1993.

**quipus** (ca. A.D. 1000) *South American Andean cultures*
A quipu is an accounting and communication system that uses knotted strings to record information. The positioning and number of the knots tied into the strings of a quipu is determined by the content of the information that is being recorded. Pre-Inca, Inca, and other indigenous culture groups in South America employed quipus for a number of purposes, including accounting and the preservation of historical data.

Although the quipus of other groups have not been well preserved, those of the Inca, who established an empire in what is now Peru in about A.D. 1000, remained intact. Because of this, more is known about the Inca quipu than those of other South American cultures. Inca quipus were quite elaborate, often being made up of over 100 individual knotted strings of many colors. These were kept in order by being tied to a main string. The Inca used quipus to record and transmit information about the quantities and types of food and other goods stored in warehouses (see also CROP STORAGE), tributes (see also TAX SYSTEMS), the output of mines, CENSUS data, and ac-

The Inca used quipus to record and transmit information. Those schooled in the art were called *quipucamayoc*. Some scholars have compared the sophisticated system of storing information to the binary system used in computer technology today. *(After Felipe Guamán Poma de Ayala.* Nueva Coronica y Buen Gobierno*)*

countings of workers and soldiers. Such accountings were kept using the decimal system. Once a *quipucamayoc*, a quipu specialist, had tied the knots, runners called *chasqui* carried it in relays along an extensive ROAD SYSTEM until it reached its destination. There another *quipucamayoc* translated the meaning of the knots.

Some quipus used knots to represent words, according to the Spanish chronicler Cieza de León. A recently surfaced Jesuit manuscript written shortly after conquest adds credence to de León's reports. Its authors claimed that some quipus contained poetry. Some anthropologists believe that quipus found in burials may have contained astrological information or data based on a system of numerology. Although the Jesuit manuscript remains to be proven authentic, such theories are both interesting and entirely possible.

Those who encoded and decoded this logical-numerical information, the *quipucamayoc*, tended to specialize in a particular type of information, such as military, population, or economic data. The knotted systems were so sophisticated that they have been said to resemble the way data is broken down, stored, and retrieved using computers in modern times. *Quipucamayoc* used hundreds of colors for their strings and needed the ability to recognize and accurately interpret them. Art historian Cesar Paternoster wrote of the quipus that they were "a harmonically organized system of visual, or visual-tactile signs that operate as an efficient substitute for writing." (See also WRITING SYSTEMS.)

Spanish priests, who believed that quipus were the work of the devil, destroyed most of them. Today about 550 remain in existence. Anthropologists continue to work to decode them. Although they have made progress in understanding the mathematical data stored on the knotted strings, many mysteries still remain.

See also ABACUS.

**Sources/Further Reading**
Ascher, Marcia. "Before the Conquest." *Math Magazine* 65 (1992).
Domenenci, Viviano and Davide Domenenci. "Talking Knots of the Inka: a Curious Manuscript May Hold the Key to Andean Writing." *Archaeology* (November/December 1996): 50–56.
Paternosto, Cesar. *The Stone and the Thread: Andean Roots of Abstract Art.* Austin: University of Texas Press, 1996.
Salmoral, Manuel Lucena. *America 1492: Portrait of a Continent 500 Years Ago.* New York: Facts On File, 1990.

**Quonset huts, American Indian influence on**
(A.D. 1941) *North American Northeast cultures*
Quonset huts are lightweight, portable buildings that are easily and quickly constructed. They are composed of a skeleton of semicircular ribs covered by corrugated steel. These buildings were invented at the beginning of World War II to house military personnel on short notice in a cost-effective manner. Many people believe that they were patterned after longhouses,

dwellings that the Iroquois and other Northeast tribes had constructed for hundreds of years before contact with Europeans. (See also APARTMENT COMPLEXES.) Although the inventors of Quonest huts never credited American Indian architects for the inspiration for these military buildings, the structure is the same as that designed by the Indians.

The Iroquois and Huron built longhouses by attaching basswood or cedar bark to a frame made from semicircular wooden saplings lashed to upright posts that had been sunk into the ground. Indians of these groups lived in the structures and also designated one longhouse as a council lodge. The semicircular shape of these longhouses allowed rain to run off their roofs easily and prevented snow buildup in winter from collapsing them. The roof was of bowed poles that were covered with bark sheeting. The Iroquois moved their village sites about every 10 to 20 years when soil quality diminished because of farming and firewood became scarce. (See also MILPA.) Because longhouses were simple to construct, making a new village was not a tremendously time-consuming task. Some of the larger Iroquois and Huron villages contained as many as 200 longhouses.

In 1941, as World War II loomed on the horizon, the U.S. Navy contracted with George A. Fuller Construction Company in New York to design fast, cheap housing that could be erected by untrained people. Architects Peter Dejongh and Otto Brandenberger sat down at the drawing board and in a few months set up a factory near Quonset Point, Rhode Island, a town with an American Indian name. (See also PLACE-NAMES.) During the war the factory produced about 170,000 Quonset huts. After the war ended, the U.S. government sold them to businesses and individuals for about $1,000 apiece. Many are still in use today, a testament to the utility and economy of a design that was first created by American Indians.

## Sources/Further Reading

Flexner, Stuart Berg. *I Hear America Talking: An Illustrated History of American Words and Phrases.* New York: Simon and Schuster, 1976.

Leinhard, John H. *Engines of Our Ingenuity, No. 1278: Quonset Huts.* URL: http://www.uh.edu/engines/epi1278.htm. Downloaded on October 21, 1999.

Nabokov, Peter and Robert Easton. *Native American Architecture.* New York: Oxford University Press, 1989.

Weatherford, Jack. *Native Roots: How the Indians Enriched America.* New York: Fawcett Columbine, 1991.

# R

**radial pulse**  See PULSE, RADIAL.

**rafts, balsa and reed**  (ca. A.D. 1000)  *South American Andean cultures*

The Inca, who established an empire in what is now Peru in about A.D. 1000, made rafts, flat-bottomed boats of BALSA WOOD. Balsa is one of the lightest woods known and continues to be used in the boat building industry today. The rafts that the Inca made were the largest floating vessels made in the pre-contact Americas. Primarily they were used to hold cargo for trading missions north of what is now Ecuador. Traders used the rafts to navigate over thousands of miles of open sea. According to contemporary accounts, these traders exchanged brightly dyed and embroidered tunics made from COTTON and cameloid fiber (see also ALPACAS; LLAMAS; VICUNAS); silver, gold, and metal objects (see also METALS, PRECIOUS; METALLURGY); shellfish DYES used to make their counters, or QUIPUS; as well as other goods. (See also TRADE.)

Rafts were made from sun-dried balsa logs (*Ochroma*) that were lashed together with vines. Power was provided by a large, square cotton sail. In addition to cargo space, the rafts included a tack house as well as a hearth where food could be prepared on long voyages. These were similar to motorized pontoon boats of today. Smaller boats made for one person were constructed of reeds. These were used primarily for fishing along the coastlines. Reed rafts were also used on larger lakes, such as Lake Titicaca.

## Sources/Further Reading

Fagan, Brian M. *Kingdoms of Gold, Kingdoms of Jade: The Americans Before Columbus.* New York: Thames and Hudson, Inc., 1991.

Malpass, Michael A. *Daily Life in the Inca Empire.* Westport, Conn.: Greenwood Press, 1996.

Unlike balsa rafts that were used for trade, single-person reed rafts, such as this one, were used by the Inca to fish along the coastline of what is now Peru. *(LC-USZ62-106341/Library of Congress)*

225

von Hagen, Victor Wolfgang. *Realm of the Incas.* New York: New American Library, 1957.

## rafts, inflatable (ca. A.D. 1000) *South American Andean and Southern cultures*

Inflatable rafts are generally used for recreational purposes today, but they are also used as safety features for large, seagoing vessels and for airplanes that may have to make an emergency landing over a body of water. The inflatable raft was also used by the ancient Inca along the lowlands of the western seaboard of South America. (The Inca established an empire in what is now Peru in about A.D. 1000.) Inca mariners invented these rafts to haul guano back to the mainland from islands off the coast that were inhabited by many birds. They used the guano for FERTILIZER.

Even though the Spaniards did not describe how these sealskin rafts were constructed, several methods could have been used, including using the inflated skins beneath a platform in order to make the vessel more buoyant and able to carry a heavier load. Jack Weatherford in his book, *Indian Givers: How the Indians of the Americas Transformed the World,* writes of the rafts, "Although not usually accorded much importance as transport vehicles, the rafts of Indians often surpassed similar constructions in other parts of the world."

The Greeks were known to have used an inflatable goatskin raft to ferry soldiers across a river as described by Xenophon (ca. 428–354 B.C.).

See also FLOTATION DEVICES.

### Sources/Further Reading

Malpass, Michael A. *Daily Life in the Inca Empire.* Westport, Conn.: Greenwood Press, 1996.

von Hagen, Victor Wolfgang. *The Royal Road of the Inca.* London: Gordon and Cremonese, 1978.

Weatherford, Jack. *Indian Givers: How the Indians of the Americas Transformed the World.* New York: Fawcett Columbine, 1988.

## raincoats See WATERPROOFING.

## raised-bed agriculture See AGRICULTURE, RAISED BED.

## religious freedom See U.S. CONSTITUTION, AMERICAN INDIAN INFLUENCE ON.

## research See MEDICAL RESEARCH; ZONED BIODIVERSITY.

## reservoirs See IRRIGATION.

## resource management See AQUACULTURE; ECOLOGY; FOREST MANAGEMENT.

## rice, wild See WILD RICE.

## rivets (ca. 200 B.C.–A.D. 600) *North American Southeast, South American Andean cultures*

Rivets are made of metal and shaped like bolts, but they have no threads. They are used as fasteners and are inserted into a hole bored through two pieces of metal. Pounding the end of the rivet without the head flattens it, fixing the two pieces of metal together. According to Maurice Daumas, author of *A History of Technology & Invention: Progress Through the Ages,* the ancient Peruvians used riveting and SOLDERING to join metals. Expert metalworkers, they also used WELDING, crimping, and other methods of joining metals. The Inca, who established an empire in what is now Peru in about A.D. 1000, also developed this technology prior to contact with Europeans.

In North America between A.D. 350 and 1000 ancient American Indians in the Southeast did riveting. They used copper rivets to repair copper plating. These ancient metalworkers obtained their copper through trade with American Indians of the southern Great Lakes region.

See also METALLURGY.

### Sources/Further Reading

Daumas, Maurice. *A History Of Technology & Invention: Progress Through the Ages, Volume I, The Origins of Technological Civilization.* New York: Crown Publishers, Inc., 1962.

von Hagen, Victor W. *Realm of the Incas.* New York: New American Library, 1957.

## road sites (trails) (precontact) *North American cultures*

North American Indians traveled along a system of trails that they deliberately cleared and consciously maintained to facilitate travel and TRADE and to serve military purposes (see also MILITARY TACTICS). Runners who conveyed news from village to village also used the trails (see also RUNNING.) Much Indian travel in the North American Northeast was done by CANOES, and the travelers laid out well-marked portage routes that connected rivers and lakes from the Hudson Bay to the Gulf of Mexico. Although the North American Indian trails were not developed to the extent of the Inca ROAD SYSTEM, they served the purpose for which they were intended and were adopted by European colonists who relied on them for travel and eventually turned them into wagon routes.

The longest and most extensive networks of trails were located east of the Appalachian Mountains and between the Appalachian Mountains and the Rocky Mountains. The Iroquois trail network in the Northeast, for example, ran from Canada to as far south to the Carolinas. Further south and west, the famous Santa Fe Trail, a route west that connected the cities of St. Louis, Missouri, and Santa Fe, New Mexico, was built on an original Indian trail that extended from the Mississippi River to the northern part of Mexico.

Some other trails designed by American Indians that were taken over by colonists include the Iroquois trail in the Mohawk Valley of Upstate New York; the Old Connecticut Path that ran between what are now Albany, New York, and Boston; the Warriors Path that later would become the Cumberland Gap and Wilderness Road in Kentucky; the Old Saulk Trail; the Susquehanna Trail; the Natchez Trace from Tennessee to Mississippi; and the Mohawk Trail in Massachusetts.

Portage routes—short trails that connected lakes and rivers or that served as detours around white water or waterfalls— were also numerous. The Mississippi River was used as a major north/south route for canoe travel, and ran east and west along tributaries, including the Ohio River, the Arkansas River, and the Missouri River. An extensive river and portage route connected what would become Montreal and the Mackinaw Straits in the Upper Peninsula of what is now Michigan. A route called the Grand Portage Route connected Lake Superior to what is now the Minnesota/Manitoba border. An offshoot of this route led to the Mississippi River.

After contact, American Indians continued to make trails, especially during the French and Indian Wars. A Lenni Lenape (Delaware) named Nemacolin helped plot and clear Braddock's Road with frontiersman Thomas Cresap in 1750. This trail connected the Monongahela and Potomac rivers. Cherokee trader Jesse Chisholm established what would become a major trail for cattle drives from Texas to Kansas railheads, the CHISHOLM TRAIL, in 1866.

Archaeologists believe that many modern roads that were not laid out by survey crews are improvements of older roads that were initially American Indian trails. Many of today's interstate highways follow routes originally planned and cleared by American Indians centuries ago.

### Sources/Further Reading

Davis, Emily C. *Ancient Americans.* New York: Cooper Square Publishers, 1975.

Hoxie, Fredrick E. *The Encyclopedia of North American Indians.* Boston: Houghton Mifflin Company, 1996.

Waldman, Carl. *Atlas of the North American Indian.* Rev. ed. New York: Facts On File, 2000.

Weatherford, Jack. *Indian Givers: How the Indians of the Americas Transformed the World.* New York: Fawcett Columbine, 1988.

**road systems** (ca. 1500 B.C.–A.D. 1500) *South American Andean, Mesoamerican, North American Southwest and Southeast cultures*

Roads serve as a way to travel easily from place to place. Unlike trails, they are planned and require great civil engineering efforts to complete. The most famous road system in the Americas is that of the Inca, whose empire was established in about A.D. 1000 in what is now Peru. Parts of the Inca road network were constructed over a system of preexisting trails left by other cultures. The advent of aerial photography and computer mapping systems has led archaeologists to the knowledge that the Inca built many more miles of roads than was previously believed. Their road system, which was at least 140,000 miles long, exceeded that of the Roman Empire both in length and construction. (The Roman road system was approximately 56,000 miles long.)

The Maya of Mesoamerica, whose culture arose is what is now the Yucatán Peninsula of Mexico in about 1500 B.C., developed an extensive road system that was paved in places. The Aztec, who established an empire in what is now Mexico in about A.D. 1100, also used the Maya road system. Further to the north, the Anasazi, who lived in Chaco Canyon located in what is now New Mexico, also established an engineered road system that linked outlying settlements to the main community, Casa Bonita. People of the Hopewell, a mound building culture that arose in the river valleys of the North American Midwest, are believed to have constructed a 60-mile road linking two communities.

The Inca road system consisted of two main arteries that ran north and south. One was located in the highlands and the other along the Pacific coast. The latter road ran from what are now northern Ecuador to southern Chile. In addition to the main roads, a number of smaller roads that branched from the main one connected villages. Although the Inca road system varied in width from 82 feet to very narrow ascents that were carved into solid rock and zigzagged up mountain slopes, road builders used standardized construction methods, leading anthropologists to believe that engineers closely supervised its planning and construction, including the construction of BRIDGES where the roadways crossed water.

The Inca built several types of bridges (or *chacas* in Quecha, the Inca language), depending on the type of terrain. Some of these bridges were cantilevered (supported by beams anchored at one end). Others included pontoon bridges, suspension bridges, and bridges with corbeled arches. (See also ARCH, CORBELED.) They used ferryboats to cross very wide rivers. For the high mountainous areas with deep ravines, the Inca built suspension bridges, one of which was 200 feet long.

When necessary, Inca engineers carved tunnels through hills. They lined some of these tunnels with stone and also built elevated causeways over marshes and shallow streams. One such causeway extended for eight miles. The Inca constructed causeways of packed earth and covered it with stone slabs. Sometimes they paved them with a cement compound. When the roads crossed desert areas, Inca engineers sank parallel lines of posts into the ground to mark the path of the road. If a road ran through populated areas, they built stone walls on each side of it. In irrigated areas or places near water, they planted shade trees and constructed small AQUEDUCTS to water them. In many places they built curbs at the sides of the road; in others the road was bordered with short walls to keep out drifting sand. Whenever possible, Inca engineers constructed straight roads, at times grading them to achieve this result. The most common method they used for constructing the road on relatively flat surfaces was to pack earth and then surface it with gravel and cement. Every $4\frac{1}{2}$ miles apart, they placed distance markers.

The Inca used their roads to link the far reaches of their empire, to transport goods, and to facilitate communication. They did not have wheeled vehicles, since there were no suitable animals to pull them. Instead, the Inca used LLAMAS as pack animals to carry tribute to the capitol city of Cuzco or to warehouses built throughout the empire. The primary purpose of the Inca roads, however, was to provide a way for runners who carried messages. (See also RUNNING.) These runners, who sometimes carried memory aids called QUIPUS, ran in relays. When they were not running, they lived in *tambos*, the Quecha word for rest-houses. Travelers also stopped at *tambos*, some of which resembled inns. The *tambos* built for the nobility, who were carried on litters, were built in cities and were specially equipped with baths and even plumbing. *Tambos* for commoners were located by the side of the road in rural areas. Each way station had sleeping quarters and a storehouse for food, clothing, supplies, footwear, and sometimes weapons and uniforms. Barracks reserved only for soldiers were located at certain points along this road.

Ironically, the high quality of the Inca road system led to the downfall of their empire at the hands of the Spanish conquistadores. An early Spanish observer remarked that conquest would have been severely hindered had the Inca not provided them with superior roads. Cieza de León, who chronicled Francisco Pizarro's expedition, wrote: "I believe there is no account of a road as great as this, running through deep valleys, high mountains, banks of snow, torrents of water, living rock, and wild rivers. Through some places it went through flat and paved; it was excavated into precipices and cut through rock in the mountains; it passed with walls along rivers and had steps and resting spots in the snows. In all places it was clean and swept free of refuse, with lodgings, storehouses, Sun temples and posts along the route. . . . Oh! can anything similar be claimed for . . . any of the powerful kings who ruled the world that they were able to build such a road or provide the supplies found on it."

In Mesoamerica the Olmec, whose culture flourished between 1700 B.C. and 400 B.C., built roads and trails that became the foundation for the road system established and further refined by the Maya. Maya culture arose in the Yucatán Peninsula in about 1500 B.C. Eventually the Maya road system crisscrossed the Yucatán Peninsula. The road that ran from Yaxuna to Coba was 60 miles long and the longest known road in the Maya system. Maya roadbuilders first built retaining walls and then filled the space between them with stone slabs. They then covered the slabs with gravel. Elizabeth P. Benson, a noted expert on Maya life and culture, suggests that the Maya used a large stone object found by archaeologists as a road roller. (The Maya independently invented WHEELS, using them for toys or religious objects.) The elevated roads that Maya roadmakers built allowed rainfall to run off the surface, an important feature in an area that received a great deal of rain. They surfaced many of their roads with cement made from burned limestone and wood ash. Maya civil engineers developed this technology independently from the Romans, who had plastered their roads with limestone and volcanic ash. The Maya called the white limestone roads *sacbe*, which means "white road" in the Maya language; it also means Milky Way. When the conquistadores asked indigenous people about the purpose of the Maya road system, they were told that the roads were sacred routes used for pilgrimages.

The Aztec, who established an empire in what is now Mexico in about A.D. 1100, built a roadway network in the Valley of Mexico. This network served to connect, their main city, Tenochtitlan, to surrounding communities. Like the Inca, the Aztec used runners to carry messages between cities.

In the North American desert Southwest, Anasazi roadbuilders constructed 500 miles of curbed roadways that connected 75 communities in Chaco Canyon, located in what is now New Mexico. Anasazi culture arose in about 350 B.C. and flourished until about A.D. 1450. The longest road in the Chaco Canyon system is 42 miles long. The roads are straight and radiate from the canyon like spokes on a wheel—evidence that they were engineered before actual construction began. They date from the 11th and 12th centuries. Anasazi roads are wider than necessary for foot traffic, some 30 feet across on relatively flat terrain. On these wide stretches of road, builders leveled earth and used rock berm to build up low spots and to line the sides of the roads. The roads narrow, however, on steep slopes where road builders carved stone stairsteps or built earth ramps, which some have compared to modern freeway on- and off-ramps.

Archaeologists are uncertain exactly why the Anasazi made these roads. Some speculate that the routes they took may have been more efficient than those of the modern roads in the canyon. Other archaeologists believe that the high points along these roadways may have been signaling stations. The Anasazi, who were known to TRADE extensively with Mesoamerican cultures, may have been influenced by road building there. Recent research indicates that Anasazi roads served a religious purpose and were integrative (binding many small communities into a single society).

Archaeologists long believed that although American Indians living further north created trails (see also ROAD SITES), they did not survey and construct roadways as the Inca, Maya, Aztec, and Anasazi had done. One known exception to this is a perfectly straight, 60-mile-long road connecting two Hopewell villages that are now the sites of the towns of Newark, Ohio, and Chillicothe, Ohio. The Hopewell, who were mound-building people, lived in the river valleys in the lower Midwest from about 100 B.C. to A.D. 400. Amateur archaeologists in the 1800s found short stretches of road in southern Ohio and speculated that they might be parts of a longer road. This was impossible to prove because the land had been disturbed by settlement and farming. However, recent study, including aerial photography, has confirmed the probable existence of a road that connected two circular Hopewell earthworks that are nearly identical in size.

## Sources/Further Reading

Bankes, George. *Peru Before Pizarro.* Oxford, England: Phaidon Press Ltd., 1977.

Benson, Elizabeth P. *The Maya World.* New York: Thomas Y. Crowell, 1967.

Deuel, Leo. *Conquistadors Without Swords: Archaeologists in the Americas.* New York: St. Martin's Press, 1967.

Fagan, Brian M. *Kingdoms of Gold, Kingdoms of Jade: The Americas Before Columbus.* New York: Thames and Hudson, Inc., 1991.

Frazier, K. *People of Chaco.* New York: Norton & Company, 1986.

Hysop, John. *The Inka Road System.* New York: Academic Press, 1984.

Kantner, John. *An Evaluation of Chaco Anasazi Roadways.* Presented to the Society for American Archaeology, 1996. URL: http://sipapu.scsb.edu/roads/index.html. Downloaded on February 7, 1999.

Lepper, Bradley T. "Tracking Ohio's Great Hopewell Road." *Archaeology* (November/December 1995): 52–56.

Malpass, Michael. *Daily Life in the Inca Empire.* Westport, Conn.: Greenwood Press, 1996.

Mason, J. Alden. *The Ancient Civilizations of Peru.* New York: Penguin Books, 1957.

Morris, Craig and Adriana von Hagen. *The Inka Empire and its Andean Origins.* New York: Abbeville Press, 1993.

National Park Service. *Chaco Culture National Historical Park New Mexico.* URL: http://www.chaco.com/parl/brochure.html. Downloaded on February 7, 2000.

Nobel, David Grant. *Ancient Ruins of the Southwest.* Flagstaff, Ariz.: Northland Publishing, 1991.

Trombold, C.D. *Ancient Road Networks and Settlement Hierarchies in the New World.* Cambridge, Eng.: Cambridge University Press, 1991.

von Hagen, Victor W. *Realm of the Incas.* New York: New American Library, 1957.

von Hagen, Victor W. *The Royal Road of The Inca.* London, England: Gordon Cremonesi, Ltd., 1976.

**rubber** See LATEX.

**running** (precontact) *North American, Mesoamerican, South American cultures*

Indigenous people throughout the Americas relied on sophisticated systems of specially trained runners to send messages to other tribes and receive news. These runners also moved goods along TRADE routes and ROAD SYSTEMS that crisscrossed the Americas. These couriers, who sometimes ran in relays, were able to cover great distances in incredibly short times. Hernán Cortés reported that not more than 24 hours passed after he landed in Chianiztlán in the spring of 1519 before couriers had taken that news to the Aztec ruler, Montezuma, who was 260 miles away.

In the northeastern part of North America, the Iroquois had a system of runners in place along the 240-mile Iroquois trail (see also ROAD SITES) that ran from near Albany to Buffalo. These Iroquois runners, who carried messages and WAMPUM belts between the tribes, were among the reasons the Iroquois were able to assume a leadership role in forming the IROQUOIS CONFEDERACY. (See also UNITED STATES CONSTITUTION, AMERICAN INDIAN INFLUENCE ON.) An early Quaker colonial observer of the time, James Emlen, reported that one of Iroquois chief Cornplanter's runners, named Sharp Shins, was able to run 90 miles in a day.

Several culture groups that lived in the Midwest also had running traditions. These included the Kickapoo, Sac (Sauk), and Menominee. The Creek of the Southeast had runners, as did the Kansa, Omaha, and Osage of the plains. According to anthropologist Truman Michelson, the Mesquaki runners, who were part of a religious society, lived a celibate lifestyle, pledged to always tell the truth, and ate meals restricted to turtle dove and quail. In the 1860s a Mesquaki runner covered 400 miles, in order to warn Sac Indians that the enemy was going to attack.

Runners for the Nomalki, a central California tribe, also ate special diets and trained daily. They retired at the age of 40. Their tribe took care of their needs after their retirement because of the service they had given. The Chemheuvi of California had a similar running GUILD. The Luiseno Mojave were reported to have had a running tradition as well. On long journeys California runners sustained themselves on CHIA seeds, a high-energy nutritional source.

Tribes of the desert Southwest also had runners. Pueblo couriers were responsible for spreading the news of the revolt against Spanish domination in 1680. The Pueblo leader Popé addressed an assembly of couriers at what is now called Taos Pueblo. In addition to instructing them orally, he gave the runners hides with picture writing on them and knotted yucca cords that served as CALENDARS. (See also QUIPUS.) The runners were instructed to untie one knot each day. When all the knots were untied, the revolt would begin. They warned at least 70 pueblo of the upcoming revolt as well as the Hopi, who lived about 300 miles away. (See also MILITARY TACTICS.) In the 1800s U.S. Army officers used Hopi runners to carry messages to the railhead (the furthest point of a railway line) because they were faster and more reliable than their own troops. (See also MILITARY CONTRIBUTIONS.)

The most well-developed running system was that of the Inca, whose empire was established in the Andean region of South America in about A.D. 1000. Although running had existed at least 500 years before this, the Inca created a formalized running system that was made up of young runners called *chasqui.* The system was developed in the mid-1400s by the ninth Inca ruler, Pachacuti Ina Yupanqui. By the reign of the 11th Inca ruler, Huayna Capac (A.D. 1493–A.D. 1528), the Inca had perfected a system of roads on which runners traveled. Inca *chasquis* came from the ruling class and were trained to run swiftly over short distances. Once they had finished training, they lived for 15-day shifts in stone huts that were spaced about

**COREON·MAIOR·IMENOR**
**HATVNCHASQVICHVRV**
**MVLLO·CHASQVI·CVRACA~**

Inca runners transported goods and carried information in relays. Using this formalized system, as a team they could cover 150 to 300 miles a day. *(After Felipe Guamán Poma de Ayala.* Nueva Coronica y Buen Gobierno)

two miles apart along the road system. The clothing, food, and other needs of the *chasqui* were provided by the mit'a or work tax. (See also TAX SYSTEMS.)

Forewarned by a blast on the conch shell horn from an approaching runner, the chasqui would leave the hut and listen to the message the approaching courier called out. Sometimes the courier might carry a QUIPU, a system of knotted colored strings that recorded information such as accounts. Other times, the runner might bear textiles with messages encoded in the designs. Once the message had been passed, the waiting runner headed immediately down the road to the next hut, where yet another runner awaited. Sometimes small, lightweight trade goods were transported in this manner as well. For example, the runners provided fresh fish for the Inca in their capital of Cuzco, high in the mountains. The Inca running system was continuous and allowed messages to be carried from 150 to about 300 miles a day depending on the terrain. The system was so efficient that after conquest, the Spaniards kept a modified version operating.

North American settlers adopted a relay method of carrying messages in the form of mail across the continent. Started shortly after the Civil War ended, this system using horses and riders was called the Pony Express. The Pony Express took 10 days to carry mail from St. Louis to San Francisco, 1,800 miles away, in 60-mile stretches. Although some historians credit the idea behind the Pony Express as being a 13th-century Chinese invention, it seems more likely that the system was inspired by American Indian relay runners.

## Sources/Further Reading

Fagan, Brian M. *Kingdoms of Gold, Kingdoms of Jade: The Americas before Columbus.* New York: Thames and Hudson, Inc., 1991.

Malpass, Michael. *Daily Life in the Inca Empire.* Westport, Conn.: Greenwood Press, 1996.

Nabokov, Peter. *Indian Running: Native American History & Tradition.* Santa Fe: Ancient City Press, 1981.

von Hagen, Victor Wolfgang. *Realm of the Incas.* New York: New American Library, 1957.

## salicin (salicylic acid) (precontact) *North American Northeast cultures*

Salicin is a chemical substance that is found in the bark of the American black willow (*Salix nigra*), also known as the pussy willow or the catkin willow. When the human body breaks down salicin, produces salicylic acid, the main ingredient in aspirin. Salicylic acid has an analgesic affect in addition to reducing fevers and inflammations. American Indian tribes living in the Northeast, where the black willow grew, boiled its bark to make a tea that they administered orally. These tribes included Montagnais, who lived in what is now Canada; the Mohegan, who lived in what is now Connecticut; and the Penobscot, who lived in what is now Maine. Besides using this tea as a pain reliever, fever reducer, and anti-inflammatory, they also used it as a diuretic and an antiseptic. The modern remedy of aspirin was discovered by Greek physician Hippocrates in the 5th century B.C. and rediscovered in 1758 by English clergyman Edward Stone, who had observed folk medicine practitioners in England prescribing tea made from another variety of willow. However, American Indians had used black willow long before contact with Europeans. They shared their pharmaceutical knowledge with American colonists, who used *Salix nigra* as a substitute for QUININE, another fever reducer, when shortages of that drug arose. Ultimately, willow tea was replaced by synthetic salicylic acids during the first part of the 20th century.

See also PHARMACOLOGY.

### Sources/Further Reading

Hutchens, Alma R. *Indian Herbology of North America.* Boston: Shambhala, 1991.
Vogel, Virgil. *American Indian Medicine.* Norman: University of Oklahoma Press, 1970.
Weiner, Michael A. *Earth Medicine Earth Food: The Classic Guide to the Herbal Remedies and Wild Plants of the North American Indians.* New York: Fawcett Columbine, 1980.

## salsa (precontact) *Mesoamerican cultures*

Salsa is an uncooked sauce composed of CHILES and TOMATOES. Both of these foods were indigenous to the Americas and were combined in a number of Mesoamerican dishes. The Aztec, who established an empire in what is now Mexico in about A.D. 1100, mixed chiles, tomatoes, and ground PUMPKIN seeds to make a sauce into which they dipped TORTILLAS. Sometimes they heated this sauce; at other times they served it cold. After conquest, ground chiles and tomatoes were called *salsa*, a Spanish word for "sauce." As Spanish and indigenous Mesoamerican cultures blended, cooks began adding the European vegetables onions and garlic as well as cilantro to salsa, making it a truly multicultural dish. Many modern Mexican cooks still use a molcajete, a rough-surfaced mortar made of volcanic rock, to grind tomatoes and chiles as their ancestors did centuries ago. These mortars are available in some speciality cookware stores in the United States as well.

### Sources/Further Reading

Coe, Sophie. *America's First Cuisines.* Austin: University of Texas Press, 1994.
University of Guadalajara. *Mexican Cuisine.* URL: http://mexico.udg.mx/cocina/ingles/home.html. Downloaded on February 7, 2000.

## salve, drawing (precontact) *North American Northeast cultures*

Drawing salve is a topical medication that is applied to an infection in order to aid in the draining of infected wounds. (See also DRAINAGE, SURGICAL AND WOUND.) The Potawatomi and many other Northeast tribes used the tar, or resin, from pine trees as a drawing salve. After warming the pine tar, they applied it to the wound, sometimes binding it on with a strip of leather. The heat served as a vasodilator and opened the pores of the skin, allowing the infected matter to drain. American Indians most frequently used WHITE PINE (*P. strobus L.*) for this purpose. This variety of pine has antibacterial properties that worked against the infection and encouraged proper healing. The Shoshone of what is now Nevada also developed this medical technique.

See also ANTIBIOTIC MEDICATIONS; MEDICINE; PHARMACOLOGY.

## Sources/Further Reading

Lust, John. *The Herb Book.* New York: Bantam Books, 1974.
Vogel, Virgil. *American Indian Medicine,* Norman: University of Oklahoma Press, 1970.

## sandals (ca. 7000 B.C.) *North American Southwest, Mesoamerican cultures*

Sandals are an open style of footwear designed so that the sole is fastened to the wearer's foot with straps. They were invented by the Paleo-Indians of the Southwest culture area of North America independently of sandals worn in other cultures. Their sandals were designed with a sling back to better hold them in place for walking. Sandals found by archaeologists in this region also had soles that cupped the heel to provide added comfort. They constructed these sandals from tough plant fibers, such as AGAVE, YUCCA, and a plant similar to yucca called rattlesnake master. Of these sandals, anthropologist Michael J. O'Brien states: ". . . shoes were made with fibrous plants that could be woven into a tough fabric used for top, bottom and sides of the footwear." American Indians plaited the fiber into cordage and wove it to form soles and straps in a manner that resembled basket weaving. (See also BASKET WEAVING TECHNIQUES.) Some of the sandals that have been found indicate that these Paleo-Indians were capable of repairing their sandals very adeptly.

Mesoamerican Indians also made and wore sandals out of fiber. Some of these had heels affixed to the soles. The Olmec, whose culture arose in the Yucatán Peninsula in about 1700 B.C., made rubber-soled footwear as well as sandals made completely of LATEX. The Maya, whose culture arose in about 1500 B.C. in what is now the Yucatán, made sandals with soles of copper; they began producing these sandals in the 14th century. Because no copper deposits exist in the area in which the Maya lived, archaeologists believe that they obtained it through TRADE. Since these copper-soled sandals are rare, it is thought they may have been used for ceremonial or ritual purposes, or perhaps for a temporary purpose, such as walking on slippery surfaces.

See also CRAMPONS; MOCCASINS; MUKLUKS; VULCANIZATION.

## Sources/Further Reading

Benson, Elizabeth P. *The Maya World.* New York: Thomas Y. Crowell, 1967.

Canby, Thomas Y. "The Search for the First Americans." *National Geographic* 156, no. 3 (September 1979): 330–363.
Fehrenbach, T. R. *Fire and Blood: A History of Mexico.* New York: Macmillan Publishing Co., Inc., 1973.
Recer, Paul. "Cave dwellers had flair for making shoes." *Rapid City Journal* (July 5, 1998).
Schele, France V. and Ralph L. Roys. *The Maya Chantel Indians of Acalan-Tixchel: A Contribution to the History and Ethnography of the Yucatan Peninsula.* Norman: University of Oklahoma Press, 1968.

**sanitation** See PLUMBING.

## sapodilla (*Manilkara zapota*) (precontact) *Mesoamerican, Circum-Caribbean cultures*

The sapodilla tree is native to the Yucatán and other parts of Mexico and the Mesoamerican Tropics. The bark of the tree produces a milky latex called chicle. Mesoamerican Indians used this latex for CHEWING GUM, as did early manufacturers of chewing gum in the United States. The Olmec, whose culture arose in the Yucatán Peninsula of what is now Mexico in about 1700 B.C., invented the process for turning LATEX sap of the sapodilla tree into rubber. Some indigenous peoples also used the sapodilla tree for lumber; it continues to be used for this purpose today. American Indians ate the sweet, brown-colored fruits the tree produces. Sapodilla fruits are eaten in the tropics in modern times. Today sapodilla is raised commercially in India, Africa, the East Indies, the Philippines, and Malaysia, as well as in tropical and subtropical regions of the Americas. It is sometimes sold in larger grocery stores in the United States and Canada as an exotic fruit.

## Sources/Further Reading

Sapodilla: New Crops Index. Purdue University Center for New Crops. URL: http://www.hort.purdue.edu/newcrop/crops/Sapodilla.html. Downloaded on November 23, 1999.
Sapodilla Fruit Facts. URL: http://www.cfrg.org/pubs/ff/sapodilla.html. Downloaded on November 23, 1999.
Weatherford, Jack. *Indian Givers: How the Indians of the Americas Transformed the World.* New York: Fawcett Columbine, 1988.

**sarcophagi** See PYRAMIDS.

**sarsaparilla** See SOFT DRINK INGREDIENTS.

## sassafras (*Sassafras albidum*) (precontact) *North American Northeast and Southeast cultures*

Sassafras is a tree that is indigenous to North America. A member of the laurel family, this tree stands from 30 to 40 feet tall and has aromatic bark, leaves, and root bark that contain a volatile oil. The name *sassafras* is believed to be a corruption of the Spanish word for "saxifrage," another plant entirely. American Indians used the root bark and bark from the sassafras tree's trunk for medicine and to flavor food. (See also FILE GUMBO.) The Cherokee used sassafras as an intestinal worm medicine (see also ANTIHELMINTIC) and for colds. The Choctaw used it as a blood thinner. The Lenni Lenape (Delaware) drank sassafras tea as a blood purifier. Sassafras served as a spring tonic for the Mohegan. The Seminole used it to cure diarrhea and vomiting as well as for a mouthwash and gargle. Both the Cherokee of the Southeast and Chippewa (Anishinabe) of the Midwest used sassafras as a beverage.

The first Europeans to learn about sassafras were a group of French Huguenots who settled in what is now Florida in the 1590s. Because they were unprepared and unfamiliar with the land, they relied on the help of Indians who lived in the area. These Indians used sassafras wood for bows and the leaves as a spice. They taught the Europeans that sassafras root bark, when made into a tea, was a tonic that prevented illness and could also be used to counter the effects of drinking bad water. The Huguenots revealed the remedy to Spanish colonizers, who then told the world about what soon would be considered a miracle tonic.

Civil War physicians used sassafras as a cure for soldiers with measles, pneumonia, bronchitis, or colds. Germans who lived in Pennsylvania drank sassafras tea to reduce fevers. The Choctaw taught settlers in Louisiana to season stews with powdered leaves, which came to be called filé. Filé gumbo is a popular Cajun dish today. European entrepreneurs used sassafras in the PATENT MEDICINES they sold (see also MEDICINES, PATENT, AMERICAN INDIAN INFLUENCE ON) and incorporated it into root beer, one of the first soft drinks sold commercially. (See also SOFT DRINK INGREDIENTS.)

## Sources/Further Reading

Moerman, Dan. American Indian Ethnobotanical Database. URL: http://www.umd.umich.edu/cgi-bin/herb. Downloaded on January 29, 1999.

Weatherford, Jack. *Indian Givers: How the Indians of the Americas Transformed the World.* New York: Fawcett Columbine, 1988.

Vogel, Virgil. *American Indian Medicine.* Norman: University of Oklahoma Press, 1970.

**saws** (ca. 1700 B.C.–400 B.C.) *Mesoamerican, South American Andean cultures*
A saw is a tool for cutting wood, metal, stone, and other materials. The Olmec invented a unique saw that was able to cut many different types of material, but it was used primarily for cutting JADE. (Olmec culture arose in about 1700 B.C. in the Yucatán Peninsula of what is now Mexico.) Jade is a very hard mineral that was highly valued by almost all South and Mesoamerican cultures. The saw was a simple one, requiring only a piece of string made of leather and an abrasive such as silica (sand) or jade dust. Olmec craftspeople scored, or scratched, the area of the stone or other material to be cut with an obsidian flint or jade blade. Next they moistened the leather "string" so that the abrasive would adhere to it. They also poured abrasive over the scored area. Then they placed the string saw over the scored area and pulled it back and forth until the material was cut. If the project was a large one, the stonemason would place wedges into the cuts and hammer on them until the stone broke. The string saw was used later by Mesoamerican cultures and by some South American Andean cultures. American Indians of South and Mesoamerica also made saws out of obsidian flint that they shaped like hacksaw blades. These saws were used much like modern saws.

See also JADE WORK; TOOLS.

## Sources/Further Reading

Coe, Michael D. *America's First Civilization: Discovering the Olmec.* Eau Claire, Wisc.: American Heritage Publishing Co. Inc., 1968.

Daumas, Maurice. *A History of Technology & Invention: Progress through the Ages, Vol. I, The Origins of Technological Civilization.* New York: Crown Publishers, Inc., 1962.

**scales** (ca. A.D. 1000) *South American Andean cultures*
Scales are devices used to weigh various materials. The Inca, who established an empire in what is now Peru in about A.D. 1000, used scales in the course of their business transactions. They invented these scales independently of those that were invented in other parts of the world. The Inca scales consisted of a beam with scale pans, or, in some cases, netting that was hung from each end. Holding the beam in the middle so that it would balance, the merchant placed the material to be weighed on the pan or in the netting on one end of the beam and placed stones on the other side. This ensured that the customer received the correct amount of whatever was being traded or sold. At least one author, suggests that scales were being used even earlier by Moche, whose culture flourished in what is now Peru from 200 B.C. to A.D. 600.

See also TRADE.

## Sources/Further Reading

Bankes, George. *Peru before Pizarro.* Oxford: Phaidon Press Limited, 1977.

Engel, Frederic Andre. *An Ancient World Preserved: Relics and Records of Prehistory in the Andes.* New York: Crown Publishers, Inc., 1981.

**scalpels** (ca. 1000 B.C.) *South American Andean, Mesoamerican cultures*
Scalpels are small, thin blades used for cutting in SURGERY. The first recorded use of scalpels in brain surgery occurred on the prehistoric coast of Peru. In all probability they were in use

long before this. These early scalpels were made of obsidian, flint, and copper. Later Moche metallurgists used silver to manufacture scalpels. Moche culture arose in what is now Peru in about 200 B.C. Their metal scalpels were shaped like fans or lobster tails, with the wide, flat end serving as the blade. The Inca, whose culture arose in about A.D. 1000 in what is now Peru, continued to make metal scalpels.

Despite advances in METALLURGY, South American and Mesoamerican surgeons, including the Aztec, who established an empire in what is now Mexico in about A.D. 1100, continued to use obsidian blades to make incisions, for a scientific reason. Obsidian can be chipped, or flaked, to a very thin edge. (See also FLINTKNAPPING.) This property enables obsidian scalpels to move through human cells rather than tearing them as a metal blade would do. An incision made with an obsidian flint blade stops bleeding almost immediately, and healing begins shortly thereafter. Only in the last half of the 20th century did Western medicine develop laser technology comparable to the obsidian scalpel used by ancient American Indian surgeons.

### Sources/Further Reading

Fernandez, Omar. *Pre-Columbian Surgery Gramna Weekly Review.* URL: http://marauder.millersv.edu/~columbus/data/art/FERNAN01.AR T. Downloaded January 21, 2000.

Ortiz de Montellano, Bernard. *Aztec Medicine, Health and Nutrition.* New Brunswick, N.J.: Rutgers University Press, 1990.

Stuart, George E. and Gene S. Stuart. *Discovering Man's Past In the Americas.* Washington, D.C.: National Geographic Society, 1969.

**scribes** See BOOKS.

**scuppernong grapes** (precontact) *North American Southeast cultures*

Scuppernong grapes are a variety of muscadine native to North America. They are extremely sweet and have a unique musky flavor. These grapes do not grow in bunches like conventional GRAPES. A sport, or mutation, of purple muscadines (*Vitis rotundifolia*), scuppernongs are tough-skinned and colored a bronze-green.

Although American Indians had eaten them for hundreds of years, the first Europeans believed to have encountered scuppernongs were the residents of Sir Walter Raleigh's Roanoke colony, who discovered what is known as the "mother vine" between 1584 and 1585. Stories about the plant grew to mythical proportions. Reportedly its trunk was two feet thick and the vines covered nearly half an acre. Civil War troops garrisoned on Roanoke Island would later report that the vine was still growing. Initially the indigenous grapes were simply called the big white grape. In 1755 they earned their current name after two hunters found an abundance of them growing

on the shores of Scuppernong Lake, in North Carolina's Tidewater area. *Scuppernong* is an Algonquian word meaning "place where magnolias grow."

Jamestown settlers made wine from scuppernongs, sending barrels of it back to London, but their backers were not impressed with their efforts. Blaming the grapes rather than the colonists' winemaking expertise, the Virginia Company sent vines from France, and the Jamestown Assembly enacted a law compelling settlers to plant 12 wine grapevines yearly or suffer severe punishment. When the imported plants died, the colonists turned to TOBACCO as a cash crop.

Not until the end of the 18th century were seeds or cuttings planted in local farms and gardens, making the scuppernong the first North American grape to be cultivated. Scuppernong wine soon became a southern tradition. By 1835 South Carolina had become the top wine producer in the United States, primarily because of the scuppernong grape. Today, although other states exceed South Carolina in wine production, the grapes grown in those areas are from European stock. South Carolina grape growers also plant a number of varieties of grapes from Europe, but the unique scuppernong wine is made from indigenous grapes.

### Sources/Further Reading

Flexner, Stuart. *I Hear America Talking: An Illustrated History of American Words and Phrases.* New York: Simon and Schuster, 1976.

North Carolina Wineries Page. URL: http://www.agr.state.nc.us/markets/commodit/horticul/grape. Downloaded on July 6, 1999.

The Winemaking Home Page/Napa Valley. *Native North American Grapes.* URL: wysiwyg://16/http://www.geocities.com/Napa Valley/1172/rotundif.html. Downloaded on July 6, 1999.

Stanley, Doris. "America's First Grape, the Muscadine." *Agricultural Research Magazine* (November 1997) URL: http://www.ars.usda.gov/is/AR/archive/nov97/musc1197.html

**scurvy cure** (vitamin C, ascorbic acid) (precontact) *North American Arctic, Subarctic, and Northeast cultures*

Scurvy is a disease that is caused by a deficiency of vitamin C. The symptoms of scurvy are cuts and bruises that are slow to heal, tender joints, inflamed gums, and loose teeth. Scurvy, which often led to death, plagued Europeans throughout history. North American Indians, whose diet was high in vitamin C-rich foods, did not have this problem to the extent that Europeans did. When it occurred, they knew how to cure it.

The first instance of American Indians sharing this knowledge with Europeans was in 1536, when French explorer Jacques Cartier's ship became ice-bound in the frozen St. Lawrence River near the Indian village that would become Montreal. (See also SETTLEMENT PATTERNS.) Twenty-five of his crewmembers subsequently died from scurvy.

Cartier wrote in his log, "out of the 110 men that we were, not ten were well enough to help the others, a thing pitiful to see." A Huron chief showed the explorer how to grind the bark of an evergreen and prepare a tea, which he advised Cartier to have his men drink every other day. Cartier called the tonic "very distasteful" but ordered his men to drink it. Within eight days their scurvy had been cured. Cartier dug up saplings of the trees, which he carried back to France and had planted in the king's garden. He also repaid the Indians' generosity by kidnapping the chief, his two sons, three other adults, and four children, all of whom died soon after they landed in France.

For all practical purposes, Europeans ignored the Indian cure. The problem of scurvy persisted until a British naval officer found that drinking lime juice would keep sailors scurvy-free. In 1795 the British navy made lime juice mandatory for British sailors. American sailors, who thought the treatment ridiculous, called them "limeys." Yet during the Civil War, army physicians diagnosed 30,000 cases of scurvy in Union soldiers, and in the late 1800s when canned milk became popular, a number of infants fell victim to a form of scurvy called Barlow's disease.

American Indians, even those whose diets did not contain large quantities of fresh fruits and vegetables, the usual source for vitamin C, did not seem to suffer from scurvy. One of the reasons for this was uncovered by a dentist, W. Price, who traveled to the Yukon Territory in the summer of 1933 in order to study the teeth of Indians whose health had not been affected by adopting the diet of non-Indians. He noticed that although most of the usual sources of vitamin C did not grow in the Yukon, and the people he studied mainly ate wild game, none of them had scurvy. When he asked how they kept themselves healthy, he was told that when hunters killed a moose, it was their custom to remove the two small balls of fat above the kidneys and cut them into small pieces, sharing them with each family member. The organs the Indians described were the adrenal glands, a rich source of ascorbic acid, another name for vitamin C.

American Indians of many tribes routinely ate the internal organs of the wild game they killed and fed dogs with the muscle meat, a practice that bewildered colonizers. Science has since shown that vitamins and minerals are highly concentrated in animals' internal organs, providing a nutritionally sound diet for people who subsisted primarily by hunting.

The 1937 Nobel Prize in medicine was awarded to Hungarian physiologist Albert Szent-Gyorgy and British chemist Sir Walter Haworth for isolating vitamin C and discovering its nutritional properties. Szent-Gyorgy had been able to unravel the mysteries of vitamin C by analyzing the adrenal glands of an ox, a source similar to the one used by North American Indians for centuries. Later, when he could no longer find adrenal glands for his experiments, Szent-Gyorgy synthesized vitamin C from PAPRIKA, a spice made from dried, ground peppers—vegetables that are indigenous to the Americas and were first cultivated by American Indians.

See also PEPPERS, SWEET AND BELL; PHARMACOLOGY.

## Sources/Further Reading

Driver, Harold E. *Indians of North America.* Chicago: University of Chicago Press, 1969.

Goldstein, Joseph L. *Basic Medical Research Award. Albert & Mary Lasker Foundation Living Library: 1996 Winners.* URL: http://laskerfoundation.com/library/1996/remarks1.html. Downloaded on January 26, 2000.

Trager, James. *The Food Chronology: The Food Lover's Compendium of Events and Anecdotes from Prehistory to Present.* New York: Henry Holt, 1995.

Weatherford, Jack. *Indian Givers: How the Indians of the Americas Transformed the World.* New York: Fawcett Columbine, 1988.

**seawalls** (pre-5000 B.C.) *North American Southeast cultures* Seawalls are structures engineered to protect the coastline from erosion caused by the action of waves. Early American Indian dwellers in the swamps and keys of what is now Florida built seawalls by piling up enormous deposits of shells. The largest of these deposits used as a sea wall was more than 10 feet high and was constructed mainly of conch shells. Located near this seawall were terraces and five mounds, including one that was shaped like a pyramid. (See also PYRAMIDS.) The archaeologist who studied this structure of shells, Frank Cushing, described it as being as level and broad as a turnpike. Cushing believed that early dwellers used shells to build up the Florida Keys (which he studied extensively), then built their dwellings on this human-made solid shell ground. The Florida Indians planted gardens in the mud-filled spaces between the shell heaps and built cisterns to catch drinking water. They also built shell enclosures that served as fish corrals into which they herded fish with canoes in order to make catching them easier.

American Indians also left extensive shell heaps, or middens, on what is now the St. John's River in eastern Florida. One such mound is 300 feet by 100 feet and rises abruptly. The American Indians who built it lived on the top of it. Archaeologists believe that Indians made these shell heaps, which may have started as refuse heaps, during the archaic period before 5000 B.C.

The Maya, whose culture arose in the Yucatán Peninsula of what is now Mexico in about 1500 B.C., were extensive seagoing traders. (See also TRADE.) They built seaport towns along the coast where bays were protected, which offered natural harbors. They built docks and piers in these ports as well as a seawall at Cerritos to form an artificial harbor.

See also AGRICULTURE; AQUACULTURE.

## Sources/Further Reading

Folsom, Franklin and Mary Elting Folsom. *America's Ancient Treasures.* 4th ed. Albuquerque: University of New Mexico Press, 1993.

Milanich, Jerald T. *Florida's Indians from Ancient Times to the Present.* Gainesville: University Press of Florida, 1998.

Wyman, Jeffries. *An Account of the Fresh-Water Shell-Heaps of the St. John's River, East Florida.* Salem, Mass.: Essex Institute Press, 1968.

**sedatives** See ANTIPASMODIC MEDICATIONS.

**seed selection** (ca. 8000 B.C.–7000 B.C.) *South American, Mesoamerican, North American cultures*

Seed selection is the agricultural practice of setting aside only seed from plants with desired characteristics for planting during the next season. Those characteristics might be hardiness to disease, a larger crop yield, or lower moisture requirements. During the thousands of years that plant cultivation moved northward from the South American tropics and Mesoamerica, American Indian farmers relied on seed selection in order to develop varieties of CORN, BEANS, SQUASH, TOMATOES, and other plants that were adapted to cooler climates and shorter growing seasons. Indian farmers who originated AGRICULTURE in the Northeast also used seed selection to develop new varieties of plants. American Indians from South to North America had developed at least 3,000 varieties of POTATOES and had domesticated at least 300 grasses by the time Columbus landed in the New World.

Corn is a crop that American Indians developed through seed selection. In as early as 5000 B.C., farmers in Mesoamerica had used selection to transform corn from a multiple-stalk plant to one with a single stalk, which made for higher yields and an easier harvest. By about A.D. 1, Indian farmers were expert corn breeders, selecting seeds to produce plants with strong stalks, longer ears, and fewer ears per stalk, which increased yields significantly. They also planted different varieties close together so that the plants would cross-pollinate and create hybrids. These farmers were aware that pollen could travel, and if certain varieties of plants were to be kept pure, they needed to be raised well away from other varieties.

Anasazi farmers in the North American Southwest further experimented with corn, selecting seeds from early maturing ears. (The Anasazi culture arose in what is now New Mexico in about 350 B.C.) The Zuni people, a southwestern Pueblo tribe that followed the Anasazi, continued this practice. Many years later, when the Latter-day Saints moved to the Southwest in the mid-1860s they learned the practice of seed saving from American Indians and adopted it into their agricultural practices.

Ancient farmers in the arid Southwest also developed a variety of bush bean that stood on its own and did not twine so that it would not have to compete with corn for moisture. Hohokam agriculturists farming along the Gila River cultivated crops in a region that, because of its intense heat, has one of the shortest growing seasons in North America. They, too, learned to develop varieties of corn, beans, and squash that were compatible with the difficult environment. Hohokam culture flourished in what is now Arizona from about 300 B.C. to A.D. 1200.

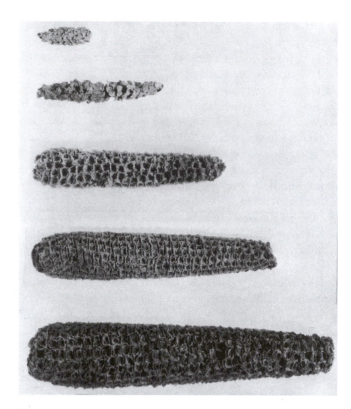

These corncobs from the Tehuacan Valley excavation in central Mexico show the evolutionary sequence of corn from 5000 B.C. to A.D. 1500. Ancient indigenous farmers who used seed selection to develop their corn crop created this evolution. *(Robert S. Peabody Museum of Archaeology. Phillips Academy, Andover, Massachusetts)*

In the northern plains of North America, Mandan, Arikira, and Hidatsa farmers developed tough, compact corn plants with tough-husked ears that developed near the ground so that they were protected from high winds and extreme weather. The seeds of this corn were resistant to rot and took only about 60 days to mature. They also developed great northern beans. White settlers in North Dakota did not attempt to raise corn until seed companies began to promote the northern flint varieties that had been developed by Indian farmers. By 1924, within less than 20 years of flint corn's general acceptance by non-Indian farmers, the acreage in North Dakota devoted to corn had increased 42 times over what it had been in 1909. Non-Indian farmers in the Great Plains and the Midwest also began growing the Hidatsa-developed great northern bean, a major agricultural crop today.

In contrast to the American Indians' ongoing quest for higher yielding and more disease-resistant crops, European knowledge of and interest in plant genetics was not strong even after the discoveries of Austrian botanist Gregor Mendel, who had experimented with peas and presented his findings about hybridization to the scientific community in 1865. His findings were not taken seriously by the scientific community until the early 1900s. American Indian agricultural research required keen powers of observation and a practical, working understanding of plant genetics. That expertise is responsible for creating many of the crops that are raised throughout the world today.

See also CHILES; COTTON; ZONED BIODIVERSITY.

**Sources/Further Reading**

Hurt, R. Douglas. *American Indian Agriculture: Prehistory to Present.* Lawrence: University Press of Kansas, 1987.

Josephy, Jr., Alvin M. *The Indian Heritage of America.* Rev. ed. Boston: Houghton Mifflin and Company, 1991.

Nabhan, Gary. *Enduring Seeds: Native American Agriculture and Wild Plant Conservation.* San Francisco: North Point Press, 1989.

Traeger, James. *The Peoples' Chronology.* New York: Holt, Reinhart Winston, 1979.

**seed treatment** See AGRICULTURE.

**separation of civil government and military** See UNITED STATES CONSTITUTION, AMERICAN INDIAN INFLUENCE ON.

**settlement patterns** (precontact) *North American, Mesoamerican, Circum-Caribbean, South American cultures* Throughout the Americas, indigenous peoples tended to locate their cities and villages in areas near streams, rivers, and lakes. This not only provided water for the residents, it also often served as sources of transportation. They selected settlement sites that could be easily defended from attack. (See also CITIES, AMERICA'S FIRST.) Once these villages had been established, the residents set about the task of clearing trails that led to other villages or cities so that TRADE could take place more easily. Many American Indian cultures cleared extensive tracts of land for AGRICULTURE. (See also MILPA.)

In Mesoamerica, when Spanish conquistador Hernán Cortés marched into the Aztec city of Tenochtitlan in 1519, he and his men encountered not only cleared land but an enormous urban infrastructure that included PYRAMIDS, houses, temples, canals, causeways with BRIDGES, dams, and busy commercial centers that were jammed with goods. Hernán Cortés and his army conquered the Aztec, whose empire had been established in about A.D. 1100, taking over the city and making its infrastructure their own.

In 1533, when Francisco Pizarro and his conquistadores began their efforts to subdue the Inca, who had established an empire in what is now Peru in about A.D. 1000, the Spaniards moved into Cuzco, the Inca capitol, claiming it for the Spanish Crown. Although shortly afterward they established their headquarters in Lima, a new city that they built on the coast, Cuzco became a colonial city. The Spaniards used stone blocks that Inca stonecutters and masons had made centuries before for the new buildings they constructed. (See also STONEMA-SONRY TECHNIQUES.) They laid out their city streets on the old Inca roads. Inca bridges were still in use in the 1800s, and some terraced fields (see also FARMING, TERRACED) that Inca farmers created are still cultivated today. The Spaniards frequently built Catholic churches on the foundations of old temples in both South and Mesoamerica.

Although some colonial North American settlements in the Northeast were established in uninhabited "wilderness" and given names borrowed from American Indian languages, many modern towns with Indian names were built on Indian village sites. (See also PLACE-NAMES.) European colonists often preferred establishing their own settlements on the site of Indian villages after they had driven away the Indian people that they encountered living there. Turning established American Indian villages into colonial settlements saved a great deal of work, since the land had been already cleared for building and farming.

Many history books state that the first Dutch governor of New Amsterdam, Peter Minuit, bought the land that would become New York City from the Manhattan for $24 worth of beads. The first time this story was recorded was in an 1877 book called *History of the City of New York* by Martha Lamb—over 250 years after the supposed purchase. In truth, the Dutch did give the Manhattan trade goods in exchange for the rights to live on part of the island. The Dutch lived on the southern end of the Manhattan Island and the Indians, unaware of the full implications of the agreement, moved northward, planting their crops in an area they called *Muscoota,* which meant "flat place." They farmed in peace for only a short time before Peter Stuyvesant, New Amsterdam's second governor, built a town there that he called Nieuw Haarlem and displaced them. Today Nieu Haarlem is known simply as Harlem (a section of New York City).

Settlers established the city of St. Louis, Missouri, across the river from the ancient city of Cahokia, which was built by the Hopewell people, whose culture flourished between 200 B.C. and A.D. 700. Before the name was changed to St. Louis, early non-Indian settlers called their "new" town Mound City. Memphis, Tennessee, was also built near the site of mounds that had been constructed by prehistoric American Indians. The city of Phoenix, Arizona, incorporated old Hohokam canals into its design. (Hohokam culture flourished between 300 B.C. and A.D. 1200.) Early Mormon farmers in central Arizona irrigated their fields with the canals the Hohokam had dug hundreds of years before. (See also IRRIGATION.) Albany, New York; Council Bluffs, Iowa; Kansas City, Missouri; and Detroit, Michigan were all originally North American Indian settlements.

North American colonists often located cities on established Indian trail routes. (See also ROAD SITES.) For example, the city of Chicago, Illinois, was founded on an Indian portage route between Lake Michigan and the Illinois River. Michigan City, Indiana, is located on Trail Creek, where Potawatomi Indian trails converged. Green Bay, Wisconsin, was once a WILD RICE gathering area for a number of tribes, including the Potawatomi.

European entrepreneurs and missionaries (as opposed to colonists) selected their settlement sites not so much for the geographical location as for their proximity to Indians. Canadian fur traders, for instance, founded Montreal next to a Huron village on the St. Lawrence River, first because of the transportation the river provided, and second because they needed close contact with Indian peoples in order to trade European-made goods for their pelts. Spanish missionaries who wished to convert Indians living in what is now California built their missions in the midst of Indian settlements. Many of these mission communities eventually became Southern California towns such as Los Angeles, Santa Barbara, and San Louis Obispo.

### Sources/Further Reading

Davis, Emily C. *Ancient Americans*. New York: Cooper Square Publishers, 1975.

Hurst, David, Jay Miller, Richard White, Peter Nabokov, and Philip Deloria. *The Native Americans*. Atlanta: Turner Publishing, Inc., 1993.

Lowen, James W. *Lies My Teacher Told Me: Everything Your American History Textbook Got Wrong*. New York: The New Press, 1995.

Stannard, David E. *American Holocaust: Columbus and the Conquest of the New World*. New York: Oxford University Press, 1992.

Weatherford, Jack. *Indian Givers: How the Indians of the Americas Transformed the World*. New York: Fawcett Columbine, 1988.

———. *Native Roots: How the Indians Enriched America*. New York: Fawcett Columbine, 1991.

Young, Bernice Elizabeth. *Harlem, the Story of a Changing Community*. New York: Simon & Schuster, Inc., 1972.

**shampoo**  See DETERGENTS.

**shinny**  See HOCKEY, FIELD AND ICE.

**shock absorbers**  See DOGSLEDS.

**shoes**  See MOCCASINS; MUKLUKS; SANDALS; SNOWSHOES.

**shovels**  (ca. 3000 B.C.)  *South American Andean, North American Northeast and Arctic cultures*

Shovels are long-handled tools for scooping or digging. The earliest record of a shovel existing in the prehistoric Americas dates around 3000 B.C.; it was made by Paleo-Indians. The Moche, whose culture began to flourish in what is now Peru in about 200 B.C., made shovels out of wood. These shovels looked like large rowboat paddles and were used for digging. The Inuit of the Arctic region of North America developed a shovel from the scapula bone of the whale. They also made a shovel of wood that resembled a scoop, or grain, shovel of today. To this they affixed a sharp, ivory blade to give the shovel a cutting edge. The Chippewa (Anishinabe) Indians of the present-day Great Lakes region also developed a shovel. It was made of wood and used for working in snow as well.

See also TOOLS.

### Sources/Further Reading

Mason, J. Alden. *The Ancient Civilizations of Peru*. Rev. ed. New York: Penguin Books. 1988.

Murdoch, John. *Ethnological Results of the Point Barrow Expedition Annual Report of the U.S. Bureau of Ethnology 1887–1888*. Washington: Government Printing Office, 1892.

Oswalt, Wendell. *Eskimos and Explorers*. Novato, Calif.: Chandler & Sharp Publishers, 1979.

**sign language**  (precontact)  *North American Great Plains and Plateau cultures*

Sign language is a way to communicate using gestures. Before contact with Europeans, American Indians living on the Great Plains developed a system of hand signs. They used this sign language to exchange information or to trade with members of culture groups who spoke a different language from their own. (See also TRADE.) Sign language was also used in order to communicate silently with speakers of the same language during hunting or raiding parties when silence was critical. Plains culture groups that are known to have used sign language include the Arapaho, Cheyenne, Pawnee, Kiowa, Crow, Osage, Comanche, Pawnee, and the Dakota, Lakota, and Nakota. The Blackfeet and the Assiniboine, also Great Plains culture groups, used sign language, as did the Plateau tribe the Nez Perce and the Ute of the Great Basin. Some historians believe that sign language is indigenous to the plains. Others believed that it may have been brought there by the Comanche or Kiowa, who had learned it in what is now Mexico.

There is no disagreement that sign language was developed to a high degree of sophistication by Plains tribes, who used over 1,000 distinct gestures to communicate words or concepts. George Frederick Ruxton, an adventurer, wrote in his account *Adventures in Mexico and the Rocky Mountains*, "The language of signs is so perfectly understood in the Western country, and the Indians themselves are such admirable sign talkers, that after a little use, no difficulty whatever exists in carrying on a conversation by such a channel."

Garrick Mallery, who studied Indian sign language in the late 1800s for the Bureau of Ethnology in the Smithsonian Institution after retiring as an army colonel, respected the sophistication of the signing system. He wrote that his studies had provided evidence of "conclusive proof that signs constitute a real language." Fur traders and mountain men who interacted with American Indians on the Plains quickly learned sign language in order to communicate with them. Later U.S. soldiers also learned signs.

Tichkematse, a Cheyenne who worked for the Smithsonian Institution, contributed immensely to the academic study of Plains sign language from 1878 to 1880. He worked with anthropologist Frank Hamilton Cushing, who made notes on the various signs and what they meant.

In the 1800s delegations of Plains Indians who traveled to Washington, D.C., to meet with the president and congressmen often utilized sign language to carry on private conversations with one another throughout the official negotiations. Late in that century, American Indian delegations visited schools for the deaf that had been established by non-Indians in the eastern part of the United States. During these visits they used Plains sign language in order to communicate with deaf mutes. Although Plains Indian "hand talk" uses some of the same gestures for particular words as does the American Sign Language that is used by people who cannot hear, many not shared. (American Sign Language, used by deaf Americans to communicate, was invented in the mid-1800s.)

See also LANGUAGE, AMERICAN INDIAN INFLUENCE ON.

### Sources/Further Reading

Clark, W. P. *Indian Sign Language*. Lincoln: University of Nebraska Press, 1982.

Farnell, Brenda. *Do You See What I Mean?: Plains Indian Sign Talk and the Embodiment of Action*. Austin: University of Texas Press, 1995.

Fronval, George and Daniel DuBois. *Indian Signals and Sign Language*. New York: Bonanza Books, 1992.

Mallery, Garrick. *A Collection of Gesture Signs and Signals of the North Americans with Some Comparisons*. Miscellaneous Publications, No. 1, Washington, D.C.: U.S. Bureau of Ethnology, 1880.

Ruxton, George F. *Adventures in Mexico and the Rocky Mountains*. New York: Harpers, 1848.

**silver** See METALS, PRECIOUS.

**sintering** (ca. 300 B.C.) *South American Andean cultures*
Sintering is the metallurgical process of fusing at least two metals together with high heat. (See also METALLURGY.) The ancient Indians in the present-day area of Ecuador invented and used this process to work platinum prior to contact with Europeans. PLATINUM has a very high melting point that was beyond what previous metalworkers could produce with their wind furnaces. (See also SMELTING.) The Ecuadorian metallurgists could generate heat high enough to melt silver or gold but not platinum. They learned to granulate platinum and silver, which were mixed together and heated. In this state the melting point of platinum was lowered, and an alloy of platinum and silver could be produced. They were then able to hammer the platinum alloy into the shape they desired. Because of this process, these metalworkers were able to produce excellent platinum objects. The final product looked as though it was made of pure platinum.

Even though the melting temperature of platinum was beyond their capability, the ancient metalworkers used their critical thinking to overcome this stumbling block. J. Alden Mason, author of the book *Ancient Civilizations of Peru*, wrote of this technique, "The discovery of ornaments of platinum on the coast of Ecuador has astounded and intrigued modern metallurgists for its melting point (about 1770 C or 3218 F) is beyond the capabilities of primitive furnaces." Platinum work was unknown in Europe until the 19th century.

See also METALS, PRECIOUS.

### Sources/Further Reading

Bergsoe, Paul. "The Metallurgy and Technology of Gold and Platinum among the Pre-Columbian Indians." *A. Ingeniorvidenska-beliege Skrifter* A, no. 44 (1937).

Mason, J. Alden. *The Ancient Civilizations of Peru*. Rev. ed. New York: Penguin Books, 1964.

*Material Issues in Layered Forming, SFFS UT '93. Sintering.* URL: http://www-rpl.stanford.edu/~rmerz/PAPER/TEXAS93/tex93.html . Downloaded on January 26, 2000.

**sisal** See AGAVE.

**skin care** See SUNSCREENS, MEDICINAL.

**skin grafts** (precontact) *North American, South American, Mesoamerican cultures*
Skin grafting is a surgical procedure during which skin is taken from one part of the body and sutured onto another part. Sometimes donor skin from another individual is used. This procedure was known and used by the precontact Indians of the Americas. South American and Mesoamerican Indians grafted scalp tissue, noses, ears, and even bones.

See also PLASTIC SURGERY; SURGERY.

### Sources/Further Reading

North Seattle Community College, 1996. *Surgery and Related Techniques*. URL: http://nsccux.sccd.ctc.edu/~contined/sdistance/nascience/sur g.html.

Vogel, Virgil. *American Indian Medicine*. Norman: University of Oklahoma Press, 1970.

**sleds, cariole** (precontact) *North American Subarctic and Arctic cultures*
Carioles are sleds that were used in the frigid northern regions by the Native peoples of North America. A cariole resembled a toboggan but had four walls of moose hide built on top. The vehicle was designed for transporting loads larger than what one person could carry and could be pulled either by dog teams or men depending on the terrain or load. It also had a carrying capacity that was larger than that of a DOGSLED or

TOBOGGAN. The wide bottom of the cariole prevented it from sinking in the snow.

The far North did not have trees to provide wood for carioles, so the Inuit used other materials, such as large bones, to make the runners and frames for the cariole sleds. In extreme emergencies the northern Native people put wet leather down and laid fish end-to-end on top of the leather. They rolled these up, shaped them like a runners, and left them on the ice until they froze, upon which they were used for sled runners. If necessary after being used for runners, the fish could eventually be thawed out and eaten.

## Sources/Further Reading

Oswalt, Wendell. *Eskimos and Explorers.* Novato, Calif.: Chandler & Sharp Publishers, 1979.

Weatherford, Jack. *Indian Givers: How the Indians of the Americas Transformed the World.* New York: Fawcett Columbine, 1988.

**sleds, dog** See DOGSLEDS.

**smelting** (ca. 200 B.C.–A.D. 600) *South American Andean cultures*

Smelting is the process of extracting metal from ore. According to Brian M. Fagan, author and archaeology professor, "Copper and gold ornaments first appeared over a broad area between southern Ecuador and Bolivia between 1500 B.C. and 200 B.C., but it was Moche metalsmiths who revolutionized metallurgy on the coast. Using only the simplest of tools, they smelted precious metals in small furnaces by blowing on the hot coals through long tubes." Moche culture arose in what is now Peru in about 200 B.C.

The Moche and later the Inca, who established an empire in what is now Peru in about A.D. 1000, used two types of small furnaces, which the Inca called *guayra*. One consisted of a ceramic pot about three feet in diameter and about two feet high. Workers used copper tubes to blow on the fire they had built inside this furnace. These tubes were about five to six feet long with an inside diameter of an inch. In order to generate enough pressure to make the fire burn hot, they made the tubes so that the end closest to the coals had a smaller diameter than the end that they blew on. The metalsmiths intentionally placed an object in the blowing tube in order to reduce its diameter. This created what is known today as the venturi effect, which increased the pressure of the air coming out of the tube. By blowing on the coals with these tubes, the Moche were able to achieve a fire that reached temperatures capable of smelting ore in very high altitudes. Without this technology, they would not have been able to smelt or keep a fire going because of the lack of oxygen at these heights.

The other method they used was a wind furnace, which was pear-shaped and had a large hole in the front for fueling it with charcoal as well as smaller holes on the back. The wind furnace was positioned so that the back faced the wind and the front faced the mountain. As the wind blew over the small holes, it provided sufficient oxygen for fire to burn hot enough to smelt ore at high altitudes.

After conquest, the Spaniards took over the Inca silver mines. Judging the Inca smelting furnaces as primitive, they imported what they considered to be advanced technology from Europe that included bellows. When they discovered that these were unable to produce fires hot enough to melt metal in the high altitudes of the Andes, they were forced to allow the Inca, who had devised specialized smelting techniques adapted to the unique environment, to continue to direct mining operations for several years.

See also ANNEALING; METALLURGY; METALS, PRECIOUS; PLATINUM; SINTERING; SOLDERING; WELDING.

## Sources/Further Reading

Bankes, George. *Peru Before Pizarro.* Oxford, England: Phaidon Press Ltd., 1977.

Engel, Frederic Andre. *An Ancient World Preserved: Relics and Records of Prehistory in the Andes.* New York: Crown Publishers, Inc., 1976.

Fagan, Brian M. *Kingdoms of Gold, Kingdoms of Jade: The Americas before Columbus.* London: Thames and Hudson Ltd., 1991.

Morris, Craig and Adriana von Hagen. *The Inka Empire And Its Andean Origins,* New York: Abbeville Press Publishers, 1993.

**smoked salmon** See FOOD PRESERVATION.

**snack foods** (precontact) *Mesoamerican; North American Great Plains, Northeast, and Southwest cultures*

Hand-held meals for eating on the go are not a 20th-century invention. American Indians were eating what would now be termed snack food long before Europeans landed in the New World. From CORN on the cob and POPCORN, to JERKY and PEMMICAN, or trail food, North American colonists quickly adopted American Indian snack foods. Spaniards who landed in Mexico found marketplace vendors selling a variety of prepared take-out foods to Aztecs, including TAMALES, TORTILLAS, and sauces. To the north, the Pueblo people of the desert Southwest also made tortillas, filling them with BEANS or meat sauce like a burrito.

See also INSTANT FOOD.

## Sources/Further Reading

Coe, Sophie. *America's First Cuisines.* Austin: University of Texas Press, 1994.

Sokalow, Raymond. *Why We Eat What We Eat: How the Encounter Between the New World and the Old Changed the Way Everyone on the Planet Eats.* New York: Summit Books, 1991.

**snakebite treatment** (precontact) *North American, South American, Mesoamerican cultures*
The snakebite treatments used by precontact American Indians throughout the Americas involved lancing the bite site and sucking out the poison or venom. Today the medical profession calls this "cupping and suction." The ancient American Indians were the first to invent this procedure and used it for snakebites as well as for spider bites and other topical infections. After contact, Europeans adopted this treatment because of its effectiveness. Small snakebite kits sold commercially and recommended through much of the 20th century that contained a lancet and rubber suction cup came about as a result of the Indian invention of the cupping and suction procedure. While recent advances have made safer snakebite kits, this remains a simple, but highly effective way to treat snakebites.

See also INSECT BITE AND BEE STING REMEDIES; MEDICINE.

**Sources/Further Reading**

Ortiz de Montellano, Bernard R. *Aztec Medicine, Health, and Nutrition.* New Brunswick, N.J.: Rutgers University Press, 1990.

U.S. National Library of Medicine. Snake Bite Treatment. URL: http://medlineplus.adam.com/ency/article/00003/trt.htm.

Vogel, Virgil. *American Indian Medicine.* Norman: University of Oklahoma Press, 1970.

Weatherford, Jack. *Indian Givers: How the Indians of the Americas Transformed the World.* New York: Fawcett Columbine, New York, 1988.

**snow creepers** See CRAMPONS.

**snow goggles** (precontact) *North American Arctic cultures*
Snow goggles are a type of eyewear that lowers the amount of light that shines into the wearer's eyes. Sunlight glaring from a vast expanse of dazzling snow would have made it impossible for Inuit hunters, fishermen, and travelers to see, were it not for their invention of snow goggles. The word for the goggles, used by Inuit people throughout Canada and Alaska, means "snow eyes" in their native language. They carved the goggles from wood, ivory, or antlers. Snow goggles completely covered the eyes, admitting just enough light from horizontal slits to allow the wearer to see. Sometimes tiny holes were drilled into the top of the goggles. Anthropologists believe that these were probably made to provide ventilation.

**Sources/Further Reading**

Murdoch, John. *Ethnological Results of the Point Barrow Expedition: Annual Report of the U.S. Bureau of Ethnology 1887–1888.* Washington: Government Printing Office, 1892.

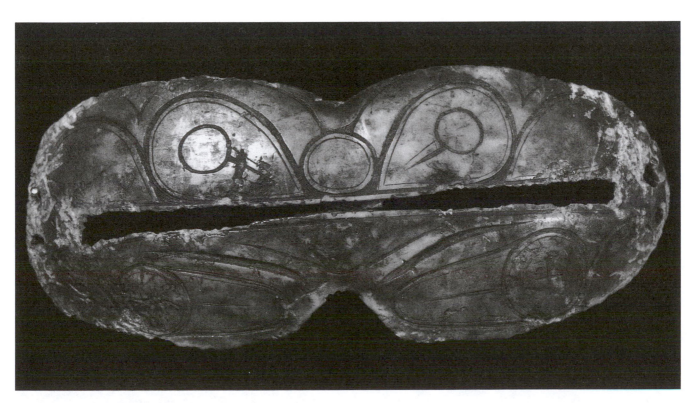

Snow goggles, such as these made from ivory from the Ipiutak site at Point Hope, Alaska, protected the wearer from snow blindness. These goggles are believed to have been made between A.D. 100 and A.D. 600. *(Neg. 121386/Photo. C. Coles/Courtesy Department of Library Services, American Museum of Natural History)*

Oswalt, Wendell. *Eskimos and Explorers.* Novato, Calif.: Chandler & Sharp Publishers, 1979.

Weatherford, Jack. *Native Roots: How the Indians Enriched America.* New York: Fawcett Columbine, 1991.

## snowshoes (precontact) *North American Arctic, Subarctic, and Northeast cultures*

Snowshoes are a type of footwear that make for easier travel in deep snow than normal footwear, such as MOCCASINS or MUKLUKS, would. American Indians from the Arctic Circle to the Great Lakes used snowshoes to aid their winter travel. They made the shoes from wooden frames laced with rawhide thongs. These shoes worked by distributing the wearer's weight over a larger area, thus preventing him or her from sinking into the snow. In addition to using them for snow travel, the Inuit also used snowshoes to cross sea ice.

American Indians in the North American Northeast constructed snowshoes by making a frame of light wood, such as spruce, and shaping it into an oval with a point on one end. The Cree and other subarctic tribes made snowshoes by bending the rounded front of the frame upward and then lacing it with netting (called *babiche*) into place. The size of snowshoes depended on the size of the wearer, but as a general rule, northeastern snowshoes were generally made to be about five times as long as they were wide. Some tribes, however, fashioned snowshoes that were shorter and more rounded, so that they almost resembled an animal's paw. American Indians made snowshoes that were fastened onto their moccasins or mukluks with leather straps. By lifting the toe and dragging the heel as they walked, snowshoe wearers made steady progress over the snow.

In the late 20th century, snowshoeing became a popular sport among outdoor people. New, high-tech snowshoes were made from lightweight metal and other materials, often no longer netted, but still based on the same age-old technology the Indians developed.

See also DOGSLEDS; SLEDS, CARIOLE; TOBOGGANS.

### Sources/Further Reading

Lowe, Warren. *Indian Giver.* Pencticton, British Columbia: Theytus Books, 1986.

Murdoch, John. *Ethnological Results of the Point Barrow Expedition: Annual Report of the U.S. Bureau of Ethnology 1887–1888.* Washington: Government Printing Office 1892.

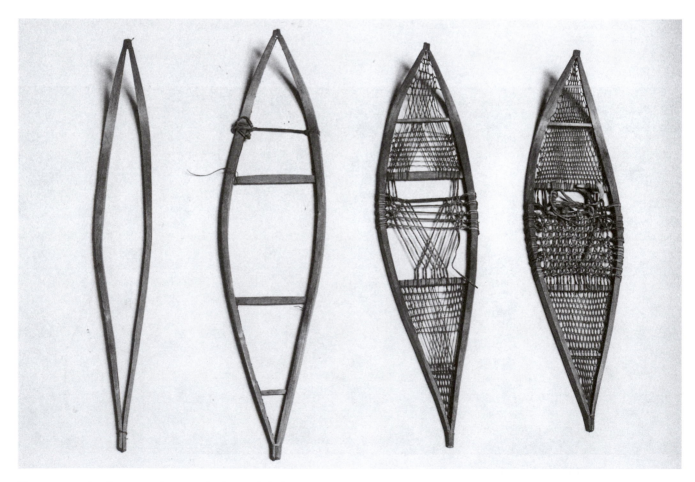

The process of making snowshoes involved using *babiche* lacing (a type of netting) and sinew lashing over a birch frame, as illustrated by the photo of Slave Indian snowshoes from about 1860. *(Canadian Museum of Civilization/image number; 74-18953)*

Oswalt, Wendell. *Eskimos and Explorers.* Novato, Calif.: Chandler & Sharp Publishers, 1979.

**snuff** (ca. 1100 B.C.) *South American Andean cultures*
Snuff is finely powdered TOBACCO, a plant that is indigenous to the Americas and was first cultivated by American Indians. Snuff was, and continues to be, taken by inhalation through the nostrils. The first use of snuff is believed to have occurred among the pre-Inca people of what is now Peru in about 1100 B.C. Snuff was used medicinally to induce sneezing in order to clear the nasal passages. The Inca, whose empire was established in what is now Peru in about A.D. 1000, used snuff as well. They called tobacco *sayri* in Quecha, the Inca language. As the cultures that had come before them had done, they took snuff for medicinal purposes rather than as a self-indulgence. The Inca also used datura seed snuff medicinally, grinding the seeds and inhaling them. The Inca produced many bone snuff tablets and snuff tubes. These tend to indicate that they used snuff regularly.

The Aztec, who established an empire in what is now Mexico in about A.D. 1100, used tobacco snuff medicinally as well. They prepared it in the same way as the Inca. Aztec physicians prescribed snuff in order to cause sneezing that would trigger a nosebleed, thereby alleviating a headache. For this purpose, they preferred using green tobacco.

The first record of snuff in Europe occurred when Jean Nicott, the French ambassador to Portugal, sent some to Catherine de Medici, queen of France, as a treatment for her son's migraine headaches shortly after 1560. By 1624 snuff was in common use as a recreational substance. It was so common that in that year Pope Urban VIII threatened those who used it with excommunication from the Catholic Church. He and other clergy believed that the sneezing caused by snuff resembled sexual ecstasy too closely. In 1637 King Louis XII of France, who used snuff, repealed restrictions on its use. Snuff use spread throughout Europe, and in 1730 the first tobacco companies, small snuff mills, were established in Virginia to meet the demand. Snuff use began to wane in the early 1800s to be replaced by CIGAR smoking.

See also CIGARS; CIGARETTES; HEADACHE MEDICATIONS; PIPES, TOBACCO.

**Sources/Further Reading**

Borio, Gene. *Tobacco Timeline: A Capsule History of Tobacco.* URL: http://www.tobacco.org/History/Tobacco/Tobacco_History.html. Downloaded on February 9, 2000.

Mason, J. Alden. *The Ancient Civilization of Peru.* Rev. ed. New York: Penguin Books. 1988.

Ortiz de Montellano, Bernard. *Aztec Medicine, Health, and Nutrition.* New Brunswick, N.J.: Rutgers University Press, 1990.

von Hagen, Victor Wolfgang. *Realm of the Incas.* New York: New American Library, 1957.

**soap** See DETERGENT.

**Socialist theory, American Indian influence on**
(A.D. 1851) *North American Northeast cultures*
Socialism is a political philosophy that regards a class-free society—in which the collective good is valued over individuality—as the ideal society. In addition to influencing the U.S. Constitution (see UNITED STATES CONSTITUTION, AMERICAN INDIAN INFLUENCE ON), the Great Law of Peace of the Iroquois League of Nations served as a major inspiration for later refinements of socialist theory (after the publication of *The Communist Manifesto* and *Das Kapital*). The Iroquois, an Iroquoian-speaking group indigenous to what is now New England, created the Iroquois League, which originally consisted of the Mohawk, Oneida, Onondaga, Cayuga, and Seneca tribes (and later the Tuscarora) between A.D. 1100 and 1450. European political philosophers Karl Marx and Friedrich Engels were influenced by the Iroquois ideas of government.

Marx and Engels, both of whom were German, lived in England. They did not have contact with the Iroquois but learned of their constitution through the work of Lewis Henry Morgan, who would later come to be known as the father of American anthropology. Morgan, who worked for the railroad industry as a lobbyist, first began studying American Indians to discover pieces of their rituals that he could use in a fraternal order he planned to found. Through the influence of his close friend Ely S. Parker, a Seneca and the first American Indian to serve as commissioner of Indian Affairs for the U.S. government, the Iroquois adopted Morgan. He spent nearly 10 years in close contact with the Iroquois people, and his writings about them were far more objective than any others until that point.

The result of his study was a comparison of the U.S. and Iroquois Constitutions called *League of the Ho-de-no-sau-nee.* This book became a classical work in anthropology after its publication in 1851 and was the first in-depth study of an American Indian social organization. In it Morgan detailed how the Iroquois had set up their government with checks and balances and equal distribution of wealth and power. Iroquois leaders were essentially servants who could be removed for any negative behavior relating to the people they served or to the office they held. Ordinary people were allowed religious and political expression, and women were allowed to participate in the political process.

Most of the thinkers in the 1800s had difficulty grasping the concept of a society without private property or social classes. Up until this time Europeans saw other cultures only in terms of European knowledge and experience. Many authors attempted to describe the American Indians with words like *feudalism* and *kingships*—concepts that were based on the European system of private property. Morgan's studies of American Indian people stood in sharp contrast to this way of thinking. His experiences with the Iroquois led him to believe that the American Indian society without private ownership of property and without class worked because it was based on family ties and kinship relationships as opposed to private ownership. At first glance the League of the Iroquois appeared more socialist in nature than democratic.

All of these concepts, and more, captivated Marx and Engels. They saw in Morgan's book a political system that worked and was, at the same time, almost their ideal of a classless and leaderless state. Among the Iroquois, the idea of private property and the competition to acquire wealth was almost unheard of. These concepts appealed the most to the two political philosophers. Marx, who had just completed *Das Kapital,* was especially intrigued. Morgan's description of Iroquois society fit into Marx's theories and was an alternative to the monarchy or the Russian czarist form of government that he was uncomfortable accepting. He felt absolute rule placed too much power in the hands of one person and produced a very unequal distribution of wealth, in addition to which the masses had few political choices or rights.

After Marx read Morgan's work, he became excited by the ideas and began writing a book incorporating Morgan's theories with his own. Marx died before he could finish the work. Before he died, he declared Morgan's scholarship a significant piece of writing that all socialists needed to read in order to understand the basis of his own theory. His notes and writings on the Iroquois were published posthumously in Russia, but it would be up to Friedrich Engels to finish the work. After Engels read Morgan's *Ancient Society,* he wrote *The Origin of Family, Private Property and the State,* published in 1884. This book would later be termed the cornerstone of modern socialist theory.

*The Origin of Family, Private Property and the State* was eventually translated into many languages for socialists around the world to study and became a primer for socialists even into the 20th century. As late as 1964, Moscow hosted a symposium of the International des Sciences Anthropologigues et Ethnologigues devoted to Morgan's theories and writings. Inadvertently, the Iroquois had contributed greatly not only to the government of the United States of America, but to that of the Union of Soviet Socialist Republics as well.

### Sources/Further Reading

Brandon, William. *The Last Americans: The Indian in American Culture.* New York: McGraw-Hill, 1974.

Farb, Peter. *Man's Rise to Civilization as Shown by the Indians of North America from Primeval Times to the Coming of the Industrial State.* New York: E.P. Dutton & Company, 1968.

Johansen, Bruce. *Native American Political Systems and the Evolution of Democracy.* Santa Fe, N.M.: Clear Light Publishers, 1998.

Weatherford, Jack. *Indian Givers: How the Indians of the Americas Transformed the World.* New York: Fawcett Columbine 1988.

**social security** See DISABILITY RIGHTS.

**soft drink ingredients** (precontact) *North American Northeast and Southeast cultures*

Soft drinks are nonalcoholic beverages; most are carbonated. Sometimes called soda, soda pop, or pop, soft drinks are a unique American invention. They were first marketed in the early 1830s by druggists as tonics or stimulants and were a part of the booming patent medicine industry. (See also MEDICINES, PATENT, AMERICAN INDIAN INFLUENCE ON.) Most early soft drink ingredients were borrowed directly from American Indians. These included sarsaparilla, SASSAFRAS, WINTERGREEN, birch, VANILLA, Jamaican ginger, and capsicum, which is obtained from CHILES. The flavorings were added after 1833, when the process for artificially carbonating water was discovered. Before that time, Americans drank soda water from naturally occurring mineral springs from which American Indians had taken water for centuries. (See also HOT SPRINGS.)

European colonists in North America made root beer from sassafras, wintergreen, and birch, plants that American Indians had used as medicines over hundreds of years. Sassafras (*Sassafras albidum*) was used by the Iroquois of the Northeast and the Cherokee and the Seminole of the Southeast as a blood purifier. The Chippewa (Anishinabe) of the Midwest and Cherokee also drank sassafras tea as a beverage. European colonists living in what became Florida used it to remedy illness caused by drinking bad water. As word spread, non-Indians began to consider sassafras tea a wonder tonic.

Like sassafras, sometimes sarsaparilla (*Smilax aristolchiifolia, S. regeli,* and *S. febrifuga*), was used in root beer. Often wild sarsaparilla (*Aralia nudicaulis*) was used as a substitute flavoring for soft drinks. Colonists consumed these sarsaparilla drinks as tonics, the same use the Algonkin, Potawatomi, Cherokee, and Chippewa had for the herb. Like many of the herbal ingredients in early soft drinks, sarsaparilla was bitter. Because of this the soft drink makers sometimes called the beverages peppers. This is how Dr. Pepper got its name.

Coca-Cola was first made from COCA leaves by Atlanta druggist John Pemberton in 1885. Coca is indigenous to South America and was originally used by pre-Inca and Inca cultures as an ANESTHETIC and a stimulant. (The Inca culture arose in what is now Peru in about A.D. 1000.) Pemberton's first name for the soft drink, French Wine of Coca, an Ideal Tonic, reflected the main ingredient. Later he added African kola nuts to his recipe. When coca was outlawed in the United States, he continued making Coca-Cola without it, but kept the name.

Today's soft drinks, originally based on American Indian remedies, have become such a way of life that, according to the National Soft Drink Association, each man, woman, and child in the United States drinks 56 gallons of them a year.

### Sources/Further Reading

Flexner, Stuart Berg. *I Hear America Talking: An Illustrated History of American Words and Phrases.* New York: Simon and Schuster, 1976.

Moerman, Dan. *American Indian Ethnobotanical Database.* URL: http://www.umd.umich.edu/cgi-bin/herb. Downloaded on January 29, 1999.

National Soft Drink Association. *Growing Up Together: The Soft Drink Industry and America.* URL: http://www.nsda.org/softdrinks/History. Downloaded on January 29, 2000.

Vogel, Virgil. *American Indian Medicine.* Norman: University of Oklahoma Press, 1970.

Weatherford, Jack. *Indian Givers: How the Indians of the Americas Transformed the World.* New York: Fawcett Columbine, 1988.

**soil rotation**   See MILPA.

**solar fire starters**   (ca. 1700 B.C.)   *Mesoamerican cultures*
A solar fire starter is a device that is able to start fires using only sunlight. The Olmec, whose culture arose in the Yucatán Peninsula of what is now Mexico in about 1700 B.C., produced a solar fire starter that worked on the basis of a reflecting surface. The Olmec fire starter had a concave surface that was highly polished. When sunlight hit the concave surface, its reflection was concentrated, producing a small, hot ray of light capable of starting a fire.

The Olmec used magnetite, hematite, and ilmentite as material for producing their fire starters. These minerals all contain iron ore. They shaped the raw material for fire starters with stone tools. Once they had achieved the desired shape of the piece, the Olmec ground and polished the fire starters so that they were highly reflective. The technology they used remains a mystery even today. The precision with which the Olmec ground the fire starters was amazing because of the even surfaces they were able to achieve as well as the symmetry in curvature. Once the material was shaped and ground, it was polished so that the material became highly reflective.

In *The Native Americans: An Illustrated History,* the authors say of the Olmec, "Their talented artisans also manufactured concave magnetite mirrors, so highly polished that today they still can be used to light a fire."

See also DRILLS, BOW.

**Sources/Further Reading**
Coe, Michael D. *America's First Civilization.* New York: American Heritage Publishing Co., Inc., 1968.

Hurst, David, Jay Miller, Richard White, Peter Nabokov, and Philip Deloria. *The Native Americans.* Atlanta: Turner Publishing, Inc., 1993.

Fiedel, Stuart J. *Prehistory of the Americas.* London: Cambridge University Press, 1987.

**soldering**   (ca. 1000 B.C.–200 B.C.)   *South American Andean cultures*
Soldering is the process that bonds or fuses at least two pieces of metal together with a metal salt—that is, a metal that has been treated with acid. (This process should not be confused with welding, which uses heat and does not require a third bonding agent.) The Chavin gold- and metalsmiths of the present-day area of Peru were able to solder gold objects together. (Chavin culture flourished from 1000 B.C. to 200 B.C.) Some of the more intricate items they soldered were life-sized gold sculptures of

South American metallurgists used soldering and other sophisticated metalworking techniques to create exquisite objects such as these gold ear spools, large earrings. Chimu craftsmen made them sometime between A.D. 900 and A.D. 1470. The Chimu lived in the northern part of what is now Peru. *(The Denver Art Museum)*

hands and arms from the elbow to the fingertips. These objects, which may have been funerary items, were hollow.

The soldering techniques these ancient metalsmiths invented relied on the use of a salt of copper and a resin. They mixed the copper salt and resin and applied it to the items to be soldered in order to prepare them. They then held the two pieces of metal in the desired position. The metallurgist applied heat until the copper salt was reduced or weakened and became metal once again. This liquid metal caused the bonding.

See also ANNEALING; METALLURGY; METALS, PRECIOUS; SINTERING; WELDING, SWEAT.

**Sources/Further Reading**
Bankes, George. *Peru Before Pizarro.* Oxford, England. Phaidon Press Limited, 1977.

Mason, J. Alden. *The Ancient Civilizations of Peru.* New York: Penguin Books, 1964.

Willey, Gordon R. *An Introduction to American Archaeology: Volume Two, South America.* Englewood Cliffs, N.J.: Prentice-Hall, 1971.

**space heaters, portable**   (ca. A.D. 1000–A.D. 1519)
*South American Andean; North American Arctic cultures*
A portable space heater is a small stove that can be moved easily from room to room to heat small areas effectively. The Inca, who established an empire in what is now Peru in about A.D. 1000, made the first known space heaters in the precontact Americas. These were about two feet high and about a foot and a half in diameter. They were made of POTTERY and shaped like a large egg with three legs on the bottom and a handle on the top. The legs kept the heater from coming into direct

contact with the floor and allowed heat to radiate in all directions. Holes made in the top also allowed heat to escape.

The Polar Inuit heated their IGLOOS with a variation of the space heater. They soaked moss in fat, then lit it with dry moss tinder that had been set afire by striking iron pyrite against quartz to make a spark. Once it was burning, they set it on a walrus shoulder blade that contained blubber. Most homes contained two of these heaters. Sometimes the Inuit hung sealskins full of snow above the heaters so that it would melt and could be used for drinking water. The Inuit of West Greenland placed drying racks above these heaters. Early explorers reported that the heaters, which also served as lamps, made the homes very warm despite below-zero temperatures outdoors.

## Sources/Further Reading

Oswalt, Wendell. *Eskimos and Explorers.* Novato, Calif.: Chandler & Sharp Publishers, 1979.
von Hagen, Victor W. *Realm of the Inca.* New York: New American Library, 1957.
———. *The Royal Road of the Inca.* London: Gordon & Cremonesi, Ltd., 1976.

**spirulina**  See BLUE-GREEN ALGAE.

**splints**  See ORTHOPEDIC TECHNIQUES.

**sports uniforms**  See BASKETBALL; HELMETS, SPORTS.

**spring, hot**  See HOT SPRINGS.

**squash  (*Cucurbita pepo, Cucurbita mosachata, Cucurbita maxima*)**  (ca. 8000 B.C.) *Mesoamerican, South American, North American cultures*
Squash is a fleshy, fruit-producing plant that is indigenous to the Americas. Varieties of the genus *Cucurbita pepo,* more commonly known as summer squash, include acorn squash, zucchini, yellow squash, and decorative GOURDS. The PUMPKIN is also classified as a *Cucurbita pepo.* Native American farmers living near what is now Oaxaca, Mexico, were the first to domesticate *Cucurbita pepo* plants. Archaeologists found domesticated squash seeds dating from 8750 to 7849 B.C. in a cave in this area. They believe squash was one of the earliest plants that American Indians domesticated. Farmers of the Eastern Woodlands of North America also domesticated *Cucurbita pepo* independently in about 2700 B.C. The word *squash* comes from a Narragansett word, *askutasquash,* meaning a "green thing that is eaten raw."

The squash variety *Cucurbita moschata* is also indigenous to what is now Mexico and was first domesticated there. Butternut squash is a variety of *Cucurbita moschata.* By about 1880

B.C., ancient farmers of the coast of what is now Peru had domesticated another type of squash, *Cucurbita maxima.* Hubbard squash is a type of *Cucurbita maxima.* These two varieties are known as winter squash today. American Indians first began cultivating winter squash in about 4000 B.C. in what is now the Mexican state of Puebla.

Mesoamerican and North American agricultural cultures depended on squash, which is an excellent source of vitamin A, as an important part of their diet. The Maya, whose culture arose in the Yucatán Peninsula of what is now Mexico in about 1500 B.C., ate all parts of the squash. Mesoamericans boiled the young fruits to eat alone. Sometimes they used squash as an ingredient in stews. More mature squashes were baked, sometimes in honey. (See also BEEKEEPING.) They ate the flowers, shoots, and leaves as vegetables and also enjoyed squash seeds, both raw and toasted. Ground squash seeds served as an ingredient in drinks, sauces, and relishes. The Aztec, who established an empire in what is now Mexico in about A.D. 1100, ate squash in many of the same ways. They also used ground squash seeds in a type of SALSA resembling the salsa that people eat today.

Squash formed an important part of the diet of the Hidatsa people who lived along the Missouri River on the northern plains. Hidatsa women would germinate seeds on grass mats and then transplant them in the soil when all danger of frost has passed. (See also TRANSPLANTING, AGRICULTURAL.) When the squash were ripe, the women sliced many of them, strung them on skewers, and hung them to dry for winter use. Others were boiled and eaten fresh. Hidatsa cooks also dried squash blossoms for winter use. When squash blossoms were still fresh, they also boiled them with fat and beans or parched corn. According to Buffalo Bird Woman, an elderly Hidatsa woman at the turn of the century, although most squash were eaten, little girls decorated the brightest colored squash for dolls.

Squash was so important to Southwest tribes that the squash blossom came to be a symbol of fertility for the Hopi. It is a common design in silver and turquoise jewelry made by southwestern Native artisans today. (See also JEWELRY, TURQUOISE AND SILVER.) Southwestern farmers, as well as Mesoamerican farmers, and those living in the Southwest, northern plains, and Eastern Woodlands of North America, planted squash in hills with CORN and BEANS. This practice, known as COMPANION PLANTING, increases crop yield by taking advantage of individual plant characteristics.

Spanish and French explorers believed that they had stumbled on melon patches when they saw American Indians' fields of squash. In the early 1500s Spaniards took seeds back to Spain. At first it was not a popular vegetable, but by the 1700s squash had spread to Italy, and Italian gardeners began growing zucchini, which would become an integral part of that nation's cuisine. When Europeans finally began growing and eating squash in the 1700s, they roasted or boiled it and ground the seeds as a substitute for almonds in the candy called marzipan. They also mixed ground seeds with water to make a drink. Sometimes they cooked squash in sugar syrup and let it dry to candy it.

See also AGRICULTURE.

## Sources/Further Reading

Coe, Sophie. *America's First Cuisines.* Austin: University of Texas Press, 1994.

Hurt, R. Douglas. *American Indian Agriculture: Prehistory to Present.* Lawrence: University Press of Kansas, 1987.

Matthews, Todd. *Thanksgiving with Reader's Digest: Gorgeous Gourds, Squash, and Pumpkins.* Reader's Digest Association. URL: http://www.rdthanksgiving.com/tasty-traditions/gourd.html. Downloaded on July 7, 1998.

*Pumpkins and Summer Squashes Cucurbita pepo. Food Museum.* URL: http://www.foodmuseum.com/hughes/pumpkin.htm. Downloaded on September 9, 1999.

Wilson, L. Gilbert. *Buffalo Bird Woman's Garden: Agriculture of the Hidatsa Indians.* Reprint. St. Paul: Minnesota Historical Society Press, 1987.

Weatherford, Jack. *Indian Givers: How the Indians of the Americas Transformed the World.* New York: Fawcett Columbine, 1988.

## staples, surgical  (precontact)  *South American Tropical Forest cultures*

Surgical staples help hold the edges of an incision or wound together so that a cut in the skin will heal with minimal scarring. Improperly closed incisions or wounds can lead to blood loss and infection. Staples serve as a replacement for suturing (sewing the wound or incision closed). Modern surgeons began using surgical staples in the 1960s. At the time this technique was considered extremely innovative because it was quicker and less cumbersome than suturing. Although surgical stapling was considered new, American Indians had invented the surgical stapling technique many years earlier. Amazonian doctors used leaf-cutting ant to hold skin together during the healing process. When a patient presented an open tear or cut on the skin, the Indian doctor would pinch the edges of the wound together so that they were closely matched. Next, he would hold the leaf-cutting ants close to the wound, so that the ant would bite down on it. Such ants were used because their large mandibles, or jaws that are shaped like pincers, could exert enough pressure on the skin to hold it together. Leaf-cutting ants are three-fourths of an inch long. Once the ants had bitten, the healer removed the ants' bodies, leaving the clamped mandibles in place like staples. They were removed when they were no longer needed.

See also ANTIBIOTIC MEDICATIONS; ASEPSIS; DEBRIDEMENT; GRANULATION; SURGERY.

## Sources/Further Reading

Adams, William R. "Aboriginal American Indian Medicine and Surgery." *Proceedings of the Indiana Academy of Science* 15, no. 1 (January 1944): 15–36.

North Seattle Community College. *Surgery and Related Techniques, Copyright, 1996.* URL: http://nsccux.sccd.ctc.edu/~continued/distance/nascience/su rg.html. Downloaded on November 4, 1999.

Vogel, Virgil. *American Indian Medicine.* Norman: University of Oklahoma Press, 1970.

## steam rooms  (sweat lodges)  (ca. 1500 B.C.)
*Mesoamerican; North American Great Plains, Northwest, Southeast, and Southwest cultures*

A steam room is an enclosed space where water is splashed onto a hot surface, such as heated rocks, in order to create steam. People in many parts of the world use steam rooms for medical reasons and for personal hygiene. American Indians in Mesoamerica built steam rooms that were attached to their houses and used them both for daily bathing and for health purposes. The steam room was so integral to Aztec life that the houses in the Aztec capitol city of Tenochtitlán each had a bathouse. (The Aztec Empire was established in what is now Mexico in about A.D. 1100.) North American Indians used sweat lodges—covered, dome-shaped structures—for the same reasons.

The Maya, whose culture arose in what is now the Yucatán Peninsula of Mexico in about 1500 B.C., called their steam rooms *temascal*. The Aztec built similar steam rooms. They made a fire inside the structure to heat rocks. When the rocks were red-hot, water was sprinkled over them.

The Aztec used the steam room and THERAPEUTIC TOUCH, or massage, before prescribing any medications or performing SURGERY. (See also PRESCRIPTIONS; PHARMACOLOGY.) Because heat is a good vasodilator, it improves circulation and dilates the pores in the skin so that toxins are more easily flushed out by perspiration. Aztec women took a steam bath immediately after they had given birth. The baby was bathed immediately after being born as well, a practice that continued for the rest of their lives. (See also HYGIENE, PERSONAL; OBSTETRICS.)

Indians throughout North America were also aware of the therapeutic value of moist heat. Indigenous people who lived in the area of present-day Virginia used the sweat lodge for many disorders and health problems. These included sore muscles, arthritis, rheumatism, and chills. Great Plains Indians also used the sweat lodge. They built the fire to heat the rocks outside and brought the rocks into the lodge when they were sufficiently hot. Indians living in what is now Canada built similar sweat lodges. The Kwakiutl, a Northwest Coast tribe, used the sweat bath for localized pain and when the nature of a disease could not be determined. The Apache, Zuni, Navajo (Dineh), and other Southwest tribes used steam baths for similar reasons. Many American Indians continue the practice today.

The Choctaw, a Southeast tribe, incorporated AROMATHERAPY with their steam baths. They steeped medicinal herbs in the water that they splashed on the rocks or burned the herbs on the rocks. These Choctaw sweat lodges were called "steam cabinets" by the early explorers. One European writer suggested that non-Indians should adopt this practice and use it at least three times a year.

According to Dr. Virgil Vogel, an expert on American Indian medicine, a member of the Lewis and Clark expedition became so disabled from chronic back pain, joint stiffness, and rheumatism that he could not move. The party stopped and built an Indian-style steam bath for him after all the European treatments failed. After drinking horse mint tea and taking steam baths, he recovered completely. (See also MINTS, BOTANICAL.)

Although long ago many ancient peoples throughout the world used steam baths, the practice died out for the most part except in the Scandinavian countries, where the sauna continued to be used regularly. Although physicians occasionally prescribed steam in order to relieve congestion or as a rheumatism cure, most modern Americans and Europeans did not use steam rooms. Recently, however, the steam room is making a comeback as people rediscover the health benefits it provides—something Indians throughout the Americas never forgot.

## Sources/Further Reading

Lowe, Warren. *Indian Giver.* Pencticton, British Columbia: Theytus Books, 1986.

Mason, J. Alden. *The Ancient Civilizations of Peru.* New York: Penguin Books, 1957.

Thompson, J. Eric S. *Maya History and Religion.* Norman: University of Oklahoma Press, 1970.

Viola, Herman J. and Carolyn Margolis. *Seeds of Change: 500 Years Since Columbus.* Washington, D.C.: Smithsonian Institution Press, 1991.

Vogel, Virgil. *American Indian Medicine.* Norman: University of Oklahoma Press, 1970.

Will, Drake W. "The Medical and Surgical Practice of the Lewis and Clark Expedition." *Journal of the History of Medicine* 14, no. 3 (July 1959): 273–97.

## stockades (forts) (precontact) *North American Northeast cultures*

Stockades are defensive enclosures built of timbers that are driven into the ground. Sometimes these barriers are called palisades. The Huron and Iroquois of the North American Northeast fortified their larger villages in this manner. According to the reports of European explorers, some of these settlements were made up of 50 buildings and were spread out over 100 acres. (See also CITIES, AMERICA'S FIRST.) Double or triple fences surrounded some Huron and Iroquois villages. Smaller villages located near the larger, stockaded ones did not have these walls. Historians believe that when danger arose, residents of the small villages took refuge behind the walls that surrounded the major towns. These American Indian stockades

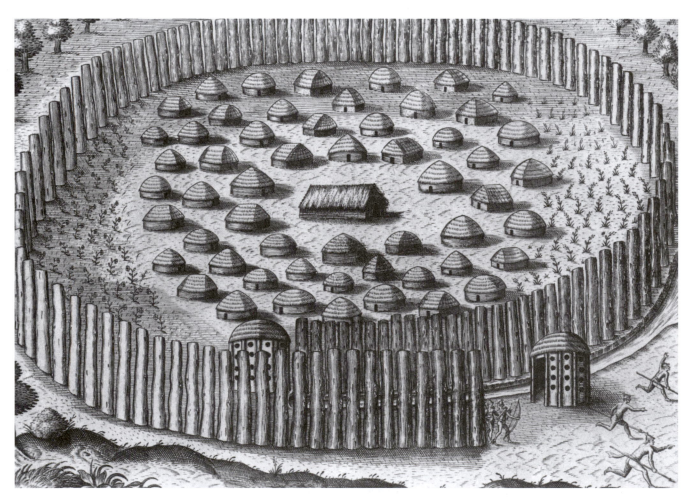

American Indians of the Northeast often fortified their villages with stockades. Early European explorers, impressed by the sophistication of their construction, compared them to castles. Theodore De Bry made this engraving of a fortified village between 1590 and 1598. *(LC-USZ62-367/Library of Congress)*

were invented independently of those that had been constructed in Europe before deforestation occurred in the 1300s (after which wood was scarce).

Unlike the square European stockades, American Indian stockade walls were oval in shape. They were constructed of long, thin wooden poles that had been sharpened at the bottom end and were then twisted into the ground a few inches from each other. Huron and Iroquois builders made this structure sturdier by weaving branches between the poles and stuffing the cracks with bark. They piled earth or tree trunks at the base to make the defense even more secure.

These American Indian forts impressed early European explorers, who compared them to castles because of their sophistication and construction. In 1535 a member of the explorer Jacques Cartier's party described the large Iroquois village of Hochelaga, which was built near what is now Montreal, Canada. He reported that the logs that made up the walls of the triple palisade were 18 feet tall and that those in the middle row were sharpened. The Iroquois at Hochelaga had constructed balconies along the middle wall where men could stand to shoot arrows or throw rocks at enemy invaders. The balconies that Cartier's men saw were a feature of most American Indian stockades. The platforms were accessed by climbing ladders made from notched logs. If an attack seemed imminent, villagers stocked the platforms, not only with rocks to use as missiles, but also with water to douse fires the enemy might set in an attempt to burn the village. Usually there was only one entrance to a palisaded village and it was barred with logs. Masters of defense, the Iroquois and Huron both preferred to locate villages in areas that were surrounded by a slight depression, so that lookouts standing on the walls' platforms could better see the enemy approaching. (See also MILITARY TACTICS.)

On his first expedition in what is now North Carolina in 1585, Sir Walter Raleigh saw an Algonquian settlement near the coast. He described it as a "village of nine houses, built of Cedar, and fortified round about with sharpe trees, to keepe out their enemies, and the entrance into it make like a turne pike very artuificially [artfully]." Some of the stockades in the area were made of logs that had been sunk three feet into the ground.

### Sources/Further Reading

Nabokov, Peter and Robert Easton. *Native American Architecture.* New York: Oxford University Press, 1989.

Trigger, Bruce G. *Case Studies in Anthropology: The Huron Farmers of the North.* New York: Holt Rinehart and Winston, 1969.

Wright, Ronald. *Stolen Continents: The "New World" Through Indian Eyes.* Reprint. New York: Houghton Mifflin, 1993.

## stonemasonry techniques (ca. 1000 B.C.)

*Mesoamerican, North American Southwest, South American Andean cultures*

Stonemasonry is the art of working with stone. It involves selecting the stone, quarrying it, cutting it to shape, carving it, and fitting it into place. American Indians of Mesoamerica, the North American Southwest, and South America all produced some form of stonework. In Mesoamerica the Olmec, whose culture arose in about 1700 B.C. in the Yucatán Peninsula of what is now Mexico, worked with basalt, a volcanic rock. Olmec stone carvers are best known for the huge basalt statues they carved. The Maya, whose culture flourished in the southern part of what is now Mexico from about 1500 B.C. to about A.D. 1450, used stones to construct elaborate temples, PYRAMIDS, and other structures. Often they carved elaborate facings for public buildings from stone. The Aztec, who established an empire in what is now Mexico in about A.D. 1100, continued this tradition. The Anasazi, whose culture arose in about 350 B.C. in what is now New Mexico, as well as in what are Utah and southern Colorado, constructed stone pueblos and towers. The Inca, who established an empire in what is now Peru in about A.D. 1000, are considered to be masters at architectural stonework. These stonemasons constructed a variety of structures, including APARTMENT HOUSES, pyramids, and field terraces. (See also FARMING, TERRACED.) Buildings they constructed centuries ago have withstood earthquakes and are still standing today.

The Olmec are thought by many art historians to be not only the first but also the greatest stone sculptors in the precontact Americas. They used basalt, jadeite (see also JADE WORK), and serpentine more frequently than other minerals. Although they produced statues that were five to six feet in height, they are best known for the massive stone pieces that they carved, some of which weigh more than 20 tons. The most famous of these statues are the huge carved heads that surround the perimeter of tombs. The Olmec also carved life-sized human figures and figures of animals, such as the jaguar. Succeeding peoples throughout precontact North, Meso-, and South America made sculptures, but they were not of the magnitude, scale, and technology of the Olmec. The Olmec also worked basalt to make conduits for water. (See also AQUEDUCTS.) They did not rely on stone for their architectural constructions.

The Maya built square stone temples atop pyramids that consisted of hundreds of steps. They used stone roofs for these temples and invented the corbelled arch (see also ARCHES, CORBELLED), which was used extensively in their architecture. They also built rectangular public buildings that they grouped around temples. Maya stonemasons made these temples and large buildings from blocks of stone that they covered with a limestone plaster in order to both set the stones and give the structures a whitewashed appearance. (See also CONCRETE.) The Maya carved stone facades to decorate their religious and civil buildings.

The Aztec also built stone pyramids, which were rebuilt frequently as they destroyed existing temples atop pyramids and built new pyramids and temples over the rubble of the old ones. Aztec stonemasons carved elaborate stone facades for their temples and also carved wooden facades that rose above the roofs of these buildings. Aztec ARCHITECTS and the stoneworkers who executed their designs tended to use more detail than the Maya had done. In addition to constructing stone buildings coated with lime, the Aztec sometimes used lime plaster or concrete to attach a decorative veneer of rock to the surface of stone buildings.

Anasazi stoneworkers built with stone throughout the Southwest. In addition to their stonework at Chaco Canyon in what is now New Mexico, most notable are their towers at Hovenweep in what is now Utah, built in about A.D. 1150. These tall structures stand like sentinels at the mouths of canyons. Made from roughly cut stones, the towers are circular, square, and D-shaped. The first European explorers to see them believed them to be castles. Although some archaeologists speculate that these towers may have been used for defense, they are not certain of the purpose for which these structures were intended. The Anasazi also used stone in their buildings in conjunction with ADOBE. Sometimes stone was used as a filler for adobe constructions. In other instances the Anasazi faced adobe buildings with stone.

The Inca, who lived in what is now Peru, and the Quecha, whom the Inca conquered, carried the art of stoneworking to its height in the New World. Because Inca buildings form such

The massive public works built by the Inca required both cooperation and specialization. Architects planned projects that were built by stonemasons. *(After Felipe Guamán Poma de Ayala.* Nueva Coronica y Buen Gobierno)

a similar pattern throughout the empire, archaeologists believe they were built according to plans and were erected by the state. One of these stone buildings, the fortress of Sadahuaman, is so large that is considered one of the largest single structures erected by indigenous people anywhere in the world. Begun in A.D. 1438 the building took 70 years and at least 30,000 workers to complete.

A great deal of planning and skill went into Inca stone constructions. In addition to building models, or maquettes, during the planning process of their construction projects, Inca stonemasons are believed to have used metal wires or tapes to determine the exact dimensions to which the stones needed to be cut. One such tape is in the archaeological museum at Cuzco. Inca stoneworkers fitted stones together precisely, in some instances carving the upper face of stones so that they would fit exactly into the preceding courses. The fit of the stones is so tight that it is impossible to push a knife blade or even a razor blade into the joints between the blocks.

The Inca used several types of masonry. Cyclopean stonework, made up of huge blocks, was used to construct the fortress and many buildings near Cuzco. These blocks weighed as much as 20 tons each. The rustic or "Pirka" type of stonework was made with rough stones. Empty spaces in the joints were filled with small stones and adobe mortar. Sometimes the adobe was mixed with LLAMA or ALPACA wool to strengthen it. Rustic masonry was used for agricultural terraces, storehouses, and homes for common people. Cellular stonework involved cutting medium-sized stones and carving them into polygons that interlocked when they were set into place. The use of cellular stonework made buildings very stable and was the most commonly used style.

The style called the Imperial Incan is the most complex and highly refined. It consists of horizontal rows of rectangular stones with joints so perfectly shaped and polished that there is virtually no space between the stones. When the Inca employed this technique, they did not use mortar except for a thin clay sealant. Some archaeologists believe that the purpose of this clay was to help the builders slide the stones into position. One characteristic of this type of masonry is the trapezoidal niches and doorways of the buildings in which it was used.

Pre-Peruvian builders preferred the hardest igneous or volcanic stones, even though the quarries that produced them might be far away from the building site. Limestone, quartzite, granite, and basalt were their favored building materials. Archaeologists have identified quarries containing stone used by the Inca. They believe that the Inca quarried these stones by chipping holes into the rock, driving wooden wedges into the cracks, and then soaking them with water. When the water froze and the wedges expanded, they caused the rock to crack. Rapid heating and cooling could have been an additional way to force the rocks to crack. Some archaeologists believe that the Inca split chunks of rock from existing fissures in the rock with bronze crowbars. (See also METALLURGY.) A system of chisels and metal wedges may have been used as well. (See also TOOLS.) The Inca discovered these quarrying techniques independently of the Egyptians and Romans.

The stonemasons' tools were made of both rock and metal. When Yale University professor Robert B. Gordon studied a collection of metal objects taken by Hiram Bingham from Machu Picchu, he found 13 instruments made of bronze. After testing and analyzing them, he concluded that twelve of them were chisels used for stonework.

Inca stonemasons are believed to have made finer cuts with SAWS consisting of wires or fine copper or bronze blades. They used these in combination with abrasives and water. Perforations in some of the rocks of Inca structures show that they were augured with some sort of DRILL BIT. Because the Inca had no draft animals, the blocks of stone were hauled from quarries by humans, probably using a complicated system of inclined planes and levels.

Once the stones had been quarried, the builders cut them into shape, dressing them with rock hammers, called *jiwaya* or *jiwayo* in Quecha, the Inca language. These hammers were made in a number of sizes, the heaviest being about 22 pounds.

The masons polished the stones with sandstone or a sand and water mixture. As the stones were set, the masons also used a sliding measuring device and a plumb bob, called a *wipayci,* to make certain they were properly aligned.

Pedro Sancho de la Hoz, one of the first Europeans to see Cuzco, the city where the Inca rulers lived, wrote: "Cuzco, because it is the capital city and the residence of the Inca nobles, is large enough and handsome enough to compare with any Spanish City." He noted the stone-paved and cobblestone streets were at right angles and that the stone lined water troughs running down the middle of them. (See also PLUMBING.)

As was the case with the mounds and other earthworks of the Mississippian Culture in North America, early archaeologists could not believe that Inca stonemasons were capable of doing such precise work. They promoted a mistaken theory that the stone structures had been constructed by an archaic culture that had disappeared long before the Inca. It was easier for them to believe this theory than to consider that American Indians had built the magnificent structures.

Inca stonemasons used a technique called cellular stonework. This involved carving blocks into polygons and setting them so that they interlocked. They cut the stones with such precision that it is impossible to push a razor blade between the blocks today. *(LC-USZ62-97754/Library of Congress)*

## Sources/Further Reading

Coe, Michael D. *America's First Civilization: Discovering the Olmec*. Eau Claire, Wisc.: American Heritage Publishing Co. Inc., 1968.

Josephy, Jr., Alvin M., ed. *America in 1492: The World of the Indian People Before the Arrival of Columbus*. New York: Random House, 1991.

Malpass, Michael A. *Daily Life in the Inca Empire*. Westport, Conn.: Greenwood Press, 1996.

Nobel, David Grant. *Ancient Ruins of the Southwest*. Flagstaff, Ariz.: Northland Publishing, 1991.

Nova Online. *Nova #2404: Secrets of Lost Empires: Inca*. URL: http://www.pbs.org/wgbh/nova/transcripts/2404inca. html. Downloaded on October 3, 1999.

Sabloff, Jeremy A. *The Cities of Ancient Mexico: Reconstructing a Lost World*. New York: Thames and Hudson, Inc., 1989.

Stuart, George E. and Gene S. Stuart. *The Mysterious Maya*. Washington, D.C.: National Geographic Society, 1977.

von Hagen, Victor Wolfgang. *Realm of the Incas*. New York: New American Library, 1957.

**storage, crop**  See CROP STORAGE.

**strawberries  (Rosaceae fragraria)** (precontact) *North American Northeast, Northwest, and Southwest cultures*
Strawberries (*Rosaceae fragraria*) belong to the rose family. The red fruits that these small plants produce are not technically berries but are instead enlarged ends of the plant's stamens. Strawberry fruits, which are sweet-tasting, are also unlike berries in that their seeds are on the outside rather than the inside of the fruits. Although the fruits are covered with an average of 200 seeds, strawberry plants reproduce by sending out runners. The strawberry is indigenous to many parts of the world including the Northeast United States, Chile, northern Europe, and Russia. American Indians who gathered wild strawberries used them primarily as a food source.

Strawberries were an important part of the diet of the Chippewa (Anishinabe) who lived in the upper Midwest and were also used for food by tribes in British Columbia. The Mescalaro Apache, who lived in the Southwest, ate strawberries that had been flavored with aspen sap. North American Indians generally ate strawberries fresh, or they dried and combined them with dried, pounded meat and animal fat to make PEM-MICAN. American Indians of the Northeast mashed strawberries and combined them with water to make a refreshing drink. They also pounded fresh strawberries and mixed them with CORNMEAL to make a type of "strawberry bread." Colonists enjoyed this dessert so much that they began making it, eventually modifying it into the strawberry shortcake that is popular today.

Strawberries formed an excellent part of the American Indian diet because they are high in vitamin C. Eight strawberries contain 140 percent of the daily requirement for that vitamin as established by the U.S. Department of Agriculture. They are also a good source of folic acid, potassium, and fiber. A cup of strawberries contains only about 50 calories.

In 1712 a French sailor took five pine, or sand, strawberry plants growing in what is now Chile to France, where a Parisian botanist crossed them with European berries to produce large fruits. (Because European strawberries were very small and seedy, they did not have a high potential to be grown commercially.) Approximately 100 years later another French botanist crossed strawberry plants native to the Northeast with a variety of wild strawberry indigenous to the Pacific Coast from South America to Alaska. This resulted in the forerunner of modern strawberries. They were reintroduced to the United States from Europe in the mid-1800s. The strawberries that are grown commercially today in every state in the United States and in every Canadian province were developed from crossbreeding North and South American strawberry plants with those native to Europe.

Today, strawberries are one of the most important small fruits grown in North America. According to the U.S. Department of Agriculture, in the United States each person eats an average of 4.85 pounds of strawberries per year. Much of the strawberry consumption is in the form of strawberry shortcake, the modern version of the Northeast American Indians' "strawberry bread."

See also BLUEBERRIES.

## Sources/Further Reading

California Strawberry Council. *Berry Good Facts*. URL: http://www.calstrawberry.com. Downloaded on October 10, 1999.

Moerman, Dan. *Native American Ethnobotany Database: Food, Drugs, Dyes and Fibers of Native North American Peoples*. URL: http://www.umd.umich.edu/cgi-bin/herb. Downloaded on September 4, 1999.

Sokalow, Raymond. *Why We Eat What We Eat: How the Encounter Between the New World and the Old Changed the Way Everyone on the Planet Eats*. New York: Summit Books, 1991.

**stretchers** (precontact) *North American Northeast and California, Mesoamerican, South American Andean cultures*
A stretcher is a device that is used for transporting injured people one at a time. It is composed of two long poles with a long piece of strong fabric stretched between them. This fabric allowed the stretcher to be folded when not in use. North American Northeast and the California tribes used stretchers. The Inca, whose culture arose in about A.D. 1000 in what is now Peru, also used stretchers to transport the wounded or ill. The poles of these stretchers were made of wood, and more than likely the cloth was made of COTTON. The Inca were noted for clothmaking (see also WEAVING TECHNIQUES.) Precontact American Indians invented the stretcher for medical use independently of any other cultures. The Inca also used litters to transport royalty. The Maya, whose culture arose in what is now Mexico in about 1500 B.C., used litters for this purpose as well.

See also MEDICINE.

**Sources/Further Reading**

Baegert, Jakob. "An Account of the Aboriginal Inhabitants of the California Peninsula." Translated by Charles Rau. *Annual Report, Smithsonian Institute, 1863–64*. Washington, D.C.: Government Printing Office, 1864–65.

Benson, Elizabeth P. *The Maya World*. New York: Thomas Y. Crowell Company, 1967.

Time-Life Books. *The Magnificent Maya*. Morristown, N.J.: Silver Burdett Company, 1993.

Vogel, Virgil. *American Indian Medicine*. Norman: University of Oklahoma Press, 1970.

**string games** See CAT'S CRADLE.

**succotash** (precontact) *North American Northeast cultures*
Succotash is a mixture of fresh or dried CORN and BEANS that was prepared by Algonquian-speaking tribes of the North American Northeast. Often they added game meats or fish as well. American Indians boiled soups such as succotash by dropping hot stones into large cooking vessels made of soapstone or wood. The Narragansett, who taught colonists to make the dish, called it *msickquatash*. European immigrants must have liked the culinary creation—they named a Rhode Island town after it, Succotash Point. They modified the soup on occasion by adding turnips, onions, and salt pork. Succotash became famous in literary circles when American author Mark Twain, in *A Tramp Abroad*, mentioned it as one of the foods he missed the most on his travels in Europe.

**Sources/Further Reading**

Plimoth on the Web. Plymouth Succotash: A Forefathers' Day Tradition. URL: http://www.plimoth.org/library/plymsuc.htm. Downloaded on January 31, 2000.

Tannahill, Reay. *Food In History*. New York: Stein and Day, 1973.

Weatherford, Jack. *Indian Givers: How the Indians of the Americas Transformed the World*. New York: Fawcett Columbine, 1988.

**suffrage, universal** See UNITED STATES CONSTITUTION, AMERICAN INDIAN INFLUENCE ON.

**sugar** See MAPLE SYRUP AND SUGAR.

**sunchokes** See JERUSALEM ARTICHOKES.

**sunflowers** (*Helianthus annus*) (ca. 3000 B.C.) *North American cultures*
Sunflowers produce large yellow flowers on stems that grow five to seven feet tall. What appears to be one huge bloom on the top of a sunflower stalk is really made up of up to 2,000 tiny flowers. Each produces a seed encased in a thin shell. Sunflowers are native to North America and were first cultivated by American Indians living in what are now Arizona and New Mexico in about 3000 B.C. Unlike wild sunflowers that have small flowers on the ends of a number of branches and produce relatively few seeds, the sunflower plants that American Indians domesticated had one main stalk topped by a large flower cluster that produced many seeds. They achieved this by a process called SEED SELECTION. Cultivation of domesticated sunflowers spread throughout many parts of North America. By 2000 B.C., American Indians living in the northeastern part of the continent were growing the seeds.

Indigenous people valued sunflowers for their seeds, which were rich in nutrients and energy-producing fats and carbohydrates. Because sunflowers have a short growing season and require relatively little attention, growing them as a food crop was an efficient way to meet dietary needs. One ounce of sunflower seeds contains 160 calories, most of them in the form of unsaturated fats. They are a good source of dietary fiber and are high in vitamin E, folate, and zinc. (See also NUTRITION.)

In the early 20th century Buffalo Bird Woman, a member of the Hidatsa tribe, told anthropologist Gilbert Wilson of the importance of sunflower seeds to her people. The Hidatsa had developed at least four varieties of sunflower plants, according to Buffalo Bird Woman. They planted this crop around fields containing other crops to form a living fence. In the fall Hidatsa women harvested the seeds by cutting the heads from the stalks before the birds ate the seeds. Then they spread them to dry around the smoke hole on the roofs of their EARTH LODGES. Once the seeds were dry, the Hidatsa placed them on a hide spread on the ground and beat them with sticks to remove the hulls. The seeds were then parched in a clay pot that ways placed among the embers of a fire.

One of the ways the Hidatsa used parched sunflower seeds was to pound them with a mortar and pestle then shape them by hand into balls. These balls were carried by hunters as an instant high-energy snack. (See also INSTANT FOODS.) American Indian cooks of many tribes added ground or whole seeds to dishes made with CORN, BEANS, or SQUASH. This was a favorite Hidatsa dish. Sometimes cooks ground sunflower seeds into flour that they mixed with water to form cakes. As many people do today, American Indians cracked the hulls and ate the seeds of sunflowers as a snack.

Oil was removed from sunflower seeds by cracking them, boiling them in hot water, and skimming the oil from the surface. This oil was used primarily as a hairdressing and a skin lotion that protected against the elements and prevented dryness. (See also SUNSCREENS, MEDICINAL.) Indigenous Americans also used various parts of the sunflower plant for medicines (see also PHARMACOLOGY) as well as for DYES. Sometimes the stalks were used as construction materials for building projects.

Spanish explorers returned to Europe with sunflower seeds in 1510. Although Europeans grew the plants, they did so for ornamental purposes rather than for food. In the late 1800s the seeds reached Russia, where people began to grow sunflowers for food and for the oil that could be produced from them. Russian farmers continued the plant breeding work that American Indians had begun and developed more domestic varieties of the plant in about 1860. Sunflowers were reintroduced to North America in the late 1800s. As American people became more conscious of how diet affects health, sunflower production boomed. By 1970 an estimated 5 million acres of U.S. fields had been planted with sunflowers. (See also AGRICULTURE.)

Oil continues to be the main product made from sunflower seeds. It is considered a premium oil because it has a mild taste, a light color, and ability to withstand high cooking temperatures, in addition to being unsaturated and containing no cholesterol. The other primary use for the seeds is as a snack food. Modern nonfood uses that have been found for the sunflower are birdseed and cattle feed. Because sunflower oil has only slightly lower energy content than diesel fuel, some researchers believe that it may someday become a diesel fuel substitute.

## Sources/Further Reading
Meyers, Robert L. and Harry C. Minor. *Sunflower: An American Native.* Department of Agronomy, University of Missouri-Columbia: Agricultural publication G4290, 1993.
National Sunflower Association. *History of the Amazing Sunflower.* URL: http://wwwsunflowerusa.com/publicinfo/history/index.html. Downloaded on March 4, 1999.
Trager, James. *The Food Chronology: The Food Lover's Compendium of Events and Anecdotes from Prehistory to Present.* New York: Henry Holt, 1995.
Weatherford, Jack. *Indian Givers: How the Indians of the Americas Transformed the World.* New York: Fawcett Columbine, 1988.
Wilson, L. Gilbert. *Buffalo Bird Woman's Garden: Agriculture of the Hidatsa Indians.* Reprint. St. Paul: Minnesota Historical Society Press, 1987.

## sunscreens, medicinal (precontact) *North American cultures*

A sunscreen is a lotion, balm, salve, or potion that is applied to exposed skin in order to prevent sunburn. Most American Indian tribes developed sunscreens. What they used for this purpose depended on what was available where they lived. For example, the Zuni, who continue to live in what is now New Mexico, used the western wallflower (*Erysimum capitatum*) as a sunscreen. They ground the wallflower and mixed it with water. They then applied this preparation to the skin to prevent and to treat sunburn. Another botanical treatment that was used by Southwest tribes to treat sunburn was aloe vera, a gel made from a type of AGAVE plant. This is an ingredient in many sunburn and skin lotions sold in pharmacies today.

In other parts of precontact North America, Indians used fats from animals and oil from fish or plants for sunscreens. Northeast tribes used oil that they obtained from SUNFLOWER seeds. American Indians who lived near PETROLEUM deposits in what is now Pennsylvania used that source for a skin protectant. A unique aspect of these sunscreens was that they served dual purposes. In the winter months they were also used to prevent exposed skin from freezing, keep the skin from drying out, and prevent wind burn.

## Sources/Further Reading
Lust, John. *The Herb Book.* New York: Bantam Books, 1974.
Vogel, Virgil. *American Indian Medicine.* Norman: University Oklahoma Press, 1970.
Weiner, Michael A. *Earth Medicine Earth Food: The Classic Guide to the Herbal Remedies and Wild Plants of the North American Indians.* New York: Fawcett Columbine, 1972.

## suppositories (precontact) *North American Northeast cultures*

A suppository is a small plug with medicinal properties. It is used by inserting it into body cavities other than the mouth. Some North American Indian tribes used suppositories made from the dogwood tree (*Cornus paniculata*). They moistened the bark and compressed it into a suppository that they inserted into the anus to treat hemorrhoids. Because the bark of the dogwood tree has astringent properties, this was an appropriate treatment. Suppositories were not the only effective way precontact American Indians treated bleeding hemorrhoids. They also used SYRINGES to inject ASTRINGENTS rectally.

## Source/Further Reading
Vogel, Virgil. *American Indian Medicine.* Norman: University of Oklahoma Press, 1970.
Weiner, Michael. A. *Earth Medicine Earth Food: The Classic Guide to the Herbal Remedies and Wild Plants of the North American Indians.* New York: Fawcett Columbine, 1972.

## surgery (ca. 1000 B.C.) *South American, North American, Mesoamerican cultures*

Surgery is the division of medicine that uses instruments and invasive techniques to treat illness, injury, and deformity. The practice of surgery had a long history in the Americas before the arrival of the Europeans. American Indian surgery was more sophisticated than that performed by the barber-surgeons of Europe at the time of contact. Although the Greeks and Romans had practiced surgery, in medieval times knowledge of their techniques was suppressed. Islamic physicians living in Spain had practiced surgery and one of them, Alvucasis, even wrote a surgical text. However, they were expelled from Spain and their discoveries ignored. By the end of the Middle Ages the most complicated documented operations that European surgeons performed were a limited number of CESAREAN SECTIONS (see also OBSTETRICS) and the removal of diseased breasts. In contrast, indigenous surgeons in South America, Mesoamerica, and North America were executing delicate and complex operations and using ANESTHETICS and ANTIBIOTIC MEDICATIONS—two practices that were not used in Europe at the time. They also practiced ASEPSIS, creating what is known today as a "sterile field" for surgeries.

The Aztec, whose empire was established in what is now Mexico in about A.D. 1100, not only performed cesarean sections but also removed cataracts from the eyes (see also CATARACT REMOVAL) as well as performing PLASTIC SURGERY.

American Indians of South America were practicing brain surgery (see also TREPHINATION), in at least 1000 B.C. (Some archeologists believe the Olmec, whose culture arose in Mesoamerica in about 1700 B.C., were successfully performing surgery long before that date.) Medical anthropologists who have studied human remains estimate that the survival rates for American Indian patients who underwent brain surgery were between 83 and 90 percent. According to anthropologist H. L. Shapiro, in the late 19th century and early 20th century only half of the brain surgery patients that non-Indian doctors operated on survived.

Evidence from POTTERY made by the Moche, a culture that arose in what is now Peru in about 200 B.C., indicated that surgeons were able to successfully amputate limbs and circumcise male infants. The Aztec performed amputations and made prosthetic limbs. North American Indian healers also performed amputations. According to author Jean Wyatt, "An amputation at the joint was performed with a knife of flint. Blood vessels were sealed with heated stones (cautery) to redness, thus arresting hemorrhage." In addition to cauterizing blood vessels, American Indians used herbal HEMOSTATS to stop bleeding. They also understood the value of the TOURNIQUETS and ASTRINGENTS, using them for the same purpose. Throughout the Americas, Indians made SCALPELS from flint, chert, or obsidian, which provided a micro-sharp edge that minimized bleeding from the incisions they made. Some cultures also made metal scalpels. (See also FLINTKNAPPING; METALLURGY.)

Besides performing amputations, American Indian physicians, reduced fractures, breaks, and dislocation of bones, both manually and by surgery. (See also ORTHOPEDIC TECHNIQUES.) They also used THORACENTESIS, carefully puncturing the chest wall to allow fluid build-up to drain. Indian healers used a similar technique, ARTHROCENTESIS, to drain fluid from the knee. They were also able to use a hollow, needlelike implement to puncture the spleen and drain it of excess fluid. They invented these procedures hundreds of years before Western medicine.

North American Indians used sutures made of human hair in order to close incisions and wounds. Healers of the Amazon basin used SURGICAL STAPLES, in the form of leaf-cutter ants, to secure the edges of an incision or wound while it healed. (See also STAPLES, SURGICAL.)

Despite their surgical discoveries and skills, American Indians uniformly fail to receive mention in medical history books. Yet colonists in North America sought out help from American Indian healers. Frontier doctors (often the local undertaker) observed American Indian medical and surgical practices and incorporated some of these techniques into their limited repertoire of treatment options. Spanish conquistadores often preferred to seek treatment from indigenous physicians rather than submit to the knives of their own barber-surgeons. The Spaniards studied the surgical techniques of the Aztec and sent written reports of them back to Europe. The infusion of information about both American Indian surgery and medicine fueled the growing scientific curiosity that marked the Renaissance.

See also ANATOMICAL KNOWLEDGE; COCA; DEBRIDEMENT; DRAINAGE, SURGICAL AND WOUND; EXCISION; HOSPITALS; MEDICAL RESEARCH; MEDICINE; PEYOTE; PHARMACOLOGY.

## Sources/Further Reading

Adams, William R. "Aboriginal American Medicine and Surgery." *Proceedings of the Indian Academy of Science* 61 (1951): 49–53.

Bankes, George. *Peru Before Pizarro.* Oxford, England: Phaidon Press Limited, 1977.

Driver, Harold E. *Indians of North America.* Chicago: University of Chicago Press, 1961.

Fernandez, Omar. "Pre-Columbian Surgery." *Gramna Weekly Review.* URL: http://marauder.millersv.edu/~columbus/data/art/FERNAN01/AR T. Downloaded on December 20, 1999.

Frederiksen, Thomas H. *Aztec Medicine-Aztec of Mexico, History Aztec Student Research Guide c. 1997–99.* URL: http://northcoast/~spdtom/a-med.html.

Hallowell, A. I. "The Bulbed Enema Syringe in North America." *American Anthropologist* 37 (1935): 708–10.

Lowe, Warren. *Indian Giver.* Pencticton, British Columbia: Theytus Books, 1986.

Mason, J. Alden. *The Ancient Civilizations of Peru.* Rev. ed. New York: Penguin Books, 1957.

Ortiz de Montellano, Bernard R. *Aztec Medicine, Health, and Nutrition.* New Brunswick, N.J.: Rutgers University Press, 1990.

Peredo, Miguel Guzman. *Medical Practices in the Ancient Americas.* Mexico City: Ediciones Euroamericanas, 1985.

Rheingold, Howard. *New Medicines from Ancient Bottles: Shaman Pharmaceuticals.* URL: http://www.well.com/user/hla/tomorrow/shaman.html. Downloaded on December 20, 1999.

Sahagun, Fray Bernardino de. *General History of the Things of New Spain.* (Florentine Codex.) Translated by Charles E. Dibble and Arthur J. O. Anderson. Santa Fe: The School of American Research and the University of Utah, Monographs of the School of American Research and the Museum of New Mexico, 1963.

Shapiro, H. L. "Primitive Surgery: The First Instance of Trephining in the Southwest." *Natural History* 27 (1927): 266.

Soustelle, Jacques. *Daily Life of the Aztec on the Eve of the Spanish Conquest.* Stanford, Calif.: Stanford University Press, 1955.

Viola, Herman and Carolyn Margolis. *Seeds of Change: 500 Years Since Columbus.* Washington, D.C.: Smithsonian Institution Press, 1991.

Vogel, Virgil. *American Indian Medicine.* Norman: University of Oklahoma Press, 1970.

von Hagen, Victor W. *Realm of the Inca.* New York: Mentor Books, 1957.

Weatherford, Jack. *Indian Givers: How the Indians of the Americas Transformed the World.* New York, Fawcett Columbine, 1988.

Wyatt, Jean. "The Roots Of North American Medicine." *Indian Life Magazine* 15, no. 3 (1994). URL: http://www.yuwiiusdinvnhii.net/articles/medroots.html

**surgery, plastic**  See PLASTIC SURGERY.


**surgical drainage**  See DRAINAGE, SURGICAL AND WOUND.


**surgical staples**  See STAPLES, SURGICAL.


**suspension bridges**  See BRIDGES.


**sweat lodges**  See STEAM ROOMS.


**sweet potatoes**  (*Ipomoea batatas*)  (ca. 2400 B.C.)
*South American Andean and Tropical Forest, Circum-Caribbean, Mesoamerican cultures*

Sweet potatoes are tropical tuberous plants not found growing wild. A thickening in the plant's roots forms the potato, where nutrients are stored. Sweet potatoes were first cultivated in the Andean regions of South America. Archeologists have found the fossilized remains of sweet potatoes that were dated from 6000 to 8000 B.C., leading them to believe that the plants were probably developed and cultivated even earlier than that. Indigenous farmers of South America developed many varieties. The Inca, who established an empire in the Andean region of what is now Peru in about A.D. 1000, called the sweet potato *batata* in Quecha, their native language. The word became *potato* in English.

Two varieties of sweet potatoes are grown today. One is moist and has reddish orange flesh; the other is drier and has yellow flesh. Although the darker sweet potatoes are often referred to as YAMS in North America, the sweet potato, which belongs to the same botanical family as the morning glory, is not related to the yam, which belongs to the lily family (*Dioscorea*). Neither are sweet potatoes related to regular POTATOES (*Solanum*). They do not have eyes, as regular potatoes do, and they are grown either from seed or cuttings. The wild potato vine that grows in the upper Midwest of the United States is sometimes called wild sweet potato. It produces a large, fleshy root that North American Indians used as a food. Botanists do not classify it as a true sweet potato.

An excellent food source, sweet potatoes produce more pounds of food per acre than any other cultivated plant. Because they contain more sugar and fats than regular potatoes do, they are more nourishing. Sweet potatoes gain their coloring from beta carotine, or vitamin A, a substance considered by modern scientists to fight against cancer. They contain almost as much beta carotine as carrots do. One-half cup of sweet potatoes contains 560 percent of the daily minimum requirement of vitamin A and half of the minimum daily requirement for vitamin C set by the U.S. government. American Indians in Mesoamerica sometimes roasted them with HONEY (see also BEEKEEPING) to produce a similar dish to the candied sweet potatoes eaten today.

By the time Columbus landed in the Caribbean, American Indians there were growing sweet potatoes. Although scholars debate whether he encountered sweet potatoes or MANIOC on his first voyage, they agree that Columbus had seen actual sweet potatoes by the fourth voyage and that he returned to Spain with samples. Spanish explorers throughout South America found American Indians cultivating sweet potatoes. Francisco Pizarro encountered them in Peru, and Vasco Nuñez de Balboa saw them in Central America.

After digging batatas from the ground, indigenous people let them cure for several days and then roasted them, producing a taste that one European said was as if the vegetable had been dipped into a jar of jam. Shortly after conquest, Fernandez de Valdez y Oviedo, a Spaniard who wrote about the indigenous peoples of the Caribbean, compared sweet potatoes to a popular candy of the day, writing that "a batata well cured and well prepared is just like fine marzipan." He returned to Spain with sweet potatoes, as did other European visitors to the New World. From Spain sweet potatoes traveled to Germany, Belgium, and England. Because they did not grow well in Europe's climate, sweet potatoes were a precious commodity and were given as gifts as late as 1577. Although they refused to eat the white potato because they believed it was poisonous, the English immediately considered the sweet potato a delicacy.

One mystery surrounding the sweet potato that continues to perplex botanists and archaeologists to this day is how the plants spread to Polynesia—including Easter Island, Hawaii, and New Zealand, where they are believed to have been cultivated starting in about A.D. 1200, long before Spanish explorers traveled there. Modern explorer Thor Heyerdahl believed that indigenous people living in what is now Peru, who were extensive traders (see also TRADE), traveled to the South Pacific on balsa rafts (see also RAFTS, BALSA), and that they introduced the sweet potato to the South Pacific. To prove that it could be done, in 1947 he constructed a balsa raft called the *Kon-Tiki* and successfully sailed it from the coast of Peru to Raroia atoll in the Tuamotu Archipelago in the South Pacific. Although he demonstrated that it was possible for pre-Inca sailors to sail across the Pacific Ocean, most scholars still do not accept his theories. Instead, many believe that either Polynesians traveled to Peru, where they obtained sweet potatoes, planting them upon return to their islands; or that an unmanned South American trade vessel ship wrecked in Polynesia.

In 1593, facing a food shortage, Chinese explorers found sweet potatoes growing on the island of Luzon. Historians believe these were originally brought there by Spanish galleons that sailed from Central America to Manila. No matter how they got there, Asians adopted sweet potatoes because they yielded three to four times as much food as rice planted on the same amount of land. China is now the world's largest producer of sweet potatoes, which are a popular ingredient in modern Chinese cuisine.

Sweet potatoes are an extremely popular food crop in tropical countries today and are second only to manioc in terms of the amount grown and consumed. Today, sweet potatoes are also a popular food in the American South, where—baked, boiled, candied, and even fried—they have become an important part of southern regional cookery.

See also AGRICULTURE; NUTRITION.

## Sources/Further Reading

Coe, Sophie. *America's First Cuisines.* Austin: University of Texas Press, 1994.

*Archaeological remains of potato and sweet potato in Peru.* URL: http://science. siu.edu/herbarium/ethnobot/archaeo2. htm. Dowloaded on March 29, 1999.

*Morning Glories! Wayne's Word.* URL: http://daphne.palomar. edu/wayne/ww0804.htm#. Dowloaded on May 22, 1999.

Weatherford, Jack. *Indian Givers: How the Indians of the Americas Transformed the World.* New York: Fawcett Columbine, 1988.

**syringes** (precontact) *Mesoamerican, North American cultures*
Syringes are medical instruments used either to inject fluids into the body or remove fluids from it. This device is responsible for saving innumerable lives throughout the world. It keeps many insulin-dependent diabetics alive and functioning and is used to inoculate or immunize people and animals against crippling, potentially fatal diseases. Scotsman Alexander Wood is credited by many medical historians with having invented the syringe in 1853. However, many years before European colonization American Indians used the syringe to inject medicine into wounds and to clean, or irrigate, them. They also used the syringe to clean ears. Virgil Vogel, an expert on American Indian medicine, writes, ". . . South American Indians used a rubber syringe in pre-Columbian times, and Gilmore claims that the animal bladder and bone syringe was in use by Indians of the United States prior to contact with Europeans." Anthropologists credit Mesoamerican cultures with inventing the first rubber-bulbed syringe. (See also LATEX; VULCANIZATION.)

North American Indians used small-animal bladders and thin, hollow bird bones to make bulbed syringes. They sharpened and beveled one end of the bone, shaping it into an object similar to a modern hypodermic needle. They then attached the unsharpened end of the bone to a small-animal bladder, which held the medication for injecting or irrigating wounds. American Indians of Mesoamerica and South America used the bird bone for a needle, but they used a rubber bulb for the medication instead of the animal bladder.

Indigenous healers also used larger syringes for administering ENEMAS, another American Indian invention. Mesoamericans devised the rubber hose that was used for the enema as well as the bulb itself. The Catawba of the North American Southeast developed a unique tubular syringe that worked by telescoping, with one tube fitting inside another, much like today's syringes.

Using the basic technology for producing syringes, the Seneca of the Northeast made a disposable nursing bottle (baby bottle). They used bear intestines that they had washed, dried, and oiled. To this they attached a "nipple" made from a bird's quill by sewing the intestine tightly around it. (Depending on the age of the infant, a different sized quill was used.) Seneca mothers filled these baby bottles with pablum made of pounded nuts and meat that had been mixed with water. Once the bottle was filled, the mother tied the open end. The mother then fed pablum to the infant by placing the quill in his or her mouth and squeezing the intestine. To a certain degree, this nursing bottle resembled the disposable nursing bottles of today.

See also MEDICINE.

## Sources/Further Reading

Hallowell, A. I. "The Bulbed Enema Syringe in North America." *American Anthropologist* 67 (1935): 708–710.

Speck, Frank G. "Catawba Medicine and Curative Practices." *Publications of the Philadelphia Anthropological Society* 1 (1937): 179–98.

Vogel, Virgil. *American Indian Medicine.* Norman: University of Oklahoma Press, 1977.

**syrup** See AGAVE; CORN SYRUP; MAPLE SYRUP AND SUGAR.

## Tabasco sauce, American Indian influence on

(A.D. 1865) *North American Southeast cultures*

Tabasco sauce is a registered trademark for the McIlhenny Company's unique blend of chile, salt, and vinegar that has been fermented in wooden barrels for three years. Although the process for making Tabasco sauce is patented, its name has come into common usage to mistakenly mean any hot pepper sauce sold in a small bottle. American Indians cultivated CHILES, the main ingredient in this sauce for thousands of years before Europeans arrived on the continent. A Choctaw cook directly inspired another brand of hot sauce, Hotter'n Hell, from the North American Southeast.

Although domesticated chiles from the Americas were adopted in many other parts of the world, consumers throughout most of the United States had no use for them. Not until the early 1800s did bottled chile sauces began to appear in New England and the mid-Atlantic. Some were British imports like Lea and Perrins Worcestershire Sauce, which contains some chile. Others were manufactured in this country. None became immediately popular.

Edmund McIlhenny, a Louisiana planter, was given "Tabasco" hot pepper seeds that were named after a river in Mexico by a friend recently returned from the Mexican War (1846–48). He planted them in his wife's garden as a conversation piece. During the Civil War, the McIlhenny family fled to Texas, leaving their plantation and the chile plants behind. On their return in 1865, they found the sugarcane crop and the saltworks on their island plantation destroyed, but volunteer pepper plants were still growing in the garden. McIlhenny subsequently began experimenting with hot pepper sauces. Finding one he liked, in 1868 he bottled a batch of the red-hot brew in 350 used cologne bottles and sold it to wholesalers for a dollar apiece. Believing his sauce should be sprinkled rather than poured on, he topped the bottles with sprinkler caps. Orders for thousands of more bottles soon poured in. By the late

1870s McIlhenny was exporting his sauce to England, and two years later he opened an office there. By 1907 Tabasco sauce was being sold in France, Germany, Italy, Belgium, Ireland, Switzerland, and India.

Hot sauce production saw a boom during the late 1800s, with many manufacturers jumping into the market. One of them was Popie Devillier, another Louisanan, who began marketing the Hotter'n Hell brand. Having run away to the lumber camps at the age of 13, he became a cook, learning the trade from a French cook and a Choctaw Indian. Relying on their influence, he created his slow-cooked hot chile sauce from eight spices.

Although competition had heated up, Tabasco sauce grew in popularity to become a household word. Chile crop failures in Louisiana prompted the McIlhenny company to diversify its chile-growing enterprises. Today, most of the crop is grown at its point of origin by farmers in Honduras, Colombia, and other Central and South American countries and shipped from there to the United States.

### Sources/Further Reading

Bradshaw, Jim. "First Tabasco Peppers Were Brought Here from Mexico." *Lafayette (LA) Daily Advertiser* (November 25, 1997).

DeWitt, Dave and Chuck Evans. *The Hot Sauce Bible*. Freedom, Calif.: The Crossing Press, 1996.

McIlhenny Company webpage. URL: http://www.tabasco.com. Downloaded on September 5, 1999.

**tactics, military** See MILITARY TACTICS.

**talk therapy** See PSYCHOTHERAPY.

**tamales** (precontact) *Mesoamerican, South American Andean cultures*

A tamale consists of CORNMEAL dough that has been wrapped around a filling and steamed. Tamales are a popular part of Mexican and southwestern cuisine. The Maya, whose culture arose in the Yucatán Peninsula of what is now Mexico in about 1500 B.C., were probably the first Mesoamericans to eat them. The Aztec, who established an empire in what is now Mexico in about A.D. 1100, also ate tamales, as did the Inca, who established an empire in what is now Peru in about A.D. 1000.

The Maya made both plain and filled tamales, wrapping them in leaves or cornhusks before steaming them. Some anthropologists believe that for one version of filled tamales, cooks spread the dough on a piece of cloth, covered it with a layer of filling, and rolled it up like a jelly roll. After this was steamed and had set, they sliced it. Maya tamale fillings included meat, fish, ground and toasted SQUASH seeds, greens, black BEANS, and eggs.

Aztec tamales were also made of cornmeal dough that had been stuffed with similar ingredients. Bernardo de Sahagun, a Spanish priest who described the wares sold in the Aztec marketplaces shortly after conquest, reported that they were filled with mushrooms, PRICKLY PEAR *tunas,* rabbit, CHILES, salt, TOMATOES, squash seeds, CORN, turkey eggs, beans, and fish. The Aztec also made fruit tamales and honey tamales (see also BEEKEEPING). Sahagun wrote of rolled tamales, which may have been similar to those made by the Maya. These tamales were steamed in *ollas,* clay cooking pots. (See also POTTERY.)

In addition to using cornmeal to make tamales, the Aztec also used a dough made from ground AMARANTH, a seed crop that they grew extensively. These amaranth tamales were used as offerings to the Aztec gods, including the god of fire Xiuhtecutli. Because the tamales were a part of indigenous religion, the Catholic church banned them, along with amaranth itself, shortly after conquest. Growing, possessing, or consuming amaranth was punishable by death. The Inca, who established an empire in what is now Peru in about A.D. 1000, made tamales from QUINOA, a cultivated seed crop that was an important part of their diet.

See also TORTILLAS; TURKEY BREEDING.

## Sources/Further Reading

Coe, Sophie. *America's First Cuisines.* Austin: University of Texas Press, 1994.

Sahagun, Fray Bernardino de. *General History of the Things of New Spain.* (Florentine Codex.) Translated by Charles E. Dibble and Arthur J. O. Anderson. Santa Fe: The School of American Research and the University of Utah, Monographs of the School of American Research and the Museum of New Mexico, 1963.

Tannahill, Reay. *Food In History.* New York: Stein and Day, 1973.

**tanning, brain (Indian tanning)** (precontact) *North American Northeast, Great Plains, Arctic, and Southeast; Mesoamerican; South American cultures*

Tanning is a method of treating hides in order to turn them into leather. Ancient cultures throughout the world developed several methods of tanning. Tanning methods developed in the Old World relied on the chemical tannin from tree bark or the mineral alum to soften and preserve leather. Although American Indians used tannin, they also developed another method that used the natural oils present in the brains of the deer and elk they hunted to create buckskin leather so soft and supple that it is considered a luxury leather today. This process, a form of oil tanning, was developed throughout the Americas by Paleo-Indians and enabled them to use leather for footgear and tools. Because of its durability and comfort, leather was an ideal material for clothing. The ability of leather to both breathe and insulate made it especially valuable as a material for clothing in cold climates.

Brain tanning produces buckskin through the oxidation of oils, causing the leather to be extremely flexible and water-resistant, more so than that tanned with tannin or alum. Untreated skins break down because they are made of collagen that is attacked by microrganisms. The impregnation and oxidation of oils

After American Indians tanned hides, they smoked the resulting leather so that it would remain soft and pliable after it dried. This photo of an Iroquois man smoking a hide was taken in Grand River, Quebec, in 1914. The American Indian tradition of brain-tanning hides continues today. *(National Archives of Canada/PA-175362/National Museums of Canada Collection)*

protects the skin. Devised by American Indians for producing buckskin thousands of years ago, this technology has remained virtually unchanged to the present time. It was adopted by colonists, many of whom also adopted the Indian style of fringed buckskin clothing (see also FRINGED CLOTHING).

First, American Indians laced the animal skin to a frame in order to stretch it. Then they carefully scraped the hair and flesh from it. Next, they coated the skin with a mixture of pulverized animal brains and water. Once they had wrung the excess brain solution from the skin, they "worked" the hide by pulling and stretching it in order to make it soft. The buckskin at this point was white in color and had the feel of flannel; were it to get wet and then dried, it would become hard again. American Indians found that by allowing smoke to penetrate the fibers of the leather, it would remain soft and pliable after it dried. They made smoke to treat hides by throwing rotten wood onto a fire. The type of wood that they used determined the color of the finished leather.

Inuit tanned their leather with urine, while American Indians who lived in the woodlands of northeastern North America developed a form of vegetable tanning. Typically, they would mix ashes from their campfires with water and then soak raw hides in the solution. This made the bits of flesh and hair easier to remove with a scraper. Next, they "worked" the hide by hand and with sticks and soaked it in a mixture of hemlock and oak bark, both of which are high in tannin. They soaked and worked the skin over a period of three months before it was finally finished.

When the European colonists arrived in North America, brain-tanned garments sewn with sinew were the standard clothing of many American Indians. Not only did the colonists often adopt this style of clothing, they began a lucrative trade in buckskin with Europe, where only the aristocrats had been allowed to wear leather before the importation of buckskin. Royalty had established huge game preserves throughout Europe and forbade hunting by commoners, so tanned hides for clothing were a luxury.

At first buckskin imported from the Americas was used for the clothing of common laborers and tradespeople, who valued it for its durability. By the mid-1700s, however, American buckskin had become the style of choice for Europe's wealthy citizens. Buckskin breeches, as well as hunting and riding gear, were made from Indian tanned leather. Between 1755 and 1773, over 2 1/2 million pounds of buckskin made by the Creek and Cherokee were shipped to England from Savannah, Georgia, just one colonial port. The first European TROUSERS, an adaptation of an American Indian style, were made of buckskin.

**Sources/Further Reading**

Daumas, Maurice, ed. *A History of Technology and Invention, Progress Through the Ages.* New York: Crown Publishers, 1969.

*History of Brain Tan: Colonial America and Renaissance Europe.* URL: http://braintan.com/articles/history/history2.html. Downloaded on January 31, 2000.

Koch, Ronald P. *Dress Clothing of the Plains Indians.* Norman: University of Oklahoma Press, 1977.

Leather Thru the Ages. URL: http://leathertown.com/Ages.htm. Downloaded on September 8, 1999.

McPherson, John. *Brain Tan Buckskin.* Randolph, Kan.: Prairie Wolf, 1986.

Paterek, Josephine. *Encyclopedia of American Indian Costume.* Denver: Colo.: ABC Clio, Inc., 1994.

**tapioca** See MANIOC.

**tarpaulins** (ca. 1700 B.C.–400 B.C.) *North American Northwest Coast, Mesoamerican cultures*

Tarpaulins are waterproof fabrics, generally made of flax, COTTON, or hemp, that are used for sails and tents and as coverings. The Olmec, whose culture arose in about 1700 B.C. in the Yucatán Peninsula of what is now Mexico, were the first to develop material water-proofed with rubber (see also LATEX). Culture groups that followed the Olmec, including the Maya (whose culture arose in what is now Mexico in about 1500 B.C.), also used these rubberizing techniques. The tribes of North America used ASPHALT for their waterproof tarpaulins.

The Olmec invented VULCANIZATION and produced many types of rubber products in addition to tarpaulins. AGAVE and cotton were used to make the cloth that was coated with rubber to make the tarpaulins. The Maya also learned to use latex to make other rubber and waterproof materials. In her book *The Maya World,* Elizabeth P. Benson writes that rubber trees ". . . provided the Maya with rubber for their balls, rain-proofing for capes, and material to be traded with the non-rubber-producing Highlands."

North American Indian tribes that had access to PETROLEUM and asphalt traded these items extensively. (See also TRADE.) Petroleum was used to coat many items to make them waterproof. The Chumash, a California tribe, made their tarpaulins out of plant fiber cloth and coated them with asphalt. They used these to cover themselves and their dwellings in rainstorms.

**Sources/Further Reading**

Benson, Elizabeth P. *The Maya World.* New York: Thomas Y. Crowell Company, 1967.

Coe, Michael D. *Mexico from the Olmecs to the Aztecs.* London: Thames and Hudson, 1994.

Shupp, Mike. *Gabrielino Material Culture.* URL: http://www.csun.edu/~ms44278/gab.htm. Downloaded on January 6, 1999.

Stuart, George E. "New Light On The Olmec." *National Geographic* 184, no. 5 (November 1993): 88–114.

**tartar removal** (precontact) *Mesoamerican cultures*

Tartar is a hard, yellowish deposit on the teeth composed of food particles and secretions that are deposited salts such as calcium carbonate. The Aztec of Mesoamerica, who established their empire in about A.D. 1100, were removing tartar from teeth in pre-Columbian times. Hundreds of years ago ancient Aztec dentists (see also DENTISTRY) removed tartar from their clients' teeth with metal instruments. In his book *Aztec Medicine, Health, and Nutrition,* Bernard Ortiz de Montellano states, "Teeth were to be polished with charcoal (a good abrasive) and salt; occasionally tartar was removed by scraping with metal tools followed by further polishing." This dental practice, although common in modern times, was not generally practiced in Europe at the time of conquest. European dentistry consisted mainly of extracting teeth.

See also DENTIFRICES, CHEWABLE; TOOTHPASTE.

## Sources/Further Reading

Driver, Harold E. *Indians of North America.* Chicago: University of Chicago Press, 1969.

Ortiz de Montellano, Bernard. *Aztec Medicine, Health, and Nutrition.* New Brunswick, N.J.: Rutgers University Press, 1990.

Vogel, Virgil. *American Indian Medicine.* Norman: University of Oklahoma Press, 1977.

**tax systems (*mit'a*)** (ca. B.C. 2000) *South American Andean, Mesoamerican cultures*

Taxes are fees or duties that are levied on people in order to support the government under which they live. Rulers have exacted taxes in the form of tribute in many parts of the world, including the Americas. In some instances American Indian taxation took a slightly different form from that practiced in other parts of the world. In general, North American Indians made voluntary contributions to the well-being of the community. Compulsory taxation developed in South America and in Mesoamerica, along with bureaucracies to administer these systems.

The oldest tax system developed in the Americas began in about 2000 B.C. in the Andean Mountains of South America. This first form of taxation, referred to as the *corvee* labor system, required people to perform work as a form of tribute. For example, the pre-Peruvian people were required to help build PYRAMIDS. The workers were divided into many different teams for the project. Those who made ADOBE bricks signed them; more than 100 different signatures or symbols have been found on adobe blocks. The *corvee* labor system was the precursor for the *mit'a* tax system that the Inca developed many years later. The Inca established an empire in what is now Peru in about A.D. 1000.

The *mit'a* system required common people to perform government service. It was their labor that enabled the Inca to expand what started as a small Andean state to a vast empire that stretched the length of western South America. This form of taxation enabled the Inca to construct huge stone structures and an enormous road system within about 200 years from the time they began this expansion. The people who lived near suspension bridges paid their taxes by building and repairing the bridges. People who lived near the vast and long Inca ROAD SYSTEM paid their tax by maintaining a section of the road.

Certain people were responsible for building way stations along the road system. Others were responsible for keeping the way stations stocked with food, supplies, and water.

In addition to allowing the creation of an extensive structure of public works, the Inca's tax system also provided for a social welfare system. (See also DISABILITY RIGHTS.) No one, even those who could not work, was allowed to go hungry. When the required work was difficult, those who performed it were protected by LABOR LAWS, as was the case with miners.

Precontact Mesoamerican cultures also had tax systems that required both work and tribute. The Maya whose culture arose in what is now Mexico in about 1500 B.C., began imposing formal tributes in about A.D. 250. City governments run by aristocratic families exacted tributes in the form of work to build religious and government buildings. In the Aztec Empire, which was established in what is now Mexico in about A.D. 1100, tribute became even more important and organized. This tribute came from individuals, but it was also exacted on TRADE, manufacturing, and AGRICULTURE.

Services that people might be required to perform under the *mit'a* system included farming, RUNNING, METALLURGY, mining, civil engineering, sanitation work, PUBLIC HEALTH, hydraulic engineering (see also IRRIGATION; PLUMBING), collecting firewood, hide TANNING, jewelry making, FEATHER-WORKING, animal herding, armor making, sewing and tailoring, weaving, charcoal making, farming, and acting as servants for the aristocracy.

Some of the common tributes required under this system included all forms of gold (see also METALS, PRECIOUS), feathers, uniforms, SANDALS, COTTON mantles, tree gums (resins), jade, silver, food, CACAO beans, weapons, flint, copper, honey (see also BEEKEEPING), spices, and jewelry.

Archaeologists believe that a similar tax system existed in North America among the mound-building culture that developed in what is now Alabama. These people built the site that is now called Moundville between A.D. 1200 and 1400. The Mound Builders, who developed the system independently of those in South America and Mesoamerica, made the paying of taxes voluntary.

The Spaniards were impressed by the efficiency of these bureaucracies and the humane way that individuals were treated. Jose de Acosta, a Jesuit priest who lived in Peru for 14 years starting in 1572, wrote in *Historia natural y moral de la Indias,* "Surely the Greeks and the Romans, if they had known the Republics of the Mexicans and the Incas, would have greatly esteemed their laws and governments." He also said that the more "profound and diligent" among the Europeans who have lived in this country have now come to "marvel at the order and reason that existed among [the native peoples]."

## Sources/Further Reading

Bankes, George. *Peru Before Pizarro.* Oxford, England: Phaidon Press Limited, 1977.

Fagan, Brian M. *Kingdoms of Gold, Kingdoms of Jade: The Americas Before Columbus.* London: Thames and Hudson Ltd., 1991.

Fiedel, Stuart J. *Prehistory of the Americas.* New York: Cambridge University, 1987.

Sharer, R. J. *The Ancient Maya.* Stanford, Calif.: Stanford University Press, 1994.

von Hagen, Victor W. *Realm of the Inca.* New York: New American Library, New York, 1957.

———. *The Royal Road of the Inca.* London: Gordon Cremonesi Ltd., 1976.

**teas, herbal**    See PHARMACOLOGY.

**terraced farming**    See FARMING, TERRACED.

**textiles**    See WEAVING TECHNIQUES.

**Thanksgiving**  (A.D. 1621)  *North American Northeast cultures*

Thanksgiving is a holiday celebrated in the United States on the fourth Thursday in November and in Canada on the second Monday in October. In the United States this holiday commemorates a feast celebrated by the Pilgrims at Plymouth Colony in October 1621. Members of the Algonquian Wampanoag band in what is now Massachusetts were an instrumental part of this feast; without them there would have been no dinner. However, the Plymouth Colony thanksgiving was not the first one on the North American continent. In 1610 Jamestown Colony settlers in Virginia held a service of thanks after an English ship arrived with food and supplies after a winter during which they had nearly starved. In 1619 the Berkeley Hundred, another group of Virginia colonists, fasted and prayed on the anniversary of their landing in what became Virginia.

The Wampanoag had set aside a time for giving thanks long before Europeans set foot on the continent. They traditionally had six thanksgiving festivals during the year, including the Maple Dance, the Planting Feast, the Strawberry Festival, the Green Corn Celebration, a harvest festival, and a mid-winter ceremony. They called the time to give thanks for the first harvest the Green Corn Celebration or ceremony. The Massachusetts gathering in 1621, however, is the one credited for inspiring the holiday that U.S. citizens now celebrate each year.

Unable to practice their religious beliefs in England, the Pilgrims had sailed to America to establish a new "kingdom of God" in 1620. Although they believed it to be their God-given destiny to live on the land inhabited by the Indians, during the first winter nearly half of them died from disease or starvation. Lost and hungry in August 1620, the colonists raided not only Indian storehouses but also graves in search of corn. Then American Indian farming advice brought the Pilgrims from the brink of starvation. Squanto, the only surviving member of the Patuxet band, who had learned to speak English when he was captured and sold into slavery, met the Pilgrims in the spring of 1621. According to historians at Plimoth Colony, he taught the Puritans to plant corn in mounds and to fertilize it with herring or shad. Other historians say he also provided the Pilgrims with deer meat and taught them which plants to use for medicinal purposes.

Following Squanto's agricultural instructions, the colonists planted 20 acres of corn and six acres of barley and peas, which they had brought with them. The barley crop, which was intended for beer making, turned out "indifferent good," and the peas were poor, but the Indian corn flourished. That fall, after hunting ducks, geese, and turkeys, the Pilgrims harvested their crops. Governor William Bradford invited Chief Massasoit, the leader of the Wampanoag band, and his people to a three-day feast to celebrate the harvest. Captain Miles Standish encouraged the feast, hoping to negotiate a treaty and cement friendly relations. Just in case the Wampanoag might have other ideas, part of the program included rifle demonstrations by the colonists. It was not intended to be an annual event. It was more public relations than actual thanksgiving, since according to Puritan doctrine, days that had been set aside for giving thanks were to be spent praying and fasting, not eating.

Chief Massasoit and the 90 men who came with him brought five deer. Approximately 50 Pilgrims attended. In addition to roasted venison, wild turkey and CORN was served, and no doubt beer as well, since that was the Pilgrims' standard drink. It is possible that SQUASH and some type of PUMPKIN pudding were also on the menu, but there is no proof of this.

According to Plimoth Plantation Foodways manager Kathleen Curtin, fruits available at the time would have been raspberries, STRAWBERRIES, GRAPES, plums, cherries, BLUEBERRIES, and gooseberries, all of which would have needed to have been dried. CRANBERRIES were indigenous to the Northeast but were not on the menu. Fish, eel, clams, lobsters, mussels, honey, MAPLE SYRUP, BEANS, and nuts would have also been available and might have been served.

The feast was not repeated the next year or in the years that followed. By 1675 the Puritans and the Wampanoag, led by Chief Massasoit's son Metacom, whom the Pilgrims called King Philip, were at war over land and conflicting values. The Puritans won the war, killing Metacom in 1676, tracking down members of the Wampanoag and other Algonquian bands, and selling those who did not escape to Canada into slavery in the Mediterranean and the West Indies.

Thanksgiving was revived in 1789, when President George Washington proclaimed November 26 to be a national day of thanksgiving. Not until 1863, however, did President Abraham Lincoln set aside the last Thursday in November as an annual celebration.

See also AGRICULTURE; BLACK WALNUTS; CLAMBAKES; HICKORY; TURKEY BREEDING.

**Sources/Further Reading**

Bradford, William. *Bradford's History of Plimoth Plantation.* Boston: Wright & Potter Printing Company, 1898.

Heath, Dwight, ed. *A Journal of the Pilgrims at Plymouth (Mourt's Relation: A Relation or Journal of the English Plantation Settled at Plymouth in New England by Certain English Adventurers Both Merchants and Others.)* New York: Corinth Books, 1963.

Plimoth-on-Web (Plimoth Plantation's Web Site). URL: http://www.plimoth.org. Downloaded on March 8, 1999.

Waldman, Carl. *Atlas of the North American Indian.* Rev. ed. New York: Facts On File, 2000.

## therapeutic touch (massage) (ca. A.D. 1000) *North American, South American, Mesoamerican cultures*

Therapeutic touch is a form of massage that is used for health rather than mere relaxation. This type of treatment was used both as a preventative measure to maintain health and as an adjunct to medical treatment. It began with alternative health practitioners in the 1960s, but it is becoming more widely accepted today. The practice of healing massage goes back hundreds of years in the precontact Americas. Both the Inca, who established an empire in what is now Peru in about A.D. 1000, and the Aztec, who established an empire in what is now Mexico in about A.D. 1100, used the practice.

The Inca used therapeutic touch to treat rheumatism and lumbago and employed it before they prescribed any invasive procedure (see also SURGERY) or medication (see also PHARMACOLOGY). They developed a special tool to enhance the massage. It resembled a small baseball bat but was about 10 inches long. They used this with a kneading or a rolling action for both superficial and deep massage, depending on the part of the body that they were treating. The Inca also developed special balms and oils for massages. The most common ingredients they used were BLUE-GREEN ALGAE and American valerian, which has antiseptic and ASTRINGENT properties.

The Aztec used therapeutic touch/massage in conjunction with the steam bath. (See also STEAM ROOMS.) Fray Bernardino de Sahagun, who described Aztec life shortly after the arrival of Hernán Cortés, wrote of Aztec physicians treating a patient that ". . . they manipulate him, they massage him." Aztec mothers were taken into the steam bath for a massage immediately after giving birth. (See also OBSTETRICS.)

Therapeutic massage is believed to have been a universal treatment among Indians of precontact North America. The Maricopa and Akimel O'odham (Pima), who lived in what is now Arizona, used it extensively for alleviating localized pain. Cherokee healers of the Southeast warmed their hands over hot coals before massaging their patients. They used massage to treat sprains, localized pain, and menstrual cramps. The Pawnee of the Great Plains crushed the black rattle pod plant and mixed it with buffalo fat to produce a balm that they rubbed into the painful area.

Another form of massage that American Indians invented is a widely accepted medical practice today. This is the Crede method of manipulation, a postpartum massage of the abdomen that helps women who have given birth to expel the placenta. It also serves to aid the uterus to begin to contract.

See also MEDICINE.

### Sources/Further Reading

Bottcher, Helmuth. *Wonder Drugs: A History of Antibiotics.* Philadelphia: J. B. Lippincott Co., 1964.

Lust, John. *The Herb Book.* New York: Bantam Books, 1974.

Ortiz de Montellano, Bernard R. *Aztec Medicine, Health, and Nutrition.* New Brunswick, N.J.: Rutgers University Press, 1990.

Sahagun, Fray Bernardino de. *General History of the Things of New Spain.* (Florentine Codex.) Translated by Charles E. Dibble and Arthur J. O. Anderson. Santa Fe: The School of American Research and the University of Utah, Monographs of the School of American Research and the Museum of New Mexico, 1963.

Vogel, Virgil. *American Indian Medicine.* Norman: University of Oklahoma Press, 1970.

Weiner, Michael A. *Earth Medicine, Earth Food: Plant Remedies, Drugs, and Natural Foods of the North American Indians.* New York: Fawcett Columbine, 1990.

## thoracentesis (precontact) *North America Northeast cultures*

Thoracentesis is a surgical procedure that involves puncturing the chest in order to allow accumulated fluid to drain. It is used to treat empyema, an infection of the pleural cavity (the area between the lungs and tissue that surrounds them.) The *pneumococcus* bacteria causes the condition that can cause up to a pint of pus to accumulate in the pleural cavity. This extra fluid causes fatigue, chest pain, dry cough, excessive sweating, weight loss, and fever. American Indians of the Great Lakes area successfully treated empyema with thoracentesis before the arrival of Europeans. These included the Sac and Fox (Mesquaki) tribe located in what is now Illinois. Sac and Fox healers punctured the pleural cavity, taking care not to puncture the lungs. This allowed the fluid to drain from the cavity and is the same technique used by modern physicians to treat empyema today. Virgil Vogel, an expert on American Indian medicine, writes: "Even as compared with their contemporary whites, they were not to be scorned. Their treatment of wounds, fractures and empyema was equal to or better than that of the white physicians of the 18th century."

See also MEDICINE; SURGERY.

### Sources/Further Reading

Stone, Eric. *Medicine Among the American Indians.* Reprint. New York: Hafner Publishing Company, 1962. (Originally published in 1932.)

Vogel, Virgil. *American Indian Medicine.* Norman: University of Oklahoma Press, 1977.

**tie-dyeing** (ikat) (ca. 900 B.C. to 200 B.C.) *South American Andean, Mesoamerican cultures*

Tie-dyeing is the process of tying off fabric or hanks of yarn before dipping them into a vat of DYE. Moche weavers dyed yarns before they were woven in order to produce complex designs in the finished textiles, in addition to tie-dyeing entire pieces of fabric. The Moche culture flourished in what is now Peru between 200 B.C. and A.D. 600.

The process of dyeing the finished fabric produced simple designs and is believed to have been developed earlier than yarn dyeing. Usually it was done with loosely woven, lightweight cloth. The most common method that dyers used was to gather small puckers in the fabric with a needle and thread, forming circle or square patterns. Sometimes Moche weavers used this dyeing technique in combination with another technique called patchwork weaving. (See also WEAVING TECHNIQUES.) In patchwork weaving the weavers removed some threads in specific areas of the fabric. They then stabilized the piece by inserting another thread or threads around the design.

When yarn, rather than finished fabric, is resist-dyed, the process is called ikat. When the hanks have been tied tightly and dipped into dye, the tied portions resist the dye. Once the yarn is dry, weavers make it into cloth. If they have carefully measured and counted the yarn before tying it, patterns appear in the finished work. Weavers dyed only the warp threads in fabric that was patterned using the ikat method. If the weaver made a miscalculation he or she sometimes used a bit of dye on a brush to touch up the design.

Today ikat continues to be used by weavers in the Andean region of Peru. Weavers in Chile and Guatemala also use this technique. Guatemalan weavers call the cloth they produce using this technique *jaspeado*. They use ikat primarily on cotton yarns that are colored with brilliant dyes. Guatemalan weavers tend to produce ikat patterns that are unique to their particular village. Shawls and other garments that they have made in this manner have become a popular fashion item in the United States.

### Sources/Further Reading

Harris, Jennifer. *Textiles: 5,000 Years.* New York: Harry Abrams, 1993.

Mason, J. Alden. *The Ancient Civilizations of Peru.* New York: Penguin Books, 1982.

Osborne, Lilly de Jongh. *Indian Crafts of Guatemala and El Salvador.* Norman: University of Oklahoma Press, 1975.

**tipis (teepees)** (precontact) *North American Great Plains cultures*

Tipis are dwellings that consist of a hide or canvas covering lashed to a conical frame of poles. *Tipi* is the Dakota, Lakota, Nakota word for "home" and has a broader meaning for these Indians than the structure it is used to identify in the English language today. Many scholars believe the cone-shaped tipi of the plains evolved from Subarctic tents that existed at least 5,000 years ago and shorter conical tents made by Woodland Indians. Most of the tribes that use tipis are known to have migrated from the Eastern Woodlands to the plains and prairie in historic times. The original plains tipi coverings were made from BISON hide.

Several distinguishing features differentiate a simple conical structure from a tipi. The floor plan of a true tipi as developed by the Indians of the northern plains is not circular but oval in shape. The structure is tilted, with the rear side steeper than the front, where the door is located, rather than being symmetrical as a cone would be. Different tribes developed various styles of tipis, depending on the arrangement of the poles. Tribes that use three poles for foundation poles, the poles on which the others are laid, include the Dakota, Lakota, Nakota, Cheyenne, Arapaho, Assiniboine, Kiowa, Atsina (Gros Ventre), Plains Cree, Mandan, Arikira, Pawnee, and Omaha. The Crow use a four-pole foundation arrangement, laying in more poles to complete the frame. Evidence from tipi rings (stones placed on the hide to anchor it on the ground) indicate that originally tipis were quite small, compared to the ones that are made and sold today.

Tipis were very energy-efficient and comfortable places to live. Since a tipi could be erected or taken down in a matter of hours, it was an extremely portable dwelling. With no flat sides, tipis were aerodynamic, allowing strong prairie winds to pass around them without being blown down. In wintertime a fire kept the dwelling warm. The smoke hole served as a ventilating system and could be opened and closed by adjusting poles that were tied to flaps, pulling air from the door and beneath the tipi cover to the outside while keeping out the elements. When the weather became bitter, snow was banked around the tipi. (In post-contact times American Indians tied canvas liners to the poles inside of the tipi to provide more insulation.)

Spanish explorer Francisco Vásquez de Coronado first saw tipis in 1540–42. They were the dwellings of a group of buffalo-hunting American Indians who wintered with the Pueblo people. Coronado wrote that their tents were made of buffalo hides arranged on a frame of poles spread apart at the bottom and tied together at the top. He described the tents as being tall and beautiful.

Don Juan Oñate, another Spanish explorer who traveled from what is now New Mexico to the southwestern plains in 1599, also encountered tipis. In what is now Texas, he described seeing tents made of tanned hides that were "very bright red and white in color and bell-shaped, with flaps and openings and built skillfully as any house in Italy." According to Oñate, the tipis were spacious but were also very portable. When the Indians had folded them, they could be loaded onto travois (drags that were, at that time, pulled by dogs) to be moved from camp to camp. According to Oñate, the tipis did not weigh over 50 pounds. Although Oñate's description is the first by a European observer that mentions smoke flaps, more than likely they were invented earlier.

Once the horse was introduced (and pulled larger travois), American Indians began making larger tipis, 15 to 20 feet across. After European settlement and actions destroyed the great buffalo herds that once roamed the North American continent, American Indians began using canvas

Tipis, the dwellings of North American Plains Indians, could be erected and dismantled within hours, so that entire villages could readily be moved. Plains Indians used hides to cover the frame of poles before contact, substituting canvas after non-Indian hunters made the buffalo nearly extinct. *(LC-USZ62-55635/Library of Congress)*

tipi covers. Because canvas is not as heavy as hide, they were able to make tipis that were 20 to 30 feet in diameter. At first the U.S. government issued this canvas, but it later stopped the practice in order to convince Indians to stay in houses on the reservations.

Non-Indians recognized the utility of the tipi. Kit Carson, who earned a reputation as an Indian fighter, insisted that explorer John Charles Frémont pack a tipi when Carson accompanied him on his first expedition that began in 1841. U.S. Army general H. H. Sibley was so impressed with the practicality of the tipi design that he incorporated it into his design for the Sibley Army tent, which was used by soldiers during the Indian Wars in the mid-1800s. Today tipis are gaining popularity throughout the world.

See also CARPENTRY TECHNIQUES; EARTH LODGES; IGLOOS.

## Sources/Further Reading
Driver, Harold E. *Indians of North America*. Chicago: University of Chicago Press, 1969.
Hassrick, Royal B. *The Sioux*. Norman: University of Oklahoma Press, 1964.
Nabokov, Peter and Robert Easton. *Native American Architecture*. New York: Oxford University Press, 1989.
Vestal, Stanley. "The History of the Tipi." In *The Indian Tipi: Its History, Construction and Use, Second Edition* by Reginald and Gladys Laubin. Norman: University of Oklahoma Press, 1977.

**tobacco (*Nicotana*)** (ca. 6000 B.C.) *Mesoamerican; North American Northeast, Southeast, and Southwest; Circum-Caribbean; South American Andean cultures*
*Tobacco* is the name given to the plants of several varieties of the species *Nicotana* and to dried leaves from these plants. The leaves are smoked, either as CIGARETTES or CIGARS or in PIPES. Powdered tobacco called SNUFF is inhaled. Tobacco belongs to the same botanical family (Solanacea) as nightshade, POTATOES, and TOMATOES. According to ethnobotanists, the two most prevalent types of tobacco (*Nicotana tabacum* and *N. rustica*) were growing in the Americas in as early as 6,000 B.C. American Indians are believed to have been cultivating tobacco by about A.D. 1. Although they used it in some social settings, indigenous peoples used tobacco primarily in ceremonies and

for medicinal purposes such as ENEMAS and wound dressings. Some American Indians also chewed it as a toothache remedy. By the time of European contact, American Indians were growing tobacco from Montreal and New England to the Amazon rain forest and the Andean regions of what is now Peru.

Methods of smoking tobacco varied from region to region. North American Indians chopped the tobacco finely and put it in bowls, drawing the smoke through a tube; thus, they were pipe smokers. The Maya, whose culture began to flourish in the Yucatán Peninsula of what is now Mexico in about 1500 B.C., and the Arawak (Taino), inhabitants of the Caribbean, rolled tobacco in tobacco leaves to form cigars. The Aztec, who established an empire in what is now Mexico in about A.D. 1100, filled reeds with tobacco, creating an ancient version of what is now termed a cigarette.

On October 15, 1492, the Arawak offered Christopher Columbus dried tobacco leaves, three days after he landed in Hispaniola. Etymologists believe the word *tobacco* comes from the Arawak word for the pipe or tube in which the tobacco was smoked. Because of the ceremonial way the Indians presented the gift of tobacco to him, Columbus speculated that the leaves were something of great value. Only when some of his crew went ashore on the island that is now called Cuba did they learn the purpose of the leaves. They reported to their captain that the Native people "drank smoke." The crew quickly took up smoking, but their captain did not.

Columbus and the explorers who followed him brought tobacco leaves and seeds back to Europe, where the plants were initially grown to be used as medicine, the same purpose for which the American Indians had grown them. In 1531 Europeans began to cultivate the crop on the island of Santo Domingo. For several decades the Spanish and Portuguese maintained a near-monopoly on the tobacco obtained from their colonies. In 1606 King Philip III of Spain went so far as to decree a death penalty for anyone caught selling tobacco to foreigners. Even so, tobacco smugglers prevailed, and tobacco use spread slowly to other European countries.

There tobacco remained a curiosity until Englishman Sir Walter Raleigh and French diplomat Jean Nicot began to popularize it in the mid-1500s. Nicot, the ambassador to Portugal, brought the plants to France in 1560 and immodestly gave them a scientific name after himself—nicotine. Raleigh tried to plant tobacco seeds he had obtained in 1578 when he had founded the Roanoke Colony, but the English climate was too cold and damp for them to flourish.

At first Europeans focused on tobacco's medicinal uses. They believed it would cure ailments ranging from bad breath to cancer. By 1571 Nicholas Monardes, a Spanish physician, had listed 36 illnesses the plant was believed to cure. At the same time European physicians were prescribing tobacco to cure worms, lockjaw, and cancer, and recreational use of tobacco was rising.

Europeans who had developed a smoking habit craved American tobacco, and the price the Spanish monopoly charged was too high. The British began a concerted effort to grow tobacco in their North American colonies for the European market. By 1617 the Jamestown Colony had tobacco planted along side the streets and marketplace. After the harvest, they shipped 20,000 pounds of it back to England. The tobacco habit spread so quickly that in the early 1600s Pope Urban VIII threatened to excommunicate people who smoked or took snuff in holy places. Physicians in England complained to King James I that people were using tobacco without a prescription. In 1610 Sir Francis Bacon wrote that smoking was a difficult habit to break. The dangers of casual tobacco use were something many American Indians groups seemed to recognize. For example, the Aikmel O'odham (Pima) and Tohono O'odham (Papago) of the North American desert Southwest grew tobacco, but only old men and old women smoked it because they believed that smoking made young men lethargic, prone to coughing, and unable to stand the cold.

As tobacco use increased in Europe, the crop became more profitable than gold for European traders and colonial farmers. In some colonies tobacco was considered so valuable that it was used as money. On occasion, New England clergymen were paid wages in tobacco. An industry sprang up around tobacco growing and curing, especially in the South. By 1776 the crop was serving as collateral on loans obtained from France to fight the Revolutionary War against Britain. Later, Lewis and Clark carried tobacco to TRADE with the Indians on their voyages up the Missouri River from 1803 to 1806.

In modern times tobacco use has gone beyond what indigenous people who first grew it ever would have imagined. Today, widespread recreational smoking has become one of the leading medical problems throughout the industrialized world. According to the American Cancer Society, 2.1 million people in industrialized countries died as a result of smoking in 1995. A major cause of heart disease, tobacco use is responsible for 30 percent of all cancer deaths.

**Sources/Further Reading**

American Cancer Society. *Cancer Facts and Figures, 1999.* URL: http://www.cancer.org/statistics/cff99/tobacco.html#intro. Downloaded on July 3, 1999.

Borio, Gene. *The History of Tobacco, 1977.* URL: http://www.historian.org/bysubject/tobacco.htm.

CNN. *A Brief History of Tobacco.* URL: http://www.cnn.com/US/9705/tobacco/history/index.html. Downloaded on July 3, 1999.

Hurt, R. Douglas. *American Indian Agriculture: Prehistory to Present.* Lawrence: University Press of Kansas, 1987.

Jeffers, H. Paul and Kevin Gordon. *The Good Cigar.* New York: Lyons and Burford Publishers, 1996.

**toboggans** (precontact) *North American Northeast cultures*
A toboggan is a long, narrow sled without runners. It is made of boards that have been curved upward to form the front of the sled. Toboggans were invented by the Chippewa (Anishinabe), who designed them for travel along footpaths. The word *toboggan* is a French mispronunciation of the Chippewa *nobugidaban,* a combination of two words meaning "flat" and

"drag." Toboggans could be pulled by people or by dogs. (See also DOG BREEDS; DOGSLEDS.) Faster and easier to make than sleds with runners, toboggans could be improvised from materials at hand when necessary.

The Chippewa, who also invented SNOWSHOES, made the sleds from hardwood that they cut during the winter. They heated the wood by boiling it and then bent the front of the sled into its characteristic curve. A piece of rawhide covered the front of the sled. The Chippewa tied loads to the toboggan with rawhide strips that were attached to hand-made cleats along the flat part of the sled. A strap extending from the back of the sled served as a brake. This was held by someone traveling behind, who pulled on it if the toboggan went out of control.

Early French explorers to the upper Midwest adopted the toboggan for hauling loads through deep snow and in places that were difficult for horses to traverse. Later non-Indian settlers in the Midwest also used toboggans for winter travel over areas where horse- or oxen-pulled wagons were impractical. Today, toboggans are used mainly for winter recreation in many parts of the world.

See also SLEDS, CARIOLE; SNOWSHOES.

## Sources/Further Reading

Geise, Paula. *Native American Indian Resources.* URL: http://indy-.fdl.cc.mn.us/~isk/food/maple.html. Downloaded on March 14, 1999.

Weatherford, Jack. *Native Roots: How the Indians Enriched America.* New York: Fawcett Columbine, 1991.

## tomatoes  (*Lycoperiscon esculentum*)

(ca. 900 B.C.–A.D. 700)   *South American Andean; Mesoamerican cultures*

Tomato plants bear succulent, somewhat acidic fruit. The tomato, whose name comes from the Nahuatl (Aztec) word *tomatl,* is native to the coast and highlands of western South America and to Mesoamerica. American Indians cultivated tomatoes in both of these regions as early as A.D. 700. They were an important food source for pre-Peruvian people and for the Maya, whose culture arose in what is now Mexico in about 1500 B.C. The Aztec, who established an empire in what is now Mexico in about A.D. 1100, are reported to have combined tomatoes with CHILES and SQUASH in a dish that resembled modern SALSA. They used thin slices of unripe tomatoes in many dishes that today would be considered CASSEROLES.

In 1527 Spanish conquistadores returned to southern Europe with tomato seeds for plants that produced yellow fruit. By 1554 the first written description of a tomato had been published in Venice. The author, a botanist named Dioscordes, called the fruit a *pomo d'oro,* or golden apple. He advised that it be eaten like eggplant, fried in oil with salt and pepper. This suggestion became the basis for Italian cuisine.

The Spaniards adopted the tomato into their cuisine, using it in gazpacho and stews. By 1698 the first cookbook to include recipes using tomatoes had been published in Naples.

As tomatoes spread throughout Europe, Italians, Spaniards, and French people came to believe that they were an aphrodisiac. Because of this widely accepted notion, the fruit became known as the southern love apple.

Most northern Europeans did not eat tomatoes and, in fact, thought they were poisonous. They called them Moor's apples or stinking golden apples. In a 1666 botanical reference published in Geneva, Dominicus Chabraeus wrote that the tomato was a malignant and poisonous plant. His belief stemmed from the fact that the tomato is a member of the nightshade family. Despite the negative opinion, some northern Europeans grew the plants as exotic ornamentals in their gardens and believed that they might have medicinal purposes. Although Germans were afraid to eat tomatoes, they used them as a poultice to treat such conditions as scabies, St. Anthony's fire, and other fluxes (diarrhea). Some herbalists advised applying tomato juice externally to treat the aches and pains of arthritis. (See also ARTHRITIS TREATMENTS.) The British refused to eat tomatoes until the 1750s, when English botanists officially designated the plant as edible.

Even though early English colonists brought tomato seeds to North America with them, they also feared what would happen if they ate them, so they planted them as ornamental landscape plants. Thomas Jefferson was one of the first non-Indians in the United States to eat tomatoes. He wrote in 1809 that he had planted them, and it is reported that he served them to his visitors. Not until the end of the Civil War did tomatoes become popular in the United States. The first ketchup was made and sold commercially by the F. & J. Heinz company in 1876, and by the 1880s salads containing tomatoes had become popular. Soon commercial breeding efforts began, and today many new varieties exist. Today the United States is the largest tomato producer. Americans eat more than 12 million tons of them each year. Each person in the United States eats an average of 18 pounds of fresh tomatoes and 70 pounds of processed tomatoes annually. Containing only 35 calories, a medium tomato provides 35 percent of the recommended daily allowance (RDA) of vitamin C and 15 percent of the RDA of vitamin A (beta carotine). Tomatoes are also rich in fiber.

## Sources/Further Reading

California Tomato Growers Association. *Tomatoes are Healthy, Versatile and Delicious.* URL: http://www.tomato.org. Downloaded on July 6, 1998.

Flexner, Stuart Berg. *Listening to America.* New York: Simon & Schuster, Inc., 1982.

Sokalow, Raymond. *Why We Eat What We Eat: How the Encounter Between the New World and the Old Changed the Way Everyone on the Planet Eats.* New York: Summit Books, 1991.

Tannahill, Reay. *Food in History.* New York: Stein and Day, 1973.

Trager, James. *The Food Chronology: The Food Lover's Compendium of Events and Anecdotes from Prehistory to Present.* New York: Henry Holt, 1995.

Weatherford, Jack. *Indian Givers: How the Indians of the Americas Transformed the World*. New York: Fawcett Columbine, 1988.

## tonic water, American Indian influence on

(ca. 1850) *South American Tropical Forest cultures*

Tonic water is a soft drink that is a popular mixer for alcoholic beverages. It contains sparkling water, sugar, and QUININE. Because of this last ingredient, tonic water originated as a malaria cure. Made from the bark of the cinchona tree, which is indigenous to the Andes of what is new Peru, quinine had been used as a fever reducer by pre-Peruvian healers. In 1638 a Spanish physician used cinchona bark to successfully treat a countess who had contracted malaria. Before this time no drugs had existed to treat this disease. Soon use of quinine, a native South American botanical medicine, spread throughout the world. Pharmacists added sugar to the preparation to make the bitter medicine more palatable. Although it began as a bonafide tonic, tonic water later became a soft drink, as did many other American Indian remedies.

See also SOFT DRINK INGREDIENTS.

### Sources/Further Reading

Hobhouse, Henry. *Seeds of Change: Five Plants that Transformed Mankind*. New York: Harper & Row, 1986.

Weatherford, Jack. *Indian Givers: How the Indians of the Americas Transformed the World*. New York: Fawcett Columbine, 1988.

## tool kits and boxes (ca. A.D. 1000) *North American Arctic cultures*

Tool kits are collections of TOOLS that are used to accomplish a task requiring more than just the use of hands. People of the Thule culture, who lived in the northern part of what is now Alaska in A.D. 1000, developed specialized tool kits to hold the numerous tools they invented. Some of these tools, such as the bow drill (see also DRILLS, BOW), were actually small machines. In addition to devising collections of tools for working snow (see also IGLOOS), the Thule developed kits for hide-working and for bone- or stoneworking. (See also FLINTKNAPPING.) They invented these kits independently of those invented in other cultures.

Sometimes the tools that formed these kits were contained in lidded BOXES carved from single pieces of wood. Other kits were kept in hide bags made with ivory handles. The tools in the kits included mauls, flint-bladed reamers, awls, whetstones for JADE WORK, twisters, scrapers, flintknappers, snow knives, SHOVELS, and picks.

### Sources/Further Reading

Josephy, Jr., Alvin M., ed. *America in 1492: The World of the Indian People Before the Arrival of Columbus*. New York: Random House, 1991.

Murdoch, John. *Ethnological Results of the Point Barrow Expedition: Annual Report of the U.S. Bureau of Ethnology 1887–1888*. Washington, D.C.: Government Printing Office, 1892.

Oswalt, Wendell. *Eskimos and Explorers*. Novato, Calif.: Chandler & Sharp Publishers, 1979.

## tools (ca. 12,000 B.C.–A.D. 1000) *North American, South American, Circum-Caribbean, Mesoamerican cultures*

Tools are hand-held instruments that are used to perform work. American Indians made a number of tools, which they invented independently of other cultures in the world. The list below includes some of the tools that American Indians developed. It is by no means comprehensive.

### 12,000 B.C.–8000 B.C.

Adzes; atlatls; BOLAS; bone NEEDLES and pins; boomerangs; choppers; engraving tools; flint knives (see also FLINTKNAPPING); manos and metates; micro blades; mortars (log); scrapers; spear points; spokeshaves; WRENCHES.

### 8000 B.C.–7000 B.C.

Awls; barbed projectile points; GOURD dippers; digging sticks; bow drills; hollow bone pipes; microliths (small cutting tools); milling stones; stone mortars; pestles and choppers; twined baskets; TRAPS.

### 6000 B.C.–5000 B.C.

Anvils; bone defleshers and bone fishhooks; bull roarers; drills; flakers; grooved stone axes; hemp cordage; hide thongs; nets; slate knives; stone gouges; hammers; hoes; net sinkers; winged atlatl weights.

### 4000 B.C.–2000 B.C.

Antler harpoon line holders; copper awls; axes, pickaxes; knives; barbed basal notched projectile points; barbed bone projectile points; barbed copper spear heads; bayonet spear heads; bone hairpins, combs, and whistles; bows and arrows; copper barbed harpoon heads; chisels; fishhooks; gouges; daggers; drills; fire-starting kits; fishing lines; fish weirs; grinding stones; HARPOONS with detachable heads; plummets; punches for making holes; slate projectile points; socketed copper axes, gouges, wedges, and spear heads; stone fishing sinkers and sinker hooks; stone tobacco pipes, toggled harpoon heads, tubes.

*Left:* American Indians invented a variety of tools to make their lives easier. Among these were copper fishhooks dating to between 5000 and 4000 B.C. made by Indians of the Great Lakes, who are considered the first metalworkers in the world. *(U.S. Bureau of Ethnography)*

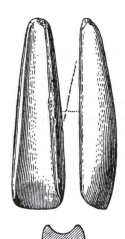

*Left:* Indigenous toolmakers created stone gouges with one face hollowed out in order to provide a curved edge when the tool was held in one hand and struck with a mallet. It was primarily American Indians of the Northeast who used them. *(U.S. Bureau of Ethnography)*

**2000 B.C.–1000 B.C.**

Abrasives, acid, beakers; clay heating balls (see also BRIQUETTES); COLANDERS; metal crowbars; crucible for melting metal (see also METALLURGY); dip nets, duck decoys; fans; FOOT PLOWS; FORCEPS; gold pins, spoons, and tweezers; hematite hammers; jug baskets; ladles; long handled sieves; pitchforks; POTTERY molds; plumb bobs; rakes; rasps; razors; RIVETS; road rollers (see also ROAD SYSTEMS); scalpels; sharktooth SAWS; SHOVELS; SOLAR FIRE STARTERS; spades; tripod containers; wind furnaces.

**1000 B.C.–A.D. 1000**

Bone sled runners; ELECTRICITY; ice creepers (see also CRAMPONS) and picks; ivory carved chains and swivels; ivory snow knives; polished slate knives; SNOW GOGGLES; stone mauls; tubular pipes.

See also BASKETWEAVING TECHNIQUES; BOWS, LAMINATED; DECOYS, DUCK; DRILLS, BOW; PIPES, TOBACCO; TOOL KITS.

**Sources/Further Reading**

Adams, R. E. W., ed. *The Origins of Maya Civilization.* Albuquerque: University of New Mexico Press, 1977.

Bankes, George. *Peru Before Pizarro.* Oxford: Phaidon Press Ltd., 1977.

Benson, Elizabeth P. *The Maya World.* New York: Thomas Y. Crowell Company, 1967.

Coe, Michael D. *America's First Civilization: Discovering the Olmec.* Eau Claire, Wisc.: American Heritage Publishing Co. Inc., 1968.

Daumas, Maurice, ed. *A History of Technology & Invention: Progress through the Ages, Volume I.* New York: Crown Publishers, Inc., 1962.

Deuel, Leo. *Conquistadors without Swords: Archaeologists in the Americas.* New York: St. Martin's Press, 1967.

Driver, Harold E. *Indians of North America.* Chicago: University of Chicago Press, 1961.

Engel, Frederic Andre. *An Ancient World Preserved: Relics and Records of Prehistory in the Andes.* Translated by Rachel Kendall Gordon. New York: Crown Publishers, Inc., 1972.

Fagan, Brian M. *Kingdoms of Gold, Kingdoms of Jade: The Americas before Columbus.* New York: Thames and Hudson Ltd., 1991.

Fehrenbach, T. R. *Fire and Blood: A History of Mexico.* New York: Macmillan Publishing Co., Inc., 1973.

Fiedel, Stuart J. *Prehistory of the Americas.* Cambridge, England: Cambridge University Press, 1987.

Gorenstein, Shirley. *Not Forever on Earth: Prehistory of Mexico.* New York: Charles Scribner's Sons, 1975.

Hazen-Hammond, Susan. *Timelines of Native American History.* New York: The Berkely Publishing Group, 1997.

Milanich, Jerald T. *Florida's Indians from Ancient Times to the Present: 12000 Years of Florida's Indian Heritage.* Gainesville: University Press of Florida, Florida's, 1998.

Morris, Craig and Adriana von Hagen. *The Inka Empire and Its Andean Origins.* New York: Abbeville Press Publishers, 1993.

Pringle, Heather. *In Search of Ancient North America: An Archaeological Journey to Forgotten Cultures.* New York: John Wiley & Sons, Inc., 1996.

Sharer, Robert J. *Daily Life in Maya Civilization.* Westport, Conn.: Greenwood Press, 1996.

Soustelle, Jacques. *Daily Life of the Aztecs on the Eve of the Spanish Conquest.* Translated by Patrick O'Brian. Stanford, Calif.: Stanford University Press, 1955.

Turolla, Pino. *Beyond The Andes: My Search for the Origins of Pre-Inca Civilization.* New York: Harper and Row Publishers, 1970.

von Hagen, Victor W. *Realm of the Incas.* New York: The New American Library, 1957.

———. *The Royal Road of the Inca.* London: Gordon Cremonesi, Ltd., London, 1976.

Weatherford, Jack. *Indian Givers: How the Indians of the Americas Transformed the World.* New York: Fawcett Columbine, 1988.

**toothache medications** See DENTISTRY.

**toothbrushes** (ca. A.D. 1100) *South American Andean, Mesoamerican cultures*

A toothbrush is a device used for cleaning the teeth. The Inca, who established an empire in what is now Peru in about A.D. 1000, and the Aztec, who established an empire in what is now Mexico in about A.D. 1100, used toothbrushes. The Inca made their toothbrushes out of the Molli tree (*Schinus molle*). The Aztec used a twig from the plant they called *tlatlauhcapatli* in Nahuatl, their language. This plant had ASTRINGENT properties so that it not only cleaned the teeth but also tightened the gums and freshened the breath. Aztec dentists (see also DENTISTRY) advised their patients to rinse their mouths with saltwater, which they also prescribed for sore throats. When tartar built up on the teeth despite good oral hygiene that included brushing, Aztec dentists removed it by scraping the teeth with a metal tool. (See also TARTAR REMOVAL.) Afterward, the dentist polished the patient's teeth.

See also CHEWABLE DENTIFRICES; HYGIENE, PERSONAL; MOUTHWASH; TOOTHPASTES AND POWDERS.

**Sources/Further Reading**

Fastlicht, Samuel. *Tooth Mutilations and Dentistry in Pre-Columbian Mexico.* Mexico City: Quintessence Books, 1971.

Ortiz de Montellano, Bernard R. *Aztec Medicine, Health, and Nutrition.* New Brunswick, N.J.: Rutgers University Press, 1990.

Peredo, Miguel Guzman. *Medical Practices in Ancient America.* Mexico City: Ediciones Euroamericanas, 1985.

Vogel, Virgil. *American Indian Medicine.* Norman: University of Oklahoma Press, 1970.

## toothpastes and powders (precontact)

*Mesoamerican, South American, North American cultures*

Toothpastes and powders are substances that are used for cleaning the teeth. They can be applied with a cloth, the fingers, or a TOOTHBRUSH. The Aztec, who established an empire in what is now Mexico in about A.D. 1100, were very health-conscious and placed emphasis on oral hygiene. One substance that the Aztec used to clean their teeth was a mixture of charcoal and salt, both mild abrasives that worked effectively to clean the teeth. The Aztec used a toothpaste made of honey and white ashes as well, applying this mixture with a piece of cotton cloth. Like the charcoal, the white ashes were abrasive. The honey provided a more pleasing taste.

The precontact Inca, who established an empire in what is now Peru in about A.D. 1000, used the bark of the Balsam of Peru (*Myroxylon pereirae*) tree. Generally the bark was used to clean the teeth, but it was an ASTRINGENT as well. (The Aztec also used this dentifrice.) The Inca also used the astringent root of a plant that resembled the dandelion to clean their teeth.

In North America, the Mesquaki, a Northeast tribe, used white clay as a toothpaste. The clay served as an abrasive and polished the teeth in addition to cleaning them.

See also DENTISTRY; DENTIFRICES, CHEWABLE; HYGIENE, PERSONAL; TARTAR REMOVAL.

**Sources/Further Reading**

Lust, John. *The Herb Book.* New York: Bantam Books, 1974.

Ortiz de Montellano, Bernard. *Aztec Medicine, Health, and Nutrition.* New Brunswick, N.J.: Rutgers University Press, 1990.

Vogel, Virgil. *American Indian Medicine.* Norman: University of Oklahoma Press, 1970.

Weiner, Michael A. *Earth Medicine, Earth Food: Plant Remedies, Drugs, and Natural Foods of the North American Indians.* New York: Fawcett Columbine, 1990.

## tops See TOYS.

## tortillas (precontact) *Mesoamerican, North American Southwestern cultures*

Tortillas are thin, unleavened breads made from CORNMEAL. This flat, round bread was a staple food of the Maya and Aztec of Mesoamerica. (Maya culture flourished in the Yucatán Peninsula of what is now Mexico from about 1500 B.C. to A.D. 1500. The Aztec established an empire in what is now Mexico in about A.D. 1100.) Maya and Aztec cooks made tortillas from dried CORN kernels that they had boiled in water mixed with charcoal or lime. This served to loosen the skins; it also increased the amount of protein the body absorbs from corn. The technical name for this process is nixtamalization. (See also HOMINY.)

Once the corn had been boiled, the tortilla makers removed the skins from the kernels by rubbing them between their hands. They crushed the corn on a stone with a stone roller (called a metate and mano) to form a paste. They then kneaded the dough and shaped it into thin, round cakes. Aztec cooks baked these on a special stone griddle, called a *comalli*, that rested over the fire. Tortillas are still made in the same way by Mexican cooks today. The Maya tortilla makers shaped their tortillas thicker than those of the Aztec. Because no Maya griddles have been found, it is believe that they cooked tortillas on or under the ashes of a fire.

Father Bernardo de Sahagun, who wrote about the Aztec shortly after conquest, detailed many types of tortillas that they prepared and ate. He wrote that in addition to being made from corn, Aztec tortillas were also made from SQUASH and from AMARANTH. Sometimes they were flavored with turkey eggs, or honey. The Aztec wrapped tortillas around a variety of foods. These fillings included CHILE sauce, TOMATOES, mush-

Tortillas were a basic ingredient in American Indian cuisine in many parts of the Americas for centuries. *(Stock Montage/The Newberry Library)*

rooms, squash, and AVOCADOS. The result was the ancestor of the modern taco, burrito, and enchilada.

## Sources/Further Reading

Coe, Sophie. *America's First Cuisines*. Austin: University of Texas Press, 1994.

Tannahill, Reay. *Food in History*. New York: Stein and Day, 1973.

**tourniquets** (precontact) *North American, Mesoamerican, South American Andean cultures*

A tourniquet is a ligature, such as a cord or a strap, that is tightened around arms or legs in order to stop the flow of blood from a wound. The use of the tourniquet was universal among precontact American Indians. They also knew to place the tourniquet between the wound and the heart. Although most culture groups used the tourniquet on arms and legs, the Inca, who established an empire in what is now Peru in about A.D. 1000, used a tourniquet around the head of a patient about to undergo TREPHINATION, or brain SURGERY. Since the head is highly vascularized, the use of the tourniquet reduced the amount of bleeding and made the surgery easier to accomplish.

## Sources/Further Reading

von Hagen, Victor W. *The Realm of the Incas*. New York: New American Library, 1957.

Weatherford, Jack. *Indian Givers: How the Indians of the Americas Transformed the World*. New York: Fawcett Columbine, New York, 1988.

**toys** (precontact) *North American, Mesoamerican, Circum-Caribbean cultures*

A toy is a child's plaything. Like parents throughout the world, American Indians provided their children with toys. Some of these were educational, while others were intended for sheer enjoyment. Several North American Indian toys, including the spinning top, the whirligig, and the "buzz," were adopted by early colonists and remained popular through the 1800s. A Mesoamerican invention, the balloon, was probably not originally used as a toy, but it was put to that purpose by Europeans. American Indians invented kites independently of Asians and stilts independently of Europeans.

Inuit parents who lived in the Arctic of North America made miniature KAYAKS and sleds (see also DOGSLEDS) for their children. They also made miniature people for small toy boats. These toys were made from ivory, fur, minerals, and wood where the latter material was available. Some small ivory animals were used as pieces for a game called fox and geese, which adults and children alike played with during long winter nights. (See also GAMES, DICE.) Inuit parents and children also played CAT'S CRADLE with string, a game that is an independent invention.

Throughout North America, Indian parents gave children miniatures of items used in their respective tribes. These educational toys prepared them for their future roles as adults.

Some of these toys that were provided for girls included dolls, miniature cradleboards, and tipis. In the Southwest, children were allowed to make small pieces of POTTERY for their use. Young girls learned domestic skills by watching the women of the tribe make doll clothing. Young boys were given small bows and arrows to learn hunting skills. The Chippewa (Anishinabe) of the Northeast made birch-bark cutouts for their children to play with by etching an image on the tree bark with a sharp fish bone and punching holes along the etched line. They then bit these perforations to make the final cutouts, which were of people, animals, CANOES, and many other subjects. Northeastern children also played with marbles in the form of round stones that they collected or that were made from the pitch of the balsam pine tree.

Indians of North America invented the spinning top, a device that has delighted children for the last few centuries. Lewis and Clark, in the records of their 1804 expedition, noted that they had observed Indians playing with the devices. "They were seen to be playing a game with a strange wedge-shaped piece of wood, which was spun with a string," they wrote. Manuel Quimper, a Spanish adventurer, also recorded seeing American Indians using a similar device. American Indians often made tops from carved stone or bone as well as wood. Tribes known to have made tops are the Sac (Sauk) and Fox (Mesquaki) of the Northeast; the Arapaho, Atsina (Gros Ventre), Crow, Dakota, and Omaha of the Great Plains; the Bannock and Shoshone of the Great Basin; the Haida, Makah, Nootka, and Tsimshian of the Northwest Coast; the Zuni and the Tewa of the Southwest; and the Inuit of the Arctic. The Maya, whose culture arose in Mesoamerica in about 1500 B.C., also played with tops.

The Arapaho, Atsina, Crow, and Dakota of the Great Plains; the Maricopa, Hopi, and Zuni of the Southwest; and the Inuit of the Arctic made a toy that ethnologists called a *buzz*. It consisted of a stone or piece of wood with a piece of sinew looped through two holes that had been made into the stone or wood. The children twisted the sinew and pulled on the ends to make the buttonlike object in the middle spin around and produce a buzzing sound.

Plains Indians made a version of the popgun for their children. This was a carved wooden tube with a plunger at one end. A child could place a small stone or other object in the barrel, push the plunger, and fire the missile. Although ethnologists are not certain that North American tribes before contact with Europeans used this, archaeologists have found similar popguns in what is now Peru that were produced before contact. Children of the Southwest cultures played with BEAN shooters.

The Olmec, whose culture arose in the Yucatán Peninsula of what is now Mexico in about B.C. 1700, were the first to make rubber balloons. Although archaeologists have not determined how these were used, they have become popular playthings for modern children. The Maya, whose culture arose near that of the Olmec in about 1500 B.C., made stilts, However, according to reports by a Spanish observer and a drawing from a Maya codex, or BOOK, these were used for religious purposes, not play. Wichita and Shoshone children did play with stilts, as did Zuni children. Some anthropologists believe that stilts evolved from the FOOT PLOW. The Maya also constructed and flew huge kites whose frames were covered with brightly colored and decorated COTTON cloth. These round kites were as large as 15 to 20 feet in diameter. Because they were so large, anthropologists believe they were used to communicate with their gods rather than as toys. The Maya also made wheeled objects, some in the shape of animals. A few of these were toys, while others were ritual objects. The Teotihuacan, who lived in Central Mexico from 150 B.C. to A.D. 650, made jointed, hollow pottery dolls that could be posed in many positions.

**Sources/Further Reading**

Maxwell, James A. *America's Fascinating Indian Heritage.* Pleasantville, N.Y.: Reader's Digest Association, 1978.
Benson, Elizabeth P. *The Maya World.* New York: Thomas Y. Crowell, 1967.
Culin, Stewart. *Games of the North American Indians.* New York: Dover Publications, 1979.
Daumas, Maurice, ed. *A History of Technology and Invention: Progress Through the Ages, Vol. I, The Origin of Technical Civilization.* New York: Crown Publishers, 1962 (English Translation, 1969).
Densmore, Francis. *Chippewa Customs.* St. Paul, Minn.: Minnesota Historical Society Press, 1979.
Garrett, Wilbur E. "La Ruta Maya." *National Geographic* 176, no. 4 (October 1989): 424–478.
Lowe, Warren. *Indian Giver.* Pencticton, British Columbia: Theytus Books, 1986.
McQuiston, Don and Debra. *Dolls & Toys of Native America: A Journey through Childhood.* San Francisco: Chronicle Books, 1995.
Ortiz de Montellano, Bernard R. *Aztec Medicine, Health, and Nutrition.* New Brunswick, N.J.: Rutgers University Press, 1990.
Schele, Linda and David Freidel. *A Forest Of Kings: The Untold Story of the Ancient Maya.* New York: William Morrow And Company, Inc., 1990.
Stuart, George. "The Timeless Vision of Teotihuacan." *National Geographic* 188, no. 6 (December 1995): 2–35.

**traction and countertraction**  (ca. 1500 B.C.–A.D. 1500) *Mesoamerican, North American cultures*
The applying of pressure or tension to one end of a fractured, broken, or dislocated limb is called traction. When an opposite pressure or tension is applied to the opposite end of the same fracture, break, or dislocation, it is called countertraction. These procedures are used to reduce, or set, bone fractures; breaks; and dislocations. Indians throughout the Americas used this orthopedic technique, including the Maya and Aztec. (Maya culture arose in the Yucatán Peninsula of what is now Mexico in about 1500 B.C. The Aztec established an empire in what is now Mexico in about A.D. 1100.) Aztec medicine authority Bernard R. Ortiz de Montellano states, "They used traction and countertraction to reduce fractures and sprains and splints to immobilize fractures." He writes that the treatment of

broken bones by the precontact American Indian physicians was ". . . possibly the most advanced aspect . . ." of their medicine.

North American Indians were reported to use a similar technique to reduce dislocations of the foot or knee by tying one end of the strap to the foot and looping the other end around a tree limb. Lying on his or her back, the injured person kept pulling on the free end of the strap to apply traction to the joint until it had popped back into place. The development of this procedure indicated that American Indians had working knowledge of the PULLEY.

See also ORTHOPEDIC TECHNIQUES.

**Sources/Further Reading**

Adams, William R. "Aboriginal American Medicine and Surgery." *Proceedings of the Indiana Academy of Science* 61 (1951): 15–36.
Ortiz de Montellano, Bernard R. *Aztec Medicine, Health, and Nutrition.* New Brunswick, N.J.: Rutgers University Press, 1990.
Peredo, Miguel Guzman. *Medical Practices in Ancient America.* Mexico City: Ediciones Euroamericanas, 1985.
Vogel, Virgil. *American Indian Medicine.* Norman: University of Oklahoma Press, 1970.

**trade**  (1000 B.C.)  *North American, South American, Circum-Caribbean, Mesoamerican cultures*
Trade is the business of buying and selling goods or exchanging them for other goods. Starting thousands of years before contact with Europeans, culture groups traded throughout the Americas. The Olmec, whose culture arose in the Yucatán Peninsula of what is now Mexico in about 1700 B.C., are considered to be the oldest Mesoamerican traders. They traded LATEX products, such as rubber BALLS and TARPAULINS. A great deal of trading occurred between neighboring tribes. The Huron farmers in the Northeast, for example, grew a surplus of CORN, which they turned into CORNMEAL and traded to tribes to the north for buffalo robes (see also BISON), fish, and winter clothing that had been embroidered with porcupine quills. The Gabrilino people, who lived near tar pits on the southern California coast, traded ASPHALT for hides or obsidian. (See also FLINTKNAPPING.) Local trade routes like these were linked to a network of other routes, forming a complex and sophisticated system of exchange that criss-crossed North, Meso- and South America. (See also ROAD SITES; ROAD SYSTEMS.)

Other traders, such as the Maya of Mesoamerica, traveled thousands of miles to trade salt from their commercial salt-making enterprises on the Yucatán Peninsula for luxury goods. (Maya culture flourished in what is now Mexico starting in about 1500 B.C.) Traders living on the Ecuadorian littoral of South America and the Arawak of the northeast coast of South America also traveled great distances to do business. In some Mesoamerican and South American culture groups, the business of trading was an established profession. For the Maya, it was not only a business but also a diplomatic career. In addition to goods, ideas, styles of artistic expression, and technology were exchanged as well.

Maya trading probably evolved between A.D. 600 and 900 in the area near Cozumel and what is now Belize. The traders' first voyages were short ones, primarily to an island about 18 miles off the coast of Belize. Within 300 years trade had begun in earnest, and the Maya had established seacoast port trading towns. The earliest and most important was Cerros in northern Belize. The town served to connect the Caribbean trade routes with those to the southern Maya lowlands that could be reached via two rivers. The Maya located other towns along the coast where bays were protected, offering natural harbors. They built docks and piers in these ports as well as a SEAWALL at Cerritos to form an artificial harbor.

The coastal Maya traded salt, shells, shark teeth, and stingray spines to inland cities many hundreds of miles from the coast. The Maya who lived in what is now Belize served as brokers in the exchange of salt, COTTON, CACAO, spices, feathers, and jaguar pelts they had obtained in the lowlands to the highlands of what is now Guatemala 500 miles away from obsidian, basalt, and jade (see also JADE WORK). Some of the obsidian had been obtained in central Mexico, about 900 miles away.

By the time the Maya established their most important city, Chichén Itzá, in the northern Yucatán peninsula, trade had intensified dramatically. Archaeologists have found jade and ceramics (see also POTTERY) from the Guatemalan highlands and turquoise (see also JEWELRY, TURQUOISE AND SILVER) from northern Mexico as well as from the North American desert Southwest in Maya archaeological sites. In addition they have found gold from what are now Costa Rica and Panama. (See also METALS, PRECIOUS.)

Much of the Maya seacoast trade depended on salt. Agricultural people living inland needed it to meet their nutritional requirements and to preserve meat. The salt beds of the northern Yucatan, the biggest in the Maya world, produced enough salt so that they were able to ship thousands of tons of it to the lowlands. Salt traders on the Pacific Coast provided salt for the highlands. Other products traded by the Maya included honey (see also BEEKEEPING), cotton and beautifully woven cloth (see also WEAVING TECHNIQUES), fish, DYES, pottery, shells, TOBACCO, manos and metates (for grinding corn), talc, volcanic ash, lime that was used in plaster and CONCRETE, bark PAPER, feathers (see also FEATHERWORKING; PARROT BREEDING), amber, cinnabar (see also MERCURY), jadeite, pyrite for MIRRORS, copal (see also AROMATHERAPY), coral, and serpentine.

By A.D. 900 to 1500, the Maya had expanded their trade network so that it was an international one that stretched many miles. Pyrite mirrors and macaw feathers from Maya traders have been found in the Southwest desert of North America. At the time of conquest nobles controlled Maya trade and marriages were arranged to further expand these business dynasties. Artists and craftspeople also traveled with the merchants, which explains the spread of styles such as post classic sculpture and styles of MURAL paintings.

The Aztec, who established an empire in what is now Mexico in about A.D. 1100, had a merchant class of traders called *pocteca*. These professional traders, armed themselves and traveled for thousands of miles to exchange goods. While Maya traders were seagoing, the Aztec primarily utilized land routes. In addition to trading items such as gold dust, copper knives, and jade for goods such as coal, VANILLA, PINEAPPLES, and CHOCOLATE, they served as spies, reporting back to the Aztec government on military establishments. They also reported on the amount of tributes that areas they traded with would be able to pay the empire. Their goods were carried by human burden carriers called *tlamemes* who were trained to carry heavy burdens with the use of a TUMPLINE starting at the age of five.

By the 1400s Nahuatl, the Aztec language, had become the language of trade throughout Mesoamerica. Long-distance merchants were given the same status as warriors and had their own court systems for dealing with disputes. They managed the bustling market places located in large cities and fixed prices. If someone stole, his or her thievery was tried in a court. Although Aztec traders had high status, they also experienced great difficulties in having to travel for months over deserts and through areas where bandits frequently attacked. Sometimes when they traveled through enemy Maya territory, traders disguised themselves to escape detection.

Long-distance trade existed in South America as well. The Arawak (Taino) and Carib Indians of the Circum-Caribbean traveled across the 1,700 miles of water between the northeast coast of South America and the Caribbean in order to trade goods. On the western coast of South America, the Inca, who established an empire in about A.D. 1000, used large BALSA WOOD rafts (see also RAFTS, BALSA) that were fitted with huge sails to travel possibly as far as the Galápagos Islands.

Only recently have some of the mysteries of Inca trade been revealed. Although Spaniards had reported in 1525 that traders had visited the port of Zacatula in west Mexico for several months before heading south, their origins remained unknown. After carefully collecting evidence, some archaeologists now believe that in precontact times the west coast of what is now Mexico was served by traders from what is now Ecuador on the northwest coast of South America. These traders would have had to travel over 2,400 miles of open sea in order to trade.

Clothing styles and the existence of very similar types of hairless dogs, pottery, and checkered textiles all indicate contact between the two cultures. Recently similarities have been documented between metallurgical techniques of Ecuador and those of West Mexico, including formulas for making copper and arsenic alloys in addition to the techniques used to manufacture the metal objects themselves. (See also METALLURGY.) The metalworkers of Mexico produced tweezers, bells, awls, and rings that closely resemble those made by the Ecuadorian metalworkers. Archaeologists have found no evidence that these metallurgical techniques gradually arose in the west part of Mexico—the metalworking appears to have arisen instantly. They believe that the two cultures first traded in about A.D. 600 to 700 and again in about 1200.

Traders from Ecuador used balsa wood rafts that had movable centerboards and rigged sails, indicating that they could make the journey across the open seas. When Spanish explorer Francisco Pizarro voyaged across the northwest coast of South America in the 1500s, he encountered a large wooden trade raft laden with beautiful textiles that merchants were trying to trade for raw spondylus shells highly prized by Andean highlands cultures. Pizarro's men, who closely examined the goods, described brightly dyed LLAMA and ALPACA garments, shirts, capes, and skirts as well as men's TROUSERS. Some of these were brightly embroidered with yarn. (See also EMBROIDERY.) The fact that west Mexican metalworking arose in the coastal areas where shells were present gives further support to the idea of frequent trade between the two distant cultures.

In North America the Inuit of the Arctic traded copper from the Coppermine River and soapstone with other Inuit living hundreds of miles away. Wood, because of its scarcity, was a valuable trade item. After contact, Inuit people were seen crossing the Bering Strait in hide boats to trade with Siberian people for objects that had been manufactured in Europe and Asia. Archaeologists believe that similar trade across the Bering Strait took place starting in about 1000 B.C. American Indians of the Northwest traded dentalia shells that they obtained from the west coast of what is now Vancouver Island. When Europeans arrived on the upper Missouri, they found the Mandan Indians had dentalia shells that had come from thousands of miles away. Southwest Indians traded with California tribes for shells, exchanging pottery and cloth for these items. Shells that California tribes traded reached as far east as the Texas panhandle. The Mojave people who lived in what is now California brokered shell beads, FISHHOOKS, and shells from Southern California Indians and pottery and textiles from Pueblo Indians in the Southwest.

The Anasazi, the ancestors of today's Pueblo Indians, and the Hohokam traded extensively with Mesoamerican merchants, obtaining BELLS and fine textiles as well as parrots. They traded turquoise to the Aztec and the Maya for these luxury goods. Some anthropologists believe that it was traders who brought the Mesoamerican ball game to North American Indians living in what is now Arizona. (See also BASKETBALL.) Plains tribes traded dried meat (see also JERKY; FOOD PRESERVATION; PEMMICAN), hide clothing (see also, FRINGED CLOTHING; TANNING, BRAIN), and MOCCASINS to farming villages along the Missouri River in exchange for corn, BEANS, SQUASH, and TOBACCO.

American Indians in the Northeast primarily used water routes when they traded, loading their CANOES with goods and sometimes traveling many miles to exchange them. The Chippewa (Anishinabe) traded copper from the southern shore of Lake Superior eastward for tobacco as well as WAMPUM, or shell beads. Catlinite, or red pipestone, that they had mined on the western edge of what is now Minnesota, was traded as far east as what is now New York State and Canada. (See also PIPES, TOBACCO.) In Canada, Ontario flint was traded to Saskatchewan and Alberta. Rocky Mountain obsidian ended up in Ohio, where the Hopewell people used it to create burial effigies.

In the Southeast, Indian traders used the Mississippi River as a trade artery. Tribes along the seacoast sold salt, made from evaporating water found at salt licks by boiling in it shallow pans over a fire. Sometimes the salt was formed into 2- to 3-pound blocks as the Maya traders further south did. Copper was also an item of trade in the Southeast.

Villages and entire tribes in different areas of North America set themselves up as commodities brokers or trading middlemen. In the Northeast the Huron served as brokers, buying corn, tobacco, and hemp from some tribes and then trading it to hunting tribes for fish and furs. When the fur trade began after European contact, they traded furs to the French for manufactured trade goods. The Iroquois developed a similar trading relationship with the Dutch. Once European trade goods began filtering into the prairies, farming tribes such as the Hidatsa on the Upper Missouri River began brokering metal pots, guns, knives, glass beads and mirrors, in exchange for hides and hide clothing. They held trade fairs that people from several tribes would attend in order to participate in the exchange. American Indian merchants in the Southeast also held trading fairs.

The first French explorers were eager to obtain furs, especially beaver, from North American Indians and were willing to trade guns and metal traps for them as well as metal cooking pots, mirrors, awls, metal NEEDLES, and a number of other useful items, including luxury goods such as glass beads. They began to participate in the already existing trade fairs, naming them *rendezvous*.

As a result of the trade for guns and traps, American Indians were encouraged to begin killing increasing number of animals for pelts. The ensuing inflation drove Indian trappers to kill more and more animals in order to receive the goods they needed. As a result, they had little time to spend on hunting for food and growing crops, which made them increasingly dependent on trade in order to make a living. The balance of trade and self-sufficiency that had worked for years in North America was suddenly turned awry.

The Spanish presence in Mesoamerica and South America also disrupted the balance of trade in those regions. In 1502 Christopher Columbus encountered Maya traders on his fourth voyage off the coast of Honduras. In his book *Historia de las Indias,* Bartolomé de Las Casas reported that the Maya's canoe was a huge one, as long as a galley and eight feet wide. A palm matting structure in the middle of the dugout kept women, children, and goods dry. Each canoe contained about 25 men. "They had in it much clothing of the kind they weave of cotton in this land, such as cloth woven with many designs and colors . . .; knives of flint, swords of very strong wood . . . and foodstuffs of the country," wrote de Las Casas.

At first the Spaniards obtained many of the botanical specimens they carried back to Europe through trade with the Indians. After conquest they had no need to trade. The conquistadores took over both the salt manufacturing and the textile weaving industries in the Yucatán. In the south they confiscated the Maya cacao plantations and gold deposits. As the Spanish subjugated the indigenous ruling class, the demand ended for luxury items that had been an important motivation for trade.

The Huron used glass beads to decorate many items. These beads were obtained in trade, often for furs and hides, with non-Indians. *(Marius Barbeau/National Archives of Canada/PA-175385/National Museums of Canada Collection)*

### Sources/Further Reading

Anawalt, Patricia. "Traders of the Ecuadorian Littoral." *Archaeology* (November/December 1997): 48–52.

Andrews, Anthony P. "America's Ancient Mariners," *Natural History* (March 1991): 72–75.

———. *Maya Salt Production and Trade.* Tucson: The University of Arizona Press, 1983.

Driver, Harold E. *Indians of North America.* Chicago: University of Chicago Press, 1969.

Hassig, Ross. *Trade, Tribute, and Transportation: The Sixteenth-Century Political Economy of the Valley of Mexico.* Norman: University of Oklahoma Press, 1985.

Karasic, Carol. *The Turquoise Trail: Native American Jewelry and Culture of the Southwest.* New York: Harry Abrams, 1993.

Sharer, Robert. *Daily Life in Maya Civilization.* Westport, Conn.: Greenwood Press, 1996.

Trigger, Bruce G. *Case Studies in Anthropology: The Huron Farmers of the North.* New York: Holt Rinehart and Winston, 1969.

**trails** See CHISHOLM TRAIL; ROAD SITES; ROAD SYSTEMS.

## transplanting, agricultural (ca. 2000 B.C.)

*Mesoamerican, North American Great Plains and Northeastern cultures*

Transplanting is the gardening technique of starting seeds in a protected environment then moving the seedlings to the garden plot or field when they are mature enough to withstand the conditions there. The Aztec, who established an empire in what is now Mexico in about A.D. 1100, started seeds on woven mats and grew them there until the plants were established before transplanting them to chinampas, or raised beds, that were surrounded by canals. (See also IRRIGATION SYSTEMS.) They used this technique to start CORN for their chinampas plots. (See also AGRICULTURE, RAISED BED.) The mats with seedlings were 20 to 30 feet long and were towed from bed to bed along canals for planting.

Transplanting was also used by the Hidatsa, an agricultural tribe that lived along the Missouri River that runs through the northern plains in what is now North Dakota. They used this technique to hasten the germination of their seeds because of the short growing season in the area where they lived. Buffalo Bird Woman, a Hidatsa woman who was an expert in the agricultural ways of her people, explained the technique she used to start SQUASH seeds to anthropologist Gilbert L. Wilson in 1917. She told him that she began by spreading a piece of buffalo robe fur side up on the floor of her EARTH LODGE. Next she covered it with wetted grass, matting the grass as she spread it over the fur. Then she mixed together sage and buck brush leaves, planting her squash seeds among the leaves, which she placed on the grass mat. She folded the mat over the leaves and then did the same with the buffalo robe, so that she had a squash bundle about 15 by 18 inches. She would hang the squash bundle from a drying pole a little to the side of the fire. At the end of two days, she would water the seeds by opening the bundle and blowing water from her mouth onto them. On the third day the seeds were an inch tall and ready for planting in the earth.

Huron women who lived in what is now called New England started their squash seeds in bark trays that they had filled with a potting soil made of moistened powdered wood. They kept these trays beside their cooking fires so that the seeds would germinate. Once the seeds had sprouted and the danger of frost was gone, they transferred the seedlings to the fields.

Because the technique of transplanting was unknown in Europe, the conquistadores marvelled at the woven mats that contained the seedlings of the Aztec farmers and mistook them for floating islands. Scholars believed this misconception until the early decades of the 20th century. Colonists in New England who observed Huron women transplanting seedlings adopted the technique for their own gardens. It remains in common use among gardeners today.

See also AGRICULTURE.

## Sources/Further Reading

Hurt, R. Douglas. *American Indian Agriculture: Prehistory to Present.* Lawrence: University Press of Kansas, 1987.

Smith, Michael E. *The Peoples of America: The Aztecs.* Cambridge, Mass.: Blackwell, 1996.

Trigger, Bruce G. *Case Studies in Anthropology: The Huron Farmers of the North.* New York: Holt Rinehart and Winston, 1969.

Wilson, L. Gilbert. *Buffalo Bird Woman's Garden: Agriculture of the Hidatsa Indians.* Reprint. St. Paul: Minnesota Historical Society Press, 1987.

**transplants, bone**   See ORTHOPEDIC TECHNIQUES.

**traps, animal**   (ca. 12,000 B.C.–10,000 B.C.)   *North American, Circum-Caribbean cultures*

The Paleo-Indians of North America devised several means of obtaining food. One was through the use of traps. The most common traps that they developed were the snare, the deadfall, and the pitfall trap. The Inuit of the Arctic region of North America used a unique spring trap to kill game. These traps were invented independently of those invented by early people in other parts of the world. In order to develop them, American Indians had to understand animal behavior. The technology of trapping was labor-saving, freeing people from having to constantly hunt. This left them time to pursue other endeavors, including AGRICULTURE. With the advent of the fur trade, American Indians began to use metal traps and guns.

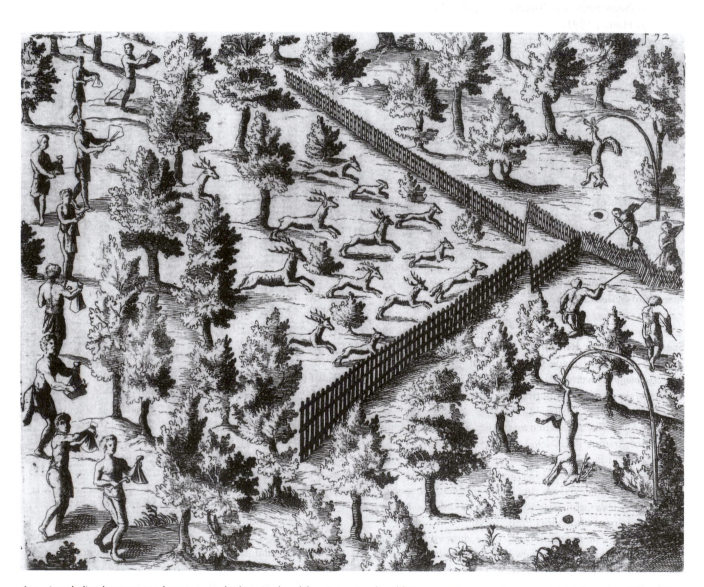

American Indian hunters used traps to make hunting less labor intensive. In addition to using snare traps, as pictured on the right of this drawing by French explorer Samuel de Champlain (made between 1603 and 1615), hunters sometimes drove game into confined areas to ensure success. Often people served as the "fences" of these pens. *(Rare Books Division, The New York Public Library Astor, Lenox and Tilden Foundations)*

The snare trap was almost a universal device among the North American Paleo-Indians to catch deer and other game animals. To make it they fashioned a rope from natural fibers. Next they made a noose at one end and tied the other to a tree. They placed these traps at the height where the animals' heads would likely be along paths and trails that those animals used. Sometimes they placed the snare on the ground to catch their prey by the feet. The noose of the snare trap was large enough so that an animal's head or feet could fit through it easily, and it was made so that it could tighten readily. When an animal unknowingly walked into the trap, it felt the pressure of the noose around its neck and attempted to flee. Struggle only tightened the noose, holding the animal securely in place until the hunter checked the trap.

The pitfall trap used by American Indians was designed to trap an animal in a large pit dug in the ground in such a way as to prevent the animal from getting out on its own. Once the pit had been dug, hunters covered it with various materials so that the animal would not see it. Sometimes they placed food on the middle of the covering. When an animal walked over the covering or tried to get the food, it would fall into the pit, from which it would be retrieved when the trapper checked the trap.

The deadfall trap that was used by North American Indians was more sophisticated. It used a large weight (usually a log or a stone) and a trigger that, when sprung, would cause the weight to fall on an animal. The animal would be killed, wounded, or immobilized. This trap used the same concept that the present-day mousetrap trigger is based upon. Hunters made the trigger from several small pieces of wood that were strong enough to support the weight. The wood pieces that formed the trigger were notched and fitted together so that they held the weight in the air. The Indians tied bait to the trigger so that when the animal tried to eat, the trigger would be sprung and the weight would fall. Hunters often placed these traps on regularly used trails, near water sources, or by naturally occurring salt licks.

The Inuit who lived in what is now Alaska used spring bait wolf traps. To make them they rolled a strip of baleen into a coil and secured it with a piece of sinew. Baleen is the thin bone strip found in the mouth of plankton-eating whales that is used to filter plankton from the water. (See also WHALING.) The Inuit covered the coil with blubber or meat in order to disguise it and to serve as a lure. They left it in the snow until it froze and they could remove the sinew. Then they placed the baited trap in an area where a wolf might be drawn to it. If this occurred, the animal would swallow the meat-covered baleen. When it thawed in the wolf's stomach, the baleen uncoiled and pierced the stomach lining. The animal would then bleed to death.

See also BOWS, LAMINATED; CAMOUFLAGE; DECOYS, DUCK; FISHNET LURES.

## Sources/Further Reading

Driver, Harold E. *Indians of North America.* Chicago: The University of Chicago Press, 1969.

Oswalt, Wendell. *Eskimos and Explorers.* Novato, Calif.: Chandler & Sharp Publishers, 1979.

**traps, fish**  See FISH TRAPS.

## trephination (brain surgery; trepanation; trepanning) (ca. 1000 B.C.) *South American, North American, Mesoamerican cultures*

Trephination is a medical procedure that is used to surgically remove parts of the skull in order to alleviate disease or provide relief for trauma to the brain. This procedure is also referred to as brain SURGERY, or a craniotomy. Even though some Neolithic (New Stone Age) people in Europe and in other parts of the world performed trephinations, their success rates for this surgery were minimal. The South American Paracas culture, which existed in what is now Peru from about 1300 B.C. to A.D. 20, independently invented trephination from that practiced in other parts of the world. According to archaeologists, while more than half of the ancient American Indian patients who underwent the procedure survived, Old World trepanners had only a 10-percent survival rate. Trephination was practiced extensively in South America. Archaeologists estimate that thousands of ancient American Indian patients underwent the procedure.

Omer Fernandez, author of the article "Pre-Columbian Surgery," states that brain surgery was being performed on a regular basis by 1000 B.C. Other writers say that the practice was older. Some believe that the Olmec, whose culture arose in the Yucatán Peninsula of what is now Mexico in about 1700 B.C., may have been the first to experiment with brain surgery. The Maya, whose culture arose in a nearby region of the Yucatán Peninsula in about 1500 B.C., are believed to have continued the process. According to Dr. Virgil J. Vogel, an expert on American Indian medicine, "The most spectacular surgery performed in pre-Columbian America was trephination (skull surgery), of which the most abundant evidence has been found in Peru, though trephined skulls have been found in several parts of the United States and Canada." The Inca who established an empire in what is now Peru in about A.D. 1000 continued the practice in South America.

Roy L. Moodie, who studied trepanning, wrote in 1927, "The Inca employed craniotomy (trepanning) scientifically, deliberately, doing it with humane purpose." There were several reasons for this procedure. The first was unbearable or unexplained headaches. Trephination was also used for a psychological condition known today as depression. It was used to repair crushing trauma to the head or to remove tumors, thereby relieving intracranial pressure. Finally, trephination was sometimes performed for superstitious or religious reasons.

Archaeologists have studied and written about South American pre-Inca trepanners the most. The majority of trephined skulls were found in the Paracas Cavernas of present-day Peru. The techniques these surgeons used were sophisticated. They anesthetized patients using PEYOTE, COCA, or hypnotism. (See also ANESTHETICS.) Surgical instruments that they used included SCALPELS made of copper, silver, gold, and various alloys of these metals. They also usedobsidian flint, chert, and quartzite blades. (See also FLINTKNAPPING.)

Once the patient had been anesthetized, the surgeon cut the scalp to produce a rectangular flap that folded out of the way. Ancient Peruvian surgeons had several options for opening the cranium (skull): cutting, sawing, scraping, or drilling. (Drilling is sometimes referred to as circular brain surgery.) The Paracas surgeons were the first in the world to use cautery in conjunction with brain surgery in order to stop excessive bleeding. To do this they heated rocks and applied them to the bleeding blood vessels. This heat caused the blood to coagulate and stop flowing. They also used TOURNIQUETS for the same purpose.

These ancient trepanners produced prostheses made of GOURD rinds and thin sheets of gold FOIL. These materials were placed over the hole left by the surgery to replace the bone that they had removed. This protected the brain while the bone grew back together. Once the operation was completed, the physician used NEEDLE and thread to sew the wound together. Almost all of the ancient American Indian physicians used gauze and COTTON in their practice; they were the first to do so. The white cotton and gauze helped to keep the wound area germ-free (see also ASEPSIS) and decreased the risk of infections. If the wound became infected, it was treated, and chances were the patient would continue to recover.

Archaeologists have found evidence that some patients survived several trepanning operations and that one person had survived five of these procedures. The survival rate of patients who underwent trepanning in the area of Cuzco was between 83 and 90 percent. During the latter half of the 19th century, despite modern medical advances, only half of the patients who underwent brain surgery at the hands of trained western physicians survived the operation. This was the same survival rate for the ancient pre-Peruvian patients of Paracas in 1000 B.C.

### Sources/Further Reading

Fagan, Brian M. *Kingdoms of Gold, Kingdoms of Jade: The Americas before Columbus.* Thames And Hudson Ltd., London, 1991.

Lowe, Warren. *Indian Giver.* Pencticton, British Columbia: Theytus Books, 1986.

Mason, J. Alden. *The Ancient Civilizations of Peru.* Rev. ed. New York: Penguin Books, 1957.

Moodie, R. L. "Injuries to the Head among pre-Columbian Peruvians." *Annals Of Medical History, Studies in Paleopathology* 21, no. 9 (1927): 298–328.

Shapiro, H. L. "Primitive Surgery: First Evidence of Trepanning in the Southwest." *Journal of Natural History American Museum of Natural History* 27 (1927): 266.

Viola, Herman J. and Carolyn Margolis. *Seeds of Change: 500 Years since Columbus.* Washington, D.C.: Smithsonian Institution Press, 1991.

Vogel, Virgil. *American Indian Medicine.* Norman: University of Oklahoma Press, 1970.

Weatherford, Jack. *Indian Givers: How the Indians of the Americas Transformed the World.* New York: Fawcett Columbine, 1988.

**trousers** (ca. 25,000 B.C.) *North American Arctic cultures*
Trousers are tailored garments made for covering the lower part of the body from the waist to the ankles. They are constructed in two sections so that each leg fits into its own portion of the garment. Although fashion historians believe that trousers originated in Asia, archaeologists estimate that Paleo-Indians in the North American Arctic were making tailored trousers as early as 25,000 B.C.

Both Inuit men and women of the Arctic and Subarctic wore fur trousers. They made them by sewing two leggings together, running a seam up the front and the rear. American Indians of the northern plains wore MOCCASINS, leggings, and breechcloths that gave the appearance of trousers from a distance. Fur trappers, traders, and colonists on the American frontier, who adopted Indian dress, began wearing buckskin trousers shortly after contact with Indians. This adaptation was necessary in an environment where hose and pantaloons or knickers were impractical. Europeans and upper class colonists did not wear full-length breeches, or trousers, until after about 1793–94 (when a more radical phase of the French Revolution made them a political statement). Trousers did not become common apparel for men until 1807. The earliest trousers were made of COTTON or buckskin and were very form-fitting.

See also MOCCASINS; MUKLUKS; PARKAS; TANNING, BRAIN.

### Sources/Further Reading

Baclawski, Karen. *The Guide to Historic Costume.* London: B.T. Batsford, Ltd., 1995.

Driver, Harold E. *Indians of North America.* Chicago: University of Chicago Press, 1969.

Paterek, Josephine. *Encyclopedia of American Indian Costume.* Denver, Colo.: ABC Clio, 1994.

Wilcox, R. Turner. *Dictionary of Costume.* New York: Charles Scribner's Sons, 1969.

**tubing, copper** (ca. 5000 B.C.–4000 B.C.) *North American Northeast, South American Andean, Mesoamerican cultures*
Tubing is a hollow cylinder. The Paleo-Indians of the present-day area of the southern Greak Lakes made copper PAN PIPES as well as tubular beads. Considered to be the first metalworkers in the world, they also produced the first copper tubing. The Chavin people in South America, whose culture arose in what is now Peru in about 900 B.C., and the people that followed them also made tubular panpipes of copper. The Inca, who established an empire in what is now Peru in about A.D. 1100, used copper tubing for their PLUMBING.

In precontact Mesoamerica the Maya, whose culture flourished in the Yucatán Peninsula of what is now Mexico in about 1500 B.C., also developed copper tubing, which they used to make hollow DRILL BITS. They used these drill bits to work stone and to prepare teeth for fillings and inlays. (See also DENTISTRY; DENTAL INLAYS.)

## Sources/Further Reading

Benson, Elizabeth P. *The Maya World.* New York: Thomas Y. Crowell Company, 1967.

Daumas, Maurice. *A History of Technology & Invention: Progress through the Ages.* New York: Crown Publishers, Inc., New York, 1962.

Fastlicht, Samuel. *Tooth Mutilations and Dentistry in Pre-Columbian Mexico.* Mexico City: Quintessence Books, 1971.

Maxwell, James A. *America's Fascinating Indian Heritage.* Pleasantville, N.Y.: Reader's Digest Books, 1978.

Morris, Craig and Adriana von Hagen. *The Inka Empire and Its Andean Origins.* New York: Abbeville Press Publishers, 1993.

**tumplines** (precontact)   *North American Northeast, California, and Southwest; Mesoamerican; South American Andean cultures*

A tumpline is a strap or sling worn across the forehead in order to help support a burden that is carried on the back. Tumplines were used by a number of culture groups throughout the Americas. Algonquian-speaking peoples of the North American Northeast used tumplines to aid in carrying canoes when they portaged them. Some linguists believe that the word *tump* is derived from the Algonquian language. The people of Mesoamerica also used tumplines to transport goods. (See also TRADE.) These carriers were trained to carry heavy burdens with the use of a tumpline starting at the age of five. Post-contact drawings of the Inca, who established an empire in what is now Peru in about A.D. 1000, show workers carrying goods with tumplines. New England colonists borrowed the practice of using tumplines from American Indians. According to *Bartlett's Dictionary of Americanisms* published in 1877, people living in the state of Maine carried packs with tumplines.

## Sources/Further Reading

Hassig, Ross. *Trade, Tribute, and Transportation: The Sixteenth-Century Political Economy of the Valley of Mexico.* Norman: University of Oklahoma Press, 1985.

Lowes, Warren. *Indian Giver.* Penticton, British Columbia: Theytus Books, 1986.

O TABA CALLE
PVCLLACOCVAMRA

Tumplines, an invention unique to the Americas, were used to help carry heavy loads. *(After Felipe Guamán Poma de Ayala.* Nueva Coronica y Buen Gobierno)

**turkey breeding** (ca. 200 B.C.)   *Mesoamerican, North American Southwest cultures*

Turkeys (*Meleagris gallopave*) are large birds that are indigenous to North America, first domesticated by the ancient people living in what is now Mexico. They are the only birds that can make the distinctive gobbling sound for which they are known. Domesticated turkey bones found in the Tehuacán Valley have been dated to 200 B.C. Aztec rulers, who oversaw an empire established in what is now Mexico in about A.D. 1100, collected turkeys as tribute. In 1430 Netzahualcouyotl, the emperor of Texcoco, collected 100 of the birds a day. So important was the turkey as a source of meat to the Aztec that they conducted a festival every 200 days in honor of the bird. During this event they spread the eggshells from which turkey chicks had hatched on the roadways as a gesture of THANKSGIVING to the god that had provided this dietary staple. Some ethnologists believe that to meet the demand for turkeys, Aztec turkey breeders developed fast-maturing breeds, beginning a trend that continues today. (Modern domesticated turkeys generally mature in 22 weeks, gaining a pound a week.)

The Anasazi of the North American desert Southwest, who flourished from about 350 B.C. to about A.D. 1250, raised domesticated turkeys as well. Many archaeologists believe that these turkeys were initially obtained from the Aztec in TRADE. Although they used them as a meat source, the Anasazi valued them more for their feathers. (See also FEATHERWORKING.) They wove feathers with cordage to make robes (see also WEAVING TECHNIQUES) and used turkey bones for making whistles, awls, and beads. As AGRICULTURE increased, the Anasazi used turkeys as a way to keep grasshoppers and other pests away from the crops. (See also INSECTICIDES.)

Archaeological evidence shows that in about A.D. 1125 the Anasazi were breeding turkeys to control feather color and diversity. They kept different types of turkeys in separate areas so that they would not crossbreed, indicating a practical knowledge of genetics. Archaeologists have found domesticated turkey remains buried with humans throughout the Southwest. At Casas Grandes, a site in northern Mexico, bodies of the dead were found wrapped in turkey-feather robes. Today's Pueblo people, the descendants of the Anasazi, believe that turkeys are teachers, and some still view them as the companions of the dead.

The Maya who lived on the Yucatán Peninsula of what is now Mexico ate turkey as well, but the variety native to their region was *Meleagris ocellata,* a wild turkey known for its beautiful plumage. Although this type of turkey was never completely domesticated, archaeological evidence indicates that the Maya may have captured wild poults and kept them penned while they fattened them. They used them in TAMALES in addition to eating them with TORTILLAS and BEANS.

The European reaction to turkey was positive. Father Bernardo de Sahagun, who tasted turkey wings prepared by Aztec cooks, wrote that turkeys were the master of meat. "It is tasty, fat and savory," he said of the bird. Turkeys were imported to Europe by Spanish explorers between 1498 and 1511. By 1541 they had reached England, where they became a popular dish. The French and Italians also raised turkeys. English colonists brought domesticated turkeys with them to Jamestown in 1604. These, along with wild turkeys that were indigenous to North America, became foundation stock for the breeds of turkeys raised commercially today.

Turkey, which was reported to have been served at the first Thanksgiving, remains the culinary centerpiece of that holiday.

The eastern wild turkey became a symbol of the first Thanksgiving. Benjamin Franklin argued that the turkey, not the eagle, should be the national bird. Wild turkeys still exist in parts of Mexico and much of the United States where they are hunted as a game bird. Although domestic birds are flightless, wild birds can fly for short distances up to 55 miles per hour and can run up to 20 miles per hour.

Consumption of domesticated turkeys, while always high, increased during the last 25 years of the 20th century, as did the health consciousness of the American public. Turkey meat is low in fat and high in protein. According to the American Turkey Federation, 285 million turkeys were produced in 1998. In 1997 each person in the United States consumed an average of 17.5 pounds of turkey.

See also ANIMALS, DOMESTICATED.

## Sources/Further Reading

Coe, Sophie. *America's First Cuisines.* Austin: University of Texas Press, 1994.

Nabhan, Gary. *Enduring Seeds: Native American Agriculture and Wild Plant Conservation.* San Francisco: North Point Press, 1989.

National Turkey Federation. *Turkey History and Trivia.* URL: www.turkey.fed.org/press/history.html. Downloaded on October 30, 1999.

Weatherford, Jack. *Native Roots: How the Indians Enriched America.* New York: Fawcett Columbine, 1991.

**turquoise**  See JEWELRY, TURQUOISE AND SILVER.

**umbrellas** (ca. 1500 B.C.–A.D. 1500) *Mesoamerican cultures*

An umbrella is a device that provides shelter from sun or rain. It consists of a small canopy or covering mounted on a small central rod, or dowel. According to Maya culture expert Elizabeth P. Benson, the Maya invented the umbrella independently of the Chinese but used it for the same purpose. (Maya culture arose in the Yucatán Peninsula of what is now Mexico in about 1500 B.C.) The Inca of South America, who established an empire in what is now Peru in about A.D. 1000, also used the umbrella. Both cultures used umbrellas long before contact with Europeans. These precontact umbrellas were made of feathers, rather than fabric as is used today. The feathers were made into a circular canopy that was then attached to a pole.

### Sources/Further Reading

Benson, Elizabeth P. *The Maya World.* New York: Thomas Y. Crowell Company, 1967.

von Hagen, Victor Wolfgang. *The Royal Road of the Inca.* London: Gordon Cremoni, Ltd., 1976.

**unconscious mind**  See FREE ASSOCIATION.

## United States Constitution, American Indian influence on   (ca. A.D. 1787) *North American Northeast cultures*

The U.S. Constitution, a document that outlines the organization of the three branches of government, defines the powers of the government in relation to that of individual states. It was framed in 1787 and was adopted in 1789. One of the most significant influences on this document was the IROQUOIS CONSTITUTION, also called the Great Law of Peace.

The Great Law of Peace was created by the Iroquois to stop neighboring tribes from fighting. The document, recorded on WAMPUM belts, formed a confederacy among the Iroquois tribes: the Oneida, Mohawk, Cayuga, Onondaga, the Seneca, and later the Tuscarora. The Iroquois place its creation between A.D. 1000 and 1400. Contemporary historians date the document at about A.D. 1450. It was conceived by Deganwidah, a man believed to be of non-Iroquoian ancestry, who traveled the southern shores of Lakes Erie and Ontario as well as up the St. Lawrence River with a Mohawk chief, Hiawatha (Hayewat-ha) in an attempt to bring peace to the warring tribes in the area. Hiawatha served as Deganwidah's spokesperson.

Colonial leaders became aware of the Iroquois Constitution during the French and Indian War from treaty and council meetings they attended with Iroquois tribes that had allied themselves with the British colonists, rather than the French. (See also MILITARY CONTRIBUTIONS.) Many scholars believe the Great Law was the longest international constitution until that time. The only possible exception to this was the unwritten English Constitution, which had its origins in the English Magna Carta. Certainly in fifteenth century Europe nothing existed to rival this American Indian constitution.

In July 1744 at a meeting between Indians and British in Pennsylvania, the Onondaga chief Canassatego aired a concern that his people had about the colonial system of government. He complained that it was virtually impossible for his Iroquois Confederacy to deal with the colonies. Each one had its own policy, administration, and way of doing things. He encouraged the colonies to form their own union, which would be stronger than the existing confederacy. He suggested that the colonists who drafted the document use the constitution of the Iroquois as an example.

## SIMILARITIES AND DIFFERENCES
## BETWEEN THE IROQUOIS CONSTITUTION
## AND THE U.S. CONSTITUTION

The Iroquois Constitution is much older than the U.S. Constitution and its amendments. Because the authors of the U.S. Constitution borrowed many principles from the Iroquois document, the two share many similarities. There are differences as well. The following chart uses portions of both constitutions to show how they are alike and different.

### HOUSE AND SENATE

**Iroquois Constitution**

"All the business of the Five Nations Confederate Council shall be conducted by the two combined bodies of Confederacy Lords. First the question shall be passed upon by the Mohawk and Seneca Lords, then it shall be discussed and passed by the Oneida and Cayuga Lords. Their decisions shall then be referred to the Onondaga Lords, (Fire Keepers) for final judgment." (Art. 9)

**U.S. Constitution**

"All legislative Powers herein granted shall be vested in a Congress of the United States, which shall consist of a Senate and House of Representatives." (Art. 1, Sec. 1)

### FILLING VACANCIES IN THE HOUSE AND SENATE

**Iroquois Constitution**

"When a Lordship title becomes vacant through death or other cause, the Royaneh women of the clan in which the title is hereditary shall hold a council and shall choose one from among their sons to fill the office made vacant. Such a candidate shall not be the father of any Confederate Lord. If the choice is unanimous the name is referred to the men relatives of the clan. If they should disapprove, it shall be their duty to select a candidate from among their own number. If then the men and women are unable to decide which of the two candidates shall be named, then the matter shall be referred to the Confederate Lords in the Clan. They shall decide which candidate shall be named. If the men and the women agree to a choice, they shall refer their action to their Confederate Lords who shall ratify the choice and present it to proper ceremony for the conferring of Lordship titles." (Art. 54.)

**U.S. Constitution**

"When vacancies happen in the Representation from any State, the Executive Authority thereof shall issue Writs of Election to fill such Vacancies." (Art. 1, Sec. 2)

### QUALIFICATIONS FOR SENATE

**Iroquois Constitution**

"The Lords of the Confederacy of the Five Nations shall be mentors of the people for all time. The thickness of their skin shall be seven spans—which is to say that they shall be proof against anger, offensive action and criticism. Their hearts shall be full of peace and good will and their minds filled with a yearning for the welfare of the people of the Confederacy. With endless patience they shall carry out their duty and their firmness shall be tempered with a tenderness for their people. Neither anger nor fury shall find lodgement in their minds and all their words and actions shall be marked by calm deliberation." (Art. 24)

**U.S. Constitution**

"No person shall be a Senator who shall not have attained to the Age of thirty Years, and be nine Years a Citizen of the United States, and who shall not, when elected, be an Inhabitant of that State for which he shall be chosen." (Art. 1, Sec. 3)

### WHEN CONGRESS SHALL MEET

**Iroquois Constitution**

"Every five years the Five Nations Confederate Lords and the people shall assemble together and shall ask one another if their minds are still in the same spirit of unity for the Great Binding Law and if any of the Five Nations shall not pledge continuance and steadfastness to the pledge of unity then the Great Binding Law shall dissolve." (Art. 4)

**U.S. Constitution**

"The Congress shall assemble at least once in every Year, and such Meeting shall be on the first Monday in December, unless they shall by Law appoint a different Day." (Art. 1, Sec. 4)

## RULES FOR HOUSES OF CONGRESS

### Iroquois Constitution

"If any Confederate Lord neglects or refuses to attend the Confederate Council, the other Lords of the Nation of which he is a member shall require their War Chief to request the female sponsors
of the Lord so guilty of defection to demand his attendance of the Council. If he refuses, the women holding the title shall immediately select another candidate for the title." (Art. 18)

"If a War Chief acts contrary to instructions or against the provisions of the Laws of the Great Peace, doing so in the capacity of his office, he shall be deposed by his women relatives and by his men relatives. Either the women or the men alone or jointly may act in such a case. The women title holders shall then choose another candidate." (Art. 39)

"No council of the Confederate Lords shall be legal unless all the Mohawk Lords are present." (Art. 6)

### U.S. Constitution

"Each House shall be the Judge of the Elections, Returns and Qualifications of its own Members, and a Majority of each shall constitute a Quorum to do Business; but a smaller Number may adjourn from day to day, and may be authorized to compel the Attendance of absent members, in such Manner, and under such Penalties as each House may provide.

Each House may determine the Rules of its Proceedings, punish its Members for disorderly Behavior, and, with the Concurrence of two-thirds, expel a Member.

. . . Neither House during the Session of Congress, shall without the Consent of the other, adjourn for more than three days, nor to any other Place than that in which the two Houses shall be sitting." (Art. 1, Sec. 5)

## FORBIDDING OF DUAL OFFICE

### Iroquois Constitution

". . . We do now crown you with the sacred emblem of the deer's antlers, the emblem of your Lordship. You shall now become a mentor of the people of the Five Nations. The thickness of your skin shall be seven spans—Which is to say that you shall be proof against anger, offensive actions and criticism. Your heart shall be filled with peace and good will and your mind filled with a yearning for the welfare of the people of the Confederacy. With endless patience you shall carry out your duty and your firmness shall be tempered with tenderness for your people. Neither anger nor fury shall find lodgement in your mind and all your words and actions shall be marked with calm deliberation. In all of your deliberations in the Confederate Council in your efforts at law making, in all your official acts, self interest shall be cast into oblivion. Cast not over your shoulder behind you the warnings of the nephews and nieces should they chide you for any error or wrong you may do, but return to the way of the Great Law which is just and right. Look and listen for the welfare of the whole people and have always in view not only the present but also the coming generations, even those whose faces are yet beneath the surface of the ground—the unborn of the future Nation." (Art. 28)

### U.S. Constitution

"No Senator or Representatives shall, during the Time for which he was elected, be appointed to any civil Office under the Authority of the United States, which shall have been created, or the Emoluments whereof shall have been increased during such time; and no Person holding any Office under the United States, shall be a member of either House during his Continuance in Office." (Art. 1, Sec. 6)

## THE PASSAGE OF LAWS

### Iroquois Constitution

"In all cases the procedure must be as follows: When the Mohawk and Seneca Lords have unanimously agreed upon a question, they shall report their decision to the Cayuga and Oneida Lords who shall deliberate upon the question and report a unanimous decision to the Mohawk Lords. The Mohawk Lords will then report the standing of the case to the Firekeepers, who shall render a decision as they see fit in case of a disagreement by the two bodies, or confirm decisions of the two bodies if they are identical. The Fire Keepers shall then report their decision to the Mohawk Lords who shall announce it to the open council." (Art. 10)

"If through any misunderstanding or obstinacy on the part of the Fire Keepers, they render a decision at variance with that of the Two Sides, the Two Sides shall reconsider the matter and if their decisions are jointly the same as before they shall report to the Fire Keepers who are then compelled to confirm their joint decision." (Art. 11).

### U.S. Constitution

". . . Every Bill which shall have passed the House of Representatives and the Senate, shall, before it become a Law, be presented to the President of the United States. If he approve he shall sign it, but if not he shall return it, with his Objections to that House in which it shall have originated, who shall enter the Objections at large on their Journal, and proceed to reconsider it. If after such Reconsideration two thirds of that House shall agree to pass the Bill, it shall be sent, together with the Objections at large, to the other House, by which it shall likewise be reconsidered, and if approved by two thirds of that House, it shall become a Law. But in all such Cases the Votes of both Houses shall be determined by yeas and Nays, and the Names of the Persons voting for and against the Bill shall be entered on the Journal of each House respectively. If any Bill shall not be returned by the President within ten Days (Sundays excepted) after it shall have been presented to him, the Same shall be a Law, in like Manner as if he had signed it, unless the Congress by their Adjournment prevent its Return, in which Case it shall not be Law. Every Order, Resolution, or Vote to which the Concurrence of the Senate and House of Representatives may be necessary (except on a question of Adjournment) shall be presented to the President of the United States; and before the Same shall take Effect, shall be approved by him, or being disapproved by him, shall be repassed by two thirds of the Senate and House of Representatives, according to the Rules and Limitations prescribed in the Case of a Bill." (Art. 1, Sec. 7)

## POWER TO DECLARE WAR

### Iroquois Constitution

"There shall be one War Chief for each Nation and their duties shall be to carry messages for their Lords and to take up the arms of war in case of emergency. They shall not participate in the proceedings of the Confederate Council but shall watch its progress and in case of an erroneous action by a Lord they shall receive the complaints of the people and convey the warnings of the women to him. The people who wish to convey messages to the Lords in the Confederate Council shall do so through the War Chief of their Nation. It shall ever be his duty to lay the cases, questions and propositions of the people before the Confederate Council." (Art. 37)

### U.S. Constitution

"The Congress shall have Power . . . to declare War, grant Letters of Marque and Reprisal, and make Rules concerning Captures on Land and Water." (Art. 1, Sec. 8)

## IMMIGRATION

### Iroquois Constitution

"The soil of the earth from one end of the land to the other is the property of the people who inhabit it. By birthright the Ongwehohwea (Original beings) are the owners of the soil which they own and occupy and none other may hold it. The same law has been held from the oldest times.

The Great Creator has made us of the one blood and of the same soil he made us and as only different tongues constitute different nations he established different hunting grounds and territories and made boundary lines between them." (Art. 73)

### U.S. Constitution

"The migration or Importation of such Persons as any of the States now existing shall think proper to admit, shall not be prohibited by the Congress prior to the Year one thousand eight hundred and eight, but a Tax or duty may be imposed on such Importation, not exceeding ten dollars for each Person." (Art. 1, Sec. 9)

## POWERS OF THE UNION VS. STATES

### Iroquois Constitution

"If a Lord of the Confederacy should seek to establish any authority independent of the jurisdiction of the Confederacy of the Great Peace, which is the Five Nations, he shall be warned three times in open council, first by the women relatives, second by the men relatives and finally by the Lords of the Confederacy of the Nation to which he belongs. If the offending Lord is still obdurate he shall be dismissed by the War Chief of his nation for refusing to conform to the laws of the Great Peace. His nation shall install the candidate nominated by the female nameholders of his family." (Art. 25)

### U.S. Constitution

"No state shall enter into any Treaty, Alliance, or Confederation; grant Letters of Marque and Reprisal; coin Money; emit Bills of Credit; make any Thing but gold and silver Coin a Tender in Payment of Debts; pass any Bill of Attainder, ex post facto Law, or Law impairing the Obligation of Contracts, or grant any Title of Nobility?" (Art. 1, Sec. 10)

## ADMISSION OF NEW STATES

### Iroquois Constitution

"When the Lords of the Confederacy decide to admit a foreign nation and an adoption is made, the Lords shall inform the adopted nation that its admission is only temporary. They shall also say to the nation that it must never try to control, to interfere with or to injure the Five Nations nor disregard the Great Peace or any of its rules or customs. That in no way should they cause disturbance or injury. Then should the adopted nation disregard these injunctions, their adoption shall be annulled and they shall be expelled." (Art. 77)

### U.S. Constitution

"New States may be admitted by the Congress into this Union; but no new State shall be formed or erected within the Jurisdiction of any other State; nor any State be formed by the Junction of two or more States, or Parts of States, without the Consent of the Legislatures of the States concerned as well as of the Congress." (Art. 4, Sec. 3)

## DUTIES TO THE FEDERAL GOVERNMENT

### Iroquois Constitution

"When a member of an alien nation comes to the territory of the Five Nations and seeks refuge and Permanent residence, the Lords of the Nations to which he comes shall extend hospitality and make him a member of the nation. Then shall he be accorded equal rights and privileges in all matters except as aforementioned." (Art. 75)

### U.S. Constitution

"The United States shall guarantee to every State in this Union a Republican Form of Government, and shall protect each of them against Invasion; and on Application of the Legislature, or of the Executive (when the Legislature cannot be convened), against domestic Violence." (Art. 4, Sec. 4)

## STATES RIGHTS

### Iroquois Constitution

"Whenever a specially important matter or a great emergency is presented before the Confederate Council and the nature of the matter affects the entire body of the Five Nations, threatening their utter ruin, then the Lords of the Confederacy must submit the matter to the decision of their people and the decision of the people shall affect the decision of the Confederate Council. This decision shall be a confirmation of the voice of the people." (Art. 20)

### U.S. Constitution

"The Citizens of each State shall be entitled to all Privileges and Immunities of Citizens in the several States." (Art. 4, Sec. 2)

## HOW LEADERS ARE SELECTED

### Iroquois Constitution

"Dekanawidah, appoint the Mohawk Lords the heads and the leaders of the Five Nations Confederacy. The Mohawk Lords are the foundation of the Great Peace and it shall, therefore, be against the Great Binding Law to pass measures in the Confederate Council after the Mohawk Lords have protested against them." (Art. 6)

### U.S. Constitution

"The executive Power shall be vested in a President to the United States of America. He shall hold his Office during the Term of four Years, and, together with the Vice President, chosen for the same Term, be elected as follows. . . ." (Art. 2, Sec. 1)

## QUALIFICATIONS FOR OFFICE OF PRESIDENT

### Iroquois Constitution

"No body of alien people who have been adopted temporarily shall have a vote in the council of the Lords of the Confederacy, for only they who have been invested with Lordship titles may vote in the council. Aliens have nothing by blood to make claim to a vote and should they have it, not knowing all the traditions of the Confederacy, might go against its Great Peace. In this manner the Great Peace would be endangered and perhaps destroyed." (Art. 76)

### U.S. Constitution

"No person except a natural born Citizen, or a Citizen of the United States, at the time of the Adoption of this Constitution, shall be eligible to the Office of the President; neither shall any Person be eligible to that Office who shall not have attained to the Age of thirty five Years and been fourteen years a resident within the United States." (Art. 2, Sec. 1)

## REMOVAL OF THE PRESIDENT FROM OFFICE/ IMPEACHMENT

### Iroquois Constitution

"If at any time it shall be manifest that a Confederate Lord has not in mind the welfare of the people or disobeys the rules of this Great Law, the men or women of the Confederacy, or both jointly, shall come to the Council and upbraid the erring Lord through his War Chief. If the complaint of the people through the War Chief is not heeded the first time it shall be uttered again and then if no attention is given a third complaint and warning shall be given. If the Lord is contumacious, the matter shall go to the council of War Chiefs. The War Chiefs shall then divest the erring Lord of his title by order of the women in whom their War Chief, and the Confederate Lords shall sanction the act. The women will then select another of their sons as a candidate and the Lords shall elect him. Then shall the chosen one be installed by the Installation Ceremony."(19)

"The expulsion shall be in the following manner: The council shall appoint one of their War Chiefs to convey the message of annulment and he shall say, "You (naming the nation) listen to me while I speak. I am here to inform you again of the will of the Five Nations' Council. It was clearly made known to you at a former time. Now the Lords of the Five Nations have decided to expel you and cast you out. We disown you now and annul your adoption. Therefore you must look for a path in which to go and lead away all your people. It was you, not we, who committed wrong and caused this sentence of annulment. So then go your way and depart from the territory of the Five Nations and from the Confederacy." (Art. 77)

### U.S. Constitution

"In Case of the Removal of the President from Office, or of his Death, Resignation, or Inability to discharge the Powers and Duties of the said Office, the Same shall devolve on the Vice President, and the Congress may by Law provide for the Case of Removal, Death, Resignation or Inability, both of the President and Vice President, declaring what Officer shall then act as President, and such Officer shall act accordingly, until the Disability be removed, or a President shall be elected?" (Art. 2, Sec. 1)

"The President, Vice President and all civil Officers of the United States, shall be removed from Office on Impeachment for, and Conviction of, Treason, Bribery, or other high Crimes and Misdemeanors." (Art. 2, Sec. 4)

## PRESIDENT AS COMMANDER IN CHIEF

### Iroquois Constitution

"Skanawatih shall be vested with a double office, duty and with double authority. One-half of his being shall hold the Lordship title and the other half shall hold the title of War Chief. In the event of war he shall notify the five War Chiefs of the Confederacy and command them to prepare for war and have their men ready at the appointed time and place for engagement with the enemy of the Great Peace." (Art. 79)

### U.S. Constitution

"The President shall be Commander in Chief of the Army and Navy of the United States, and of the Militia of the several States, when called into the actual Service of the United States; he may require the Opinion, in writing, of the principal Officer in each of the executive Departments, upon any Subject relating to the Duties of their respective Offices, and he shall have Power to grant Reprieves and Pardons for Offences against the United States, except in Cases of Impeachment." (Art. 2, Sec. 2)

## STATE OF THE UNION ADDRESS

### Iroquois Constitution

"It shall be the duty of the Lords of each brotherhood to confer at the approach of the time of the Midwinter Thanksgiving and to notify their people of the approaching festival. They shall hold a council over the matter and arrange its details and begin the Thanksgiving five days after the moon of Disko-nah is new. The people shall assemble at the appointed place and the nephews shall notify the people of the time and place. From the beginning to the end the Lords shall preside over the Thanksgiving and address the people from time to time." (Art. 100)

### U.S. Constitution

"He [the President] shall from time to time give to the Congress Information of the State of the Union, and recommend to their Consideration such Measures as he shall judge necessary and expedient; he may, on extraordinary Occasions, convene both Houses, or either of them, and in Case of Disagreement between them, with Respect to the Time of Adjournment, he may adjourn them to such time as he shall think proper; he shall receive Ambassadors and other public Ministers; he shall take Care that the Laws be faithfully executed, and shall Commission all the Officers of the United States." (Art. 2, Sec. 3)

## TREASON

### Iroquois Constitution

"If a nation, part of a nation, or more than one nation within the Five Nations should in any way endeavor to destroy the Great Peace by neglect or violating its laws and resolve to dissolve the Confederacy, such a nation or such nations shall be deemed guilty of treason and called enemies of the Confederacy and the Great Peace." (Art. 92)

### U.S. Constitution

"Treason against the United States, shall consist only in levying War against them, or in adhering to their Enemies, giving them Aid and Comfort. No Person shall be convicted of Treason unless on the Testimony of two Witnesses to the same overt Act, or on Confession in open Court." (Art. 3, Sec. 3)

## AUTHORITY OF THE FEDERAL GOVERNMENT

### Iroquois Constitution

"Five Arrows shall be bound together very strong and each arrow shall represent one nation. As the five arrows are strongly bound this shall symbolize the complete union of the nations. Thus are the Five Nations united completely and enfolded together, united into one head, one body and one mind. Therefore they shall labor, legislate and council together for the interest of future generations." (Art. 57)

### U.S. Constitution

"This Constitution, and the Laws of the United States which shall be made in Pursuance thereof; and all Treaties made, or which shall be made, under the Authority of the United States, shall be the supreme Law of the Land; and the Judges in every State shall be bound thereby, any Thing in the Constitution or Laws of any State to the Contrary notwithstanding." (Art. 6)
Constitution

## CONSTITUTIONAL AMENDMENTS

### Iroquois Constitution

"If the conditions which shall arise at any future time call for an addition to or change in this law, the case shall be carefully considered and if a new beam seems necessary or beneficial, the proposed change shall be voted upon and if adopted it shall be called, 'Added to the Rafters.'" (Art. 16)

### U.S. Constitution

"The Congress, whenever two thirds of both Houses shall deem it necessary, shall propose Amendments to this Constitution, or, on the Application of the Legislatures of two thirds of the several States, shall call a Convention for proposing Amendments, which, in either Case shall be valid to all Intents and Purposes, as Part of this Constitution, when ratified by the Legislatures of three fourths of the Several States, or by Conventions in three fourths thereof, as the one or the other Mode of Ratification may be proposed by the Congress; Provided as the one or the other Mode of Ratification may be proposed by the Congress; Provided that no Amendment which may be made prior to the Year One thousand eight hundred and eight shall in any Manner affect the first and fourth Clauses in the Ninth Section of the first Article; and that no State, without its Consent, shall be deprived of its equal Suffrage in the Senate." (Art. 5)

## CONSTITUTION AS SUPREME LAW OF THE LAND

### Iroquois Constitution

"Before the real people united their nations, each nation had its council fires. Before the Great Peace their councils were held. The five Council Fires shall continue to burn as before and they are not quenched. The Lords of each nation in future shall settle their nation's affairs at this council fire governed always by the laws and rules of the council of the Confederacy and by The Great Peace." (Art. 25)

### U.S. Constitution

"The Ratification of the Conventions of nine States, shall be sufficient for the Establishment of this Constitution between the States so ratifying the Same." (Art. 7)

## FREEDOM OF RELIGION, SPEECH, AND THE PRESS

**Iroquois Constitution**

"The rites and festivals of each nation shall remain undisturbed and shall continue as before because they were given by the people of old times as useful and necessary for the good of men." (Art. 99)

**U.S. Constitution**

"Congress shall make no law respecting an establishment of religion, or prohibiting the free exercise thereof, or abridging the freedom of speech, or of the press; or the right of the people peaceably to assemble, and to petition the Government for a redress of grievances." (Amend. 1)

## NO UNAUTHORIZED ENTRY INTO HOMES

**Iroquois Constitution**

"A certain sign shall be known to all the people of the Five Nations which shall denote that the owner or occupant of a house is absent. A stick or pole in a slanting or leaning position shall indicate this and be the sign. Every person not entitled to enter the house by right of living within it upon seeing such a sign shall not approach the house either by day or by night but shall keep as far away as his business will permit." (Art. 107)

**U.S. Constitution**

"No soldier, shall, in time of peace be quartered in any house, without the consent of the Owner, not in time of war, but in a manner to be prescribed by law." (Amend. 3)

## VACANCIES IN SENATE AND HOUSE

**Iroquois Constitution**

"A bunch of a certain number of shell (wampum) strings each two spans in length shall be given to each of the female families in which the Lordship titles are vested. The right of bestowing the title shall be hereditary in the family of the females legally possessing the bunch of shell strings and the strings shall be the token that the females of the family have the proprietary right to the Lordship title for all time to come, subject to certain restrictions, hereinafter mentioned." (Art. 17)

**U.S. Constitution**

"When vacancies happen in the representation of any State in the Senate, the executive authority of such State shall issue writs of election to fill such vacancies: *Provided,* That the legislature of any State may empower the executive thereof to make temporary appointments until the people fill the vacancies by election as the legislature may direct." (Amend. 16)

The Iroquois Constitution prevented government interference in everyone's daily lives and enhanced individual freedom. It also separated the civilian government from military and religious affairs; allowed many different religions and faiths to coexist; and recognized the importance of one's religious belief, no matter what its content or origin. Section 99 of the Iroquois Constitution stated outright the guarantee of religious freedom: "[t]he rites and festivals [religious practices] of each nation shall remain undisturbed and shall continue as before because they were given by the people of old times as useful and necessary for the good of men."

Benjamin Franklin became familiar with the Iroquois political system and its leaders as the official Pennsylvania colony printer. In that capacity he printed the minutes of their meetings. As a result of this, he began to develop an interest in Indians. The Pennsylvania colony asked him to be their first Indian commissioner. This became Franklin's first diplomatic job, a position he held through the 1750s. From that time he became a staunch advocate of the Iroquois Constitution. In 1754 he asked colonial delegates at the Albany Congress to follow the example of the Iroquois and their constitution. They ignored his advice for some 30 years.

As his contact with the League of the Iroquois continued, Franklin became convinced of the uniqueness and genius of their government compared to those of Europe. He recognized that the Iroquois Constitution contained many features absent in other governments at the time, including a ban on the forced entry by the government into citizen's homes, the freedom of political and religious expression, recall and impeachment of corrupt leaders, and the insurance that elected officials were never masters but remained servants of their constituents. Impressed by the Iroquois model, he publicly advocated that a federal union of the colonies be based on the principles of their constitution. Thomas Jefferson also acknowledged that he preferred the American Indian concept of liberty over the European monarchy system. (However, the colonial leaders did not completely agree with the Iroquois provisions for the fair distribution of wealth or participation of women in politics, concepts that would later be adopted by Frederick Engels in his blueprint for communism and socialism.)

At the Albany convention that convened in 1754, the colonists were faced with the task of forging an agreement that would retain them to retain their individuality and at the same time operate as a unified whole. James de Lancy, the acting governor of New York, invited Tiyanoga, an Iroquois leader, to inform the delegates about the structure of the Iroquois Confederacy. At the two-week convention's end Benjamin Franklin was requested to write a formal plan based on the discussion that had occurred there.

When he later presented his plan, which would form the basis for the Articles of Confederation, he expressed admiration for the Iroquois form of government, pointing out "the strength of the League which has bound our Friends the Iroquois together in a common tie which no crisis, however grave, since its foundation has managed to disrupt."

In fact, Franklin's plan contained many of the core concepts in the Iroquois Constitution, including how power would be wielded and ceded and how each colony would maintain sovereignty and at the same time retain an equitable federal union that would operate in a just manner for all parties involved. The influence of the Iroquois was evident in the Articles of Confederation that were ratified in 1781 and later the U.S. Constitution, which grew out of these articles.

The story of the influence of the Iroquois Constitution on the founding fathers and the United States Constitution is one that is still not generally known. On September 16, 1987, the U.S. Senate passed a resolution officially stating that the U.S. Constitution was modeled after the Iroquois Constitution, the Great Law of Peace. In truth, without the Iroquois, the U.S. government might be far different.

See also SOCIALIST THEORY, AMERICAN INDIAN INFLUENCE ON.

**Sources/Further Reading**

Barrero, Jose, ed. *Indian Roots of American Democracy.* Ithaca, New York: Cornell University Press, 1992.

Brandon, William. *The Last Americans: The Indian in American Culture.* New York: McGraw-Hill, 1974.

Grinde, Donald and Bruce Johansen. *Exemplar of Liberty: Native America and the Evolution of Democracy.* Los Angeles: American Indian Studies, UCLA, 1991.

Miller, Robert J. "American Indian Influence on the United States Constitution and its Framers." *American Indian Law Review* 18 (1993): 133–160.

Weatherford, Jack. *Indian Givers: How the Indians of the Americas Transformed the World.* New York: Fawcett Columbine, 1988.

**urban development**  See CITIES, AMERICA'S FIRST.

**urban planning** (ca. 1700 B.C.)  *North American Southeast, South American Andean, Mesoamerican cultures*
Urban planning involves the design of cities to improve quality of life. Some of the issues that urban planners must take into account are population density, transportation, environmental issues, and sanitation. Many of the earliest cities throughout the Americas showed evidence of urban design. (See also CITIES, AMERICAS'S FIRST.) The planning that went into these urban environments rivaled and often surpassed that of the Old World.

The Olmec, whose culture arose in what is now the Yucatán Peninsula of Mesoamerica in about 1700 B.C., were among the first to plan their cities. They apparently chose the sites based on their cosmological beliefs. Once they had chosen a city site, they cleared the land and began building temples and PYRAMIDS. Olmec cities were laid out around a central plaza that contained religious and administrative buildings. (See also CIVIC CENTERS.) In order to ensure that water was readily available, city administrators had it piped into the communities through basalt AQUEDUCTS. These aqueducts were entirely enclosed in stone so that the water remained fresh. (See also PLUMBING.) Because the Olmec had few natural resources, they had to develop TRADE routes to and from their communities. (See also ROAD SYSTEMS.) According to author and archaeology professor, Brian M. Fagan, "The countless inter-village paths and trade routes carried tropical foods, animal pelts, and feathers to the highlands had come into being centuries before the Olmec." The Olmec improved these and adapted them to their own needs.

The Maya, whose culture began to flourish in approximately the same area of Mesoamerica in about 1500 B.C., utilized much of what they learned from the Olmec and greatly refined their urban planning skills. Many authorities credit the Maya with building and developing one of the finest precontact civilizations in the Americas. They were excellent mathematicians (see also BASE 20 MATHEMATICAL SYSTEM), astronomers (see also ASTRONOMY), engineers, and ARCHITECTS; the architects were under the control of the nobles. As the Olmec did, the Maya built central plazas and courts. They also built their OBSERVATORIES in a central location and added residences situated around these. Most buildings and streets in Maya communities were aligned geometrically according to Maya cosmological beliefs and astronomical references. They selected the sites for their cities according to these criteria as well. As a result, they were not always located near natural resources, which meant that the Maya had to develop water and transportation systems. They built dams to conserve water for the dry times of the year, and their stone and plaster houses were built on graded plaster pavements so that water would drain into cisterns when it rained. (See also WATER CONSERVATION.) The roofs of these houses were constructed in similar fashion. Each house had its own water tank or reservoir for personal use. The Maya also transported solid wastes to designated areas for burial. (See also PLUMBING.)

The Aztec, who established an empire in what is now Mexico in about A.D. 1100, were also great urban planners who learned from their predecessors and improved on it. The Aztec constructed their cities around plazas. Aztec urban planners focused on the area of sanitation, building sophisticated aqueducts to provide water to the households for personal use. These aqueducts supplied water year-round. The Aztec also found another method for dealing with water and solid wastes. Certain merchants sold fresh drinking water; others were responsible for transporting solid wastes out of the community. The government hired at least 1,000 workers to keep the cities clean. They also built causeways over swamps to improve transportation in and out of the city.

In South America the Inca, who established an empire in about A.D. 1000, also built plazas around which the rest of the city arose. The Inca who lived high in the Andes Mountains were able to utilize their environment in a remarkable way. Since many of their cities were erected on mountaintops, they built terraces along the sides of the mountains for agricultural purposes. This increased the small amount of land available for farming. (See also AGRICULTURE; FARMING, TERRACED.) The terraces were stepped so that when one area was watered, the excess would run onto the next terrace. They also built aqueducts that were stone-lined and carried fast-moving water throughout the community. Such aqueducts were built in the center of each street and were very efficient in providing water to each resident.

The Inca were masters at public works and specialized in building roads. During their empire they built over 140,000 miles of roads made of stone and plaster across highlands and lowlands. They also built way stations, or rest stops, along their roads and stocked them with supplies from food to weapons. These way stations also provided sleeping rooms for travelers. Inca urban planners also built many BRIDGES to make travel easier. According to archaeologist Victor W. Von Hagen, the Inca built hanging bridges hundreds of years before the Europeans.

Like the Mesoamericans, the Hopewell, whose culture arose in the river bottomland of the North American Midwest in about 300 B.C., laid their cities out using astronomical events to align streets and buildings. Although they did not build pyramids, as the Maya and Olmec did, they did construct enormous mounds of earth that required the cooperation of the entire community to complete. Households were grouped around small plazas that defined neighborhoods. Each neighborhood contained a sweat lodge (see also STEAM ROOMS) and a community meeting hall, as well as community storage buildings.

The Anasazi of the North American Southwest, whose culture arose in about 350 B.C., also showed evidence of urban planning in their cities. Most of their pueblos (the Spanish word for towns) are laid out in an east-to-west direction. Pueblos tended to be built as a collection of units, standardized groups of 15 or so dwellings or workrooms, a plaza, and a kiva (a round ceremonial structure). In order to ensure the city's survival, the Anasazi built check dams in order to provide water for washing and drinking. (See also IRRIGATION SYSTEMS.) They made farming terraces, roads, and towers that some archaeologists believe may have been signaling stations. According to landscape architect Jon Bryan Burley, the urban planning of the Anasazi may provide answers for problems that plague urban planners today: ". . . the Anasazi and existing Puebloan cultures present a lifestyle that has relevance to the development of a global community. The Puebloan lifestyle is an example, acting as precedent, illustrating how a diverse set of Paleo-Indians adopted some common conventions to survive in a resource limited biosphere."
See also STONEMASONRY TECHNIQUES.

## Sources/Further Reading

Adams, Richard E. W. "Rio Azul. Lost City of the Maya." *National Geographic* 169, no. 4 (April 1986): 420–450.

Benson, Elizabeth P. *The Maya World.* New York: Thomas Y. Crowell Company, 1967.

Bankes, George. *Peru Before Pizarro.* Oxford: Phaidon Press Limited, 1977.

Burley, Jon Bryan. *Anasazi Site Planning: Historic Precedents, Modern Constructs, and Multicultural Dynamics.* URL: http://www.ssc.msu/edu/~lacj/historypapers/Burley3/. Downloaded on September 24, 1999.

Fagan, Brian M. *Kingdoms of Gold, Kingdoms of Jade: The Americas Before Columbus.* London: Thames And Hudson, Ltd., 1991.

Iseminger, William. "Mighty Cahokia." *Archaeology* (May/June 1996): 30–37.

Schele, Linda and David Freidel. *A Forest of Kings: The Untold Story of the Ancient Maya.* New York: William Morrow And Company, Inc., 1990.

Stuart, George E. and Gene S. Stuart. *The Mysterious Maya.* Washington, D.C.: National Geographic Society, 1977.

Townsend, Richard F. *The Aztecs.* London: Thames And Hudson, Ltd., 1992.

von Hagen, Victor W. *Realm of the Inca.* New York: The New American Library, 1957.

———. *The Royal Road of the Inca.* London: Gordon Cremonesi Ltd., 1976.

**vanilla** (precontact) *Mesoamerican cultures*
Vanilla is a flavoring extract made from the bean of one of two species of orchid plants, also called vanilla, indigenous to Mesoamerica. The first variety (*Vanilla planifolia* or *V. fragrans*) is the most commonly used. The second (*V. pompana Schiede*) is cultivated less often because the flavor that its beans produce is not as well liked today. Vanilla vines, which thrive in a hot, moist climate, climb to a height of several feet, using trees as supports. The plants flower once a year. The seedpods that are produced when the flower dies form the basis of vanilla. Looking somewhat like a string bean, they contain millions of seeds. American Indians were the first to discover the flavorful properties of these two varieties out of over 90 varieties of orchids and to domesticate them. They cultivated vanilla and pollinated the flowers by hand. Today vanilla is primarily used as a flavoring for desserts.

Just as cacao must be processed before it becomes CHOCOLATE, vanilla beans must be cured to bring out their vanillin, the essential oil that produces the flavor. The indigenous people of Mesoamerica discovered this four-step process. First, they wilted the beans to begin the enzyme-producing reactions that provide the flavor. Next, they heated the beans to speed the flavor production and prevent them from fermenting or rotting. This also turned the pods their characteristic dark brown color. Next, they dried the pods at room temperature. Finally, they conditioned them by putting them in closed BOXES for about three months.

The Aztec, whose empire was established in what is now Mexico in about A.D. 1100, called ground vanilla beans *tlilxochitl*, which means "black pods." They used vanilla to flavor *chocolatl*, a drink made from the roasted and ground seeds of the CACAO tree. Vanilla beans were so valued that they were one of the ways in which common people paid tribute to the Aztec emperors. (See also TAX SYSTEMS.)

The first Spaniards to write about Mesoamerica, including Bernal Diaz and Bernardino de Sahagun, described vanilla. The latter, a Fransciscan friar, wrote in 1529 that in addition to being used to flavor chocolate drinks, the flavoring was sold in the marketplaces. Although the Spaniards imported vanilla beans to Europe, where they were used to flavor chocolate, which the Spaniards also borrowed from the Aztec, vanilla-processing factories were not established in Europe until the late 1700s. Before this time Europeans did not understand the steps required to make the pods and seeds taste and smell like vanilla. The curing process was kept secret by the indigenous people of what by then had become Veracruz, Mexico.

Europeans used vanilla for medicinal purposes, valuing it as a nerve stimulant. They also believed it was an aphrodisiac, perhaps because of the name the Spaniards had given the plant, *vaina,* which meant both "pod" and "vagina." Europeans used vanilla to flavor TOBACCO, another plant they adopted from American Indians, and a flavoring for food. Vanilla extract, an alcohol-based flavoring, was not invented until 1847. The flavor became such an integral part of European cooking that in 1921 the Academy of Sciences and Gastronomic Arts in Paris honored the ancient American Indians who had discovered the orchids from which vanilla favoring comes and the process for making it.

By the mid-1800s vanilla was introduced to Indonesia. Today it is grown in tropical countries throughout the world. Madagascar produces large amounts of vanilla, but the largest crop of vanilla comes from the state of Veracruz in Mexico, where the plants continue to be grown by the Totonac Indian people.

**Sources/Further Reading**
Coe, Sophie. *America's First Cuisines.* Austin: University of Texas Press, 1994.

King, Steven R., Ph.D. *Foods That Changed the World. Ethnobotany.* URL: http://www.accessexcellence.org/RC/Ethnobotany. October 3, 1999.

Shanks Extracts—History of Vanilla. URL: http:/www.shanks.com/aboutvanilla/history.htm. Downloaded on October 3, 1999.

Weatherford, Jack. *Indian Givers: How the Indians of the Americas Transformed the World.* New York: Fawcett Columbine, 1988.

**vegetable tanning** See TANNING, BRAIN.

**ventilation systems** (ca. 1000 B.C.–200 B.C.) *South American Andean cultures*

A ventilation system is designed to convey air through ducts or shafts. The precontact Chavin people, whose culture flourished in what is now Peru from about 1000 B.C. to about 200 B.C., were one of the first American Indian cultures to build ventilation systems in their buildings. They built PYRAMIDS and what archaeologists believe to be ceremonial buildings in the northern Peruvian highlands. The most notable of these buildings is called the Castillo (castle) because of its resemblance to a castle. This building, made of cut stone (see also STONEMASONRY TECHNIQUES) and built without windows or chimney holes, was approximately 235 feet by 235 feet square and 45 feet high. It had three stories and contained ramps, stairs, rooms, galleries, a maze of walls, and a unique ventilating system composed of horizontal and vertical ducts built into the solid stone. This system still conveys fresh air throughout the Chavin temple today.

**Sources/Further Reading**

Mason, J. Alden. *The Ancient Civilizations of Peru.* Rev. ed. New York: Penguin Books, 1988.

Willey, Gordon R. *An Introduction to American Archaeology, Volume Two: South America.* Englewood Cliffs, N.J.: Prentice-Hall, Inc., 1971.

**vicunas (Viguna vicugna)** (precontact) *South American Andean cultures*

Vicunas, mammals indigenous to South America are the smallest members of the Camelidae family and are related to LLAMAS and ALPACAS. Weighing between 75 and 140 pounds, vincunas are adapted to high altitudes, living at about 12,000 feet above sea level at the snow line of the Andes. Although vicunas were not domesticated, as llamas and alpacas were, they are believed to be the wild progenator of the alpaca, which American Indians selectively bred beginning about 4000 B.C. Vicunas served as a food source and provided fur for indigenous people living in the central Andean region of South America for thousands of years. Today garments woven from vicuna fiber are considered luxury items throughout the world.

Vicuna fiber is long, fine, soft, and lustrous. The underbellies of vicunas are white, and the upper body varies from a reddish yellow to a deep tan to a reddish brown in color. Because of their superior fiber qualities, they were highly valued by indigenous Americans of the Andes, who used them in their textiles. (See also WEAVING TECHNIQUES.) Vicuna hunts, which were held annually, were community endeavors among these people. Since vicunas have excellent eyesight and are fast runners, they were easily able to elude solo hunters. Hundreds of people would turn out to frighten vicuna herds into rope traps. Once they had trapped the animals, they killed the older and younger vicunas for their fur and meat while shearing animals of breeding age with obsidian blades. (See also FLINTKNAPPING.) After the shearing, they set them free to reproduce. The Inca, who established an empire in what is now Peru in about A.D. 1000, called these vicuna hunts *chacu* in Quecha, their language. Only the Inca nobility were allowed to wear cloth made from vicuna fleece. Commoners caught wearing such garments were executed.

After conquest, wealthy Europeans began wearing the lightweight, soft, and warm coats and scarves made from vicuna fiber. By the 1960s poaching, spurred by high prices paid for vicuna fleece, nearly caused the vicunas' extinction; their numbers dwindled from the millions to about 10,000. As a result the animals were placed on the endangered species list. In 1979 the governments of Argentina, Bolivia, Chile, Ecuador, and Peru developed an agreement for vicuna management and conservation, called the Vicuna Convention, prohibiting international trade in raw wool. Trade in finished garments and textiles made from vicuna fibers was still allowed, providing the articles were marked with proof that the wool was obtained from live animals. Because of these efforts, the vicuna population had grown to about 100,000 by 1992. At the same time the herds were growing, indigenous people in Peru, unable to hunt and sheer vicuna, endured extreme poverty. In 1993 the government, in conjunction with Grupo Inca, a Peruvian textile mill, reinstituted the *chacu* system without the butchering. In 1998 nearly 200 *chacus* were held throughout Peru. A typical harvest of fleece from one vicuna is four ounces, making it the world's most expensive animal fiber. Today vicuna wool brings about $225 a pound in the world market.

**Sources/Further Reading**

Coe, Sophie. *America's First Cuisines.* Austin: University of Texas Press, 1994.

Hoffman. Vicunas: Bearers of the Golden Fleece. URL: http://www.bonnydoonalpacas.org/vicunart.htm. Downloaded on November 5, 1999.

Salmoral, Manuel Lucena. *America 1492: Portrait of a Continent 500 Years Ago.* New York: Facts On File, 1990.

Species Fact Sheets—Defenders of Wildlife. URL: http://www.defenders.org/cfacvicu.html. Downloaded on November 5, 1999.

**vinegar** See AGAVE.

**vitamin C** See SCURVY CURE.

**vitamins** See NUTRITION.

**vulcanization** (ca. 1700 B.C.) *Mesoamerican cultures*
Vulcanization is the process of adding chemicals to LATEX in order to make the sap that is obtained from the rubber tree (*Hevea brasiliensus*) easier to shape into objects. Vulcanization also ensures that these objects will keep their shape in warm temperatures and will not crack in cold ones. The Olmec, whose culture arose in the Yucatán Peninsula of what is now Mexico in about 1700 B.C., were the first people in the world to make rubber from both *Hevea brasiliensus* and a variety of the SAPODILLA tree (*Manilkara zapota van Royen*). The Olmec made many objects from rubber, including BALLS, SANDALS, waterproofed PONCHOS, TARPAULINS, BALLOONS, and hollow rubber bulbs for SYRINGES that were used to administer medicine. In order to accomplish this, they devised a way to process latex, very similar to that patented by chemist Charles Goodyear in 1844. (He added sulfur to latex to produce the same effect that the Olmec did.)

To cure the rubber, the Olmec built a fire of palm nuts. The smoke from these nuts, most often from the uricuri palm, contained acetic acid and phenols that cured the rubber. Next they built a funnel-shaped chimney over the fire to concentrate the smoke. They made objects such as waterproof shoes or bottles by holding a clay form in the smoke and carefully pouring latex over it until 20 to 25 thin coats had been applied.

They varied the proportions of the mixture depending on what the rubber was to be used for. If the rubber was to be made into hard game balls, then they added more phenols and acetic acid to the sap. If the rubber was to be used for WATERPROOFING, less of these chemicals was mixed with the latex sap so that it remained softer and more liquid. Today, especially in the Amazonian area of South America, some indigenous people still make rubber by hand. They mix the sulfur and latex sap and pour it over a stick being held over a heat source. When it is cool enough to handle, workers form the rubber into blocks for selling or trade.

Charles Goodyear experimented for 10 years before stumbling on the process of adding sulfur to rubber that is called vulcanization today. First he added nitrate, but that did not work. Then he purchased the right to use sulfur to treat latex from another inventor who had begun experiments with that chemical. By accident, Goodyear spilled the mixture on a hotplate and discovered a process American Indians had known about for thousands of years. Before that time rubber items were primarily curiosities in Europe and the United States because they melted in warm temperatures.

## Sources/Further Reading

Coe, Michael D. *Mexico from the Olmecs to the Aztecs.* London: Thames and Hudson, 1994.

Stern, Theodore. *The Rubber-Ball Games of the Americas. Monographs of the American Ethnological Society, No. 17.* New York: J. J. Austin, 1950.

Stuart, George E. "New Light on the Olmec." *National Geographic* 184, no. 5 (November 1993): 88–114.

# W

**wahoo (*Evonymus atropurpurea*)** (precontact) *(North American Great Plains and Northeast cultures*

Wahoo is a shrub found along the rivers from Montana to the eastern United States. It grows in moist areas, especially in open-wooded places. American Indians used wahoo for several purposes, but its most valuable use was as a heart medication based on the plant's digitalis-like effect. American Indians of the Northeast and Great Plains of North America prepared wahoo by boiling the bark in water to make a tea that, when drunk, worked to increase the heart's effectiveness by increasing the strength of its contractions. This improved the circulation and urinary output. Wahoo also served as a treatment for edema (swelling due to fluid retention) and congestive heart failure. Winnebago (Ho-Chunk) women used wahoo for problems associated with the uterus. North American Indians introduced wahoo to the early European colonists, who adopted and used it as a diuretic and a heart medication. (American hemp and DOGBANE, two other botanical remedies used by North American Indians, exert a similar action on the heart.) See also HEMP, AMERICAN.

## Sources/Further Reading

Hutchens, Alma R. *Indian Herbology of North America.* Boston: Shambhala, 1991.

Lust, John. *The Herb Book.* New York: Bantam Books, 1974.

Vogel, Virgil. *American Indian Medicine.* Norman: University of Oklahoma Press, 1970.

Weiner, Michael A. *Earth Medicine Earth Food: The Classic Guide to the Herbal Remedies and Wild Plants of the North American Indians.* New York: Fawcett Columbine, 1980.

**wampum** (A.D. 200) *North American Northeast cultures*

*Wampum* is a Narragansett world for shell beads. The Algonquian-speaking tribes of the North American Northeast who strung these beads or wove them into belts used them for several purposes. Wampum belts served as a way to record agreements and to bind truth to the oral understandings that had been made. One such belt symbolized the founding of the Iroquois Confederacy, and as such it was considered sacred. This confederacy was a formal alliance between the Oneida, Onondaga, Mohawk, Cayuga, and the Seneca. (They were later joined by the Tuscarora.) At times American Indians also used wampum as a way to send messages. After contact, wampum also functioned as a medium of exchange, or MONEY.

To make wampum, Indians gathered spiral shells during the summer. They cut the spirals into cylinders about an eighth of an inch in diameter and a quarter of an inch long. They then ground the quahog, whelk, or mussel shells to shapes, polished them; and drilled the centers with stone drill bits. Wampum makers made two colors of beads—white and purple Quahog shells were scarcer than whelk shells; thus when wampum was used as currency in postcontact times, purple beads were generally assigned twice the value as white beads. When wampum was used to record agreements or send messages, these beads were woven into a belt or a sash on a bow LOOM. Wampum belt makers used sinew and plant fiber for the warps and wefts.

Although some authors claim that the Iroquois were the first to make wampum beads and string or weave them, it is more likely to be the Narragansett, since they lived near the coastline while the Iroquois lived inland. The oldest wampum beads found by archaeologists in northeastern North America were made in about 2500 B.C. While some historians believe that older wampum belt in existence today is one made by the Micmac Nation and given to the Catholic Church to symbolize the concordance between the Holy See and the Indian people (it is kept in the Vatican today), another wampum belt may actually be older. It is the Hiawatha Belt, which was created to memorialize the creation of the Iroquois League, or Haudenosaunee. (See also UNITED STATES CONSTITUTION,

AMERICAN INDIAN INFLUENCE ON; IROQUOIS CONSTITU-
TION.) The constitution of the Iroquois League was recited orally
but was also recorded on a series of wampum belts. (See also
AMERICAN HISTORY, RECORDED.)

The Iroquois Constitution explained the meaning of one
of the belts: "A bunch of wampum shells on strings, three spans
of a hand in length, the upper half of the bunch being white
and the lower half black [purple], and formed from equal contributions of the men of the Five Nations, shall be a token that
the men have combined them into one head, one body and one
thought and it shall also symbolize their ratification of the
peace pact of the Confederacy, whereby the Lords of the Five
Nations have established the Great Peace." In this particular
belt, the white shells represented the women and the dark shells
represented the men.

Another famous wampum belt is the Covenant Chain Belt,
which recorded a 1794 treaty between the 13 colonies that made
up the new U.S. government and the six nations that made up the
Iroquois League of nations (the Tuscarora had become the sixth
nation in 1722. This agreement was called the Covenant Chain.)
The belt that commemorated it is called the Great Chain. Figures representing the colonies and the League are depicted holding a wampum belt, symbolizing that the agreement was
permanent and could not be broken. When wampum belts such
as these were used to convey messages, they were carried from village to village by runners. (See also RUNNING.) In good messages, white beads predominated. If the news were solemn or
sorrowful, most of the beads on the belt were purple.

The European colonists quickly adopted wampum as a
form of currency in their trade with American Indians and with
each other, since metal coins were scarce in the early colonies.

Once the colonists introduced metal DRILL BITS to the Northeast tribes, the Narragansett and Pequot began mass-produc-
ing wampum beads. Mohican and Mohawk people served as
wampum brokers throughout this time, trading the beads to
tribes in the west and the north. (See also TRADE.) Wampum,
the first currency in North America, remained legal tender in
the colonies until the late 1600s. On the frontiers, it was used
until the mid-1700s. The strung beads were measured in six-
foot lengths called fathoms. These were assigned value in terms
of British currency.

Colonists were not above counterfeiting wampum by
dying white shell beads purple to double their value, a practice
some Indians took up as well. So common was counterfeiting
that colonial governments passed laws to control the manufacture of wampum and establish penalties for counterfeiting it.
Some colonists protected themselves against being cheated by
accepting only white wampum. At the end of the 1600s, silver
money began to slowly replace wampum. By the start of the
French and Indian War in the mid-1700s, American Indian demand for wampum had decreased and, fearing economic col-
lapse, the colonies made a concerted effort to coin metal
money.

## Sources/Further Reading

Federici, Richard and Elaine. *Wampum—America's First Currency.* URL: http://www.mohicanpress.com/mo08017.
html. Downloaded on October 22, 1999.

Giese, Paula. *Wampum Treaties, Sacred Records.* URL:
http://indy4.fdl.cc.mn.us/art/beads/wampum.html.
Downloaded on October 22, 1999.

Martien, Jerry and Gary Synder. *Shell Game: A True Account of
Beads and Money in North America.* San Francisco: Mercury House, 1996.

Oneida Indian Nation. *Wampum Belt Fact Sheet.* August 4,
1997.

Prindle, Paula. *Native Tech: Wampum History and Background.*
URL: http://www.nativeweb.org/Native Tech/wampum/
wamphist.htm. Downloaded on October 22, 1999.

Speck, F. *Functions of Wampum Among the Eastern Algonkian.*
Germantown, New York: Periodicals Service Company,
1974.

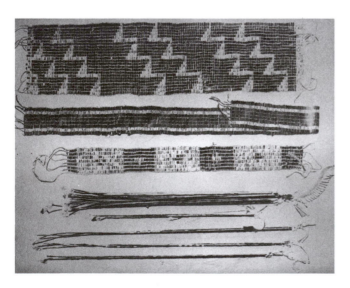

Tribes of the Northeast used wampum belts and strings of
wampum beads such as those pictured above to record treaties
and other important information. Early colonists adopted
wampum, but they changed its purpose, using it as a medium of
exchange. *(Photograph No. NWDNS-106-IN-18A National Archives and
Records Administration at College Park)*

**warehouses**  See CROP STORAGE.

**water conservation**  (precontact) *South American
Andean, North American Southwest, Mesoamerican cultures*
Water conservation is the systematic protection and controlled
usage of water. American Indians who did not live near sources
of abundant water found ways to limit their use of this natural
resource while practicing sustainable AGRICULTURE at the same
time. When water was used for growing crops, they developed
irrigation methods that minimized the amount of water that
would be lost through evaporation or seeping into the soil. (See
also IRRIGATION SYSTEMS.)

The Anasazi, whose culture began to flourish in the North American desert Southwest in about 350 B.C., built walled terraces that were arranged like stair steps on hillsides. These small terraces, where they grew crops, trapped runoff from rains, giving it time to sink into the soil. Excess water ran down to the next terrace to water another plot, ensuring minimal waste. When the area of these tiny plots that were scattered throughout the Southwest is added, the total comes to thousands of acres. Pre-Peruvian farmers living in the Andes of South America used a similar method of terracing to conserve water. (See also FARMING, TERRACED.)

In Arizona and Utah, the Anasazi placed rocks in lines to form borders on sloping land, both to slow runoff and to hold the soil in place. At Beaver Creek in Utah, Anasazi farmers arranged oblong, flat stones in rows around their crops in order to prevent wind damage and to conserve soil moisture that would have been lost through evaporation. The Anasazi built dikes, called check dams, at the top of watercourses, diverting water where it was needed. They also used ditches to conduct runoff to crops. Many of these were lined with stones to prevent water from seeping into the soil. The Hohokam, whose culture arose in what is now Arizona in about 300 B.C., lined their irrigation ditches with a clay and limestone mixture for the same purpose.

In Mesoamerica the Olmec, whose culture arose in about 1700 B.C. in the Yucatán Peninsula of what is now Mexico, carved water conduits out of basalt to bring water to their cities. This practice not only served to keep the water cleaner than it would have been had it traveled through dirt ditches, it also conserved water that would have been lost through soil seepage. The Olmec covered these stone conduits with basalt caps that served the dual purpose of keeping the water free from impurities and guarding against water loss due to evaporation. In South America the Inca, who established an empire in what is now Peru in about A.D. 1000, also built covered stone water conduits. (See also PLUMBING.)

The Maya, whose culture arose in the Yucatan area of what is now Mexico in about 1500 B.C., chose the locations of their cities based on astronomical and religious criteria. As a result, these cities were often located far from sources of drinking water. Maya architects planned their cities so that the large plazas (see also CIVIC CENTERS), which were finished with a type of CONCRETE called *sacbe,* tilted slightly. This allowed rainwater to drain into the limestone cisterns they had built. Some Maya residences had roofs that were slanted in the same manner and also drained into cisterns.

## Sources/Further Reading

Coe, Michael D. *America's First Civilization: Discovering the Olmec.* New York: American Heritage Publishing Co., 1968.

Donkin, R. A. *Agricultural Terracing in the Aboriginal New World.* Tucson: University of Arizona Press, 1979.

Hurt, R. Douglas. *American Indian Agriculture: Prehistory to Present.* Lawrence: University Press of Kansas, 1987.

Mason, J. Alden. *The Ancient Civilizations of Peru.* Rev. ed. New York: Penguin Books, 1988.

Sabloff, Jeremy A. *The Cities of Ancient Mexico: Reconstructing a Lost World.* New York: Thames And Hudson, 1989.

**waterproofing** (ca. 1700 B.C.) *Mesoamerican, North American California cultures*
Waterproofing is the process of applying a water-repellent substance to woven items such as textiles and baskets. The Olmec, whose culture arose in the Yucatán Peninsula of what is now Mexico in about 1700 B.C., were the first people in the world to use rubber waterproofing. They collected sap from certain trees (see also LATEX) and converted it to rubber through a process called VULCANIZATION. Charles Goodyear, the inventor who patented vulcanizing in 1844, was pushed into rediscovering this process when the rubber on the latex-treated waterproof mailbags he had earlier sold the U.S. Post Office melted in hot weather. The Olmec, who had invented the predecessor of Goodyear's process, successfully applied rubber coatings to both cloth and baskets more than 3,000 years before Goodyear stumbled on the technique. They were able to waterproof items such as bottles, ropes, SANDALS, TARPAULINS, PONCHOS, capes, and baskets (see also BASKETWEAVING TECHNIQUES).

The American Indians of North America waterproofed many items as well. ASPHALT, a naturally occurring PETROLEUM product, was the substance they used for this purpose. The Chumash, a California tribe, used it to caulk CANOES and baskets. (The Pomo, another California tribe that is considered by many to be the finest basket weavers in the Americas, wove baskets so tightly that they could hold water without an asphalt coating.) Other North American culture groups waterproofed hides by coating them with animal fat.

## Sources/Further Reading

Coe, Michael D. *Mexico from the Olmec to the Aztecs.* London: Thames and Hudson, 1994.

Maxwell, James A. *America's Fascinating Indian Heritage.* Pleasantville, N.Y.: Reader's Digest Books, 1978.

Porter, Frank W. *The Art of Native American Basketry.* Westport, Conn.: Greenwood Press, 1990.

Scarborough, Vernon L. and David R. Wilcox, eds. *The Mesoamerican Ballgame.* Tucson: University of Arizona Press, 1991.

Shupp, Mike. *Gabrielino Material Culture.* URL: http://www.csun.edu/~ms44278/gab.htm. Downloaded on January 6, 1999.

**way stations** See ROAD SYSTEMS.

**weaving techniques** (ca. 5000 B.C.–4000 B.C.) *South American Andean, Mesoamerican, North American Northwest Coast and Southwest cultures*
Weaving is the creation of cloth, or textiles, from fiber. The finest cloth produced by American Indians came from South America. Archaeologists believe that this is where weaving

began in the Americas. (Textiles found in the Andes are as old as 5000 to 3000 B.C. Weaving was invented independently from that in the Indus Valley of what is now India in about 3000 B.C. Evidence exists that weaving may actually have begun in what is now Ecuador one to two thousand years earlier than in the Andes. This would date it much earlier than the invention of weaving in the Old World. Because textile samples disintegrate with time, relatively few have been found in humid climates. To piece together the history of weaving in the Americas, archaeologists must rely on murals or statues in these locations that depict people wearing clothing made from cloth or on pottery decorated by pressing cloth into the clay to make a pattern.

Because the climate of the Andes is dry, a number of burial cloths have been preserved. (See also MUMMIES.) These huge cloths woven of COTTON were the most well-developed visual form of art in the Chavin culture that arose in the region in about 200 B.C. Weavers spun this cotton into yarn with a drop spindle. Many of the large cloths were finger-woven from this yarn, or twined without the benefit of a loom. Others were netted, but some were woven on LOOMS made up of breast and warp beams, bobbins, and shed sticks. Weavers made cloth on these looms that was woven to size with a selvage (the edge of a fabric woven so that it will not ravel) on each side. They dyed textiles from this period with vivid colors. (See also DYES.) These antique textile samples show a range of more than 200 shades of color, indicating that the earliest weavers were masters of dying. Often they edged their fabrics with a technique known as needle knitting. (See also KNITTING.) Several hundred years later, Andean weavers were working not only with cotton but with fibers from ALPACAS, LLAMAS, VICUNAS, and guanacos as well. They used these fibers in their natural states or dyed them.

Moche weavers who lived on the northern coast of what is now Peru began weaving slit tapestries between A.D. 200 and 600. They also used a technique of discontinuous warps and wefts in which material was woven on a scaffold of threads that were pulled when the piece was completed in order to make openwork fabric. They wove brocades as well and decorated some of the material they wove with feathers. (See also FEATHERWORKING.) During this period they began using finer threads to create their fabrics. According to modern textile experts, by 400 B.C. Andean weavers had discovered every technique known to weavers today. By A.D. 700 weavers of the Nazca of what is now Peru had begun to create tapestry shirts. Over the next centuries weavers added IKAT (tie-dyed yarn) to their repertoire of decorative techniques, which they applied to fabrics. (See also TIE-DYEING.)

The Inca, who established an empire in what is now Peru in about A.D. 1100, developed what constituted a factory system for the manufacture of cloth. The rulers distributed fiber to weavers who were obligated to make cloth for tribute as well as clothing for their own families. (See also TAX SYSTEMS.) Most of the weaving that was done as tribute was made into army uniforms that were stored in warehouses throughout the empire.

In at least one Inca city, Huanuco Pampa, a large area was dedicated solely to cloth production. The Inca used both a backstrap loom and a standing loom with a vertical frame. They used the latter for making what was called *cumbi* cloth. This was the best cloth, reserved for wear by royalty and ceremonial burning. Sometimes weavers wove gold fibers into this fabric. *Cumbi* cloth also served political purposes. When the Inca conquered another group of people, they gave the rulers *cumbi* cloth. By accepting the gift, the conquered people officially accepted Inca rulership over them.

Mesoamerican weavers used backstrap looms to produce fabric. Not as many ancient textiles have been found in Mesoamerica as have been found in South America. However, some examples of Maya weaving have been found at Chichén Itzá and others have been found in dry caves. The earliest textiles woven by the Maya, whose culture arose in about 1500 B.C., were from white and brown cotton. Sometimes they wove rabbit fur and feathers into the fabric. They also used AGAVE and YUCCA to produce sturdier cloth. At the same time that Maya weavers began dying cloth and yarn, they developed patterns including checks and tapestry. Maya weavers also invented end-to-end warp locking, double-cloth, twill, gauze, weft-wrap, openwork, brocade, and looped-weft weaving. They embellished the material they had made with EMBROIDERY and by painting designs on it. Archaeologists believe some fabric may have been printed with pottery stamps and cylinders. They also believe that Maya weavers practiced the art of batik (wax-resist dying).

The finest Maya fabrics served as dowry payments or as wrappings for the dead. These fabrics also served as tribute in the Aztec Empire, which was established in what is now Mexico in about A.D. 1100. The Maya traded their textiles to the Aztec as well as other culture groups. Spaniards, the first Europeans to see their work, praised it as being equal to the finest fabrics available in Europe. The brightly colored fabrics that are produced by the Maya of Guatemala and Chiapas, Mexico, today are part of a Mesoamerican weaving tradition that stretches centuries into the past, as are the rugs woven near Oaxaca, Mexico. Weavers of the area made cloth on backstrap LOOMS, sewing them together to make blankets before European contact. Afterward, they adopted the horizontal loom of the Spaniards and began weaving the blankets and rugs in one piece.

Throughout North America, indigenous people produced textiles by finger weaving for thousands of years. The technique of finger weaving includes plaiting, crocheting, knitting, braiding, looping, knotting, coiling, and netting. The Tsimshian tribe of the Northwest Coast in what is now British Columbia made Chilkat blankets, dramatically designed textiles with abstract geometric patterns (see also ABSTRACT ART, AMERICAN INDIAN INFLUENCE ON) and long fringe (see also FRINGED CLOTHING). Tribal leaders wore these blankets, which took a year to make, as ceremonial garb. Weavers constructed the warp of the blanket from shredded cedar bark and the double wefts from mountain goat fur. Although women spun the yarn and wove the blankets, men made the looms and provided the goatskins from which the fiber for the blankets was obtained. One blanket typically required the hair from three goatskins to make. Men also made the abstract designs of figures such as eagles and bears, drawing them on pattern boards. The technique spread to the Tlingit tribe through trade and marriage. Flathead (Salish) weavers, who also lived on the Northwest coast, used goat, cattail fluff, and fur from specially bred dogs (see also DOG BREEDS) to make white blankets.

In the Plateau region the Nez Perce fingerwove mats as well as hats and bags from cornhusks that were twined. After contact, they overlaid the cornhusks with wool. The warps were suspended from a horizontal bar and the weaver worked from the bottom to the top. In the Northeast the Chippewa (Anishinabe) and the Iroquois fingerwove bags, mats, and sashes from rushes and CATTAILS. The Iroquois sometimes wove WAMPUM beads into sashes on a bow loom. After European contact and the introduction of commercial yarns, both Northeast and Southeast cultures began fingerweaving items such as sashes and bags.

In about A.D. 700 the Anasazi of the Southwest used bark, plant fibers, such as agave and yucca to fingerweave sashes, PONCHOS, and SANDALS. They suspended warp threads from a loop of string in a form of fingerweaving that was a step beyond basketry but not yet loom weaving. Sometimes they imprinted these fabrics on wet clay to make designs in their POTTERY. After the Anasazi began growing cotton, they began weaving with backstrap looms. Between A.D. 1050 and 1300, Anasazi weavers began using a vertical blanket loom to weave intricate blankets of cotton. Their descendants, the Pueblo people, continued this tradition. Pueblo weavers were mainly men and they wove to provide textiles for their own people.

When the Pueblo people sought refuge from the Spaniards among the Navajo (Dineh), Navajo women learned their blanket-weaving techniques. By the 1700s these women were weaving blankets from cotton as well as from wool obtained from sheep that the Spaniards had brought to the Americas. In 1795 Fernando de Chacon, the Spanish governor of New Mexico, praised the work they produced, saying they "work their wool with more delicacy and taste than the Spaniards." At first these Navajo weavers primarily made dresses and blankets for themselves. By the 1800s they were making striped "chiefs' blankets" that they traded to other tribes for at least 10 buffalo hides (see also BISON) for one blanket. One Spanish writer of the time

In this 1933 Bureau of Indian Affairs photograph, a Navajo woman from the Ganado district weaves a rug. (Photograph No. NRIS-75-PAO50-NAVRUG3/National Archives and Records Administration—Pacific Alaska Region, Seattle)

assessed the Navajo blankets as the most valuable product of the province. (See also TRADE.)

In 1863, when the Navajo were seen as a threat to white settlers, they were relocated in Bosque Redondo, a barren prison camp–like place, in southern New Mexico. Their forced relocation is known as the Long Walk. During the five years they remained there, the U.S. Army destroyed Navajo sheep herds and burned the Navajo's blankets. Upon their release, the U.S. government paid the Navajo annuity payments in yarns and dyes. Navajo weavers began making rugs using geometric patterns they had not used previously. (See also GEOMETRY.) White traders—most notably John Lorenzo Hubbel, who ran a post at Ganado in what is now Arizona—encouraged the weavers to increase production. These blankets and rugs were sold to tourists and collectors. Navajo weaving has evolved over time and varies from family to family and from weaver to weaver. Each rug takes about 240 hours of weaving to complete. Authentic Navajo rugs are considered collectors' items today and are sold for very high prices.

## Sources/Further Reading

Alaskan Center Home Page. *The Chilkat Blanket.* URL: http://alaskan.com/docs/blanket.html. Downloaded on October 20, 1999.

Burger, Richard L. *Chavin and the Origins of Andean Civilization.* London: Thames and Hudson, 1992.

Harris, Jennifer, ed. *Textiles: 5,000 Years.* New York: Harry N. Abrams, Inc., Publishers, 1993.

Kaufman, Alice and Christopher Selser. *The Navajo Weaving Tradition, 1650 to the Present.* New York: E.P. Dutton, Inc., 1985.

Kent, Kate Peck. *Navajo Weaving Three Centuries of Change.* Santa Fe, N.M.: School of American Research Press, 1985.

Malpass, Michael. *Daily Life in the Inca Empire.* Westport, Conn.: Greenwood Press, 1996.

Schevill, Margot Blum, Janet Catherine Berlo, and Edward B. Dwyer, eds. *Textile Traditions of Mesoamerica and the Andes: An Anthology.* Austin: University of Texas Press, 1996.

Winter, Mark. *Navajo Textiles: Primitive Art.* URL: http://indianvillage.com/stories/Primitive Art.htm. Downloaded on October 20, 1999.

**wedges**  See TOOLS.

**weirs**  See FISH TRAPS.

**welding, sweat**  (ca. 1000 B.C.)  *South America Andean cultures*

Welding is the process of joining metals together through the application of heat. Long before contact with Europeans, the Chavin, whose culture arose in the Andes in about 1000 B.C., invented welding. Their invention is referred to as *sweat welding.* They used this technique to produce three-dimensional objects of silver and gold. (See also METALLURGY.) The ancient Chavin metalsmiths learned that by placing the edges of metals together and applying high heat, they melted together. An interesting aspect of this invention was that placing two metals together caused the melting point of the metal with the higher melting point to be lowered. This allowed metalworkers to work with PLATINUM, which has a melting point much higher than any precontact furnace was capable of producing. (See also SINTERING; SMELTING.) These ancient Andean metalsmiths also discovered how to join metal by SOLDERING, crimping, stapling, and using interlocking tabs.

## Sources/Further Reading

Bankes, George. *Peru Before Pizarro.* Oxford: Phaidon Press Limited, 1977.

Engel, Frederic Andre. *An Ancient World Preserved: Relics and Records of Prehistory in the Andes.* New York: Crown Publishers, Inc., 1976.

Fagan, Brian M. *Kingdoms of Gold, Kingdoms of Jade: The Americas before Columbus.* London: Thames and Hudson Ltd., 1991.

Material Culture and Technology 2. URL: http://webf0164.ntx.net/huacaso/page21.htm. Downloaded on January 12, 2000.

Morris, Craig and Adriana von Hagen. *The Inka Empire and Its Andean Origins.* New York: Abbeville Press Publishers, 1993.

**wet suits**  See FLOTATION DEVICES.

**whaling**  (precontact)  *North American Northeast, Northwest, and Pacific Coast cultures*

Whaling is the practice of hunting and killing whales, large marine mammals. American Indians living along the east and west coasts of what is now the United States made good use of an occasional whale that beached along the shoreline and occasionally ventured out after whale, but only Arctic groups and two tribes who lived along the coast of what is now British Columbia—the Makah and the Nootka—routinely took to the open sea in order to hunt whales. These huge mammals provided them with meat, oil, baleen for traps, and bone for TOOLS. They braided the sinew that they obtained from whales into rope and used the intestines as containers. Because their sustenance depended on whaling, these groups of American Indians devised sophisticated techniques to hunt whale.

Despite the fact that most whaling histories credit 10th-century Basque fishermen as the first open-sea whalers, the Inuit people in Alaska and Greenland had been venturing to sea in their *umiaks,* or hide boats, for centuries before this time. To kill the whales, they used toggle-headed HARPOONS with slate points fixed to heavy rawhide lines. They typically tied two sealskin floats to the lines. When they paddled close to a whale, the hunters thrust the harpoon and twisted it so that the detachable point would hold and come off the shaft. Then they threw the floats over board. As the huge animal (about 33 feet long and weighing 30 or more tons) dove and resurfaced, the whalers thrust more harpoons with floats attached to the lines into its side. The floats marked where the animal was when it dove underwater and also made it tire quickly by providing added resistance in the water. After the hunters had killed the whale with a harpoon or spear thrust to the heart, the floats kept it buoyant so that they could butcher it in the water. Even though the hunters were experts, whale hunting was dangerous because a harpoon point could come loose from the whale and snap back into the umiak, or the whale might decide to resurface directly beneath the boat. For this reason some Inuit whalers wore inflatable suits. (See also FLOTATION DEVICES.)

The Makah and the Nootka conducted their whale hunts from large wooden CANOES led by a chief harpooner, whose position had been handed down from his father. The harpoons these hunters used were tipped with mussel shell points with curved bone spurs affixed at the bottom, ensuring that the harpoon would not come loose. In general, the whaling techniques of the Makah and the Nootka were similar to those of American Indian whalers of the Arctic. When the whale had died, they towed it to the beach and butchered it. As was the custom with Inuit whaling crews, the first choice of the meat went to the whaling crew chief, who then divided the rest among his helpers and the people in the community.

Whaling by non-Indians was not organized on such a large scale until the 1600s, when Dutch crews began hunting for whales in the North Atlantic Ocean and off the east coast of the United States. At first colonial whaling crews began hunting off the coastline of Nantucket and then New Bedford, Massachusetts. At the height of what was called "on-shore hunting" in 1726, whalers took 86 whales in one season in Nantucket alone. The record catch was 11 in one day. Incessant hunting depleted the supply of whales, and it became necessary for whalers to venture into the open waters of the Atlantic and Pacific oceans on voyages that generally lasted for three to six weeks and could even last for several years.

The American whaling industry that was to serve as the inspiration for Herman Melville's famous novel *Moby-Dick* was fueled by consumer demand for whale oil that was used to light homes. The killing of the first sperm whale in 1712, along with the discovery that its head contained a reservoir of oil that burned more brightly than any other substance at the time, spurred the killing of even more whales. In addition to providing light, sperm whale oil was also used to lubricate machinery as well as clocks and watches, firearms and sewing machines. It was also used for tanning and in the manufacture of cosmetics. (Today a liquid made from JOJOBA is generally used to replace sperm whale oil, which became illegal in 1972.) A waxy substance called spermaceti, which was also located in the whale's head, or case, made exceptional candles that burned without odor. A third substance, ambergris, formed the basis for perfumes.

Within 100 years, so many whales had been killed that they were becoming scarce and the cost of long whaling voyages

had become prohibitive. The start of the Civil War and the discovery of PETROLEUM in Pennsylvania in 1859, a resource American Indians had known of for centuries, marked the decline of the whaling industry. Between 1871 and 1876, 46 whaling ships went down in Arctic waters, convincing many whalers to choose another profession.

During the 1800s, despite the decline in the demand for whale oil, whale baleen was still sold. This strong and flexible material from the mouths of toothless whales is used to filter plankton. American Indians had used baleen for wolf TRAPS and for BASKETS. (See also BASKET WEAVING TECHNIQUES.) Non-Indians used it for corset stays, hoops for skirts, and for scientific and medical instruments. The invention of the explosive harpoon in 1868 made it possible for U.S. whalers to harvest 90 million pounds of baleen in the 1900s. Whalers, who often killed whales solely for that substance, and frequently left the carcasses to rot in the ocean. By 1924, primarily because whales had become nearly extinct, the U.S. whaling industry was no longer economically viable.

In 1971 the U.S. Congress passed a law prohibiting whaling and the importation and use of whale products. However, commercial whaling by countries such as Japan, Norway, Iceland, and Russia posed a continuing threat to the survival of the whale. Global efforts to protect the whale have included the establishment of the International Whaling Commission and a moratorium on commercial whaling that went into effect in 1985. The commission has allowed exemptions for small-scale whaling carried out by traditional methods for subsistence purposes. In 1997 the U.S. government presented the International Whaling Commission with a request from the Makah tribe of Washington State to be allowed to hunt gray whales "for cultural uses and subsistence needs." The last Makah whaling had taken place 70 years previously. Despite resistance from some members of the commission, the Makah won approval to take up to five whales a year for five years. In 1998, they held their first hunt in years.

## Sources/Further Reading

Bryant, Peter. "Whaling and Fishing." *Biodiversity and Conservation*. URL: http://darwin.bio.uci.edu/~sustain/bio65/lec04/b65lec04.htm History of Whaling. Downloaded February 20, 1997.

Maxwell, James A. ed. *America's Fascinating Indian Heritage*. Pleasantville, N.Y.: Reader's Digest Books, 1978.

Murdoch, John. *Ethnological Results of the Point Barrow Expedition: Annual Report of the U.S. Bureau of Ethnology 1887–1888*. Washington D.C.: Government Printing Office, 1992.

Oswalt, Wendell. *Eskimos and Explorers*. Novato, Calif.: Chandler & Sharp Publishers, 1979.

**wheels** (ca. 1200 B.C.–A.D. 900) *Mesoamerican cultures*
Wheels are solid cylindrical disks that are attached to an axle. In places other than the Americas, wheels were used on carts that were pulled by draft animals. Despite the fact that there were

no animals present in the Americas suitable to serve as draft animals, the indigenous people of Mesoamerica independently invented the wheel—the presence of which has been held by scholars to be the true test of whether a society was a civilization. In other parts of the world, the invention of the wheel allowed animals to pull heavier burdens than they would have been able to do if they had carried them or dragged them over the ground. The Mesoamerican wheel is believed to have been developed by the Maya, whose culture flourished from about 1500 B.C. to about 1500 A.D. and is still in existence today.

In the 1880s archaeologists found wheeled pottery figurines in what are now El Salvador and Mexico. These wheeled objects, which probably were funerary items, have been dated to between 1200 B.C. and A.D. 900. At the time of the initial discovery, anthropologists assigned the wheeled artifacts little or no significance, perhaps because to do so would have indicated that American Indians did, indeed, have a civilization. Not until 1944, when archaeologists found more wheeled artifacts at burial sites near what is now Tampico and Vera Cruz, Mexico, did scholars begin to study them seriously.

These wheeled POTTERY statuettes depict animal figures including deer, jaguars, and monkeys. The most common animals that are portrayed are DOGS. (See also DOG BREEDS.) Some of the animal figures can be converted from an animal form into a platform. This may indicate that the object was designed for carrying something. Not only did American Indians invent a wheel and wheeled objects, but archaeologists have found that the people who created the pottery figures used at least three ways to attach wheels to objects. Some archaeologists believe that these ancient inventors may have developed the

The two wheeled toys or funerary objects above were found in Veracruz. They date to the classic period of Mesoamerican prehistory. Made from pottery, they depict what appear to be dogs, although features of bats are also present. Today they are part of the collection of the National Museum of Anthropology in Mexico City. *(David Hixon)*

idea for the wheels on the pottery figurines from the spindle, a device used by the Maya (and other cultures throughout the world), to spin yarn from fiber. (See also WEAVING TECHNIQUES.)

## Sources/Further Reading

Boggs, Stanley H. "Salvadorian Varieties of Wheeled Figurines." *Contributions to Mesoamerican Anthropology, Pub, No. 1.* Miami: Institute of Maya Studies of the Museum of Science, 1973.

Borhequi, Stephan F. "Wheels and Man," *Archaeology* 23 (January 1970): 24.

Farb, Peter. *Man's Rise to Civilization.* New York: E.P. Dutton, 1968.

Miller, Mary and Karl Toube. *The Gods and Symbols of Ancient Mexico and the Maya.* New York: Thames and Hudson, 1993.

**white pine  (*Pinus strobus*)** (precontact)  *North American Northeast cultures*

The American white pine is an evergreen tree that is native to the northeastern part of North America. This tree served as a kind of pharmacy for North American Northeast culture groups. (See also PHARMACOLOGY.) After contact, the British harvested the trees, using them for masts on sailing ships. In addition to using white pine for their own ships, the British sold white pine that they had harvested in North America throughout Europe.

For hundreds of years before the arrival of the British, Northeast Indians including the Menominee, Mohegan, Montagnais, and Chippewa (Anishinabe) used white pine as a cough and cold treatment, for treating wounds and sores, as a decongestant, and as an expectorant. White pine also served as an ASTRINGENT to stop internal bleeding. White pine tar has a tannin content of 10 percent, making it a good chemical HEMOSTAT.

Northeast tribes also made a tea from the needles from this tree to treat and prevent scurvy, a vitamin C deficiency. (See also SCURVY CURE.) This use continues among the Indians of New England today. White pine needles contain five times the vitamin C found in an equal weight of lemons. The needles are also high in vitamin A, which helps to prevent night blindness and maintain resistance to infections, in addition to promoting normal growth and development. Because of its antioxidant properties, white pine may also be an anticancer agent. American colonists adopted these medicinal uses of white pine, and physicians routinely used it as a cold remedy. From 1916 to 1965, the plant was listed in the *National Formulary,* a pharmacopoeia that served as an officially sanctioned drug reference for physicians.

Because white pines grow to extraordinary heights of up to 200 feet tall, they made excellent masts. Before the British navy began using white pine, it purchased lumber for ships' masts from the Baltic region and spliced them, which made them vulnerable to breaking under stress. Soon British shipping companies began using the white pines. The importation of this tree impacted the European lumber economy like American silver and gold impacted the world economy.

## Sources/Further Reading

Vogel, Virgil. *American Indian Medicine.* Norman: University of Oklahoma Press, 1970.

Weatherford, Jack. *Native Roots: How The Indians Enriched America.* New York: Fawcett Columbine, 1991.

Weiner, Michael A. *Earth Medicine, Earth Food: Plant Remedies, Drugs, and Natural Foods of the North American Indians.* New York: Fawcett Columbine, 1990.

**white potatoes**  See POTATOES.

**wild rice  (*Sisania aquatica*)**  (precontact)  *North American Northeastern cultures*

Wild rice (*Sisania aquatica*) is a seed-bearing plant that grows about 8 to 12 feet tall in water three to eight feet deep. Thou-sands of varieties of this plant are native to the upper Midwest of North America. The term *wild rice* is really a misnomer. The Chippewa (Anishinabe), Assiniboine, and Potawatomi tribes of the upper Great Lakes region cultivated it for centuries, sowing as much as a third of the crop in the marshes where it naturally grew. The Assiniboine weeded their rice fields to increase yields. Wild rice made up as much as 25 percent of the caloric intake of these tribes. The rice was so valued that territorial disputes erupted between the Chippewa and the Dakota over possession of the wild rice stands in the lakes of Minnesota. The Chippewa called the rice *manomin,* or "good berry." The first part of the word refers to *Manido,* the spirit giver whom the Chippewa believe gave the rice to the people. French voyagers later called the rice *folle avenoine,* or "wild oats."

American Indian women, who were responsible for harvesting the rice, went into the rice fields in CANOES to tie the stalks into sheaves about two weeks before the main harvest that took place in late summer. When the rice was ripe, they cut these sheaves then knocked the rice grains from the sheaves. Some of

The Anishinabe women in this watercolor made in 1867 by Seth Eastman harvested wild rice as their ancestors had done for centuries. Two of the women bend the tall stalks and beat them with paddles to loosen the rice while the other paddles the canoe. (*Stock Montage/The Newberry Library*)

Wild rice continued to be an important American Indian crop after contact. This picture of Paul Buffalo and his wife parching the wild rice they had harvested was taken in 1937. *(Photograph No. NRE-75-COCH(PHO)-1494/Department of the Interior, 1937/National Archives and Records Administration—Central Plains Region)*

this rice, called green rice, was eaten immediately. Most of it was allowed to dry in the sun or on a frame made of green branches placed over a low fire. When it was sufficiently dry, the Indians parched it so that the husks would be easier to remove. Placing the rice in a wooden container and gently pounding on it with long-handled wooden poles removed the husks. Indian women placed the rice in birch-bark trays and tossed it into the air to winnow it. They then hung the winnowed rice grains in a skin bag over a fire in order to dry them further.

In the 1960s non-Indians who had discovered a market for wild rice as a gourmet food item began harvesting it in flat-bottom wooden boats that crushed the reeds. Taking all of the rice they could find, they prevented the rice stands in the lakes from reseeding, and as a result rice production diminished. Today rice grown on state-owned water legally must be harvested using traditional American Indian methods. The White Earth Band of Chippewa (Anishinabe) harvests and sells wild rice in order to fund its land recovery project.

Most "wild" rice sold in stores is commercially grown on private land. Farmers flood the rice fields before they seed the

rice and drain them before harvesting the rice with flotation combines.

See also AGRICULTURE; FOOD PRESERVATION.

### Sources/Further Reading

Giese, Paula. *Native American Indian Resources.* URL: http://indy4.fdl.cc.mn.us/~isk/food/wildrice.html. Downloaded on September 7, 1998.

Hurt, R. Douglas. *American Indian Agriculture: Prehistory to Present.* Lawrence: University Press of Kansas, 1987.

Vennum, Thomas. *Wild Rice and the Ojibway People.* St. Paul: Minnesota Historical Society Press, 1988.

### wintergreen (ground tea, mountain tea, *Gaultheria procumbens*) (precontact) *North American Northeast culture groups*

Wintergreen (*Gaultheria procumbens*) is a low-growing shrub with white flowers and red fruit. Its leaves are the source of an oil, methyl salicylate. that is used as a flavoring for chewing gum and candy today. Wintergreen is indigenous to the northeastern United States and also grows in England. American Indians used wintergreen both as food and as medicine.

Northeast tribes used wintergreen as a food, eating the berries raw or cooking them and brewing the leaves into a tea that was used as a beverage and a medicine. These berries were sometimes called *deer berries*. The Iroquois dried the berries and shaped them into cakes for storage. Later they would soak these cakes in water and either cook the berries as a sauce or mix them with CORNMEAL to make a pudding. Chippewa (Anishinabe) cooks added the leaves to a number of dishes as a seasoning. The eastern Cherokee chewed wintergreen leaves as a form of CHEWING GUM, as a treatment for tender gums and as a breath freshener. (See also CHEWABLE DENTIFRICES.)

Methyl salicylate, found in wintergreeen, is both an ANTISEPTIC and an analgesic, and wintergreen teas were used by the Cherokee to treat colds. The Chippewa drank wintergreen tea as a tonic in the spring and fall and also used it to treat colds when the need arose, as did the Iroquois. The Lenni Lenape (Delaware) made poultices of wintergreen leaves to treat rheumatism, in addition to drinking wintergreen tea for the same condition. The Iroquois and the Potawatomi had a similar ARTHRITIS TREATMENT. Methyl salicylate is used in external arthritis medicines today. Although oil of wintergreen is used as a flavoring, ingesting this volatile oil in large amounts can cause poisoning.

See also ANESTHETICS; MINTS, BOTANICAL; PHARMACOLOGY.

## Sources/Further Reading

Brooklyn Botanic Garden. *Metropolitan Plants: Wintergreen.* URL: http://www.bbg.org/nymf/encyclopedia/eri/gau0020a.htm. Downloaded on November 5, 1999.

Moerman, Dan. *Native American Ethnobotany Database: Food, Drugs, Dyes and Fibers of Native North American Peoples.* URL: http://www.umd.umich.edu/cgi-bin/herb. Downloaded on November 5, 1999.

## witch hazel (*Hamamelis virginiana*) (precontact)
*North American Northeast cultures*
Witch hazel (*Hamamelis virginiana*) is a tall shrub that grows in eastern North America. It is best known for the ASTRINGENT property of its leaves. American Indians used it for this purpose and also as a sedative. It was used both externally and internally. Some of the American Indian tribes that used witch hazel were the Mohawk, Menominee, Potawatomi, and Stockbridge (as the Mahican bands that lived near/in Stockbridge, Massachusetts were known). Tribes of the Iroquois mixed witch hazel tea with MAPLE SYRUP and used it as a tonic.

Externally, witch hazel was used to treat poison ivy irritations, other skin irritations, minor burns, insect bites, stings, and bruises. (See also INSECT BITE AND BEE STING REMEDIES.) It was also effective in treating hemorrhoids and certain eye inflammations. Internally, it was used as a gargle and mouthwash for catarrh (sore throat with bleeding) and bleeding gums. Another use for this herb was as an antidiarrheal. It was effective in stopping diarrhea. However, one of the most important uses of witch hazel was as a HEMOSTAT. Witch hazel is very effective in stopping bleeding both internally and externally.

European colonists readily adopted witch hazel into their medicine and sold it at pharmacies. The early Europeans to the New World used witch hazel for the same reasons American Indians did. Today witch hazel remains a common home remedy as well as a cosmetic (it is often used as a facial astringent). Colonists also used the branches of the witch hazel as divining rods when they to sought the location of water before drilling wells.

See also PHARMACOLOGY.

## Sources/Further Reading

Hutchens, Alma R. *Indian Herbology of North America.* Boston: Shambhala, 1991.

Vogel, Virgil. *American Indian Medicine.* Norman: University of Oklahoma Press, 1970.

Weiner, Michael A. *Earth Medicine, Earth Food: Plant Remedies, Drugs, and Natural Foods of the North American Indians.* New York: Fawcett Columbine, 1990.

## women's rights (ca. A.D. 1000–A.D. 1400) *North American Northeast cultures*
The Iroquois League of the Five Nations, an alliance that was established by the Onondaga, Oneida, Seneca, Mohawk, and the Cayuga, (and later the Tuscarora), allowed women full political participation. Although men made the decisions, women held the power to veto them as well as to appoint men to positions of authority within the league (see also IROQUOIS CONSTITUTION).

The Iroquois were a matrilineal society, with lineage being traced through the women, and a matriarchial society, with property and clan affiliation being owned and passed on through women. According to the Iroquois Constitution, women "shall own the land and the soil. Men and women shall follow the status of the mother." In Iroquois society women were considered the head of the longhouses in which they lived. (See also APARTMENT COMPLEXES.) They were responsible for agricultural activities as well as for ceremonial activities, while male activities consisted of hunting, war, and intertribal relations. This arrangement ensured that men and women had different roles but equal status. Some historians believe that before the Iroquois League was established, women may have held dominant roles in their respective tribes.

Women of other American Indian tribes often did serve as spokespersons for their people. That began to change dramatically with the arrival of Europeans in the Americas. European colonists did not believe that women could be leaders, so they insisted on communicating only with men from the tribes they encountered regarding matters of state. Nevertheless, American Indian women continued to play a vital role in the life of their people.

Although the framers of the U.S. Constitution borrowed heavily from the Iroquois Constitution to establish the principles of democracy set forth in that document, they did not include female suffrage. (See also UNITED STATES CONSTITUTION, AMERICAN INDIAN INFLUENCE ON.)

## Sources/Further Reading

Alan, Paula Gunn. *The Sacred Hoop.* Boston: Beacon Press, 1992.

Fagan, Brian M. *Kingdoms of Gold, Kingdoms of Jade: The Americans Before Columbus.* New York: Thames and Hudson, Inc., 1991.

Josephy, Jr., Alvin M., ed. *America in 1492: The World of the Indian People Before the Arrival of Columbus.* New York: Random House, 1991.

Stannard, David E. *American Holocaust: Columbus and the Conquest of the New World.* New York: Oxford University Press, 1992.

**wrenches** (ca. 8000 B.C.) *North American Great Plains culture*

Wrenches are tools that are used to grip, twist, or turn an object. The first wrench produced in Americas was invented by the Paleo-Indians of what is now Montana. It was made of bone, about 18 inches long, with a handle about an inch and a half in diameter. It was shaped much like a large box-end wrench and resembled a large, flat needle. The "eye" hole in this wrench was about an inch in diameter. Paleo-Indians used it for straightening foreshafts of their spears and atlatls by gripping the projectile point to bend the shaft. This tool would only work on green wood. Paleo-Indians inserted the bent green wood into the eye of the wrench until the wrench was over one end of the bend. Then the wrench handle or the shaft could be used like a lever, straightening the shaft.

## Sources/Further Reading

Canby, Thomas Y. "The Search for the First Americans." *National Geographic* 156, no. 3 (September 1977): 330–363.

Fiedel, Stuart J. *Prehistory of the Americas.* Cambridge, England: Cambridge University Press, London, 1987.

**writing systems** (ca. 600 B.C.) *North American, South American Andean, Mesoamerican cultures*

Writing is a system of communication using conventional markings. Indigenous peoples throughout the precontact Americas used a writing system called pictograms to record information and wrote information with varying degrees of sophistication. These writing systems ranged from the simple petroglyphs (rock drawings) of ancient North American Paleo-Indians to the complex written language system of the Maya that was capable of recording anything spoken in the Maya language. These writing systems were developed independently from those in other parts of the world.

Pictograms are drawings made for the purpose of communication rather than art. They are primarily used as a way to remember oral traditions. They can also be a way to record history or to communicate simple information with others. Pictograms in the form of petroglyphs and incised bones have been found throughout the Americas. The Chippewa (Anishinabe) used a bone or stone stylus to impress details of their Midewiwin (Medicine Society) healing rituals, including songs, herbal knowledge, and initiation rites, on bark. The Chippewa also kept tallies and genealogical records on birch-bark scrolls. Great Plains Indians used pictograms on their hide winter counts to create a historical record. (See AMERICAN HISTORY, RECORDED.)

Other groups of American Indians developed more abstract symbols to represent information they wished to communicate. The Iroquois, for example, used WAMPUM beads woven into sashes and belts to record tribal alliances. In South America the Inca Empire, which was established in what is now Peru in about A.D. 1000, used the QUIPU, a system of knotted strings, to transmit information. They also used patterned textiles to the same effect.

Mesoamerican cultures developed a more sophisticated writing system that used pictures to represent objects, actions, or individuals. The writing of the Mesoamericans recorded historical events, kept accounts of government tributes and land holdings, and was used to calculate mathematical problems. These writings also recorded and predicted astronomical and weather events and helped to bring spiritual meaning to everyday life. More complex than originally thought, these languages, which were recorded in the form of stone carvings and books, continue to be studied by archaeologists. Although each of the Mesoamerican written languages was different, they shared common patterns.

The earliest known complex and abstract writing practiced in Mesoamerica was that of the Zapotec, whose culture arose in the area that is now Oaxaca, Mexico, in about 500 B.C. They developed a writing system that was partly pictographic and partly phonetic (using symbols to represent sounds in the oral language). The Zapotec used writing to record history and to express and reinforce the status of rulers. The Olmec, whose culture arose in the Yucatán Peninsula of what is now Mexico in about A.D. 1700, also developed writing. The earliest example of this was found on a stone stelae dated about 31 B.C. at Monte Albán.

Maya writing contains more abstract symbols, most of which were phonetic symbols used to represent sounds or syllables. These symbols are called hieroglyphs, or glyphs. In addition to phonetic symbols, the Maya, whose culture arose in what is now Mexico in about 1500 B.C., used logographs, pictures that stood for an entire word or a concept specific to the oral language of the culture—much like Americans today use the ampersand, "&". They used pictographs as well. Because the pictographs were not language-specific, these symbols could be read and understood throughout Mesoamerica, serving in effect as a universal language. Maya writing, like that of the Olmec and the Zapotec, included a way of representing numbers. About 700 of the 800 known Maya glyphs are logographs. About 100 are phonoglyphs, used to spell out words. Modern linguists have identified Maya glyphs that represent parts of speech, as well as those that represent prefixes or suffixes. The Maya collected their writings into BOOKS, as did the Aztec, who established an empire in what is now Mexico in about A.D. 1100. The Aztec used more pictograms than the Maya. The most common glyphs that they used symbolized place-names. Archaeologists believe that Aztec writings were meant primarily as mnemonic (memory) devices to aid them in accurately recalling information.

See also MAPS, FIRST AMERICAN; PAPER.

## Sources/Further Reading

Closs, Michael T., ed. *Native American Mathematics.* Austin: University of Texas Press, 1986.

Schele, Linda and Peter Matthews. *The Code of Kings: The Language of Seven Sacred Maya Temples and Tombs.* New York: Charles Scribner and Sons, 1998.

Smith, Michael E. *The Peoples of America: The Aztecs.* Cambridge, Mass.: Blackwell, 1996.

Sharer, Robert. *Daily Life in Maya Civilization.* Westport, Conn.: Greenwood Press, 1996.

# X

## xeriscaping (precontact) *Mesoamerican, South American, North American cultures*

*Xeriscaping* is a modern word that was coined by combining *xeros,* which means "dry" in Greek, with the word *landscaping.* It refers to a landscaping technique with the primary goal of conserving water. (See also WATER CONSERVATION.) People who practice xeriscaping in their lawns and gardens use plants that are indigenous to their area. They try to cluster plants with similar water requirements together so that they will flourish with spot-watering. Another principle of xeriscaping is to make certain the slope of the land does not encourage water runoff or evaporation. Careful xeriscaping can reduce water use by 30 to 80 percent. Although it has been given a modern name, this environmentally conscious way of planting is a technique that was routinely practiced by American Indian farmers for centuries before contact with Europeans.

American Indians not only planted crops that were indigenous to the areas in which they lived, they developed new varieties that were even better suited to temperature and water conditions by a process called SEED SELECTION. COMPANION PLANTING, the practice of growing several crops together, such as CORN, BEANS, and SQUASH, resulted in ground cover that slowed the evaporation of moisture from the soil and slowed the growth of weeds at the same time. Unlike Europeans who planted crops in rows, American Indians planted crops in middens, or hills, which necessitated only spot-watering rather than watering an entire field. Often they planted crops on flood plains, taking advantage of natural flooding to provide both moisture and soil nutrients for the plants. Finally, when irrigation was used as it was in the desert Southwest of what is now the United States and in Mesoamerica, American Indian farmers were careful to conserve water.

See also AGRICULTURE; IRRIGATION SYSTEMS.

### Sources/Further Reading

Driver, Harold E. *Indians of North America.* Chicago: University of Chicago Press, 1969.

Hurt, R. Douglas. *American Indian Agriculture: Prehistory to Present.* Lawrence: University Press of Kansas, 1987.

Nabhan, Gary. *Enduring Seeds: Native American Agriculture and Wild Plant Conservation.* San Francisco: North Point Press, 1989.

## "X-ray art" (ca. 19th century) *North American Northwest Pacific Coast cultures*

X rays are a way modern medicine uses to see the interior bone structure of the body. American Indians in the area of what is now Oregon developed a distinctive art form that modern archaeologists call "X-ray art" (although it does not use actual X rays). The Wishram and Washo tribes carved human and animal figurines of bone and wood that showed the skeletal system from the outside of the body. In addition to being used on carved spoons and bowls, the design also was used in basketry (see also BASKETWEAVING TECHNIQUES). These carvings emphasize the bones of the face and chest more than those located on the rest of the body. Modern scholars do not know the purpose of this artwork, but they agree that it demonstrates that these Indians possessed a working knowledge of human anatomy.

See also ANATOMICAL KNOWLEDGE.

### Source/Further Reading

Maxwell, James A. *America's Fascinating Indian Heritage.* Pleasantville, New York: Reader's Digest Books, 1978.

# Y

**yams (Dioscorea)** (precontact) *Mesoamerican, Circum-Caribbean, South American Tropical Forest cultures*

Yams are indigenous to tropical areas of the world, including Central America, the Caribbean, and parts of South America, West Africa, and the Pacific Islands. The plants are climbing vines with heart-shaped leaves. Yam plants produce underground tubers that, in turn, develop buds, or "eyes," that grow new plants like white POTATOES do. In the United States, SWEET POTATOES are often mistakenly called yams. However, they belong to a different family (Ipomoea) than do yams. Sweet potatoes do not have eyes, as yams do, and their skin is thinner and smoother than that of yams.

True yams can grow to an enormous size, measuring as long as six feet and weighing as much as 150 pounds. American Indian peoples living in the tropics of the Americas depended upon a number of varieties of yams as a food source. Today, yams continue to serve as a source of nutrition, and are also used by the pharmaceutical industry to produce synthetic steroids.

Some varieties of yams that are indigenous to the Americas contain poisonous chemicals called saponins that foam in water. These chemicals break down red blood cells and irritate the mucous membranes. Scientists believe that cold-blooded animals such as fish are especially susceptible to the effects of saponin. Although American Indians living in the tropics did not eat these varieties of yams, they used them to obtain other food: fish. Scrapings or slices of these poisonous yams were spread over water where fish were present. The saponins stunned the fish but did not taint the meat, making this a safe and highly efficient method of fishing. (See also FISHING, CHEMICAL.)

The science of synthesizing steroids owes its existence to this indigenous technology. Modern organic chemists studied indigenous fishing practices in order to find a plant source from which steroids could be synthesized. Initially pharmaceutical manufacturers used the adrenal glands of animals to produce steroids such as cortisone. It took 40 oxen to manufacture enough to treat a patient for one day. By the late 1930s cortisone cost $100 a gram. The chemists found that several varieties of American yams, including *Dioscorea floribunda, D. composita, and D. mexicana,* contained large amounts of diosgenin, a steroidal glycoside.

Although diosgenin is not identical to human steroids in its raw state, this natural plant steroid is made up of molecules containing the four carbon rings that are contained in all steroids, including cortisone, the sexual hormones testosterone and progesterone, and cholesterol. Several steps are required in order to make steroids from yams, which are an inexpensive source of medicine for thousands of people. These steroids are responsible for the treatment of many illnesses today, including asthma, bursitis, tendinitis, arthritis, rheumatism, hemorrhoids, lupus, and Addison's disease. They also serve as the basis of the synthetic hormones used in birth control pills. (See also CONTRACEPTION, ORAL.) The pharmaceutical industry uses them to produce muscle-building anabolic steroids, synthetic derivatives of the male sex hormone testosterone; and to make synthetic dehydroenpiandrosterone, or DHEA, which works in the same way as a hormone secreted by the human adrenal glands. It is believed by some to help with weight loss and to slow the aging process. The United States imports 60,000 tons of yams from Mexico each year in order to manufacture birth control pills. About 70 to 80 percent of the raw materials for today's steroid drugs come from yams that are now commercially grown in southern Mexico.

See also ARTHRITIS TREATMENTS; PHARMACOLOGY.

**Sources/Further Reading**

Coe, Sophie. *America's First Cuisines.* Austin: University of Texas Press, 1994.

Heiser, Charles B. *Seed to Civilization: The Story of Food.* Cambridge: Mass.: Harvard University Press, 1990.

Mowrey, Daniel B. *Herbal Tonic Therapies*. New York: Random House, 1996.

*Steroids that Foam in Water*. *Wayne's Word*. URL: http://daphne.palomar.edu/wayne/plsept96.htm. Downloaded on May 22, 1999.

Taylor, Norman. *Plant Drugs that Changed the World*. New York: Dodd, Mead & Company, 1965.

**yuca** See MANIOC.

**yucca** (precontact) *North American Southwest cultures*
Yucca, a genus of the Liliacae, or lily family, is a plant that is indigenous to the northern part of what is now Mexico, arid regions of Mesoamerica, and the desert Southwest of what is now the United States. The plants grow up to 40 feet tall and consist of a woody stem surrounded by tufts of long, stiff leaves. The most well-known varieties of yucca plants are the Spanish bayonet and the Joshua tree. Indigenous peoples living in the Southwest; Baja California; and the northern deserts of Mexico cultivated yucca plants for food, medicine, and fiber. Because of its usefulness, yucca probably was of greater economic value to the Pueblo tribes than was any other plant in the area. Today yucca is grown throughout the warm regions of the United States as an ornamental plant. It is an important part of XERISCAPING (gardening with minimal water) in the southwestern United States.

Southwestern American Indians ate the petals of yucca flowers raw or in salads and boiled as a vegetable. The Hopi roasted yucca fruit in earth ovens. The Apache mixed pinon nuts with yucca fruit to make a pudding. The Hopi ate boiled yucca fruit with CORN dumplings. Yucca pods were picked green and then roasted and peeled before being eaten. Sometimes yucca fruits were dried and stored throughout the winter. Because they were sweet, the Apache boiled them into a syrup that they then brushed on other vegetables they were drying. Once the Navajo (Dineh) and some Pueblo people had removed seeds from ripe yucca fruit, they boiled the fruits until they had made a thick jam that they shaped into rolls and ate throughout the winter. These were possibly the world's first fruit roll-ups. The Akimel O'odham (Pima) ate dried banana yucca fruits as candy. Yucca fruits were also commonly used to make beverages by a number of tribes. The Apache boiled the leaves in stews. Today, Pueblo people continue to eat roasted yucca fruit. While not a popular food item for non-Indians, the yucca's roots are used in the production of some root beers. (See also SOFT DRINK INGREDIENTS.)

American Indians used yucca to treat arthritis and rheumatism. (See also ARTHRITIS TREATMENTS.) One of the reasons why tea made from the roots and leaves of these plants may have worked to alleviate pain is that they contain saponins, steroidlike substances that boost the body's production of cortisone. Yucca root was also used as shampoo or a soap (see also DETERGENTS) and also as a cream that was applied to treat rashes. The soap made from yucca root was so mild that Zuni washed newborn babies in it. Yucca shampoo is still used by American Indians throughout the Southwest because of the shine it imparts to hair. Yucca is also an ingredient in some commercial shampoos sold in stores today.

American Indians soaked yucca leaves in water and then pounded them with stones to obtain fiber, which they twined into cordage to make cloth, belts, baskets, ropes, rope ladders, and SANDALS. When prehistoric Pueblo people wove with yucca fiber, they sometimes incorporated rabbit fur into the textiles they made. (See also WEAVING TECHNIQUES.) The Hopi and Rio Grande Pueblo people used yucca fiber for paintbrushes with which they applied coloring to POTTERY. The Navajo made brushes from yucca fiber tied in bundles, which they used to clean their metates, or corn-grinding stones. They also tied wooden slats together with yucca fiber in order to make temporary SNOWSHOES. The use of yucca to make cloth continued after conquest. During World War I, factories made 8 million tons of burlap from the fiber of the Spanish Bayonet for the war effort. Wood from the Joshua tree was also used during both World War I and II to make splints that were applied to broken bones. (See also ORTHOPEDIC TECHNIQUES.)

**Sources/Further Reading**

American Desert Plants, Inc. *Did You Know This?* URL: http://www.desertplants.com/html_pages/didyou.html. Downloaded on November 21, 1999.

Brandt, Roger. *Recent and Historic Uses of Plants Found in the Death Valley Region*. URL: http://www.ivnet.net/pupfish/plnt-use.htm. Downloaded on November 21, 1999.

Driver, Harold E. *Indians of North America*. Chicago: University of Chicago Press, 1969.

Dunmire, William W. and Gail D. Tierney. *Wild Plants of the Pueblo Province: Exploring Ancient and Enduring Uses*. Santa Fe: Museum of New Mexico Press, 1995.

Moerman, Dan. *Native American Ethnobotany Database: Food, Drugs, Dyes and Fibers of Native North American Peoples*. URL: http://www.umd.umich.edu/cgi-bin/herb. Downloaded on November 21, 1999.

Ramsay, Marylee and John Richard Schrock. "The Yucca Plant and the Yucca Moth." *The Kansas School Naturalist* 38, no. 2 (1998): 1–9.

# Z

**zero** (ca. 31 B.C.) *Mesoamerican cultures*
The zero is a numerical symbol that serves as a position notation, or placeholder. In calculation it behaves like a natural number. Without the zero, division and fractions are impossible. Many scholars credit the Hindu with inventing the zero. However, the Olmec, whose culture arose in Mesoamerica in about 1700 B.C., invented the zero independently from the same concept that was invented in India in about A.D. 595 and the Mesopotamian zero that is thought to have been invented much earlier. Mesoamerican scholars believe that the Olmec were using the zero sometime near 31 B.C. This is the earliest date the Olmec carved into stone that has been found by archaeologists; however, logic dictates they were developing and using the concept well before this time. At the same time they were creating the concept of zero, the Olmec invented the CALENDAR, a bar and dot numerical system, and WRITING. The Maya, whose culture arose in the same region as the Olmec and flourished longer than Olmec culture, borrowed the concept of the zero from them. Evidence found on Maya stone carvings and in books shows them to have been sophisticated mathematicians who used the zero to figure CALENDAR dates, perform astronomical calculations, and keep accounts.

See also BASE 20 MATHEMATICAL SYSTEM.

## Sources/Further Reading

Benson, Elizabeth P. *The Maya World*. New York: Thomas Y. Crowell Company, 1967.

Closs, Michael T., ed. *Native American Mathematics*. Austin: University of Texas Press, 1986.

Coe, Michael D. *America's First Civilization: Discovering the Olmec*. Eau Claire, Wisc.: American Heritage Publishing Co., Inc., 1968.

Mexico History—The Preclassic Period, The Olmec. URL: http://www.mexconnect.com/mex_/hpreclassic.html. Downloaded on September 25, 1999.

Schele, Linda and Freidel, David. *A Forest of Kings: The Untold Story of the Maya*. New York: William Morrow and Company, Inc., 1990.

**zinnias (*Zinnia elegans*)** (precontact) *Mesoamerican cultures*
Zinnias (*Zinnia elegans*) are one of the three most popular garden flowers today. They are characterized by showy composite blossoms and are indigenous to the area that is called Mexico today. The blooms that zinnias produce vary in color, including white, yellow, gold, orange, copper, crimson, purple, and maroon blossoms. The Aztec, who established an empire in what is now Mexico in about A.D. 1100, held flowers in high regard. They cultivated several varieties of zinnias. Spaniards brought the first zinnias to Europe in 1753. The plants were named after botany professor, J. G. Zinn. In 1796 the first *Zinnia elegans* variety was brought to Europe from Mexico. This variety quickly became popular and is the stock to which all modern garden zinnias owe their start.

See also DAHLIAS; MARIGOLDS; POINSETTIAS.

## Sources/Further Reading

Michigan State University Extension. *Zinnia Elegans*. URL: http://www.msue.msu.edu/son/mod21/21000280.html. Downloaded on January 29, 2000.

Parsons, James A. "Southern Blooms: Latin America and the World of Flowers." *Queen's Quarterly* 99, no. 3 (1992): 542–561.

**zoned biodiversity** (ca. A.D. 595) *Mesoamerican, South American Andean culture groups*
Zoned biodiversity is the practice of systematically planting crops in various locations in order to provide for a number of

growing conditions, including soil composition, drainage, temperature, available sunlight, and rainfall. Modern agronomists urge farmers to use this practice as a form of crop failure insurance and to diversify the genetic makeup of crops. It also serves to counter 20th century farming methods that rely heavily on chemical fertilizers and pesticides that have reduced the varieties of crops that are grown. The agricultural strategy of zoned biodiversity is not a modern one. It was practiced extensively by ancient farmers of both Meso- and South America, who used it to ensure consistent yields and to experiment to find optimal growing conditions for specific varieties of plants.

At Machu Picchu high in the Andes, the Inca, who established their empire in what is now Peru in about A.D. 1000, planted what appear to be experimental plots. These were established at a number of altitudes and angles in relationship to the sun. This practice allowed them to grow very high yields of POTATOES and CORN and to develop a number of varieties that were suited to different soils and climates. (See also SEED SELECTION.) The Hohokam, whose culture arose in what is now Arizona in about 300 B.C., also planted crops in a variety of soils and sunlight conditions. This practice, which they began using in about A.D. 595, not only helped develop new types of plants, it also served as a form of crop insurance. The more widely varied the environments the crops could be planted in, the less chance existed that drought or disease would wipe out an entire crop.

See also AGRICULTURE, FARMING, TERRACED; DOUBLE CROPPING.

## Sources/Further Reading

Hurt, R. Douglas. *Indian Agriculture in the Americas: Prehistory to Present.* Lawrence: University Press of Kansas, 1988.

Weatherford, Jack. *Indian Givers: How the Indians of the Americas Transformed the World.* New York: Fawcett Columbine, 1988.

Wiseman, James. "The Art of Gardening: Eating Well at a Mesoamerican Pompeii." *Archaeology* (January/February 1998): 12–14.

**ZOOS** (ca. A.D. 1100–A.D. 1519) *Mesoamerican cultures*
*Zoo* is an abbreviated term for *zoological gardens,* parklike areas where animals are exhibited for the education and amusement of visitors. The Aztec, who established an empire in what is now Mexico in about A.D. 1100, created extensive gardens that contained all of the flora and fauna found in the Aztec Empire. Some of these specimens had been given to the emperor Montezuma as gifts. Others were brought by his order. Although zoos were located throughout Montezuma's realm, the

three best-known were located in the cities of Tlalelolco, Texcoco, and Iztapalapán. The gardens contained medicinal plants as well as decorative ones. Aztec physicians used these plants to conduct MEDICAL RESEARCH. Some of the animals kept in the Aztec zoological gardens were foxes, jaguars, wildcats, and wolves. The zoos also contained different types of lizards and snakes. Probably this is the first time that Hernán Cortés and his men saw a rattlesnake in one of the zoological gardens. In their reports of their visits to the Aztec zoos, the Spaniards mention seeing a snake with a "sounding rattle on it."

The Izatapalapán zoological garden had human-made canals, ponds, lakes, and waterfalls. The garden could be entered by boat from a lake. Montezuma went to great lengths to re-create the natural environments for the fish and fowl he had at the gardens. The lakes, canals, and ponds were filled with either salt water or freshwater to accommodate the fish and fowl that came from each of those habitats. The garden was so well planned that both types of canals and ponds could be drained for cleaning and refilled again by AQUEDUCTS without disturbing the fish or birds.

This zoological garden had an aviary (an enclosure for holding birds) that the Aztec called *totocalli,* which meant "the house of birds." The aviary was built as a half-shelter so that the birds could be protected from the rain. The birds that lived there were fed the diet they ate in their natural habitats—fish, worms, or grain. The zoological garden at Izatapalapán was so large that 300 employees worked in the aviary alone. Some of these workers were specialists who treated the sick birds—much like today's veterinarians.

The garden at Izatapalapán also contained amusements, including a large maze. Guest facilities and baths were also built in the garden. They were designed so that visitors could walk outside on balconies to view the plants and animals. When the emperor could not obtain certain plants and animals that he desired, he had them made of gold, silver, and jewels. These were often placed in smaller gardens. The Spaniards marveled at the opulence to the point that life-sized CORN plants were made of gold and the corn silk was made of silver. Nothing of this type and scale existed in Europe at the time.

See also GARDENS, BOTANICAL; GARDENS, HERB.

## Sources/Further Reading

Coe, Sophie. *America's First Cuisines.* Austin: University of Texas Press, 1994.

Ortiz de Montellano, Bernard R. *Aztec Medicine, Health, and Nutrition.* New Brunswick, New Jersey: Rutgers University Press, 1990.

Soustelle, Jacques. *Daily Life of the Aztecs on the Eve of the Spanish Conquest.* Stanford, Calif.: Stanford University Press, 1961.

# Appendix A: Tribes Organized by Culture Area

## North American Culture Areas

### Arctic Culture Area
Aleut
Inuit

### California Culture Area
Achomawi (Pit River)
Akwaala
Alliklik (Tataviam)
Atsugewi (Pit River)
Bear River
Cahto (Kato)
Cahuilla
Chilula
Chimariko
Chumash
Costanoan (Ohlone)
Cupeño
Diegueño (Ipai)
Esselen
Fernandeño
Gabrieliño
Huchnom
Hupa
Ipai (Diegueño)
Juaneño
Kamia (Tipai)
Karok
Kitanemuk
Konomihu
Lassik
Luiseño
Maidu

Mattole
Miwok
Nicoleño
Nomlaki
Nongatl
Okwanuchu
Patwin (subgroup of Wintun)
Pomo
Salinas
Serrano
Shasta
Sinkyone
Tolowa (Smith River)
Tubatulabal (Kern River)
Vanyume
Wailaki
Wappo
Whilkut
Wintu (subgroup of Wintun)
Wintun
Wiyot
Yahi
Yana
Yokuts
Yuki
Yurok

### Great Basin Culture Area
Bannock
Chemehuevi
Kawaiisu
Mono
Paiute
Panamint

Sheepeater (subgroup of Bannock and Shoshone)
Shoshone
Snake (subgroup of Paiute)
Ute
Washoe

### Great Plains Culture Area
Arapaho
Arikara
Assiniboine
Atsina (Gros Ventre)
Blackfeet
Blood (subgroup of Blackfeet)
Cheyenne
Comanche
Crow
Hidatsa
Ioway
Kaw
Kichai
Kiowa
Kiowa-Apache
Mandan
Missouria
Omaha
Osage
Otoe
Pawnee
Piegan (subgroup of Blackfeet)
Plains Cree
Plains Ojibway
Ponca
Quapaw
Sarcee

311

Sioux (Dakota, Lakota, Nakota)
Tawakoni
Tawehash
Tonkawa
Waco
Wichita
Yscani

**Northeast Culture Area**
Abenaki
Algonkin
Amikwa (Otter)
Cayuga
Chippewa (Ojibway, Anishinabe)
Chowanoc
Conoy
Coree (Coranine)
Erie
Fox (Mesquaki)
Hatteras
Honniasont
Huron (Wyandot)
Illinois
Iroquois (Haudenosaunee)
Kickapoo
Kitchigami
Lenni Lenape (Delaware)
Machapunga
Mahican
Maliseet
Manhattan (subgroup of Lenni
   Lenape or Wappinger)
Massachuset
Mattabesac
Meherrin
Menominee
Miami
Micmac
Mingo (subgroup of Iroquois)
Mohawk
Mohegan
Montauk
Moratok
Nanticoke
Narragansett
Nauset
Neusiok
Neutral (Attiwandaronk)
Niantic
Nipmuc
Noquet
Nottaway
Oneida
Onondaga
Ottawa
Otter (Amikwa)

Pamlico (Pomeiok)
Passamaquoddy
Paugussett
Penacook
Penobscot
Pequot
Pocomtuc
Poospatuck (subgroup of Montauk)
Potawatomi
Powhatan
Raritan (subgroup of
   Lenni Lenape)
Roanoke
Sac
Sakonnet
Secotan
Seneca
Shawnee
Shinnecock (subgroup of Montauk)
Susquehannock
Tobacco (Petun)
Tuscarora
Wampanoag
Wappinger
Weapemeoc
Wenro
Winnebago (Ho-Chunk)

**Northwest Coast
Culture Area**
Ahantchuyuk
Alsea
Atfalati
Bella Coola
Cathlamet
Cathlapotle
Chastacosta
Chehalis
Chelamela
Chepenafa (Mary's River)
Chetco
Chilluckittequaw
Chimakum
Chinook
Clackamas
Clallam
Clatskanie
Clatsop
Clowwewalla
Comox
Coos
Coquille (Mishikhwutmetunne)
Cowichan
Cowlitz
Dakubetede
Duwamish

Gitskan
Haida
Haisla
Heiltsuk
Kalapuya
Kuitsh
Kwakiutl
Kwalhioqua
Latgawa
Luckiamute
Lumni
Makah
Miluk
Muckleshoot
Multomah (Wappato)
Nanaimo
Nisga
Nisqually
Nooksack
Nootka
Puntlatch
Puyallup
Quaitso (Queets)
Quileute
Quinault
Rogue
Sahehwamish
Samish
Santiam
Seechelt
Semiahmoo
Siletz
Siuslaw
Skagit
Skilloot
Skykomish
Snohomish
Snoqualmie
Songish
Squamish
Squaxon (Squaxin)
Stalo
Swallah
Swinomish
Takelma (Rogue)
Taltushtuntude
Tillamook
Tlingit
Tsimshian
Tututni (Rogue)
Twana
Umpqua
Wappato (Multomah)
Wasco
Watlala (Cascade)
Yamel

Yaquina
Yoncalla

**Plateau Culture Area**
Cayuse
Chelan
Coeur d'Alene
Columbia (Sinkiuse)
Colville
Entiat
Flathead (Salish)
Kalispel
Klamath
Klickitat
Kootenai (Flathead)
Lake (Senijextee)
Lillooet
Methow
Modoc
Molalla
Nez Perce
Ntlakyapamuk (Thompson)
Okanagan
Palouse
Pshwanwapam
Sanpoil
Shuswap
Sinkaietk
Sinkakaius
Skin (Tapanash)
Spokan
Stuwihamuk
Taidnapam
Tenino
Tyigh
Umatilla
Walla Walla
Wanapam
Wauyukma
Wenatchee
Wishram
Yakama

**Southeast Culture Area**
Acolapissa
Adai
Ais
Akokisa
Alabama
Amacano
Apalachee
Apalachicola
Atakapa
Avoyel
Bayogoula
Bidai

Biloxi
Caddo
Calusa
Caparaz
Cape Fear
Catawba
Chakchiuma
Chatot
Chawasha (subgrop of Chitimacha)
Cheraw (Sara)
Cherokee
Chiaha
Chickasaw
Chine
Chitimacha
Choctaw
Congaree
Coushatta
Creek
Cusabo
Deadose
Eno
Eyeish (Ayish)
Griga
Guacata
Guale
Hitchiti
Houma
Ibitoupa
Jeaga
Kaskinampo
Keyauwee
Koroa
Lumbee
Manahoac
Miccosukee (subgroup of Seminole)
Mobile
Monacan
Moneton
Muklasa
Nahyssan
Napochi
Natchez
Occaneechi
Oconee
Ofo
Okelousa
Okmulgee
Opelousa
Osochi
Pasacagoula
Patiri
Pawokti
Pee Dee
Pensacola
Quinipissa

Santee (Issati)
Saponi
Sawokli
Seminole
Sewee
Shakori
Sissipahaw
Sugeree
Taensa
Tamathli
Tangipahoa
Taposa
Tawasa
Tekesta
Timucua
Tiou
Tohome
Tunica
Tuskegee
Tutelo
Waccamaw
Washa (subgroup of Chitimacha)
Wateree
Waxhaw
Winyaw
Woccon
Yadkin
Yamasee
Yazoo
Yuchi

**Southwest Culture Area**
Akimel O'odham (Pima)
Apache
Coahuiltec
Cocopah
Halchidhoma
Halyikwamai
Havasupai
Hopi
Hualapai
Jumano (Shuman)
Karankawa
Keres (Pueblo Indians)
Kohuana
Maricopa
Mojave
Navajo (Dineh)
Piro (Pueblo Indians)
Pueblo
Quenchan (Yuma)
Shuman (Jumano)
Sobaipuri
Tewa (Pueblo Indians)
Tiwa (Pueblo Indians)

Tohono O'odham (Papago)
Towa (Jemez, Pueblo Indians)
Yaqui
Yavapai
Yuma (Quechan)
Zuni

**Subarctic Culture Area**
Ahtena (Copper)
Beaver (Tsattine)
Beothuk
Carrier
Chilcotin
Chipewyan
Cree
Dogrib
Eyak
Han
Hare (Kawchottine)
Ingalik
Kolchan
Koyukon
Kutchin
Montagnais
Nabesna
Nahane
Naskapi
Sekani
Slave (Slavery,
    Etchaottine)
Tahltan
Tanaina
Tanana
Tatsanottine (Yellowknife)

Tsetsaut
Tutchone (Mountain)

**MESOAMERICAN CULTURE AREA***
Aztec (Mexica-Nahuatl)
Maya
Mixtec
Olmec
Toltec
Zapotec

**CIRCUM-CARIBBEAN CULTURE AREA (WEST INDIES AND PORTION OF CENTRAL AMERICA)**
Arawak
Boruca
Carib
Ciboney
Ciguayo
Coiba
Corobici
Cuna
Guaymi
Guetar
Jicaque
Lucayo
Matagalpa
Mosquito
Paya

Rama
Silam
Sumo
Taino
Talamanca
Ulva
Voto
Yosco

**SOUTH AMERICAN CULTURE AREAS***

**Andean Culture Area**
Achuari
Aguaruna
Chavin
Chimu
Inca
Jivaro
Mapuche
Moche
Nazca
Quecha

**Southern Culture Area**
Guarani
Mapuche

**Tropical Forest (Amazon Basin) Culture Area**
Arawak
Carib
Tupi

* These lists do not attempt to include all groups in the area. They do, however, include a mix of ancient and modern peoples.

# APPENDIX B: MAPS

### MAPS

# North American, Mesoamerican, and Circum-Caribbean Indian Culture Areas

| | |
|---|---|
| ⋅⋅⋅ Arctic | Northeast |
| California | Northwest Coast |
| Circum-Caribbean | Plateau |
| Great Basin | Southeast |
| Great Plains | Southwest |
| Mesoamerican | Subarctic |

## Arctic Culture Area

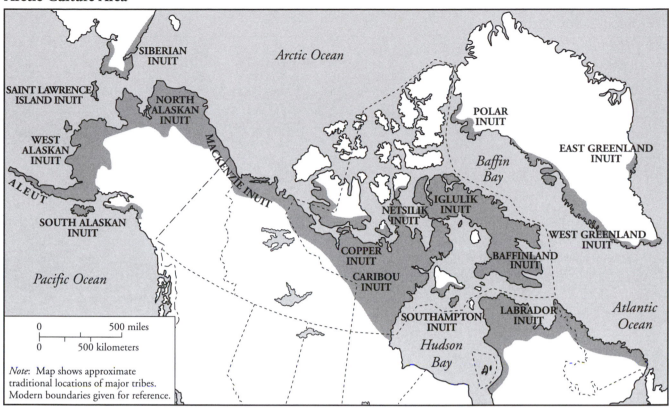

SIBERIAN INUIT

SAINT LAWRENCE
ISLAND INUIT

NORTH
ALASKAN
INUIT

WEST
ALASKAN
INUIT

ALEUT

SOUTH ALASKAN
INUIT

*Arctic Ocean*

POLAR
INUIT

*Baffin
Bay*

EAST GREENLAND
INUIT

MACKENZIE INUIT

NETSILIK
INUIT

IGLULIK
INUIT

WEST GREENLAND
INUIT

COPPER
INUIT

CARIBOU
INUIT

BAFFINLAND
INUIT

*Pacific Ocean*

SOUTHAMPTON
INUIT

LABRADOR
INUIT

*Atlantic
Ocean*

*Hudson
Bay*

0     500 miles

0     500 kilometers

*Note*: Map shows approximate
traditional locations of major tribes.
Modern boundaries given for reference.

## Subarctic Culture Area

*Arctic Ocean*

KOYUKON

INGALIK

TANAINA   TANANA
     KUTCHIN

NABESNA   HAN    HARE
AHTENA

TUTCHONE

TAGISH

DOGRIB

TATSANOTTINE

TAHLTAN   NAHANE

TSETSAUT    SLAVE     CHIPEWYAN

SEKANI

CARRIER    BEAVER

THOMPSON

CHILCOTIN

WESTERN
WOODS
CREE

*Hudson
Bay*

NASKAPI

EAST MAIN
CREE

*Pacific
Ocean*

SWAMPY
CREE

WEST
MAIN
CREE

MONTAGNAIS

BEOTHUK

CHIPPEWA

TÊTE DE
BOULE
CREE

ALGONKIN

*Atlantic
Ocean*

0     500 miles

0     500 kilometers

*Note*: Map shows approximate
traditional locations of major tribes.
Modern boundaries given for reference.

## Northeast Culture Area

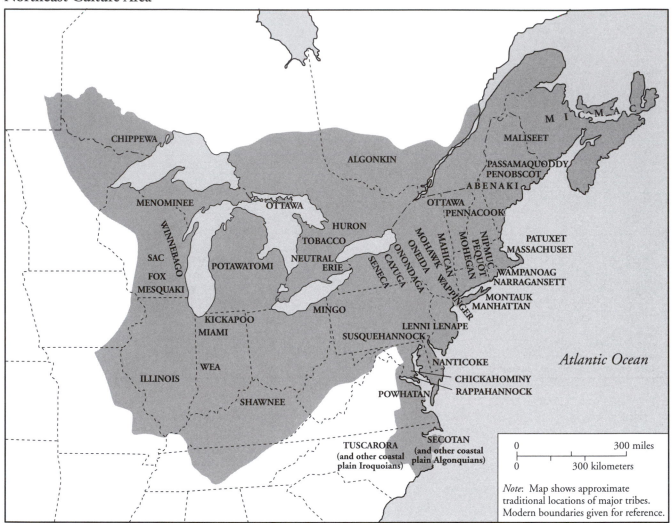

CHIPPEWA

ALGONKIN

MICMAC

MALISEET

PASSAMAQUODDY
PENOBSCOT
ABENAKI

MENOMINEE

OTTAWA

OTTAWA
PENNACOOK

WINNEBAGO

HURON

TOBACCO

NIPMUC
PEQUOT
MOHEGAN

PATUXET
MASSACHUSET

SAC

FOX

MESQUAKI

POTAWATOMI

NEUTRAL
ERIE

MOHAWK
ONEIDA
ONONDAGA
CAYUGA
SENECA

MAHICAN
WAPPINGER

WAMPANOAG
NARRAGANSETT

KICKAPOO
MIAMI

MINGO

LENNI LENAPE

MONTAUK
MANHATTAN

SUSQUEHANNOCK

WEA

ILLINOIS

NANTICOKE

CHICKAHOMINY
RAPPAHANNOCK

Atlantic Ocean

SHAWNEE

POWHATAN

TUSCARORA
(and other coastal
plain Iroquoians)

SECOTAN
(and other coastal
plain Algonquians)

0          300 miles
0      300 kilometers

*Note*: Map shows approximate
traditional locations of major tribes.
Modern boundaries given for reference.

## Southeast Culture Area

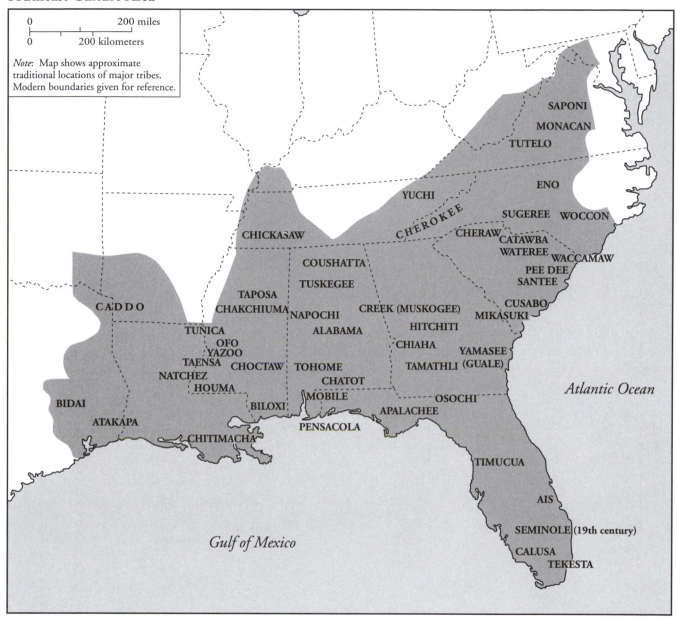

0    200 miles

0    200 kilometers

*Note*: Map shows approximate
traditional locations of major tribes.
Modern boundaries given for reference.

SAPONI

MONACAN

TUTELO

ENO

YUCHI

CHEROKEE

SUGEREE   WOCCON

CHICKASAW

CHERAW

CATAWBA

WATEREE   WACCAMAW

COUSHATTA

PEE DEE

TUSKEGEE   SANTEE

TAPOSA

CHAKCHIUMA   CUSABO

CADDO   CREEK (MUSKOGEE)   MIKASUKI

NAPOCHI

TUNICA   ALABAMA   HITCHITI

OFO   CHIAHA

YAZOO   YAMASEE

TAENSA   CHOCTAW   TOHOME   TAMATHLI   (GUALE)

NATCHEZ   CHATOT

HOUMA

MOBILE   *Atlantic Ocean*

BIDAI   BILOXI   OSOCHI

APALACHEE

ATAKAPA   PENSACOLA

CHITIMACHA

TIMUCUA

AIS

*Gulf of Mexico*   SEMINOLE (19th century)

CALUSA

TEKESTA

## Great Plains Culture Area

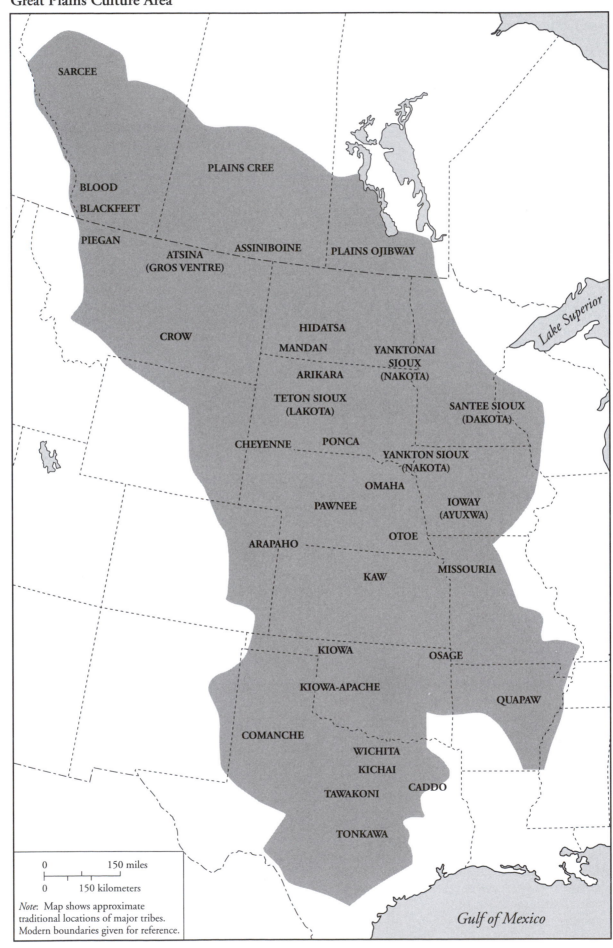

SARCEE

PLAINS CREE

BLOOD
BLACKFEET
PIEGAN
ATSINA
(GROS VENTRE)
ASSINIBOINE
PLAINS OJIBWAY

Lake Superior

CROW

HIDATSA
MANDAN
ARIKARA
TETON SIOUX
(LAKOTA)
YANKTONAI
SIOUX
(NAKOTA)
SANTEE SIOUX
(DAKOTA)

CHEYENNE
PONCA
YANKTON SIOUX
(NAKOTA)
OMAHA
PAWNEE
IOWAY
(AYUXWA)
ARAPAHO
OTOE
MISSOURIA
KAW

KIOWA
OSAGE
KIOWA-APACHE
QUAPAW

COMANCHE
WICHITA
KICHAI
CADDO
TAWAKONI

TONKAWA

| 0 | 150 miles |
| 0 | 150 kilometers |

*Note*: Map shows approximate
traditional locations of major tribes.
Modern boundaries given for reference.

*Gulf of Mexico*

## Plateau Culture Area

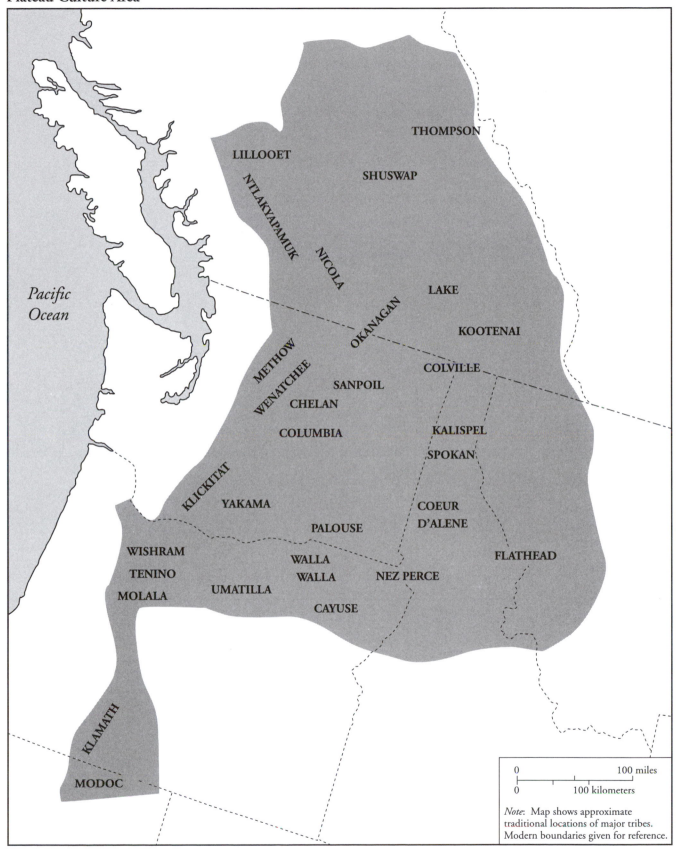

*Pacific Ocean*

THOMPSON

LILLOOET

SHUSWAP

NTLAKYAPAMUK

NICOLA

LAKE

OKANAGAN

KOOTENAI

METHOW

COLVILLE

WENATCHEE

SANPOIL

CHELAN

COLUMBIA

KALISPEL

SPOKAN

KLICKITAT

YAKAMA

COEUR
D'ALENE

PALOUSE

FLATHEAD

WISHRAM

WALLA

TENINO

WALLA

NEZ PERCE

MOLALA

UMATILLA

CAYUSE

KLAMATH

MODOC

| 0 | | 100 miles |
|---|---|---|
| 0 | | 100 kilometers |

*Note*: Map shows approximate traditional locations of major tribes. Modern boundaries given for reference.

## Great Basin Culture Area

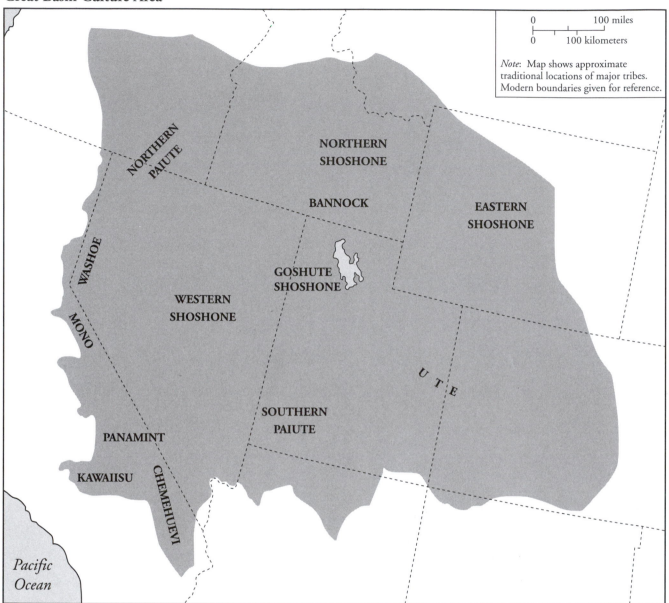

0         100 miles

0       100 kilometers

*Note*: Map shows approximate traditional locations of major tribes. Modern boundaries given for reference.

NORTHERN PAIUTE

NORTHERN SHOSHONE

BANNOCK

EASTERN SHOSHONE

WASHOE

GOSHUTE SHOSHONE

WESTERN SHOSHONE

MONO

U T E

SOUTHERN PAIUTE

PANAMINT

KAWAIISU

CHEMEHUEVI

*Pacific Ocean*

## Northwest Coast Culture Area

EYAK

T L I N G I T

HAIDA

NISGA

TSIMSHIAN

BELLA
COOLA
HEILTSUK

KWAKIUTL
COMOX
SEECHELT
NOOTKA
PUNTLATCH
SQUAMISH
NANAIMO
SEMIAHMOO
COWICHAN
LUMNI
MAKAH
NOOKSACK
QUILEUTE
SKAGIT
QUINAULT
CLALLAM
CHEHALIS
CHIMAKUM
COAST SALISH
TWANA
DUWAMISH
CHINOOK
SNOQUALMIE
CLATSOP
PUYALLUP
KWALHIOQUA
NISQUALLY
CLATSKANIE
COWLITZ
TILLAMOOK
SILETZ
YAQUINA
ALSEA
KALAPUYA
SIUSLAW
COOS
UMPQUA
TAKELMA
TUTUTNI
CHASTACOSTA

## California Culture Area

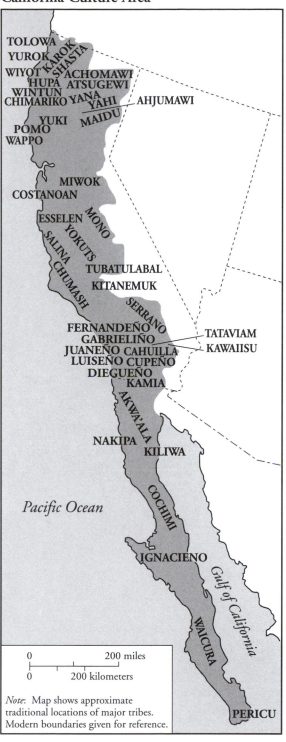

TOLOWA
YUROK
KAROK
SHASTA
WIYOT
ACHOMAWI
HUPA
ATSUGEWI
WINTUN
CHIMARIKO
YANA
YAHI
AHJUMAWI
MAIDU
YUKI
POMO
WAPPO

MIWOK
COSTANOAN

ESSELEN
MONO
YOKUTS
SALINA
TUBATULABAL
CHUMASH
KITANEMUK
SERRANO
FERNANDEÑO
TATAVIAM
GABRIELIÑO
KAWAIISU
JUANEÑO
CAHUILLA
LUISEÑO
CUPEÑO
DIEGUEÑO
KAMIA
AKWA'ALA
NAKIPA
KILIWA

*Pacific Ocean*

COCHIMI

*Gulf of California*

IGNACIENO

WAICURA

PERICU

## Southwest Culture Area

HUALAPAI

HAVASUPAI

HOPI

JICARILLA
APACHE

MOJAVE

NAVAJO

HALCHIDHOMA

TIWA
TEWA

YAVAPAI

TOWA

PECOS

MARICOPA

ZUNI

KERES

YUMA

TIWA

COCOPAH

PIRO

WESTERN
APACHE

MIMBRENO
APACHE

TOHONO
O'ODHAM

MESCALERO
APACHE

CHIRICAHUA
APACHE

AKIMEL
O'ODHAM

SUMA

Gulf of California

OPATA

JUMANO

SERI

CAHITA

JOVA

CONCHO

YAQUI

LIPAN
APACHE

TEPAHUE

TARAHUMARA

VAVROHIO

KARANKAWA

MAYO

TOBOSO

ZOE

COMANITO

NIO

COAHUILTEC

LAGUNERO

GUASAVE

TEPEHUAN

ZACATEC

BOCALOS

TAMAULIPEC

Gulf
of
Mexico

JANAMBRE

PISONES

NEGRITO

HUICHOL

Pacific Ocean

TEPECANO

JONAZ

COLOTLAN

GUACHICHIL

GUAMARES

TEUL

PAME

| 0 | | 150 miles |
|---|---|---|
| 0 | | 150 kilometers |

*Note*: Map shows approximate
traditional locations of major tribes.
Modern boundaries given for reference.

# Mesoamerican Culture Area

Gulf of Mexico

TAHUE
ACAXEE
XIXIME
CORA
TECUAL
CAZCAN
TAMAULIPEC

HUASTEC
TEPEHUA
TOTONAC

TECUEXE
CUYUTEC
COCA
SAYULTEC
MAZATEC
TAMAZULTEC
CHICHIMECA
TOLTEC

XOCOTEC
PAMPUCHIN
TECO
TARASCAN
OTOMI
MATLAZINCA
CHUAHCOMECA
NAHUATL
OCUILTECA
CUITLATEC
MATLAME
MAZATEC
POPOLOCA
TLAXCALAN
(AZTEC)
IXCATEC

YUCATÁN
MAYA

TUXTEX
TEPUZTEC
TEPETIXTEC
TLATZIHUIZTEC
CUYUMATEC
TLAPANEC
CHINANTEC
MIXTEC
TEZCATEC
AMUSGO
TRIQUE
MIXE
ZAPOTEC
MIXTEC
ZOQUE
TOJOLABAL
TZELTAL

CHONTAL
CHOL
LACANDON
MAYA

CHATINO
HUAVE
CHIAPANEC
CHICOMUCELTEC
TZOTZIL
MOTOCINTLEC
TAPACHULTEC
AGUACATEC
QUICHE
XINCA
KANJOBAL
KEKCHI
POKOMAM
ACHI
CHUJ

CHORTI
LENCA
CHOLUTEC

TARASCAN

Pacific Ocean

NAHUATLATO
PIPIL
SUBTIABA
TACACHO
MANGUE
NICARAO
BAGAZ
OROTINA

0        300 miles
0        300 kilometers

*Note*: Map shows approximate traditional locations of major tribes. Modern boundaries given for reference.

## Circum-Caribbean Culture Area

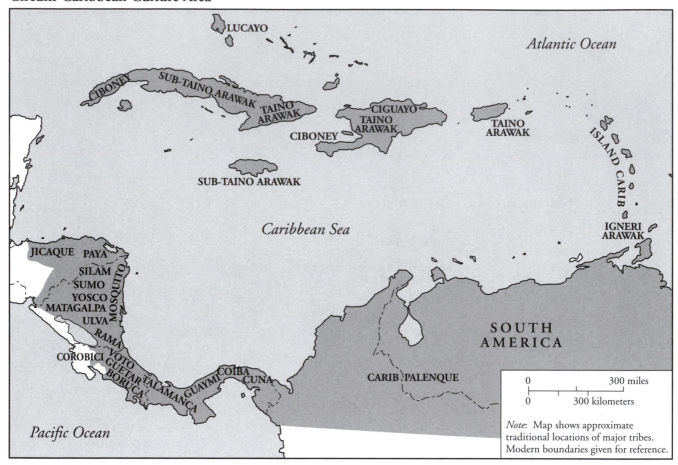

Ancient Civilizations of the Southwest

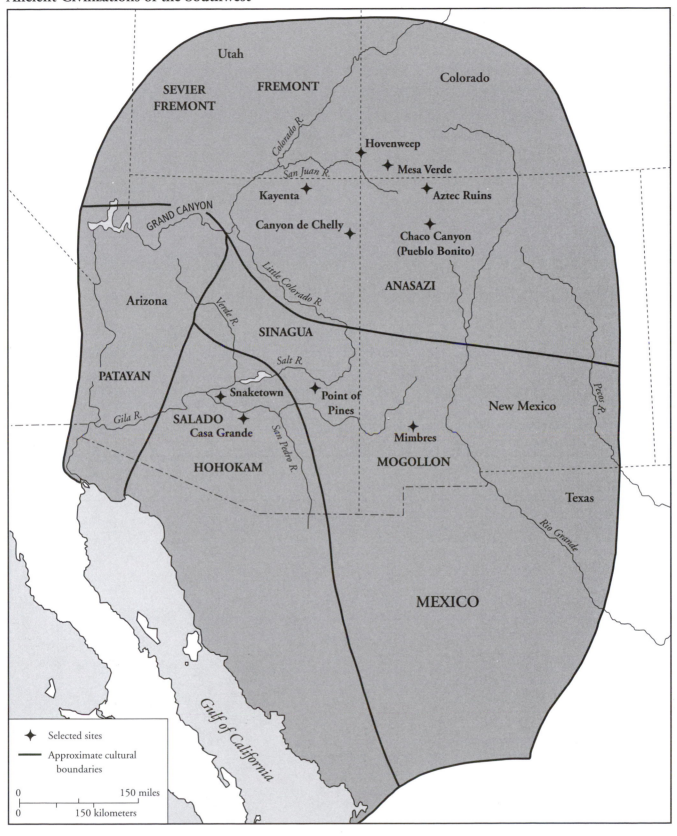

Utah

SEVIER
FREMONT

FREMONT

Colorado

*Colorado R.*

Hovenweep

Mesa Verde

*San Juan R.*

Kayenta

Aztec Ruins

GRAND CANYON

Canyon de Chelly

Chaco Canyon
(Pueblo Bonito)

*Little Colorado R.*

Arizona

ANASAZI

*Verde R.*

SINAGUA

*Salt R.*

PATAYAN

Snaketown

Point of
Pines

New Mexico

*Pecos R.*

*Gila R.*

SALADO

Casa Grande

*San Pedro R.*

Mimbres

HOHOKAM

MOGOLLON

Texas

*Rio Grande*

MEXICO

✦ Selected sites

— Approximate cultural
boundaries

0        150 miles

0     150 kilometers

*Gulf of California*

## Aztec Empire and Neighboring States

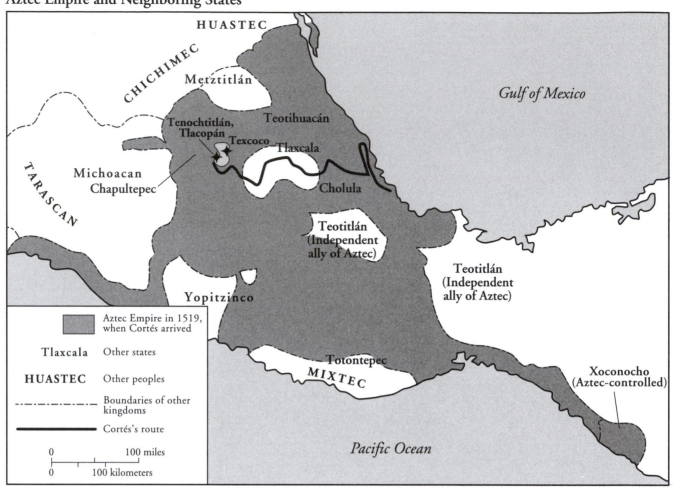

HUASTEC

CHICHIMEC

Metztitlán

Teotihuacán

Tenochtitlán, Tlacopán

Texcoco

Tlaxcala

Michoacan
Chapultepec

Cholula

TARASCAN

Gulf of Mexico

Teotitlán
(Independent
ally of Aztec)

Teotitlán
(Independent
ally of Aztec)

Yopitzinco

Totontepec

MIXTEC

Xoconocho
(Aztec-controlled)

Pacific Ocean

> Aztec Empire in 1519,
> when Cortés arrived
>
> **Tlaxcala**  Other states
>
> **HUASTEC**  Other peoples
>
> Boundaries of other
> kingdoms
>
> Cortés's route
>
> 0        100 miles
> 0     100 kilometers

## Olmec Civilation

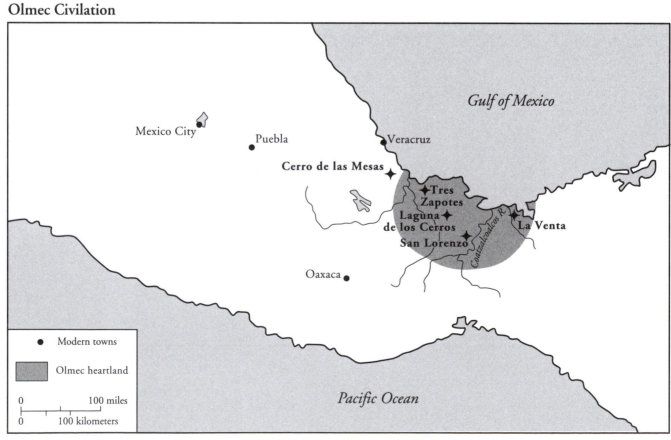

Gulf of Mexico

Mexico City

Puebla

Veracruz

**Cerro de las Mesas**

**Tres
Zapotes**

**Laguna
de los Cerros**

**San Lorenzo**

*Coatzalcoalcos R.*

**La Venta**

Oaxaca

Pacific Ocean

> •  Modern towns
>
>    Olmec heartland
>
> 0        100 miles
> 0     100 kilometers

# Maya Civilization

- ● Modern cities
- ✦ Ancient Mayan sites
- ▨ Izapan culture
- –··– Modern nations and borders

0 ——— 100 miles
0 ——— 100 kilometers

**Isla Cerritos** ✦

**Dzibilchaltún** ✦

● Mérida

**Chichén Itzá** ✦

**Coba** ✦

Isla Cozumel

**Kabah** ✦
**Uxmal** ✦
**Labna**
**Savil**

**Tulum** ✦

● Campeche

**Edzna** ✦

NORTHERN LOWLANDS

**Becan** ✦
**Río Bec** ✦

*Hondo R.*

**Calakmul** ✦

**Lamana** ✦

**El Mirador** ✦
**Nakbe** ✦

**San José** ✦

● Belize City

**Palenque** ✦

**Uaxacrun** ✦
**Tikal**

**Holmul** ✦
**Barton Ramie** ✦

SOUTHERN LOWLANDS

**Piedras Negras** ✦

**Taxchilan** ✦

**Altar de Sacrificos** ✦

**Bonampak** ✦

MEXICO

BELIZE

**Naco** ✦

GUATEMALA

NORTHERN HIGHLANDS

HONDURAS

**Copán** ✦

SOUTHERN HIGHLANDS

**Izapa** ✦

Guatemala City ●

**Kaminaljuyú** ✦

**Monte Alto** ✦

EL SALVADOR

**Ancient Mesoamerican City-States**

Legend:
- ● Mesoamerican cities of 20,000 or more at some time between
- ■ Tikal, ca. 600–1000
- ○ Cholula, ca. 1000–1250
- △ Texcoco, ca. 1250–1500

0 — 400 miles
0 — 400 kilometers

*Gulf of Mexico*

*Caribbean Sea*

*Pacific Ocean*

Tula(■)●
Tenochtitlán(△) Teotihuacán(■)
Calixtlahuaca(■) Texcoco(△)
Azcapotzalco(■○△)
Tzintzuntzán(△) Pátzcuaro(△) Tlaxcala(△)
Xochicalco(■) Cholula(■○△)
Tilantongo(■) Zaachila(△)
Monte Albán(■) Mitla(△)

Dzibalchaltún(■)
Tícoh(△)
Mayapán(○●) Chichén Itzá
Uxmal(■○△) ■○△
Mani (■△)

Tikal(■)
Piedras Negras(■)●

Utatlán(△)
Copán(■○)
Iximché(△)

South American Culture Areas

CIRCUM-CARIBBEAN

CARIB
PALENQUE

TUPI
ARAWAK

AGUARUNA
ACHUARI
JIVARO

CARIB

ARAWAK

TUPI

CHIMU

INCA

TROPICAL FOREST

ANDEAN

EASTERN
HIGHLANDS

GUARANI

GUARANI

CENTRAL AND SOUTHERN

MAPUCHE

PAMPAS

TIERRA DEL FUEGO

**ANDEAN**  Culture areas

PAMPAS  Regions

**MAPUCHE**  Tribes and peoples

———————  Approximate culture
area boundaries

----------  Approximate regional
boundaries

0 ———————— 800 miles

0 ———————— 800 kilometers

*Note:* See the Circum-Caribbean map for
the entire scope of the culture area.

# Inca Civilization

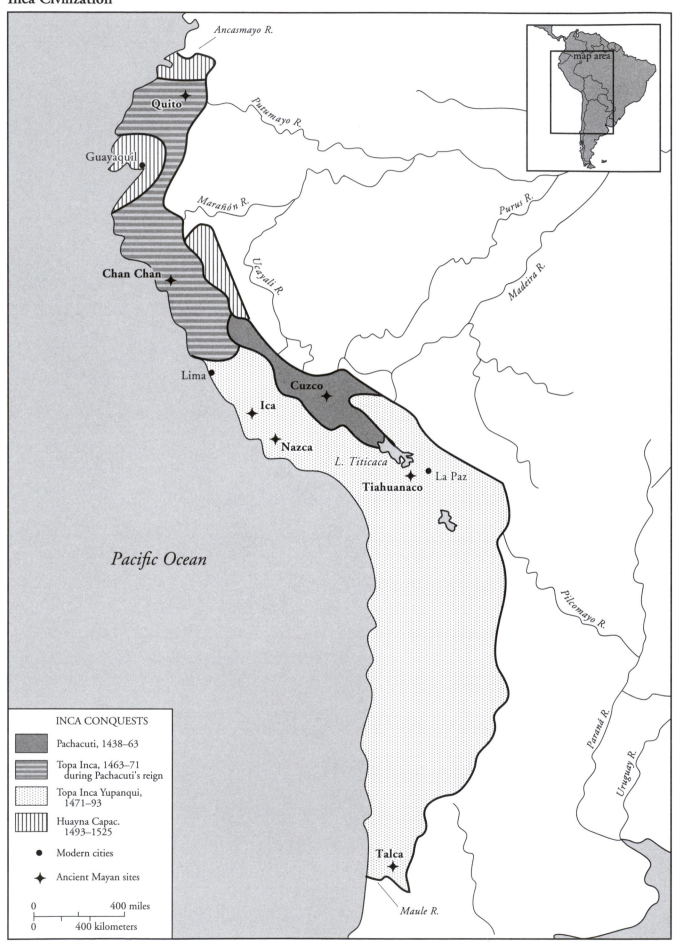

*Ancasmayo R.*

*Putumayo R.*

**Quito**

Guayaquil

*Marañón R.*

*Purus R.*

*Ucayali R.*

*Madeira R.*

**Chan Chan**

Lima

**Cuzco**

**Ica**

**Nazca**

*L. Titicaca*

La Paz

**Tiahuanaco**

*Pacific Ocean*

*Pilcomayo R.*

*Paraná R.*

*Uruguay R.*

**INCA CONQUESTS**

Pachacuti, 1438–63

Topa Inca, 1463–71 during Pachacuti's reign

Topa Inca Yupanqui, 1471–93

Huayna Capac. 1493–1525

● Modern cities

✦ Ancient Mayan sites

**Talca**

0      400 miles

0      400 kilometers

*Maule R.*

map area

# GLOSSARY

The following are definitions of medical or technical terms that appear in the text. As these terms appear in numerous entries, it is hoped that this glossary will be a helpful resource to the reader.

**abscess**   Caused by infection, an abscess is a collection of dead white blood cells, bacteria (germs), tissue debris, and protein that is surrounded by a membrane.

**ague**   *Ague* is an outdated term for malaria, a mosquito-borne illness characterized by periods of chills, fever, and sweating.

**alkaloid**   An alkaline substance that is taken from an animal or plant source is called an alkaloid. When alkaloids are mixed with acid, they produce a salt. These salts are used for medical purposes. Two common alkaloids are nicotine and morphine.

**amino acid**   An amino acid is a compound that is found in animals and in plants. These compounds are sometimes called the building blocks of protein. Amino acids are also the end product of protein digestion.

**analgesic**   An analgesic is a pain-relieving medicine.

**anesthetize**   To anesthetize is to create a partial or total lack of feeling, with or without the loss of alertness.

**annealing**   Annealing is the process of heating metal to a high temperature and allowing it to cool slowly. This reduces brittleness and strengthens the metal.

**anti-inflammatory**   An anti-inflammatory is a substance that reduces inflammation, an area that is marked by heat, pain, redness, and swelling. Inflammation can be caused by injury or by infection.

**antispasmodic**   An antispasmodic relieves spasms, uncontrollable and sudden muscle movements caused by an injury or irritation.

**antitussive**   An antitussive is a medicine that relieves or prevents coughing.

**apothecary**   *Apothecary* is an outdated term for a druggist or pharmacist, a tradesperson who specialized in selling medicines to customers.

**arterial**   *Arterial* refers to the arteries, blood vessels that carry blood away from the heart.

**asepsis**   Asepsis is the state or condition of being without infection, germs, or any form of life. Another word for asepsis is sterile.

**astringent**   An astringent is a chemical or agent that causes binding, drawing together, or constricting. It is generally used to slow or to stop the loss of blood or bodily fluids.

**binomial**   *Binomial* is the Latin word meaning two names. The binomial system of scientific classification uses two names (the genus name and the species name) for the plants and animals it names.

**biodegradable**   The quality of a substance that allows it to be naturally broken down into simpler chemical compounds over time is called biodegradable. Plant and animal substances are more biodegradable than are mineral and many human-made substances because they decompose more quickly.

**biopharmaceuticals**    Medicines, or drugs, that are derived from plants are called biopharmaceuticals.

**bronchodilator**    A bronchodilator is a medication that relaxes the bronchial tubes, the airways that enter the lungs. When this occurs, breathing becomes easier.

**cardiac**    *Cardiac* refers to something that is near or pertaining to the heart.

**cathartic**    A treatment or medication that produces a bowel movement is called a cathartic.

**cautery (cauterize)**    Cautery is a medical treatment that involves applying a heated instrument to a wound in order to prevent infection. On occasion, blood vessels may be cauterized in order to stop bleeding.

**chlorophyll**    Chlorophyll is a plant substance responsible for photosynthesis, a process that combines water and carbon dioxide to form oxygen and sugar. Chlorophyll causes the green color common to most plants.

**coagulate**    When a substance coagulates, it changes from a fluid to a more solid state. Blood coagulation (clotting) is what causes wounds to stop bleeding.

**collagen**    Collagen is a strong protein compound that is produced by all living organisms. In animals and in humans it is found in tendons, bones, skin, cartilage, ligaments, and connective tissue.

**concave**    When a surface is concave, it is rounded and hollow, or indented.

**congestive heart failure**    This serious medical condition is caused by the inability of the heart to maintain blood flow throughout the body.

**convex**    A convex surface is one that is evenly rounded and protrudes outward.

**cranial**    Cranial refers to the cranium, the part of the skull that covers the brain.

**debridement**    The act of removing dead or damaged tissue in a wound is called debridement.

**dehydration**    Dehydration refers to the loss of bodily fluid that occurs when fluid output exceeds fluid intake. It can also mean removing water from a substance.

**dementia**    *Dementia* is a general term used to describe memory loss and confused thinking. It can be caused by physical or psychological problems.

**diaphoretic**    A medical treatment that causes an increase in sweating is called a diaphoretic.

**diphtheria**    Diphtheria is a highly contagious disease that has a sudden onset. The symptoms of diphtheria are a gray or yellow-white coating on the tonsils or on the throat. Sometimes a coating forms on the skin as well. People die from diphtheria when the coating comes loose and sticks in the throat and blocks the airway. Because vaccines have been developed against diphtheria, it is a rare disease today.

**diuretic**    A diuretic is a substance that causes an increased output of urine from the body.

**dropsy**    *Dropsy* is an old medical term that is no longer in use. It refers to an excess accumulation of fluid in body tissue, a condition called *edema* today.

**dysentery**    Certain disorders of the intestines due to inflammation of the inner lining are called dysentery. Dysentery is characterized by intestinal spasms, pain and diarrhea as well as the passing of blood or mucous.

**edema**    Edema is an excess accumulation of fluid in the tissues of the body. It can occur in a localized area or in several parts of the body at the same time.

**electrolytes**    Substances that carry an electric current when they are dissolved in fluid are called electrolytes. In the human body they can be found in cells, tissue fluid, and blood. The main electrolytes in the body are chlorine, potassium, and sodium.

**emetic**    An emetic is an agent that, when swallowed, causes a person to vomit.

**ethnobotanist**    An ethnobotanist studies the ways in which people in various cultures use plants in their lives.

**ethnographer**    An etographer studies culture. Ethnologist is another word for ethnographer.

**expectorant**    An agent that causes a person to cough or spit up mucous from the lungs is called an expectorant.

**febrifuge**    *Febrifuge* is an old word for a treatment or medicine that reduces fevers.

**flexion**    A decrease in the angle between two bones forming a joint is called flexion. This word can also mean the ability of material to bend or the act of bending.

**gangrene**    When bone or tissue dies because of a lack of a blood supply, the condition is called gangrene. It can also be caused by injury, inflammation, and bacteria (germs).

**glycoside**    A substance found in plants that can be changed to a sugar is called a glycoside.

**gout**    Gout is a disorder that causes inflammation of joints. Usually it begins in the feet and knees.

**halitosis**   A condition that causes bad breath is called halitosis.

**hematite**   Hematite is a brick red to blackish-red colored mineral that is the main ore of iron.

**hemorrhoids**   Hemorrhoids are bleeding veins around the rectum. This condition causes itching and discomfort.

**hemostat**   A medication, agent, or tool used for slowing or stopping blood flow is called a hemostat.

**horticulturists**   Individuals trained in the art or science of planting flowers, fruits, vegetables, herbs, and other plants are known as horticulturists.

**hydrophobia**   *Hydrophobia* literally means a strong fear of water. Usually it is used as a synonym for the disease rabies (during the latter stages of which one is unable to drink).

**legumes**   A legume is a plant with a pod that splits into two valves (halves) with the seeds connected to the lower edge of one of the valves. Peas and beans are examples of legumes.

**lye**   Lye is an alkali substance that is produced by boiling wood.

**malleable**   A substance capable of being formed or shaped by pressure or hammering is said to be malleable.

**maul**   A maul is a heavy hammer with a long handle used to drive wedges or stakes.

**microorganisms**   A very small, living body that cannot be seen with the eyes is called a microorganism.

**molars**   The back teeth that are used for grinding are called molars.

**morbid matter**   This term refers to tissue that is diseased or decayed.

**mucosa**   Moist tissue that lines body cavities and hollow organs of the body is called mucosa.

**neuralgia**   *Neuralgia* refers to a very sharp and severe pain that occurs around some nerve pathways.

**neurotransmitter**   A chemical substance that is produced and released by nerve cells is called a neurotransmitter. This substance passes between cells in order to convey sensation and information.

**olfactory**   *Olfactory* describes the ability to sense smell.

**opacities**   A cloudy matter or substance that forms in the front of the eyes is known as an opacity. This substance prevents people from seeing clearly or from seeing at all. A cataract is an opacity.

**oxytocic**   An oxytocic is a substance or agent that strengthens a woman's contractions during labor and hastens birth.

**pathogen**   A substance or microorganism capable of causing a disease is called a pathogen. Bacteria, or germs, and viruses are pathogens.

**pathology**   *Pathology* is used to refer to diseases. It can also mean the study of the causes and nature of diseases.

**peristalsis**   Muscle movement in the throat, stomach, and intestines that moves matter in one direction is called peristalsis. It is a necessary part of digestion.

**petroglyphs**   Line drawings or carvings found on rock are known as petroglyphs.

**pleural cavity**   The word *pleura* is Greek and means "side" or "rib." In the body the area between the covering on the lungs and the chest wall is known as the pleural cavity.

**poultice**   A hot, wet, thick plaster, often placed between two pieces of fiber or cloth, and then applied to the skin to relieve pain or congestion is called a poultice.

**premolars**   The teeth located between the canines and the molars are called premolars.

**pulmonary**   *Pulmonary* is a word used to refer to anything involving or concerning the lungs.

**renal**   *Renal* refers to anything involving or concerning the kidneys.

**rheumatism**   This is a general term used to describe stiffness, inflammation, muscle soreness, and pain in bone joints and related structures.

**suture**   To suture is to sew two pieces of tissue together.

**tartar**   Tartar is the hard material that forms on teeth due to poor oral hygiene.

**tensile**   Tensile is an adjective that describes the ability of material to be lengthened or stretched.

**vasoconstrictor**   An agent or medication that causes the inside diameter of a blood vessel to become smaller is a vasoconstrictor.

**vasodilation**   The enlarging of the inside diameter of a blood vessel due to an agent or chemical is known as vasodilation.

# CHRONOLOGY

## PRECONTACT

The following entries are believed to have existed in the Americas before European contact. Although some were in use for hundreds of years before Europeans arrived in North America, Mesoamerica, and South America, many are believed to have been used by American Indians much longer than that.

agave
allspice
antiasthmatic medication
antibiotic medications
antihelmintics
antiviral medications
aquaculture
arthritis treatments
arthrocentesis
asepsis
astringents
balsa wood
beekeeping
bison
blackberries
black walnuts
blueberries
bows, laminated
boxes
Brazil nuts
bunk beds
calls, animal and bird
camouflage
canoes
caramel corn

cascara sagrada
cashews
casseroles
cat's cradle
caucus
cayenne
chewable dentifrices
chewing gum
chia
chili
cigarettes
civic centers
clambakes
coca
cochineal
cocoa
codes
companion planting
compulsory education
consensus management
contraception, oral
cornbread
cornmeal
corn, parched
corn syrup
cradleboards
cranberries
crop storage
curare
curry, American Indian influence on
dahlias
debridement
decoys, fish (olfactory)
deodorants
detergents

diapers, disposable
distillation
diuretics
dogbane
dogsleds
double cropping
drainage, surgical and wound
dreamwork psychology
dumplings
dyes
earache treatments
ecology
enemas
ephedra
evaporative cooling
eyes, medical treatment of
farina
filé gumbo
fishhooks, multiple
fishing, chemical
fishing, ice
fishnet lures, olfactory
flotation devices
food coloring
food preservation
foot plows
foxglove
free association
fringed clothing
games, dice
games, footbag
gardens, herb
gastroenteritis treatment
goiter prevention
gold panning

grapes
guacamole
guaiacum
guinea pigs
hair conditioners
hammocks
harpoons
headache medications
hickory
hockey, field and ice
holistic health
hominy
hospitals
hot springs
hygiene, personal
igloos
indigestion medications
indigo
insect bite and bee sting remedies
insecticides
insect repellents
instant foods
insulation, home
ipecac
ironwork
jackstraws
jalap
jerky
Jerusalem artichoke
jicama
jojoba
kayaks
lacrosse
lady's slipper
language, American Indian influence
    on
lighthouses
mahogany
maple syrup and sugar
maps, first American
maracas
medicine
megaphones
military tactics
milkweed
mints, botanical
moccasins
morning glories
mouthwash
mukluks
musical instruments
nasturtiums
nutrition
obstetrics
orchards
papayas

parkas
passion fruit
pawpaws
pecans
pemmican
persimmons
pharmacology
pineapples
place-names
poinsettias
ponchos
prescriptions
prickly pear cacti
pulleys
quinine
rheas
road sites
running
salicin
salsa
salve, drawing
sapodilla
sassafras
scuppernong grapes
scurvy cure
settlement patterns
sign language
skin grafts
sleds, cariole
snack foods
snakebite treatments
snow goggles
snowshoes
soft drink ingredients
staples, surgical
stockades
strawberries
stretchers
succotash
sunscreens, medicinal
suppositories
syringes
tamales
tanning, brain
tartar removal
tipis
toboggans
toothpastes and powders
tortillas
tourniquets
toys
tumplines
 umbrellas
vanilla
vicunas
wahoo

water conservation
whaling
white pine
wild rice
wintergreen
witch hazel
xeriscaping
yams
yucca
zinnias

**B.C.**

**25,000**
trousers

**13,000**
bolas

**13,000–10,000**
animals,
    domesticated

**12,000–10,000**
traps

**12,000–A.D. 1000**
tools

**11,000**
flintknapping

**10,000–5000**
dog breeds

**8000**
asphalt
basket weaving
    techniques
gourds
needles
peyote
potatoes
pumpkins
squash
wrenches

**8000–7000**
agriculture
avocados
corn
irrigation systems
seed selection
milpa

**7000**
peppers, sweet or bell
sandals

**7000–5500**
chiles

**6000**
tobacco

**6000–5000**
cotton

**5200–3400**
beans

**5000**
annealing
calabash
embalming
mummies
pins, straight
seawalls

**5000–4000**
axes, copper
chisels
drill bits
jewelry, metal
metallurgy
tubing, copper
weaving techniques

**5000–3000**
fertilizers
fishhooks

**4000–2000**
fish traps

**4000**
alpacas

**3900**
peanuts

**3500**
llamas

**3400**
amaranth

**3000**
adobe
carpentry techniques
manioc
pottery
pyramids
quinoa
shovels
sunflowers

**2500**
popcorn

**2400**
sweet potatoes

**2000**
arrowroot

cattails
forest management
looms
pipes, tobacco
tax system
transplanting, agriculturally

**1900–1400**
foil, metal

**1900–300**
metals, precious

**1800**
embroidery

**1700**
aqueducts
balls
farming, terraced
mirrors
solar fire starters
urban planning
vulcanization
waterproofing

**1700–400**
featherworking
mosaics
optical technology, basics of
plumbing
tarpaulins
saws
zero

**1500**
agriculture, raised bed
astronomy
fans
kaolin
mercury
steam rooms

**1500–A.D. 1500**
blowguns
board games
murals
road systems
traction and countertraction

**1300**
medicine kits

**1200**
cities, America's first
geometry
jade work
wheels

**1100**
snuff

**1000**
anesthetics
basketball
bells
compass
crampons
decoys, duck
dental inlays
dentistry
gold plating
latex
orthopedic techniques
paper
scalpels
stonemasonry techniques
surgery
trade
trephination

**1000–200**
pan pipes
soldering
ventilation systems

**900–200**
tie-dyeing

**900–A.D. 700**
tomatoes

**600**
writing systems
calendars

**600–A.D. 200**
briquettes

**400**
knitting

**300**
helmets, sports
hydralics
platinum
sintering

**300–A.D. 300**
concrete

**200**
cacao
jewelry, turquoise and silver
metal casting
turkey breeding

**200–A.D. 600**
electricity
electroplating
rivets
smelting
welding, sweat

**100**
ducks, muscovy
lost-wax casting technique

**31**
American history, recorded
base 20 mathematical system

## A.D.

**1**
apartment complexes
chocolate
colanders
guava
marigolds

**100–110**
etching, acid

**200**
wampum

**300**
arches, corbeled

**500**
popcorn poppers

**595**
zoned biodiversity

**600**
almanacs
architects

**600–1400**
disability rights

**660**
books

**700**
earth lodges

**800**
excision
money
observatories, astronomical

**850**
keros
parrot breeding

**900–1000**
abacus

**1000**
acoustics
bridges
census
cigars

decoys, fish (visual)
drills, bow
freeze-drying
mining, placer
quipus
rafts, balsa
rafts, inflatable
scales
therapeutic touch
tool kits and boxes

**1000–1400**
Iroquois Constitution

**1000–1519**
labor laws
blue-green algae
space heaters

**1100**
achiote
anatomical knowledge
antispasmodic m
    edications
barbershops
canals, shipping
cataract removal
gardens, botanical
guilds
headache, knowledge of
    etiology
intramedullar nails
pills
plant classifications
public health
pulse, radial
toothbrushes

**1100–1519**
aromatherapy
barbecues
medical research
nurses, nursing
phlebotomy
plastic surgery
psychotherapy
public drunkenness laws
zoos

**1101**
hemostats

**1200**
forceps

**1300**
hydraulics

**1415**
petroleum

**CONTACT**

**1513**
paprika, American Indian influence
    on

**1600**
hemp, American

**1621**
Thanksgiving

**1689**
military contributions

**1700**
granulation
isolation

**1710**
Appaloosa horse breed

**1800**
"X-ray art"

**1850**
tonic water, American Indian
    influence on

**1787**
United States Constitution, American
    Indian influence on

**1793**
medicines, patent, American Indian
    influence on

**1851**
Socialist theory, American Indian
    influence on

**1852**
potato chips

**1865**
Tabasco sauce, American Indian
    influence on

**20th century**
Boy Scouts of America, American
    Indian influence on

**1930**
abstract art, American Indian
    influence on

**1938**
diabetes medication
Erickson's developmental stages,
    American Indian influence on

**1941**
Quonset huts, American Indian
    influence on

# BIBLIOGRAPHY AND FURTHER READING

Adair, John. *The Navajo and Pueblo Silversmiths.* Norman: University of Oklahoma Press, 1994.

Adney, Tappan and Howard I. Chapelle. *Bark Canoes and Skin Boats of North America.* Washington, D.C.: Smithsonian Institution Press, 1993.

Altieri, Miguel. *Agro-ecology: The Science of Sustainable Agriculture.* Boulder, Colo.: Westview Press, Inc., 1995.

Anawalt, Patricia Rieff. *Indian Clothing Before Cortes: Mesoamerican Costumes from the Codices.* Norman: University of Oklahoma Press, 1981.

Anderson, Kat. *Before the Wilderness: Environmental Management by Native Californians.* Menlo Park, Calif.: Ballena Publishers, 1993.

Andrews, Jean. *Peppers: The Domesticated Capsicums.* Arlington: University of Texas Press, 1995.

Aveni, A. F., ed. *Archaeoastronomy in the New World: American Primitive Astronomy.* London: Cambridge University Press, 1982.

Axelrod, Alan. *Chronicle of the Indian Wars from Colonial Times to Wounded Knee.* New York: Prentice Hall, 1993.

Bankes, George. *Peru Before Pizarro.* Phaidon Press Limited, Oxford, England, 1977.

Barriero, Jose, ed. *Indian Roots of American Democracy.* Ithaca, New York: Cornell University Press, 1992.

Beal, Merrill D. *I Will Fight No More Forever: Chief Joseph and the Nez Perce War.* New York: Ballantine Books, 1966.

Benson, Elizabeth P. *The Maya World.* New York: Thomas Y. Crowell Company, 1967.

Blanchard, Kendall and Alyce Cheska. *The Anthropology of Sport, an Introduction.* South Hadley, Mass.: Bergin Garvey Publishers, 1985.

Booth, Annie L. and Harvey M. Jacobs. *Environmental Consciousness—Native American Worldviews and Sustainable Natural Resource Management: An Annotated Bibliography.* Chicago: Council of Planning Librarians, 1988.

Brandon, William. *The Last Americans: The Indian in American Culture.* New York, McGraw-Hill, 1974.

Brotherson, Gordon. *Painted Books from Mexico.* London: British Museum Press, 1995.

Burger, Richard L. *Chavin and the Origins of Andean Civilization.* London: Thames and Hudson, 1992.

Cajate, Gregory. *Native Science: Natural Laws of Interdependence.* Santa Fe: Clear Light Publishers, 2000.

Calloway, Colin G. *Crown and Calumet: British-Indian Relations, 1983–1815.* Norman: University of Oklahoma Press, 1987.

Carmody, Delise Lardner and John Tully Carmody. *Native American Religions: An Introduction.* New York: Paulist Press, 1993.

Clark, W. P. *Indian Sign Language.* Lincoln: University of Nebraska Press, 1982.

Closs, Michael P., ed. *Native American Mathematics.* Austin: University of Texas Press, 1986.

Coe, Michael D. *America's First Civilization: Discovering the Olmec.* New York: American Heritage Publishing Co., Inc., 1968.

———. *Mexico from the Olmecs to the Aztecs.* London: Thames and Hudson, 1994.

Coe, Michael D. and Richard A. Diehl. *In the Land of the Olmecs: The Archaeology of San Lorenzo Tenochtitlan, Vol. 1.* Austin: University of Texas Press, 1980.

Coe, Sophie. *America's First Cuisines.* Austin: University of Texas Press, 1994.

Cooper, Emmanuel. *A History of Pottery.* New York: St. Martin's Press, 1972.

Culin, Stewart. *Games of the North American Indians.* Reprint. Lincoln: University of Nebraska Press, 1992.

Curtis, Natalie. *The Indians' Book.* New York: Harper & Brothers, 1907.

Davis, Emily C. *Ancient Americans.* New York: Cooper Square Publishers, 1975.

Davis, Nigel. *The Ancient Kingdoms of Peru.* New York: Penguin, 1998.

Deloria, Vine, Jr. *God Is Red: A Native View of Religion.* Golden, Colo.: Fulcrum, 1994.

Densmore, Frances. *How Indians Use Wild Plants for Food, Medicine and Crafts.* New York: Dover Publications, Inc., 1974.

———. *Chippewa Customs.* Washington, D.C.: Government Printing Office, 1929.

Domenenci, Viviano and Davide Domenenci. "Talking Knots of the Inka: a Curious Manuscript May Hold the Key to Andean Writing." *Archaeology* (November/December 1996): 50–56.

Donkin, R. A. *Agricultural Terracing in the Aboriginal New World.* Tucson: University of Arizona Press, 1979.

Driscoll, Bernadette. *The Spirit Sings: Artistic Traditions of Canada's First Peoples.* Toronto: McClelland and Stewart, 1987.

Driver, Harold E. *Indians of North America.* Chicago: University of Chicago, 1969.

Duke, James A. *Handbook of Energy Crops.* Unpublished, 1983. URL: http:www.hort.purdue.edu/newcrop/duke_energy/.

Dunmire, William W. and Gail D. Tierney. *Wild Plants of the Pueblo Province: Exploring Ancient and Enduring Uses.* Santa Fe: Museum of New Mexico Press, 1995.

Engel, Frederic Andre. *An Ancient World Preserved: Relics and Records of Prehistory in the Andes.* New York: Crown Publishers, Inc., 1976.

Fagan, Brian M. *Kingdoms of Gold, Kingdoms of Jade: The Americas Before Columbus.* New York: Thames and Hudson, Inc., 1991.

Farb, Peter. *Man's Rise to Civilization as Shown by the Indians of North America from Primeval Times to the Coming of the Industrial State.* New York: E. P. Dutton & Company, 1968.

Farnell, Brenda. *Do You See What I Mean?: Plains Indian Sign Talk and the Embodiment of Action.* Austin: University of Texas Press, 1995.

Fastlicht, Samuel. *Tooth Mutilations and Dentistry in Pre-Columbian Mexico.* Mexico City, Mexico: Quintessense Books, 1971.

Fiedel, Stuart J. *Prehistory Of The Americas.* Cambridge, England: Cambridge University Press, 1987.

Flexner, Stuart Berg. *I Hear America Talking: an Illustrated History of American Words and Phrases.* New York: Simon and Schuster, 1976.

Folsom, Franklin and Mary Elting Folsom. *America's Ancient Treasures.* 4th ed. Albuquerque: University of New Mexico Press, 1993.

Francis, Lee. *Native Time: A Historical Time Line of Native America.* New York: St. Martin's Press, 1996.

Fronval, George and Daniel DuBois. *Indian Signals and Sign Language.* New York: Bonanza Books, 1992.

Gabriel, Kathryn. *Gambler Way: Indian Gaming in Mythology, History and Archaeology in North America.* Boulder, Colo.: Johnson Publishing, 1996.

Geist, Valerius. *Buffalo Nation: History and Legend of the North American Bison.* New York: Voyageur Press, 1998.

Grae, Ida. *Nature's Colors: Dyes from Plants.* New York: Macmillan Publishing Company, Inc., 1974.

Grinde, Donald and Bruce Johansen. *Exemplar of Liberty: Native America and the Evolution of Democracy.* Los Angeles: American Indian Studies, UCLA, 1991.

Hagen, Victor Wolfgang von. *Realm of the Incas.* New York: New American Library, 1957.

———. *The Aztec Man and Tribe.* New York: New American Library, 1961.

Haines, Francis. *The Buffalo: The Story of American Bison and Their Hunters from Prehistoric Times to the Present.* Norman: University of Oklahoma Press, 1995.

Harris, Jennifer, ed. *Textiles, 5,000 Years.* New York: Harry N. Abrams, Inc. Publishers, 1993.

Hassig, Ross. *Trade, Tribute, and Transportation: The Sixteenth-Century Political Economy of the Valley of Mexico.* Norman: University of Oklahoma Press, 1985.

Hazen-Hammond, Susan. *Timelines of Native American History: Through the Centuries with Mother Earth and Father Sky.* New York: Berkeley Publishing Company, 1997.

Heiser, Charles B. *Seed to Civilization: The Story of Food.* Cambridge, Mass.: Harvard University Press, 1990.

Hirshfelder, Arlene and Martha Kreipe de Montano. *The Native American Almanac—A Portrait of Native America Today.* New York: Prentice Hall, 1993.

Hobhouse, Henry. *Seeds of Change: Five Plants that Transformed Mankind.* New York: Harper & Row, 1986.

Hook, Jason. *American Indian Warrior Chiefs.* Dorset, England: Firebird Books, 1989.

Hoskin, Michael, ed. *Cambridge Illustrated History of Astronomy.* New York: Cambridge University Press, 1997.

Hoxie, Frederick E., ed. *Encyclopedia of North American Indians.* New York: Houghton Mifflin Company, 1996.

Hughes, J. Donald. *North American Indian Ecology.* El Paso: University of Texas Press, 1983.

Hurst, David, Jay Miller, Richard White, Peter Nabokov, and Philip Deloria. *The Native Americans.* Atlanta: Turner Publishing, Inc., 1993.

Hurt, R. Douglas. *American Indian Agriculture: Prehistory to Present.* Lawrence: University Press of Kansas, 1987.

Hysop, John. *The Inka Road System.* New York: Academic Press, 1984.

Irwin, R. Stephen. *The Providers: Hunting and Fishing Methods of the North American Natives.* Surry, British Columbia, 1984.

Jeffers, H. Paul and Kevin Gordon. *The Good Cigar.* New York: Lyons and Burford Publishers, 1996.

Jennings, Francis. The *Founders of America: How Indians Discovered the Land, Pioneered in It, and Created Great Classical Civilizations; How They Were Plunged into a Dark Age by Invasion and Conquest; and How They Are Now Reviving.* New York: W. W. Norton, 1993.

Johansen, Bruce. *Forgotten Founders.* Boston: Harvard Common Press, 1987.

———. *Native American Political Systems and the Evolution of Democracy.* Santa Fe, N.M.: Clear Light Publishers, 1998.

———. *Forgotten Founders.* Ipswich, Mass: Gambit, Inc. Publishers, 1982.

Josephy, Jr., Alvin M., ed. *America in 1492: The World of the Indian People Before the Arrival of Columbus.* New York: Random House, 1991.

Karasic, Carol. *The Turquoise Trail: Native American Jewelry and Culture of the Southwest.* New York: Harry Abrams, 1993.

Kent, Kate Peck. *Navajo Weaving Three Centuries of Change.* Santa Fe, N. M.: School of American Research Press, 1985.

Kidwell, Clara S. and Peter Nabokov. "Directions in Native American Science and Technology." In *Studying Native America: Problems and Prospects,* edited by Russell Thornton. Madison, Wis.: The University of Wisconsin Press, 1998.

Kopper, Philip. *The Smithsonian Book of North American Indians before the Coming of the Europeans.* Washington, D.C.: Smithsonian Books, 1986.

Krupp, E. C. *Echoes of the Ancient Skies: The Astronomy of Lost Civilizations.* New York: Harper and Row, 1983.

Krupp, E. C., ed. *In Search of Ancient Skies.* New York: Doubleday & Company, 1978.

Laubin, Reginald and Gladys. *American Indian Archery.* Norman: University of Oklahoma Press, 1980.

Lawlor, Robert. *Sacred Geometry: Philosophy and Practice.* London: Thames and Hudson, 1992.

Lowe, Warren. *Indian Giver.* Pencticton, British Columbia: Theytus Books, 1986.

Lowen, James W. *Lies My Teacher Told Me: Everything Your American History Textbook Got Wrong.* New York: The New Press, 1995.

Lust, John. *The Herb Book.* New York: Bantam Books, 1974.

MacFarlan, Allan and Paulette MacFarlan. *Handbook of American Indian Games.* Dover Books: New York, 1958.

Malone, Patrick M. *The Skulking Way of War: Technology and Tactics among the New England Indians.* New York: Madison Books, 1991.

Malpass, Michael A. *Daily Life in the Inca Empire.* Westport, Conn.: Greenwood Press, 1996.

Martien Jerry and Gary Snyder. *Shell Game: A True Account of Beads and Money in North America.* San Francisco: Mercury House, 1996.

Mason, J. Alden. *The Ancient Civilizations of Peru.* Rev. ed. New York: Penguin Books, 1988.

Mason, Otis Tufton. *American Indian Basketry.* New York: Dover Publications, 1989.

Maxwell, James A. *America's Fascinating Indian Heritage.* Pleasantville, N.Y.: Reader's Digest Books, 1978.

McQuiston, Don and Debra. *Dolls & Toys of Native America: A Journey through Childhood.* San Francisco: Chronicle Books, 1995.

Melanich, Jerald T. *Florida's Indians from Ancient Times to the Present: 12,000 Years of Florida's Indian Heritage.* Gainesville, Fla.: University Press of Florida, 1998.

Miller, Robert J. "American Indian Influence on the United States Constitution and its Framers." *American Indian Law Review* 18 (1993): 133–160.

Moerman, Dan. *Native American Ethnobotany Database: Food, Drugs, Dyes and Fibers of Native North American Peoples.* URL: http://www.umd.umich.edu/cgi-bin/herb.

Morales, Edumundo. *The Guinea Pig: Healing, Food and Ritual in the Andes.* Tucson: University of Arizona Press, 1995.

Morris, Craig and Adriana von Hagen. *The Inka Empire and Its Andean Origins.* New York: Abbeville Press Publishers, 1993.

Moseley, Michael. *The Inca and their Ancestors.* London: Thames and Hudson, 1992.

Murdoch, John. *Ethnological Results of the Point Barrow Expedition: Annual Report of the U.S. Bureau of Ethnology 1887–1888.* Washington: Government Printing Office, 1892.

Nabhan, Gary. *Enduring Seeds: Native American Agriculture and Wild Plant Conservation.* San Francisco: North Point Press, 1989.

Nabokov, Peter and Robert Easton. *Native American Architecture.* New York: Oxford University Press, 1989.

Nabokov, Peter. *Indian Running: Native American History & Tradition.* Santa Fe: Ancient City Press, 1981.

Nies, Judith. *Native American History: A Chronology of a Culture's Vast Achievements and Their Links to World Events.* New York: Ballantine Books, 1996.

Nobel, David Grant. *New Light on Chaco Canyon.* Santa Fe: School of American Research, 1985.

———. *Ancient Ruins of the Southwest: An Archaeological Guide.* Flagstaff, Ariz.: Northland Publishing, 1991.

Northrop, Stuart A. *Turquoise and Spanish Mines in New Mexico.* Albuquerque: University of New Mexico Press, 1975.

Ortiz de Montellano, Bernard. *Aztec Medicine, Health, and Nutrition.* New Brunswick, N.J.: Rutgers University Press, 1990.

Oswalt, Wendal N. *Eskimo and Explorers.* Novato, Calif.: Chandler & Sharp, 1979.

Page, Thomas. *The Civilization of the American Indians.* New York: Crescent Books, 1979.

Parsons, James A. "Southern Blooms: Latin America and the World of Flowers." *Queen's Quarterly* 99, no. 3 (1992): 542–561.

Paterek, Josephine, Ph.D. *Encyclopedia of American Indian Costume.* Denver, Colo.: ABC-Clio, Inc., 1994.

Paternosto, Cesar. *The Stone and the Thread: Andean Roots of Abstract Art.* Austin: University of Texas Press, 1996.

Peredo, Miguel Guzman. *Medical Practices in Ancient America.* Mexico City: Ediciones Euroamericanas, 1985.

Peterson, James B. *A Most Indispensable Art: Native Fiber Industries from Eastern North America.* Knoxville: University of Tennessee Press, 1996.

Porter, Frank W. *The Art of Native American Basketry.* Westport, Conn.: Greenwood Press, 1990.

Prindle, Tara. *NativeTech:Games.* URL: http://www.nativeweb.org/NativeTech. Downloaded April 13, 2001.

Readers's Digest Association. *Mysteries of the Ancient Americas.* Pleasantville, N.Y.: Reader's Digest Books, 1986.

Sabloff, Jeremy A. *The Cities of Ancient Mexico: Reconstructing a Lost World.* New York: Thames and Hudson, 1989.

Sahagun, Fray Bernardino de. *General History of the Things of New Spain.* (Florentine Codex.) Translated by Charles E. Dibble and Arthur J. O. Anderson. Santa Fe: The School of American Research and the University of Utah, Monographs of the School of American Research and the Museum of New Mexico, 1963.

Salaman, Redcliffe N. *The History and Social Influence of the Potato.* Cambridge, England: Cambridge University Press, 1949.

Salmoral, Manuel Lucena. *America in 1492: Portrait of a Continent 500 Years Ago.* New York: Facts On File, 1990.

Salvador, Ricardo. "Maize." In *The Encyclopedia of Mexico: History, Culture and Society.* Chicago: Fitzroy Dearborn Publishers, 1997.

Sauer, Carl Otwin. *Early Spanish Main.* Berkeley: University of California Press, 1966.

Scarborough, Vernon L. and David R. Wilcox, eds. *The Mesoamerican Ballgame.* Tucson: University of Arizona Press, 1991.

Schele, Linda and David Freidel. *A Forest Of Kings: The Untold Story of the Maya.* William Morrow and Company, Inc., New York, 1990.

Schele, Linda and Peter Matthews. *The Code of Kings: The Language of Seven Sacred Maya Temples and Tombs.* New York: Charles Scribner and Sons, 1998.

Schevill, Margot Blum, Janet Catherine Berlo, and Edward B. Dwyer, eds. *Textile Traditions of Mesoamerica and the Andes: An Anthology.* Austin: University of Texas Press, 1996.

Schultes, R. and R. Raffauf. *The Healing Forest.* Portland, Oregon: Dioscordes Press, 1990.

Schwartz, Marion. *A History of Dogs in the Early Americas.* New Haven, Conn.: Yale University Press, 1997.

Sharer, Robert. *Daily Life in Maya Civilization.* Westport, Conn.: Greenwood Press, 1996.

Smith, Bruce D. *Rivers of Change, Essays on Early Agriculture in Eastern North America.* Washington, D.C.: Smithsonian Institution Press, 1993.

———. *The Emergence of Agriculture.* New York: Scientific American Library, 1995.

Smith, Michael E. *The Peoples of America: The Aztecs.* Cambridge, Mass.: Blackwell 1996.

Sokalow, Raymond. *Why We Eat What We Eat: How the Encounter Between the New World and the Old Changed the Way Everyone on the Planet Eats.* New York: Summit Books, 1991.

Soustelle, Jacques. *Daily Life of the Aztecs on the Eve of the Spanish Conquest.* Stanford, Calif.: Stanford University Press, 1961.

Stahl, P. W. and Presley Norton. "Precolumbian Animal Domestication from Salango, Ecuador." *American Antiquity* 52, no. 2 (1987): 382–391.

Stannard, David E. *American Holocaust: Columbus and the Conquest of the New World.* New York: Oxford University Press, 1992.

Stone, Eric. *Medicine among the American Indians.* Reprint. New York: Hafner Publishing Company, 1962.

Symington, Fraser. *The Canadian Indian.* Toronto: McClelland and Stewart, 1969.

Tannahill, Reay. *Food in History.* New York: Stein and Day, 1973.

Taylor, Norman. *Plant Drugs that Changed the World.* New York: Dodd, Mead, and Company, 1965.

Trager, James. *The Food Chronology: The Food Lover's Compendium of Events and Anecdotes from Prehistory to Present.* New York: Henry Holt, 1995.

Trigger, Bruce G. *Case Studies in Anthropology: The Huron Farmers of the North.* New York: Holt Rinehart and Winston, 1969.

Trigger, Bruce G. and Wilcomb E. Washburn, eds. *The Cambridge History of the Native Peoples of the Americas: Vol. I, Part I, North America.* New York: Cambridge University Press, 1996.

Turolla, Pino. *Beyond the Andes: My Search for the Origins of Pre-Inca Civilization.* New York: Harper & Row Publishers, 1970.

Vennum, Jr., Thomas. *American Indian Lacrosse: Little Brother of War.* Washington, D.C.: Smithsonian Institution Press, 1994.

———. *Wild Rice and the Ojibway People.* St. Paul: Minnesota Historical Society Press, 1988.

Viola, Herman and Carolyn Margolis. *Seeds of Change: 500 Years Since.* Washington, D.C.: Smithsonian Institution Press, 1991.

Vogel, Virgil. *American Indian Medicine.* Norman: University of Oklahoma Press, 1977.

Waldman, Carl. *Atlas of the American Indian.* Rev. ed. New York: Facts On File, 2000.

Warhus, Mark. *Another America: Native American Maps and the History of Our Land.* New York: St. Martin's Press, 1997.

Weatherford, Jack. *Indian Givers: How the Indians of the Americas Transformed the World.* New York: Fawcett Columbine 1988.

———. *Native Roots: How the Indians Enriched America.* New York: Fawcett Columbine, 1991.

Weiner, Michael A. *Earth Medicine, Earth Food: Plant Remedies, Drugs, and Natural Foods of the North American Indians.* New York: Fawcett Columbine, 1990.

Wilson, L. Gilbert. *Buffalo Bird Woman's Garden: Agriculture of the Hidatsa Indians.* Reprint. St. Paul: Minnesota Historical Society Press, 1987.

# ENTRIES BY TRIBE, GROUP, OR LINGUISTIC GROUP

This list refers only to the tribes mentioned in the entries contained in this book. Because of space constraints, many entries list one or two tribes from a particular culture group area. The list below is not intended as a comprehensive list of the accomplishments of particular American Indian tribes that are many and beyond the scope of this book to detail.

### ADENA

abstract art
agriculture
irrigation systems

### ACHUAR

blowguns

### AGUARUNA

blowguns

### AHJUMAWI

fish traps (weirs)

### AKIMEL O'ODHAM (PIMA)

adobe
chia
insect repellents
irrigation systems
place-names
therapeutic touch (massage)
tobacco
yucca

### ALEUT

place-names

### ALGONQUIAN-SPEAKING TRIBES

language, American Indian influence
 on
pipes, tobacco
place-names
tumplines

### ALGONKIN

agriculture
beans
bunk beds
calls, animal and bird
canoes
maple syrup
soft drink ingredients

### ANASAZI

adobe
apartment complexes
architects
astronomy
calendars
cities, America's first
civic centers
cotton
crop storage
farming, terraced
geometry
insect repellents

irrigation systems
jewelry, turquoise and
 silver
looms
musical instruments
observatories
parrot breeding
pipes, tobacco
popcorn
pottery
prickly pear cacti
road systems
seed selection
stonemasonry techniques
urban planning
water conservation
weaving techniques

### APACHE

cat's cradle
drainage, surgical and wound
 (Mescalero)
granulation (Mescalero)
military contributions
moccasins
peyote (Lipan)
place-names (White Mountain)
steam rooms
strawberries (Mescalero)
yucca

## APALACHEE

agriculture
double cropping
milpa

## ARAPAHO

diapers, disposable
games, footbag
sign language
tipis
toys

## ARAWAK

aquaculture
arrowroot
chiles
language, American Indian influence on
peanuts
popcorn
tobacco
trade

## ARIKARA

earth lodges
insulation, home
seed selection
tipis

## ASSINIBOINE

tipis
sign language

## ATSINA (GROS VENTRE)

games, footbag
mints, botanical
tipis
toys

## AYUXWA

place-names

## AZTEC (MEXICA)

abacus
abstract art
achiote
agave
agriculture
almanacs
amaranth

American history, recorded
anatomical knowledge
anesthetics
antibiotic medications
antispasmodic medications
aquaculture
architects
aromatherapy
arthritis treatments
arthrocentesis
base 20 mathematical system
astronomy
avocados
balls, rubber
barbecues
barbershops
basketball
blowguns
blue-green algae
board games
books
cacao
calendars
canals, shipping
casseroles
chewable dentifrices
chewing gum
chiles
chili
chocolate
cigarettes
cities, America's first
civic centers
cochineal
compulsory education
concrete
corn
corn, parched
cornmeal
cotton
crop storage
dahlias
debridement
dentistry
deodorants
distillation
dog breeds
ducks, muscovy
dumplings
dyes
earache treatments
embroidery
enemas
ephedra
excision
eyes, medical treatment of

farming, terraced
fast foods
featherworking
fertilizers
flintknapping
food preservation
forceps
free elections
gardens, botanical
gastroenteritis treatments
geometry
gold panning
guilds
hair conditioners
headache, knowledge of etiology
helmets, sports
hemostats
hominy
hospitals
hygiene, personal
indigestion medications
instant foods
jade work
jewelry, turquoise and silver
language, American Indian influence on
lost-wax casting technique
maps, first American
marigolds
medical research
medicine
metallurgy
metals, precious
morning glories
mosaics
mouthwash
musical instruments
nurses/nursing
nutrition
observatories, astronomical
obstetrics
orchards
paper
parrot breeding
peyote
pharmacology
phlebotomy
pills
pipes, tobacco
place-names
plant classifications
plumbing
poinsettias
ponchos
popcorn
pottery

## CHIPPEWA (OJIBWAY, ANISHINABE)

antispasmodic
    medications
astringents
caramel corn
decoys, fish (olfactory)
dyes
hair conditioners
hemp, American
insulation, home
lacrosse
lady's slipper
language, American Indian
    influence on
maple syrup and sugar
megaphones
mints, botanical
moccasins
mouthwash
obstetrics
place-names
plastic surgery
sassafras
shovels
snowshoes
soft drink
    ingredients
strawberries
toboggans
toys
trade
weaving techniques
white pine
wild rice
wintergreen
writing systems

## CHOCTAW

blowguns
chewable dentifrices
codes
cornmeal
file gumbo
lacrosse
military contributions
place-names
steam rooms
Tabasco sauce, American Indian
    influence on

## CHUMASH

asphalt
tarpaulins

waterproofing

## CLOVIS

flintknapping

## COLVILLE

mints, botanical

## COMANCHE

black walnuts
codes
eyes, medical treatment of
fringed clothing
moccasins
sign language

## COXCALTAN

chiles

## CREE

mints, botanical
persimmons
snowshoes
tipis (Plains Cree)

## CREEK

antihelmintics
antispasmodic medications
civic centers
diuretics
double cropping
hickory
lacrosse
military contributions
tanning, brain

## CROW

fringed clothing
games, footbag
sign language
tipis

## CUNA

cashews

## DIEGUEÑO

chia

detergents

## FLATHEAD (SALISH)

cat's cradle
dog breeds (Western Salish)
dyes
insect repellents
mints, botanical
weaving techniques

## FOLSOM

flintknapping

## FOX

astronomy
cat's cradle
lacrosse
thoracentesis
toys

## GABRIELIÑO

chewing gum
trade

## GUARANI

language, American Indian influence
    on
pineapples

## HAIDA

architects
canoes
carpentry techniques
jackstraws (pick up
    sticks)
toys

## HIDATSA

beans
corn, parched
double cropping
earth lodges
fertilizers
food preservation
insulation, home
milpa
seed selection
squash
sunflowers

trade
transplanting, agricultural

## HOHOKAM

adobe
agriculture
architects
basketball
beans
cities, America's first
civic centers
cotton
crop storage
etching, acid
irrigation systems
jewelry, turquoise
    and silver
seed selection
settlement patterns
trade
water conservation
zoned biodiversity

## HOPEWELL

abstract art
agriculture
irrigation systems
pipes, tobacco
road systems
settlement patterns
trade
urban planning

## HOPI

adobe (pre-Hopi)
antispasmodic
    medications
board games
calendars
cotton
jewelry, turquoise
    and silver
running
squash
toys

## HUASTEC

milpa

## HUICHOL

peyote

## HUPA

cat's cradle (string games)

## HURON

agriculture
cities, America's first
dreamwork psychology
indigestion medications
isolation
pipes, tobacco
psychotherapy
Quonset huts, American Indian
    influence on
scurvy cure
settlement patterns
stockades
transplanting, agricultural

## ILLINI

eyes, medical treatment of
place-names

## INCA

abstract art
acoustics (pre-Inca, Inca)
agriculture
alpacas
American history, recorded
anesthetics
aqueducts
architects
arrowroot
balsa wood
bridges
calendars
census
cities, America's first
civic centers (pre-Inca)
coca
crop storage
disability rights
dog breeds
farming, terraced
fertilizers
food coloring
food preservation
forceps
freeze-drying
goiter prevention
gold panning
gold plating
guinea pigs
hydraulics

instant foods
irrigation systems
jerky
kaolin
labor laws
latex
llamas
mercury
metal casting
metallurgy
mining, placer
musical instruments
nasturtiums
nutrition
observatories, astronomical
orchards
orthopedic techniques (pre-Inca)
pan pipes
passion fruit
place-names
platinum (pre-Inca)
plumbing
ponchos
popcorn
potatoes
pottery
quinine
quinoa
quipus
rafts, balsa
rafts, inflatable
road systems
running
scales
scalpels
snuff
soft drink ingredients
space heaters, portable
stonemasonry techniques
stretchers
sweet potatoes
tamales
tax systems
therapeutic touch
toothbrushes
toothpastes and powders
tourniquets
trade
trephination
tubing, copper
tumplines
urban planning
vicunas
water conservation
writing systems
zoned biodiversity

## INUIT

abstract art
bolas
bows, laminated
calls, animal and bird
camouflage
cat's cradle
compulsory education
cradleboards
crampons
dog breeds
dogsleds
earth lodges
flotation devices
games, footbag
games, dice
harpoons
igloos
ironwork
jackstraws
kayaks
metallurgy
mukluks
parkas
shovels
sleds, cariole
snow goggles
snowshoes
space heaters, portable
toys
trade
traps
trousers
whaling

## INUPIAQ

cranberries
insect bites and bee sting remedies

## IROQUOIS

agriculture
antispasmodic medications
apartment complexes
black walnuts
caucus
cities, America's first
corn
cornbread
corn, parched
dreamwork psychology
dumplings
dyes
free association
hemp, American

insect repellents
Iroquois Constitution
Jerusalem artichokes
lacrosse
League of Nations, American Indian
    influence on
military contributions
petroleum
place-names
popcorn
psychotherapy
Quonset huts, American Indian
    influence on
running
sassafras
stockades
trade
United States Constitution, American
    Indian influence on
wampum
weaving techniques
wintergreen
women's rights

## KANSA

place-names
running

## KAROK

detergents
insecticides

## KAW

place-names

## KAWAIISU

chia
detergents

## KERES

ephedra

## KICKAPOO

running

## KIOWA

fringed clothing
mints, botanical
sign language

tipis

## KOOTENAI (FLATHEAD)

insect repellents
mints, botanical
moccasins

## KWAKIUTL

cat's cradle
hemostats
steam rooms

## LENNI-LENAPE (DELAWARE)

antispasmodic medications
cranberries
military tactics
place-names
wintergreen

## LUSIEÑO

running

## MANDAN

earth lodges
games, footbag
insulation, home
seed selection
tipis
trade

## MAKAH

antibiotic medications
whaling

## MALAMUTE

dog breeds

## MALISEET

pills

## MANHATTAN

settlement patterns

## MAPUCHE

bolas
ponchos

## MARICOPA

therapeutic touch
toys

## MAYA

abacus
abstract art, American Indian
    influence on
agriculture
agriculture, raised bed
American history, recorded
aquaculture
arches, corbeled
architects
aromatherapy
arrowroot
astronomy
avocados
balls, rubber
balsa wood
barbecues
base 20 mathematical system
basketball
beans
beekeeping
blowguns
board games
books
cacao
calendars
cat's cradle
chewing gum
chiles
chocolate
cigars
cities, America's first
cochineal
colanders
concrete
cornmeal
cotton
crop storage
dental inlays
dentistry
dog breeds
drill bits, metal
drills, bow
ducks, muscovy
embroidery
fans
farming, terraced
featherworking
flintknapping
food coloring
food preservation

geometry
helmets, sports
hominy
indigestion medications
insect repellents
instant foods
jade work
jewelry, turquoise and silver
jicama
lighthouses
mercury
milpa
mummies
murals
musical instruments
orchards
paper
parrot breeding
pipes, tobacco
pottery
prescriptions
pulleys
pyramids
road systems
sandals
squash
steam rooms
stonemasonry techniques
stretchers
tamales
tarpaulins
tax systems
tobacco
tomatoes
tortillas
toys
traction and countertraction
trade
trephination
tubing, copper
turkey breeding
umbrellas
urban planning
water conservation
weaving techniques
women's rights
writing systems

## MENOMINEE

astringents
calls, animal and bird
decoys, fish (olfactory)
enemas
indigestion medications
lacrosse

lady's slipper
mints, botanical
mouthwash
obstetrics
running
white pine

## MESQUAKI (FOX)

astringents
astronomy
black walnuts
cat's cradle
earache treatments
gastroenteritis treatments
lacrosse
lady's slipper
milkweed
obstetrics
running
thoracentesis
toothpastes and powders
toys

## MIAMI

eyes, medical treatment of
lacrosse
military tactics

## MICMAC

moccasins

## MISSISSIPPIAN CULTURE

calendars
cities, America's first
civic centers
pyramids
road systems

## MIXTEC

books
chocolate
gold panning
jewelry, turquoise and silver
metallurgy
metals, precious

## MOCHE

adobe
American history, recorded
annealing

aqueducts
bells
cities, America's first
dog breeds
electricity
electroplating
excision
foil, metal
geometry
gold plating
irrigation systems
lost-wax casting
    technique
metallurgy
mosaics
musical
    instruments
popcorn poppers
pottery
pyramids
scales
scalpels
shovels
surgery
tie-dyeing

## MOGOLLON

farming, terraced

## MOHAWK

agriculture
corn
Iroquois Constitution
lady's slipper
military contributions
potato chips
socialist theory, American Indian
    influence on
U.S. Constitution, American Indian
    influence on
wampum
women's rights

## MOHEGAN

earache treatments
mints, botanical
mouthwash
salicin
white pine

## MOHICAN

wampum

## MOJAVE

running

## MONTAGNAIS

salicin
white pine

## MOUND BUILDERS

agriculture
calendars
cities, America's first
civic centers
irrigation systems
pipes, tobacco
pyramids
road systems
settlement patterns
tax systems
trade
urban planning

## MUSCOGEAN

place-names

## MUSKOGEE

hickory

## NARRAGANSETT

black walnuts
moccasins
place-names
squash
wampum

## NATCHEZ

civic centers
diuretics
milkweed

## NAVAJO (DINEH)

abstract art
arches, corbeled
codes
dyes
ephedra
geometry
jewelry, turquoise and silver
looms
military contributions

milkweed
mints, botanical
moccasins
place-names
steam rooms
weaving techniques
yucca

## NAZCA

abstract art, American Indian
    influence on
calendars
embroidery
geometry
knitting, needle
pan pipes

## NEZ PERCE

Appaloosa horse breed
dyes
embroidery
looms
military tactics
sign language
weaving techniques

## NOMALKI

running

## NOOTKA

carpentry techniques
whaling

## OLD COPPER CULTURE

annealing
chisels
fishhooks
jewelry, metal
tubing, copper

## OLMEC

American history, recorded
aqueducts
architects
balls, rubber
base 20 mathematical system
basketball
cities, America's first
civic centers
compasses

settlement patterns
soft drink ingredients
wild rice
wintergreen

## POVERTY POINT CULTURE

briquettes

## POWHATAN

language, American Indian influence on
moccasins

## PUEBLO/PUEBLOAN

abstract art
adobe
detergents
ephedra
fast foods
geometry
jewelry, turquoise and silver
military tactics
pottery
toys
weaving techniques
yucca

## QUAPAW

military contributions

## QUECHUA

architects
kaolin
latex
nasturtiums
stonemasonry
    techniques

## QUINAULT

obstetrics

## RAPPAHANNOCK

arthritis treatments

## SAC (SAUK, SALK)

astronomy
cat's cradle
lacrosse
thoracentesis
toys

## SEMINOLE

blowguns
evaporative cooling
lacrosse
sassafras

## SENECA

agriculture
astronomy
Iroquois Constitution
League of Nations, American Indian
    influence on
petroleum
socialist theory, American Indian
    influence on
syringes
U.S. Constitution, American Indian
    influence on
wampum

## SHAWNEE

military tactics

## SHOSHONE

asepsis
calls, animal and bird
contraception, oral
eyes, medical treatment of
indigestion medications
insecticides
mints, botanical
orthopedic techniques
place-names
toys

## SHUAR

blowguns

## SHUSWAP

mints, botanical

## SICAN

keros
money

## SIOUX
## (DAKOTA, LAKOTA, NAKOTA)

antiviral medications
astronomy
black walnuts

Boy Scouts of America, American
    Indian influence on
cat's cradle
codes
decoys, fish (visual)
diuretics
dyes
Erikson's developmental stages,
    American Indian influence on
gastroenteritis treatment
granulation
lacrosse
lady's slipper
mints, botanical
orthopedic techniques
pipes, tobacco
place-names
sign language
tipis
toys

## STOCKBRIDGE

witch hazel

## TATAVIAM

chia

## TAINO

arrowroot
barbecues
canoes
chiles
corn
cotton
hammocks
language, American Indian influence
    on
trade

## TARAHUAMARA

chia
peyote

## TEWA

military tactics
toys

## THOMPSON

mints, botanical
plant classifications

# ENTRIES BY GEOGRAPHICAL CULTURE AREA

pumpkins
Quonset huts
salicin
salve, drawing
sassafras
scurvy cure
seed selection
shovels
snack foods
snowshoes
Socialist theory, American Indian
    influence on
soft drink ingredients
squash
stockades
strawberries
stretchers
succotash
sunflowers
suppositories
Thanksgiving
tobacco
toboggans
transplanting, agricultural
tubing, copper
United States Constitution, American
    Indian influence on
wahoo
wampum
whaling
wild rice
wintergreen
witch hazel
women's rights

## Northwest Coast Culture Area

anatomical knowledge
anti-asthmatic medication
antibiotic medications
antihelmintics
architects
boxes
canoes
carpentry techniques
cascara sagrada
cat's cradle
diabetes medication
dogbane
fishhooks, multiple
fishing, chemical
fish traps
goiter prevention
harpoons
hemostats
insect repellents
insecticides

jackstraws
looms
needles
snack foods
strawberries
tobacco
whaling
"X-ray art"

## Plateau Culture Area

Appaloosa horse breed
cascara sagrada
decoys, duck
embroidery
fishing, chemical
fringed clothing
hair conditioners
hockey, field and ice
insect repellents
insecticides
looms
military tactics
mints, botanical
plant classifications
sign language

## Southeast Culture Area

agriculture
antihelmintics
antispasmodic medications
arthritis treatments
beans
black walnuts
blowguns
briquettes
calendars
canoes
chewable dentifrices
cities, America's first
civic centers
codes
companion planting
corn
cornbread
cornmeal
detergents
dogbane
diuretics
evaporative cooling
file gumbo
fish traps
forest management
gardens, herb
gourds
granulation
grapes

hockey, field and ice
hickory
hominy
indigestion medications
indigo
insect repellents
irrigation systems
Jerusalem artichokes
lacrosse
lady's slipper
milpa
mints, botanical
pan pipes
pawpaws
peanuts
pecans
persimmons
pins, straight
pipes, smoking
pumpkins
pyramids
rivets
sassafras
scuppernongs
seawalls
seed selection
soft drink ingredients
squash
strawberries
sunflowers
Tabasco sauce, American Indian
    influence on
tax systems
tobacco

## Southwest Culture Area

adobe
agave
agriculture
anti-asthmatic medication
antibiotic medications
antispasmodic medications
apartment complexes
architects
arthritis treatment
astronomy
basketball
beans
board games
calendars
cat's cradle
chia
chiles
chili
cities, America's first
civic centers

# Entries by Subject

## AGRICULTURAL TECHNIQUES

agriculture, raised bed
beekeeping
companion planting
crop storage
double cropping
farming, terraced
fertilizers
foot plows
gardens, botanical
gardens, herb
irrigation systems
milpa
orchards
seed selection
seed treatment
transplanting, agricultural
xeriscaping

## ARCHITECTURE

adobe
apartment complexes
arches, corbeled
architects
concrete
earth lodges
evaporative cooling
igloos
insulation, home
lighthouses
pyramids
Quonset huts, American Indian
    influence on
stockades

stonemasonry techniques
tipis
ventilation systems

## ART

abstract art, American Indian influence
    on
featherworking
jade work
jewelry, turquoise and silver
mosaics
murals
pottery
weaving
"X-ray art"

## ASTRONOMY

almanacs
astronomy
calendars
observatories, astronomical

## CARPENTRY

balsa wood
boxes
canoes
carpentry techniques
mahogany

## CERAMICS

jar lids, twist-on

kaolin
keros
mugs
popcorn poppers
pottery

## CIVIL ENGINEERING

aqueducts
bridges
canals, shipping
civic centers
irrigation systems
plumbing
seawalls
urban planning

## CLOTHING/FOOTWEAR

crampons/snow creepers
flotation devices
fringed clothing
goggles, snow
moccasins
mukluks
parkas
ponchos
sandals
snow goggles
snowshoes
trousers

## CULTIVATED CROPS

achiote

mercury (cinnabar,
quicksilver)
metal casting
metallurgy
metals, precious
mining, placer
needles
pins, straight
platinum
rivets
silver
sintering
smelting
soldering
tubing, copper
welding, sweat

**MILITARY SCIENCE**

camouflage
codes
military contributions
military tactics
Quonset huts, American Indian influence on
stockades

**MUSIC**

acoustics
bells
maracas
musical instruments
pan pipes

**PERSONAL HYGIENE**

barbershops
cattails
deodorants
detergent
diapers, disposable
hair conditioners
hygiene, personal
insecticides
insect repellents
jojoba
mouthwash
public health
steam rooms
yucca

**PHARMACOLOGY**

agave
anesthetics

antiasthmatic medication
antibiotic medications
antihelmintics
antispasmodic medications
antiviral medications
astringents
cascara sagrada
cattails
coca
curare
diabetes medication
diuretics
dogbane
ephedra
foxglove
gastroenteritis treatments
goiter prevention
guaiacum
headache medications
hemp, American
indigestion medications
insect bite and bee sting
remedies
ipecac
jalap
kaolin
lady's slipper
medicines, patent, American Indian
influence on
milkweed
mints, botanical
pharmacology
pills
prescriptions
prickly pear cacti
quinine
salicin
salve, drawing
sassafras
wahoo
witch hazel

**POLITICAL/SOCIAL SCIENCE**

Boy Scouts of America, Indian
influence on
caucus
census
cities, America's first
compulsory education
consensus management
disability rights/social
welfare
free elections
Iroquois Constitution
labor laws

League of Nations, American Indian
influence on
public drunkenness laws
public health
settlement patterns
Socialist theory, American Indian
influence on
tax systems
U.S. Constitution, American Indian
influence on
women's rights

**PSYCHOLOGY**

dreamwork psychology
Erikson's developmental stages,
American Indian influence on
free association
psychotherapy

**SCIENCE**

anatomical knowledge
astronomy
ecology
electricity
gardens, botanical
medical research
plant classifications
zoned biodiversity
zoos

**TECHNOLOGY**

asphalt
blowguns
bows, laminated
cacao
compasses
distillation
embalming
etching, acid
freeze-drying
hominy
hydraulics
insect repellents
insecticides
latex
mirrors
mummies
optical technology, basics of
paint rollers
paper
petroleum
pulleys
solar fire starters

# INDEX

Page locators in **boldface** indicate main entries. Page locators in *italic* indicate photographs or illustrations. Page locators followed by *m* indicate maps. Page locators followed by *g* indicate glossary entries. Page locators followed by *c* indicate chronology.

## A

abacus **1**, 28
abscess 333*g*
abstract art **1–2**
achiote **2**, 31, 92, 110, 118
Achuar 35
acid etching **101–102**
Ackerknecht, Erwin H. 217
Ac ko mok ki (Blackfeet chief) 165
Acoma 100
Acosta, Jose de 261
acoustics **2–3**
Adams, Thomas 55
Adena 1, 6, 141, 344*g*
adobe **3–5,** *4*
  in America's first cities 61
  in apartment complexes 17
  in civic centers 62
  and concrete 68
  and home insulation 138, 139
  in stonemasonry 250
*Adventures in Mexico and the Rocky Mountains* (George Frederick Ruxton) 238
agave **5**
  as antibiotic 15
  in basket-weaving 30
  and bridges 41
  distillation of 84
  and hammocks 126
  as medicinal sunscreen 254
  and public drunkenness laws 217
  in sandals 232
agriculture **5–8.** *See also* cultivated crops

America's first cities 60
animal traps 276
astronomy 24
beekeeping **32**
botanical gardens **117**
companion planting **66–67**
crop storage *77,* **77–78**
double cropping **88–89**
fertilizers **105–106**
foot plows *111,* **111–112**
herb gardens **117–118**
hydraulics 132
irrigation systems **140–142,** *141*
milpa **175–176**
orchards **190**
raised-bed **8–9,** 19, 105
seed selection *236,* **236–237**
settlement patterns 237
slash-and-burn **175–176**
terraced farming **103–104,** *104*
transplanting **275–276**
and turkey breeding 279
water conservation and 294
xeriscaping **306**
Aguaruna 35
ague 333*g*
Ahjumawi 108
Akimel O'odham (Pima)
  chia 55
  cotton 74
  insect repellents 137
  irrigation systems 142
  massage (therapeutic touch) 263
  place-names 205
  tobacco 266
  tobacco pipes 204

yucca 308
Alaska
  architects in 20
  dice games 116
  dogsleds 87–88
  earth lodges 95
  forest management 113
  harpoons 126
  home insulation 138
  jackstraws 143
  tool kits in 268
Albany Congress 287
Albers, Josef 2
Aleut 205
Alexander the Great 74
Algonkin
  beans 31
  bird/animal calls 46
  bunk beds 42
  canoes 48
  soft drink ingredients 244
  tobacco pipes 204
Algonquian-speaking tribes
  agriculture 7
  caucus 53–54
  contributions to place-names 205, 206
  hickory 129
  influence on English language 155
  maple syrup/sugar 163
  pecans 197
  succotash 253
  Thanksgiving 262
  tumplines 279
  wampum 293
alkaloid 333*g*

Allen, Johnny 87
allspice **9,** 59, 99
almanacs **9–10,** 24, 39
aloe vera 5, 254
alpacas **10,** 151, 291
Alta Vista 146, 179
Alvarado, Pedro de 11
Alvucasis 254
Amadas, Philip 122
amaranth 4, **10–11,** 110, 259
Amazon Basin
  achiote 2
  blowguns 35
  Brazil nuts 41
  camouflage 47
  carpentry 49
  cashews 51
  chemical fishing 107
  gold panning 120
  ipecac 139
  maracas 165
  milpa 176
  pharmacology 202
  pineapples 203
  precious metals 172
  surgery 255
  surgical staples 247
Amazon rain forest 266
Amazon River 78, 156
Amazon Valley 162
America, South. *See* South America
American history, recorded **11,** *12,* 181
*American Indian Medicine* (Virgil Vogel)
  American hemp 128